DEMOCRATIC GOVERNANCE AND INTERNATIONAL LAW

Prior to the end of the Cold War, the word "democracy" was rarely used by international lawyers. Few international organizations supported democratic governance, and the criteria for recognition of governments took little account of whether regimes enjoyed a popular mandate. But the events of 1989–91 profoundly shook old assumptions. *Democratic Governance and International Law* attempts to assess international law's new-found interest in fostering transitions to democracy. Is an entitlement to democratic government now emerging in international law? If so, what are its normative foundations? How have global and regional organizations encouraged transitions to democracy, and are their efforts consistent with their constitutional frameworks? How should international law react to elections in which profoundly anti-democratic parties win the vote? In this collection, leading legal scholars grapple with these and other questions to assess the future of international law on this most domestic of questions.

Gregory H. Fox is Assistant Professor of Law at Chapman University School of Law.

Brad R. Roth is Assistant Professor of Legal Studies and Political Science and Adjunct Professor of Law at Wayne State University.

DEMOCRATIC GOVERNANCE AND INTERNATIONAL LAW

EDITED BY

GREGORY H. FOX AND BRAD R. ROTH

PUBLISHED BY THE PRESS SYNDICATE OF THE UNIVERSITY OF CAMBRIDGE
The Pitt Building, Trumpington Street, Cambridge, United Kingdom

CAMBRIDGE UNIVERSITY PRESS
The Edinburgh Building, Cambridge CB2 2RU, UK   www.cup.cam.ac.uk
40 West 20th Street, New York, NY 10011-4211, USA   www.cup.org
10 Stamford Road, Oakleigh, Melbourne 3166, Australia
Ruiz de Alarcón 13, 28014 Madrid, Spain

© Cambridge University Press 2000

This book is in copyright. Subject to statutory exception
and to the provisions of relevant collective licensing agreements,
no reproduction of any part may take place without
the written permission of Cambridge University Press.

First published 2000

Printed in the United Kingdom at the University Press, Cambridge

Typeface Monotype Baskerville 11/12.5 pt.   *System* QuarkXPress™   [SE]

A catalogue record for this book is available from the British Library

Library of Congress Cataloguing in Publication data

Democratic governance and international law / edited by Gregory H. Fox
& Brad R. Roth
p.   cm.
ISBN 0 521 66095 5 hardback – ISBN 0 521 66796 8 paperback
1. International law – Political aspects.   2. Democracy.   I. Fox,
Gregory H., 1961– .   II. Roth, Brad R.
KZ1250.D46   2000
341–dc21   99-40257   CIP

ISBN 0 521 66095 5 hardback
ISBN 0 521 66796 8 paperback

Contents

List of contributors	*page* viii
List of acknowledgments	xii

Introduction: the spread of liberal democracy and its implications for international law   1
Gregory H. Fox & Brad R. Roth

PART I   THE NORMATIVE FOUNDATIONS OF A RIGHT TO POLITICAL PARTICIPATION

1 Legitimacy and the democratic entitlement   25
Thomas M. Franck

2 The right to political participation in international law   48
Gregory H. Fox

3 Democracy and the body of international law   91
James Crawford

PART II   DEMOCRACY AND INTER-STATE RELATIONS

4 Democratic legitimacy and the recognition of States and governments   123
Sean D. Murphy

5 Constitutionalism and democratic government in the inter-American system   155
Stephen J. Schnably

6 Government networks: the heart of the liberal democratic order   199
Anne-Marie Slaughter

PART III   DEMOCRACY AND THE USE OF FORCE

7   Sovereignty and human rights in contemporary
    international law   239
    W. Michael Reisman

8   "You, the People": pro-democratic intervention in
    international law   259
    Michael Byers & Simon Chesterman

9   Pro-democratic intervention by invitation   293
    David Wippman

10 The illegality of "pro-democratic" invasion pacts   328
    Brad R. Roth

11 International law and the "liberal peace"   343
    John M. Owen, IV

PART IV   DEMOCRATIZATION AND CONFLICTING IMPERATIVES

12 Intolerant democracies   389
    Gregory H. Fox & Georg Nolte

13 Whose intolerance, which democracy?   436
    Martti Koskenniemi

14 Democratic intolerance: observations on Fox and Nolte   441
    Brad R. Roth

15 A defense of the "intolerant democracies" thesis   445
    Gregory H. Fox & Georg Nolte

16 Democracy and accountability: the criss-crossing paths
    of two emerging norms   449
    Steven R. Ratner

PART V   CRITICAL APPROACHES

17 Evaluating democratic progress   493
    Brad R. Roth

18 What kind of democracy does the "democratic
    entitlement" entail?   517
    Jan Knippers Black

19 International law, democracy, and the end of history 532
   Susan Marks

Index 567

Contributors

JAN KNIPPERS BLACK is a professor in the Graduate School of International Policy Studies at the Monterey Institute of International Studies in California and a senior associate member of St. Anthony's College, Oxford. Previously, she served as research professor of public administration at the University of New Mexico and as senior research scientist and chair of the Latin American research team in the Foreign Affairs Studies Division of American University. She has authored or edited and co-authored nine books, most recently, *Latin America, Its Problems and Its Promise* (3rd rev. edn, 1998), *Development in Theory and Practice: Paradigms and Paradoxes* (2nd rev. edn, 1999), and *Recycled Rhetoric and Disposable People: The Globalization of Insecurity* (1999).

MICHAEL BYERS is Associate Professor of Law at Duke University. From 1996–99 he was a Fellow of Jesus College, Oxford. He is the author of *Custom, Power and the Power of Rules* (1999) and the editor of *The Role of Law in International Politics* (1999).

SIMON CHESTERMAN is a doctoral candidate at Magdalen College, Oxford. His thesis, on humanitarian intervention, is being supervised by Professor Ian Brownlie. He has recently published articles on war crimes, theories of human rights, and euthanasia.

JAMES CRAWFORD is Whewell Professor of International Law in the University of Cambridge and the Director of the Lauterpacht Research Centre for International Law. He is a member of the International Law Commission and its Special Rapporteur on State Responsibility. His inaugural lecture at Cambridge was on the subject of "Democracy in International Law" (1993).

GREGORY H. FOX is an Assistant Professor of Law at Chapman University Law School. He has been a Senior Fellow at the Orville H.

Schell, Jr. Center for International Human Rights at Yale Law School and an Adjunct Professor of Law at New York University Law School. His publications include "Strengthening the State," *Indiana Journal of Global Legal Studies*, and "Self-Determination in the Post-Cold War Era: A New Internal Focus?" *Michigan Journal of International Law*.

THOMAS FRANCK is the Murray and Ida Becker Professor of Law at New York University Law School and Director of its Center for International Studies. Professor Franck is the author of *Fairness in International Law and Institutions* (1995, 1997). He is President of the American Society of International Law (1998–2000) and has litigated before the International Court of Justice.

MARTTI KOSKENNIEMI is a Professor of International Law, University of Helsinki and Director, The Erik Castrén Institute of International Law and Human Rights. Former Counsellor (legal adviser) Ministry for Foreign Affairs of Finland. He is the author of *From Apology to Utopia: The Structure of International Legal Argument* (1989). He is currently working on a book of essays on international legal history.

SUSAN MARKS is a University Lecturer in the Faculty of Law, University of Cambridge, and a Fellow of Emmanuel College. She teaches, and writes on, international law and human rights law. In recent publications, as well as in a forthcoming book, she addresses the interrelation of democracy and international law.

SEAN D. MURPHY is an Associate Professor of Law at George Washington University in Washington, D.C. He served from 1987 to 1995 in the U.S. Department of State Office of the Legal Adviser and from 1995 to 1998 as Legal Counselor at the U.S. Embassy in The Hague. He is the author of *Humanitarian Intervention: The United Nations in an Evolving World Order* (1996), which was awarded the 1997 Certificate of Merit by the American Society of International Law.

GEORG NOLTE is Professor of International Law at the University of Goettingen. From 1987 to 1999 he was a Fellow at the Max Planck Institute for Comparative Public Law and International Law. During this time he taught at the universities of Leipzig (1990–91), New York (1992), Saarbruecken (1998–99) and Regensburg (1999). He is the author of *Eingreifen auf Einladung (Intervention upon Invitation)* (Springer 1999) as well as a number of articles on international law, comparative constitutional law, and comparative administrative law.

JOHN M. OWEN, IV is Assistant Professor of Government and Foreign Affairs at the University of Virginia. He has held post-doctoral fellowships at Harvard and Stanford. He is the author of *Liberal Peace, Liberal War, American Politics and International Security* (1997), and of "The Canon and the Cannon," *International Security* 23, no. 3 (Winter 1998/99).

STEVEN R. RATNER is Professor of Law at the University of Texas School of Law. He was recently a member of the UN Secretary-General's Group of Experts charged with making recommendations regarding accountability of the Khmer Rouge for their atrocities in the 1970s, and was also a Fulbright Senior Scholar in the Organization for Security and Cooperation in Europe Regional Research Program. He is the author (with Jason Abrams) of *Accountability for Human Rights Atrocities in International Law Beyond the Nuremberg Legacy* (1997), which was awarded the 1998 Certificate of Merit by the American Society of International Law, and the author of *The New UN Peacekeeping: Building Peace in Lands of Conflict After the Cold War* (1995), as well as numerous articles.

W. MICHAEL REISMAN is McDougal Professor of Law at Yale, the co-Editor in-Chief of the *American Journal of International Law*, Counselor of the American Society of International Law, a member of the Advisory Committee on International Law of the Department of State and the Vice-Chairman of Policy Sciences, Inc. He has served as the President of the Inter-American Commission on Human Rights and has advised governments on international law matters.

BRAD R. ROTH is Assistant Professor of Legal Studies and Political Science at Wayne State University in Detroit. He served in 1996 as a Visiting Professor of Law at the University of California at Berkeley. He is the author of *Governmental Illegitimacy in International Law* (1999), which was awarded the 1999 Certificate of Merit by the American Society of International Law, as well as articles on sovereignty, constitutionalism, and democracy.

STEPHEN J. SCHNABLY is Professor of Law at the University of Miami. He has served as counsel or expert witness in human rights cases before the Inter-American Commission on Human Rights and U.S. courts. He is a co-author of *International Human Rights Law & Practice: Cases, Treaties & Materials* (1997), and author of the *Rights International Companion to Property Law* (2000), as well as articles on constitutional law and international human rights law.

ANNE-MARIE SLAUGHTER is J. Sinclair Armstrong Professor of International, Foreign, and Comparative Law and Director of Graduate and International Legal Studies at Harvard Law School. Her most recent publications are (with Laurence Helfer) "Toward a Theory of Effective Supranational Adjudication," *Yale Law Journal* (1997) and (with Andrew Tulumello and Stepan Wood) "International Law and International Relations Theory: A New Generation of Inter-Disciplinary Scholarship," *American Journal of International Law* (1998). She is working on a book about government networks.

DAVID WIPPMAN is Associate Professor of Law at Cornell Law School. He served as a Director in the Office of Multilateral and Humanitarian Affairs in the National Security Council from June 1998 to June 1999. He is the editor of and a contributor to *International Law and Ethnic Conflict* (1998).

Acknowledgments

A number of chapters included in this collection have been adapted by the contributors from work previously published. We gratefully acknowledge the permission that the previous publishers have granted us to reprint here portions of the following publications:

Jan Knippers Black, "For Richer and Poorer: South America's Tenuous Social Truce," *Latin American Perspectives* 87 (1995), pp. 81 ff., adapted by permission of Sage Publications, Inc., which holds copyright.

Gregory H. Fox, "The Right to Political Participation in International Law," *Yale Journal of International Law* 17 (1992), pp. 539 ff., adapted by permission of the Yale Journal of International Law, Inc., which holds copyright.

Gregory H. Fox and Georg Nolte, "Intolerant Democracies," *Harvard International Law Journal* 35 (1995) pp. 1 ff., adapted by permission of the President and Fellows of Harvard College, who hold copyright.

Thomas M. Franck, *Fairness in International Law and Institutions* (Oxford: Clarendon Press, 1995), excerpts adapted by permission of Oxford University Press, which holds copyright.

Martti Koskenniemi, Brad R. Roth, Gregory H. Fox, and Georg Nolte, "Responses," *Harvard International Law Journal* 37 (1996), pp. 231 ff., adapted by permission of the President and Fellows of Harvard College, who hold copyright.

Susan Marks, "The End of History? Reflections on Some International Legal Theses," *European Journal of International Law* 8 (1997), pp. 449 ff., adapted by permission of the European Journal of International Law, which holds copyright.

Sean D. Murphy, "Democratic Legitimacy and the Recognition of States and Governments," *International & Comparative Law Quarterly* 48 (1999), pp. 545 ff., adapted by permission of the British Institute of International and Comparative Law, which holds copyright.

Acknowledgments

John Owen, "How Liberalism Produces the Democratic Peace," *International Security* 19 (1994), pp. 87 ff., adapted by permission of the President and Fellows of Harvard College and the Massachusetts Institute of Technology, who hold copyright.

Steven Ratner, "New Democracies, Old Atrocities: An Inquiry into International Law," *Georgetown Law Journal* 87 (1999), pp. 707 ff., adapted by permission of Georgetown University and Georgetown Law Journal, which hold copyright.

W. Michael Reisman, "Sovereignty and Human Rights in Contemporary International Law," *American Journal of International Law* 84 (1990), pp. 866 ff., and "Haiti and the Validity of International Action," *Am. J. Int'l L.* 89 (1995), pp. 82 ff., adapted by permission of the American Society of International Law, which holds copyright.

Brad R. Roth, "Evaluating Democratic Progress: a Normative Theoretical Approach," *Ethics & International Affairs* 9 (1995), pp. 55 ff., adapted by permission of the Carnegie Council on Ethics and International Affairs, which holds copyright.

Brad R. Roth, *Governmental Illegitimacy in International Law* (Oxford: Clarendon Press, 1999), excerpts adapted by permission of Oxford University Press, which holds copyright.

Stephen J. Schnably, "The Santiago Commitment as a Call to Democracy in the United States: Evaluating the OAS Role in Haiti, Peru, and Guatemala," *University of Miami Inter-American Law Review* 25 (1994), pp. 393 ff., adapted by permission of the University of Miami, which holds copyright.

Anne-Marie Slaughter, "The Real New World Order," *Foreign Affairs* 76 (1997), pp. 183 ff., adapted by permission of the Council on Foreign Relations, which holds copyright.

David Wippman, "Military Intervention, Regional Organizations and Host-State Consent," *Duke Journal of Comparative & International Law* 7 (1996), pp. 209 ff., excerpts adapted by permission of the Duke Journal of Comparative and International Law, which holds copyright.

David Wippman, "Treaty-Based Intervention: Who Can Say No?" *University of Chicago Law Review* 62 (1995), pp. 607 ff., adapted by permission of the University of Chicago, which holds copyright.

Introduction: the spread of liberal democracy and its implications for international law

Gregory H. Fox and Brad R. Roth

I DEMOCRATIC GOVERNANCE AND INTERNATIONAL LAW

Prior to the events of 1989–91, "democracy" was a word rarely found in the writings of international lawyers. Most scholars, and certainly most States, accepted the 1987 view of the American Law Institute that "international law does not generally address domestic constitutional issues, such as how a national government is formed."[1] Apart from its use in resolutions repudiating "alien, colonial, and racist" domination, the term "democratic" appeared in collective pronouncements as a mere platitude, so abstract as to encompass opposite interpretations. Although human rights instruments such as the International Covenant on Civil and Political Rights (ICCPR) had long provided for a right to political participation, the diversity (and, in the case of Cold War participants, mutual hostility) of governmental systems in the international "community" had precluded consensus on the specifications of this right.[2] Moreover, any assertion of a determinate "right to democratic governance" would have suggested criteria of governmental legitimacy at odds with the "effective control" doctrine that had long prevailed in the recognition practices of most States and intergovernmental organizations.

The United Nations, an organization founded on the principle of the sovereign equality of ideologically diverse States, seemed an unlikely vehicle to further a specific mode of internal governance. Although the UN had an extensive history of monitoring elections and referenda in States emerging from colonialism, it did not send a monitoring mission

---

[1] American Law Institute, *Restatement (Third) of the Foreign Relations Law of the United States*, § 203, comment e (1987).
[2] *See generally* Henry J. Steiner, "Political Participation as a Human Right," *Harvard Hum. Rts. Y.B.* 1 (1988), p. 77. The impression that participatory rights could not transcend ideological conflict was reinforced by the US Government's invocations of that right in support of Cold War policies. *See, e.g.*, Cynthia Brown, ed., *With Friends Like These: The Americas Watch Report on Human Rights & US Policy in Latin America* (New York: Pantheon Books, 1985), pp. 3–23.

to a sovereign State until the 1990 elections in Nicaragua.[3] Even after the UN Security Council began using its long-dormant Chapter VII powers to address humanitarian catastrophes arising from civil conflict, there seemed little prospect that the organization would get into the business of imposing solutions to internal power struggles, let alone that it would invoke liberal–democratic criteria in dictating outcomes. Regional intergovernmental organizations, despite occasional rhetorical commitments to political democracy,[4] appeared scarcely more disposed to enter the fray.

Whatever one is to make of developments in the 1990s, it is now clear that international law and international organizations are no longer indifferent to the internal character of regimes exercising effective control within "sovereign" States. In region after region, political change has swept through the former bastions of authoritarian and dictatorial rule, offering the promise, if not always the reality, of democratization, and this development has been reflected in international institutions. The status and determinacy of the right to political participation have been enhanced by pronouncements of the ICCPR Human Rights Committee,[5] the European and Inter-American Commissions on Human Rights,[6] the Organization of American States (OAS),[7] the Organization for Security and Cooperation in Europe (OSCE),[8] and the

---

[3] *See* Yves Biegbeder, *International Monitoring of Plebiscites, Referenda and National Elections* (Dordrecht: Martinus Nijhoff, 1994).

[4] The 1948 Charter of the Organization of American States declares that "representative democracy is an indispensable condition for the stability, peace and development of the region." The 1950 European Convention for the Protection of Human Rights and Fundamental Freedoms states in its preamble that "an effective political democracy is essential to the protection of fundamental freedoms."

[5] Human Rights Committee, General Comment 25 (57), UN Doc. CCPR/C/21/Rev.1/Add.7 (1996); Bwalya v. Zambia, Commun. No. 314/1988, UN Doc. CCPR/C/48/D/314/1988 (1993), *reprinted* in *Hum. Rts. L.J.* 14 (1993), p. 408 (opining against the barring of electoral candidates who are not members of the ruling party).

[6] *See* Greek Case, 1969 YB. Eur. Conv. on H.R. 179, 180 (Eur. Comm'n. of Hum. Rts.); Case of the Socialist Party and Others v. Turkey, Case No. 20/1997/804/1007 (ECHR 1998); *Mexico Elections Decision*, Cases 9768, 9780, 9828, Inter-Amer. Comm'n on Hum. Rts. 97, 108, OEA/Ser.L/V/11.77, doc. 7, rev. 1 (1990).

[7] *See* AG/RES 1080 (XXI-0/91) (5th plen. sess., June 5, 1991) ('Representative Government" resolution coinciding with the "Santiago Commitment to Democracy and the Renewal of the Inter-American System"); OEA/Ser.P/AG/Doc.11 (XVI-E/92) (Dec. 14, 1992) (Charter amendment providing for suspension from participation in the OAS General Assembly of a state whose democratically elected government is forcibly overthrown).

[8] *See* Conference on Security and Co-operation in Europe, Document of the Moscow Meeting, Oct. 3, 1991, paras. 17.1, 17.2, ILM 30 (1991), pp. 1670, 1677 (condemning forces seeking to overthrow a freely and fairly elected government and pledging to "support vigorously, in accordance with the Charter of the United Nations," the "legitimate organs" of that State).

UN General Assembly.[9] The UN and other intergovernmental organizations have invested heavily in the crafting and monitoring of electoral processes in many nations across the globe.[10] On two occasions, the international community has responded vigorously to military coups against elected governments, endorsing the use of external armed force to restore the deposed governments of Jean-Bertrand Aristide in Haiti in 1994 and Ahmad Tejan Kabbah in Sierra Leone in 1998.[11] So commonly espoused is the commitment to democratic institutions that the UN Secretary-General could assert in 1997 as "an established norm" the view that "military coups against democratically elected Governments by self-appointed juntas are not acceptable."[12]

In 1999, the UN Commission on Human Rights, by a vote of 51-0 with two abstentions (China and Cuba), promulgated a resolution affirming that "democracy fosters the full realization of all human rights," and enumerating a list of "rights of democratic governance" that includes familiar ICCPR rights as well as "transparent and accountable governmental institutions."[13] The resolution is entitled "Promotion of the Right to Democracy," although the inclusion in the title of the term "right to democracy," mentioned nowhere in the text, was itself the subject of a separate vote that drew 12 nays and 13 abstentions, with several States expressing doubts as to democracy's legal status as a right.[14]

Regardless of whether the Commission ever reaches consensus on this question, its increasingly frequent call for States to "democratize" made it virtually inevitable that the Commission would address the status of democracy directly.[15] In the same 1999 session, for example, the

---

[9] *See, e.g.*, GA Res. 45/150 (1990) (on "Enhancing the effectiveness of the principle of periodic and genuine elections"). [10] *See generally*, Biegbeder, *supra* note 3.
[11] *See* SC Res. 940 (1994) (authorizing armed intervention in Haiti); UN Doc. S/PRST/1998/5 (Security Council Presidential Statement welcoming the removal of the Sierra Leonean junta); SC Res. 1162 (1998) (commending ECOWAS after the fact for its role in the Sierra Leonean transition).
[12] Annual Report of the Secretary-General on the Work of the Organization, UN Doc A/52/1, para. 37 (1997).
[13] UNCHR Res. 1999/57, paras. 1 and 2, U.N. Doc. E/CN.4/RES/1999/57 (April 27, 1999).
[14] U.N. Doc. E/CN.4/1999.SR.57 (April 27, 1999), paras. 8–9 (India), 15 (Pakistan), 20 (Mexico), 22–23 (Cuba), 29 (Russian Federation), 40 (Indonesia), 42 (China).
[15] In the 1999 session alone such language appeared in the following country-specific resolutions: UNCHR Res. 1999/8, para. 7, UN Doc. E/CN.4/Res/1999/8 (April 23, 1999) (Cuba); UNCHR Res. 1999/9, para. 7, UN Doc. E/CN.4/Res/1999/9 (April 23, 1999) (Afghanistan); UNCHR Res. 1999/15, para. 1(c), UN Doc. E/CN.4/Res/1999/15 (April 23, 1999) (Sudan); UNCHR Res. 1999/17, para. 7(c), UN Doc. E/CN.4/1999/17 (April 23, 1999) (Myanmar); UNCHR Res. 1999/18, para. 9(c), UN Doc. E/CN.4/Res/1999/18 (April 23, 1999) (Federal Republic of Yugoslavia, Republic of Croatia and Bosnia/Herzegovina; UNCHR Res. 1999/19,

Commission commended Nigeria for its "successful holding of free and fair elections, on the basis of democratic principles. . . ."[16] This followed on its call in the prior year for Nigeria "to take concrete and credible steps to restore democratic government without delay."[17] The many caveats expressed by States voting for the "Right to Democracy" resolution may arguably have the effect of exposing a hollowness at the core of resolutions such as these. On the other hand, in context, it seems clear that most of the Commission's calls for "democratization" in particular countries refer to elections and to rights associated with those elections being considered "free and fair."

There can be little doubt that this unprecedented international attention to the internal governing structures of States has significant implications for the current content and future direction of international law. There remains substantial disagreement, however, as to what those implications are.

At the core of this book is the question of whether there can meaningfully be said to be, in Thomas Franck's pioneering words, a "democratic entitlement" in international law.[18] This question prompts a series of further questions as to the purported norm's content, justification, and consequences. For example, is the concept of democracy amenable to embodiment in an international legal standard? Does the "democratic entitlement" require States to permit overtly anti-democratic forces to contest for power? Does the much-touted (and much-debated) observation that democracies do not go to war with one another (the so-called "democratic peace" thesis) enhance the legal basis for promoting the spread of democracy? To what extent have intergovernmental organizations such as the Organization of American States affirmed the promotion of democracy within member States as a legitimate (or imperative) function? Has democratic governance emerged in State

---

Footnote 15 *(cont.)*
  para. 8, UN Doc. E/CN.4/RES/1999/19 (April 27, 1999) (Equitorial Guinea); UNCHR Res. 1999/56, para. 8(d), UN Doc. E/CN.4/RES/1999/56 (April 27, 1999) (Democratic Republic of Congo); UNCHR Res. 1999/76, para. 13, UN Doc. E/CN.4/RES/1999/76 (April 28, 1999) (Cambodia); UNCHR RES. 1999/77, para. 1, UN Doc. E/CN.4.RES/1999/77 (April 28, 1999) (Haiti). For a list of General Assembly resolutions along the same lines, *see* Gregory H. Fox, "Self-Determination in the Post-Cold War Era: A New Internal Focus?" *Mich. J. Int'l L.* 16 (1995), 733, p. 753 n.98.

[16] UNCHR Res. 1999/11, para. 4, UN Doc. E/CN.4/Res/1999/11 (April 23, 1999).
[17] UNCHR Res. 1998/64, para. 3(f), UN Doc. E/CN.4/Res/1998/64 (April 21, 1998).
[18] Thomas M. Franck, "The Emerging Right to Democratic Governance," *Am. J. Int'l L.* 86 (1992), p. 46.

practice as a criterion for the recognition of States and governments? Does the goal of promoting democracy qualify the legal duty of non-intervention in the internal affairs of States?

In exploring some of the central aspects of the relationship between democratic governance and international law, this book reflects a diversity of scholarly interpretations. The editors, who hold sharply contrasting views on some of the most salient issues, have selected contributions that reveal the logic of competing approaches, and that generate dynamic tension rather than harmony. The book as a whole seeks not to provide definitive answers, but to raise questions, and to lay a sound scholarly foundation for future debate.

II DEMOCRATIZATION AND THE INTERNATIONAL SYSTEM

It once seemed incontrovertible that, given the range of ideologies and institutional structures of member States, the international system was, by its very nature, neutral on the subject of the internal character, let alone legitimacy, of domestic regimes. The recent wave of democratization, however, has had ramifications for the conduct of international organizations, and consequently for international law.

The end of the Cold War occasioned a challenging new role for international organizations as architects for the rebuilding of shattered States in the developing world. In countries from Nicaragua to El Salvador to Cambodia to Angola to Bosnia, it has become almost a given that international organizations will culminate their efforts at national reconciliation with the holding of democratic elections. Not once has the international community proposed that a new, post-conflict government be chosen in any other way.[19]

What began as an adjunct to conflict resolution has grown to a broader, institutionalized, legitimating function. Many international organizations now maintain permanent electoral assistance divisions. In 1996 the United Nations Electoral Assistance Division received requests

---

[19] *See* Report of the Secretary-General, Support by the United Nations System of the Efforts of Governments to Promote and Consolidate New or Restored Democracies, UN Doc. A/53/554 & corr. 1 (1998); Sonia K. Han, Note, "Building a Peace that Lasts: the United Nations and Post-Civil War Peace Building," *N.Y.U. J. Int'l L. & Pol.* 26 (1994), p. 837. Nonetheless, in Bosnia's Republika Srpska, the international community has shown a willingness to override electoral outcomes where these have threatened to obstruct the implementation of the peace accord. *See, e.g.*, R. Jeffrey Smith, "Firing of Bosnian Serb President Fuels Tension," *The Washington Post* (Mar. 7, 1999), A21.

for aid from twenty-four member States, most of them in Africa, and most without the former predicate of a recently ended civil war.[20] Between 1990 and 1995 the European Union (EU) provided electoral assistance to forty-four different countries.[21] Similar statistics could be quoted for the OAS and the Office for Democratic Institutions and Human Rights of the OSCE. Many of these missions end with the organization determining whether the elections have been conducted according to criteria of fairness that have essentially achieved boilerplate status.[22] Necessarily, a determination as to whether an election was conducted properly speaks to the legitimacy of the purported victor's mandate to govern.

Such judgments sharply contradict the traditional international law maxim that the selection of national leaders is quintessentially a matter of exclusive domestic jurisdiction.[23] At the same time, such developments must be seen in context: international organizations are now involved in virtually every aspect of national policy-making, from budgeting priorities to labor issues to the eradication of official corruption. It is not self-evident that a great legal distance exists between weighing in on these important questions of policy and having a say in the selection of policy-makers themselves.

As notions of democratic legitimacy diffuse throughout the international legal system, one can identify at least four broad justifications for democratization as a concern of the international law. A crucial feature of these justifications is that they do not simply repeat pro-democratic arguments found in political theory. While some overlap with political theory is certainly evident, these arguments also reflect the distinctive interests of the international legal system. The arguments therefore address not only the well-being of those living within democratic systems, but the interests of outsiders as well.

The first justification is a perceived connection between competitive multiparty elections and the range of other internationally protected human rights. For reasons of Cold War politics – relating primarily to

---

[20] *Electoral Assistance Activities of the United Nations System* (Electoral Assistance Division, United Nations Department of Political Affairs, 1996), p. 5.

[21] Report from the Commission on the Implementation of Measures Intended to Promote Observance of Human Rights and Democratic Principles, COM(96)672 (1997), p. 6.

[22] These are set out in detail in the UN Center for Human Rights' *Human Rights and Elections: A Handbook on the Legal, Technical and Human Rights Aspects of Elections* (Geneva: United Nations, 1994).

[23] As Oppenheim stated in the first edition of his treatise: "The Law of Nations prescribes no rules as regards the kind of head a State may have. Every State is, naturally, independent regarding this point, possessing the faculty of adopting any Constitution according to its discretion," Lasa Oppenheim, *International Law* vol. 1, (1905), p. 403.

the impossibility of agreement that free and fair elections were a human right on par with core norms such as the right against torture – these two categories have been consistently described in discrete terms: democracy *and* human rights.[24] Nonetheless, international organizations increasingly assert that a commitment to the principles of choice, transparency and pluralism that mark political democracy is essential to securing an institutionalized protection of other human rights.[25] This is hardly a new insight: the mutually reinforcing nature of broad political participation and individual freedom has been a major theme in Western political thought over the past two centuries.[26]

Second, democratization is increasingly regarded as a means of preventing internal armed conflict, which in the 1990s has been unrivaled as the leading form of deadly strife.[27] Democratization is said to address the exclusionary politics lying at the heart of civil conflicts. As UN Secretary-General Kofi Annan has stated, "in the absence of genuinely democratic institutions, contending interests are likely to seek to settle

[24] *See* Vienna Declaration and Programme of Action, UN Doc A/Conf. 157/23, para. 8 (1993) ("[t]he international community should support the strengthening and promoting of democracy, development and respect for human rights"); Annual Report of the Secretary-General on the Work of the Organization, UN Doc. A/52/1, paras. 22 ff. (section of report entitled "Governance, Human Rights and Democratization"); Case C-268/94, Portuguese Republic v. Council of the European Union, 1996–12 ECJ Rep. 6177, 6217 (1996) (Article 130(2) of the EC Treaty "demonstrates the importance to be attached to respect for human rights and democratic principles"); Case 10.956, Inter-Am. Comm'n Hum. Rts. (Mexico), *reprinted in Annual Report of the Inter-American Commission on Human Rights, 1993* (1994), pp. 259, 269 ("[t]he close relationship between representative democracy as a form of government and the exercise of the political rights so defined, also presupposes the exercise of other fundamental rights"); Final Declaration and Action Plan on Human Rights and Democracy of the Council of Europe's Second Summit Meeting of Heads of State and Governments 1997 (1997), *reprinted in Int'l Hum. Rts. Rep.* 5 (1998), p. 581 (reaffirming "attachment to the fundamental principles of the Council of Europe – pluralist democracy, respect for human rights, the rule of law").

[25] Report of the Secretary-General: Supplement to Reports on Democratization, UN Doc. A/51/761 (Annex), para. 3 (1996) ("the practice of democracy is increasingly regarded as essential to progress on a wide range of human concerns and to the protection of human rights"); Inter-American Commission on Human Rights, *Ten Years of Activities 1971–81* (1982), p. 337 ("the democratic context is the necessary element for the establishment of a political society where human rights can thrive to their fullest").

[26] *See, e.g.,* James Madison, *The Federalist,* nos. 39, 51, *in* Michael Kammen, ed., *The Origins of the American Constitution: A Documentary History* (New York: Penguin Books, 1986), pp. 180–86, 202–12; Benjamin Constant, "The Liberty of the Ancients Compared with That of the Moderns," *in* Benjamin Constant, Biancamaria Fontana, trans., *Political Writings* (Cambridge University Press, 1988) pp. 307, 323; John Stuart Mill, "Considerations on Representative Government," *in Utilitarianism, On Liberty, and Considerations on Representative Government* (London: J. M. Dent and Sons Ltd., 1972), p. 171.

[27] In approving an electoral monitoring mission at the end of a long and brutal civil war in Liberia, for example, the Security Council declared "that the holding of free and fair elections as scheduled is an essential phase of the peace process in Liberia" SC Res. 1100 (1997). *See also* SC Res. 1116 (1997) (same).

their differences through conflict rather than through accommodation."[28] In the Secretary-General's words, "democratization gives people a stake in society. Its importance cannot be overstated, for unless people feel that they have a true stake in society lasting peace will not be possible."[29]

Third, and relatedly, democratization has been asserted as a key to peace among States. The widely reported finding that democratic States do not go to war with one another, though not uncontroversial in its particulars,[30] has led many to link the international community's security interests to the promotion of democratic governance within States.

Finally, a range of emerging international norms, unrelated to democratization, have come to rely upon implementation through democratic processes. Three examples of this phenomenon can be found in the international efforts to protect the environment, to fight official corruption, and to promote the rights of indigenous peoples.[31] In each of these cases, instruments establishing the regimes provide for the maximum degree of popular participation in formulating strategies for implementing a State's international obligations. The instruments also require the sort of transparent decision-making processes and free flow of information that are typical of democratic systems.[32]

International organizations have used the limited carrots and sticks available to tie progress in democratization to receipt of various international entitlements. Such devices have included links between democratization and recognition of new States and governments,[33] the withholding of development assistance to States unwilling to pursue democratic reforms,[34] and the conditioning of full membership in the

---

[28] Report of the Secretary-General: The Causes of Conflict and the Promotion of Durable Peace and Sustainable Development in Africa (1998), para 77.   [29] *Ibid.*, para. 78.
[30] For a collection of scholarly articles on both sides of the "democratic peace" controversy, *see* Michael E. Brown, Sean M. Lynn-Jones and Steven E. Miller, eds., *Debating the Democratic Peace* (Cambridge, Mass.: The MIT Press, 1996).
[31] For an extended discussion of these points, *see* Remarks of Gregory H. Fox, "Implementing Democratization: What Role for International Organizations?" *ASIL Proc.* 91 (1997), pp. 356, 360–62.
[32] The United Nations Economic Commission for Europe, for example, has devoted an entire treaty to the participatory aspects of environmental law-making. *See* Convention on Access to Information, Public Participation in Decision-Making and Access to Justice in Environmental Matters, UN Doc. ECE/CEP/43 (1998). Article 1 provides that in order to protect the right of every person to live in a healthy environment, "each Party shall guarantee the rights of access to information, public participation in decision-making, and access to justice in environmental matters in accordance with the provisions of this Convention."   [33] *See infra*, chapter 4.
[34] Stephen Haggard and Steven B. Webb, eds., *Voting for Reform: Democracy, Political Liberalization and Economic Adjustment* (New York: Oxford University Press, 1994); Leila L. Frischtak, *Governance Capacity and Economic Reform in Developing Countries*, World Bank Technical Paper no. 254 (1994).

EU, OAS and MERCOSUR on the maintenance of political democracy.[35] One of the most interesting forms of this new conditionality is the EU's predicating its adherence to new treaty obligations on other parties' observance of democratic norms. All new EU treaties specify observance of democratic principles as an essential element of the accord, a material breach of which would permit the Union to suspend compliance with its treaty obligations.[36]

Moreover, in the cases of Haiti (1991-94) and Sierra Leone (1997-98), intergovernmental organizations not only denied delegation credentials to military regimes that seized power from elected governments, but also took direct action to reverse the coups by means of external armed force. The Security Council directly authorized intervention in the former case, and gave indirect, *post hoc* authorization to a regional organization in the latter.[37]

In the *Tinoco* Arbitration, William Howard Taft famously held that "non-recognition [of governments] on the ground of illegitimacy of origin was not a postulate of international law and did not secure general acquiescence."[38] Intervening events, however, have cast doubt on this conventional wisdom, and have raised the question of the emergence of a right to democratic governance in international law. Such an emergent right, if established, is so thoroughly at odds with traditional

---

[35] The Maastricht Treaty on European Union provides that democracy and respect for human rights, as set forth in the European Convention on Human Rights, shall be pre-conditions for membership in the European Union Treaty on European Union, Title I(F), ILM 31 (1992) pp. 247, 256. The Washington Protocol to the OAS Charter provides for the suspension from the General Assembly of any member State whose democratically constituted government has been overthrown by force. OAE/Ser.P, AG/doc.11 (XVI-E/92) rev. 1 (1992). MERCOSUR's 1996 Protocol of Ushuaia provides that any disruption of democracy in a member State may lead to the suspension of that State's right to participate in MERCOSUR organs and a suspension of its rights under the preferential trade instruments promulgated by the organization. *Protocol de Ushuaia Sobre Compromiso Democrático en el Mercosur, la Republica de Bolivia y la Republica de Chile*, Arts. 4 & 5 (1996), *available at* <www.idrc.ca/lacro/investigacion/mercosur2.html>. The member States of MERCOSUR are Argentina, Brazil, Paraguay, and Uruguay.

[36] *On the Inclusion of Respect for Democratic Principles and Human Rights in Agreements between the Community and Third Countries*, COM(95)215 (1995). Democratic principles are defined by reference to the Helsinki Final Act, Aug. 1, 1975, ILM 14, p. 1292, and the OSCE Charter of Paris, Nov. 21, 1990, ILM 30 (1991), p. 190. *See* Barbara Brandtner and Allan Rosas, "Human Rights and the External Relations of the European Community: an Analysis of Doctrine and Practice," *Eur. J. Int'l L.* 9 (1998), pp. 468, 473-77.

[37] *See* note 11 *supra*. Though it is far from established that the forcible removal of democratic regimes *per se* authorizes the Security Council to declare a "threat to the peace" under Article 39 of the UN Charter, thereby suspending a State's Article 2(7) entitlement to freedom from "intervention in matters essentially within the domestic jurisdiction," there can now be no question that a crisis provoked by an interruption of democratic processes can lead to such a Security Council response.   [38] Great Britain v. Costa Rica, 1923-24 Ann. Dig. Pub. Int'l L. Cas. 34, 37 (1923).

conceptions of State sovereignty as to augur a major transformation of the ground rules of the international system.

III THE DEMOCRATIC ENTITLEMENT THESIS: SCOPE AND CONSEQUENCES

Because the assertion of a "democratic entitlement" in international law is grounded in the right to political participation as established in Article 21 of the Universal Declaration of Human Rights (UDHR), Article 25 of the ICCPR, and the counterpart articles of regional human rights instruments, the questions posed by the thesis may, at first glance, appear confined to the human rights treaty system. As that system provides for only the most limited of remedies and notoriously lacks efficacious enforcement mechanisms, one might well imagine that the specification of its requirements in respect of political participation, as in respect of freedom of speech or religion or association, would be a development of limited significance to international law, organization, and relations overall.

Yet the right to political participation, at least as interpreted through the lens of the democratic entitlement, is unlike other human rights, for its individual enjoyment is inseparable from its collective effect. One participates in politics not solely (and usually not principally) for the fulfillment derived from the activity, but for the opportunity to affect the exercise of power in the polity. From the liberal–democratic perspective, to have the individual right to political participation is to have the collective right to oust a political leadership that fails to garner the support of at least a plurality of one's fellows. Article 21 of the UDHR, in a manner strikingly dissimilar to that of the document's other Articles and that of the ICCPR, speaks not merely of the individual right to take part in government, but also of the principle that "[t]he will of the people shall be the basis of the authority of government."[39]

If the very basis of the authority of government can be said to rest, as a matter of international law, on the fulfillment of liberal–democratic participatory standards, the consequences will be wide-ranging. Indeed, if the sovereignty affirmed and protected by the international system is understood to be popular sovereignty, and popular sovereignty is understood to be predicated upon liberal democracy, the potential result is a

---

[39] GA Res. 217 (III) (1948).

revolutionary transformation of the full array of international norms, from norms governing recognition of States and governments to those governing the use of force. Thus, the most pointed interpretation of the democratic entitlement, espoused in chapter 7 by W. Michael Reisman, would permit unilateral armed intervention across State boundaries to depose a regime that has usurped an electoral mandate.

It is by no means clear that the argument for a democratic entitlement need be taken to such a conclusion. Nonetheless, the democratic entitlement thesis generates a progression of path-breaking legal conclusions that has no clear stopping point.

The progression can be elaborated as follows. The democratic entitlement thesis expressly embodies two assertions:

(1) The right to political participation, however deliberately vague its specifications in human rights instruments that were adopted prior to the recent wave of liberal–democratic transitions, has now acquired a determinate content grounded in liberal–democratic institutional practices.

(2) The right entails not merely the existence of appropriate participatory mechanisms, but also a determinate relationship between the mandated participatory mechanisms and the actual exercise of political power. As in the UDHR, but not the ICCPR, the individual right to cast a vote reflecting uncoerced choice is organically connected to the proposition that "[t]he will of the people shall be the basis of the authority of government." The regime has a duty not merely to allow individuals "to take part in government" through a consultative process, but also a duty to subject itself to the popular will – *i.e.*, to allow itself to be voted out of power.

From these two assertions, one can well infer a third:

(3) The sovereignty affirmed by the international legal system belongs to the people, and can be cognizably asserted on the people's behalf only where the government conforms to the right to political participation; therefore, measures to implement democratic rights, undertaken by foreign States collectively and/or individually, need not respect the sovereign prerogatives of governments that violate those rights. This is especially so where a "free and fair election" has actually taken place, and those elected have been denied, or ousted from, office by force of arms.

The third assertion is, of course, the critical one. Though they have not unambiguously embraced it, the early works of the democratic entitlement school hint at it.[40] Acceptance of the third assertion is, perhaps, not necessarily compelled by acceptance of the first and second, but it is the logical next step.

The third assertion leaves open the practical question of how to further democratic development across borders. It does not necessarily mandate de-recognition of regimes that fail to abide by international standards; proponents of the democratic entitlement neither assert as *lex lata* nor propose *de lege ferenda* a mechanistic rule by which certificates of recognition, IGO delegation credentials, and diplomatic and trade relations are automatically to be denied to violators. Still less does the democratic entitlement thesis predict that measures will be taken to intervene in any particular State's internal affairs, whether by intrusive political or economic measures (e.g., covert funding of opposition groups in violation of municipal law, or secondary boycotts to disrupt a State's trade relations) or by forcible measures (e.g., supply of insurgents or outright invasion).[41] Given the realities of international relations, none of these measures is likely to be used routinely against non-democratic governments.

What the democratic entitlement thesis does suggest, however, is that whereas intrusive political, economic, and military measures would previously have been excluded as violative of international law, they may now be included on the menu of lawful options for foreign powers seeking – collectively or perhaps even unilaterally – to implement democratization in a recalcitrant State. While limitations on aggressive promotion of democracy would continue to arise from considerations of efficacy and prudence, the bars traditionally posed by international law would be, at a minimum, open to question. In an international system that has repeatedly affirmed the sovereign right of each State to be free from the coer-

---

[40] Gregory Fox has characterized the extent of the legal implications of a regime's violation of the right as "an open question," but hints that "a regime that bases its legitimacy on nothing more than the fact that it holds power exercises no 'sovereign' authority to object" to international enforcement. Gregory H. Fox, "The Right to Political Participation in International Law," *Yale J. Int'l L.* 17 (1992), pp. 539ff., at p. 595. Thomas Franck has proposed "that legitimate governments should be assured of protection from overthrow by totalitarian forces through concerted systemic forces after – and *only* after – the community has recognized that such an exigency has arisen." Franck, *supra* note 18, p. 91 (emphasis in original). Others writing in this vein have been far less cautious. *See, e.g.*, Anthony D'Amato, "The Invasion of Panama was a Lawful Response to Tyranny," *Am. J. Int'l L.* 84 (1990), p. 516.

[41] In his seminal article, Thomas Franck warns that efforts to implement the democratic entitlement need "to be uncoupled, in the clearest fashion, from a long history of unilateral enforcement of a tainted, colonialist 'civilizing' mission"; he thus urges that "all states unambiguously renounce the use of unilateral, or even regional, *military* force to compel compliance. . . ." (Franck, *supra* note 18, p. 84 [emphasis in original]).

cive interferences of others in its choice of political, economic, social, and cultural systems,[42] this alone is a revolutionary proposition.

Adherents of the democratic entitlement characterize it as an "emerging" right. They understand full well that undemocratic regimes continue to be tolerated in the international community. They do not assert that collective practice and *opinio juris* as yet manifest any legal *duties* of foreign States and intergovernmental organizations to adopt specific democracy-promoting measures. They are aware that expediency will ever undermine consistency in efforts to promote democracy. They insist, however, that the legal door is now open to determined efforts to spur democratization, and that the failure to do good everywhere should not be seen as a bar to doing good anywhere.

IV MISGIVINGS ABOUT THE DEMOCRATIC ENTITLEMENT

Although many observers have expressed doubts about the democratic entitlement, there have been few scholarly efforts to examine it skeptically at length.[43] The case against the democratic entitlement rests in part on a narrower reading of the source material cited as evidence of the "emerging norm" and on a recitation of the countervailing collective practices and pronouncements that highlight the continued inviolability of the "essence" of domestic jurisdiction.[44] Intrusive international involvement in the establishment of democratic procedures has been accompanied either by consent of the target State's effective government or by extraordinary circumstances, and intergovernmental bodies have often expressly disavowed any general principle licensing the imposition of such procedures on sovereign States.[45]

More profoundly, however, skepticism of the democratic entitlement may be grounded in a more open-textured interpretation of the concept of popular sovereignty than the one embraced by the entitlement's proponents. The argument for such an interpretation can be rendered as follows.

---

[42] *See* GA Res 2625 (XXV) (1970) (the "Friendly Relations Declaration").
[43] The most elaborate exception is the work of one of the co-editors of this volume. *See* Brad R. Roth, *Governmental Illegitimacy in International Law* (Oxford University Press, 1999).
[44] *See ibid.*, pp. 321–44.
[45] *See, e.g.*, GA Res. 49/180 (1994) (emphasizing that absent a State's request for electoral assistance, electoral matters are essentially within the domestic jurisdiction); *see also* Boutros Boutros-Ghali, *An Agenda for Democratization* (New York: United Nations, 1996), pp. 1, 3 (UN Secretary-General notes that "individual states decide if and when to begin democratization" and that the new emphasis on democratization "does not imply a change" in the traditional principle of non-intervention).

One can acknowledge that, within the scheme of the United Nations system, sovereignty ultimately belongs to peoples and not to governments, and still question whether a liberal–democratic institutional structure is the ultimate and indispensable vehicle of popular will. Indeed, in reducing popular will to the outcome of specified processes, adherents of the "emerging right to democratic governance" neither worship empirical popular will nor own up to the consequences of an inherently teleological – and therefore ideological and controvertible – enterprise.

On the one hand, no empirical account of popular satisfaction with an authoritarian system would satisfy the democratic entitlement. It would not be sufficient even for a dictatorship to hold a verifiably honest plebiscite on the continuation of dictatorial rule, since the "proper conditions" for the exercise of popular will require a remaking of authoritarian institutions to allow for knowing, willing, and intelligent collective choice. Putting aside the problem that liberal–democratic structures may not alone establish the requisites of a collective choice that is genuinely knowing (based on good information), willing (not merely a choice among options imposed by the will of elites or by circumstance), and intelligent (taken in circumstances that allow for proper reflection, including widely available education, a robust societal marketplace of ideas, and the absence of distortive economic pressures), the posited "conditions of choice" require the very institutional transformation – perhaps an irreversible one – about which the populace was supposed to be empowered to choose. And even then, adherents of the democratic entitlement would not take no for an answer, on the ground that the present majority cannot legitimately vote to deny the democratic right to future instantiations of the polity.[46] Though justifiable from the standpoint of a particular comprehensive worldview, this is a rather presumptuous approach to popular self-determination.

On the other hand, the calculated effort to specify the democratic entitlement without express reference to wider social goals entails a contradiction. In defining democracy in essentially procedural terms, the democratic entitlement school follows the contemporary comparative politics literature in rejecting teleological definitions that render democratic performance inherently unmeasurable by social science techniques.[47] Yet political scientists justify this sterile definition, so much

---

[46] *See, e.g.*, Gregory H. Fox and Georg Nolte, "Intolerant Democracies," chapter 12 of this volume.
[47] *See, e.g.*, Samuel Huntington, *The Third Wave: Democratization in the Late Twentieth Century* (Norman, Okla.: University of Oklahoma Press, 1991), pp. 5–13.

at odds with the term's role in both classical theory and popular morality, by purporting (perhaps not always ingenuously) to lighten the term's normative baggage – that is, by identifying democracy as, at most, one of many political virtues.[48] The democratic entitlement school restores to the term "democracy" its former normative weight as the *sine qua non* of governmental legitimacy, but not its former complexity as a realization of substantive ends and, thus, an object of ideological contestation.

Not only are there, as everyone concedes, other perceived first-order political virtues besides "procedural democracy," but the many who have yet to adopt the whole of the liberal–democratic worldview (and, more troublingly yet, even some of those who have) frequently perceive the former virtues to be achievable, in certain circumstances, only at the expense of the latter. Majorities occasionally choose – if, perhaps, unwisely – to eschew or to void liberal-democratic procedures where these appear to jeopardize other virtues.

On such occasions, one can always posit a "higher" popular will, at odds with empirical manifestations, that embodies the "objective" interests of the populace, perhaps locating the "true" collective decision in customary practice or an heroic revolutionary moment. Yet for the democratic entitlement to have recourse to such devices, it must take its place alongside every other variant of political messianism. It must accept the insight that what ultimately count as democratic are such acts as are calculated to bring about a "truly" democratic social reality, the insight that inspires the bearers of a substantive political faith (liberal democrats included)[49] to eschew procedural niceties as needed. Perhaps the liberal–democratic faith is the true faith – it unquestionably has a better track record than all the rest – but it is hard to argue that a genuine international consensus has emerged on this point.

From the standpoint of those skeptical of the democratic entitlement, then, what remains is a partisan vision dressed up as international law, thereby to supply a rationale for meddling in the internal affairs of foreign political communities. When one affirms that the term "democracy" demarcates the moral high ground in political struggle, one must also acknowledge that the word encompasses the universe of political virtues as variously perceived, at which point democracy's presence or absence largely ceases to be an empirical question. This acknowledg-

---

[48] See ibid., p. 10.
[49] Note the substantial support among liberal democrats for Algeria's 1992 coup that nullified the Islamic fundamentalist electoral victory, for Russia's 1993 sending of troops to disperse the elected legislature, and so on.

ment should, arguably, lead the international actor to fall back on the principle of respect for the internal processes, however ragged, of countries not one's own.

To be sure, some consensus has emerged, at least, as to what democracy *is not*. One need only invoke "Democratic Kampuchea" to point out that the existence of twilight does not refute the distinction between day and night.[50] But the "democratic" merits of real-life political struggles in diverse lands are seldom so reliably judged from abroad, let alone reliably judged on the basis of a mechanistic application of procedural criteria. Or so an opponent of the democratic entitlement may contend.

V THE STRUCTURE OF THE COLLECTION

In the chapters of this collection, leading authors grapple with the effects on international law of the global trend toward democratic structures of governance. Although no one volume can provide comprehensive treatment of the wide range of issues that this theme presents, the coverage is expansive.

The first part of the book explores the systemic foundations of the right to political participation in international law. The first two contributors, Thomas M. Franck and Gregory H. Fox, wrote two of the earliest contributions to what has become the "democratic entitlement school."[51] In their chapters, Franck and Fox trace international attention to political participation from its origin in the principle of self-determination and in vague and neglected provisions of human rights instruments. They then examine its current embodiment in the practices of intergovernmental organizations that exhort States to democratize, that conduct increasingly routinized election monitoring, and that respond to the usurpation of electoral mandates. These chapters consider the prospects for more aggressive implementation of the right to political participation, as well as the limits imposed by other norms. James Crawford follows with an assessment of the place of a right to democracy in the body of international legal doctrine. He analyzes potential implications of the emergence of a "democratic entitlement" for a wide

---

[50] The constitution of Democratic Kampuchea indeed dutifully provided for an elected legislature (Arts. 5–7), proclaimed "complete equality among all Kampuchean people" (Art. 13) and described various aspects of Cambodian society as "democratic" in three separate articles (Arts. 1, 13 and 21). *Reprinted in* François Ponchaud, *Cambodia Year Zero* (New York: Holt, Rinehart and Winston, 1978), p. 199.   [51] *See* Franck, *supra* note 18; Fox, *supra* note 40.

range of questions that not long ago were regarded as definitively settled, such as the legal capacity of an undemocratic, but effective, regime to undertake transactions that will remain binding on the State after the regime's demise.

The second part deals with the effect of the recent democratization developments on inter-State relations. Sean D. Murphy assesses the extent to which the trend has affected recognition practices. He finds that democratic norms have begun to affect, though they by no means dominate, the criteria for recognition of both States and governments. Stephen J. Schnably examines in detail the recent practice of one intergovernmental organization, the Organization of American States, which has proclaimed a commitment to the furtherance and preservation of democracy within its member States, a policy that has achieved uneven results. Anne-Marie Slaughter explores the ways in which democratization has contributed to the emergence of a "transgovernmental" order, one in which domestic governmental institutions of democratic States cooperatively address transboundary problems such as environmental degradation, organized crime, and terrorism.

The third part deals with democracy and the use of force. W. Michael Reisman argues that traditional conceptions of State sovereignty that operate to shield dictatorial regimes are "anachronistic," and that non-intervention norms must give way, in appropriate circumstances, to foreign uses of force – even unilateral ones – that vindicate popular will. In contrast, the succeeding chapter by Michael Byers and Simon Chesterman takes exception to Reisman's suggestion that a pro-democratic agenda permits States to use force in a manner not, in their view, contemplated by the United Nations Charter. David Wippman offers a variation on the theme of pro-democratic intervention, analyzing the legal effect of "invitation" of the legitimate government of a State and exploring the prospect of "treaties of guarantee" that might provide advance consent to restore a democratic system in the event of its ouster by *coup d'état*. Brad R. Roth argues, *contra* Wippman, that such "pro-democratic invasion pacts" would be void *ab initio* as violations of peremptory norms of the international system. John M. Owen explores the implications for the international system of the "democratic peace" thesis – the assertion that democracies do not go to war with one another. Although identifying strong empirical connections between a State's liberal ideology and peacefulness toward other States perceived as like-minded, he cautions that international organizations should not thereby acquire a mandate to create liberal polities through force of arms. Such a crusade, he warns, may produce unintended and self-defeating consequences.

The fourth part deals with the problems posed by conflicting imperatives. The chapter by Gregory Fox and Georg Nolte examines the question of whether such democratic values as are affirmed in international law require toleration of political forces that would, if given the opportunity, destroy the democratic system itself. Fox and Nolte respond in the negative, provoking two brief critical comments, by Martti Koskenniemi and Brad Roth, that take the opportunity to raise questions about the "democratic entitlement" itself. These comments, in turn, draw a Fox–Nolte rejoinder. Lastly in this part, Steven R. Ratner examines the potential tension between furthering smooth transitions to democracy and assuring accountability for human rights violations committed under outgoing authoritarian regimes.

The fifth and final part is devoted to approaches critical of the democratic entitlement. Brad Roth cautions that the current literature tends to exaggerate the extent of democratic progress in certain countries, thereby encouraging unwarranted support for their governments, while at the same time failing to appreciate political achievements of a different nature. Jan Knippers Black notes the failure of the new democracies to provide genuine empowerment for broad sectors of their populations. Susan Marks warns that assertions of a democratic entitlement are distorted by a "liberal millenarianism" that obscures the depth and complexity of the democratic ideal.

VI CONCLUSION

As the essays in this volume make clear, analyzing a right to democratic governance involves substantially more than predicting the future of recent democratic transitions. To be sure, the contours of a democratic entitlement will be shaped by the same political forces affecting every rule of international law.[52] But the democratic entitlement involves indeterminacy of an entirely different order, for the putative right embodies a marriage of law and politics that is in many ways unprecedented in international law. The entitlement is not simply law *affected by* politics. It is law that penetrates and regulates the very essence of political life, both domestically and internationally.

[52] For a fascinating discussion of how customary norms are shaped by asymmetrical power structures, *see* Michael Byers, *Custom, Power and the Power of Rules: International Relations and Customary International Law* (Cambridge University Press, 1999).

Domestically, the democratic entitlement sets out a theoretical blueprint for the proper allocation of national political power. In so doing it assumes a critical degree of trust and cooperation on the part of all factions participating in democratic institutions. While Fox and Nolte argue in chapter 12 that democracies may defend themselves against uncooperative anti-democratic actors by restricting their participation in elections, the uncertain record of democratic transitions in Africa, Central Europe, and Central Asia suggests that political actors determined to subvert democratic institutions will usually succeed in doing so. The democratic entitlement thus appears to envision, for its success, a change not only in political institutions but in political cultures as well.[53] It was for this reason that the 1990 UN Observer Mission to Haiti warned the General Assembly that "there is no democratic tradition in Haitian politics . . . [and] violence has always been the means of settling conflicts and choosing leaders."[54] The governmental paralysis that followed "restoration" of Haitian democracy in 1994 appeared to confirm the monitors' prescience. Such vagaries of domestic politics are usually relevant to international norms only to the extent that they facilitate or impede state compliance with their terms. In the case of the democratic entitlement, however, domestic politics and the terms of compliance are one and the same.

Internationally, the democratic blueprint translates into a legal standard of regime legitimacy. Where a regime is considered illegitimate according to democratic theory, other States face a stark choice. If they continue business as usual with an undemocratic regime, they implicitly affirm its capacity to act as agent for the State – that is, to serve as the State's legitimate government. In that case, the democratic entitlement will have failed to make normative inroads into the political dynamic of inter-State relations. The norm will likely suffer as a result, taking on more the hue of a political aspiration than a binding guideline.

Alternatively, States may incorporate democratic legitimacy criteria into their foreign policies and refuse to carry on relations with undemocratic regimes. This was the approach of many States toward the apartheid regime in South Africa: until majoritarian elections were held, any

---

[53] The Secretary-General has observed, "democratization must begin with an effort to create a culture of democracy – a political culture, which is fundamentally non-violent and in which no one party or group expects to win or lose all the time." Support by the United Nations System of the Efforts of Governments to Promote and Consolidate New or Restored Democracies, UN Doc. A/51/761 (Annex), p. 7 (1996).

[54] First Report of the United Nations Observer Group for the Verification of the Elections in Haiti, UN Doc. A/45/870 (Annex), p. 9 (1990).

interaction with the regime was seen as an improper validation of its authority to act.[55] What if this were adopted as a global strategy toward all undemocratic regimes? As James Crawford, Michael Byers and Simon Chesterman describe in chapters 3 and 8, the consequences of effectively disenfranchising the world's non-democratic regimes would be almost unimaginable. International politics as it is now practiced would effectively halt. While proponents of a democratic entitlement would surely respond that no State (or the United Nations) is likely to adopt such a rigid legitimism, it is hard to dispute that a principle of non-recognition flows quite naturally from the internal logic of the democratic entitlement. Once again, political conflict is not exogenous to but inherent in the entitlement itself.

Two other aspects of the entitlement also bring political considerations to the fore. First, the view that democratic regimes are best able to implement a range of other international legal obligations[56] ties much of the case for the entitlement to realization of these other normative goals. But these other legal regimes may fail for a host of reasons unrelated to the democratic nature of participating States. Environmental norms, for example, while increasingly reliant on implementation strategies that utilize democratic political institutions, may be opposed by industry groups, may be perceived as inimical to appropriate rates of development, or may clash with other normative goals such as free trade. If these arguments succeed and schemes such as international environmental cooperation experience temporary or long-term failures, it will be the political power of those making the countervailing arguments that will contribute to undermining the case for the democratic entitlement.

Second, the democratic entitlement is often described as a necessary precondition to social progress in a wide range of other areas – protection of human rights, economic development, cultural diversity, etc.[57] On this view, democratization sits atop a hierarchy of normative goals.

---

[55] The myriad of international sanctions against the apartheid regime are detailed in I. E. Sagay, *The Southern African Situation and the Eventual Triumph of International Law* (Lagos, Nigeria: Nigerian Institute of Advanced Legal Studies, 1991), pp. 34–36. In a 1991 resolution the General Assembly set out the conditions for South Africa's reentry into international society: "only the total eradication of apartheid and the establishment of a non-racial, democratic society based on majority rule, through the full and free exercise of adult suffrage by all the people in a united and non-fragmented South Africa, can lead to a just and lasting solution to the situation in South Africa." GA Res. 46/130 (1991).   [56] *See* text accompanying notes 24–32, *supra*.

[57] "Because democratic Governments are freely chosen by their citizens and held accountable through periodic and genuine elections and other mechanisms, they are more likely to promote and respect the rule of law, respect individual and minority rights, cope effectively with social conflict, absorb migrant populations and respond to the needs of marginalized groups." Support by the United Nations System, *supra* note 53, p. 6.

But constructing such a hierarchy is as much an empirical statement of causation – a State must be democratic in order to achieve certain other normative objectives – as it is a ranking of values. And as an empirical statement it is susceptible to being proven false: Cuba has achieved remarkably high literacy rates; infant mortality in Singapore is among the world's lowest; ethnic conflict in Eastern and Central Europe was largely quiescent during the Communist era, etc. While these counter-examples are clearly debatable, it is the very prospect of debate that contributes to politicizing the democratic entitlement. The value of enforcing the entitlement as a legal rule becomes subject to the outcome of discussions involving highly complex issues of local culture, political economy and resource allocation. If democracy is thereby understood as a contingent value, then a legal rule embodying democratic principles will suffer from perpetual contingency as well.

In analyzing the normative possibilities of a democratic entitlement, the chapters that follow ask whether this extraordinary degree of politicization can be overcome. Will the broad community of States accept a Manichean rule that postulates a right way and a wrong way for governments to relate to their citizens and for States to relate to one another? This question cannot be answered simply by predicting a triumph of the democratic ideal, the "liberal millenarianism" described by Susan Marks in chapter 19. Reliance on political trends will not stand in for a rigorous legal analysis that investigates systemic consequences of a democratic norm.

An exercise in hindsight makes this point clear. In April 1917, former Secretary of State Elihu Root gave an address to the American Society of International Law, of which he was then President, entitled "The Effect of Democracy on International Law."[58] Speaking only a few weeks after American entry into the First World War, and brimming with Wilsonian optimism, Root argued that the forward march of democracy then evident would remove the fundamental cause of international conflict – the territorial ambitions of dynastic rulers. To Root, the trajectory of history was clear, as he listed country after country in which democratic reforms were taking hold. These included Russia, which he described as "engaged in establishing the new self-control of that vast Empire upon the basis of universal suffrage and republican institutions."[59] Root argued that because "democracies are absolutely dependent for their existence upon the preservation of law," respect for

---

[58] *Proc. Am. Soc. Int'l L.* 11 (1917), p. 2.
[59] *Ibid.* at p. 5. Root also described China as "throwing off the domination of the Manchu [and] striving to accustom her long-suffering and submissive millions to the idea of a constitutional right." *Ibid.*

international law would arise as a natural corollary to the spread of democracy. The designs of autocracies, by contrast, could not be constrained by the consensual and self-enforcing tools of international society: "The Congresses of Westphalia, of Vienna, of Berlin, and a multitude of others less conspicuous have sought to curb the evil through settings limits upon power by treaty. They have all failed."[60] Only change at the national level would bring lasting peace between nations:

> The progress of democracy . . . is dealing with the problem by destroying the type of government which has shown itself incapable of maintaining respect for law and justice and resisting the temptations of ambition, and by substituting a new form of government which in its nature is incapable of proceeding by the same methods, and necessarily responds to different motives and pursues different objects from the old autocratic offenders. Only when that task has been substantially accomplished will the advocates of law among nations be free from the inheritance of the former failure.[61]

This early articulation of the democratic peace thesis is as notable for its omissions as it is for the naïveté of its predictions. Root did not describe ways in which international law might encourage transitions to democracy. Nor did he assess the implications of its adopting political democracy as a normative goal. He appears to have assumed that the spread of democracy would portend little change in the direction or content of international rules. His focus was rather on the enhanced appeal and respect for existing international law that would come about once autocratic governments had given way to popularly elected regimes. The spread of democracy, in Root's view, was fundamentally a political question but one with important consequences for international law.

It is the goal of this collection to address the democratic entitlement directly as a legal question. Politics, we have noted, is ever present. But only by understanding how political democracy can be conceived as a legal obligation, whether existing normative structures can accommodate a right to democratic governance, and, if not, what sort of reforms would be needed, will wholesale reliance on political factors be avoided. Root, speaking in the midst of war and at the dawn of a truly global American foreign policy, may be forgiven for his misplaced optimism. But it is imperative that contemporary international lawyers eschew reliance on pure politics and focus their unique analytical tools on the idea of a legal right to democratic governance. This collection is an attempt to add their essential voice to what has become a vigorous global debate.

[60] *Ibid.* at p. 7.   [61] *Ibid.*

PART I

The normative foundations of a right to political participation

CHAPTER I

Legitimacy and the democratic entitlement
Thomas M. Franck

I DEVELOPING OVERLAPPING CONSENSUS

In the world that emerged after the collapse of the Fascist and Communist ideologies, the principal cause of war has become unfairness and anomie. How the means of a good life are distributed among peoples and persons and whether people and persons are adequately consulted in the decisions that determine their life-prospects: these are the principal determinants of war and peace.

The role of the State, in an era of increasing transnationalization of big decisions and of the localization of subsidiary ones, is to serve as the forum for that organized social discourse, leading to a high degree of consensus regarding *what is fair*. That consensus is essential to the avoidance of war: in particular, *civil war*, the principal form of belligerence in the new era.

The most important instrument for developing overlapping consensus is the voting booth. Attention must therefore be paid to democracy as a right protected by international law and institutions. Democracy does not provide a guarantee against civil war. It merely provides the only known process by which a genuine social discourse can proceed among persons legitimately representing the spectrum of opinions and interests in a community or *polis*. Without it, there can be decisions. There can even be negotiation and discourse. But there can never be a genuine social convergence.

"Democracy," as etymology suggests, concerns the role of people in governance. The right to democracy is the right of people to be consulted and to participate in the process by which political values are reconciled and choices made. Some aspects of this right are therefore, nowadays, encompassed in human rights instruments. Rights to free speech, press, religion, and assembly are examples of associational and discursive entitlements which are already formulated in conventions.

Even more recently, we have seen the emergence, specifically, of an internationally constituted right to electoral democracy that builds on the human rights canon, but seeks to extend the ambit of protected rights to ensure meaningful participation by the governed in the formal political decisions by which the quality of their lives and societies are shaped.

II THE CONSENT OF THE GOVERNED

More than two centuries have elapsed since the signatories of the U.S. Declaration of Independence endorsed two radical propositions. The first is that citizens should have "unalienable rights" protected by governments which derive "their just powers from the consent of the governed." We may call this the "democratic entitlement." In declaring this right, the authors were uninhibited by any trace of cultural modesty, baldly asserting its equal application to persons at all times and in all places. The second proposition, perhaps less noted by commentators, is that a nation earns "separate and equal station" in the community of states by demonstrating "a decent respect to the opinions of mankind." The authors of the Declaration evidently believed that the legitimacy of the new Confederation of American States was not established solely as a consequence of the *de facto* transfer of power from Britain to its colonies, but also required further acknowledgment by "mankind." This may be seen as a prescient glimpse of the power of the community of nations to validate government by consent, and invalidate all other governance.

For two hundred years, these two notions – that the right to govern depends on governments having met both the democratic entitlement of the governed and also the standards of the community of states – have remained a radical vision. This radical vision, while not yet fully encapsulated in law, is now rapidly becoming a normative rule of the international system. The "opinions of mankind" have begun in earnest to require that governments, as a prerequisite to membership in the community of nations, derive "their just powers from the consent of the governed." Increasingly, governments recognize that their legitimacy depends on meeting normative expectations of the community of States. Democracy is thus on the way to becoming a global entitlement, one which may be promoted and protected by collective international processes.

The UN Secretary-General, Kofi Annan, has succinctly put it thus:

"It is increasingly recognized that good governance is an essential building block for meeting the objectives of sustainable development, prosperity and peace . . . [G]ood governance comprises the rule of law, effective state institutions, transparency and accountability in the management of public affairs, respect for human rights, and the meaningful participation of all citizens in the political process of their countries and in decisions affecting their lives."[1]

III THE EMERGENCE OF AN INTERNATIONAL LEGAL ENTITLEMENT

While democracy has long been a right of people in some nations, enshrined in their constitutions and traditions and enforced by their judiciary and police, this has not been true universally. That democracy is *becoming* an entitlement in international law and process is due in part to the very recent political reality of a burgeoning pro-democracy movement within the States that constitute the world community. Most remarkable is the extent to which an international law-based entitlement is now urged by governments, themselves. This is a cosmic but unmysterious change. For nations surfacing from long and tragic submergence beneath bogus "people's democracy" or an outright dictatorship, the legitimation of power is a basic but elusive reform. As of late 1997, approximately 130 national governments were legally committed to permit open, multiparty, secret-ballot elections with a universal franchise. Most had joined this trend within the previous decade.[2] While a

---

[1] Report of the Secretary-General on the work of the Organization, GAOR, 52nd Sess., Supp. No. 1 (A/52/1), 1997, p. 5, para. 22.
[2] This enumeration was compiled by reference to reports in the *N.Y. Times* and the *Country Reports on Human Rights Practices*, prepared by the Department of State for the appropriate committees of Congress. States which currently make legal provision for determining their governments by recourse to multiparty secret ballot elections are: Albania, Andorra, Angola, Antigua and Barbuda, Argentina, Australia, Austria, Bahamas, Bangladesh, Barbados, Belarus, Belgium, Belize, Benin, Bolivia, Bosnia, Botswana, Brazil, Bulgaria, Canada, Cape Verde, Central African Republic, Chile, Colombia, Comoros, Congo, Cook Islands, Costa Rica, Côte d'Ivoire, Croatia, Cyprus, Czech Republic, Denmark, Djibouti, Dominica, Dominican Republic, Ecuador, Egypt, El Salvador, Eritrea, Estonia, Finland, France, Gabon, Gambia, Georgia, Germany, Greece, Grenada, Guatemala, Guinea, Guyana, Hungary, Honduras, Iceland, India, Ireland, Israel, Italy, Jamaica, Japan, Kazakhstan, Kenya, Kiribati, Korea (South), Latvia, Lesotho, Liberia, Liechtenstein, Lithuania, Luxembourg, Macedonia, Madagascar, Malawi, Malaysia, Mali, Malta, Marshall Islands, Mauritius, Mexico, Micronesian Federation, Moldova, Mongolia, Morocco, Mozambique, Namibia, Nauru, Nepal, Netherlands, New Zealand, Nicaragua, Niger, Norway, Pakistan, Panama, Papua New Guinea, Paraguay, Peru, Philippines, Poland, Portugal, Romania, Russia, San Marino, Sao Tome, Senegal, Serbia, Seychelles, Singapore, Slovakia, Slovenia, Solomon Islands, South Africa, Spain, Sri Lanka, St. Kitts, St. Lucia, St. Vincent,

few may arguably be democratic in form rather than substance, most are, or are in the process of becoming, genuinely open to meaningful political choice. Many of these new regimes want, indeed need, to be validated by being seen to comply with global standards for free and open elections. This is new and important.

The almost-complete triumph of Humeian, Lockean, Jeffersonian, Montesquieuian, or Madisonian notions of democracy (in Latin America, Africa, Eastern Europe, and to a lesser extent in Asia) may well prove to be the most profound event of the twentieth century, and will in all likelihood create the fulcrum on which the future development of global society will turn. It is the unanswerable response to claims that free, open, multiparty, electoral parliamentary democracy is neither desired nor desirable outside a small enclave of Western industrial States.

The question is not whether democracy has swept the boards, but whether global society is ready for an era in which *only* democracy and the rule of law will be capable of validating governance. This may be a venerable philosophical issue, known to Plato,[3] but it is also a functional question which can be, and is now being, stated in global legal terms. Are we witnessing the evolution of an international rule system which defines the minimal requisites for a democratic process to exercise power? What norms will such a rule system encompass? Is the international community capable, consensually, of developing an institutional and normative framework for monitoring fulfillment of those requisites? Is the community of nations able collectively to recognize and to sanction noncompliance?

In other words, it is now time to ask whether the community of nations is ready to assume systematic responsibility for a new task of dazzling importance and complexity: the validation of governance in member states. Do we have, or are we in the process of evolving, a legit-

---

Footnote 2 (*cont.*)
Sweden, Switzerland, Tajikistan, Tanzania, Thailand, Tonga, Trinidad, Tunisia, Turkey, Tuvalu, Ukraine, United Kingdom, Uruguay, Vanuatu, Venezuela, Western Samoa, Zambia, Zimbabwe. Several more States, such as Ethiopia, are committed to free, multiparty elections but have not yet enacted the necessary constitutional or legislative fiat. It must also be conceded that there are borderline cases, such as Morocco (included) and Jordan (not included), Kenya (included), Singapore (included) and Serbia (included), as well as several former Soviet States which were not included. The somewhat subjective judgment, here, pertains to whether the elections were decisive, depending on various factors. In the large majority of cases, however, the decision to include or exclude is not seriously in doubt. It should be recalled, however, that the test for inclusion is whether the legal system establishes free and secret elections. Whether these are conducted fairly is another question.

[3] Plato's effort, in the *Statesman*, the *Laws* and the *Republic*, to define the extent to which a ruler's legitimacy is validated by wisdom, on the one hand, and by his subordination to the laws on the other, is analyzed *in* G. Sabine, *A History of Political Theory* (rev. edn. 1953), pp. 67–105.

imate international system of rules and processes for requiring and monitoring the compliance of nations with a new global democratic order?

IV TWO LEGITIMACIES

These questions, in turn, raise two separate issues of legitimacy which, although related, should not be confused. First, there is the legitimacy of national *governments*. Secondly, there is the legitimacy of the increasing *international validation* of the governance, and the rules and processes of that validation. It is the latter issue which is of primary interest to the international lawyer (although the importance stems from its manifest connection with the legitimacy of governments). We are witnessing a sea change in international law, as a result of which the legitimacy of each government will one day be measured definitively by international rules and processes. We are not quite there yet, but the outlines are emerging of such a new world, in which the citizens of each State will look to international law and organization to guarantee them fair access to political power and participation in societal decisions. For some people, this will be no more than an embellishment of existing rights already protected by domestic constitutional order. For others, it will be a dream come true.

Citizens, however, will not be the only beneficiaries. We have observed that the prime motivation for democratic entitlement is the need of governments for validation. Without validation, the task of governance is fraught with difficulty. In other words, validation is prized as evidence of a regime's legitimacy. Legitimacy, in turn, is the quality of a rule – or of a system of rules, or a process for making or interpreting rules – which by its manifest fairness pulls those addressed towards voluntary compliance.

In Western democracies legitimacy has been achieved largely by subjecting the political process to rules, which are often immutably entrenched in an intrepid constitution. In such States the fairness of the electoral process is monitored by credible local actors ranging from perceptive judges to investigative journalists. Thus a lucky few nations have succeeded in evolving their own legitimate means of validating the process by which the people choose those to whom they entrust the exercise of power. To achieve such a system of autochthonous validation, those who hold or seek political power have made a farsighted bargain comparable to John Locke's social compact:[4] to facilitate governing they have surrendered control over the nation's validation process to various

---

[4] *See* John Locke, *Two Treatises of Government*, W. Carpenter, ed. (New York: Dutton, 1966), pp. 119–20, 164–66.

others such as national electoral commissions, judges, an inquisitive press, and above all to the citizenry acting at the ballot box. These decide collectively whether the requisites for democratic entitlement have been met by those who claim the right to govern. This process bestows legitimacy, giving back to those who govern far more power than they surrendered.

Unfortunately, in many nations no such bargain was struck. Those who claim to govern cannot demonstrate that they have fulfilled the requirements of democracy, even if they purport to recognize that obligation. Senegal affords a recent example. In 1988, when elections were widely perceived to have been rigged, the victors' claim to power was not legitimated and they failed to secure the consent of the governed.[5] The promise of stability was not realized. In such circumstances, governments, even traditionally xenophobic ones, turn increasingly to the international system for observers in order to validate elections. What they seek is legitimation by a global standard monitored by processes of the international system. Requests in 1994 by Malawi, South Africa, Mexico, and Belarus for observers to attend their presidential or parliamentary elections are a few recent and notable instances of this remarkable trend.[6] Governments seek such validation to avoid the alternative: persistent challenges to authority by coups, counter-coups, instability and stasis, and in order to obtain the essential societal acquiescence. Having failed to create the prerequisites for autochthonous validation, they look to the rules and organs of the international system to codify the prerequisite of democratic governance and to certify their compliance. To quote once again UN Secretary-General Kofi Annan:

> The value that Member States attach to democratization is reflected in the large number of requests the United Nations receives for electoral assistance – no fewer than eighty in the past five years. United Nations electoral assistance seeks in the first instance to enhance the effectiveness of international observers in making assessments regarding the legitimacy of an electoral process and its outcomes, and to recommend election-related policy changes through dialogue with the Government, political parties and the civil society . . . [T]he United Nations also emphasizes the importance of building the domestic institutional capacity of Member States in constitutional and electoral law reforms and strengthening Governments' own institutional capacities to organize elections.[7]

---

[5] US Department of State, 102d Cong., 1st Sess., Country Reports on Human Rights Practices for 1990; Report submitted to the Committee on Foreign Relations, US Senate and the Committee on Foreign Affairs, House of Representatives (Comm. Print 1991), 322–23.
[6] Malawi: *N.Y. Times*, June 21, 1994, at A8; South Africa: *N.Y. Times*, Jan. 15, 1994, at A3; Mexico: *N.Y. Times*, May 13, 1994, at A6; Belarus: *N.Y. Times*, June 24, 1994, at A9.
[7] Report of the Secretary-General on the work of the Organization, 1997, *supra* note 1, at p. 7, para. 38.

All these activities on the part of the international system in such inherently domestic affairs of States would have been unthinkable a decade ago. Yet all were undertaken at the specific request of States with the consent of a responsible UN organ. Thus, in 1996-97, elections were observed in Algeria, Ghana, Madagascar, Mali, and Yemen; further electoral assistance was also provided to Bangladesh, the Comoros, Gambia, Guyana, Haiti, Liberia, Mali, and Mexico.[8]

V LEGITIMATING THE INTERNATIONAL REGIMES

The international system responds no longer solely out of moral or ideological commitment to an expanding ambit of human rights, but now also out of self-interest. As global and regional institutions assume powers which were once the sole preserve of sovereign States – for matters now perforce transnational, such as environmental pollution, nonproliferation of nuclear weapons, and the prevention of breaches of the peace – it is very much to the advantage of such institutional endeavors that their initiatives be perceived as legitimate and fair. This cannot be achieved if any significant number of the participants in the decision-making process are palpably unresponsive to the views and values of their own people. In the legitimacy of national regimes resides the legitimacy of the international regime. The UN that raises and allocates several billion dollars annually for general and specific purposes of the global village cannot pretend to do so legitimately if the States parties to these allocations are out of touch with their own tax-paying citizenry.

The capacity of the international community to extend legitimacy to national governments, however, depends not only on its capacity to monitor an election or to recognize the credentials of a regime's delegates to the UN General Assembly, but also on the extent to which such international validating activity has evolved from the *ad hoc* to the normative: that is, the degree to which the process of legitimation has itself become legitimate. Do the global rules and processes for democratic validation have the indices of legitimacy? In other words, is a consistent, determinate set of standards evolving by which the international system can extend, or withhold, validation of national processes of popular consultation and participation? In the international context, legitimacy is achieved if, or to the extent that, those addressed by a rule, or by a rule-making institution, perceive the rule or institution to have come into being and to operate in accordance with generally accepted principles

[8] *Ibid.*

of right process.⁹ Are we developing a global canon of legitimate rules and procedures by which to judge the democracy of nations?[10]

VI ORIGINS OF THE DEMOCRATIC ENTITLEMENT

The process leading up to the birth of a democratic entitlement began with chapters XI and XII of the UN Charter. The latter bestowed on the UN an express legal right to intervene in and validate the democratic process within trust territories. The General Assembly soon also found grounds for exercising a supervisory role in colonial elections and referenda immediately prior to independence. This gradually became an accepted element in legitimizing such crucial transitions. Thus, UN observers oversaw in 1965 the referendum establishing a new constitution for the Cook Islands,[11] and in 1968 observed the pre-independence referendum and elections in Spanish Equatorial Guinea.[12] Similar monitoring by the UN occurred during the referendum on the future status of West New Guinea (West Irian) in 1969,[13] and during the November 1980 elections in the New Hebrides, then under French and British administration, which led to the creation of independent Vanuatu.[14]

As the colonial era drew to a close, the significance of the UN's election-monitoring role, instead of declining, appears to have increased. This is partly because the last cases of decolonization were among the most difficult. In these, a UN "honest broker" role proved indispensable.

A remarkable example is UNTAG, the UN transitional administration which acted as midwife in the birth of an independent Namibia. This was formerly the German colony known as South West Africa, and had been under South African administration since Germany's defeat in World War I. It was set on the road to independence by the General Assembly's symbolic termination of South Africa's mandate in 1966. A

---

[9] Thomas M. Franck, *The Power of Legitimacy Among Nations* (Oxford: Clarendon Press, 1990) p. 19.
[10] Legitimacy, in this as in all other contexts, is a matter of degree. Some rules and institutions enjoy more legitimacy than others.
[11] GA Res. 2005, UN GAOR, 19th Sess., Supp. No. 15, at 7, UN Doc. A/5815 (1965); *Report of the United Nations Representatives for the Supervision of the Elections in the Cook Islands*, UN Doc. A/5962 and Corr.1 (1965).
[12] GA Res. 2355, UN GAOR, 22nd Sess., Supp. No. 16, at 54, UN Doc. A/6716 (1968); *United Nations Mission for the Supervision of the Referendum and the Elections in Equatorial Guinea*, UN Doc. A/7200/Add.4, Annex V and Annex VI (1968). Independence was formally achieved on Oct. 12, 1968.
[13] GA Res. 1752, UN GAOR, 17th Sess., Supp. No. 17, at 70, UN Doc. A/5217 (1963); *Report of the Secretary-General regarding the Act of Self-determination in West Irian*, UN Doc. A/7641 (1969).
[14] GA Res. 34/10, UN GAOR, 34th Sess., Supp. No. 46, at 199, UN Doc. A/34/46; *Report of the United Nations Mission to Observe the Elections in the New Hebrides*, UN Doc. A/34/852 (1980).

landmark advisory opinion of the International Court of Justice confirmed that termination,[15] and, in 1978 a decision of the Security Council established the parameters for the territory's political development and democratic entitlement.[16] It took another decade, however, for the political climate in South Africa to change sufficiently to permit international implementation of self-determination through a UN-supervised vote. By then it had become difficult to take the lid off the pressure cooker without an explosion. Tribal and racial rifts were potential obstacles to a peaceful transition.

UNTAG was created by the Security Council precisely to prevent a pre-independence civil conflict, and it monitored the final months of South African administration and supervised the elections immediately prior to independence. It not only monitored a vote, but also took responsibility for maintaining peace, overseeing the South African military withdrawal, and assisting in the drafting of a new constitution. It helped achieve the rapid repeal of discriminatory legislation, implementation of an amnesty, and the return of political refugees; it was instrumental in ensuring the peaceful and fair election preceding independence. Deploying more than 7,000 military and civilian personnel at a cost of $373 million, it prepared the November 1989 elections and conducted them so successfully that a situation fraught with risk became a model of political transformation.[17]

While chapters XI and XII laid the legal groundwork for an entitlement of peoples – dependent peoples – to democratic governance, a further large step towards realization of the democratic entitlement was the General Assembly's adoption of the Universal Declaration of Human Rights on December 10, 1948.[18] As a mere resolution, it did not claim binding force, yet it was passed with such overwhelming support, and such prestige has accrued to it in succeeding years, that it may be said to have become a customary rule of State obligation. More to the point, its text manifests remarkable determinacy, specifically recognizing a universal right to freedom of opinion and expression (Article 19) as well as peaceful assembly and association (Article 20). The specificity of the Declaration has helped make it a landmark of continuing importance and recognized legitimacy.

---

[15] Namibia (SW. Africa) Case, 1971 ICJ 3 (Advisory Opinion of January 26).
[16] SC Res. 435 (1978). It did not authorize the sending of UNTAG until 1989. SC Res. 628 (1989); SC Res. 629 (1989).
[17] *Namibia, Independence at Last*, 27 UN Chronicle, no. 2 (June 1990), at p. 4. Namibia formally achieved independence on March 21, 1990. *Ibid.*
[18] GA Res. 217A, UN GAOR, 3rd Sess., at p. 71, UN Doc. A/810 (1948).

The entitlements first prescribed by the Declaration are repeated with even greater specificity in the Covenant on Civil and Political Rights.[19] Spelled out in that treaty are specific rights to freedom of thought (Article 18) and of association (Article 22). Article 19(2) is a particularly important component of the democratic entitlement. It states:

> Everyone shall have the right to freedom of expression; this right shall include freedom to seek, receive and impart information and ideas of all kinds, regardless of frontiers, either orally, in writing or in print, in the form of art, or through any other media of his choice.

While Article 19(2) is subject to restriction by law where "necessary . . . [f]or the protection of public order . . . or of public health or morals,"[20] these restrictions, like the rule itself, are subject to case-by-case review by the quasi-judicial Human Rights Committee of independent experts.[21] Rights to opinion, expression, and association are contained in Articles 18, 19 and 22.

When the Civil and Political Rights Covenant entered into force, the democratic entitlement entered a new phase. It established discursive rights of political participation, pioneered in connection with colonies and now made universally applicable by the Covenant. It shifted the prior focus, from "peoples" to persons and from decolonization to personal political participatory entitlements in independent nations. It entitles peoples in all States to free, fair, and open participation in the democratic process of governance chosen by each State.

The establishment of the Human Rights Committee to monitor compliance and give opinions incrementally increases the determinacy of the new norms. Borrowing from the earlier experience of colonial self-determination, when oversight committees such as the General Assembly's Special Committee on Non-Self Governing Territories monitored the performance of colonial powers, the Covenant imposes reporting requirements on States. Now, however, reports and complaints are made not to a political body but to an independent panel of experts, increasing the likelihood that the review procedure will be perceived as fair. Since the Covenant came into force, reporting and scrutiny have been formalized and depoliticized to an extent. Case-by-case applications of the norms have been welded to the process. This adumbration

---

[19] International Covenant on Civil and Political Rights, Dec. 16, 1966, p. 999 UNTS 171, *reprinted in* 6 ILM (1967) p. 368 (*entered into force* Mar. 23, 1976) [hereinafter ICCPR].   [20] *Ibid.* at Art. 19(3).
[21] *See* Dominic McGoldrick, *The Human Rights Committee* 461 (Oxford: Clarendon Press, 1991).

is gradually imbuing the Covenant's provisions with a perceptible aura of legitimacy which few governments are willing to ignore.[22]

VII RECENT SURGE OF THE ENTITLEMENT

In the years since the fall of Communism, these earlier initiatives have been augmented by UN supervision of democratic participation in crucial political decisions. This has become increasingly routine in situations of civil conflict in independent states. In 1992, UN observers validated Eritrea's plebiscite on secession from Ethiopia.[23] By the mid-nineties it had become commonplace for independent nations like Mexico or South Africa to ask to have their elections monitored by the UN and regional organizations.

The monitoring of elections in States riven by civil strife received its first major impetus when the UN was asked to monitor elections in Nicaragua. In August 1987 five Central American presidents signed the Esquipulas II agreement, which was a blueprint for restoring peace and ensuring legitimacy in that State. It called for free, internationally monitored elections, and, on March 3, 1989, the Nicaraguan Foreign Minister requested the Secretary-General to establish an observer mission to verify the fairness of his nation's forthcoming vote.[24] The General Assembly had already authorized the Secretary-General to assist the Esquipulas process in appropriate ways,[25] but that resolution had made no specific mention of election monitoring. Nevertheless, the Secretary-General thought he had "sufficient legislative basis" to comply with Nicaragua's request.[26] As a result, he established ONUVEN on July 6, 1989,[27] an initiative approved by the Security Council three weeks later.[28]

The active, far-reaching role of the UN observers in Nicaragua clearly illustrates how much the groundrules for international election monitoring had evolved in practice from the days of observing decolonizing votes in British Togoland or Ruanda-Urundi. The observers

---

[22] As of 1999, 144 States were parties to the Covenant. Multilateral Treaties Deposited with the Secretary-General, ST/LEG/SER.E, *available* at <http://www.un.org./Depts/Treaty/final/ts2/newfiles/part_boo/iv_4.html>.
[23] GA Res. 47/114 (1992) and UN Doc. A/47/544 (1992).
[24] *See* The Situation in Central America: Threats to International Peace and Security and Peace Initiatives, UN Doc. A/44/642, at p. 2 (1989).
[25] GA Res. 24, UN GAOR, 43rd Sess., Supp. no. 49, at p. 27, UN Doc. A/43/49 (1989).
[26] UN Doc. A/44/304, at p. 2 (1989).   [27] UN Doc. A/44/375 (1989).
[28] SC Res. 637 (1989).

deployed by the Secretary-General did not merely monitor voting. They actively observed the activities of the Supreme Electoral Council in drafting and implementing new laws applicable to nominating, campaigning, and related activities. Observers were deployed throughout the electoral campaign and involved themselves in mediating disputes between candidates concerning access to funding, the media, and even to the streets. They oversaw the rights of political parties to organize and campaign, verified the campaigners' right of access to radio, television, and newspapers, and investigated numerous charges of abuses and irregularities which might have undermined the legitimacy of the outcome.[29] At the final stage, ONUVEN observed the voting and established its own projection of results.[30] Commenting on these varied functions, the head of ONUVEN, Elliot Richardson, noted that his group had decided early in its career "that responsibility for verification of the electoral process demanded more than merely recording the process, more than monitoring, and could not stop short of actively seeking to get corrected whatever substantial defects had been discovered."[31]

On October 10, 1990 the UN established ONUVEH, the mission to oversee the Haitian elections. This was controversial, being seen by some States as a potential precedent entitling the international community to monitor anywhere. While the same might have been said of ONUVEN, Nicaragua was different in that its long civil war could be said to have given rise to a threat to the peace sufficient to rationalize an exceptional UN role in validating those national elections as part of an internationally brokered peace process. In Haiti's case, there was no such obvious connection to international peace. Instead, the UN was invited to oversee elections by the Haitian Transitional Government.[32] In normative terms, Haiti was the first instance in which the UN, acting on the request of an independent national government, intervened in an electoral process solely to validate the legitimacy of the outcome.

Despite misgivings, ONUVEH was launched with the imprimatur of the General Assembly.[33] Once again, the monitors' authority extended far beyond overseeing the ballot count. Their first report noted Haiti's lack of democratic traditions and its long history of totalitarianism and

---

[29] *See, e.g.,* The Situation in Central America: Threat to International Peace and Security and Peace Initiatives, UN Doc. A/44/927 (1990) (Fifth Nicaragua Report). *See also* UN Doc. A/44/642 (1989) (First Report); UN Doc. A/44/834 (1990) (Second Report); UN Doc. A/44/917 (1990) (Third Report); UN Doc. A/44/921 (1990) (Fourth Report).
[30] Fifth Nicaragua Report, *supra* note 29.   [31] *Ibid.* at p. 3.   [32] UN Doc. A/44/965 (1990).
[33] GA Res. 45/2 (1990).

violence, much of it government-inspired and some of it quite recent.[34] In preemptive response to this problem, the Assembly authorized the recruiting of observers "with solid experience in the public order field."[35] As ONUVEH soon discovered, the "first task . . . was to help create a psychological climate conducive to the holding of democratic elections. . . . In this they were assisted by a radio and television campaign conducted by an ONUVEH information team. . . . [They] inquired into difficulties encountered by the registration and polling stations in registering voters and into irregularities reported to them. They attended political meetings . . . and monitored radio and television broadcasts to make sure that all candidates had equal access to the mass media."[36]

Although the Secretary-General, in his final report on ONUVEH, expressed satisfaction with the fairness of the electoral process and the role played by the UN, he also noted the formidable obstacles lying ahead for Haitian democracy, and advocated "launching a civil education campaign on the importance of the parliament and local authorities."[37] This is a long-term task, but ONUVEH had been given an operational life of only two months. With prescience, the Secretary-General warned that, if electoral democracy is to be more than a one-time event in the history of a State with little experience in such matters, a far more sustained effort would have to be made under the auspices of the community of nations. When his advice was ignored, the anticipated consequences ensued.

Since then, UN monitoring or observation nevertheless has been authorized in a growing number of post-colonial situations: Eritrea,[38] Cambodia,[39] Mozambique,[40] and (most significantly) South Africa, to which in 1994 the UN sent 1,800 electoral observers.[41] Notably, the mandate of the UN in implementing the 1996 accords that ended decades of civil war in Guatemala – a role including but not limited to building democracy – made provision for verification of implementation until the year 2000.[42]

The monitoring of elections has also been taken up by regional organizations. The Organization of American States has been especially

---

[34] First Report of the United Nations Observer Group for the Verification of the Elections in Haiti, UN Doc. A/45/870, at 9–10 (1990). [35] GA Res. 45/2, para. 1(d) (1990).
[36] United Nations Electoral Assistance to Haiti, UN Doc. DPI/1120 (1991).
[37] Electoral Assistance to Haiti: Note by the Secretary-General, UN Doc. A/45/870/Add.1, at 23 (1991). [38] SC Res. 47/114 (1992). [39] SC Res. 745 (1991); SC Res. 717 (1991).
[40] SC Res. 782 (1992); SC Res. 797 (1992). [41] SC Res. 894 (1994).
[42] Report of the Secretary-General on the work of the Organization, 1997, *supra* note 1, p. 18, para. 122.

active, beginning with the despatch of a 435-person commission to Nicaragua in 1990 to observe 70 percent of polling sites.[43] A major OAS presence was also mounted during the Haitian elections,[44] not only as poll-watchers but also to assist in drafting the electoral law and in organizing voter registration.[45] Over the past few years, OAS monitors have observed elections in, *inter alia*, Surinam, El Salvador, Paraguay, Panama, and Peru.[46] In the post-1989 transition from Communism in Eastern Europe, regional monitoring has also played an important part. Members of the Organization for Security and Co-operation in Europe (the OSCE) have sent missions to play a role in various elections, beginning with Bulgaria's 1990 election.[47]

On a non-governmental level, several members of the US Congress and other OSCE legislatures observed the Bulgarian and Czech electoral campaigns to ensure fairness,[48] as did their counterparts from other Western European parliaments. Non-governmental organizations (NGOs), too, have become professional global electoral monitors. Emissaries of the Council of Freely Elected Heads of Government of the Carter Center in Atlanta, Georgia, have observed many elections, including the crucial 1990 Nicaraguan and 1991 Zambian polls.[49] The US National Democratic Institute for International Affairs has monitored elections in dozens of countries since 1986.[50] At least half a dozen teams of such foreign observers, including experts from the US, the Philippines, Japan, and the Commonwealth, monitored parliamentary elections in Bangladesh on February 27, 1991.[51] International observers from Canada, France, Germany, and the US verified the propriety of elections held in Benin in March 1991.[52] Sixty-five representatives of NGOs observed the independence referendum conducted in Latvia on March 3, 1991.[53]

It is likely that such activity will increase. Elliot Richardson, head of

---

[43] *N.Y. Times* (Feb. 23, 1990), at A3. [44] OEA/Ser.G/CP/RES.537, doc. 805 (1990).
[45] Report of the Secretary-General on the Assistance the Organization is Giving to the Provisional Government of Haiti in its Electoral Process, OEA/Ser.G/CP/Doc. 2108 at p. 1 (1990).
[46] OEA/SerD/III-42 at p. 33 (1992); OEA/Ser.D/III-44 at p. 49 (1994); OEA/Ser.D/III-46 at p. 44 (1996). [47] *N.Y. Times* (June 6, 1990), at A10.
[48] Thomas S. Kahn, "Bulgaria's Different Pathway," *Christian Science Monitor*, June 22, 1990, at p. 18. Helsinki Watch also sent monitors. *N.Y. Times* (June 11, 1990), at A1. For the first democratic election in Czechoslovakia *see N.Y. Times* (June 10, 1990), sec. 1, A31.
[49] *N.Y. Times* (Aug. 9, 1989), at A13; *N.Y. Times* (Nov. 1, 1991), A3.
[50] *National Democratic Institute for International Affairs, Response to United Nations General Assembly Resolution 45/150: Developing a United Nations Elections Assistance Capability*, at p. 2 (1991).
[51] *N.Y. Times* (Feb. 28, 1991), at A5. [52] *N.Y. Times* (Mar. 12, 1991), at A11.
[53] *Financial Times* (Mar. 4, 1991), at p. 14.

the UN Observers in Nicaragua, predicted that "the United Nations is likely in the future to be called upon for similar assignments in other countries."[54] As Professor Michael Reisman has recently observed, "results of such elections serve as evidence of popular sovereignty and become the basis for international endorsement of the elected government."[55]

In addressing the Forty-Fifth General Assembly, President George Bush proposed the establishment of a standing UN electoral commission to assist a requesting nation in guaranteeing that its elections are free and fair.[56] The Secretariat has responded with an Electoral Assistance Division which, together with the United Nations Development Programme, provides technical assistance to States needing help in organizing and conducting elections.[57] The Secretary-General has also prepared guidelines to help member States which are considering a request for such assistance or for monitoring, supervising, or verifying an election. These make it clear that UN participation depends upon the requesting government demonstrating the basic requisites for fairness: "that political parties and alliances enjoy complete freedom of organization, movement, assembly and expression without hindrance or intimidation" and that these conditions are to be verified by "observer teams" stationed in "regional or provincial capitals." The observers must be free to "establish regular contacts with political parties and social organizations at the national and local levels" and to carry out "a programme of village and municipality visits throughout the country" in order, among other objectives, to "verify the observance by all parties of the stipulations of the electoral law and any code of conduct that might have been agreed upon among the parties or established by the electoral authorities."[58] Thus, the requesting State is put on notice that its application for validation of an election by international monitoring will not be considered unless the requisites for electoral democracy have been agreed and the prospects for their effective implementation are favorable.

---

[54] Fifth Nicaragua Report, *supra* note 29, at p. 3 (1990).
[55] W. Michael Reisman, "Sovereignty and Human Rights in Contemporary International Law," *Am. J. Int'l L.* 84 (1990), pp. 868–69.   [56] *N.Y. Times* (Oct. 2, 1990), at A12.
[57] Enhancing the effectiveness of the principle of periodic and general elections, Report of the Secretary-General, UN Doc. A/47/668/Add.1 (November 24, 1992), p. 10, para. 28. Strengthening the role of the United Nations in enhancing the effectiveness of the principle of periodic and genuine elections and the promotion of democratization, UN Doc. A/52/129, December 12, 1997.   [58] *Ibid.*, Addendum, at p. 4, para. 13.

It is likely that the practice of requesting international electoral monitoring will become a routine part of national practice, particularly useful when the democratic legitimacy of a regime is in question. Of course, there are still hard-core abstainers, such as the totalitarian governments of Myanmar, North Korea, and China. However, their number is diminishing. The government formed in May 1991 after the end of the civil war in Ethiopia immediately undertook to conduct "free, democratic and internationally monitored elections" within a year.[59] At about the same time, the insurgents who took power in Eritrea committed themselves not to secede from Ethiopia until after a UN-monitored plebiscite.[60] What is remarkable is not that in particular cases the democratic process has been monitored and declared legitimate, but rather that such recourse to international legitimation through election monitoring is becoming the rule rather than the exception.

A recent UN Secretariat study, noting the rising demand for monitoring, has started to set out the juridical, institutional, administrative, and fiscal parameters for an expanded UN electoral monitoring service.[61] The OAS Secretariat has provided a companion regional study.[62] These begin the conceptually difficult task of sifting through the increasing body of practice to clarify the meaning of the normative concept signaled by the phase "democratic entitlement." These data make it strikingly apparent that international election monitoring cannot be limited merely to guaranteeing citizens' right to cast a vote, but must also ensure a far broader basket of democratic rights, of the type described in the text of the Civil and Political Rights Covenant and the Charter of Paris.

A study which seeks to connect the dots of practice with lines of enunciated principle must also look at those instances in which election monitoring has been denied. For example, in 1990 the Secretary-General refused to monitor the Romanian elections on the ground that his participation had not been authorized by the General Assembly or Security Council. Perhaps even more persuasive was the objection that he had not been invited to participate early enough in the process, before the outgoing regime had established the rules and methods by which the election campaign was to be conducted.[63] In 1991 the Secretary-General also rejected requests for election monitoring made by Lesotho and

---

[59] *N.Y. Times* (May 29, 1991), at A6.   [60] *N.Y. Times* (June 22, 1991) at A3.
[61] *Principles for United Nations Observance of Elections*, Confidential Memorandum, June 6, 1989.
[62] OEA/Ser.G/CP/RES.421, doc. 606 (1985).
[63] *See* "UN Says it Won't Monitor Romanian Elections," Reuters News Service, NEXIS, CURRENT Library (January 25, 1990).

Zambia, again on the public ground that he was unauthorized, in the absence of special circumstances, to engage in the monitoring of elections in sovereign States, but also on the private ground that the effectiveness of his participation had not been sufficiently assured.

There is reason for such caution. Commentators have rightly warned that the monitoring of voting alone may place observers in the position of legitimating an electoral victory which was not fairly achieved. This need not imply fraud or repression but, more likely, the effect on free choice of the continuing "normal" operation of entrenched social and political institutions.[64] While no observation process can reach back into a nation's history to extirpate the impacted roots of social and cultural inequalities, observers can do – and have done – more than simply watch tellers count ballots. To make citizens' rights to free and open elections a legitimate entitlement, its parameters need to be clear and specific. To that end, a robust repertory of practice, an explicit canon of principles, and an institutional framework for implementation is developing which is capable of increasing the determinacy of the entitlement. Some of this recapitulation of the lessons learned in field-practice is being undertaken by non-governmental organizations.[65]

Apparent failures such as the monitoring missions in Angola and (for quite different reasons) in the Western Sahara are fortunately exceptions, more than offset by the credible and path-breaking operations culminating in fair elections in difficult situations such as Namibia, Cambodia, Nicaragua, and El Salvador. As the entitlement becomes an accepted norm, a lengthy international law debate will end. Do governments validate international law or does international law validate governments? The answer is becoming apparent: each legitimates the other.

VIII VALIDATION AND MONITORING

The validation of governments by the international system is rapidly being accepted as an appropriate role of the United Nations, the regional systems and, supplementarily, for NGOs. Democracy and human rights are now requirements for admission of new member

---

[64] Leslie Gelb, "The Free Elections Trap," *N.Y. Times* (May 29, 1991), at A23.
[65] *See, e.g.*, the Special Edition, Electoral Assistance Activities From January 1, 1992 to June 30, 1993, Electoral Assistance Network, EAU/DPA (1993). *See also* M. Hodgson, "When to Accept, When to Abstain: A Framework for UN Election Monitoring," 25 *N.Y.U. J. Int'l L. and Pol.* 25 (1992), p. 137.

States into the European Union, as enumerated by the Maastricht Treaty. Indeed, the European Court of Human Rights has held that "democracy is without doubt a fundamental feature of the European public order."[66] A recent study conducted by the Netherlands Minister of Foreign Affairs gives expression to the new normative expectation. It asks: what can reasonably be expected of a European State seeking to join the European Communities and the Council of Europe? It answers that applicant States "must be plural democracies; they must regularly hold free elections by secret ballot; they must respect the rule of law; [and] they must have signed the European Convention on Human Rights and Fundamental Freedoms..."[67] Such an international test for validation of governance and entry into a society of nations would have been unthinkable even a decade ago; in the new Europe it is considered unexceptionable. Some comparable rule should, and undoubtedly will, become the standard for participation in the multinational institutions of the global community.

As a step in this direction, the UN General Assembly might adopt and adapt the specific guidelines set out in the OSCE's Copenhagen Declaration and Paris Charter and declare these applicable to Article 25 of the Civil and Political Covenant. The Human Rights Committee in any event is likely to interpret Article 25 in accordance with the Copenhagen and Paris principles, but it would be better if this were specifically endorsed by a resolution of the Assembly. Such a resolution would, among other benefits, guide and assist the Human Rights Committee in more effectively monitoring compliance by the large majority of States party to that global instrument. It would also help to make more determinate the content of the evolving customary law applicable to national political practices. By bringing the evolution of UN practice approximately into line with that of the OSCE, the emerging democratic entitlement would attain greater specificity and coherence.

How coherent is the new normative canon of the democratic entitlement? The democratic entitlement rests on the still-radical principle that the community of States is empowered to compose and apply codes which regulate the conduct of governments towards their own citizens.

---

[66] Case of United Communist Party of Turkey and Others v. Turkey (133/1996/752/951), Judgment of the European Court of Human Rights (January 30, 1998), para. 45.
[67] Letter from the Minister for Foreign Affairs (H. van den Broek) to the Advisory Committee on Human Rights and Foreign Policy (June 20, 1990), *reprinted in Netherlands Advisory Committee on Human Rights and Foreign Policy, Democracy and Human Rights in Eastern Europe*, at pp. 30–31 (1990).

Legitimacy and the democratic entitlement

The very idea of general international monitoring of elections in sovereign States still arouses passionate ire, not only among the increasingly isolated totalitarian regimes, but also among some nations with long memories of humiliating interventions by States bent on "civilizing" missions. While they are willing to see the international community engage in occasional monitoring of elections to end a civil war or regional conflict, they accept this only as a necessary exception, not as a normal manifestation of a universal democratic entitlement.

The prospect of such dissent was clearly foreshadowed in 1990 when the Assembly considered the proposal to establish ONUVEH, the observer group to monitor Haiti's elections. Here, a link between election monitoring and peace was much harder to demonstrate since no armed hostilities were underway. ONUVEH was therefore created in the face of significant opposition from several UN members, notably China, Cuba, and Colombia.[68] The long spectre of US hemispheric interventions was invoked in the Assembly's corridors. It was said that the UN was becoming a front for the neo-colonial ambitions of the US and other North Atlantic members of the Rich Man's Club, invoking electoral rights to divert attention from the rights of the poor to food. Several months elapsed before suspicions were assuaged by diplomatic assurances that the Haitian case, too, would set no general precedent. Cuba, in the Assembly's debate prior to the vote authorizing ONUVEH, spoke emphatically against "any attempt to use this United Nations resolution or activity as a pretext for interfering in the internal affairs of Haiti . . ."[69] and stressed that "elections . . . can never be regarded as a matter affecting international peace and security . . ."[70] Mexico also went on record as rejecting any precedential value in the authorization of ONUVEH.[71] These States contended that UN election monitoring in an independent nation is unlawful *per se*, in the absence of exceptional peace-making exigencies. That this attitude is changing, however, has been demonstrated by the astonishing request of Mexico, only three years later, for international observers to monitor its own Presidential elections to assuage the suspicions of its electorate.

The International Court of Justice has rebuffed the claim that monitoring is intrusive, and thus unlawful *per se*. In the 1986 Nicaragua

---

[68] The Security Council failed to reach consensus on the issue, with China threatening to veto in the Security Council and Cuba and Colombia in the General Assembly arguing that election monitoring in an independent state, unrelated to a threat to the peace, constituted a violation of Article 2(7) of the Charter. *See* UN Doc. A/45/PV.29 (1990).   [69] *Ibid.* at p. 62.
[70] *Ibid.* at pp. 58–60.   [71] *Ibid.* at pp. 64–65.

decision, in connection with commitments made by the Sandinista government to abide by democratic electoral standards, the Court stated that it

> cannot discover, within the range of subjects open to international agreement, any obstacle or provision to hinder a State from making a commitment of this kind. A State, which is free to decide upon the principle and methods of popular consultation within its domestic order, is sovereign for the purpose of accepting a limitation of its sovereignty in this field. This is a conceivable situation for a State which is bound by institutional links to a confederation of States, or indeed to an international organization.[72]

It is also clear that no legal impediments prevent voluntary international election monitoring as a means of protecting the emerging right of all peoples to free and open electoral democracy. However, this is not to say that any *duty* yet obliges States to have their elections internationally validated. Although we have noted that the OSCE process in Europe seems poised to pioneer such a general duty, even there the duty has not, as yet, been explicitly imposed on all members. In the international community, while there may be a duty under Article 25 of the Civil and Political Rights Covenant (as in its regional and customary law analogues) to permit free and open elections and to subject national compliance to review by the Human Rights Committee, there is still no obligation to permit election monitoring by international or regional organizations. Indeed, any effort to transform an election monitoring *option*, exercisable at the discretion of each government, into an *obligation* owed by each government to its own people and to the other States of the global community is likely to be resisted. It must be admitted, however, that a "rule" which only applies voluntarily may have less legitimacy and may be seen as less fair than one that is of general application.

This was demonstrated when the General Assembly tiptoed around the democratic entitlement at its session in the fall of 1990. Passing two somewhat incongruent resolutions, one of which restates the democratic entitlement and commends monitoring[73] while the other emphasizes State sovereignty, affirming "that it is the concern solely of peoples [of each State] to determine methods and to establish institutions regarding the electoral process, as well as to determine the ways for its implementation according to their constitutional and national legislation"[74] and

---

[72] Military and Paramilitary Activities in and against Nicaragua (Nic v. US), 1986 ICJ 14, at 131 (Judgment of June 27, 1986).   [73] GA Res. 45/150 (1991), paras. 2, 3, 8, 10, 11.
[74] GA Res. 45/151 (1990), para. 2.

urging all States "to respect the principle of noninterference in the internal affairs of States."[75] The General Assembly has continued to pass versions of these two resolutions in the years since 1991.[76]

Opponents fear mostly that the monitoring process will be used to reimpose a form of neo-colonialism under the banner of democracy. That fear must be addressed, but it must also be put in perspective. History has warned, repeatedly, that the natural right of all people to liberty and democracy is too precious and too vulnerable to be entrusted entirely to those who govern. True, as John Stuart Mill has warned, the moral fiber of a nation may be weakened if it relies on the intervention of outsiders, rather than its own efforts, to achieve liberation.[77] However, given the technological edge which contemporary dictators enjoy over their own citizens, the chances of successful self-liberation have declined since Mill's day. Uganda's President Godfrey L. Binaisa, after the overthrow of Idi Amin's bloody junta, quite properly chided the General Assembly's delegates for their indifference to the plight of his nation's people. "In light of the clear commitment set out in . . . provisions of the Charter," he said, "our people naturally looked to the United Nations for solidarity and support in their struggle against the fascist dictatorship. For eight years they cried out in the wilderness for help; unfortunately, their cries seem to have fallen on deaf ears." Acerbically, Binaisa observed that "somehow, it is thought to be in bad taste or contrary to diplomatic etiquette to raise matters of violations of human rights by member States within the forums of the United Nations."[78]

In an age in which an effective confrontation with entrenched auto-

---

[75] *Ibid., para. 4.*
[76] On December 12, 1997, the General Assembly again passed two different resolutions. The first, entitled *Respect for the Principles of National Sovereignty and Non-Interference in the International Affairs of States in Their Electoral Process*, reaffirms that "any activities that attempt, directly or indirectly, to interfere in the free development of national electoral processes, in particular in the developing countries, or that are intended to sway the results of such processes, violate the spirit and letter of the principles established in the Charter and in the Declaration on Principles of International Law concerning Friendly Relations and Cooperation among States in accordance with the Charter of the United Nations." GA Res. 52/119 (1997). The second resolution, entitled *Strengthening the Role of the United Nations in Enhancing the Effectiveness of the Principle of Periodic and Genuine Elections and the Promotion of Democratization*, commends "the electoral assistance provided to Member States" and recommends that "the Electoral Assistance Division continue to provide post-election assistance, as appropriate, to requesting States and electoral institutions, in order to contribute to the sustainability of their electoral processes." GA Res. 52/129 (1997).
[77] John Stuart Mill, *Dissertations and Discussions: Political, Philosophical and Historical* (1873), vol. III, pp. 238–63. [78] UN Doc. A/34/PV.14, at pp. 4–6 (1979).

46   *The normative foundations of a right to political participation*

crats may be nearly impossible without the direct or indirect support of the international community or neighboring States, inhibitions about interference in the "domestic jurisdiction" of States seem less persuasive than they used to be. "We are arriving at the conclusion," Soviet Foreign Minister Boris D. Pankin observed in 1991, "that national guarantees [of human rights] are not sufficient. So we have to review the principle of non-interference in affairs of other governments."[79] To this end, the post-coup Declaration of Human Rights and Freedoms, adopted on September 5, 1991 by the Soviet Congress of People's Deputies, states that "Every person possesses natural, inalienable and inviolable rights and freedoms. They are sealed in laws that must correspond to the universal declaration of human rights, the international covenants on human rights and other international norms and this Declaration."[80] The OAS foreign ministers' resolution of June 5, 1991 is to the same effect[81] as are the OSCE heads' Paris Charter[82] and Moscow Document.[83]

IX COLLECTIVE ENFORCEMENT V. UNILATERALISM

It thus appears that there is increasing support (even, or perhaps *especially*, among former totalitarian States) for the proposition that the democratic entitlement, abetted by links with other basic human rights and the accompanying international monitoring of compliance, has trumped the principle of non-interference. What validly remains of past inhibitions against interference in national sovereignty is a concern that such intervention be, and be seen to be, *bona fide* aid to democratic self-governance. Thus, actions to reenforce or reinstate democratic rule taken on behalf of the international system and in accordance with its legitimate collective decision-making procedures are likely to be generally welcomed, whereas unilateral acts by a State, unauthorized by its global (or regional) peers, will be treated with deserved suspicion and alarm. The 1989 US intervention in Panama stands as a sharp procedural contrast to the international decision to intervene against the junta

---

[79] *N.Y. Times* (Sept. 10, 1991), A13.   [80] *N.Y. Times* (Sept. 7, 1991), A5.
[81] *Resolution on Representative Democracy*, OEA/Ser. P/AG/RES.1080 (XXI-0/91).
[82] Conference on Security and Co-operation in Europe: Charter of Paris For a New Europe and Supplementary Document to Give Effect to Certain Provisions of the Charter, Nov. 21, 1990, *reprinted in* 30 ILM 190, Preamble, 193 (1991).
[83] Conference on Security and Co-operation in Europe: Document of the Moscow Meeting on the Human Dimension, Emphasizing Respect for Human Rights, Pluralistic Democracy, the Rule of Law, and Procedures for Fact Finding. Moscow (Oct. 13, 1991), *reprinted in* 30 ILM 1670 (1991).

in Haiti. International "jurying" of a decision of this sort carries far different resonance than does unilateral action.

This was undoubtedly in the minds of the representatives of States to the United Nations Human Rights Commission when they voted unanimously to condemn the military government of Myanmar for failing to carry out its promise to return that country to democratic, civilian rule.[84] The junta's refusal to allow the elected legislature to meet and its arrest of many parliamentary leaders was perceived as not merely a domestic but an international issue, warranting a collective judgment and response from those empowered by the international community to make such judgments.

Despite the Security Council's 1994 decision to authorize the use of force against Haiti's junta,[85] the international community still undoubtedly provides a slower, less decisive recourse for supporting embattled democrats within nations than does unilateral intervention by a powerful (and self-interested) State. This argument for unilateralism, however, fails to take into account the costs of unilateralism to the project of gradually developing community-based institutional responses to the problem of totalitarian usurpations. Such costs might be acceptable, if there were no real prospect of gradually developing, in the institutions of global governance, a multilateral approach unfreighted by the baggage of unilateralism. That, however, as this essay seeks to demonstrate, is not the case. Monitoring, of various degrees of rigor and performed by a panoply of multilateral institutions, has become quite normative in the span of a decade, and is accepted by States at the hands of quite intrusive instrumentalities and processes backed by legitimate multilaterally bestowed authority. If that authority is less persuasive than the US Marine Corps, it is at least an accruing asset. If monitoring evolves into a universal obligation, perhaps consequences will attach even to a refusal to be monitored. As Professor Buergenthal observed about the effect of the Copenhagen Declaration and the Paris Charter, there is bound to evolve a "linkage of human rights to other questions (trade, security, environment, etc.) . . . Linkage permits the participating States . . . to condition their bilateral and multilateral relations in general upon progress in the human dimension sphere."[86] The authority that grows out of such linkages may even prove to have greater staying power in the long run than did US military power in some of its most recent deployments.

[84] *N.Y. Times* (Mar. 7, 1991), at A14.   [85] SC Res. 940 (1994).
[86] Thomas Buergenthal, "CSCE Human Dimension: The Birth of a System," *Collected Courses of the Academy of European Law* 1, no. 2 (1992), p. 43.

CHAPTER 2

The right to political participation in international law

Gregory H. Fox

I INTRODUCTION

Is international law prepared to accept a right to democratic governance? To answer this question one would need to examine the many facets of international law potentially affected by a principle of democratic legitimacy: recognition of States and governments, the accreditation of delegates to international organizations, the use of force, treaty law, etc. But such an inquiry into the *consequences* of a democratic right would be a rather sterile enterprise if one had not first asked whether the right itself has achieved a firm legal grounding. Does international law in fact speak to the ways in which citizens choose their leaders? Is the right confined to treaty law or is support to be found in State practice as well? Do efforts by international organizations to foster transitions to democracy constitute norm-generating State practice? And is relevant *opinio juris* confined to regions of the world in which democratic government is already well established?

These questions about the *sources* of a democratic right immediately raise another, more complex question: when inquiring into the normative status of a "right to democratic government," what, precisely, is one looking for? If "democracy" is understood in consequentialist terms as one or another comprehensive visions of "the good life," then the relevant sources of law would be potentially infinite.[1] All manner of political, social, economic, environmental, and other rights could potentially contribute to democracy so defined. International law clearly has not cohered around such an all-encompassing notion of a democratic society.

---

[1] Such a broad conception of democracy is described in Thomas Christiano, *The Rule of the Many* (Boulder, Colo.: Westview Press, 1996). According to the Canadian Supreme Court, "[d]emocracy is not simply concerned with the process of government ... [but] is fundamentally connected to substantive goals." In the Matter of Section 53 of the Supreme Court Act, R.S.C., 1985, C. S-26 And in the Matter of a Reference by the Governor in Council Concerning Certain Questions Relating to the Secession of Quebec from Canada, as set out in Order in Council P.C. 1996–1497, Dated September 30, 1996 (1998).

International law has, however, come to understand "democracy" in narrower, more process-oriented terms. Perhaps recognizing the limited ability of outsiders to affect broad political change within States, international actors have come to use the term "democracy" to mean the essential procedures by which a democratic society functions.[2] The distinctive essence of democratic government is popular sovereignty – the notion of citizen consent to the exercise of coercive power within a state.[3] It is the appeal to popular consent, above all else, that differentiates democracy from theories of political authority grounded in alternative sources of legitimation – dynastic continuity for monarchies, a divine mandate for theocracies, etc. While democratic consequentialists argue persuasively that a whole range of civil rights and social prerequisites may be necessary for *meaningful* popular consent, the fact of consent still lies at the heart of their theories.

In the modern State, popular consent is made manifest through competitive elections. International law's modest approach to democratization, therefore, has focused on electoral processes.[4] This in no way suggests that other political or social rights are not seen as essential to the process of democratization; the UN Secretary-General, in particular, has argued that democratization must begin but cannot end with competitive elections.[5] And as noted elsewhere in this volume, "human rights" are frequently described by international actors in contradistinction to "democracy."[6] What this view does suggest is that international actors understand elections as the essential framework through which other "democratic" goals are to be effectuated. In a world of highly diverse states, achieving consensus on even this minimal understanding of democracy would be a remarkable event.

In accordance with this understanding, the instruments and practice

---

[2] "The term 'democratization' is used here to denote a process by which an authoritarian society becomes more participatory." Report of the Secretary-General, Support by the United Nations System of the Efforts of Governments to Promote and Consolidate New or Restored Democracies, UN Doc. A.51/512 (1996), para. 5.

[3] "[T]he concept of representative democracy is founded upon the principle that it is the people who have political sovereignty." *Annual Report of the Inter-American Commission on Human Rights 1990–1991*, OEA/Ser.L/V/II.79, rev. 1, doc. 12 (1991).

[4] In a resolution entitled "Strengthening the Role of the United Nations in Enhancing the Effectiveness of the Principle of Periodic and Genuine Elections and the Promotion of Democratization," GA Res. 52/129 (1997), the General Assembly commended the UN for assisting in "the continuation and consolidation of the democratization process in certain Member States requesting assistance." It then went on to describe that assistance solely by reference to aspects of the electoral process. *Ibid.* para. 5.

[5] *See, e.g.,* Report of the Secretary-General, Support by the United Nations System of the Efforts of Governments to Promote and Consolidate New or Restored Democracies, UN Doc. A/52/513 (1997), para. 30.   [6] *See* Introduction, text accompanying note 24.

surveyed in this chapter will be those concerned with "free and fair" elections. The chapter begins with a review of how international law approached questions of regime legitimacy before a guarantee of political participation entered the law of human rights. It will then survey the human rights treaties in which a right to participation is set out, as well as the relevant jurisprudence of treaty bodies. It will then review the practice of multilateral election monitoring and conclude that a right to political participation has established a firm grounding in both treaty law and international practice.

II THE EMERGING INTERNATIONAL LAW OF PARTICIPATORY RIGHTS

A *Participatory rights before 1948: the reign of statism*

All of human rights law presents a challenge to traditional notions of State sovereignty. In this sense the right to political participation is unexceptional. But participatory rights involve not only specific limits on State sovereignty in given areas, but the more fundamental question of who holds sovereign authority within a State. For most of recent history "the sovereign" has been that person or group actually wielding political power. The right to participation rejects this *de facto* control test by asserting that the mass of citizens is the ultimate repository of sovereignty.

If participatory rights were merely a theory of democratic legitimacy then international law would not enter the discussion. But they are not merely theory: they are, as this section will show, treaty-based obligations owed to other States. Participatory rights have thereby "internationalized" previously domestic questions of regime legitimacy. By presenting the identity of "the sovereign" as a question of international law, these rights have granted to other State parties the capacity to judge the adequacy of popular participation.

The traditional exclusion of participatory rights from international law can be explained by two sets of factors; those generic to all human rights norms and others specific to the right itself. The generic reasons are well known. The international law of human rights emerged following the Second World War.[7] Before then, "apart from a few anomalous cases, in which individuals were allowed to vindicate their rights directly

---

[7] *See generally* Louis Sohn, "The New International Law: Protection of the Rights of Individuals Rather Than States," *Am U. L. Rev.* 32 (1982), pp. 1, 9–17 (discussing development of international law of human rights).

The right to political participation in international law

on the basis of a special international agreement, individuals were not subjects of rights and duties under international law."[8] States in the nineteenth century, caught increasingly in the throes of aggressive nationalism, saw their domestic political institutions as essential components of a unique national culture. In order to protect these institutions from external pressures, the dominant States of Europe shaped an international law that carved out an exclusive sphere of domestic jurisdiction.[9] A fortress-like conception of State sovereignty endowed governments with "a monopoly over fundamental political decisions, as well as over legislative, executive and judicial powers."[10]

An individual right to participate in government did not and could not arise in this international legal climate. The manner in which States chose their leaders formed a central feature of the protected domestic sphere.[11] Statism found its ultimate expression during the eighteenth and nineteenth centuries in the conception of nations as autonomous moral beings which, in the selection of their leaders, gave expression to their national personalities.[12] Vattel, who conceived of political societies as morally engaged, described the national sovereign as "the moral person" of his State. Once chosen, a sovereign became "the depository of the obligations relative to government" and other persons, while not "absolutely ceasing to exist in the nation, act thence wards only in him and by him."[13] To condemn the process of choosing a leader, therefore, was to impugn the character of the nation itself.

Two more specific factors also contributed to the late emergence of participatory rights in international law. The first is that national elections did not become commonplace until the mid-nineteenth century.[14]

---

[8] *Ibid.* at p. 9.   [9] *See* Matthew S. Anderson, *The Ascendancy of Europe* (1972), pp. 140–50.
[10] Helmut Steinberger, "Sovereignty," *in* Rudolf Bernhardt, ed., *Encyclopedia of Public International Law* 10 (1987), pp. 397, 404.
[11] Henry Wheaton's views were typical of international lawyers of this period: "The perfect independence of every sovereign State in respect to its political institutions, extends to the choice of the supreme magistrate and other rulers, as well as to the form of government itself." Henry Wheaton, *Elements of International Law* (2d ann. edn., Boston, Mass.: Little Brown, 1863), p. 135.
[12] *Ibid.* at p. 132 ("Every state, as a distinct moral being, independent of every other, may freely exercise all its sovereign rights in any manner not inconsistent with the equal rights of other states. Among these is that of establishing, altering, or abolishing its own municipal constitution of government.") Professor Tesón has termed this view the "Hegelian Myth." Fernando Tesón, *Humanitarian Intervention: An Inquiry into Law and Morality* (1988), pp. 53–76.
[13] I. Emmerich de Vattel, Joseph Chitty, ed. (Philadelphia, Penn.: T. and J. W. Johnson, 1849) *The Law of Nations* (1759), ch. IV, p. 40.
[14] *See* Alan F. Hattersley, *A Short History of Democracy* (Cambridge University Press, 1930), p. 161; Leslie Lipson, *The Democratic Civilization* (New York: Oxford University Press, 1964), p. 79; Stein Rokkan, *Citizens, Elections, Parties: Approaches to the Comparative Study of the Processes of Development* (New York: McKay, 1970), pp. 84–85.

An international requirement of free and fair elections could not reasonably be expected to arise until elections in individual states became the norm. Until the mid-twentieth century, however, many States were still engaged in national debates over the nature, power, and extent of representative institutions.[15] Even in 1948, when participatory rights were first formally expressed in the Universal Declaration, full adult suffrage was less than a generation old in many European countries.[16]

The second reason concerns the treatment of unelected governments by the international community. Governments which obtain power in violation of participatory rights (*i.e.*, without holding proper elections) do so illegally. Presumably, such governments would themselves be considered illegal.[17] For most of recent history, however, the international law of recognition has paid little or no attention to the manner in which

---

[15] Although several European states had functioning parliamentary bodies in the seventeenth and eighteenth centuries, the size of their electoral base appears negligible by modern standards. Hattersley, *supra* note 14, pp. 120–40. In mid-eighteenth century Britain, for example, no more than one in twenty citizens was eligible to vote for the House of Commons. Lipson, *supra* note 14, p. 80. Only after the twin upheavals of the French Revolution and the Napoleonic wars did representative institutions begin to proliferate and the base of suffrage expand. Hattersley, *supra* note 14, pp. 161–62. In Belgium, which gained independence in 1830, the first constitution established a bicameral parliament with suffrage limited to men over twenty-five years of age who paid a minimum tax. Universal male suffrage was not introduced until 1893. Thomas F. Mackie and Richard Rose, *The International Almanac of Electoral History* (3rd rev. edn., Washington, DC: Congressional Quarterly, 1991), p. 39. In France, universal male suffrage for a Constituent Assembly was not instituted until 1848. *Ibid.* at pp. 130–31. In the Netherlands a States-General was introduced in 1848; 11 percent of the adult male population was eligible to vote. Universal male suffrage did not appear until 1917. *Ibid.* at p. 322. In Norway the constitution of 1814 enfranchised about 28 percent of the adult male population; suffrage for virtually all males over 25 was introduced in 1898. *Ibid.* at p. 356. In Spain the constitution of 1812 tempered royal power by enacting broad franchise provisions, but a series of coups disrupted the work of parliament. *Ibid.* at pp. 385–86. In the United Kingdom the Reform Act of 1832, much heralded as broadening the base of representation, increased the parliamentary electorate from 2.7 percent to 4.4 percent of the population. Successive reform bills in 1867 and 1884 gave the vote to most adult males. Until 1948 university graduates and businessmen were allowed two votes each. *Ibid.* at pp. 438–39; Hattersley, *supra* note 14, pp. 164–65; Lipson, *supra* note 14, pp. 80–81. In the United States, members of the presidential electoral college were not chosen by direct election in all States until 1860. Mackie and Rose, *supra*, p. 456. Senators were chosen by state legislatures until 1913, and poll taxes were only eliminated by constitutional amendment in 1964. US Const. amends. XVII, XXIV.

[16] Women became entitled to vote on equal standing with men on the following dates: Austria (1920); Belgium (1948); France (1944); Germany (1919); Greece (1956); Italy (1948); the Netherlands (1919); Norway (1913); Portugal (1968); Spain (1931); Sweden (1921); United Kingdom (1928); United States (1920). Mackie and Rose, *supra* note 15, *passim*.

[17] To argue otherwise one must defend the proposition that the process of selecting a regime can be legally separated from the regime actually selected. Participatory rights, however, are instrumental: they serve as a means by which citizens make their views known and felt in the formulation of national policy. If citizens are excluded from the political process, those rights would not have been instrumental in achieving anything. This delineation of a "proper" process creates a threshold of legitimacy that all governments must meet.

The right to political participation in international law

regimes are chosen. Rather, States have generally been free to conduct relations with governments which, under a scheme of participatory rights, would likely be regarded as pariahs.[18]

B *The nature and scope of post-war treaty-based participatory rights*

Participatory rights first appeared in multilateral instruments following the Second World War. These human rights instruments guarantee the right to political participation primarily by requiring parties to hold fair elections at regular intervals. During this era, the United Nations also began to monitor elections and plebiscites in colonial territories and newly independent states. A review of the treaty-based requirements reveals a comprehensive set of international standards governing critical aspects of the electoral process.

1 The international covenant on civil and political rights

The International Covenant on Civil and Political Rights (Political Covenant), which entered into force in 1976, is the most widely subscribed treaty guaranteeing participatory rights.[19] Article 25 is the principal provision on political rights in the Covenant, and contains three broad guarantees relevant to this discussion: non-discrimination, the right to participate in public affairs, and the right to free elections:

Every citizen shall have the right and the opportunity, without any of the distinctions mentioned in article 2 and without unreasonable restrictions:
(a) To take part in the conduct of public affairs, directly or through freely chosen representatives;
(b) To vote and to be elected at genuine periodic elections which shall be by universal and equal suffrage and shall be held by secret ballot, guaranteeing the free expression of the will of the electors;
(c) To have access, on general terms of equality, to public service in his country.[20]

---

[18] For a thorough discussion of recognition issues, *see* chapter 4 of this volume.
[19] As of March 12, 1999 there were 144 States parties to the Political Covenant. United Nations, Multilateral Treaties Deposited with the Secretary-General, Status as of March 12, 1999. *Available at* <www.un.org/depts/treaty/bible.htm>.
[20] Article 25 is the successor to Article 21 of the Universal Declaration of Human Rights, which provides:
  1. Everyone has the right to take part in the government of his country, directly or through freely chosen representatives.
  2. Everyone has the right of equal access to public service in his country.
  3. The will of the people shall be the basis of the authority of government; this will shall be expressed in periodic and genuine elections which shall be by universal and equal suffrage and shall be held by secret vote or by equivalent free voting procedures.

a Non-discrimination Article 25 provides that the rights it contains shall be enjoyed "without any of the distinctions mentioned in Article 2 of this Covenant and without unreasonable restrictions." Article 2 forbids any restrictions that discriminate against citizens on the basis of an explicitly prohibited characteristic.[21] The phrase "without unreasonable restrictions" implies that some restrictions on participation not based on prohibited distinctions are "reasonable" and therefore permissible. The drafters of the Political Covenant included this phrase to permit the denial of suffrage to minors, convicts, the mentally ill, and those not meeting residency requirements, and to permit the existence of certain limitations on the right to hold public office, such as a requirement of professional training.[22] The drafters apparently did not consider such "reasonable" restrictions "discriminatory,"[23] but did not intend the standard of reasonableness to sanction the egregious forms of discrimination set out in Article 2.[24] While Article 25's non-discrimination language is directed explicitly at individuals, it may also be read to prohibit states from discriminating against political parties embracing a particular ideology.[25]

b The right to take part in public affairs Paragraph (a) of Article 25 guarantees the right to "take part in the conduct of public affairs directly or

---

[21] Article 2 provides that all rights shall be respected "without distinction of any kind." Explicitly prohibited distinctions include "race, color, sex, language, religion, political or other opinion, national or social origin, property, birth or other status."

[22] *See* UN GAOR, 3d Comm., 16th Sess., 1097th mtg, (1961), p. 105; UN GAOR 3d Comm., 16th Sess., 1096th mtg. (1961), p. 179 [hereinafter Third Committee, 1096th Meeting]; Summary Record of the 365th Meeting, UN ESCOR Commission on Human Rights, 9th Sess., 365th mtg. (1953), pp. 5, 15–16 [hereinafter Commission on Human Rights, 365th Meeting]; Summary Record of the 364th Meeting, UN ESCOR Commission on Human Rights, 9th Sess., 364th mtg. (1953), p. 6 [hereinafter Commission on Human Rights, 364th Meeting]; Summary Record of the 363d Meeting, UN ESCOR Commission on Human Rights, 9th Sess., 363d mtg. (1953), pp. 12, 15, 16 [hereinafter Commission on Human Rights, 363d Meeting].

[23] *See* Commission on Human Rights, 363d Meeting, *supra* note 22, p. 16 (statement of Mr. Jevremovic, Yugoslavian delegate) (describing restrictions such as those based on mental deficiency as "reasons of a non-discriminatory character"); Commission on Human Rights, 365th Meeting, *supra* note 22, p. 13 (statement of Mr. Cassin, French delegate) (similar).

[24] *See* Annotation by Secretary-General of the Draft International Covenants on Human Rights, UN GAOR, 10th Sess., Supp. No. 19, (1955) [hereinafter Annotation by Secretary-General].

[25] While the Human Rights Committee has been careful to describe Art. 25 as providing rights to individuals and not groups – evidently in an effort to distinguish its refusal to consider similar claims of group entitlement under Article 1 of the Covenant – it has effectively extended the non-discrimination requirement to parties as well. In the Committee's view, freedom of association is an "essential condition . . . for the effective exercise of the right to vote and must be fully protected." Human Rights Committee, General Comment 25 (Dec. 7, 1996), para. 4.

through freely chosen representatives." Since paragraph (b) requires genuine, periodic elections, paragraph (a) must contemplate additional means of influencing public policy. While paragraph (a) does not identify the types of public bodies to which it applies, and the drafters rejected a proposal that would have applied to "all organs of authority," the Human Rights Committee has stated that the article "covers all aspects of public administration, and the formulation and implementation of policy at international, nation, regional and local levels."[26]

c Requirements concerning elections Although paragraph (b) presents some of the most difficult interpretative questions in Article 25, the drafters spent little time discussing its central terms. Paragraph (b) guarantees the right to vote "at genuine periodic elections which shall be by universal and equal suffrage and shall be held by secret ballot, guarantee[ing] the free expression of the will of the electors." The drafters generally agreed that the requirements of universal and equal suffrage and a secret ballot meant that each vote must count equally.[27] However, they left to individual States the question of whether votes would have equal effect, largely a matter determined by whether a country follows a proportional representation or a simple majority electoral system.[28] The drafters of the Universal Declaration also briefly discussed whether ballot secrecy was appropriate for States with a high percentage of illiterate voters,[29] and the majority concluded that ballot secrecy was a fundamental aspect of a fair election and should be retained.[30]

Given Cold War tensions, it is not surprising that the drafters failed to clarify whether the guarantee of a "genuine election" to establish "the free expression of the will of the electors" required party pluralism. During the Cold War this proved to be the most intractable point of division in the application of Article 25. While Western States have long maintained that single-party elections are incompatible with genuine

---

[26] *See* Annotation by Secretary-General, *supra* note 24, p. 173. [27] *Ibid.*
[28] *See, e.g.*, Commission on Human Rights, 364th Meeting, *supra* note 22, pp. 8, 15 (statement of Mr. Cassin, French delegate).
[29] *See* Summary Records of Meetings of 3d Committee, UN GAOR 3d Comm., 3d Sess., 132d mtg. at p. 450, (1948) [hereinafter Third Committee, 132d Meeting] (statement of Mr. Saint-Lot, Haitian delegate); *ibid.* at p. 455 (statement of Mr. Garcia Bauer, Guatemalan delegate).
[30] *See* Third Committee, 132d Meeting, *supra* note 29, p. 450 (statement of Mr. Sandifer, US delegate); *ibid.* at p. 459 (statement of Mr. Watt, Australian delegate); *ibid.* at p. 463 (statement of Mr. Pavlov, Soviet delegate). The Universal Declaration provides in Article 21(3) for a secret ballot "or equivalent free voting procedures." This language was not retained in the Political Covenant, thus establishing secret balloting as the sole legitimate method of voting.

56   *The normative foundations of a right to political participation*

choice, socialist States did not share this view.[31] During the Covenant's long drafting process (1948–66), this debate spread to other regions. Several African leaders (most prominently Tanzanian President Julius Nyerere) argued in the 1960s that the existence of multiple political parties was not a prerequisite to genuine electoral choice.[32] Others argued that multiple parties would bring violence and perhaps civil war to states in which different ethnic groups, forced together by colonial-era boundaries, would seize on competitive elections as a means of exploiting pre-existing divisions.[33]

The Political Covenant's *travaux préparatoires* barely address this issue. The Human Rights and Third Committees spent little time debating the meaning of the term "genuine," and did not discuss the specific question of party pluralism. The only attempt to define a "genuine" election came late in the drafting process, when the Chilean delegate stated that "[t]he adjective 'genuine' had been used to guarantee that all elections

---

[31] For example, the Soviet delegate argued that "in his country, the bourgeois class had ceased to exist. There thus remained only workers and peasants, and the Communist Party by itself was capable of looking after their interests." UN GAOR 3d Comm., 3d Sess., 134th mtg. at p. 471 (1948) [hereinafter Third Committee, 134th Meeting] (statement of Mr. Pavlov, Soviet delegate). He argued further that "[u]nder the prevailing system [in the Soviet Union], there was no justification for the creation of other parties." *Ibid.* These statements occurred during the debate over the Universal Declaration.

[32] *See, e.g.*, Julius K. Nyerere, "Democracy and the Party System" (1962) in *Freedom and Unity: A Selection from Writings and Speeches, 1952–66* (New York: Oxford University Press, 1966); *see also* International Comm'n of Jurists, ed., *Human Rights in a One-Party State* (1978); Yougindra Khushalani, "Human Rights in Africa and Asia," *Hum. Rts. L.J.* 4 (1983), pp. 403, 417; Simbi V. Mubako, "Zambia's Single-Party Constitution – A Search for Unity and Development," *Zambia L.J.* 5 (1973), 67, pp. 80–3. For a more recent view, *see* Ibbo Mandaza and Lloyd Sachikonye eds., *The One Party State and Democracy: The Zimbabwe Debate* (1991).

[33] *See, e.g.*, Pius Msekwa, "The Doctrine of the One-Party State in Relation to Human Rights and the Rule of Law," in *Human Rights in a One-Party State* (London: Int'l Comm'n Jurists, 1978), 22, pp. 22–23. Togo, for example, defended its one-party system in response to queries from the UN Human Rights Committee as follows:

> [P]luralism which had been instituted at the time of independence had rapidly degenerated, giving rise to a plethora of parties based on ethnic units, each serving its own interests. This had engendered a civil war mentality. The Togolese People's Rally had proved to be the best means of achieving national unity and solidarity. The concept of "rally" implied respect for the individual and for diversity of opinions, the single Party being a forum where citizens could engage in dialogue and freely express their points of view. (Report of the Human Rights Committee, UN GAOR, 44th Sess., Supp. no. 40, pp. 60–61, (1989) [hereinafter Report to 44th Session].)

See also Report of the Human Rights Committee, UN GAOR, 45th Sess., Supp. No. 40, p. 121 (1990) [hereinafter Report to 45th Session] (statement of Zairian delegate) ("The limitation to three political parties had been chosen to avoid the repetition of the tragic experience of the years 1960–65 when unrestricted multipartism caused serious difficulties and involved the death of more than half a million people.")

of every kind faithfully reflected the opinion of the population and to protect the electors against government pressure and fraud."[34] The text itself supports this interpretation. A parenthetical clause providing for universal and equal suffrage and secret ballot, and the phrase "guaranteeing the free expression of the will of the electors," follow the requirement of "genuine periodic elections." The latter phrase appears to be describing the first: that is, a "genuine periodic" election is one which guarantees the "will of the electors," freely expressed. On this view, if the electorate did not have the opportunity to express its opinion by casting a vote for a particular candidate or party, the election would not be "genuine."[35]

This interpretation suggests that Article 25, as originally drafted, did not prohibit one-party States *per se*. Single-party elections would run afoul of the Chilean formula only if (1) public opinion in a State were actually divided on important political issues, and (2) if a single party did not permit candidates representing each faction to stand for election. A single party of homogeneous views would accurately reflect the "free expression of the will of the electors" if there were no divisions in public opinion. Similarly, if divisions did exist but the various factions within a party gave voice to all major points of view, additional parties would be unnecessary.

The Human Rights Committee, which reviews parties' adherence to the Political Covenant, has consistently expressed skepticism that "genuine" one-party elections are possible.[36] In 1993 the Committee faced the issue directly and, in a little-publicized decision, abandoned its case-by-case approach and held that one-party systems impose inherent limitations on genuine electoral choice. The decision came in an

---

[34] Third Committee, 1096th Meeting, *supra* note 22, p. 180.

[35] The Inter-American Commission on Human Rights, for example, has concluded that an "authentic election" occurs when there exists "some consistency between the will of the voters and the result of the election." Mexico Elections Decision, Cases 9768, 9780, 9828, Inter-Am. C.H.R. 97, 108, OEA/ser. L/V/11.77, doc. 7, rev. 1 (1990). The Commission based this opinion upon the American Convention on Human Rights, whose provisions on participatory rights it has described as "fundamentally coincid[ing]" with Article 25 of the Political Covenant. *Ibid.* at p. 107.

[36] Upon receipt of a State party's periodic report, the Human Rights Committee usually questions State delegates as to whether opposition parties are permitted, the extent to which those parties are allowed to operate freely, and whether any parties have been banned. *See, e.g.*, Report to 45th Session, *supra* note 33, p. 13 (Yemen); *ibid.* at p. 38 (Portugal); *ibid.* at p. 47 (Chile); *ibid.* at p. 52 (Argentina); *ibid.* at p. 95 (Nicaragua); *ibid.* at p. 104 (Vietnam); Report to 44th Session, *supra* note 33, at p. 28 (Mexico); *ibid.* at pp. 57, 61 (Togo); Report of the Human Rights Committee, UN GAOR, 42d Sess., Supp. no. 40, at p. 22, UN Doc. A/42/40 (1987) (Poland); *ibid.* at p. 38 (Tunisia); *ibid.* at p. 57 (Senegal).

individual petition filed by Peter Chiiko Bwalya, a Zambian citizen, who had attempted to stand for parliamentary election as a member of an opposition party.[37] The party was banned under Zambia's one-party constitution, and Bwalya alleged that the authorities had "prevented him from properly preparing his candidacy and from participating in the electoral campaign."[38] Bwalya alleged further that in retaliation for his candidacy he was dismissed from his job, expelled from his home, and ultimately detained for thirty-one months on charges of belonging to the banned party.[39] These actions, Bwalya claimed, violated Article 25 of the Covenant. The Committee agreed:

> The Committee notes that the author, a leading figure of a political party in opposition to the former President, has been prevented from participating in a general election campaign as well as from preparing his candidacy for this party. This amounts to an unreasonable restriction on the author's right to "take part in the conduct of public affairs" which the State party has failed to explain or justify.
>
> In particular, it has failed to explain the requisite conditions for participation in the elections. Accordingly, it must be assumed that Mr. Bwalya was detained and denied the right to run for a parliamentary seat in the Constituency of Chifubu merely on account of his membership in a political party other than that officially recognized; in this context, the Committee observes that restrictions on political activity outside the only recognized political party amount to an unreasonable restriction of the right to participate in the conduct of public affairs.[40]

Three years later, the Committee issued a General Comment on Article 25 in which it reiterated and expanded on its holding in Bwalya.[41] The Committee first noted the centrality of the electoral processes outlined in Article 25 to an effective democratic system: "Article 25 lies at the core of democratic government based on the consent of the people and in conformity with the principles of the Covenant."[42] Given this link between popular consent and governmental authority, the Committee

---

[37] Communication No. 314/1988, UN Doc. CCPR/C/48/D/314/1988 (1993).
[38] Ibid., para. 2.1.   [39] Ibid., para. 2.3.
[40] Ibid., para. 6.6. For reasons that are unclear, the Committee located the violation of Article 25 in sub-section (a), addressing the general right to "take part in the conduct of public affairs," rather than sub-section (b), which deals directly with elections.
[41] General Comment 25, *supra* note 25. *See also* Annual Report of the Human Rights Committee, UN Doc. A/52/40, para. 120 (1997) (Committee "welcomes the positive political evolution of Gabon toward a multi-party and pluralist democracy"); Annual Report of the Human Rights Committee, UN Doc. A/51/40, para. 191 (1996) (addressing Zambia, the Committee "welcomes the introduction of a multi-party system of government as well as efforts undertaken by the State party to strengthen democratic institutions and the multi-party system").
[42] General Comment 25, *supra* note 25, para. 1.

emphasized the need for electoral systems to minimize distortions of popular views. While the Committee acknowledged that Article 25 does not envision any particular form of electoral system, it noted that "any system operating in a State party must . . . guarantee and give effect to the free expression of the will of the electors."[43]

Having established broad electoral choice as a principle animating Article 25, the Committee proceeded to address restrictions on party activities from three different perspectives. First, addressing the rights of voters, the Committee stated that "[p]arty membership should not be a condition of eligibility to vote, nor a ground of disqualification."[44] Second, regarding candidates, "[t]he rights of persons to stand for election should not be limited unreasonably by requiring candidates to be members of parties or of specific parties."[45] Finally, in setting out other political rights necessary for meaningful political participation, the Committee stated that "[t]he right to freedom of association, including the right to form and join organizations and associations concerned with political and public affairs, in an essential adjunct to the rights protected by article 25."[46] This is so, the Committee concluded, because "[p]olitical parties and membership in parties play a significant role in the conduct of public affairs and the election process."[47]

2 The First Protocol to the European Convention on Human Rights

The European Convention on Human Rights itself contains no provisions on participatory rights. However, Article 3 of the First Protocol to the Convention provides: "The High Contracting Parties undertake to hold free elections at reasonable intervals by secret ballot, under conditions which will ensure the free expression of the opinion of the people in the choice of the legislature." Article 3 is therefore substantially narrower in scope than Article 25 of the Political Covenant, as it does not require universal suffrage or "genuine" elections, does not prohibit discrimination, and does not mention equal access to public service. Finally, Article 3 does not discuss political participation as an individual right, but rather addresses the obligations of States parties.

The European Commission and Court of Human Rights have disregarded these literal shortcomings, however, and have interpreted Article 3 to provide guarantees substantially similar to those contained in the Political Covenant. They have done so by viewing the Protocol's language through the lens of the European states' common democratic

---

[43] *Ibid.*, para. 21.   [44] *Ibid.*, para. 10.   [45] *Ibid.*, para. 17.   [46] *Ibid.*, para. 26.   [47] *Ibid.*

heritage.[48] Unlike the UN Human Rights Committee, which rarely ventures beyond treaty language in its decisions on participatory rights, European tribunals have adduced extra-textual participatory rights that reflect the common expectations of states parties to the Convention.

An example is Article 3's application to elections for "the legislature." The European Court has held that a legislature "does not necessarily mean the national parliament: the word has to be interpreted in the light of the constitutional structure of the state in question."[49] The Court will apply Article 3 to political institutions so as to ensure that "effective political democracy" is maintained.[50] In a remarkable decision applying this principle, the Court found that the European Parliament, which is established by separate multilateral treaty, has become sufficiently involved in the legislative process of the European Union to constitute a "legislature" for purposes of Article 3.[51] Individuals living in states of the EU (or in dependent territories thereof) thus have a right under the European Convention to vote for members of the European Parliament.[52]

a Rights concerning elections Although Article 3 appears to impose a duty on States rather than bestow rights on individuals,[53] both the Commission and the Court have found the Protocol to contain an implicit guarantee of individual rights.[54] This interpretative leap has quite practical roots: to deny all voters and candidates standing to bring claims under Article 3 would foreclose the most effective means of

---

[48] The European Convention declares in its preamble that the governments of Europe "are likeminded and have a common heritage of political traditions, ideals, freedom and the rule of law." The European Court of Human Rights has made clear that this commonality is founded in democratic principles, holding that "[d]emocracy is without doubt a fundamental feature of the European public order," and that democracy "appears to be that only political model contemplated by the Convention and, accordingly, the only one compatible with it." United Communist Party of Turkey and Others v. Turkey, E.H.R.R. 26 (1998), p. 121, para. 45.

[49] Matthews v. United Kingdom, App. No. 24833/94 (1999), para. 40.

[50] *Ibid.*, para. 43.   [51] *Ibid.*, para. 54.   [52] *Ibid.*, para. 65.

[53] As a report of the Council of Europe stated in 1968:

[Article 3] does not guarantee that the individual shall enjoy a certain right . . . The individual as citizen has at most the "right" to expect the Contracting States to hold such elections, thus fulfilling the obligation assumed when ratifying the European Convention. But he can on no account deduce from the actual wording of the clause his own right to vote or his right as a citizen to take part in such elections.

Council of Europe, Report of the Council of Europe to the International Conference on Human Rights, 1968 (1968), section 5.

[54] Matthews, *supra* note 49; Mathieu-Mohin and Clerfayt v. Belgium, *Eur. Ct. Hum. Rts.* 113 (ser. A) (1987), pp. 22, 23; W. v. Belgium, *Eur. Comm'n Hum. Rts. Dec. & Rep.* 2, (1975), p. 116.

bringing denials of political rights before adjudicatory bodies of the Council of Europe. The Court has drawn on a number of sources to conclude that Article 3 protects "subjective rights of participation – the 'right to vote' and the 'right to stand for election to the legislature.'"[55]

Neither of these rights is unconditional. The Court has devised a multifaceted test to evaluate limitations on political rights: "[C]onditions [cannot] curtail the rights in question to such an extent as to impair their very essence and deprive them of their effectiveness . . . In particular, such conditions must not thwart 'the free expression of the opinion of the people in the choice of the legislature.'"[56] The "free expression" requirement, the Court explained, "implies essentially – apart from freedom of expression (already protected under Article 10 of the Convention) – the principle of equality of treatment of all citizens in the exercise of their right to vote and their right to stand for election."[57]

However, the Court has also held that states may restrict the rights to vote and to stand for election so long as the limitations are not arbitrary, disproportionate, or thwart "the free expression of opinion of the people in the choice of legislature."[58] Thus, limitations with substantial public policy justifications and minimal impact on the representative nature of legislatures have been upheld. Convicted prisoners serving jail sentences may be disqualified from voting,[59] as may imprisoned conscientious objectors.[60] The Commission has also upheld various residency requirements.[61] In interpreting the right to stand for election, the Commission has upheld State subsidies to parties that attain a certain percentage of the vote,[62] minimum signature requirements for a party to appear on a ballot,[63] and prohibitions against members of one legislative body standing for election to another.[64] The Commission also seems to follow an unexpressed *de minimis* rule: laws such as those excluding parties unable to muster 500 signatures are considered unlikely to alter the outcome of an election, and are therefore permissible.[65] Such an approach toward

---

[55] Mathieu-Mohin, *supra* note 54, pp. 22–23. [56] *Ibid.* [57] *Ibid.*, at 24.
[58] Gitonas and Others v. Greece, *Eur. Ct. H. R. 1997–IV* (1997), para. 44.
[59] X v. Federal Republic of Germany, App. No. 2728/66, *Eur. Comm'n Hum. Rts. Dec. & Rep.* 25 (1967), pp. 38, 40.
[60] H v. The Netherlands, App. No. 9914/82, *Eur. Comm'n Hum. Rts. Dec. & Rep.* 33 (1983), pp. 242, 245–46.
[61] X v. United Kingdom, App. No. 7730/76, *Eur. Comm'n Hum. Rts. Dec. & Rep.* 15 (1979), p. 137; X. v. United Kingdom, App. No. 7566/76, *Eur. Comm'n Hum. Rts. Dec. & Rep.* 9 (1976), p. 121.
[62] X v. Federal Republic of Germany, App. No. 6850/74, *Eur. Comm'n Hum. Rts. Dec. & Rep.* 5 (1976), pp. 90, 93. [63] *Ibid.* at 94.
[64] M v. United Kingdom, App. No. 10316/83, *Eur. Comm'n Hum. Rts. Dec. & Rep.* 37 (1984), pp. 129, 135. [65] *See* X v. Federal Republic of Germany, *supra* note 62, p. 94.

small political movements is consistent with the Court's longstanding view that Article 3 does not require a system of proportional representation; each party need not receive seats in the legislature in proportion to its percentage of the popular vote.[66] These rulings are in keeping with the wide margin of discretion afforded State parties in structuring their electoral systems.[67]

The Court's most far-reaching decisions on permissible limitations have arisen out of Turkey's repeated banning of political parties that advocate an accommodation with Kurdish separatist forces.[68] Two of these banned parties – the United Communist Party of Turkey and the Socialist Party – challenged the bans as violations of Article 11 of the European Convention, which guarantees freedom of association.[69] While the Court found that Turkey had in both cases been pursuing the legitimate aim of preserving national security,[70] the extreme remedy of banning entire parties was deemed not "necessary in a democratic society." Neither party, the Court found, advocated violence or in any other way posed a threat to the democratic process. To the contrary, both offered dialogue and negotiation as alternatives to the government's military campaign against Kurdish forces.[71] The bans, the Court concluded, contravened this very "democratic" approach to the Kurdish problem:

> one of the principal characteristics of democracy is the possibility it offers of resolving a country's problems through dialogue, without recourse to violence, even when they are irksome. Democracy thrives on freedom of expression. From that point of view, there can be no justification for hindering a political group solely because it seeks to debate in public the situation of part of the State's population and to take part in the nation's political life in order to find, according to democratic rules, solutions capable of satisfying everyone concerned.[72]

---

[66] Mathieu-Mohin, *supra* note 54, pp. 23–24.
[67] Gitonas, *supra* note 58, para. 39. In the Matthews case the Court stated: "the choice of electoral system by which the free expression of the opinion of the people in the choice of legislature is ensured – whether it be based on proportional representation, the 'first-past-the-post' system or some other arrangement – is a matter in which the state enjoys a wide margin of appreciation." Matthews, *supra* note 49, para. 64.
[68] The legitimacy of party bans is discussed more fully in chapter 12 of this volume.
[69] Case of Socialist Party and Others v. Turkey, 1998–III (1998); United Communist Party of Turkey and Others v. Turkey, *supra* note 48. Because the Court in both cases held the bans to be in violation of Article 11, it did not reach the question of whether Article 3 of Protocol 1 had been breached. Socialist Party, para. 57; Communist Party, para. 64.
[70] Socialist Party, para. 36; Communist Party, para. 41.
[71] Socialist Party, para. 46; Communist Party, para. 57. [72] Communist Party, para. 57.

The Court held to this position despite Turkey's assertion that its very national identity was at stake. The Turkish Constitutional Court, in the case of the Socialist Party, had found proposals for accommodation with Kurdish aspirations for autonomy to threaten "the unity of the Turkish nation and the territorial integrity of the State."[73] In the Court's view, this was not sufficient justification for a ban:

> the fact that such a political programme is considered incompatible with the current principles and strictures of the Turkish State does not make it incompatible with the rules of democracy. It is of the essence of democracy to allow diverse political programmes to be proposed and debated, even those that call into question the way a State is currently organized, provided they do not harm democracy itself.[74]

b Non-discrimination Article 3 of the first Protocol does not contain an anti-discrimination provision, but the Commission has adjudicated claims of electoral discrimination under Article 14, the general anti-discrimination clause in the European Convention.[75] As with Article 2 of the Political Covenant, Article 14 of the European Convention forbids discrimination on any ground whatever. However, the European Court has held that Article 14 does not provide a remedy against all instances of inequality.[76] The Court's test focuses instead on the reasons for differential treatment, asking whether:

> [T]he facts found disclose a differential treatment; . . . the distinction does not have a legitimate aim, i.e., it has no objective and reasonable justification having regard to the aim and effects of the measure under consideration; and . . . there is no reasonable proportionality between the means employed and the aim sought to be realized.[77]

The test's initial criterion concerns not only facially discriminatory laws, but those laws that affect similarly situated persons differently. The British Liberal Party, in a challenge to Britain's simple majority electoral

---

[73] Socialist Party, para. 47.   [74] *Ibid.*
[75] *See* Liberal Party v. United Kingdom, App. No. 8765/79, *Eur. Comm'n Hum. Rts. Dec. & Rep.* 21 (1980) p. 211 (reviewing claim that simple majority electoral system constitutes discrimination based on political opinion and party affiliation); Lindsay v. United Kingdom, App. No. 8364/78, *Eur. Comm'n Hum. Rts. Dec. & Rep.* 15 (1970), p. 247 (reviewing similar claim in regard to elections for European Parliament).
[76] Case Relating to Certain Aspects of the Laws on the Use of Languages in Belgium (Belgian Linguistics Case), *Eur. Ct. Hum. Rts.* 6 (ser. A) (1968), p. 34.
[77] Geillustreerde Pers N.V. v. The Netherlands, App. No. 5178/71, *Eur. Comm'n Hum. Rts. Dec. & Rep.* 8 (1976), pp. 5, 14–15.

system, claimed that the dominant parties' refusal to adopt a proportional system constituted discrimination based on political opinion and party affiliation.[78] The Commission agreed that the system functioned to the Party's detriment, but found that the simple majority electoral system passed other elements of the test, and so was not *per se* discriminatory.[79]

The second criterion, whether an "objective and reasonable justification" supports differential treatment, has been the crucial issue in most claims under Article 14. Review of this standard requires the Court or Commission to strike a "fair balance between the protection of the interests of the community and respect for the rights and freedoms safeguarded by the Convention" when reviewing a State's justifications for differential treatment.[80] In the Liberal Party Case, the Commission found no Article 14 violation, reasoning that "[t]he simple majority system is one of the two basic electoral systems. It is or has been used in ma[n]y democratic countries. It has always been accepted as allowing for the 'free expression of the opinion of the people' even if it operates to the detriment of small parties."[81] This decision suggests that the Commission will view distinctions which have long been part of Europe's common political heritage as "objective and reasonable."

The third criterion, proportionality, has received somewhat less attention from the European Court and Commission, perhaps because the question of whether a restriction is reasonably proportional to its goal can only be determined on a case-by-case basis.

3 *The American Convention on Human Rights*

Article 23 of the American Convention explicitly tracks Article 25 of the Political Covenant, varying only in minor respects.[82] Yet despite textual similarities, the unique problems in the region have sent the

---

[78] Liberal Party, *supra* note 75, pp. 211, 221.   [79] *Ibid.*, at 221.
[80] *See* Belgian Linguistics Case, *supra* note 76, p. 44.   [81] *See* Liberal Party, *supra* note 75, p. 225.
[82] Article 23 provides:

(1) Every citizen shall enjoy the following rights and opportunities:
   (a) to take part in the conduct of public affairs, directly or through freely chosen representatives;
   (b) to vote and to be elected in genuine periodic elections, which shall be by universal and equal suffrage and by secret ballot that guarantees the free expression of the will of the voters; and
   (c) to have access, under general conditions of equality, to the public service of his country.
(2) The law may regulate the exercise of the rights and opportunities referred to in the preceding paragraph only on the basis of age, nationality, residence, language, education, civil and mental capacity, or sentencing by a competent court in criminal proceedings.

The right to political participation in international law 65

Inter-American Commission on Human Rights in its own interpretive directions. Unlike both the UN Human Rights Commission and the European tribunals, the Inter-American Commission has not focused on elucidating particular treaty terms. In the years prior to the democratic transitions of the late 1980s, the reports often concerned states in which ruling parties had entirely suspended representative government and engaged in widespread violations of other human rights.[83] Many of these reports describe attempts to manipulate elections that rather clearly violate Article 23, such as fraud, intimidation, and misuse of government property during election campaigns. Few of the reports contain a close textual analysis of the American Convention.

The Commission's review of the 1990 Mexican elections is its most significant decision on participatory rights, holding that violations of these rights are emphatically a matter of international concern.[84] Mexico argued that "no Article of the Convention gives it the competence to rule in the states parties' internal political processes."[85] The Commission rejected this view, holding quite sensibly that to adopt Mexico's position would render Article 23 rights unenforceable. "Any mention of the right to vote and to be elected would be mere rhetoric if unaccompanied by a precisely described set of characteristics that the elections are required to meet."[86]

According to the Commission, the central issue under Article 23 is whether an election is "authentic." The Commission has defined an "authentic" election as one occurring in the context of "a legal and institutional structure conducive to election results that reflect the will of the voters."[87] Thus, excessive government intrusions into the political

---

[83] *See* Report on the Situation of Human Rights in Haiti, OEA/ser.L/V/II.77, doc. 18, rev. 1, at pp. 9–27 (1991) [hereinafter Second Haiti Report]; Report on the Situation of Human Rights in Panama, OEA/ser.L/V/II.76, doc. 16, rev. 2, at pp. 47–61 (1989) [hereinafter Panama Report]; Report on the Situation of Human Rights in Haiti, OEA/ser.L/V/II.74, doc. 9, rev. 1, at pp. 53–105 (1988) [hereinafter First Haiti Report]; Report on the Situation of Human Rights in Paraguay, OEA/ser.L/V/II.71, doc. 19, rev. 1, at pp. 93–113 (1987) [hereinafter Paraguay Report]; Report on the Situation of Human Rights in Chile, OEA/ser.L/V/II.66, doc. 17, at pp. 253–83 (1985) [hereinafter Chile Report]; The Situation of Human Rights in Cuba: Seventh Report, OEA/ser.L/V/II.61, doc. 29, rev. 1, at pp. 25–37 (1983) [hereinafter Cuba Report]; Annual Report of the Inter-American Commission on Human Rights 1979–80, OEA/ser.L/V/II.50, doc. 13, rev. 1, at pp. 120–24 (1980) [hereinafter 1979–80 Annual Report] (reviewing status of human rights in Uruguay).   [84] Mexico Elections Decision, *supra* note 35, p. 97.
[85] *Ibid.*, at p. 9.   [86] *Ibid.*, at p. 10.
[87] Panama Report, *supra* note 83, p. 47; *see also* Mexico Elections Decision, Inter-Am. C.H.R. at p. 108 ("[t]here must be some consistency between the will of the voters and the result of the election. In the negative sense the characteristic implies an absence of coercion which distorts the will of the citizens").

process warps and delegitimizes electoral outcomes,[88] and States should strive to prevent "a disproportionate presence of the government" in electoral activities.[89] An authentic election, therefore, is one in which no barriers, such as intimidation, fraud, and harassment, come between the popular will and electoral results. If necessary, an independent electoral commission should verify voting rolls, tabulate ballots, and monitor campaign conduct.[90]

The most important prerequisite to an authentic election is the absence of coercion or intimidation of voters.[91] The Commission has concluded that one-party States are inherently coercive, and by implication such States are incapable of holding authentic elections.[92] The Commission argues that pluralism prevents individuals or groups from acquiring monopolies on political power.[93] The absence of pluralism results in governments that are estranged from the views of their citizens, and therefore do not embody an "authentic" popular choice.[94]

4 Other international instruments guaranteeing participatory rights

a The African Charter on Human and Peoples' Rights Article 13 of the African Charter guarantees participatory rights, but because it lacks specific standards regarding elections its utility remains unclear. Article 13 provides that "[e]very citizen shall have the right to freely participate in the government of his country, either directly or through freely chosen representatives, in accordance with the provisions of the law." The "freely chosen" requirement implies a right to vote without coercion or intimidation. However, unlike the Political Covenant or the European Convention, the African Charter fails to stipulate that an electoral choice must reflect the free expression of the electors' will or the opinion of the people. The absence of such a provision suggests that Article 13 may permit one-party elections. The "freely chosen" clause could require merely an absence of coercion in any election, including one

---

[88] 1979–80 Annual Report, *supra* note 83, p. 124; Chile Report, *supra* note 83, p. 282; Panama Report, *supra* note 83, p. 115; Paraguay Report, *supra* note 83, p. 113.
[89] Mexico Elections Decision, *supra* note 35, p. 112. [90] Panama Report, *supra* note 83, pp. 48–57.
[91] Second Haiti Report, *supra* note 83, p. 10; Mexico Elections Decision, *supra* note 35, p. 108; Cuba Report, *supra* note 83, p. 37 (noting that party restrictions impede "the existence of healthy ideological and party pluralism, which is one of the basis of a democratic system of government").
[92] *See* Cuba Report, *supra* note 83, p. 35 ("[T]he intolerance of the groups in power toward any form of political opposition represents the principal limitation on participation").
[93] Inter-American Comm'n on Hum. Rts., Ten Years of Activities 1971–81, p. 334 (1982); Mexico Elections Decision, *supra* note 35, p. 107.
[94] Chile Report, *supra* note 83, p. 282; 1979–80 Annual Report, *supra* note 83, pp. 122–24.

involving pre-selected parties or candidates. Article 13 also lacks provisions addressing discrimination, universal suffrage, and a secret ballot. Finally, the reservation that rights need only be respected "in accordance with the provisions of the law" suggests that Article 13 requires nothing more of States than what is already provided by their national constitutions. If so, then Article 13 would be almost entirely useless as an international standard by which each State is to measure the legality of its actions.

Despite these textual ambiguities, the African Commission on Human Rights has issued a series of remarkably forthright and unqualified statements in support of electoral democracy. Perhaps because Article 13 is not well suited to condemning unelected (or dubiously elected) governments, the Commission has followed the lead of the Inter-American Commission and eschewed a detailed elucidation of textual terms. Its statements have come as broad declarations in resolutions, and not in individual cases.[95] These statements are perhaps the most effective articulation of democratic principles in a continent where the problems of democracy frequently involve not, as in Europe, variations on a set of shared assumptions, but direct attacks on democratic institutions and their supporters.

In a "Resolution on the Military," for example, the Commission declared that "the best government is one elected by, and accountable to the people."[96] It called upon "incumbent military governments to hand over political power to democratically elected governments without prolonging their incumbencies and unnecessarily delaying the return to democratic civilian rule."[97] Applying these principles to a military coup in The Gambia, the Commission reaffirmed "the fundamental principle that all governments should be based on the consent of the people freely expressed by them and through their chosen representatives and that a military government is a clear violation of this fundamental principle of democracy."[98] It condemned the coup as "a flagrant and grave violation of the right of the Gambian people to freely choose their government."[99] Similarly, the Commission called on the then-military

---

[95] Responding to several individual petitions against Malawi, however, the Commission spoke favorably of "important political changes" in the country: "Multiparty elections have been held, resulting in a new government. The Commission hopes that a new era of respect for the human rights of Malawi's citizens has begun." Communs. 64/92, 68/92 & 72/92, Opinion of Nov. 3, 1994 (16th Ord. Sess.), *reprinted in Hum. Rts. L.J.* 18 (1997), p. 29.
[96] "Resolution on the Military," *Eighth Annual Activity Report of the Commission on Human and Peoples' Rights, 1994–95*, Thirty-First Ordinary Session, June 26–28, 1995, Addis Ababa, Ethiopia, p. 39.
[97] *Ibid.*, p. 39.   [98] "Resolution on The Gambia," *in ibid.*, p. 42.   [99] *Ibid.*

government of Nigeria "to respect the right of free participation in government... and hand over the government to duly elected representatives of the people without unnecessary delay."[100] And in a resolution assessing the overall "Human Rights Situation in Africa," the Commission expressed alarm at "the possible resurgence of the illegal seizure of the reins of government in Africa," and called upon "all African Governments to ensure that elections and electoral processes are transparent and fair."[101]

b Organization for Security and Co-operation in Europe Accords The Organization for Security and Co-operation in Europe (OSCE), previously the CSCE, has adopted three documents containing lengthy and highly detailed provisions on participatory rights. The three documents represented the culmination of a long negotiating process which began with the 1975 CSCE Final Act (generally referred to as the Helsinki Accords).[102] While CSCE States did not intend for the Helsinki process to produce legally binding treaties,[103] provisions in these subsequent agreements read as obligatory rather than merely hortatory standards.

For example, the Copenhagen Document, concluded on June 29, 1990, begins with a number of broad statements affirming the importance of representative government.[104] It then describes a comprehensive set of requirements for all electoral systems.[105] The document also sets standards for the observation of elections, a provision intended to "enhance the electoral process."[106] Another important OSCE endorsement of participatory rights appears in the Charter of Paris, signed on November 21, 1990.[107] The Charter also creates an institutional struc-

[100] "Resolution on Nigeria," *in ibid.*, p. 40.
[101] "Resolution on the Human Rights Situation in Africa," *in ibid.*, pp. 42–3.
[102] Conference on Security and Co-operation in Europe Final Act (Helsinki Accords), Aug. 1, 1975, 14 ILM (1975), p. 1292.
[103] *See* Alexander C. Kiss and Mary F. Dominick, "The International Legal Significance of the Human Rights Provisions of the Helsinki Final Act," *Vand. J. Transnat'l L.* 13 (1980), p. 293 (describing history of CSCE process).
[104] Document of the Copenhagen Meeting of the Conference on the Human Dimension of the Conference on Security and Co-operation in Europe, June 29, 1990, pmbl., 29 ILM (1990), pp. 1305, 1307 ("[The signatories] welcome the commitment expressed by all participating States to the ideals of democracy and political pluralism as well as their common determination to build democratic societies based on free elections and the rule of law").
[105] *Ibid.*, paras. 5.1–5.4, 29 ILM at p. 1308.   [106] *Ibid.*, para. 8, 29 ILM p. 1310.
[107] CSCE Charter of Paris for a New Europe, 30 ILM (Nov. 21, 1990), pp. 190, 193 (preamble). The Charter succinctly provides that signatories "undertake to build, consolidate and strengthen democracy as the only system of government of our nations." *Ibid.*

The right to political participation in international law 69

ture to oversee their implementation by establishing an Office for Free Elections.[108]

The OSCE dramatically strengthened the normative force of its standards in October 1991 through the Moscow Document.[109] Drafted following the attempted Soviet coup, the Moscow Document condemns "unreservedly forces which seek to take power from a representative government of a participating State against the will of the people as expressed in free and fair elections."[110] In the event of a coup against an elected regime, the Document directs member States not to recognize the usurping force.[111] This commitment appears to repudiate the time-honored *de facto* control test, under which any government in control of a nation is recognized by other States. In its place, the Moscow Document substitutes a Wilsonian notion of democratic legitimacy.[112]

5 Summary of treaty-based norms

The preceding review of global and regional treaty systems reveals that a free, fair, and legally sufficient election consists of the following four elements: (1) universal and equal suffrage; (2) a secret ballot; (3) elections at reasonable periodic intervals; and (4) an absence of discrimination against voters, candidates, or parties. For many years, however, the treaty bodies elucidating the texts in which these standards appear either issued equivocal rulings or did not speak at all to important issues such as party pluralism. Moreover, if the claim is to be made that participatory rights have migrated beyond the strict confines of human rights treaties and entered general customary law, additional evidence of State practice is needed. Some scholars have criticized the announcement of new human rights based on little more than verbal support.[113] Actual State practice, these critics contend, is as essential to customary law here as it is elsewhere. The next sections will address this problem by reviewing the practice of monitoring referenda, plebiscites, and, most importantly, national elections. Election monitoring provides critical support for the participatory norms now firmly established as a matter of treaty law.

---

[108] *Ibid.*, Art. 1, § 6, 30 ILM, p. 195.
[109] Conference on Security and Co-operation in Europe, Document of the Moscow Meeting on the Human Dimension, Emphasizing Respect for Human Rights, Pluralistic Democracy, the Rule of Law, and Procedures for Fact-Finding, Oct. 3, 1991, 30 ILM (1991), p. 1670.
[110] *Ibid.*, para. 17.1., 30 ILM, p. 1677.   [111] *Ibid.*
[112] *See* the discussion of democratic legitimacy as a basis for recognition in chapter 4 of this volume.
[113] *See, e.g.*, Philip Alston, "Conjuring up New Human Rights: A Proposal for Quality Control," *Am. J. Int'l L.* 78 (1984), p. 607.

III INTERNATIONAL ELECTION MONITORING: THE ELABORATION AND ENFORCEMENT OF PARTICIPATORY RIGHTS

The United Nations has monitored a variety of elections in the post-war era, developing standards for "free and fair" balloting that approximate quite closely the participatory rights set out in the Political Covenant and other instruments. None of the UN's early monitoring in colonial territories was undertaken to vindicate a right to political participation. These votes were rather viewed in purely instrumental terms as effectuating colonial peoples' right to self-determination.

Recently, however, as election monitoring has entered the mainstream of UN assistance to developing countries, a link to treaty-based participatory rights has emerged. UN missions have implicitly affirmed the interpretations of participating rights first articulated by human rights treaty bodies. They have also cast themselves as enforcing a right to political participation.

A Election monitoring prior to 1945

Regular national elections did not become common in Europe until the mid-nineteenth century, and so it is not surprising that foreign observers monitored few elections before the First World War. While foreign observers monitored several plebiscites on national self-determination during this period,[114] these early votes did not generate a consistent set of criteria by which to judge elections.

Plebiscites held after 1918 produced a more consistent set of monitoring criteria. The Treaty of Versailles provided for referenda in ten territories of mixed ethnic composition.[115] The treaty did not establish specific election guidelines, requiring only that troops from the various interested States be evacuated from the plebiscite zones and that the "freedom, fair-

---

[114] *See* Lawrence T. Farley, *Plebiscites and Sovereignty* 4 (1986) (noting instances of pre-World War I election monitoring). Several well-known plebiscites on the unification of Italian provinces were held from 1848 to 1870. Other plebiscites of a similar nature included the following: Moldavia and Wallachia (1857), the Ionian Islands (1863), St. Thomas and St. John in the West Indies (1866), St. Bartholomew in the West Indies (1877), and Norway (1905). *See generally* Sarah Wambaugh, *A Monograph on Plebiscites with a Collection of Documents* (1920), pp. 58–169 (discussing early plebiscites).

[115] Treaty of Versailles, June 28, 1919, 225 Consol.T.S. 189, 2 Bevans 43. Plebiscites were held in Schleswig (1920), Allenstein and Marienwerder (1920), Klagenfort Basin (1920), Upper Silesia (1921), Sopron (1921), and the Saar Territory (1935). The Allies planned but did not carry out plebiscites in Teschen, Spisz, and Orava. *See generally* Wambaugh, *supra* note 114, pp. 46–411.

The right to political participation in international law 71

ness and secrecy" of the ballot be ensured.[116] Instead, the Allied Plebiscite Commissions developed their own standards to implement the treaty requirements, the first electoral criteria promulgated by a multilateral body. The Commissions' first task was to establish order. They did so by establishing supervisory control over their zones and enforcing penalties for intimidation, bribery, fraud, and other offenses connected with registration and voting.[117] They then granted the franchise to the inhabitants of a territory without regard to sex, property ownership, or literacy.[118] Groups on both sides of the ballot question campaigned with only modest restrictions,[119] and voting occurred by secret ballot.[120] These minimal requirements, while embryonic, have remained the core of more comprehensive standards adopted in the UN era.

B *Monitoring under the United Nations system*

The recognition of a right to self-determination in the UN Charter[121] and subsequent General Assembly resolutions[122] vastly increased the scope of monitoring by international bodies. The new right required the development of mechanisms to ascertain the preferences of peoples emerging from colonialism. Rather than deferring to the decisions of local leaders or colonial powers, the United Nations sought to follow democratic standards in the decolonization process.

1 Monitoring the era of decolonization

The drafters of the UN Charter intended the right of self-determination to apply primarily to colonial territories.[123] The Charter, for example,

---

[116] Treaty of Versailles, *supra* note 115, Art. 88 (Annex Art. 3) (Upper Silesia); *see also ibid.*, Art. 49 (Annex Art. 34) (Saar Basin); Art. 97 (East Prussia); Art. 109 (Schleswig).
[117] *See* Wambaugh, *supra* note 114, pp. 442–54, 482; D. W. Bowett, *United Nations Forces: A Legal Study* (1964), pp. 8–11.   [118] Wambaugh, *supra* note 114, pp. 474–77.
[119] *Ibid.*, pp. 468–69. The sole exception occurred in Sopron, where the Allied Plebiscite Commission prohibited "propaganda" of any kind. *Ibid.*, at p. 468. This regulation was, however, widely ignored in practice. *Ibid.*, pp. 285–86.
[120] *Ibid.*, p. 481.
[121] UN Charter, Art. 1(2) (declaring United Nations to be dedicated to "develop[ing] friendly relations among nations based on respect for the principle of equal rights and self-determination of peoples"); *ibid.*, Art. 55 (same).
[122] *See, e.g.*, Declaration on the Granting of Independence to Colonial Countries and Peoples, GA Res. 1514 (1960) (declaring that all peoples "have the right to self-determination; by virtue of that right they freely determine their political status and freely pursue their economic, social and cultural development").
[123] *See* Gregory H. Fox, "Self-Determination in the Post-Cold War Era: A New International Focus?" *Mich. J. Int'l L.* 16 (1995), 733, p. 739.

requires member States to "develop self-government" in their "non-self-governing territories" and to "take due account of the political aspirations of the peoples, and to assist them in the progressive development of their free political institutions."[124] In 1953 the General Assembly adopted a resolution outlining criteria for the achievement of "self-government" and proposed a number of alternatives to colonial status.[125] These were to be chosen by the people of a territory through democratic means.[126] In 1960 the General Assembly further clarified the meaning of "non-self-governing" by reaffirming the popular sovereignty requirements of the 1953 resolution:[127] self-government by integration with an independent State, for example, was to be achieved "through informed and democratic processes, impartially conducted and based on universal adult suffrage."[128] These principles guided the organization of plebiscites in a number of non-self-governing[129] and trust territories.[130] In all but one case (West Irian) the plebiscite commissioner reported to the Secretary-General that the vote was conducted freely and fairly.[131]

[124] UN Charter Art. 73(b).   [125] GA Res. 742 (VIII) (1953).
[126] *See ibid.* pt. 1(B)(1) (full independence requires "[c]omplete freedom of the people of the Territory to choose the form of government which they desire"). The resolution also declared that States wishing to establish "other separate systems of self-government" ascertain the opinion of the population through "informed and democratic processes". *Ibid.* pt. 2(A)(1). A territory forming an association with another State must make constitutional provision for "[u]niversal and equal suffrage, and free periodic elections, characterized by an absence of undue influence over and coercion of the voter or of the imposition of disabilities on particular political parties." *Ibid.*, pt. 3(C)(1). The resolution explains "an absence of undue influence and coercion" by listing such factors as the existence of more than one political party in the territory, a secret ballot, the absence of martial law, and freedom to criticize the incumbent government. *Ibid.*   [127] GA Res. 1541 (XV) (1960).   [128] *Ibid.*, Annex Principle IX(b).
[129] *See, e.g.*, UN Doc. A/AC.109/664 (1981) (Turks and Caicos Islands); (Annex) (1980) (New Hebrides); (West New Guinea), UN Doc. A/7723 Annex I (1969) (West Irian), UN Doc. A/5962 (1965) (Cook Islands).
[130] The UN Trusteeship Council is charged with the administration of the colonies of defeated World War II powers, and the territories formerly under League of Nations mandate UN Charter Art. 77 (1). In order to further the trust territories' "progressive development towards self-government or independence" in accordance with "the freely expressed wishes of the peoples concerned," UN Charter Art. 76, the Council has dispatched missions to observe eight plebiscites or elections. *See* UN TCOR, 53d Sess., Supp. No. 2, at 1, UN Doc. T/1885 (1986) (Palau, Trust Territory of the Pacific Islands); UN Doc. T/1860 (1984) (Federated States of Micronesia, Trust Territory of the Pacific Islands); UN Doc. T/1771 (1976) (Northern Mariana Islands, Trust Territory of the Pacific Islands); UN Doc. A/4994 (1961) (Ruanda-Urundi); UN Doc. T/1564 (1961) (Western Samoa) [hereinafter Western Samoa Report]; UN Doc. A/4314 (1959) (Cameroons Under United Kingdom Administration); UN Doc. A/3957 (1958) (Togoland Under French Administration); UN Doc. T/1258 (1956) (Togoland Under British Administration).
[131] *See, e.g.*, Cook Islands Report, *supra* note 129, pp. 149, 151. ("I was satisfied that the people were able to exercise their rights, while the Observers and I were in the Territory, prior to and during polling in complete freedom . . . [T]he counting of the votes was correct and the reporting of the results was accurate.") For a discussion of the West Irian episode, *see* Gregory H. Fox, "The Right to Political Participation in International Law," *Yale J. Int'l L.* 17 (1992), 539, at p. 575–6.

In many cases, the General Assembly went beyond general statements of support for democratic procedures and outlined specific monitoring standards. For example, the General Assembly sought to "ensure full respect for democratic freedoms . . . [and] universal adult suffrage" for the plebiscite in Equatorial Guinea.[132] The General Assembly likewise urged Britain to abolish a regime based upon emergency powers and declare an amnesty for all imprisoned and exiled political workers in Rwanda-Urundi, in order that the population of the territory could "resume normal, democratic political activity before the elections."[133] It also took issue with local leaders and recommended voting by universal adult suffrage in French Togoland and Western Samoa.[134]

Colonial-era monitoring culminated in the 1989 UN mission to Namibia, which in many ways served as a bridge to later monitoring in sovereign States.[135] In Namibia the United Nations made certain that clear standards for electoral participation were articulated throughout the planning process. As the elections approached, UN observers consistently refused to permit the South African administering authorities to deviate from those standards. The mission's success in light of the South African challenge, as well as its completion during a surge of post-Cold-War optimism, lent the mission enormous precedential value. A host of even more complex UN missions soon followed.

[132] GA Res. 2355 (1967).   [133] GA Res. 1579 (1960).
[134] GA Res. 1182 (1957) (Togoland under French Administration). In Western Samoa, the Trusteeship Council and Samoan leaders disagreed on whether the franchise should be restricted to heads of families in deference to Samoan tradition. The Council argued that Samoa should follow "the normal practice of secret ballot for legislative elections," Western Samoa Report, *supra* note 130, at p. 5, and the General Assembly eventually resolved that the elections should be conducted by universal adult suffrage. See GA Res. 1569 (1960).
[135] The territory of present-day Namibia became a German protectorate in the nineteenth century, and came under South African control through military conquest in 1915. This arrangement was confirmed in 1920 by the League of Nations, and continued under the aegis of the United Nations following World War II. In 1948 South Africa granted Namibian whites direct representation in its parliament and threatened to annex the territory as a fifth province. *See generally* National Democratic Institute for International Affairs, *Nation Building: The UN and Namibia* (1990), pp. 10–11. The International Court of Justice ruled in 1950 that South Africa had no right to alter the mandate unilaterally. International Status of South-West Africa, 1950 ICJ 128 (July 11). The General Assembly formally revoked the mandate in 1966 and placed the territory under direct UN supervision. *See* GA Res. 2145 (1966). The ICJ upheld these actions in 1971. *See* Legal Consequences for States of the Continued Presence of South Africa in Namibia (South West Africa). Notwithstanding Security Council Resolution 276 (1970), 1971 ICJ 6 (Jan. 26). That same year the Southwest Africa People's Organization (SWAPO) began an armed rebellion against South African occupation, which lasted until the declaration of a cease-fire in July 1988. *See* Principles for a Peaceful Settlement in Southwestern Africa, Approved by the South African Government on July 18, 1988, *reprinted in* Nation Building, *supra*, p. 117. SWAPO agreed to this settlement in August 1988. *See* Letter Addressed to the Secretary-General, UN Doc. S/20129 (1988).

The United Nations began to lay the groundwork for democratic self-rule in Namibia in the mid-1970s. In 1976 the Security Council adopted Resolution 385, calling for "free elections in Namibia under supervision and control of the United Nations."[136] The Security Council developed a comprehensive settlement plan for the territory in 1978, which created a transitional working group to facilitate "the early independence of Namibia through free election[s]."[137] In 1982 the five-member Western Contact Group, which had mediated disputes among the various parties, negotiated a set of electoral guidelines with South Africa to implement the 1978 plan. These guidelines stipulated that specific voting rights would be guaranteed to all adult Namibians.[138]

In 1989, UN representatives and South African administrators began to negotiate a legal framework for elections based on these guidelines. The concessions obtained by the United Nations were remarkable. South Africa agreed to a general amnesty for all Namibian political prisoners and to repeal all "discriminatory or restrictive laws" and regulations which might inhibit a free and fair vote.[139] South Africa also agreed to a party registration system that permitted any political organization to field candidates if it could obtain two thousand signatures and pay a modest deposit.[140] As the election approached, UN observers helped repatriate exiled Namibians, obtain the release of political prisoners, and register voters and parties.[141]

---

[136] S C Res. 385 (1976).   [137] S C Res. 435 (1978).
[138] The guidelines stated:

> Every adult Namibian will be eligible, without discrimination or fear of intimidation, from any source, to vote, campaign and stand for election to the Constituent Assembly. Voting will be by secret ballot, with provisions made for those who cannot read or write. The date for the beginning of the electoral campaign, the date of elections, the electoral system, the preparation of voter rolls and the respects of electoral procedures will be promptly decided upon so as to give all political parties and interested persons, without regard to their political views, a full and fair opportunity to organize and participate in the electoral process.
> Full freedom of speech, assembly, movement and press shall be guaranteed.
> The electoral system will seek to ensure fair representation in the Constituent Assembly to different political parties which gain substantial support in the election.

> Letter Dated July 12, 1982 from the Representatives of Canada, France, The Federal Republic of Germany, The Kingdom of Great Britain and Northern Ireland and the United States of America Addressed to the Secretary-General UN Doc. S/15287 (1982) (Annex), p. 1.

[139] *See* Nation Building, *supra* note 135, pp. 27–28. The repealed laws restricted "Communist" political dissent, banned or limited activities by certain political organizations, suspended various rights under a state of emergency decree, authorized detention without trial, and imposed a curfew through much of the territory. *Ibid.* at 28.   [140] *Ibid.* at p. 31.

[141] *See ibid.* at pp. 37–42. The most contentious discussions concerned a new electoral law proposed by South Africa, which compromised ballot secrecy by labeling ballots with voters' identification numbers, rejected local (and allegedly faster) tabulation of ballots, and denied observation

The right to political participation in international law 75

The November 1989 election was a resounding success. Ten different parties or coalitions of parties appeared on the ballot.[142] Ninety-seven percent of eligible voters cast ballots, and seven parties obtained seats in the seventy-two-member Constituent Assembly.[143] The Secretary-General's Special Representative certified that the electoral process had "at every stage, been free and fair."[144] In February 1990 the Namibian Constituent Assembly unanimously adopted a new constitution which incorporated the electoral principles approved by the Security Council in 1989.[145]

2 Monitoring in the post-colonial era
Following the end of the colonial era – a demise which UN electoral monitoring had helped facilitate – a second phase began on the heels of the Namibia mission. In July 1989 the Secretary-General agreed to oversee elections in Nicaragua. For the first time the United Nations would observe elections in an independent state. While decolonization could no longer supply a rationale for UN involvement in elections, the new missions applied and advanced the same criteria of fairness evident in the colonial era. These criteria, it appeared, had not simply been technical procedures confined to a narrow and now defunct UN enterprise, but standards relevant to the elections many States were obligated to hold under human rights instruments. For international lawyers, the

---

posts at polling places to political parties. *Ibid.* at p. 32. The Security Council responded to this law by asking the Secretary-General to ensure that all electoral legislation conformed to the principles enunciated by the Western Contact Group and to "internationally accepted norms for free and fair elections." S C Res. 640 (1989).

[142] Further Report of the Secretary-General Concerning the Implementation of Security Council Resolution 435 (1978) Concerning the Question of Namibia. UN Doc. S/20967 (1989), p. 2.

[143] Nation Building, *supra* note 135, pp. 57, 64.   [144] *Ibid.* at p. 110.

[145] Article 17 of the Namibian Constitution provides:
(1) All citizens shall have the right to participate in peaceful political activity intended to influence the composition and policies of the Government. All citizens shall have the right to form and join political parties and, subject to such qualifications prescribed by law as are necessary in a democratic society, to participate in the conduct of public affairs, whether directly or through freely chosen representatives.
(2) Every citizen who has reached the age of eighteen (18) years old shall have the right to vote and who has reached the age of twenty-one (21) years to be elected to public office, unless otherwise provided herein.
(3) The rights guaranteed by Sub-Article (2) hereof may only be abrogated, suspended or be impinged upon by Parliament in respect of specified categories of persons on such grounds of infirmity or on such grounds of basic public interest or morality as are necessary in a democratic society. Namib. Const. Art. 17.

The influence of the Political Covenant on Article 17 is evident in the last phrases of sub-section (1), which quote from Article 25(a) of the Political Covenant almost verbatim. The Namibian Constitution goes farther, however, by making participatory rights non-derogable. Namib. Const. Art. 24(3).

76   *The normative foundations of a right to political participation*

critical question concerns the normative relation between multilateral monitoring and treaty-based participatory rights. We will address this issue after reviewing practice evident in this second phase of UN monitoring, beginning with missions to Nicaragua and Haiti.

a The Nicaragua mission The Nicaragua mission originated in the Esquipulas II Agreement, an August 1987 pact among the presidents of five Central American countries.[146] The Agreement, which outlined a broad framework for peace in the region, called on the five States to hold "free, pluralistic and fair elections" by June 1988 and invited the United Nations, the OAS, and other states to send observers.[147] The United Nations agreed to assume a role in November 1988.[148] In February 1989, President Daniel Ortega announced elections in Nicaragua and invited Secretary-General Javier Perez de Cuellar to send a monitoring team. The Secretary-General accepted the invitation in July and announced the formation of the United Nations Observer Mission to Verify the Electoral Process in Nicaragua (ONUVEN).[149]

The Secretary-General was initially circumspect in describing ONUVEN's tasks, declaring that the mission should not "be construed as any kind of value judgement as to the laws in force in Nicaragua governing the electoral process."[150] However, the comprehensive "terms of reference" that served as the mission's mandate required ONUVEN to verify that the election was "equitable," "free," without hindrance or intimidation, and "proper,"[151] all determinations calling on the UN

---

[146] *See* Letter dated August 27, 1987 from the Permanent Representatives of Costa Rica, El Salvador, Guatemala, and Nicaragua to the United Nations Addressed to the Secretary-General, UN Doc. A/42/521 (1987).   [147] *Ibid.*   [148] GA Res. 43/24, para. 6 (1989).

[149] *See* Letter dated July 5, 1989 from the Secretary-General Addressed to the Permanent Representative of Nicaragua to the United Nations, UN Doc. A/44/375 (1989) [hereinafter SG's Nicaragua Letter]. The mission eventually issued five detailed reports: First Report of the United Nations Observer Mission to Verify the Electoral Process in Nicaragua to the Secretary-General, UN Doc. A/44/642 (1989) [hereinafter First Nicaragua Report]; Second Report to the Secretary-General by the United Nations Observer Mission to Verify the Electoral Process in Nicaragua, UN Doc. A/44/834 (1989); Third Report to the Secretary-General by the United Nations Observer Mission to Verify the Electoral Process in Nicaragua, UN Doc. A/44/917 (1990); Fourth Report to the Secretary-General by the United Nations Observer Mission to Verify the Electoral Process in Nicaragua, UN Doc. A/44/921 (1990) [hereinafter Fourth Nicaragua Report]; Fifth Report to the Secretary-General by the United Nations Observer Mission to Verify the Electoral Process in Nicaragua, UN GAOR, 44th Sess., Agenda Item 34, UN Doc. A/44/927 (1990) [hereinafter Fifth Nicaragua Report].

[150] SG's Nicaragua Letter, *supra* note 149, p. 2.

[151] Establishment and Terms of Reference of the United Nations Observer Mission to Verify the Electoral Process in Nicaragua, The Situation in Central America, UN GAOR, 44th Sess., Annex I, Agenda Item 34, app. p. 3, (1989) [hereinafter Terms of Reference].

observers to make value judgments about the fairness of Nicaragua's electoral laws. A review of the UN terms of reference and of ONUVEN's five reports reveals that the United Nations indeed took specific positions on two important issues: party pluralism and the conduct of the Supreme Electoral Council.

ONUVEN's terms of reference required it to "verify that political parties enjoy complete freedom of organization and mobilization, without hindrance or intimidation by anyone [and to] verify that all political parties have equitable access to State television and radio in terms of both the timing and the length of broadcasts." [152] Furthermore, the government agreed to repeal certain statutes (concerning, for example, conscription, public safety, and police duties) and to promulgate a new electoral law.[153] ONUVEN concluded that the resulting guidelines were "sufficiently open to ensure that the elections [would] take place in an atmosphere of free competition."[154] In particular, it approved of the procedures for the formation of political parties and their acquisition of legal status.[155]

Second, the UN observers reviewed the conduct of the Supreme Electoral Council (CSE), which directed all aspects of the electoral process.[156] ONUVEN was called upon to verify that "political parties are equitably represented in the [CSE] and its subsidiary bodies."[157] The National Assembly elected the five members of the Council in June 1989: two from the Sandinista party, two from opposition parties, and one "eminent person."[158] ONUVEN reviewed over one hundred CSE resolutions on issues such as electoral ethics, donations from abroad, registration of absentee voters and a timetable for the elections. It reported that an "[a]nalysis of these resolutions does not reveal bias towards the governing party."[159] ONUVEN continued to monitor the Council throughout the campaign and on the eve of the elections concluded, "[t]here has been evidence of broad-mindedness, flexibility and a determination to ensure – as far as possible – the greatest possible participation of political groups in the electoral process."[160]

Finally, while the UN terms of reference did not explicitly direct ONUVEN to monitor polling places and the tabulation of ballots,

---

[152] Ibid.   [153] First Nicaragua Report, *supra* note 149, p. 6.
[154] Fourth Nicaragua Report, *supra* note 149, p. 7.
[155] *See* First Nicaragua Report, *supra* note 149, p. 17.
[156] First Nicaragua Report, *supra* note 149, p. 6. The Nicaraguan Constitution established the CSE as a fourth branch of government, independent of the executive, legislative, and judiciary.
[157] Terms of Reference, *supra* note 151, p. 3.   [158] First Nicaragua Report, *supra* note 149, p. 7.
[159] Ibid. at 9.   [160] Fourth Nicaragua Report, *supra* note 149, p. 8.

ONUVEN assumed these to be among its most important tasks.[161] As a further safeguard against fraud, ONUVEN devised a formula to project the outcome based on approximately 17 percent of precinct returns. This so-called "quick count," held on February 25, 1990, deviated by less than 1 percent from the official results, according to which the victorious UNO party won 55 percent and the Sandinistas 40 percent of the vote in the presidential election.[162]

b The Haiti mission The second request for monitoring in an independent State came from Haiti. The Haitian government had attempted to hold elections in 1987, but outbreaks of violence and voter intimidation led to their cancellation even before the polls closed.[163] The next three years saw a succession of military-backed governments take power, followed by a provisional civilian government.[164] In June 1990 Ertha Pascal Trouillot, President of the provisional regime, requested the Secretary-General to send a UN team to monitor elections scheduled for December 16 of that year.[165] President Trouillot requested the mission to undertake several specific duties:

[O]bservation and verification of the elections, covering the entire electoral process, particularly registration of voters on the electoral rolls, registration of candidatures, freedom of expression and freedom of political parties to mobilize, respect for the equality of candidates in the electoral campaign, and independent verification of the outcome of the vote . . . .[166]

The General Assembly adopted an authorizing resolution on October 12, 1990,[167] despite some States expressing concerns over the lack of a clear mandate[168] and interference in Haiti's internal affairs.[169] While the

[161] Nicaragua had requested electoral observers to verify the process "at every stage and in all electoral districts." Terms of Reference, *supra* note 151, at p. 3.
[162] Fifth Nicaragua Report, *supra* note 149, pp. 10, 21.
[163] Council of Freely-Elected Heads of Gov't & National Democratic Inst. for Int'l Affairs, *The 1990 General Elections in Haiti* (1991), pp. 32–33.
[164] First Report of the United Nations Observer Group for the Verification of the Elections in Haiti, UN Doc. A/45/870 (1990), Annex, p. 10 [hereinafter First Haiti Report].
[165] Letter dated July 17, 1990 from the Permanent Representatives of the Bahamas, Colombia and Haiti to the United Nations Addressed to the President of the General Assembly, UN Doc. A/44/965/Add. 1 (1990), p. 1. [166] *Ibid.* [167] GA Res. 45/2 (1990).
[168] UN Doc. A/45/PV.29 (1990), p. 61 (statement of Cuban delegate).
[169] Cuba, which supported the resolution, spoke against "any attempt to use this United Nations resolution or activity as a pretext for interfering in the internal affairs of Haiti, a fraternal country." *Ibid.* at p. 62. National elections, Cuba stated, "can never be regarded as affecting international peace and security" and so cannot involve a breach of the Charter leading to collective action. *Ibid.* at p. 58–60. The Mexican delegate likewise argued that "sending this mission will not set a precedent in respect of the domestic jurisdiction of States . . . [E]lectoral processes lie within the domain in which domestic legislation in each State is sovereign." *Ibid.* at pp. 64–65.

mission (the United Nations Observer Group for the Verification of the Elections in Haiti (ONUVEH)) never received a formal mandate akin to the Nicaraguan "terms of reference," President Trouillot's request effectively served that purpose. In substance, the mission scrutinized virtually the same core of participatory rights at issue in Nicaragua and Namibia.

The mission faced a formidable task. As ONUVEH noted in its first report, "there is no democratic tradition in Haitian politics... [and] violence has always been the means of settling conflicts and choosing leaders."[170] The elections also faced logistical barriers. There was no permanent register of voters, forcing the government to draw up new voter rolls for each election.[171] Further, candidate registration procedures proved too complex, causing many potential candidates to be disqualified for filing incorrect or incomplete documentation.[172]

ONUVEH monitored compliance with the rights listed in President Trouillot's request. It reported that individuals representing "all shades of opinion" entered the elections, despite the cumbersome and confusing candidate registration procedures.[173] While instances of double registration partially marred the voter registration process, in ONUVEH's view precautions taken against double voting vitiated the problem.[174] ONUVEH concluded that apart from an attack on an opposition rally late in the campaign (for which no particular group was ever found responsible), the process operated smoothly and the electoral authorities functioned in an impartial manner.[175]

Yet ONUVEH's success was short-lived. Supporters of former President Duvalier attempted a coup against President-elect Aristide on January 6, 1991. The army quickly defeated this uprising but officers staged a second and successful coup on September 29, forcing President Aristide to flee the country. The international community reacted swiftly, with the monitored elections providing a powerful basis for condemning the military's actions. OAS foreign ministers, hastily convened in Washington on October 13, 1991, declared that the coup "represent[ed] disregard for the legitimate Government of Haiti, which was constituted by the will of its people freely expressed in a free

---

[170] First Haiti Report, *supra* note 164, p. 9.   [171] *Ibid.* at p. 14.   [172] *Ibid.* at p. 17.
[173] *Ibid.* at p. 19.   [174] *Ibid.* at pp. 14–16.
[175] *Ibid.* at pp. 19, 23. ONUVEH, together with an OAS observer team, used the same "quick count" of election results that it employed successfully in Nicaragua. ONUVEH released its projections to the Haitian electoral council and the major candidates in order to dissuade any fraud in the tabulation process. *Ibid.* at p. 13. It projected (with a six-point margin of error) that Jean-Bertrand Aristide would win the presidency with 66.4 percent of the vote. According to the official returns, Aristide received 67.5 percent. *Ibid.* at pp. 12, 14.

80   *The normative foundations of a right to political participation*

and democratic electoral process under international observation."[176] The Ministers recommended that all OAS member States sanction the military government by suspending their economic and commercial ties to Haiti.[177] One week later, the UN General Assembly passed a resolution urging UN member States to join the OAS embargo.[178] The resolution referred to the Aristide regime as "legitimate" and the coup as "illegal," thus reinforcing the OAS position that the disregard of democratic procedures in Haiti constituted an international wrong. Other chapters in this collection detail subsequent multilateral efforts to restore President Aristide to office.

C The mainstreaming of multilateral election monitoring

The Namibian, Nicaraguan, and Haitian missions led to a vast expansion of United Nations electoral assistance.[179] An optimism seemed to pervade the UN that with the ideological polarities and alliances of the Cold War now gone, the organization could begin to make real progress in fostering open and democratic governance in the developing world. In some cases, monitored elections were part of comprehensive efforts to rebuild societies recovering from long civil wars, an enterprise the Secretary-General described as "post-conflict peace-building."[180] In others, democracy was seen not as a means of reconciling old combatants but as a path away from one or another form of authoritarian rule. In both cases, the Secretary-General has regarded electoral assistance as aiding in establishment of the democratic institutions contemplated by human rights instruments.[181]

---

[176] Support to the Democratic Government of Haiti, MRE/RES1/91, corr. 1, at 2, OEA/ser.F/V.1 (October 3, 1991). The resolution further declared that the OAS would recognize representatives of the Aristide government "as the only legitimate representatives of Haiti." *Ibid.*
[177] *Ibid.*   [178] GA Res. 46/7 (1991), para. 3.
[179] The United Nations web site contains extensive documentation on UN electoral assistance activities, both past and present. See <www.un.org/Depts/dpa/docs/eadhome.htm>. *See also*, Thomas Carothers, "The Observers Observed," *J. of Democ.* 8 (1997), p. 17; Timothy C. Evered, *United Nations Electoral Assistance and the Evolving Right to Democratic Governance* (Livingston, N.J., Center for UN Reform Education, 1996); Douglas Lee Donoho, "Evolution or Expediency: the United Nations Response to the Disruption of Democracy," *Cornell Int'l L. J.* 29 (1996), p. 329.
[180] An Agenda for Peace, UN Doc. A/47/277 – S/24111, paras. 55–59 (1992). *See generally*, Sonia K. Han, Note, "Building a Peace That Lasts: The United Nations and Post-Civil War Peace-Building," *N.Y.U. J. Int'l. L. & Pol.* 26 (1994), p. 837.
[181] Report of the Secretary-General, *Enhancing the Effectiveness of the Principle of Periodic and Genuine Elections*, UN Doc. A/46/609, para. 76 (1991). *See also*, UN Centre for Human Rights, Human Rights and Elections (United Nations 1994), pp. 4–5 (describing "United Nations human rights standards regarding elections" solely by reference to human rights instruments).

In 1992, pursuant to a General Assembly resolution, the Secretary-General established the Electoral Assistance Division within the Secretariat as the "focal point" for electoral matters.[182] The Division processes requests for assistance from member States and maintains a staff of experts in electoral procedures. The vast bulk of UN assistance "takes the form of relatively small-scale, technical assistance activities that do not require a specific mandate from the General Assembly or the Security Council."[183] A select number of more ambitious missions, however, have been of sufficient scope and political sensitivity to require advanced approval by UN political organs. These larger missions typically come as part of social reform projects – often following negotiated ends to civil wars – that involve fundamental reorganization of States' political institutions. They are also not infrequently accompanied by heightened political tensions, as former adversaries in war reverse the Clausewitzian dictum and continue their battles in the political arena.

Both the scope of these larger missions and their approval by UN political organs render their articulation of electoral standards especially noteworthy. By the mid-1990s, these burgeoning international standards had been repeated so frequently that the particulars of any given election monitoring mission had become essentially uncontroversial. The Secretary-General reported in 1994 that "[i]n providing electoral assistance in over fifty cases to date, the United Nations has never received a complaint from a Member State regarding interference in its internal affairs."[184]

The independence of national electoral authorities, for example, was a central concern of many missions.[185] Liberia, for example, held elections in 1997 after several years of brutal civil war, occupation by a

---

[182] GA Res. 46/137 (1991). *See* Evered, *supra* note 179, p. 8; "Context and Objectives of UN Electoral Assistance," *available at* <www.un.org/depts/dpa/docs/website5.htm>.

[183] "Main Types of Assistance Activities," *available at* <www.un.org/depts/dpa/docs/website3.htm>.

[184] Report of the Secretary-General, *Enhancing the Effectiveness of the Principle of Periodic and Genuine Elections*, UN Doc. A/49/675 (1994), para. 3.

[185] *See, e.g.*, Report of the Secretary-General on the Request to the United Nations to Observe the Referendum Process, UN Doc. A/47/544, para. 11 (1992) (mission in Eritrea to "monitor and evaluate the operations and impartiality of the referendum authorities at all levels"); Further Report of the Secretary-General on the United Nations Angola Verification Mission (UNAVEM II), UN Doc. S/23671, para. 28 (1992) [hereinafter Angola Report] (Angola electoral observers to "monitor and evaluate the operations and impartiality of electoral observers at all levels.") Even when formal missions are not underway, the neutrality of electoral authorities is a central concern of UN human rights monitors. *See* Report of the Secretary-General, Situation of Human Rights in Cambodia, UN Doc. A/52/489, para. 49 (1997) ("[a] crucial ingredient in a free and fair election is an independent electoral commission.")

regional peace-keeping force and the assassination of several leaders.[186] Given the level of mistrust among the combatants turned political rivals, the Secretary-General emphasized that one of the main factors determining whether the Liberian elections would be free and fair was "the efficiency and credibility of the organization and conduct of the elections by the Independent Elections Commission."[187] When the Secretary-General approved the results of elections held in July 1997, much of the basis for his conclusion rested on the impartiality shown by the Elections Commission.[188]

A second issue of concern to UN monitors has been equal access to the media.[189] Especially in states where major media outlets are controlled by the central government, United Nations monitors have focused on whether opposition candidates are accorded equal time on television and radio and in newspapers.[190] UN monitors have taken great pains to document the degree of access afforded non-incumbents and have frequently brought biased coverage or wholesale exclusion of certain views to the attention of national electoral authorities.[191]

By far the most normatively challenging issue faced by UN monitors has been the question of party pluralism. We have seen how all human rights treaty bodies addressing the question have eventually found pluralism to be an essential aspect of free choice. Similarly, despite intense ideological debate in the decades before UN monitoring became

---

[186] Twenty-Third Progress Report of the Secretary-General on the United Nations Observer Mission in Liberia, UN Doc. S/1997/478, para. 30 (1997).   [187] *Ibid.*
[188] *See* Twenty-Fourth Progress Report of the Secretary-General on the United Nations Observer Mission to Liberia, UN Doc. S/1997/643, paras. 18–30 (1997).
[189] *See* Situation of Human Rights in Cambodia, *supra* note 185, para. 51 ("[f]air and equal access to the media is another crucial requirement of a free and fair election"); Secretary-General's Twenty-Third Report on Liberia, *supra* note 186, para. 30 (fairness of Liberian election to be determined in part by whether there exists "access by all political parties to the media, in particular to radio time"); Final Report of the Secretary-General on the Question of South Africa, UN Doc. S/1994/717, para. 98 (1994) (concluding that "media coverage of the electoral process was balanced and did not disadvantage any one political party").
[190] *See* Report of the Secretary-General on the Activities of the ONUSAL Electoral Division, UN Doc. S/1994/179, para. 26 (1994) (while UN observer mission to El Salvador received several complaints of governmental favoritism in media access, it concluded that "all the parties are being granted access to the media").
[191] *See* John Marston, "Cambodian News Media in the UNTAC Period and After," *in* Steve Heder and Judy Ledgerwood, eds., *Propaganda, Politics, and Violence in Cambodia* (Armonk, N.Y., M. E. Sharpe, 1996), p. 208 (detailing UNTAC efforts to ensure balanced media coverage during 1993 Cambodian elections); Report of the Secretary-General on the United Nations Operation in Mozambique (ONUMOZ), UN Doc. S/24892, para. 36 (1992) [hereinafter Mozambique Report] (in order to verify equal access to the media, UN mission to Mozambique tasked to "verify the distribution of broadcasting time between parties, the content of news broadcasts and the fairness of tariffs").

The right to political participation in international law 83

widespread, international observers have consistently placed the freedom to organize parties at the center of their determination of whether an election is free and fair.[192] The UN Centre for Human Rights states in its training manual for election monitors that "[p]olitical pluralism is seen today as an essential element in providing a real choice to the electors."[193] As we have seen, this was a central concern of the Namibian, Nicaraguan, and Haitian missions. Subsequent missions have gone to great lengths to investigate both the conduct of the government toward parties and the conduct of parties toward each other.[194] The United Nations Operation in Mozambique undertook the following:

> In order to verify that political parties and alliances enjoy complete freedom of organization, movement, assembly and expression without hindrance and intimidation, the electoral component would establish offices in each provincial capital, with an adequate number of observer teams at each of them. The latter would establish contact with political parties and social organizations at the national and local levels and would visit villages and municipalities throughout the country. They would attend all important political rallies and other relevant activities, and verify the observance by all parties of the electoral law and any code of conduct that might be agreed between the parties or established by the electoral authorities.[195]

It is not simply happenstance that UN electoral missions continually highlight certain aspects of electoral processes as crucial to determinations of fairness. To be sure, each mission has varied greatly in context, in the degree of cooperation demonstrated by the participants, and, perhaps most crucially, the extent to which other States take a genuine interest in the election's outcome. But as missions proliferate the criteria of fairness employed by the missions has become standardized. Whereas in early missions the nature of a fair election was often an *ad*

---

[192] *See, e.g.*, Peace Accords for Angola, UN Doc. S/22609 (Annex), at p. 47 (1991) (electoral standards for Angola, adopted by UN mission as its terms of reference, provide that "[a]ll political parties and interested persons will have the opportunity to organize and to participate in the elections process on an equal footing, regardless of their political position"); Twenty-Fourth Report on Liberia, *supra* note 188, para. 21. (in determining fairness of electoral process, Secretary-General reports that "all eligible Liberians had been afforded a fair opportunity to vote for the political party of their choice.")
[193] Human Rights and Elections, *supra* note 181, para. 79.
[194] In El Salvador, for example, representatives of the UN Observer Mission ONUSAL reported that "[p]eriodic meetings with political parties were held at the central and local levels in order to discuss ongoing problems and viable solutions." Report of the Secretary-General on the Activities of the ONUSAL Electoral Division, UN Doc. S/1994/304, para. 4 (1994).
[195] Report of the Secretary-General on the United Nations Operation in Mozambique (ONUMOZ), UN Doc. S/24892, para. 35 (1992).

hoc determination, or one understood only by consulting a variety of documents (peace agreements, resolutions by UN political organs authorizing a mission, reports of the Secretary-General, etc.), later missions have drawn on this experience to reduce the question of fairness to boilerplate. The following mandate has guided an increasing number of UN missions with only minor variations in language and form:

(a) To verify the impartiality of the National Elections Commission and its organs in all aspects and stages of the electoral process;
(b) To verify that political parties and alliances enjoy complete freedom of organization, movement, assembly and expression, without hindrance and intimidation;
(c) To verify that all political parties and alliances have fair access to State mass media and that there is fairness in the allocation of both the hour and duration of radio and television broadcasts;
(d) To verify that the electoral rolls are properly drawn up and that qualified voters are not denied identification and registration cards or the right to vote;
(e) To report to the electoral authorities on complaints, irregularities and interferences reported or observed, and, if necessary, to request the electoral authorities to take action to resolve and rectify them, as well as conducting its own independent investigation of irregularities;
(f) To observe all activities related to the registration of voters, the organization of the poll, the electoral campaign, the poll itself and the counting, computation and announcement of the results;
(g) To participate in the electoral education campaign.[196]

With a normative foundation in treaty law and an increasingly rich body of practice under its belt, election monitoring has entered the mainstream of United Nations activities. The purposes animating any given electoral mission will vary with context. But this diversity of objectives makes the uniformity of method even more significant. What constitutes a "free and fair" election is now a rather mundane question, one virtually devoid of ideological or serious interpretive ambiguities.

---

[196] This version of the boilerplate is taken from the mandate of the UN mission to Mozambique para. 32. A virtually identical list of factors guided UN missions to Angola, El Salvador, Eritrea, and South Africa. *See* Angola Report *supra* note 185, para. 22; Report of the Secretary-General on the Request to the United Nations to Observe the Referendum Process, UN Doc. A/47/544, para. 7 (1992); Report of the Secretary-General on the Activities of the ONUSAL Electoral Division, UN Doc. S/1994/304, para. 2 (1994); Report of the Secretary-General Concerning Arrangements for United Nations Monitoring of the Electoral Process in South Africa and Coordination of Activities of Internal Observers, UN Doc. A/48/845–S/1994/16, para. 57 (1994).

D *Election monitoring and treaty norms: the legal effect of the new regime*

What is the relationship between the practice of UN election monitoring and human rights instruments creating participatory rights? Can the former provide any assistance in refining the latter?

1 Using mission standards to interpret treaties

The preceding sections suggest that two distinct but parallel systems of participatory standards now operate in the international community. The first consists of norms in global and regional human rights treaties, including the decisions and reports of specialized tribunals. The second consists of criteria employed by UN election monitors. The standards adduced by the latter are strikingly similar to the former. From the League-supervised plebiscites of the 1920s to the UN boilerplate mandates of the 1990s, international observers have made essentially the same demands of elections they monitor: the process must be supervised by an independent electoral authority, party activity must not be limited or disrupted, ballot secrecy must be maintained, suffrage must be universal for adult residents, access to the media must not be restricted, and fraud in voting and ballot tabulation must be prevented. These requirements all consistently match the texts of the major human rights treaties, and many echo holdings of the UN Human Rights Committee, the European Court and Commission of Human Rights, and the Inter-American Commission.

Despite this *logical* intersection between the systems,[197] no *formal* linkage exists between these two sources of law. Treaty-based participatory rights have not explicitly formed the basis for any observer mission, and the mission reports generally do not refer to human rights instruments. Neither do regional or global treaty systems provide for election monitoring as an enforcement mechanism. But our analysis need not end here. According to the Vienna Convention on the Law of Treaties, evidence of the "ordinary meaning" of treaty terms may be derived from sources not formally linked to a treaty.[198] The ordinary meaning of a term is presumably one that does not vary with the context of its use but which rather has acquired a universal understanding. The terminol-

---

[197] *See* W. Michael Reisman, "International Election Observation," *Pace Y.B. Int'l L.* 4 (1992), p. 1, 25 ("[t]he rich body of electoral observation practice now available provides a source for clarifying what exceptional norms have emerged, how they have adapted themselves to the diverse circumstances presented in election observation, and what social goals animate them.")

[198] Vienna Convention on the Law of Treaties, May 23, 1969, Art. 31(1), 1155 UNTS pp. 331, 340.

ogy of participatory rights has now achieved such status. While during the Cold War terms such as "genuine" elections gave rise to unresolvable ideological debates, that divisiveness is now fading. A new, more uniform terminology is evident in the following trends: (1) more States have ratified instruments protecting participatory rights; (2) regional bodies from Europe, Latin America, and Africa have pursued virtually identical agendas of consolidating electoral democracy; (3) leaders' credibility in describing their States as "democratic" turns increasingly on the judgments of international actors; (4) the criteria of fairness applied by UN monitors has become so widely accepted that their terms are repeated virtually verbatim from mission to mission; and (5) all parties to the major human rights conventions also have voted to establish the UN monitoring missions[199] and to approve reports detailing participatory rights scrutinized by the observers.[200] Through this State practice the language of electoral fairness has become both more universal and more uniform.

Not only is there now an emerging horizontal uniformity of understanding (among multilateral actors), but a nascent vertical uniformity is evident as well. We have seen in States such as Namibia that new national constitutions are incorporating international participatory standards almost word-for-word.[201] New and widely active NGOs seek to mold national electoral laws to conform with international instruments.[202] Widespread cross-pollination of standards is occurring on both planes.

---

[199] *See, e.g.*, Special Economic and Disaster Relief Assistance: Electoral Assistance to Haiti, UN Doc. A/45/870/Add.1 (1991) (Haiti); Terms of Reference, *supra* note 151 (Nicaragua); Question of the Turks and Caicos Islands, GA Res. 35/25 (1980); Question of the New Hebrides, GA Res. 34/10 (1979); Question of Niue, GA Res. 3155 (1973); Question of American Samoa Gilbert and Ellice Islands, Guam, New Hebrides, Pitcairn, St. Helena, Seychelles and Solomon Islands, GA Res. 3156 (1973); Supervision of the Elections to be Held in the Cook Islands, GA Res. 2005 (XIX); GA Res. 1579 (1960) (Rwanda-Urundi); GA Res. 1569, *supra* note 134 (Western Samoa); GA Res. 1350 (1959) (Northern Cameroons); GA Res. 1182, *supra* note 134 (French Togoland); GA Res. 944 (1955) (British Togoland).

[200] *See, e.g.*, GA Res. 45/15 (1991) (Nicaragua); GA Res. 3285 (1974) (Niue); GA Res. 3288 (1974) (Gilbert and Ellice Islands); Report of the Fourth Committee, UN GAOR, 23d Sess., 1692d plen. mtg. (1968), p. 22 (Equatorial Guinea); GA Res. 2064 (1965) (Cook Islands); GA Res. 1626, (1961) (Western Samoa) (1959); GA Res. 1253 (1958) (French Togoland). In almost every case these resolutions were passed by unanimous votes or by consensus. [201] *See supra* note 146.

[202] *See, e.g.*, National Democratic Institute for International Affairs, *Mission Statement*, available at <www.ndi.crg/mission.htm>; International IDEA, *Objectives*, available at <www.int-idea.se/institute/1-01.html>; *Charter of the Association of African Election Authorities*, available at <www.ifes.org/afrassoc/charter.htm>; *Charter of the Association of Asian Election Authorities*, available at <www.ifes.org/asiaassocsite/charter/charter.htm>; *Charter of the Association of Caribbean Electoral Organizations*, available at <www.ifes.org/caribbean/charter5.htm>.

2 Sovereignty and the right to political participation

Despite evident agreement on standards, a sense still lingers that the way in which States choose their leaders is an essentially domestic matter and should remain so. Some would draw on language in General Assembly resolutions to argue that any distinction between elected and non-elected regimes would compromise the principle of state equality.[203] This view labels criticism of national governments as an intervention into domestic affairs and contends that an essential purpose of international law is to preserve the diversity of national systems.[204]

Whatever its rhetorical appeal, this view of sovereignty is flawed as a legal proposition on at least three levels. First, opponents of participatory rights rely upon an overboard conception of sovereign discretion. In their most extreme moments the opponents seem to suggest that participatory rights are inherently beyond the reach of international law.[205] But given that every major human rights instrument includes an article on political participation, these critics carry an immense burden to show that rights concerning elections cannot become the subject of a treaty obligation. Certainly this argument did not persuade the International Court in the Nicaragua case:

> The Court cannot discover, within the range of subjects open to international agreement, any obstacle or provision to hinder a State from making a commitment of this kind. A State, which is free to decide upon the principle and methods of popular consultation within its domestic order, is sovereign for the purpose of accepting a limitation of its sovereignty in this field.[206]

Second, it is difficult to understand how an argument of sovereign discretion in regard to participatory rights would not also apply to other

---

[203] *See* Respect for the Principles of National Sovereignty and Non-Interference in the Internal Affairs of States in Their Electoral Processes, GA Res. 45/151 (1990). This resolution invokes Article 2(7) of the UN Charter, appeals to States to stop financing political parties or candidates in other States, and declares that "there is no single political system or single model for electoral processes equally suited to all nations and their peoples." Most importantly, it asserts that any "extraneous" attempt to "interfere in the free development of national electoral processes, in particular in the developing countries . . . violates the spirit and letter of the principles established in the Charter" and the Declaration on Friendly Relations.

[204] *See e.g.*, Pact of the League of Arab States, Mar. 22, 1945, Art. 8, 70 UNTS 237, 254 ("Every member State of the League shall respect the form of government obtaining in the other States of the League, and shall recognize the form of government obtaining as one of the rights of those States, and shall pledge itself not to take any action tending to change that form"); Charter of the Organization of American States, Apr. 30, 1948, Art. 13, 2 UST 2394, T.I.A.S. no. 2361, 119 UNTS 3, 56 ("[e]ach State has the right to develop its cultural, political and economic life freely and naturally").

[205] *See*, for example, Mexico's claim to this effect before the Inter-American Commission on Human Rights, at text accompanying notes 84–86, *supra*.

[206] Military and Paramilitary Activities (Nicar. v. US), 1986 ICJ 4, 131 (June 27).

human rights norms. Both sets of rights find expression in the same binding instruments using the same mandatory language of obligation. Nothing in the text or *travaux* of the Political Covenant, for example, suggests the drafters intended obligations regarding elections to be any less binding or immediate.[207] Both sets of rights address the relationship between governments and their citizens. Both are subject to compliance review by multilateral bodies. And both find justification in conceptions of individual dignity and autonomy routinely invoked by a broad range of international bodies.

The fact that participatory rights were once a purely domestic concern does not affect the binding nature of a State's treaty obligation. Domestic jurisdiction is fluid, definable only by reference to international law, including treaty law.[208] Thus, elections are not some immutable mainstay of the domestic sphere. States cannot appeal to the previously domestic nature of their obligations to avoid sanctions for breach of treaty.[209]

---

[207] The Spanish delegate noted in the final debate over the Political Covenant that "some people considered that the principle of universal and equal suffrage should be introduced gradually because of the low educational level in some countries," but argued that gradual enforcement was "unacceptable and should not be included in a legal instrument such as the draft Covenant" 3rd Committee, 1096th Meeting, *supra* note 22, p. 180. No provision on gradual implementation was included. According to one commentator,

> [n]othing in Article 25 or in other text of the Covenant justifies a distinction between the clarity or immediacy of a state's duties under that Article and, say, its duty to refrain from torture. Citizens of a party to the Covenant would have a valid claim under international law if their government had seized power and abolished elections.

Henry J. Steiner, "Political Participation as a Human Right," *Harv. Hum. Rts. Y.B.* 1 (1988), p. 77, p. 131.

In the Mexican cases, the Inter-American Commission concluded that gradual implementation of participatory rights "would condition the existence of human rights on 'the circumstances and situation of each country,' leaving the whole legal system in a precarious state." Mexico Elections Decision, Cases, *supra* note 35, p. 118.

[208] *See, e.g.*, Advisory Opinion no. 4, Tunis & Morocco Nationality Decrees, 1923 P.C.I.J. (ser. B) no. 4, at p. 24 (Feb. 7) ("The question of whether a certain matter is or is not solely within the jurisdiction of a State is an essentially relative question; it depends on the development of international relations."); *see also* C. G. Fenwick, "The Scope of Domestic Questions in International Law," *Am. J. Int'l L.* 19 (192), pp. 143, 144; Lawrence Preuss, "Article 2, paragraph 7 of the Charter of the United Nations and Matters of Domestic Jurisdiction," *Hague Recueil des Cours* 74 (1994), pp. 553, 567; C. H. M. Waldock, "The Plea of Domestic Jurisdiction Before International Legal Tribunals," *Brit. Y.B. Int'l L.* 31 (1954), pp. 96, 110.

[209] *See* The S. S. Wimbledon (Gr. Brit., Fr., Italy, Japan, and Pol. v. Ger.), 1923 P.C.I.J. (ser. A) no. 1, at p. 25 (Aug. 17) (enforcing provision of Versailles Treaty over German claim of preexisting sovereign rights); Interpretation of Peace Treaties with Bulgaria, Hungary, and Romania, 1950 ICJ pp. 65, 70–71 (Mar. 30) (holding that interpretation of treaty is by its nature question of international law); *see also* Tunis & Morocco Nationality Decrees, 1923 P.C.I.J. (ser. B) no. 4, at p. 24. ("[I]n a matter which, like that of nationality, is not in principle, regulated by international law, the right of a State to use its discretion is nevertheless restricted by obligations which it may have undertaken towards other States.")

Third, a shift in the locus of sovereignty undermines arguments against participatory rights based on an infringement of sovereignty. For a non-democratic regime to claim that participatory rights violate its national sovereignty begs the question of whether that regime has legitimate authority to make such a statement. When the will of the people is the basis of the authority of government, regimes that thwart the will of the people will lack legitimacy. The participatory rights provisions of the human rights conventions have succeeded in extending this notion of legitimacy from the domestic to the international sphere. It is still an open question as to how far this principle should be extended. But if political participation is to have any meaning as an internationally enforceable right, the community of states must be empowered to prescribe standards detailing how participation is to occur and to insist that parties to the major treaties adopt these standards as law. A regime that bases its legitimacy on nothing more than the fact that it holds power exercises no "sovereign" authority to object to such prescriptions.

IV CONCLUSION

The particulars of a human right to political participation, once a flashpoint for grand ideological battles, now appear rather pedestrian. That receipt of an electoral mandate bestows legitimacy upon governments, that genuine choice in an election requires multiple political parties, that incumbent regimes cannot monopolize the mass media during a campaign, and that the other elements of fair elections must be provided, all seem to flow inevitably from treaties announcing a commitment to representative government. It is becoming increasingly difficult to find either states or international institutions that argue as a matter of principle that factors such as these should be excluded from the definition of a "free and fair" election.

It is the seemingly mundane nature of this emerging consensus that is its most remarkable feature. In 1988 Henry Steiner observed that the right to political participation "expresses less a vital concept meant to universalize certain practices than a bundle of concepts, sometimes complementary but sometimes antagonistic."[210] The right, he noted, functioned less as a model of conduct than as a "weapon of rhetorical battle" through which "each of the world's ideological blocs, infusing the right with its own understandings, attacks the others for violating those understandings."[211] In Thomas Franck's terminology, the legitimacy of

---

[210] Steiner, *supra* note 207, p. 77. [211] *Ibid.*

the right suffered from its lack of determinacy.[212] This indeterminacy no longer exists. While one must not overstate the case, the list of sources from which the right draws clarity is impressive: global and regional human rights treaties, over forty years of UN election monitoring reports, opinions of the United Nations Human Rights Committee and three regional tribunals, and two new CSCE instruments which count among their signatories all the former Soviet bloc nations.

In sum, parties to the major human rights conventions have created an international law of participatory rights. They have agreed to open their political institutions to inspection for the purpose of ensuring minimum standards of procedural fairness. In the process, the nineteenth century concept of the State has undergone a substantial change: international notions of legitimacy are no longer oblivious to the origin of governments, but have come to approximate quite closely those domestic conceptions embodied in theories of popular sovereignty. In Professor Reisman's words, "[i]nternational law still protects sovereignty, but – not surprisingly – it is the people's sovereignty rather than the sovereign's sovereignty."[213]

This does not, however, diminish the importance of the State itself. On the contrary, treaties such as the Political Covenant exist as profound reaffirmations of the State as the essential forum of political activity and expression. In its new role as ombudsman, the international community simply ensures that a State will act in the interests of all its citizens.

---

[212] *See* Thomas M. Franck, *The Power of Legitimacy Among Nations* (New York: Oxford University Press, 1990), pp. 50–66.

[213] W. Michael Reisman, "Sovereignty and Human Rights in Contemporary International Law," *Am. J. Int'l L.* 84 (1990), pp. 866, 869.

CHAPTER 3

*Democracy and the body of international law**
James Crawford[1]

I AN OUTLINE OF THE PROBLEM

It is often said that democracies do not wage war on each other, and conflict researchers, looking at wars over the last 200 years, have confirmed that this is broadly true.[2] Admittedly, "the clash of conflicting interests between States governed on democratic principles is not necessarily less serious than between those under less popular forms of government."[3] Democracies seem able, however, to resolve such clashes by means other than war. Perhaps we might "diminish . . . and finally . . . extinguish war between nations"[4] by developing international law and international institutions so as to reinforce democratic government, to deter attempts to overthrow it, and even to reinstate it in cases where it has been wrongfully overthrown. So far attempts at collective security have concentrated on the avoidance of international armed conflict, with rather limited concern for the internal conditions within States which are a major cause of war. Perhaps we need some form of collective democratic security?

An initial difficulty, no doubt, is that of definition. There can be different ideals or legitimate versions of democracy: is one particular ideal or version to be externally imposed? On the other hand, international law

---

* © Professor James Crawford, 1994.
[1] This is the basis of an Inaugural Lecture delivered at the University of Cambridge on March 5, 1993. The author thanks Hugo Caminos, Maxwell Gaylard, Rein Mullerson, Matthew Neuhaus, and Michael Reisman for their assistance in providing information. A post-script, written for this volume, follows this chapter as a *Reprise*. This assesses reaction to the original lecture and surveys developments since its publication.
[2] E. Weede, "Some Simple Calculations on Democracy and War Involvement," *Journal of Peace Research* 29 (1992), p. 377. The same is not true of covert action: D. P. Forsythe, "Democracy, War and Covert Action," *ibid.*, p. 385.
[3] A. Perce Higgins, "International Relations and International Law," in *Studies in International Law and Politics* (Cambridge University Press: 1928), p. 1 at pp. 10–11.
[4] To quote the terms of the bequest by William Whewell (1866) creating the Chair of International Law at Cambridge.

is already seeking to reach some agreement on an agreed minimum content of, or at least an agreed minimum standard for, democracy. The major human rights treaties spell out in some detail the essentials of democracy, understood as the right of all citizens to participate in the political life of their societies. The International Covenant on Civil and Political Rights provides in Article 25 that every citizen has the right to take part in the conduct of public affairs, directly or through freely chosen representatives. This includes in particular "the right to vote and to be elected at genuine periodic elections." The elections must be by universal and equal suffrage, and must be held by, secret ballot "in circumstances which guarantee the free expression of the will of the electors."[5] At the regional level, Article 25 has counterparts in Article 3 of Protocol 1 of the European Convention on Human Rights,[6] and in Article 23 of the American Convention on Human Rights.[7] It is also reflected, although to a lesser extent, in the African Convention on Human and Peoples' Rights.[8] The language of Article 25 goes back to Article 21 of the Universal Declaration of Human Rights of 1948, which adds the proposition that "the will of the people shall be the basis of the authority of government."[9]

That the will of the people is to be the basis of the authority of government is as good a summary as any of the basic democratic idea. But the idea of democracy reflected in the International Covenant, in the Universal Declaration, and in other instruments is not a simple majoritarian one. It is a reflection of the idea that every person, whether a member of a majority or a minority, has basic rights, including rights to participate in public life. Thus the authority of a government, elected by a majority, to conduct for the time being the public affairs of the society

---

[5] *UN Treaty Series*, vol. XMIX, p.171. There are more than 120 States parties to the ICCPR, a sharp increase since 1985, when there were 81.

[6] European Convention on Human Rights (ECHR), Protocol 1, March 20, 1952, *UN Treaty Series*, vol. CCXIII, p. 262, Art. 3 (undertaking by States parties to hold free elections). Cf. ECHR, Art. 16 (restrictions on the political activity of aliens permitted).

[7] American Convention on Human Rights, November 22, 1969 (AMR), *Int'l Legal Materials* 9 (1970), p. 673.

[8] African Charter on Human and Peoples' Rights, June 26, 1981 (AFR), *ibid.*, 21 (1982), p. 58, Art. 13 ("the right to freely participate in the government of his country, either directly or through freely chosen representatives in accordance with the provisions of the law"). It is not clear whether the qualifying phrase "in accordance with the provisions of the law" applies only to the method of choice of representatives or to the right to participate itself.

[9] GA Res. 217A(III), December 10, 1948. Reisman regards Art. 21 as "declaratory of customary international law" and as substituting for "the sovereignty of the sovereign the sovereignty of the people": W. M. Reisman, "Sovereignty and Human Rights in Contemporary International Law," *Am. J. Int'l L.* 84 (1990), pp. 866ff at p. 867.

is a *consequence* of the exercise of the rights of participation in public life of all citizens, whether they belong to the majority or the minority. The capacity of the government to limit or derogate from the rights of a minority is limited, even in times of public emergency.[10]

This is why human rights courts have not given much independent meaning to the qualifying phrase "necessary in a democratic society," which occurs in the limitation article in the various human rights treaties.[11] That phrase might have been used as a way of relativizing human rights defined at the international level, of allowing local modifications deemed necessary in a given democratic society. No doubt the findings of human rights courts and commissions are context-dependent. It has been necessary to look carefully at the circumstances of the alleged breach in the circumstances of the society concerned. But in the end a democratic society, as envisaged in the human rights treaties, is one which respects the basic rights of its members.[12]

Some societies are tolerant, plural, or relatively homogeneous, and have settled ideas of the proper limits of government. It may be appropriate in such societies to rely on majority institutions to protect individuals. That was Dicey's view of the protection of individual liberty in the

---

[10] It should be noted that the right to participate is nonderogable under AMR (Art. 27(2)) and AFR (which has no derogation clause), but is derogable in time of public emergency under ICCPR (Art. 4) and ECHR (Art. 15). For discussion, see S. R. Chowdhury, *Rule of Law in a State of Emergency* (London: Pinter Publishers, 1989), at p. 250; J. Oraá, *Human Rights in States of Emergency* (Oxford: Clarendon Press, 1992), at p. 101.

[11] That phrase occurs in the ICCPR in Arts. 14(1) (closed trials), 21 (peaceful assembly) and 22(2) (freedom of association). It is more frequently used in the ECHR: see Arts. 6(1) (closed trials), 8(2) (private and family life), 9(2) (manifestations of religion or beliefs), 10(2) (freedom of expression), 11(2) (peaceful assembly); Protocol 4, Art. 2(3) (right to leave a country). Cf. also AMR, Arts. 15 (peaceful assembly), 16(2) (freedom of association), 22(3) (freedom of movement and residence); 29(c) (savings clause for "other rights or guarantees . . . derived from representative democracy as a form of government"). On the other hand the term does not appear at all in the AFR.

[12] On a number of occasions the European Court has held that laws with strong support within the relevant community (as manifested by elections or referenda) none the less violated the Convention, and has given little or no weight to the factor of local preference. *See, e.g.*, Open Door and Dublin Well Woman v. Ireland (1992), ECHR, Series A, no. 249, p. 25, where the Court referred briefly to "pluralism, tolerance and broadmindedness" as characteristics of a democratic society. Some of the dissenting judges pointed out that the law in question had recently been affirmed by national referendum ("eminently democratic process"): *ibid.*, pp. 32 (Judge Cremona), 35 (Judge Matscher). For other examples of the reluctance to legitimate governmental conduct as "necessary in a democratic society" see Lingens v. Austria (1986), ECHR, Series A, no. 103; Oberschlick v. Austria (1991), ECHR, Series A, no. 204; Funke v. France (1993), ECHR, Series A, no. 256A; Kokkinakis v. Greece (1992), Series A, no. 260A. Cases on the other side of the line (but equally lacking detailed analysis of the concept of a democratic society) include Leander v. Sweden (1987), ECHR, Series A, no. 116; Hadjianastassiou v. Greece (1992), Series A, no. 252.

United Kingdom.[13] For a long time his view was generally accepted, and it is still influential. It is one major reason why the United Kingdom still does not have an enforceable bill of rights.

Whatever the position may be in particular societies, the majoritarian theory is untenable in the context of the protection of human rights internationally. At the international level the point of human rights is not merely to relate the individual to public power, but to protect him or her from abuses of public power, including abuses supported by a majority. There is no international consensus on the values of tolerance and pluralism, or on the proper role, of the State, which would secure individual liberty without express protection such as that contained in the various human rights treaties.

In addition to Article 25 of the International Covenant, the idea of democracy is also reflected in Article 1. Under Article 1, all peoples have the right of self-determination. By virtue of that right, it is said, "they freely determine their political status and freely pursue their economic, social and cultural development."[14] This suggests that self-determination is a continuing matter, not a once-for-all constitution of the State. Thus in addition to its familiar role in the decolonization process, Article 1 can be read as affirming the self-direction of each society by its people, and thus as affirming the principle of democracy at the collective level.[15] This is certainly the view taken by the United Nations Human Rights Committee. The Committee identifies as the beneficiaries of self-determination the people of existing states. It equates their right of self-determination with the existence within the State of a continuing system of democratic government based on public

---

[13] For analysis of Dicey's approach see T. R. S. Allan, "Legislative Supremacy and the Rule of Law: Democracy and Constitutionalism," *Cam. L. J.* 44 (1985), p. 111, esp. pp. 129–41; P. P. Craig, *Public Law and Democracy in the United Kingdom and the United States of America* (Oxford, Clarendon Press, 1990), ch. 2.

[14] Among the regional human rights treaties, Art. 1 is reflected only in AFR, Art. 20.

[15] In this context the words of the Friendly Relations Declaration (GA Res. 2625 (xxv), October 24, 1970) are often cited. In elaborating the principle of equal rights and self-determination of peoples, the Declaration states that:

> Nothing in the foregoing paragraphs shall be construed as authorizing or encouraging any action which would dismember or impair, totally or in part, the territorial integrity or political unity of sovereign and independent States conducting themselves in compliance with the principle of equal rights and self-determination of people as described above and *thus possessed of a government representing the whole people belonging to the territory without distinction as to race, creed or colour.* (Emphasis added.)

This certainly implies that the principle extends to internal self-determination so as to produce the result referred to in the words italicized: on the other hand the paragraph is a savings clause, and the "foregoing paragraphs" do not, explicitly at least, so provide.

participation. It denies that self-determination involves a right to secede.[16]

Until recently, provisions such as Article 25, or Article 1 if it is understood as a sort of collective right to democratic institutions, were honored more in the breach than in the observance. In the mid-1980s, only about a third of all the countries of the world could be described as democratic, and a still smaller proportion had long-standing and stable democratic structures. Moreover under the rights conception of democracy, it is not enough that the government of the day have been elected, in the comparatively recent past, at a general election. Democracy implies a range of rights to participate in public life, effective freedom of speech, the opportunity to organize political parties and other groups, and so on. In many countries, notoriously, such rights and opportunities have been lacking. A particular point is the denial of voting rights to women in many countries, and of an effective political voice to women in many more.

Thus it is hardly surprising that under international law (apart from treaties), there was no general endorsement of a principle of democracy. There was no requirement that the government of a State, to be a government, should have been democratically elected or even that it should have the general support of its people. As Oppenheim pointed out in 1905, the actual control of a government over the apparatus of the State has been treated as sufficient.[17] Jefferson's famous reference to the "will of the people substantially declared" has not been taken literally.[18]

Moreover other features of classical international law were deeply undemocratic, or at least were capable of operating in a deeply undemocratic way. Six examples may be given.

First, international law assumes that the executive has comprehensive power in international affairs. Generally the Head of State and the Minister for Foreign Affairs have plenary powers to make international

---

[16] *See* A. Cassese, "The Self Determination of Peoples," in L. Henkin, ed. *The International Bill of Rights* (New York: Columbia University Press, 1987), at pp. 92, 96–98, 101–02, 111–13; D. McGoldrick, *The Human Rights Committee* (Oxford: Clarendon Press, 1991), at pp. 247–58, for reviews of the Committee's approach to Art. 1. Generally on self-determination *see* J. Crawford, *The Creation of States in International Law* (Oxford: Clarendon Press, 1979), at pp. 84–106; T. Franck, "The Emerging Right to Democratic Governance," *American Journal of International Law*, 86 (1992), p. 46, at pp. 52–63.

[17] L. Oppenheim, *International Law* (1st edn., Longman, 1905), vol. I, at pp. 403, 405.

[18] US recognition practice, in particular, has relied to some extent on the criterion of popular support for a new but unconstitutional government, but not consistently: *see, e.g.*, M. Whiteman, *Digest of International Law* (Washington, D.C.: US Government Printing Office, 1963), vol. II, at pp. 46, 68–74, 261–2; L. T. Galloway, *Recognizing Foreign Governments. The Practice of the United States* (Washington, D.C.: American Enterprise for Public Policy Research, 1978), at pp. 139–45.

commitments on behalf of the State, and to agree to and apply rules of international law which may affect the rights or claims of individuals without their consent, and even without their knowledge.[19]

Second, it is established that national law, no matter how democratically established, is not an excuse for failure to comply with international obligations.[20] At one level the rule is obvious, and would seem to have no adverse implications for democratic government. After all if an obligation exists at the international level, it cannot be the case that a law of one State can release that State from the obligation. At another level, however, the rule creates significant problems of democratic control. If an international obligation arises, apart from a treaty, there may have been no direct process of commitment to the obligation either by parliament or by elected leaders. In some countries treaties, or certain classes of treaties, require the approval of parliament, but many consensual obligations in international law (executive agreements, memoranda of understanding, to say nothing of less formal unilateral commitments) fall outside the scope of such procedures. In common law countries such as the United Kingdom there are no formal constitutional constraints at all on the executive: the process of ratification of treaties is a purely executive act. Moreover if the executive enters into a treaty or commits the State in some other way, parliament may have little real choice but to enact the laws necessary to give effect to the obligation. It is true that practices of consultation have developed which seek to involve parliament at an early stage, or at least to keep it informed. But these are practices not laws, and do not eliminate the difficulty. Thus if the British Government had ratified the Maastricht Treaty despite the passage of an amendment relating to the Social Chapter, that might have presented problems of legality under United Kingdom law, but it would have been effective *vis-à-vis* the other members of the Community.[21]

The third potentially undemocratic rule relates to the important question of remedies. The executive government has virtually exclusive control over the availability of international remedies. The individual has no autonomous procedural rights in international law. In many cases rights of individual petition are based on an optional clause or an

---

[19] *See, e.g.*, Vienna Convention on the Law of Treaties, May 23, 1969: *UN Treaty Series*, vol. MCLV, p. 331, Art. 7(2)(a).
[20] The rule is enunciated in the context of treaty obligations by Art. 27 of the Vienna Convention on the Law of Treaties. For the equivalent rule in the context of non-treaty obligations, see ILC Draft Articles on State Responsibility, Part 1, Art. 4; Part 2, Art. 6, bis(3).
[21] R. v. Secretary of State for Foreign Affairs, ex parte Rees-Mogg (QBD, July 30, 1993), noted *New Law Journal* 143 (1993), p. 1153; cf. Blackburn v. Attorney-General, [1971] 2 All ER 1380.

optional protocol, and may be to that extent precarious. This is true both of the right of individual communication under the International Covenant, and of the right of individual petition to the European Commission under the European Convention.

Fourth, the principle of non-intervention extends to protect even non-democratic regimes in relation to action taken to preserve their power against their own people. At least, that has been the traditional understanding.

Fifth, the principle of self-determination is not permitted to modify established territorial boundaries. Nor, on the whole, has it replaced the traditional rules for determining territorial disputes. Those rules are based largely on the political history of the territory concerned rather than on the current wishes of its inhabitants. The ninth edition of *Oppenheim's International Law* suggests that "the injection of a legal principle of self-determination into the law about acquisition and loss of territorial sovereignty" amounts to a "fundamental change."[22] But it does not spell out what specific changes have been produced, outside the colonial context, and the recent cases involving territorial disputes in Africa and Central America have bypassed the principle of self-determination in the interests of stability.[23]

Sixth, the powers of a government to bind the State for the future seem to be virtually unlimited. International law recognizes the general authority of a government over the State as a continuing entity. That can be seen, for example, from the well-known *Tinoco* arbitration.[24] A military regime in Costa Rica seized power but was eventually overthrown and replaced by an elected government. The new government disputed its liability to pay for debts incurred by the military regime. The case went to arbitration, where it was held that the successor government was bound by all the acts of its predecessor, on the basis that the predecessor regime was firmly established, and that its legitimacy or constitutionality were irrelevant.[25]

It is significant that that rule has rarely been challenged, even by successor governments with much to gain from a successful challenge and

---

[22] *Oppenheim's International Law*, R. Y. Jennings and A. Watts, eds. (9th edn., Longman, 1992), vol. I, p. 715.
[23] Burkina Faso/Mali Frontier Dispute, 1986, ICJ, p. 554, para. 25; Land, Island and Maritime Frontier case (El Salvador/Honduras, Nicaragua intervening), 1992, ICJ.
[24] (1923), *Reports of International Arbitral Awards*, vol. I, p. 369.
[25] For more recent applications of the principle that a government in control of the State can commit it internationally *see, e.g.*, Short v. Islamic Republic of Iran (1987), 82 ILR p. 149; cf. Yeager v. Islamic Republic of Iran (1987), 82 ILR p. 179.

with no sympathy for their predecessor or its foreign supporters. The most important example of such a challenge was the rejection by the post-1917 Revolutionary Government of Russia of continuity with the prerevolution Tsarist regime. That rejection was based on special grounds which did not challenge a general rule of governmental succession, and anyway was modified after a few years.[26] Not the least of the ironies surrounding the dissolution of the Soviet Union is the fact that the Russian Federation argued that it is the same legal person as the Soviet Union, and based that argument to some extent on the continuity of the Soviet Union with prerevolutionary Russia.[27]

In its earlier manifestations, it is not surprising that international law had these six characteristics, since its own primary characteristic was as a law of co-ordination of the activities of potentates, principalities, and powers. Before 1928, or perhaps 1945, international law made no final attempt to outlaw war, which was, as Lord McNair said in his inaugural lecture, "extra-legal rather than illegal."[28] Modern international law has changed in this crucial respect – that is to say, it now purports to protect the existence and territorial integrity of States. Earlier (pre-1945) international law could be defended, in a perhaps back-handed way, by the argument that it was, in a fundamental sense, *descriptive*. It did not underwrite regimes or even States; it merely accepted them while they continued. Not underwriting them, it could legitimately be argued that it did not assume any responsibility for quality control, any more than seismology exists to encourage "good" earthquakes.

Formally, that position had changed by 1945, when the United Nations Charter prohibited the use of force in international relations except in self-defence or with the authorization of the Security Council. For example it was on this basis that the Security Council took action to restore "the sovereignty, independence and territorial integrity of Kuwait," and the authority of what it described as "the legitimate Government of Kuwait."[29] For a long time, however, the

---

[26] T. A. Taracouzio, *The Soviet Union and International Law* (New York: Macmillan, 1935), at pp. 21–25; D. P. O'Connell, *State Succession in International Law and Municipal Law* (Cambridge University Press, 1967), vol. I, at pp. 19–20; Crawford, *supra* note 16, at pp. 405–6.
[27] The continuity of Russia with the former Soviet Union was asserted in the Agreement establishing the Commonwealth of Independent States, Alma Ata, December 21, 1991. *Int'l Legal Materials* 31 [1992], p. 138 and has been accepted by UN organs and by foreign courts (*see, e.g. The Kherson*, [1992] 2 Lloyd's Rep. 261). For discussion, *see* R. Mullerson, "The Continuity and Succession of States by Reference to the Former USSR and Yugoslavia," *Int'l & Comp. L.Q.*, 42 (1993), p. 473.
[28] A. D. McNair, "Collective Security," *Year Book*, 17 (1936), pp. 150ff, at p. 152.
[29] SC Res. 662 (1990) (adopted 15–0). See *International Legal Materials* 29 (1990), p. 1325, for this and other Security Council resolutions on Kuwait.

consequences of the change brought about by the United Nations Charter were limited. The six rules of international law referred to above remained essentially unchanged. Indeed some of them were reinforced.

This can be seen from the decision of the International Court in the Nicaragua case in 1986.[30] In that case, Nicaragua claimed that the assistance given by the United States to the *contras* was an unlawful use of force by the United States against Nicaragua, or at least an unlawful intervention in its internal affairs. The United States claimed that it was justified in supporting the *contras* for a number of reasons, including the breach by the Nicaraguan Government of commitments about the composition of the government and the installation "of a truly democratic government that guarantees peace, freedom and justice."[31]

In fact the Nicaraguan Government had been elected in 1984, in elections observed by a range of individuals and non-governmental organizations.[32] The major United States complaint against it related to the internal and external policies subsequently adopted by the Sandinista Government, although the State Department also rejected the 1984 elections as unfair. Rather than examining the question of compliance with the various commitments made by the Sandinistas as a condition of coming to power, the Court took another tack. It said:

> The assertion of the commitment raises the question of the possibility of the State binding itself by agreement in relation to a question of domestic policy, such as that relating to the holding of free elections on its territory. The Court cannot discover, within the range of subjects open to international agreement, any obstacle . . . to hinder a State from making a commitment of this kind. A State, which is free to decide upon the principle and methods of popular consultation within its domestic order, is sovereign for the purpose of accepting a limitation of its sovereignty in this field.[33]

It went on to point out that the OAS Charter referred to "the effective exercise of representative democracy" only as an aspect of "solidarity" and as a "high aim." Given this unspecific language it rejected the view

---

[30] Military and Paramilitary Activities in and against Nicaragua (Nicar. v. USA), 1986 ICJ, p. 14, para. 194.
[31] The specific commitments on which the United States relied are set out in the dissenting opinion of Judge Schwebel: ICJ (1986), p. 14, at pp. 398–401. The majority opinion referred to them only in general terms: *ibid.*, p. 130 ("questions such as the composition of the government, its political ideology and alignment, totalitarianism, human rights, militarization and aggression").
[32] On the 1984 elections in Nicaragua see *Keesing's Contemporary Archives* 30 (1984), pp. 33269–72.
[33] 1986 ICJ, at p. 131.

that Nicaragua actually undertook a commitment to organise free elections, and that this commitment was of a legal nature . . . [T]he Court cannot find an instrument with legal force . . . whereby Nicaragua has committed itself in respect of the principle or methods of holding elections.[34]

This aspect of the Court's decision is rather unsatisfactory. Nicaragua was a party both to the International Covenant and to the American Convention, both of which contain clear commitments with respect to the principle of free elections and their regularity, although not with respect to precise issues of timing or method. The Court professed itself "unable to find" such commitments: one can only say that it did not look very hard. To be fair, it was unaided in its search by any assistance from the United States, which did not appear at the stage of the merits and which did not rely either on the International Covenant or on the American Convention, no doubt because it was at that time a party to neither. The Court also made the point that any question of compliance with commitments made towards the OAS was not a matter for specific enforcement by the United States, and certainly not by way of forcible intervention.[35]

The Court's negative reaction even to the idea that Nicaragua was subject to international supervision or accountability in the conduct of elections reflects the emphasis of traditional international law on non-intervention in the internal affairs of States. The holding of free elections was treated still as essentially a matter of "domestic policy." Clearly, the Court was reluctant to accept that established international law might have changed. This is quite apart from the controversial question of the means used by the United States to enforce any commitment that might have been made.

In many other respects, however, international law has changed. It is increasingly concerned with issues which impinge on what were once considered matters of domestic policy. The potentially undemocratic aspects of the traditional international law rules are only heightened by this. Rules which draw lines between societies may be less problematic, from the point of view of democratic principle, than rules which deal with the internal life of those societies. International law is increasingly concerned with the second as well as the first.

Since 1986 the world has itself undergone vast changes. In particular there has been a significant change in the democratic balance. In

---

[34] *Ibid.*, pp. 131–32. But see the separate opinion of Judge Ago (*ibid.*, pp. 186–87) for justified doubts on this point.   [35] *Ibid.*, pp. 132–33.

the last decade the proportion of States with democratic systems, however fragile or tentative, has increased sharply – a process beginning in Southern Europe, extending to Latin America and Eastern Europe, the Soviet Union and many of its former republics, and even to East Asia.[36] In Africa, according to one analysis, there were only four democracies, as against forty States with apparently stable non-democratic regimes, in 1989. By 1992, the number of democracies had increased to eighteen, and the number of non-democracies was reduced to twelve. Significantly, there had also been a great increase (from three to twenty-two) in the number of regimes in a stage of transition to democracy.[37] No doubt this is all fragile and reversible, but it is also, in the words of the noted African commentator Ali Mazrui, an "unmistakable" trend.[38]

With this change has come a new stress on democracy as a value, even a dominant value, in national and international affairs.[39] The same is

---

[36] There is now an enormous literature on these developments. *See, e.g.*, G. A. O'Donnell and P. C. Schmitter, *Transitions from Authoritarian Rule* (Baltimore, Md.: The Johns Hopkins University Press, 1986); J. Higley and R. Gunther, *Elites and Democratic Consolidation in Latin America and Southern Europe* (Cambridge University Press, 1991); S. D. Huntingdon, *The Third Wave: Democratization in the Late Twentieth Century* (Oklahoma, Okla.: University of Oklahoma Press, 1991); G. Pridham, *Encouraging Democracy: The International Context of Regime Transition in Southern Europe* (Leicester University Press, 1991); A. Przesvorski, *Democracy and the Market: Political and Economic Reforms in Eastern Europe and Latin America* (Cambridge University Press, 1991); and the essays in D. Held, ed., *Prospects for Democracy. North, South, East, West* (Cambridge, Ma.: Polity Press, 1993), part IV.

[37] *See* H. M. McFrerson, "Democracy and Development in Africa," *Journal of Peace Research* 29 (1992), p. 241, at p. 242. *See* also the annual Freedom House surveys: e.g., *Freedom in the World: Political Rights and Civil Liberties 1990–91* (New York: Freedom House, 1991).

[38] A. A. Mazrui, "Planned Governance and the Liberal Revival in Africa: The Paradox of Anticipation," *Cornell Int'l L. J.* 25 (1992), p. 541.

[39] A sample of the literature in political science and international relations includes: D. Held, *Models of Democracy* (Cambridge, Mass.: Polity Press, 1987); G. Duncan, ed., *Democracy and the Capitalist State* (Cambridge University Press, 1989); D. Held, "Democracy, the Nation State and the Global System," in D. Held, ed., *Political Theory, Today* (Cambridge, Mass.: Polity Press, 1991), p. 97; F. Fukuyarna, *The End of History. and the Last Man* (London: Penguin, 1992); J. Dunn, ed., *Democracy: The Unfinished Journey* (Oxford University Press, 1992); E.-O. Czempiel, "Governance and Democratization," in J. N. Rosenau and E.-O. Czempiel, eds., *Governance without Government: Order and Change in World Politics* (Cambridge University Press, 1992), p. 250; R. Bartley *et al.*, eds., *Democracy and Capitalism: Asian and American Prospectives* (Singapore: Institute of South-East Asian Studies, 1993); Held, ed., *supra* note 36. On democratic principles in different religious traditions *see, e.g.*, A.Y. al-Hibri, "Islamic Constitutionalism and the Concept of Democracy," *Case Western Reserve J. Int'l L.* 24 (1992), p. 1. For feminist perspectives *see, e.g.*, S. Mendus, "Losing the Faith: Feminism and Democracy," in Dunn, *supra*, p. 207; A. Phillips, "Must Feminists Give up on Liberal Democracy?" in Held, *supra* note 36, p. 93. More-or-less sceptical accounts include N. Chomsky, *Deterring Democracy* (London: Vintage, 1992); O. M. Fiss, "Capitalism and Democracy," *Michigan J. Int'l L.*, 13 (1992), p. 908; B. Parekh, "The Cultural Particularity of Liberal Democracy," in Held, *supra* note 36, p. 156.

true of the law regulating those affairs.[40] References to democracy, which a generation or even a decade ago would have been regarded as political and extralegal, are entering into the justification of legal decision-making in a new way.

At the national level, two examples may be given. In 1992 the High Court of Australia invalidated a federal law prohibiting paid political advertising during election campaigns, on the basis that the constitutional requirement of parliamentary elections implied that the conditions for free elections, including freedom of speech and of the press, could not be infringed.[41] In February 1993 the House of Lords held that a local council could not sue for defamation, because to protect the reputation of public agencies such as councils by the law of defamation would unduly affect freedom of speech in a democratic society.[42] It is doubtful if either case would have been decided the same way fifteen years ago.[43] It is no accident that in both cases reference was made, alongside the idea of democracy, to international human rights treaties.

At the international level also, concern for democracy as a principle has deepened. This prompts the question to what extent international law may be moving in the direction of underpinning democracy, of taking seriously the democratic principles referred to in Articles 1 and 25 of the International Covenant, of giving effect to the proposition in Article 21 of the Universal Declaration that "the will of the people shall be the basis of the authority of government"?

---

[40] For international law perspectives (mostly North American), see esp. Franck, *supra* note 16; G. H. Fox, "The Right to Political Participation in International Law," *Yale J. Int'l L.*, 17 (1992), p. 539. Other accounts include H. Steiner, "Political Participation as a Human Right," *Harvard Hum. Rts. Y. B.*, 1 (1988), p. 77; Panel, "The Human Right to Participate in Government: Towards an Operational Definition," *Proc. Am. Soc. Int'l L.* (1988), p. 505; T. Meron, "Democracy and the Rule of Law," *World Affairs*, 153 (1990), p. 23; Panel, "National Sovereignty Revisited: Perspectives on the Emerging Norm of Democracy in International Law," *Proc. Am. Soc. Int'l L.* 86 (1992), p. 249; A. Rosas and J. Helgesen, eds., *The Strength of Diversity: Human Rights and Pluralist Democracy* (Dordrecht: Martinus Nijhoff, 1992). For public law perspectives *see*, *e.g.*, K. E. Klare, "Legal Theory and Democratic Reconstruction: Reflections on 1989," *U. Brit. Columbia L. Rev.* 25 (1991), p. 69; R. F. and H. J. Taubenfeld, "Some Thoughts on the Problems of Designing Stable Democracies," *Int'l Law.* 24 (1990), p. 689; G. Ress, "The Constitution and the Requirements of Democracy in Germany," in C. Starck, ed., *New Challenges to the German Basic Law* (Baden-Baden: Nomos Verlag, 1991), p. 111.

[41] Australian Capital Television Pty. Ltd. v. Commonwealth of Australia no. 2 (1992), 108 ALR 577. Cf. also Nationwide News Pty. Ltd. v. Wills (1992), 108 ALR 681.

[42] Derbyshire County Council v. Times Newspapers Ltd., [1993] 1 All ER 1011 (HL), affirming [1992] 3 All ER 65.

[43] In the Australian case there is no doubt that the decision would have been different: *see* Attorney General for Australia, ex rel. McKinlay v. Commonwealth of Australia (1975), 50 ALJR 279.

II DEVELOPING INTERNATIONAL LAW IN PRO-DEMOCRATIC DIRECTIONS

In one sense, there has been a great deal of development, as the following examples show:

(1) There is a developing practice of election monitoring by international organizations such as the UN and the OAS, as well as non-governmental organizations. This has occurred both in colonial territories and, more recently, in independent States.

The holding of plebiscites for elections to determine the future of a colonial or non-self-governing territory is a long-established practice.[44] A recent and successful example was the pre-independence election in Namibia, where the role of non-governmental organizations was crucial in creating an atmosphere in which 97 percent of the electors cast a vote.[45] It remains to be seen whether the same process will be allowed to occur in the Western Sahara,[46] or for that matter East Timor.[47]

Even more significant has been the development of election monitoring in independent States. The United Nations Observer Mission to Verify the Electoral Process in Nicaragua in 1989 was the first occasion where a public international organization monitored an election in an independent State.[48] It was followed in 1900 by the monitoring of the election in Haiti, though with less happy results.[49] The Commonwealth

---

[44] Franck, *supra* note 16, pp. 69–71.
[45] SC Res. 628 (1989). For the background see Namibia advisory opinion, 1971 ICJ, p. 6; Fox, *supra* note 40, pp. 576–79.
[46] As envisaged by SC Res. 690 (1991). For the background see Western Sahara advisory opinion, ICJ Reports, 1975, p. 12; T. M. Franck, "The Stealing of the Sahara," *Am. J. Int'l L.* 70 (1976), p. 694.
[47] The issue of self-determination underlies proceedings brought by Portugal against Australia before the ICJ: *see* case concerning East Timor, 1991, ICJ p. 9; C. Chinkin, "The Merits of Portugal's Claim Against Australia," *U. New South Wales L. J.* 15 (1992), p. 423. From the East Timorese perspective *see* J. Ramos Horta, *Funu. The Unfinished Saga of East Timor* (New Jersey: Red Sea Press, 1987); J. G. Taylor, *Indonesia's Forgotten War* (London: Zed Books, 1991).
[48] See Fox, *supra* note 40, pp. 597–83. Generally see Panel, "International Observation of Elections," *Proceedings of the American Society of International Law* 84 (1990), p. 375; J. M. Ebersole, "The United Nations' Response to Requests for Assistance in Electoral Matters," *Virginia J. Int'l L.*, 33 (1992), p. 91; W. M. Reisman, "International Election Observation," *Pace U. Sch. L. Y.B. Int'l L.* 4 (1992), p. 1; D. Stoelting, "The Challenge of UN Monitored Elections in Independent Nations," *Stanford J. Int'l L.* 28 (1992), p. 371.
[49] See OAS Res. MRE/RES 3/92, May 17, 1992; GA Res. 47/20B, 23 April 1993; SC Res. 841 (1993). It should be noted that the Security Council, though expressly acting under chapter VII of the Charter in imposing a mandatory trade embargo on Haiti, did so on the combined basis that a request to that effect by the Haitian Permanent Representative and the action taken by the OAU and the General Assembly together defined "a unique and exceptional situation warranting extraordinary measures." No precedent was evidently intended to be created but on the other hand the Council was clearly operating on the basis of a principle of legitimacy in taking action against what it described as a "*de facto*" regime. See Fox, *supra* note 40, pp. 583–86; Franck, *supra* note 16, pp. 72–74.

104   *The normative foundations of a right to political participation*

Secretariat has also played an active role in monitoring elections, and the preparations for elections, in independent Commonwealth countries.[50]

In some cases this involvement has extended to creating the conditions for free elections and for the establishment of democratic rule, as with the United Nations operation in Cambodia, the long-term success of which also remains to be seen.[51]

(2) There are moves to institutionalize these functions, for example the Office of Fair Elections created by the Paris Charter of the Conference on Security and Co-operation in Europe in 1991 (CSCE),[52] and the Organization of American States Resolution on Representative Democracy of the same year.[53] In 1992 the United Nations General Assembly provisionally endorsed guidelines for election observation. Electoral assistance under the guidelines would be offered "on a case-by-case basis . . . recognizing that the fundamental responsibility for ensuring free and fair elections lies with Governments."[54]

(3) The various human rights courts and commissions have also begun to deal with these issues. For example the first case under Article 3 of Protocol 1 of the European Convention was decided by the European

---

[50] In the period 1990–93, Commonwealth Observer Groups have observed and reported on elections in the following countries: Malaysia (1990 general elections); Bangladesh (1991 Parliamentary elections); Zambia (1991 Presidential and National Assembly elections); Guyana (1992 general and regional elections); Kenya (1992 Presidential, parliamentary and civic elections); Seychelles (Constitutional Commission elections [July 1992], Constitutional referendum [November 1992], Presidential and National Assembly elections [July 1993]); Lesotho (1993 general election). In each case a report of the Observer Group was published by the Commonwealth Secretariat.

[51] For the Paris Agreement on Cambodia of October 21, 1991, see *Int'l Legal Mat.*, 31 (1992), p. 174.

[52] *Int'l Legal Mat.* 30 (1991), p. 190. For the Report of the CSCE Seminar of Experts on Democratic Institutions (Oslo, November 1991) see *Int'l Legal Mat.* 31 (1992), p. 374.

[53] OEA/Ser.P/AG/Res. 1080 (XXIO/91); Franck, *supra* note 16, pp. 65–66. In an exchange of correspondence with the UN Secretary-General concerning their respective competences in relation to the situation in Haiti, the Secretary-General of the OAS asserted that one of the "unique features" of the OAS was "the promotion and consolidation of democracy . . . yet another valuable contribution of the region to the development of international law, although this does not imply any claim of universal applicability for these distinctive features": OEA/Ser.F/V.i, MRE/INF.15/92, July 25, 1992.

[54] GA Res. 47/138, December 18, 1992 (adopted 141–0:20), paras. 4, 9. On the same day the General Assembly adopted a countervailing resolution on "Respect for the principles of national sovereignty and noninterference in the internal affairs of States in their electoral processes": GA Res. 47/130 (99–45:16). Res. 47/130 reflects reservations on the part of many Third World States, who fear that the new emphasis on democratic standards will be used to justify or excuse interference in their affairs. It also reflects the older equation of self-determination with non-intervention in the case of independent States, as to which see Crawford, *supra* note 16, p. 102. On the other hand the level of support for these implicitly competing resolutions has been changing: cf. GA Res. 46/137 (134–4:13) and GA Res. 46/130 (102–40:13), both of December 17, 1991; GA Res. 45/150 (129–8:9) and 45/151 (111–29:11), both of December 18, 1990. For comment, see Fox, *supra* note 40, p. 587; Franck, *supra* note 16, p. 82.

Court in 1986. That case involved complex arrangements for the decentralization of Belgium having regard to the interests of the different linguistic groups.[55] This follows the earlier action by the European Commission in the *Greek* case,[56] which signaled the departure of Greece from democratic standards, and which played a role in the suspension of Greece from the Council of Europe until those standards were reinstated. The Inter-American Commission on Human Rights has also been dealing with these issues, for example in a case involving a complaint by three Mexican citizens dealing with electoral fraud.[57] In that case – in apparent contrast to the International Court in the *Nicaragua* case – the Commission refused to accept the argument that these matters were essentially domestic.

(4) At the universal level the Human Rights Committee has been dealing with a range of cases under the Optional Protocol involving restrictions on, and in most cases flagrant violations of, the political rights in Article 25.[58] The Committee is also drafting a general comment on Article 25: the draft comment points out that Article 25 is "called to guarantee democratic political systems in States parties to the Covenant," stresses the close relationship between Articles 1 and 25, and notes that arbitrary deprivation of citizenship for the purposes of avoiding or diminishing the political rights of individuals would violate Article 25. The Committee doubts whether any form of one party State could comply with Article 25.[59]

There are a number of further elements in the debate. It is sometimes

---

[55] Case of Mathieu-Mohin and Clerfayt (1987), ECHR, Series A, No. 113. The Court held that, although Art. 3 was in form an inter-State undertaking, it vested rights in the citizens concerned (*ibid.*, p. 15). It went on succinctly to outline its approach to Art. 3: on the positive side a universal right to vote and to stand for election on a basis of equality in any body which constitutes a "legislature" under the constitutional structure of the State in question; on the negative side, a wide margin of appreciation in the legislature as to the system of representation and of voting, a system to be judged "in the light of the political evolution of the country concerned," but subject to the overriding principle that the system must ensure "the free expression of the opinion of the people in the choice of the legislature." *See ibid.*, pp. 16–17, and for comment, Merrills, *Brit. Y. B. Int'l L.* 58 (1987), p. 466. For a review of the Commission's practice under Protocol 1, Art. 3, see Council of Europe, *Digest of Strasbourg Case Law relating to the European Convention on Human Rights* (Cologne: Carl Heymanns, 1985), vol. v, pp. 829–67.

[56] Yearbook of the European Convention on Human Rights, 11 (1968), part 2, p. 690, at p. 730; *ibid.* 12 (1969), part 2, *passim*; *Int'l Legal Mat.* 14 (1975), p. 313.

[57] Mexico Elections Decision (Cases 9768, 9780, 9829) (1990), cited by Fox, *supra* note 40, p. 794. And see D. Shelton, "Representative Democracy and Human Rights in the Western Hemisphere," *Hum. Rts. L. J.* 12 (1991), p. 353.

[58] E.g., Mpandanjila v. Zaire (No. 138/1983), reproduced in UN, Selected Decisions of the Human Rights Committee under the Optional Protocol, UN Doc. CCPR/C/OP/2, vol. II, p. 164; Mpaka-Nsusu v. Zaire (No. 157/1983), *ibid.*, p. 187.

[59] Draft General Comments (Article 25) 1993.

argued that a State may justifiably use armed force to overthrow a despotic government in another State. There were overtones of this idea in the so-called Reagan doctrine, and in the use of armed force by the United States in Grenada and Panama. The idea has found at least some support from commentators within and even outside the United States. For example it has been argued that the essential justification for the United States action in Panama was that it was taken "in support of the democratic process," since it was directed against a regime which had been voted out of office but which refused to give up power, and since the intervention was followed by the holding of free elections after the American withdrawal.[60]

No-one can regret the fall of a Noriega, or for that matter a Pol Pot. But there are serious problems with the idea that democracy can be installed by the unilateral assertion of external force. The first problem, from the perspective of international law, is simply that the vast majority of governments, including the vast majority of democratic governments, do not accept that view. The Grenada and Panama interventions were roundly condemned by the United Nations and the Organization of American States respectively,[61] and it is significant that in its official justifications in each case the United States did not rely on the democratic argument, as distinct from a number of other arguments such as the protection of its nationals. Nor for that matter did Tanzania, when it took justified action against the Amin regime.[62]

There is also the problem that this asserted right to intervene has so far been exercised in a quite arbitrary way – in Panama but not elsewhere, in Nicaragua but not elsewhere. Moreover other countries taking action which might have seemed justified on similar grounds – Vietnam in Cambodia, to take one possible example[63] – have been subject to vigorous and sustained criticism, not least by the United States. As Bowett has pointed out, the "nations of the world will not accept international

---

[60] E. Lauterpacht QC, *The Times*, December 23, 1989, p. 11. Similarly A. D'Amato, "The Invasion of Panama was a Lawful Response to Tyranny," *Amer. J. Int'l L.* 84 (1990), p. 516; D. W. Alberts, "The United States Invasion of Panama: Unilateral Military Intervention to Effectuate a Change in Government: A Continuum of Lawfulness," *Transn. L. Contempo. Prob.* 1 (1991), p. 259.
[61] As to Grenada: GA Res. 38/7, November 2, 1983 (108–9:27). As to Panama: OAS Res. CP/ Res. 534 (800/89), December 22, 1989.
[62] See J. Crawford, "Self-Determination outside the Colonial Context," in W. J. A. Macartney, ed., *Self-Determination in the Commonwealth* (Aberdeen University Press, 1988), p. 1, at p. 10, and references there cited.
[63] E.g. GA Res. 34/22, November 14, 1979, and subsequent annual resolutions. See G. Klintworth, *Vietnam's Intervention in Cambodia in International Law* (Canberra: AGPS, 1989). On human rights violations under the post-1979 regime, see Lawyers' Committee for Human Rights, *Kampuchea: After the Worst* (New York, 1985).

rules that yield a different answer to the question of whether an action is legal depending on the identity of the actor."[64] It was just such considerations that led the International Court to reject the idea that the United States had any "special responsibility" to enforce any democratic commitments the Nicaraguan Government may have made to the OAS when it came to power. The Court refused to "contemplate the creation of a new rule opening up a right of intervention by one State against another on the ground that the latter has opted for some particular ideology or political system."[65]

This consideration is reinforced by the essential point that democracy is not something which can be installed by foreign force in a few days. It is not necessary to agree with the motives or program of those carrying out a *coup d'état* – for example that in Fiji in 1987[66] to see the potentially destabilizing effect of external intervention, or of the threat of such intervention. After the event, especially in cases where the intervention was on a major scale or lasted for a considerable time, it can be very difficult to re-establish local legitimacy.

No doubt the strength of the international reaction to interventions of this kind will vary, depending on the consequences. That point was made by W. V. Harcourt, in a discussion of the experience of intervention during the nineteenth century. He referred to intervention as "a high and summary procedure which may sometimes snatch a remedy beyond the reach of law . . . [I]ts essence is illegality, and its justification is its success. Of all things, at once the most unjustifiable and the most impolitic is an unsuccessful Intervention."[67] Subsequent success, while it may mitigate, is not a test of legality. On the contrary a rule of legality for pro-democratic invasions would deny to the people concerned – the alleged beneficiaries of the rule – any opportunity to state their own views on the events.[68]

---

[64] D. W. Bowett, "International Incidents: New Genre or New Delusion?," *Yale J. Int'l L.* 12 (1987), pp. 386ff, at p. 388.   [65] 1986 ICJ, p. 133. Cf. also Corfu Channel case, 1949 ICJ, p. 4, at p. 35.
[66] As to which see V. Lal, *Fiji: Coups in Paradise, Race, Politics and Military Intervention* (London: Zed Books, 1990); R. M. Kiwanuka, "On Revolution and Legality in Fiji," *Int'l & Comp. L. Q.,* 37 (1988), p. 961; M. R. Islam, "The Proposed Constitutional Guarantee of Indigenous Governmental Power in Fiji: An International Legal Appraisal," *California Western J. Int'l L.* 19 (1988), p. 107.
[67] "Neutrality or Intervention?" in *Letters by Historicus on Some Questions of International Law* (London, Macmillan, 1863), p. 41.
[68] See the debate between W. M. Reisman, "Coercion and Self-determination: Construing Charter Article 2(4)," *Am. J. Int'l L.* 78 (1984), p. 642, and O. Schachter "The Legality of Pro-Democratic Invasion," *ibid.*, p. 645. See also T. J. Farer, "The United States as a Guarantor of Democracy in the Caribbean Basin: Is There a Legal Way?," *Hum. Rts. Q.* 10 (1988), p. 157; J. A. R. Nafziger, "Self-Determination and Humanitarian Intervention in a Community of Power," *Denver J. Int'l L. & P.,* 20 (1991), p. 9; K. Ryan, "Rights, Intervention and Self-Determination," *ibid.*, p. 55.

Despite this, there is scope for developing institutions at the international level which will reinforce democracy, and which may even, by mutual agreement, help to shore up democratic institutions against internal challenge. It is through international organizations, including regional organizations acting within the framework of part VIII of the Charter, and not by unilateral intervention, that these problems should be tackled.

A second issue goes to the very existence of a clearly undemocratic government – existence in the sense of international capacity to represent the State. It has been argued that disputes over the credentials of a government to represent the State should be resolved by applying democratic standards rather than the standard of effective control, at least in cases where "the results of a UN-monitored election are overturned and an incumbent regime refuses to yield power,"[69] but possibly in other cases also.

This idea has some attraction, especially since its focus is on an organized collective response rather than unilateral military action. In particular it might be written into the procedures for United Nations supervision of elections, so that everyone has notice of the possible consequences – although there are so far no signs of this happening. But if the suggestion is that the continued recognition of a regime as a government should be made dependent on its continued acceptance of democratic standards, there are problems with it. In particular it leaves little or no room for maneuver, for nuance, in situations where maneuver and nuance may well be necessary. In many cases little is to be gained from denying the existence of a group actually in control in the institutions of State, whether or not they have recently won, or would ever win, an election. Of course there is no need to jump to the conclusion that mere occupation of the parliament building, or of the American embassy, is enough to make a government. A State may temporarily lack a government – as for example in Somalia.[70] If the consequence is that the extra-territorial property of the State is quarantined until a secure government emerges, so much the better. But transitional situations are one thing: the refusal to deal with established authorities is another. No doubt there may be room for symbolic gestures – for example, the refusal of Hungarian credentials by the United Nations for some years after 1956.[71] On the other

---

[69] Fox, *supra* note 40, p. 603.
[70] As Hobhouse J. held *in* Republic of Somalia v. Woodhouse, Drake & Carey (Suisse) SA, [1992] 3 WLR 744, noted in *Cam. L. J.* 52 (1993), p. 4.
[71] R. Higgins, *The Development of International Law through the Political Organs of the United Nations* (Oxford University Press, 1963), at pp. 158–59.

hand, failure to deal with established regimes may only harm the people whom it is intended to assist – as may have been the case in Haiti.[72]

This is not to suggest a mere capitulation to force, or even to power growing *slowly* out of the barrel of a gun. There are things that can be done. Philip Allott has remarked, in the context of his thoroughgoing critique of present international law, that the system lacks a principle or theory of representation.[73] That is perhaps not quite true. International law has a theory of representation. This is the theory that an established government stands for, and has responsibility for, the State and its people for all or virtually all purposes. The theory is simple, but not necessarily simple-minded. One underlying justification is that third parties, who are after all not supposed to intervene in the internal affairs of a State, are entitled to rely on whatever government is securely established in a State as being the entity with which they can deal.

But that justification goes only so far. Third parties are no doubt entitled to call on the established government of a given territory to respect the rights of those in the territory. Responsibility in this sense arises from control. But it is not intervention to deal with the government of a State on a consensual basis, even if the dealing – whether in the form of arms sales or bribes to officials to obtain some concession or special treatment – is in no sense in the interests of the people of the State, and even though this must be obvious to the participants. The difficulty with the all-or-nothing solution of non-recognition of an effective but undemocratic government is that it avoids holding those who have made the decisions responsible for their acts. Where there is power there should be responsibility, including legal responsibility.

This does not, however, end the argument. One possibility – which has had little or no consideration compared with either forcible intervention or blanket non-recognition – might be to develop a system under which third parties dealing with a grossly unrepresentative regime would be required to take the risk of doing so. This would apply both to States and to private parties, including corporations. It would put them on notice that if they wish to deal with a regime lacking any legitimacy or popular support, they would take the risk of the review of the transaction by a subsequent representative government.

No doubt the details would have to be worked out, including some provision for notice to third parties, some specification of the triggering conditions, and especially some provision for dispute settlement. There

---

[72] *See* M. Cerna, "The Case of Haiti before the OAS," *Proc. Am. Soc. Int'l L.* 86 (1992), p. 378.
[73] P. Allott, *Eunomia. New Order for a New World* (Oxford University Press, 1990), at pp. 306–10, 372–75.

is a problem, increasingly common in international law, of the formulation of ever more complex rules in the absence of proper procedures for dispute settlement. This is one major reason for the attraction of simple rules, free of exceptions – idiot rules, as Franck calls them.[74] Such rules are determinate, even though they may not do justice in every case. By contrast the development of law in complex societies has seen a constantly increasing refinement, and international law has shared in this.

This suggestion – which, if the *Tinoco* case is right, does not represent the status quo – is not without some analogy in international law. Long-term transactions of a territorial trustee, or of a belligerent occupant, may be subject to this form of review. In the *Nauru* case the International Court seems to have accepted the principle of review of the acts of a trustee affecting the beneficiary prior to the independence of the territory concerned.[75]

At a deeper level, there is an analogy with the different rules relating to the competence of the State which are embedded in the law of treaties and State responsibility. State responsibility is dependent primarily on factual control.[76] On the other hand, the making of treaty commitments by a government is now dependent, to a limited but significant extent, on compliance with fundamental constitutional procedures. That rule is contained in Article 47 of the Vienna Convention on the Law of Treaties of 1969. When it was adopted it came as a surprise to many commentators, used to thinking of the primacy of international law over national law, or at least of their radical separation. But there is a common interest in the stability of treaties, and unconstitutional treaties are unlikely to be stable. The same could be said for unconscionable transactions with wholly undemocratic regimes.

III CONCLUSIONS

This is only an initial survey of some of the issues that are raised by the question whether and to what extent international law endorses, or is even consistent with, democratic principle. Other issues relevant to this theme include:

---

[74] T. M. Franck, *The Power of Legitimacy among Nations* (New York: Oxford University Press, 1990), at p. 74.
[75] 1992 ICJ, p. 240. The case was settled in August 1993 without giving the Court the opportunity finally to rule on this issue.
[76] I. Brownlie, *State Responsibility* (Oxford: Clarendon Press, 1983), at pp. 1656, 1756, 1778, with references to the work of the ILC and to arbitral jurisprudence.

(1) the problem of democratic accountability for the conduct of foreign policy;[77]
(2) the question whether individuals and groups are bound by, as well as beneficiaries of, human rights law, and how that can be reconciled with democratic tenets.[78] In this context it is worth noting that even Sir Hersch Lauterpacht, the great early proponent of international human rights, accepted that the rule that individuals have no independent position in international law was a matter of "moral principle." Presumably the basis of this "moral principle" is the fact that individuals have little or no role — and certainly no formal role — in making international law.[79] The problem has become all the more urgent in view of the revival of the idea of international criminal trials;[80]
(3) the relationship between democratic principle and respect for minority rights,[81] as well as the position of indigenous peoples in those countries where there are surviving indigenous societies;[82]

---

[77] *See, e.g.,* A. Cassese, ed., *Parliamentary Foreign Affairs Committees: The National Setting* (New York: Oceana, 1982); P. R. Trimble, "Foreign Affairs Law and Democracy," *Michigan L. Rev.* 91 (1990), p. 1371; Symposium, "Parliamentary Participation in the Making and Operation of Treaties," *Chicago-Kent L. Rev.* 67 (1991), p. 293.

[78] *See* M. Forde, "Nongovernmental Interference with Human Rights," *Brit. Y. B. Int'l L.* 56 (1985), p. 153; N. S. Rodley, "Can Armed Opposition Groups Violate Human Rights?" in K. E. Mahoney and P. Mahoney, *Human Rights in the Twenty-first Century* (Dordrecht: Martinus Nijhoff, 1992), p. 297; C. M. Vázquez, "Treaty-based Rights and Remedies of Individuals," *Columbia L. Rev.* 92 (1992), p. 1082; J. J. Paust, "The Other Side of Right: Private Duties under Human Rights Law," *Harvard Hum. Rts. J.* 5 (1992), p. 51. The Inter-American Commission of Human Rights has on several occasions condemned violations of the American Convention by "groups": Press Release No. 8/92, July 22, 1992 (Peru), Press Release No. 2/93, February 17, 1993 (Colombia).

[79] E. Lauterpacht, ed., *International Law, being the Collected Papers of Hersch Lauterpacht* (Cambridge University Press, 1970), vol. I, p. 141. But Sir Hersch referred also to "numerous exceptions which the practice of States has already grafted" on to that principle, and went on to argue that individuals are, and should be, "the true subjects of international law" (*ibid.*, p. 148) — although without addressing the question how they should contribute to its making.

[80] *See* International Law Commission, Revised Report of the Working Group on the Draft Statute for an International Criminal Court, A/CN.4/L.490 & Add.1, July 19, 1993; SC Res. 827, May 25, 1993.

[81] The Declaration on the Rights of Persons belonging to National or Ethnic, Religious and Linguistic Minorities, adopted by GA Res. 47/135, December 18, 1992, refers to the promotion of minority rights "within a democratic framework based on the rule of law" (Preamble, para. 6), but does not expressly address this issue in the operative paragraphs. Cf. however Arts. 2(2) (right to participate effectively in public life), 8(4) (reservation of territorial integrity of States). For text see *Int'l Legal Materials,* 32 (1993), p. 912. Cf. European Charter for Regional or Minority Languages, Strasbourg, November 5, 1992 (*European Treaty Series,* No. 148), which refers to "the principles of democracy and cultural diversity within the framework of national sovereignty and territorial integrity" (Preamble, para. 6). *See* further P. Thornberry, *International Law and the Rights of Minorities* (Oxford: Clarendon Press, 1991), esp. part IV.

[82] *See, e.g.,* Australian Law Reform Commission 31, *The Recognition of Aboriginal Customary Laws* (Canberra: AGPS, 1986), vol. II, ch. 39; I. Brownlie, *Treaties and Indigenous Peoples* (Oxford: Clarendon Press, 1992), esp. ch. 2; Thornberry, *supra* note 81, Part VI; M. E. Turpel, "Indigenous Peoples' Rights of Political Participation and Self-determination," *Cornell Int'l L. J.* 25 (1992), p. 579.

(4) the issue of democratization of international organizations, both global[83] and regional – in the European context, the issue of democratization of the European Community (the so-called democratic deficit),[84] and the role of the democratic idea as a contested term in the Maastricht Treaty.[85]

Another and most important element concerns the growing role of non-governmental organizations in this field.[86]

Let me conclude with a few provisos. The first is, obviously, that democracy is not everything. It is a procedural principle which embodies a substantive value, and both the substantive value and the effectiveness of the procedures which are used to embody it remain under challenge. It is easy to overstate the depth or durability of the democratic revival, although we can be hopeful about it. Democratic regimes can violate rights, especially of minorities.[87] There is the problem of public alienation from political structures and political parties, evidenced for example by the declining membership of political parties in many countries. There are countervailing factors such as the growth of fundamentalism and of ethnic conflict. At a time of greater possibilities and expectations there are greater problems. These problems should put an end to the facile millenarianism that was an immediate product of 1989. Someone once asked the Chinese leader Chou En-Lai to assess the consequences of the French revolution of 1789. He said it was too

---

[83] *See, e.g.,* D. Archibugi, "The Reform of the UN and Cosmopolitan Democracy: A Critical Review," *Journal of Peace Research* 30 (1993), p. 1.

[84] *See, e.g.,* R. Beiber, "Democratic Control of European Foreign Policy," *European Journal of International Law,* 1 (1991), p. 148, at p. 151. The European Court of Justice has made the most of its few opportunities in this field, and of the Parliament's limited role: e.g. Roquette Frères v. Council of the European Communities, [1984/4] ECR 3333 (failure to consult Parliament as required by Treaty invalidates measures adopted by the Council).

[85] Treaty on European Union, Maastricht, February 7, 1992. The Treaty makes no essential change in the position of the European Parliament, although it is given a greater role in relation to grievances and maladministration, and there are changes to electoral arrangements (Arts. 137–138e as amended). The term "democracy" is referred to in the preamble. Title 1, Art. A, describes the Treaty as regulating relations between member States and their peoples. Art. F stipulates that member States' governmental systems ("founded on the principles of democracy") are to be respected: this appears to be a declaratory, not a normative, provision. Title 2 inserts a new Part dealing with citizenship of the Union, but voting rights do not extend to voting for national as distinct from municipal elections. Art. 130u (Development Cooperation) provides that community policy should contribute "to the general objectives of developing and consolidating democracy and the rule of law" (i.e., democracy for others). Similarly Title v, Art J.1(2). That is all.

[86] E.g., the Democratic Audit of the United Kingdom: see D. Beetham, *Auditing Democracy in Britain* (London: University of Essex Human Rights Centre, Democratic Audit Paper No.1 1993). *Generally see* A. M. Micon and B. Lindsnaes, eds., *The Role of Voluntary Organizations in Emerging Democracies* (Copenhagen: Danish Centre for Human Rights, 1993).

[87] E.g. the Peruvian counter-insurgency: see A. Cornell and K. Roberts, "Democracy, Counterinsurgency and Human Rights: The Case of Peru," *Hum. Rts. Q.* 12 (1990), p. 529.

soon to tell. Whether or not that is true of 1789, it is certainly true of 1989.

Obviously this is a difficult area, acutely difficult, and the role of international law in responding to it is correspondingly difficult. The difficulty was encapsulated by Sir Henry Maine, who asked how "when the forces at work are so enormous . . . shall they be controlled, diminished, or reduced by a mere literary agency?"[88] If international law is a merely literary agency the question is unanswerable.

But international law in its relationship with practice is better described as an intellectual activity, carried out for practical purposes, though in more or less literary form. And an increasing proportion of our activity, our property, our social structures is intellectual rather than material. In his inaugural lecture, Sir Robert Jennings said: "It is obvious today that a community of rival sovereignties, which claim to be above the law or which, while professing submission to it, in fact refuse to recognize its supremacy, cannot escape self-destruction. The only mechanism by which a viable international society of States can be reached is through effective submission to a developing international law."[89] If that was obvious in 1958, it is even more obvious now.

And what should be noted is Sir Robert's reference to "a developing international law." Amid vast political change international law cannot but change. It is interesting to note that John Westlake – often viewed as the prototype of a positivist international lawyer – was not content with the definition of international law as "the body of rules prevailing between States," but saw it also in broader terms, as "human action not internal to a political body."[90] He would have accepted that what was "internal" or domestic to a particular political body could change with time, and is a relative matter. And this is because the emphasis of his definition was on "rules of action" which develop and change. The difficulty is to envision appropriate forms of change, and at the same time to hold to those aspects of international law which embody the stable outcomes of the interaction between peoples, societies, and their governments over many years.

---

[88] H. S. Maine, *Int'l Law* (The Whewell Lectures, 1887; London: John Murray, 1888), at p.7.
[89] R. Y. Jennings, "The Progress of International Law," *Brit. Y. B. Int'l L.* 34 (1958), p. 334, at p. 355.
[90] "Introductory Lecture" (October 17, 1888) in L. Oppenheim, ed., *The Collected Papers of John Westlake* (Cambridge, 1914), p. 393, at p. 393. It is true that in his "Chapters on the Principles of International Law" (1894), in *Collected Papers*, vol. 1, p. 1, he gave the more conventional definition, but he immediately qualified it by saying that international law could also be described "as the body of rules governing the relations of a State to all outside it," and his later discussion retains some of the more dynamic approach of his Introductory Lecture.

Democracy in international law – a reprise[91]

The paper reprinted here was a contribution to a continuing debate about the role of democratic ideas in international law. In its origins it was an inaugural lecture at Cambridge – but time moves on, and there have been significant developments since 1993. Indeed they raise the question whether the modified skepticism at the role of the democratic principle, expressed in 1993, should itself be modified, or even abandoned. Without repeating what is said in the other chapters of this book, some further comments are called for.

A preliminary point relates to the idea of "modified skepticism." A number of people, influenced perhaps by its title, seem to have taken the lecture as a straightforward proclamation of democratic values. In fact it made a number of points, not all in the same direction. First, it argued that in international human rights law, the "right to democracy" is not prior, still less primordial, that it is not a right which trumps others, so much as coexists with them. Indeed it would be truer to say that "the authority of a government, elected by a majority, to conduct for the time being the public affairs of the society is a *consequence* of the exercise of the rights of participation in public life of all citizens, whether they belong to the majority or the minority." In other words, democracy is as much the product of the exercise of civil and political rights (and in the longer term, of economic, social, and cultural rights), as it is the precondition for them. This being so, democracy is no justification for a violation of other fundamental human rights, and derogations in the interests of a "democratic society" have only a limited reach.

Secondly, it pointed out, not only that many "features of classical international law were deeply undemocratic, or at least were capable of operating in a deeply undemocratic way," but also that there were reasons for this, not limited to the crude fact that until recently, a major-

---

[91] My thanks to Greg Fox and Roger O'Keefe for their assistance with information and research.

ity of States in the world were not democratic even in the limited sense envisaged by Article 25. These "undemocratic" features of international law (such as the general rule that unconstitutional treaties bind the State[92]) apply, and with good reason, even as between two States which are in all respects democracies. There is not, as some writers like to imagine, one code of international law for democracies and another for lesser States outside that pale. The international normative system seeks to advance at the same time a range of partly incompatible goals – international peace and security (as a minimum the absence of armed conflict between or on a large scale within States), non-intervention, human rights, security of transactions, and many others, and to do so as far as possible on a universal basis. In such a system, not very many rights trump, and those that do are of a limited and largely negative kind – such as the right not to be subject to genocide or aggression.

Thirdly, it noted, and welcomed, the various developments in the direction of a collective democratic guarantee, but doubted how far this had yet gone, or even how far it could go at the universal level, in the absence of parallel institutional developments. Changes in the normative framework – for example, in the rule that a firmly established regime in control of the territory of the State constitutes the government of the State – may even be counter-productive.[93] But, in any event, they have not yet been generally accepted. Nor has the so-called right of unilateral intervention in another State to install a democratic regime. But there is room for a more subtle understanding of what constitutes effective government, incorporating and reinforcing the old idea of the will of the people substantially declared – and perhaps for a principle of *ex ante* ratification, by a genuinely representative government, of actions taken against a previous undemocratic regime within that State.

Against this background, it is useful to mention briefly three problems with the development of the right to democracy under general international law, with all the consequences such a right could have.[94] They are, first, the very tentative level of articulation of such a right since 1966; secondly, the inconsistencies in State practice, even in recent times, and thirdly, the difficulty of the "margin of appreciation," which includes the

---

[92] Vienna Convention on the Law of Treaties, 1969, Art. 46.
[93] A government denied standing to sue is unlikely to be willing to be sued, and the same goes for other manifestations of responsibility.
[94] For discussion of some further questions see James Crawford and Susan Marks, "The Global Democracy Deficit: An Essay in International Law and its Limits," in D. Archibugi, D. Held, M. Kohler, eds., *Re-Imagining Political Community. Studies in Cosmopolitan Democracy* (Cambridge: Polity Press, 1998), p. 72.

problem of making legal judgments about political institutions in what are usually difficult transitional situations.

ARTICULATING DEMOCRATIC RIGHTS AT THE UNIVERSAL LEVEL

Article 25 of the ICCPR proclaims the right to participate in one's own government as a fundamental human right, but there has been little follow-up action at the universal level since.[95] The first resolution of the Commission on Human Rights on the subject of the Right to Democracy was adopted on April 27, 1999, by a vote of 51 to 0, with Cuba and China abstaining. The resolution recalls

> the large body of international law and instruments . . . which confirm the right to full participation and the other fundamental democratic rights and freedoms inherent in any democratic society.[96]

It emphasises the reciprocal links between democracy and other human rights, and affirms a series of "rights of democratic governance" which include most of the key civil and political rights, but also some additional elements, such as "transparent and accountable government institutions" (para. 2(f)). The various human rights organs and agencies are requested "to pay due attention, within their mandates, to those elements of democratic governance outlined in paragraph 2."

As a whole the resolution is rather anodyne, and anyone reading it against the background of the "large body of international law and instruments" referred to would think it unremarkable. But in fact the debate on it was long and controversial.[97] A Cuban resolution to delete the term "right to democracy" from the title gained some support: it was defeated by 12–28 with 13 abstentions. Many speakers expressed concern that the right to democracy would become a further excuse for intervention in internal affairs: in the words of the Indian delegate, since democracy is "a form of government rising from the people . . . [it cannot] be proposed from outside." Pakistan was concerned the right to democracy might be used to validate foreign occupation of territory, contrary to the right of self-determination: as its suggestion the original United States draft was amended to incorporate a reference to the right of self-determination.

---

[95] The Human Rights Committee's General Comment (1994) adds relatively little to the debate.
[96] E/.CN.4/1999/L.55/Rev.2, Preamble, para. 6.
[97] The following account of the debate is taken from Comm'n Hum. Rts. Press Release, HR/CN/99/61, 27.04.1999.

Some delegations had difficulty with the underlying idea of a "right to democracy" even within a single, undisputed political community. Russia noted that there "were some doubts as to the concept of the right to democracy from a purely legal point of view," and thought it "premature to introduce this concept in inter-governmental documents," an idea which does not sit well with Article 25 of the ICCPR itself. Indonesia, while "not challenging the principle of democracy," thought it "questionable whether it could be considered as a right." China claimed to accept the principle, but criticized the resolution, and in particular the term "right to democracy," as "premature and . . . not balanced." The Chinese delegate stressed that different traditions lead to different forms of democracy, having regard to "the differing historical, social and economical backgrounds of countries"; the failure of the resolution to recognize this was the reason for China's abstention.

ARTICULATING DEMOCRATIC RIGHTS IN STATE PRACTICE SINCE 1993

In State practice since 1993, there has been a marked inconsistency in the treatment accorded the various undemocratic governments, from wholesale regional intervention in Sierra Leone and Liberia, to limited measures of disapproval and economic sanctions in Myanmar and Nigeria, to toleration or acceptance (as with the Kabila government in Congo/Zaïre and or that of Buyoya in Burundi), and even to complicity (as with the "preventive" coup in Algeria). The Security Council has on occasions authorized action under Chapter VII which was taken with a view to restoring democratic legitimacy, or bolstering up an elected government against internal opposition: the most significant case so far remains that of Haiti in 1993, where a genuine principle of democratic legitimacy was applied, as was seen above. But that case can be justified on narrower grounds, as incidental to an earlier certification by the United Nations of the result of an election to restore democratic rule. Against such an outcome, military control of a State in the short term does not make the controllers into a legitimate government, and this was widely recognised even before Security Council resolution 841 (1993).[98]

---

[98] *See, e.g.,* on Sierra Leone, Security Council resolutions 1132 (1997), October 8, 1997; 1156 (1998), March 16, 1998; 1171 (1998), June 5, 1998; 1181, June 13, 1998 and subsequent resolutions on UNOMISIL.

The fact remains that relevant United Nations resolutions treat as the government in place established but unelected military regimes in many countries (e.g., Myanmar, Algeria). For example, GA Resolution 52/137 of March 3, 1998, on the Situation of Human Rights in Myanmar, recalls Article 21(3) of the Universal Declaration, with its affirmation that "the will of the people shall be the basis of the authority of government," and calls in a particularized way for "the full and early restoration of democracy" – but refers throughout to "the Government of Myanmar" (whose authority is certainly not the will of the people of Myanmar).[99]

All this suggests that elective democracy in itself is still not regarded as a necessary prerequisite to governmental legitimacy. Rather, it seems that democratic government is still seen as one – even if a privileged – means of achieving a complex of established civil and political rights, and as one – not necessarily privileged – indicator of the existence of an established government in an existing State.[100]

THE JUSTICIABILITY PROBLEM

Some further light is shed on the problem of justiciability by the decision of the European Court of Human Rights in *Matthews v. United Kingdom* (Application no. 24833/94, February 18, 1999). The issue was whether residents of Gibraltar, who were not entitled to vote in elections for the European Parliament, had suffered a breach of their rights under Article 3 of Protocol No. 1, which provides for "the free expression of the opinion of the people in the choice of the legislature." Under the EU treaties Gibraltar is treated as part of the EU for some but not for all purposes, and the exclusion of Gibraltar from the electorate for the EU Parliament was expressly provided for in European legislation adopted well before the conclusion of the Maastricht Treaty. The Maastricht Treaty substantially increased the powers of the European Parliament, which had earlier been held not to be a "legislature" for the purposes of Article 3, and the Court in *Matthews* took the view that the position under the Maastricht Treaty was different. Applying the principle of effectiveness to the guarantee of "effective political democracy," it held that the new powers of the European Parliament were such as to convert it into a "legislature" within the meaning of Article 3.

[99] See also Comm'n Hum. Rts. Resolutions 1997/64, 1998/63, and many others.
[100] See generally B.R. Roth, *Governmental Illegitimacy in International Law* (Oxford: Clarendon Press, 1999), for a subtle analysis of the issues.

As to the context in which the European Parliament operates, the Court is of the view that the European Parliament represents the principal form of democratic, political accountability in the Community system. The Court considers that whatever its limitations, the European Parliament, which derives democratic legitimation from the direct elections by universal suffrage, must be seen as that part of the European Community structure which best reflects concerns as to "effective political democracy."[101]

Moreover this was true even in relation to Gibraltar, despite the limitations on the powers of the European Parliament there.[102] Nor was the position affected by the "local requirements" of a dependent territory under Article 56(3) of the Convention, in the absence of any "compelling" justification to the contrary.

Though the Court, in the passage quoted above, was evidently assessing the position in a straightforward and serious manner, the passage is not without its ironies. Even if it is true, or at least is becoming true, that "the European Parliament represents the principal form of democratic, political accountability in the Community system," it does not follow that the European Parliament is a legislature within the meaning of Article 3 of Protocol 1, still less that it is a legislature for Gibraltar. And even if, despite its limitations, the European Parliament "must be seen as that part of the European Community structure which best reflects concerns as to 'effective political democracy'," is it entailed – that is to say, entailed by the system of European human rights – that the European Parliament should become more than it is, whether that means more "powerful" or more "democratic"? It seems that a certain vision of European integration is being driven, in part at least, by a certain vision of European human rights.

But however that may be, the principal issue in the case for present purposes was whether the denial of a European parliamentary vote to Gibraltarians fell within the scope of the margin of appreciation, which has previously played such an important role in decision-making in relation to democratic rights – as it did indeed in the case of *Mathieu-Mohin and Clerfayt* [(1987) ECHR Series A, No. 113]. Of particular relevance to the margin of appreciation in *Matthews* were two facts: first, that the electorate was far too small to justify its own seat in the Parliament, and secondly, that to attach Gibraltarians to a European Parliament constituency in the United Kingdom would have been completely unacceptable to Spain, whose consent was and is required to such a change in the law.

---

[101] Judgment, para. 52. [102] *Ibid.*, para. 53.

The Court was unmoved by such considerations. It said:

> in the present case the applicant, as a resident of Gibraltar, was completely denied any opportunity to express her opinion in the choice of the members of the European Parliament. The position is not analogous to that of persons who are unable to take part in elections because they live outside the jurisdiction, as such individuals have weakened the link between themselves and the jurisdiction. In the present case . . . the European Community forms part of the legislature in Gibraltar, and the applicant is directly affected by it. In the circumstances of the present case, the very essence of the applicant's right to vote, as guaranteed by Article 3 of Protocol, was denied.[103]

Accordingly it held (by 15–2) that there had been a breach of Article 3.

Only Judges Freeland and Jungwiert dissented, on the basis that the European Parliament was not, even after Maastricht, a legislature for the purposes of Article 3, and certainly not a legislature for Gibraltar. More fundamentally, in their view "a particular restraint should be required of the Court when it is invited, as it is here, to pronounce on acts of the European Community or consequent to its requirements, especially when those acts relate to a matter so intimately concerned with the operation of the Community as elections to one of its constitutional organs." This was even more so when in practice there was nothing whatever the United Kingdom could do to change the electoral situation of Gibraltar, having regard to the dispute with Spain over the territory.

Resolving the situation may present difficulties, since Spain (itself a party to Protocol 1) may veto any solution Britain may propose within the framework of the European Union, yet it is the United Kingdom which is responsible, *de facto* and *de jure*, for compliance with Article 3 in relation to Gibraltar. But the case has larger implications too, in that it suggests, at least for the European Court, a much more activist mode of applying the right to democratic participation. As with other fields, it may be that large reliance on the margin of appreciation as a means of avoiding scrutiny is a transitional phenomenon, and that the right of democratic participation is gaining increasing purchase. On the other hand, this was not a case (as was *Mathieu-Mohin and Clerfayt*) where a difficult situation was addressed by a, perhaps arguable, solution: the population of Gibraltar had no means of participating in European elections, so that once it was concluded that the European Parliament was part of their "legislature," there was little or no room for the margin of appreciation.

[103] *Ibid.*, paras. 64–65.

PART II

Democracy and inter-State relations

CHAPTER 4

Democratic legitimacy and the recognition of States and governments

Sean D. Murphy

In a seminal 1992 article, Thomas Franck postulated the emergence in international law of a right to democratic governance.[1] Franck argued that, increasingly, the acceptance of a government by other States turns on whether the government governs with the consent of its people.

In supporting this notion, Franck pointed to events such as the 1991 effort by Haitian military and police authorities to overthrow the elected President of Haiti, Jean-Bertrand Aristide. Although those authorities exercised complete control over Haiti, the international community condemned the coup leaders, refused to engage in normal diplomatic relations with them or to seat their representatives at international organizations, and instead continued to recognize the exiled President Aristide as representing the legitimate government of Haiti. Severe economic and ultimately military sanctions were imposed on Haiti, and finally, in 1994, the coup leaders were forced to relinquish power. President Aristide then returned to Haiti to complete his term as President.

The reaction to the Haitian crisis may be important evidence that the international community finds relevant, at least in certain situations, that governing authorities have not been democratically elected. But does this incident, and other examples of State practice, support the proposition set forth by Franck?

The first and most fundamental element in legal relations between States is whether a particular political community is "recognized" as a State, for only in this way can that community engage as a State in legal relations with other States. A second critical element concerns which political authorities within a State are "recognized" as representing the State in the conduct of its foreign relations. It is through those legal rela-

---

[1] Thomas M. Franck, "The Emerging Right to Democratic Governance," *Am. J. Int'l L.* 86 (1992), 46.

tions that the State can lawfully request military support from other States; can lawfully refuse entry to foreign military forces; can lawfully negotiate and conclude international agreements; can avail itself of other rights accorded sovereigns under international law and vindicate those rights before available international fora; and can demand respect by other States of sovereign acts exercised within its territory, including the enactment and enforcement of civil and criminal laws.

If it can be shown that one of the criteria in "recognition" practice by States is whether the entity is democratic, this would be powerful evidence that democracy is on its way to becoming a global entitlement. When political authorities within a territory seek to have the territory recognized as a new State, does the international community consider it important that democratic institutions exist within the territory? Similarly, when political authorities within a State seek recognition as the government of that State, does the international community consider it important that they came to power through the consent of those they govern? And, to the extent that democracy is relevant in the recognition of new States and governments, does that relevance reflect the existence of a *legal* norm, as opposed to some other norm that is political or discretionary in nature?[2]

I DEMOCRACY AND RECOGNITION OF STATES

From the Peace of Westphalia to the advent of modern democratic States in the late eighteenth century, recognition practice did not concern itself with democratic legitimacy as we know it today. Since the rise of modern democratic States, however, the relationship between those who govern and those governed, at times, has had a powerful effect on the formation and recognition of States.

---

[2] For purposes of the following discussion, it is important to bear in mind the different faces of "recognition." As already mentioned, the heart of "recognition" is the acknowledgment by States of the legal capacity of a new State or government to avail itself of international rights and obligations. That acknowledgment may be express, such as when states openly declare that they "recognize" a State or government, or it may be tacit, such as when States quietly enter into diplomatic relations or otherwise engage in acts that make clear their intention toward the new entity. In many important cases, some States recognize a new entity while others do not; in other cases, even if recognition is not accorded, some type of special status may develop. A further face of "recognition" occurs when a new State is granted admission to an international organization or when an organ of an international organization accepts the credentials of the delegates of a new government. Yet another face concerns the effects of recognition (or non-recognition) on rights and obligations within a State's national legal system (e.g., litigation in the State's courts), an area unaddressed in this chapter. At any given time, one or more of these faces may be lacking, but the core issue of "recognition" remains whether it can be said that States accept the legal capacity of the new entity.

A Traditional theory and past practice

Under traditional international legal theory, an entity aspiring to be recognized as a new State first had to meet certain factual conditions, which did not expressly include the existence of democratic institutions within the entity, nor the consent of the population to the creation of the State. The aspiring entity had to have: (1) a defined territory; (2) a permanent population; (3) an effective government; and (4) the capacity to enter into relations with other States.[3] For the most part, these conditions continue to be taught today as the fundamental elements of the recognition of States.

With respect to the third condition – historically the existence of an "effective" government – the emphasis has been on the control that the government exercises over the relevant territory, to the exclusion of other entities. James Crawford's review of State practice indicates that the degree of control necessary may be a function of the manner in which the government came to power; if the Statehood is "opposed under title of international law," then a relatively high degree of control may be necessary, whereas if the prior sovereign in the territory has consented to the creation of a new State under a government, then a relatively lower degree of control by the government may be tolerable in finding Statehood.[4] Either way, "effective control" has not traditionally required democratic consent. In part, this is attributable to the interest of the international community in promoting other values, such as non-intervention.

Manifestations of consent have not, however, been entirely ignored. First, a high degree of consent by the people of a new State to the authority of the new government has sometimes been taken as an indication of a high degree of control by that government, thus bolstering the case for recognition under the traditional criteria.

Second, although global human rights instruments, such as the 1948 Universal Declaration of Human Rights, which sets forth "the right to take part in the government of [one's] country,"[5] and the 1966

---

[3] The standard point of departure on these conditions is the 1933 Montevideo Convention on the Rights and Duties of States, *LNTS* 165 (1936), 19. *See also* J. L. Brierly, *The Law of Nations*, H. Waldock, ed., 6th edn. (Oxford University Press, 1963), p. 137. *See generally* Stefan Talmon, *Recognition of Governments in International Law: With Particular Reference to Governments in Exile* (Oxford University Press, 1998); Colin Warbrick, "Recognition of States: Recent European Practice," in Malcolm D. Evans, ed., *Aspects of Statehood and Institutionalism in Contemporary Europe* (Hanover, N.H.: Dartmouth University Press, 1996), p. 9.
[4] James Crawford, *The Creation of States in International Law* (Oxford Clarendon Press, 1979), pp. 44–45.
[5] Universal Declaration of Human Rights, Article 21(1), GA Res. 217A, *United Nations General Assembly Official Records*, 3rd Sess., pt. 1 at p. 71, UN Doc. A/810 (1948).

International Covenant on Civil and Political Rights, which sets forth rights to participate in public affairs and free elections,[6] did not expressly deal with democratic legitimacy as a part of the process of State formation, at times they served as important benchmarks when States weighed recognition of a new State. For instance, the anti-apartheid values of the international community permitted near universal non-recognition of Southern Rhodesia when it declared independence in November 1965.[7]

Third, efforts to give effect to the self-determination of peoples in the colonial context have frequently had recourse to referenda, for the purpose of asking persons permanently residing within a designated "Non-Self-Governing Territory" whether they wish to establish an independent State with its own government.[8] A referendum solely on the issue of whether the population wishes to establish a new State is not in itself the same as the establishment of a democratic government in the new State, yet it injects notions of popular will into the process of State creation.

Nonetheless, self-determination of peoples has not meant unrestricted deference to popular will in regions seeking to assert themselves as independent States. Various regions such as Basque in Spain,[9] Biafra in Nigeria,[10] Katanga in the Congo,[11] Turkish-dominated northern Cyprus,[12] and others all fell short in their quest for recognition. This

---

[6] International Covenant on Civil and Political Rights, Article 25, Dec. 16, 1966, *UNTS* 999 (1976), p. 171.

[7] *See* International Convention on the Suppression and Punishment of the Crime of Apartheid., Nov. 30, 1973, *UNTS* 1015 (1973), p. 243; International Convention on the Elimination of All Forms of Racial Discrimination, Mar. 7, 1966, *UNTS* 660 (1966), p. 195; Vera Gowlland-Debbas, *Collective Responses to Illegal Acts in International Law: United Nations Action in the Question of Southern Rhodesia* (Boston, Mass.: Martinus Nijhoff, 1990), pp. 273–361. On the General Assembly's refusal to accept the credentials of the delegates of South Africa's apartheid government, *see* Dan Ciobanu, "Credentials of Delegations and Representation of Member States at the United Nations," *Int'l Comp. L.Q.* 25 (1976), 351.

[8] P. K. Menon, *The Law of Recognition in International Law* (Lewiston, N.Y.: Edwin Mellon Press, 1994), p. 39; H. M. Blix, "Contemporary Aspects of Recognition," *Recueil des Cours d'Académie de Droit International* 130 (1970–II), p. 636.

[9] The Basque separatist group ETA began violent actions in 1968 in an effort to secede from Franco's Spain. After Franco's death in 1975, Spain became a democratic country and, over time, the four Basque provinces achieved considerable self-governance under a new system of regional autonomy, which gradually weakened violence by the separatist movement. Nevertheless, as of 1997, the largest party in the region remains the Basque Nationalist Party, which runs the regional government and seeks a separate Basque State. *See* "The Basques: A Murder Too Far," *The Economist* (July 19, 1997), p. 30.

[10] *See* David A. Ijalaye, "Was 'Biafra' at Any Time a State in International Law?" *Am. J. Int'l L.* 65 (1971), p. 551.

[11] Georges Abi-Saab, *The United Nations Operation in the Congo 1960–64* (Oxford University Press, 1978).

[12] Suzanne Palmer, "The Turkish Republic of Northern Cyprus: Should the United States Recognize it as an Independent State?" *Boston Univ. Int'l L.J.* 4 (1986), 423.

failure was not due to lack of popular support in the relevant region but, rather, due to other factors, including a presumption of international law that often runs against self-determination: the principle of *uti possidetis*.

Uti possidetis arose from an international consensus that States created through decolonization should normally maintain the external colonial borders existing at the time of their independence,[13] regardless of whether those borders made any sense in terms of the tribal, ethnic, religious, or political affiliations of those who had been colonized. Over time, the principle has been referred to in non-colonial contexts and with respect to both historical external and internal boundaries. The attraction of the principle lies in its promotion of stability, by disfavoring unpredictable and excessive fragmentation. At the same time, however, the principle can disfavor the creation of a new State from a region in which the majority of the people wish to secede, simply because that region has no historical boundaries. Although associated with the period of decolonization, the principle retains vitality in contemporary times with respect to recognition of new States in non-colonial contexts, as will be discussed in the next section.

In the Declaration on Friendly Relations,[14] the General Assembly interpreted the principle of self-determination in a manner that disfavored secession *so long as* the government of a State is "representing the whole people belonging to the territory without distinction as to race, creed, or colour." At the same time, when regions have fought to secede from an existing State (e.g., Tibet from China, Kashmir from India, or Kurdistan from Iraq, Turkey, Iran, and Syria), the international community has been reluctant to recognize a new State, in part because it would transform the situation from one of internal conflict to one of international armed aggression, thereby raising considerably the gravity of the situation. This concern no doubt has detracted from shaping attitudes favoring formation of new States based purely on notions of self-rule.

Although recognition of States as such has not traditionally revolved around democratic principles, a limited number of inter-governmental organizations have established admissions and credentials procedures that turn on the existence of democratic institutions within a State. For

---

[13] Case Concerning Frontier Dispute (Burkina Faso/Mali), 1986 ICJ, p. 565.
[14] Declaration on Principles of International Law Concerning Friendly Relations and Co-Operation Among States in Accordance with the Charter of the United Nations, Oct. 24, 1970, General Assembly Resolution 2625 (XXV), *United Nations General Assembly Official Records*, 25th Sess., Supp. No. 28 at 121 (annex), UN Doc. A/8028 (1970).

instance, the Statute of the Council of Europe (COE), which entered into force in 1949, provides that members "must accept the principles of the rule of law and of the enjoyment by all persons within its jurisdiction of human rights and fundamental freedoms..."[15] Consequently, in considering admission of a new member, the COE assesses the member's commitment to democracy, as evidenced not just by the existence of elections but by the presence of a stable political process that accords rights to minority groups.[16]

However, for the most part, international organizations have not established admissions procedures that turn on the existence of democratic institutions in the emerging State. For instance, although one of the purposes of the United Nations is to "develop friendly relations among nations based on respect for the principle of equal rights and self-determination of peoples,"[17] this aspiration has not precluded the admission of States that were non-democratic, nor would such conditionality appear permissible under the UN Charter.[18] Consequently, for decades after enactment of the Charter numerous States were admitted to the United Nations and to other international organizations that were not democratic.

B Contemporary practice

There is certainly no evidence today that States refuse to recognize the existence of another State simply because it has a non-democratic form of government. Determining whether a State is "democratic" requires

[15] Statute of the Council of Europe, May 5, 1949, Article 3, *UNTS* 87 (1953), 103. *See* Hans Winkler, "Democracy and Human Rights in Europe: A Survey of the Admission Practice of the Council of Europe," *Austrian J. Pub. Int'l L.* 47 (1995), 147.
[16] *See, e.g,* Recommendation 1338 (1997) on the Obligations and Commitments of the Czech Republic as a Member State, pt. IV, *Council of Europe Parliamentary Assembly, 1997 Ordinary Session*, (Sept. 22–26, 1997), p. 1.   [17] UN Charter, Art. 1(2).
[18] The Charter provides that membership is open to all "peace-loving States" which accept the obligations of the Charter and which, in the judgment of the United Nations, are able and willing to carry out those obligations. UN Charter, Art. 4(1). The International Court of Justice advised that it was illegal to impose any additional conditions on States seeking membership. Advisory Opinion on the Conditions of Admission of a State to Membership in the United Nations (Charter, Art. 4), 1948 ICJ, pp. 62–65; *see also* Advisory Opinion on the Competence of the General Assembly for the Admission of a State to the United Nations, 1950 ICJ p. 4.
   Recently, the Court also rejected arguments by Serbia (Yugoslavia) that Bosnia–Herzegovina was incapable of becoming a party to the Genocide Convention because it achieved independence through a process that violated the principles of equal rights and self-determination. Rather than consider whether Bosnia–Herzegovina's statehood ran afoul of fundamental human rights, the Court simply noted that the Genocide Convention was open to "any Member of the United Nations." Case Concerning Application of the Convention on the Prevention and Punishment of the Crime of Genocide (Bosnia and Herzegovina v. Yugoslavia), 1996 ICJ, para. 19.

the application of subjective criteria, but most studies would regard at least 25 percent of States today as having non-democratic governments (e.g., China) and perhaps another 25 percent of States today as having only partially democratic governments, in the sense that the accountability of the government to its people is qualified.[19] Yet both tiers (non-democratic and partially democratic) of States enjoy widespread recognition as States by the international community.[20] The international community acknowledges their right to be members of international organizations[21] and their right to avail themselves of the benefits and protections of international law.

Even when a State's government lapses from being democratic to non-democratic, the international community continues to respect the international legal status of the State (as opposed to its government), although certain economic or diplomatic sanctions might be imposed on the State. For instance, through an amendment to its Charter that entered into force in September 1997, the Organization of American States became the first regional organization to permit suspension of a member whose government takes power through undemocratic means.[22] However, in doing so, the OAS does not question the existence of the State.

Further, to the extent that there is concern about the failure of a democratic State to allow a minority group to participate in the democratic process, the international community does not promote those rights by non-recognition of the State, with an eye toward carving up the State to protect particular minority groups.[23] Rather, the international commu-

---

[19] *See, e.g.,* David Potter *et al.,* eds., *Democratization* (Malden, Mass.: Polity Press/Open University, 1997), pp. 1, 38.

[20] For instance, although the United States places considerable emphasis on democratic legitimacy in the conduct of its foreign policy, the United States nevertheless recognizes (and maintains diplomatic relations with) numerous States that are non-democratic, including Afghanistan, Algeria, Burma, China, Oman, Saudi Arabia, and Syria. Even non-democratic States with which the United States does not have diplomatic relations are recognized as independent States, such as Cuba, Iran, Iraq, Libya, and North Korea. *See* "Fact Sheet: Independent States and Dependencies as of August 20, 1996," *US Dept. of State Dispatch,* 7 (Aug. 26, 1996), p. 433.

[21] *See, e.g.,* Yves Beigbeder, *International Monitoring of Plebiscites, Referenda and National Elections: Self-Determination and Transition to Democracy* (Dordrecht and Boston, Mass.: Martinus Nijhoff, 1994), p. 94.

[22] *See* Marian Nash (Leich), "Contemporary Practice of the United States Relating to International Law," *Amer. J. Int'l L.* 88 (1994), 719. Suspension requires a two-thirds majority vote in the OAS General Assembly.

[23] Of course, the international community acknowledges a State's right to hold referenda on whether it should fragment into smaller States, as recently occurred in the Caribbean state of St Kitts and Nevis. Serge F. Kovaleski, "Secession Move Fails on Caribbean Island," *Washington Post* (Aug. 11, 1998), A18.

nity favors maintaining the integrity of the State, while promoting minority rights by monitoring and reporting on the situation, with reference to the extensive array of human rights instruments. In some situations, minority rights to democratic access may be protected explicitly by an international instrument.[24]

The most interesting developments in contemporary practice concerning recognition of States and democratic legitimacy relate to the former Soviet Union, which broke up after 1989, and the former Yugoslavia, which broke up after 1991.

1 The former Soviet Union

The fragmentation of the Union of Soviet Socialist Republics (USSR) after 1989 resulted in the establishment of several new States. In December 1989, the Congress of the USSR People's Deputies found that the July 1939 Molotov–Ribbentrop Accords, by which the USSR first occupied and then annexed the Baltic States (Estonia, Latvia, and Lithuania), were contrary to international law.[25] On this basis, the Baltic States held referenda in early 1991 on whether to seek independence; the overwhelming response was positive, so the Baltic States then waged a successful campaign for full independence.[26] The State Council of the Soviet Union released the Baltic States and recognized their independence on September 6, 1991. The Baltic States were then admitted to the United Nations on September 17, 1991.

The presence of democratic institutions within the Baltic States does not appear to have been a significant factor in promoting foreign recognition. Indeed, many States would have preferred to see the Baltic States stand down from pursuing their political independence, due to fears of what a disintegrated Soviet Union would entail.[27] At the same time, it should be noted that Western States had never recognized the legal validity of the Soviet incorporation of the Baltic States. Thus, there was no need for those States to recognize the existence of new Baltic States, although ultimately most Western States issued statements noting that the Baltic States had reacquired political independence.

With respect to the dissolution of the remainder of the Soviet

---

[24] *See, e.g.,* Hungary–Romania Treaty on Understanding, Cooperation, and Good Neighborliness, (Sept. 16, 1996) Articles 15–16, *reprinted in* 36 ILM (1997), pp. 348–50 (requiring protections for the rights of ethnic Hungarians living in Romania and ethnic Romanians living in Hungary, including the right to effective participation in the political life of their country).
[25] Evans, *supra* note 3, pp. 19–21; Antonio Cassese, *Self-Determination of Peoples* (Cambridge University Press, 1995), pp. 258–61.   [26] Cassese, *supra* note 25, p. 262 n.9.
[27] *Ibid.*, p. 264.

Union,[28] some of the constituent republics during the course of 1991 held referenda on whether to secede. All (except Kazakhstan) then proceeded to proclaim their independence during 1991, except that Russia proclaimed itself as the successor State to the former Soviet Union.[29] Virtually all other States then recognized the republics of the former Soviet Union as new States and they were admitted as members of the United Nations.[30]

A notable development in this recognition practice was the approach taken by the United States and by the Foreign Ministers of the European Community. The United States announced that, in addition to the traditional criteria for recognition of States, recognition should only be accorded in light of, *inter alia*, the prospective State's adherence to democracy and the rule of law, including respect for the Helsinki Final Act and the Charter of Paris.[31] Shortly thereafter, in December 1991, the European Community issued a "Declaration on the Guidelines on the Recognition of New States in Eastern Europe and in the Soviet Union." In that declaration, the European Community and its member States said that they:

affirm their readiness to recognise, subject to the normal standards of international practice and the political realities in each case, those new States which, following the historic changes in the region, *have constituted themselves on a democratic basis*, have accepted the appropriate international obligations and have committed themselves in good faith to a peaceful process and to negotiations.[32]

The Declaration then set down general conditions requiring the new State: (1) to respect the UN Charter, the Helsinki Final Act, and the Charter of Paris, "especially with regard to the rule of law, *democracy* and

---

[28] Armenia, Azerbaijan, Belorussia, Georgia, Kazakhstan, Kirghizia, Moldavia, Russia, Tajikistan, Turkmenistan, Ukraine, and Uzbekistan.

[29] *See* Decision by the Council of Heads of State of the Commonwealth of Independent States, (Dec. 21, 1991), para. 1 *reprinted in* 31 ILM (1992), p. 151 (all former Soviet republics except Georgia establishing a commonwealth of independent states); *see also* Yehuda Z. Blum, "Russia Takes Over the Soviet Union's Seat at the United Nations," *Euro. J. Int'l L.* 3 (1992), 354; Ralph Gaillard, Jr., "The Baltic Republics," *Washington Post* (Sept. 3, 1991), A12.

[30] Azerbaijan, Armenia, Kazakhstan, Krygyzstan, Moldova, Tajikistan, Turkmenistan, and Uzbekistan were admitted as members of the United Nations on March 2, 1992. Georgia was admitted on July 31, 1992. Belarus and Ukraine were original UN members and consequently did not require admission upon obtaining independence. Russia assumed the membership of the former Soviet Union, taking over the former Soviet seat in the General Assembly and its permanent membership in the Security Council.

[31] "Testimony by Ralph Johnson, Deputy Assistant Secretary of State for European and Canadian Affairs (Oct 17, 1991)," *Foreign Policy Bulletin* 2 (Nov.-Dec. 1991), p. 42.

[32] "Declaration on the Guidelines on the Recognition of New States in Eastern Europe and in the Soviet Union," Dec. 16, 1991, *reprinted in* 31 ILM (1992), pp. 1486-87.

human rights" (emphasis added); (2) to guarantee rights for ethnic and national groups and minorities; (3) to respect existing borders; (4) to accept relevant arms control commitments; and (5) to commit to settle by agreement all questions regarding State succession and regional disputes. The European Community[33] and United States[34] recognized the Statehood of the republics of the former Soviet Union based on these principles.

The US Statement and EC Declaration were quite significant; they expressly conditioned recognition on the basis of democratic rule. Yet, the EC Declaration was also predicated on "the normal standards of international practice and the political realities in each case," which provided ample opportunity to suppress the emergence of new States from regions within the Soviet republics. For instance, secessionist forces in Nagorno–Karabakh, a province in western Azerbaijan containing a 75 percent ethnic Armenian majority, by 1994 had gained complete control of the region, in the process forcing out almost the entire minority population. Although Nagorno–Karabakh has held democratic elections, it has not been recognized by any other State, including its principal supporter, Armenia.[35]

2 *The former Yugoslavia*

Prior to its dissolution, the former Yugoslavia consisted of six republics (Bosnia–Herzegovina, Croatia, Serbia, Slovenia, Macedonia, and Montenegro) and two autonomous regions (Kosovo and Vojvodina). These republics and regions all had their own local governments; in addition, there was a federal government directed by a Presidential Council (or collective presidency), whose chairmanship rotated among the heads of the republics and autonomous regions.[36]

In late 1990, Slovenia and Croatia proclaimed that federal law would no longer be supreme in their republics, and Slovenia held a referendum in which the vast majority of Slovenians voted for independence. When the chairmanship of the collective presidency failed to rotate from a

---

[33] Evans, *supra* note 3, p. 23.
[34] *See* "President Bush Welcomes Commonwealth of Independent States, (December 25, 1991)," *Foreign Pol. Bulletin* 2 (Jan.-Apr. 1992), 12. For the US Government's attitude on various issues relating to the break-up of the former Soviet Union and the former Yugoslavia, *see* Edwin Williamson and John Osborn, "A US Perspective on Treaty Succession and Related Issues in the Wake of the Breakup of the USSR and Yugoslavia," *Vir. J. Int'l L.* 33 (1993), p. 261 (views of former State Department Legal Adviser and his Special Assistant).
[35] *See* David Rieff, "Nagorno–Karabakh: Case Study in Ethnic Strife," *Foreign Affairs* 76 (Mar.-Apr. 1997), 118.
[36] Marc Weller, "The International Response to the Dissolution of the Socialist Federal Republic of Yugoslavia," *Amer. J. Int'l L.* 86 (1992), p. 569.

Serb to a Croat leader in May 1991, Croatia held a referendum in which the vast majority of Croats voted for independence. On June 25, both Slovenia and Croatia declared their independence, prompting the Serb-dominated federal armed forces to move against militias in both republics. To add confusion to the situation, Serbia claimed that it was protecting Serbs within Croatia who did not wish to secede.

Thus, by the summer of 1991, there were two Yugoslav republics – Croatia and Slovenia – with defined territories, permanent populations, somewhat effective (but not unchallenged) governments, and a capacity to enter into foreign relations seeking recognition as independent States. The European Community, the CSCE, and the United States all initially hoped to maintain the integrity of Yugoslavia as a single State. On July 7, EC mediators brokered an agreement for the withdrawal of federal forces to their barracks in Slovenia, as well as the disarmament of the Slovenian militia. In turn, Croatia and Slovenia suspended their declarations of independence. An EC plan to deploy armed forces into the region, however, was thwarted, since it was viewed as legally necessary to have the consent of the Serb-dominated federal government, which was not forthcoming.

As violence continued over the summer, primarily in Croatia, the EC began to doubt the wisdom of maintaining a single State of Yugoslavia. On August 27, the EC issued a declaration in which it called upon the parties to the conflict in Yugoslavia to submit their differences to an Arbitration Commission of five members chosen from the Presidents of the Constitutional Courts of EC countries. After four of the eight members of the Yugoslav collective presidency decided in early October that they alone would conduct the affairs of federal Yugoslavia, Croatia and Slovenia reinstated their declarations of independence. At the same time, after a meeting in The Hague of the EC, Serbian, and Croatian representatives, the participants agreed that recognition of those republics seeking independence would be granted "in the framework of a general agreement" having the following components: (1) a loose association or alliance of sovereign or independent republics; (2) adequate arrangements to be made for the protection of minorities, including human rights guarantees and possibly special status for certain areas; and (3) no unilateral changes in borders. It should be noted that these EC-generated criteria for recognition went somewhat beyond the traditional criteria, but, at the same time, did not include a requirement that democratic institutions exist within the new States. In November 1991, Macedonia declared its independence.

Although in early November, the EC tabled a "general agreement" that fleshed out the three components set forth above, the agreement was not acceptable to Serbia. At this point, the interest in recognition shifted to establishing conditions that each republic had to meet whether there was agreement among all relevant parties or not. Consequently, the EC issued a December 1991 Declaration containing the guidelines on recognition, as discussed above.[37] Each Yugoslav republic was invited to state by December 23 whether it sought recognition as a State and, if so, whether it agreed to the EC conditions.[38] Bosnia–Herzegovina, Croatia, Macedonia, and Slovenia all responded affirmatively, submitting documentation to show that they had met the EC conditions.

The EC-sponsored Arbitration Commission, under the chairmanship of Robert Badinter, issued a series of opinions over the course of late 1991 relevant to the EC's decisions on recognition.[39] The Badinter Commission found that Yugoslavia was in the process of dissolution and that it was up to those republics that wished to work together to form within the existing borders of Yugoslavia "a new association endowed with the democratic institutions of their choice."[40] Further, even before individual republics were recognized as States, it was deemed appropriate to accord them certain protections arising out of international law, including norms relating to the use of force, based on existing internal

---

[37] Declaration on Guidelines, *supra* note 32, p. 1486. In addition, each State had to pledge that it had no territorial claims against any neighboring EC State and that it would not use a name that implied such claims. This condition was prompted by Greece's concerns regarding potential territorial claims by Macedonia. Greece believed even the name "Macedonia" implied territorial ambitions toward Greece, since its northernmost province is also named Macedonia. "Macedonia: Next on the List," *The Economist* (Feb. 8, 1992), 46.

[38] Declaration on Yugoslavia, Dec. 16, 1991, *reprinted in* 31 ILM (1992), pp. 1485–86.

[39] The Arbitration Commission was established by the Peace Conference to address issues arising in connection with the break-up of Yugoslavia. Judges were chosen from the Constitutional Courts of Belgium, France, Germany, Italy, and Spain.

During 1992, the Arbitration Commission rendered ten opinions, some of which are discussed below. Opinion 1 considered the criteria of public international law for the establishment of a State, adopted the declaratory theory of recognition, and concluded that Yugoslavia was in the process of dissolution. Opinion 2 asserted that the right of self-determination must not involve changes to existing frontiers, although discrete minorities within States are entitled to protection. Opinion 3 stated that the external frontiers of Yugoslavia must be respected, that the internal boundaries between Serbia and Bosnia and between Serbia and Croatia had to be respected in the absence of any agreement to vary them, and that these boundaries became frontiers protected by international law. Opinions 4 to 7 considered the applications of international recognition submitted by Bosnia, Croatia, Macedonia, and Slovenia. Opinion 10, issued in July 1992, determined that the Federal Republic of Yugoslavia (Serbia and Montenegro) was a new State which cannot be considered the sole successor of the former Socialist Federal Republic of Yugoslavia.

[40] Conference on Yugoslavia, Arbitration Commission Opinion No. 1, para. 3, *reprinted in* 31 ILM (1992), p. 1494.

boundaries.[41] According to the Badinter Commission, the principle of *uti possidetis* was alive and well and applicable to Yugoslavia notwithstanding the non-colonial context. While the principle of self-determination and other human rights norms served to protect minority groups within existing units of a federal State (e.g., Serbs in Croatia or Serbs in Bosnia–Herzegovina), they did not support forcible actions to modify existing internal borders. Individuals of such minority groups could choose to reject allegiance to a new State, but could not collectively choose to secede.[42]

In early January 1992, the Arbitration Commission considered the applications of the Yugoslav republics for EC recognition. While it found that Slovenia had met the EC conditions and recommended that Slovenia be recognized,[43] the Arbitration Commission found that Croatia had not taken sufficient steps under its constitution to protect minorities in satisfaction of the EC recognition requirements.[44] Nevertheless, the EC decided to proceed with the recognition of both Slovenia and Croatia on January 15, 1992.

The Arbitration Commission found that Macedonia had met the EC's recognition criteria,[45] but the EC did not decide to proceed with recognition of "Macedonia" due to resistance by Greece. Instead, the EC issued a declaration making clear that a State had come into existence, which allowed EC States on their own to decide to recognize that State. On April 7, 1993, however, the UN Security Council approved UN membership for Macedonia under the provisional name of the "Former Yugoslavia Republic of Macedonia."[46]

---

[41] Conference on Yugoslavia, Arbitration Commission Opinion No. 3, Jan. 11, 1992, *reprinted in* 31 ILM (1992), p. 1499.
[42] Conference on Yugoslavia, Arbitration Commission Opinion No. 2, Jan. 11, 1992, *reprinted in* 31 ILM (1992), p. 1497.
[43] Conference on Yugoslavia, Arbitration Commission Opinion No. 7, Jan. 11, 1992, *reprinted in* 31 ILM (1992), p. 1512.
[44] Conference on Yugoslavia, Arbitration Commission Opinion No. 5, Jan. 11, 1992, *reprinted in* 31 ILM (1992), p. 1503.
[45] Conference on Yugoslavia, Arbitration Commission Opinion No. 6, Jan. 11, 1992, *reprinted in* 31 ILM (1992), p. 1507.
[46] SC Res. 817 (1993). The erratic application of the EC Guidelines has been noted:

> The political character of the recognition decisions is clear in the reactions of three states. Slovenia was a State and satisfied the Guidelines; it was recognised. Croatia was a State but did not satisfy the Guidelines; nonetheless, it was recognised. This demonstrates the political nature of the Guidelines; they could be dispensed with so long as the entity claiming statehood was a State. Macedonia was a State and satisfied the Guidelines; it was not recognised. It could have been: the non-recognition decision here is an act of policy (and was later overturned when states voted for Macedonia's admission to the UN). (Evans, *supra* note 3, pp. 29–30.)

With respect to Bosnia–Herzegovina, the Arbitration Commission found that the popular will within Bosnia–Herzegovina to establish an independent State had not been clearly established since there had been no internationally supervised referendum, open to all citizens without discrimination, on independence.[47] Bosnia–Herzegovina proceeded to hold a referendum on March 1, 1992, in which – despite the boycott by Bosnian Serbs (a substantial minority) – an overwhelming majority opted for independence. On April 6, the EC decided to recognize Bosnia–Herzegovina.

The Arbitration Commission's finding on Bosnia is interesting in that the EC conditions had not required such a referendum. Perhaps this attention to the referendum should be viewed as, in the words of one commentator, "reflecting an additional criterion for recognition of Statehood in cases of secession, based on the principle of self-determination and on considerations of general international law, including human rights law."[48] While this may be the case, the particular circumstances of the Badinter Commission finding should be kept in mind; Bosnia–Herzegovina was a republic, on the verge of a civil war, containing three sizable ethnic groups, any two of which outnumbered the third, and which had close links to neighboring republics. Calling for a referendum on secession was particularly appropriate in such a case and might, or might not, be considered essential in other cases.

Most States followed the EC in its recognition of Croatia, Slovenia, and Bosnia–Herzegovina. On April 7, the United States announced that it recognized the three new States, but, like the EC, did not yet recognize Macedonia. The United States did not specify the criteria on which its recognition was based, but did indicate that it thought the democratic expression from the referenda in each country in favor of independence was relevant.[49] On May 18, the Security Council recommended (without a vote) that the three States be admitted to the United Nations. Consistent with the UN Charter and the 1948 *Admissions* case (discussed in note 18 above), the issue of democratic institutions, and even of referenda in favor of independence, was not expressly a factor in this decision. Rather, the President of the Security Council, for each of the new States, issued a simple statement noting "with great satisfaction [the new State's] solemn commitment to uphold the Purposes and Principles of

---

[47] Conference on Yugoslavia, Arbitration Commission Opinion No. 4, Jan. 11, 1992, *reprinted in* 31 ILM (1992), p. 1501.   [48] Weller, *supra* note 36, p. 593.
[49] The United States asserted that it was recognizing the three new States "because we are satisfied that these states meet the requisite criteria for recognition. We acknowledge the peaceful and democratic expression of the will of citizens of these States for sovereignty." "US Recognition of Former Yugoslav Republics," *US Dept. of State Dispatch* 3 (Apr. 13, 1992), p. 287.

the Charter of the United Nations, which include the principles relating to the peaceful settlement of disputes and the non-use of force, and to fulfil all the obligations contained in the Charter."[50] On May 22, the General Assembly by acclamation then admitted the three States to membership.[51]

Despite international recognition of the State of Bosnia, the viability of the new State remained in doubt from 1992 to late 1995. Due to the severe ethnic warfare, it was unclear whether Bosnia would break apart, with Bosnian Serb territory merging with Serbia and Bosnian Croat territory merging with Croatia. In late 1995, the war was brought to a close under the Dayton Peace Accords, which were signed not just by the leaders of Bosnia, Croatia, and Serbia, but also by a representative of the European Union and the leaders of France, Germany, Russia, the United Kingdom, and the United States. The Dayton Accords provided, *inter alia*, that Bosnia "shall continue its legal existence under international law as a State, with its internal structure modified as provided herein and with its present internationally recognized borders." Further, Bosnia "shall be a democratic State, which shall operate under the rule of law and with free and democratic elections."[52]

In April 1992, the federal Yugoslav authorities in Belgrade announced the existence of a "Federal Republic of Yugoslavia" consisting of the borders of the republics of Serbia and Montenegro, and further declared that it was the successor to the rights and obligations of the Socialist Federal Republic of Yugoslavia (SFRY).[53] On May 12, 1992, the EC stated that recognition of this new State (whether as a successor or not) was contingent on its compliance with various conditions, including

---

[50] For Croatia, SC Res. 753, *United Nations Security Council Official Records*, 47th Sess., 3076th meeting at p. 115, UN Doc. S/INF/48 (1992); Statement by the President of the Security Council, United Nations Document S/23945 (1992), *ibid*. For Slovenia, SC Res. 754, *United Nations Security Council Official Records*, 47th Sess., 3077th meeting at p. 115, UN Doc. S/INF/48 (1992); Statement by the President of the Security Council, United Nations Document S/23946 (1992), *ibid*. For Bosnia–Herzegovina, SC Res. 755, *United Nations Security Council Official Records*, 47th Sess., 3079th meeting at p. 116, UN Doc. S/INF/48 (1992); Statement by the President of the Security Council, United Nations Document S/23982 (1992), *ibid*.

[51] GA Res. 46/236, *United Nations General Assembly Official Records*, 46th Sess., Supp. No. 49A at p. 5, UN Doc. A/46/49/Add.1 (1992) (Slovenia Admission); General Assembly Resolution 46/237, *United Nations General Assembly Official Records*, 46th Sess., Supp. No. 49A at p. 5, UN Doc. A/46/49/Add.1 (1992) (Bosnia–Herzegovina Admission); General Assembly Resolution 46/238, *United Nations General Assembly Official Records*, 46th Sess., Supp. No. 49A at p. 5, UN Doc. A/46/49/Add.1 (1992) (Croatia Admission).

[52] Constitution of Bosnia and Herzegovina, Article 1, *reprinted in US Dept. of State Dispatch, Supplement* 7 (Mar. 1996), 25.

[53] *See* Letter dated April 27, 1992 from the Chargé d'Affaires AI. of the Permanent Mission of Yugoslavia to the United Nations Addressed to the President of the Security Council, UN Doc. S/23877 (1992), annex.

withdrawal of federal military forces from Bosnia, the facilitation of humanitarian relief, and respect for human rights and the rights of minorities.[54] Democratic legitimacy was not at issue, in that the political authorities in Serbia and Montenegro operated throughout this period on the basis of democratic elections. On July 4, 1992, the Arbitration Commission decided that the Federal Republic of Yugoslavia was a new State, but that it could not be considered the sole successor to the SFRY.[55] Thereafter, the Security Council asserted that this new State could not claim UN membership on the basis of the prior UN membership of the former Yugoslavia. In light of this, the General Assembly decided that the new State would have to apply for membership before it could participate further in the work of the General Assembly.[56]

The recognition practice of the international community with respect to the break-up of the former Yugoslavia clearly contained notions of democratic legitimacy that went beyond the traditional requirements for Statehood. At the same time, critics have charged that the international community's recognition practice was wholly inappropriate; on the one hand, the State of Bosnia was recognized even though the traditional requirements for Statehood (e.g., a stable population and a government in effective control of the State's territory) had not been met; on the other hand, Macedonia exhibited the characteristics of a State but for a long time was left with an uncertain status.[57]

---

[54] *See* Letter dated May 12, 1992 from the Permanent Representatives of Belgium, France, and the United Kingdom to the United Nations Addressed to the President of the Security Council, UN Doc. S/23906 (1992), annex. For the position of the United States, *see* Letter dated May 5, 1992 from the Permanent Representative of the United States to the United Nations Addressed to the President of the Security Council, UN Doc. S/23879 (1992).

[55] Conference on Yugoslavia, Arbitration Commission Opinion No. 10, July 4, 1992, para. 5, *reprinted in* 31 ILM (1992), p. 1525. Interestingly, the Commission found that recognition was "purely declaratory" and was not a requirement for the creation of a State.

[56] For the Security Council, see SC Res. 777, *United Nations Security Council Official Records*, 47th Sess., 3116th meeting at p. 34, UN Doc. S/RES/777 (1992) (adopted by twelve votes, with China, India, and Zimbabwe abstaining). The Security Council previously had noted that Serbia and Montenegro's claim to continue automatically the UN membership of the former Yugoslavia "has not been generally accepted." SC Res. 757, *United Nations Security Council Official Records*, 47th Sess., 3082d meeting at p. 13, UN Doc. S/RES/757 (1992). For the General Assembly, *see* GA Res. 47/1, *United Nations General Assembly Official Records*, 47th Sess., 7th plenary meeting, Supp. No. 49, at p. 12, UN Doc. A/47/49 (1992) p. 197.

For the debate on the legal right of Serbia and Montenegro to continue as a member of the United Nations based on the membership of the former Yugoslavia, *compare* Yehuda Z. Blum, "UN Membership of the 'New' Yugoslavia: Continuity or Break?" *Amer. J. Int'l L.* 86 (1992), 830; *with* "Correspondents' Agora: UN Membership of the Former Yugoslavia," *Amer. J. Int'l L.* 87 (1993), 240.

[57] *See* Raju Thomas, "Self-Determination and International Recognition Policy," *World Affairs* 160 (1997), p. 17; Robert M. Hayden, "Bosnia's Internal War and the International Criminal Tribunal," *The Fletcher Forum of World Affairs* 22 (Winter/Spring 1998), p. 45.

Democratic legitimacy and recognition 139

In sum, notions of democratic legitimacy are certainly present in contemporary practice concerning recognition of States. However, the evidence of these notions is not uniform, and it derives exclusively from the practice of States that are themselves democratic. Further, there is no effort by even democratic States to apply these notions to existing States where governments lack legitimacy.

II DEMOCRACY AND RECOGNITION OF GOVERNMENTS

A Traditional theory and past practice

Under traditional international legal theory, the establishment of a new government through normal, constitutional processes within a State does not result in questions regarding the recognition of the government; the new government is entitled to all the rights and obligations accorded under international law. By contrast, an entity that comes to power through non-constitutional means is not automatically accorded such rights and obligations. Rather, its status as the government of the State is in doubt until such time as it is widely recognized by other States.[58]

The central (and often determinative) issue for a State when deciding whether to recognize a newly formed government has been whether the new government is in "effective control" of its State (sometimes referred to as the "*de facto* control test").[59] "Effective control" has largely been measured by the degree to which the government commands the obedience of the people within the State. Although in a given case there may be extremely complicated facts concerning what factions control what portions of a territory, the "effective control" test is a relatively simple one, and allows States to proceed pragmatically in their relations with the new government.

The decision by States to recognize a new government, however, has not always been dictated simply by whether the new government passes the effective control test. For instance, capital-exporting States, such as the United States, at one time found relevant whether the new government had declared its willingness to honor the international obligations

---

[58] *See generally* M.J. Peterson, *Recognition of Governments: Legal Doctrine and State Practice, 1815–1995* (New York: St. Martin's Press, 1997).

[59] *See, e.g.*, H. Lauterpacht, *Recognition in International Law* (Cambridge University Press: 1947), p. 98; Hans Kelsen, *General Theory of Law and State* (Cambridge, Mass.: Harvard University Press, 1949 [1945]), pp. 228–29.

of its predecessor, including debt obligations, before granting recognition, even if the new government was effectively in control of its State.[60] Further, States often refused to recognize a government's authority over territory that the government had acquired through aggression. And, as will be discussed further below, historically States have also found relevant the political nature of the new government, including the degree to which it is democratic.

European monarchies in the late seventeenth and eighteenth centuries made it their policy not to recognize democratic revolutionary governments, because such governments represented a threat to the status quo. Initially prompted by the French Revolution, this reactionary policy was one of the driving purposes of the Holy Alliance after the Congress of Vienna in 1815.[61]

Over time, monarchical views fell into disfavor, displaced by Kantian notions of republican government, and this had an effect on the manner in which at least democratic States regarded other States. In the United States, Thomas Jefferson declared that "[i]t accords with our principles to acknowledge any Government to be rightful which is formed by the will of the nation, substantially declared."[62] Yet, for Jefferson, the "will of the nation" was not necessarily expressed through democracy; he accepted that States may engage in foreign relations through a monarchy.[63] Consequently, State practice during this period, including US practice, regarded "the will of the people" as present simply by a population's tacit acquiescence to a government in effective control of a State.

The first part of the twentieth century did not see radical inroads for notions of democracy in the practice of recognizing governments.[64] There were exceptions, however. As in many areas of his foreign policy,

---

[60] *See* L. Thomas Galloway, *Recognizing Foreign Governments: The Practice of the United States* (Washington, D.C.: American Enterprise Institute for Public Policy Research, 1978), pp. 21–24.
[61] *See* René Albrecht-Carrié, *A Diplomatic History of Europe Since the Congress of Vienna*, revised edition (New York: Harper and Row, 1973).
[62] *Quoted in* Marjorie M. Whiteman, *Digest of International Law*, 15 vols. (Washington, D.C. US Government Printing Office, 1963), vol. II, pp. 68–69; Lauterpacht, *supra* note 59, pp. 125–26.
[63] Whiteman, *supra* note 62, p. 69.
[64] For an example of this, see a 1913 US Department of State memorandum reported in Green Haywood Hackworth, *Digest of Int'l. L.*, 13 vols. (Washington, D.C. US Government Printing Office, 1940), vol. I, p. 176 (Although there must be "general acquiescence" of the people, the "form of government has not been a conditional factor" in US recognition practice; "in other words, the *de jure* element of legitimacy of title has been left aside, probably because liable to involve dynastic or constitutional questions hardly within our competency to adjudicate, especially so when the organic form of government has been changed, as by revolution, from a monarchy to a commonwealth or vice versa").

US President Woodrow Wilson injected some notions of democracy into US recognition practice. The Mexican Revolution that began in 1911, pitted urban middle classes and agrarians, led by Francisco Madero, against the country's wealthy elite.[65] Madero succeeded in ousting Mexico's dictator, Porfirio Diaz, but the Mexican military, led by General Victoriano Huerta, staged a *coup d'etat* and executed Madero. While the European powers recognized the new government of Huerta, Wilson was appalled and refused to do so, not only imposing economic sanctions but ultimately occupying Veracruz with military forces. Wilson's support allowed the revolutionary forces to gain strength. Huerta was forced from power in 1914 and the revolution resumed its course. In 1917, Venustiano Carranza was installed as President under a new constitution, which was built upon agrarian, land, church, and oil reforms of the Mexican revolution. In that regard, it is important to note that US and British firms at this time controlled 90 percent of the Mexican oil industry and virtually all of Mexico's railroads, yet Wilson eschewed recognition of a military regime – whose control of the country offered security for those investments – in favor of a radical revolution, explaining: "I am willing to get anything for an American that money and enterprise can obtain, except the suppression of the rights of other men."[66]

Wilson's distaste for military suppression of the constitutional democracies that had emerged in Latin and South America led him to endorse the 1907 Tobar Doctrine, named for Ecuador's foreign minister Carlos Tobar. Under the Tobar Doctrine, States of the Western hemisphere were to deny recognition to governments that might come to power pursuant to non-constitutional means. Wilson applied the doctrine when considering recognition of new governments in the Dominican Republic, Ecuador, Haiti, Cuba, Portugal, and the Soviet Union.[67]

---

[65] Thomas J. Knock, *To End All Wars: Woodrow Wilson and the Quest for a New World Order* (Oxford University Press, 1992), pp. 25–30; Jules Davids, *America and the World of Our Time: United States Diplomacy in the Twentieth Century* (New York: Random House, 1970), pp. 37–42.

[66] "Woodrow Wilson Address of July 4, 1914," *quoted in* Knock, *To End All Wars*, *supra* note 65, p. 28. The Government of Mexico was only recognized in 1923 by Wilson's successor, primarily on the basis of Mexico's willingness to protect US nationals and property in Mexico. Hackworth, *supra* note 64, p. 176.

[67] Galloway, *Recognizing Foreign Governments*, *supra* note 60, pp. 27–29; *see also* Division of Historical Policy Research, Department of State, *The Problem of Recognition in American Foreign Policy, Research Project No. 174* (US Department of State, 1950), pp. 35–45; Taylor Cole, *The Recognition Policy of the United States Since 1901* (Baton Rouge, La.: Louisiana State University, 1928); Frederic Paxson, *The Independence of South-American Republics: A Study in Recognition and Foreign Policy* (Philadelphia, Penn.: Ferris and Leach, 1903).

However, the Tobar Doctrine proved difficult to maintain in practice; by definition, the issue of recognition of a new government only arises in situations where non-constitutional change has occurred, and in those situations the new regime establishes a new constitution that purports to (and may even in terms of democracy) legitimize its existence. Consequently, Wilson's approach did not have an enduring effect on US government practice or that of other States. In the famous 1923 *Tinoco Arbitration*, US Chief Justice (and former President) William Howard Taft found that international obligations incurred by a non-recognized government that had assumed power unconstitutionally were nevertheless binding on its successor, an acknowledgment that the existence of such governments could not be denied by other States.

Indeed, the whole idea of States "recognizing" a new government of a State is anathema to those States that see it as an insulting interference in national affairs. The 1930 Estrada Doctrine, named for the Mexican Foreign Secretary Genaro Estrada, stands for the proposition that the manner in which a new government comes to power is wholly a matter of national concern.[68] As such, States should not seek to influence the outcome of an internal power struggle by granting or withholding recognition. The Estrada Doctrine is attractive, not just for the reason stated by Mr. Estrada, but also because many States view it as politically difficult to announce publicly, one way or another, whether they "recognize" a new government, and would prefer simply to open diplomatic channels or otherwise develop relations with the new government without issuing a pronouncement that could be construed as approval of the new government. In such instances, determination of the legal effects of the new relationship is often left to national courts, which must pass upon the legal rights and obligations of the new government in the absence of a clear statement of recognition.

Due to the refusal of a substantial number of States to accept Western notions of democracy, the recognition practices of international organizations (e.g., the practice of the UN Credentials Committee), and international law more generally, have traditionally not specified democracy as a linchpin of governmental legitimacy.[69] Indeed, dozens of non-democratic governments were fully represented at the various conferences that spawned the human rights treaties now pointed to as evidencing an emerging right of democratic governance.

---

[68] *See* Philip C. Jessup, "The Estrada Doctrine," *Amer. J. Int'l L.* 25 (1931), p. 719.
[69] *See, e.g.,* Bernard R. Bot, *Nonrecognition and Treaty Relations* (Dobbs Ferry, N.Y.: Oceana Publications, Inc., 1968), p. 25.

B Contemporary practice

As has been fully documented elsewhere, the international community in recent years has been significantly involved in ending civil conflict within States through a process of national reconciliation that includes UN monitored elections.[70] Once elections occur, recognition of the new government by other States is virtually automatic.

However, as is the case regarding recognition of States, the international community does not refuse to recognize governments simply by virtue of their being non-democratic. China is the premier example of a State whose non-democratic, communist government is fully recognized within the international community, to the point of its representatives participating not just in the work of the United Nations generally but also as a permanent member of the Security Council. Yet there are dozens of other non-democratic States that also are generally recognized by the international community – mostly in Africa and the Middle East – and that participate fully in the work of international organizations. Even the United States, which in recent years has emphasized the importance of democracy in its foreign policy, recognizes and maintains diplomatic relations with several non-democratic States.[71] Understandably, the many non-democratic governments that continue to exist globally do not conduct their recognition practice so as to disfavor other non-democratic governments.

The continuing recognition of non-democratic governments by democratic governments cannot be explained as vestiges of history anomalously "grandfathered in" amidst contemporary pro-democratic practice. Consider, for instance, the case of China. From its assumption of effective control of the Chinese mainland in 1949 until 1971, the Beijing-based communist government was not generally recognized as the government of China outside the communist bloc States. Rather, the Taiwan-based (also non-democratic) nationalist government was recognized by most States as the government of China. General recognition of the Beijing-based government occurred only recently, in 1970–71, when representatives of the communist Chinese government were (at the expense of the now de-recognized Taiwan authorities) permitted to participate in the work of the United Nations on behalf of China. Thus,

---

[70] Gregory Fox, "The Right to Political Participation in International Law," *Yale J. Int'l L.* 17 (1992), pp. 570–87.
[71] "Fact Sheet: Independent States and Dependencies as of August 20, 1996," *US Dept. of State Dispatch* 7 (Aug. 26, 1996), p. 433.

the international community has in recent years affirmatively recognized the non-democratic government in Beijing as the legitimate government of China.[72]

Even more recently, the international community fully accepted transfer of governance of the democratically governed Hong Kong from the democratic United Kingdom to non-democratic China on July 1, 1997.[73] On its first day in power, the Beijing-appointed legislature voted to restrict public demonstrations (prompting activists to take to the streets demanding free and fair legislative elections immediately),[74] and within days established a new electoral system that was expected to limit sharply the ability to elect pro-democracy candidates.[75]

China is not the only example of contemporary recognition of non-democratic governments.[76] After the reunification of Vietnam in 1975, the communist government of the Socialist Republic of Vietnam gradually gained widespread global recognition, although it experienced some setbacks when it invaded Cambodia in 1978.[77] The United States held back recognition of Vietnam's communist government for many years, but ultimately normalized diplomatic relations in July 1995. In doing so, the United States emphasized the progress that had been made with the communist government in recovering the remains of US soldiers missing in action in Vietnam, but was silent on the government's lack of democratic legitimacy.[78]

In short, in determining whether to recognize another government, States do not find the democratic quality of the government as decisive;

---

[72] *See, e.g.,* "Chronicle of State Practice," *Asian Y.B. Int'l L.* 2 (1992), p. 298 (Israel–China diplomatic relations established in 1992).

[73] The reversion of Hong Kong to China was agreed to by the United Kingdom and China in a Sino–British Joint Declaration on the Question of Hong Kong, signed on December 19, 1984.

[74] Velisarios Kattoulas, "A New Order Takes Its Place in Hong Kong," *Int'l Herald Trib.* (July 2, 1997), p. 1. By contrast, Spain has been unsuccessful in its efforts to have Gibraltar revert to Spanish control, no doubt largely because Gibraltar's population of 30,000 prefer to remain a UK colony. Barbara Crossette, "As It Seeks New Status, Island Helps a UN Panel," *N.Y. Times* (June 8, 1997), p. 19. Some sixteen other territories remain classified by the United Nations as colonies: American Samoa, Anguilla, Bermuda, British Virgin Islands, Cayman Islands, East Timor, the Falklands, Guam, Montserrat, New Caledonia, Pitcairn, Tokelau, Turks and Caicos, St. Helena, US Virgin Islands, and Western Sahara.

[75] Edward A. Gargan, "Hong Kong Scraps Its Voting System," *Int'l Herald Trib.* (July 9, 1997), p. 1.

[76] *See, e.g.,* "Chronicle of State Practice," *Asian Y.B. Int'l L.* 1 (1991), p. 283 (Philippines–North Korea diplomatic relations established in 1991).

[77] *See, e.g., ibid.* at p. 281 (Belgium–Vietnam diplomatic relations downgraded in 1978 and then upgraded in 1991); "Chronicle of State Practice," *Asian Y.B. Int'l L.* 3 (1993), p. 281 (South Korea–Vietnam diplomatic relations established in 1993).

[78] "US Normalizes Diplomatic Relations with Vietnam," *US Dept. of State Dispatch* 6 (July 10, 1995), p. 551; Marian Nash (Leich), "Contemporary Practice of the United States Relating to International Law," *Am. J. Int'l L.* 90 (1996), 79.

other factors are taken into consideration as well. The stated reason for recognizing the government may be that the transition to democracy is better achieved by engaging in relations with the non-democratic government, rather than by isolating it. Indeed, the willingness to recognize a non-democratic government is not necessarily detrimental to the best interests of its people; respectable arguments are made by respectable commentators that a democratic form of government is not the best form for some States depending on their stage of economic and political development.[79] At the same time, such recognition may be for non-altruistic reasons, such as seeking trade opportunities.

Actions by a non-democratic government against the flowering of democracy also do not necessarily trigger non-recognition of that government. Chinese treatment of dissidents seeking democratic change, including the treatment of student protestors in Tiananmen Square, has not led to non-recognition of the Chinese government. More recently, the violent crushing of pro-democracy demonstrations in Kenya in July 1997 led to no significant reaction by the international community in terms of non-recognition.[80]

US efforts to direct sanctions against the non-democratic government of Cuba through the Helms–Burton Act[81] was roundly condemned by the international community as an effort by the United States to dictate its foreign policy to other States. Yet that foreign policy, on its face, was an effort to pressure a non-democratic government by inhibiting "trafficking" in property owned by US nationals that was confiscated by the government, *until such time as the government transitioned toward democracy*.[82] The international reaction to the Helms–Burton Act confirms the belief of many States that they are entitled to recognize and engage in trade relations with a non-democratic government.[83]

---

[79] Robert D. Kaplan, "Was Democracy Just a Movement?" *The Atlantic Monthly* (Dec. 1997), p. 55. Efforts by the United Nations to promote democracy have been extensive, but have not included systematic non-recognition of non-democratic governments. Beigbeder, *International Monitoring*, pp. *supra* note 21, 91–118. For some recent efforts by the General Assembly and the Secretary-General to promote the transition to democracy not by isolating non-democratic states and governments but, rather, by working with them and other relevant actors, see *Y.B. UN 1995* (Boston, Mass.: Martinus Nijhoff, 1997), pp. 293–95.

[80] James C. McKinley, Jr., "Moi Keeps Foes at Bay," *Int'l Herald Trib.* (July 10, 1997), p. 1.

[81] Cuban Liberty and Democratic Solidarity (LIBERTAD) Act of 1996, Pub L. nos. 104–114, 110 Stat. 785 (1996).

[82] "Promoting a Peaceful Transition to Democracy in Cuba," *US. Dept. of State Dispatch* 7 (July 15, 1996), p. 364.

[83] The reaction to the Helms–Burton law is unfortunate in that imposing risks on third parties, including companies, that deal with a non-democratic government has been advanced as an attractive alternative to the more draconian measure of blanket non-recognition of that government. James Crawford, "Democracy and International Law," *Brit. Y.B. Int'l L.* 64 (1993), p. 113.

When a non-democratic regime is ousted without outside involvement, the new regime typically promises to undertake elections at some future point, thereby promoting recognition by foreign governments. This provides some evidence that there is a belief by many States within the international community that democracy is the preferred form of government. For instance, when rebel forces under Laurent Kabila ousted Zaire's dictator Mobutu Sese Seko in 1997, Kabila established the "Democratic Republic of the Congo," promised elections by 1999, and secured widespread international recognition of his government. However, Kabila's promise of elections was shortly followed by the banning of political party activity and public rallies, to muted criticism from abroad.[84] Thus, the aspiration for democracy is not always borne out in practice and, when it is not borne out, the consequences that flow often do not include a withdrawal of recognition of the new government.

If there is an emphasis on democratic legitimacy in the recognition of governments, it arises primarily in situations where a democratic government is internally overthrown by non-democratic (often military) authorities. As mentioned at the beginning of this chapter, Haiti is an important potential precedent for an emerging norm of democratic governance. The 1990 election of President Aristide was usurped by Haitian military and police authorities in 1991, but despite the complete control of the new regime, the international community rallied around Aristide, refusing to recognize the legitimacy of the *de facto* government in Haiti, and instead gradually increasing sanctions until Aristide was restored to power in 1994. Arguably, this is the first step in the creation of a new international legal norm of non-recognition of governments that overthrow democratic governments. Similar coordinated actions by States, albeit on a much less dramatic scale, have occurred since that time, such as the reaction to the threat to democracy in Sao Tome and Principe in August 1995,[85] in Niger in January 1996,[86] and in Paraguay in April 1996.[87] The 1991 Moscow Meeting of the Conference on the Human Dimension of the CSCE issued a statement affirming that participating States "will support vigorously, in accordance with the Charter

---

[84] Howard W. French, "The Honeymoon is Over for Kabila," *Int'l Herald Trib.* (July 14, 1997), p. 9.
[85] *See, e.g.*, "Condemnation of Military Coup in Sao Tome and Principe," *US Dept. of State Dispatch* 6 (Aug. 28, 1995), p. 665; "US Welcomes Restoration of Government of Sao Tome and Principe," *ibid.*
[86] *See, e.g.*, "US Suspends Assistance to Niger Following Military Coup," *US Dept. of State Dispatch* 7 (Feb. 12, 1996), p. 44.
[87] *See, e.g.*, "Hemispheric Support for Democracy in Paraguay," *US Dept. of State Dispatch* 7 (Apr. 22, 1996), p. 203.

of the United Nations, in case of overthrow or attempted overthrow of a legitimately elected government of a participating State by undemocratic means, the legitimate organs of that State upholding human rights, democracy and the rule of law."[88]

However, it is difficult to see that the international community has taken the second step of crystallizing this notion as a legal norm, or is even over time moving toward such a legal norm. Some situations that might help support the emergence of such a norm are clouded by the complexity of their circumstances; often the reaction of the international community is in the nature of a withdrawal of economic benefits, or perhaps the imposition of economic sanctions, but not a refusal to recognize the new government.[89] Rather than isolate the *de facto* government through a comprehensive process of non-recognition, the reaction often is to maintain diplomatic relations with the new government, but with a policy that seeks to promote reestablishment of democratic rule.

Consider the case of Cambodia. Hun Sen's Cambodian People's Party (CPP) ran Cambodia as a communist one-party State throughout the 1980s. In 1993, elections were held in Cambodia under UN supervision, resulting in a coalition government, headed by First Prime Minister Norodom Ranariddh (the son of the Head of State, King Norodom Sihanouk) and Second Prime Minister Hun Sen. In July 1997, Prince Ranariddh was deposed by Hun Sen, who then appointed Ung Huot as First Prime Minister. The initial reaction by the international community to the coup was negative, but also somewhat muted.[90] In September

---

[88] Document of the Moscow Meeting of the Conference on the Human Dimension of the CSCE, Oct. 3, 1991, Article II, para. 17.2, *reprinted in* 30 ILM (1991), p. 1670.

[89] For instance, US legislation in recent years has precluded the provision of US foreign assistance to any country whose elected head of government is deposed by military coup or decree. *See, e.g.,* 1996 Foreign Operations, Export Financing, and Related Programs Appropriations Act, Section 508, Public Law 104–07, 110 Stat. 704, 723 (1996), which provides:

> None of the funds appropriated or otherwise made available pursuant to this Act shall be obligated or expended to finance directly any assistance to any country whose duly elected Head of Government is deposed by military coup or decree: *Provided*, That assistance may be resumed to such country if the President determines and reports to the Committees on Appropriations that subsequent to the termination of assistance a democratically elected government has taken office.

The US Congress probably could not constitutionally require the President not to recognize a foreign government, since the US Constitution allocates to the President the power to "receive Ambassadors and other Public Ministers," US Constitution, Art. II, sec. 3.

[90] "The Tigers' Fearful Symmetry," *The Economist* (July 19, 1997), p. 53 (noting tepid reactions in the West); "Cambodia: The Last Battle?" *The Economist* (Aug. 23, 1997), p. 44 ("Prince Ranariddh has been touring the world, appealing for help. He has received little more than the occasional kind word.")

1997, the UN Credentials Committee refused to accept credentials signed by King Sihanouk (presenting a delegation headed by Hun Sen and Ung Huot), but also refused to accept the credentials of Prince Ranariddh (in exile in France, presenting a delegation headed by himself). On the one hand, most donor States suspended non-humanitarian aid, the World Bank pulled back from starting new projects, and the Association of South East Asian Nations (ASEAN) suspended Cambodia's application for admission.[91] On the other hand, States did not impose comprehensive economic sanctions and continued to maintain diplomatic relations with the new government through their embassies in Phnom Penh. The Hun Sen regime allowed internationally monitored elections in July 1998, but the regime's victory was the product of its control over the election infrastructure, the national media, and local administration.[92]

Consider also the recent situation in West Africa with respect to Nigeria, Sierra Leone, and Liberia. A several-year process of transitioning to civilian rule in Nigeria was to culminate in the election of a civilian president in June 1993. The election was held and it appeared that Chief MKO Abiola won, but before the formal results could be announced, the existing military-backed government annulled the election. By November, the military's strongman, General Sani Abacha, formally assumed control of the country, and proceeded to engage in significant human rights abuses, including executions of dissidents. Exactly one year after the elections were annulled, General Abacha placed the apparent winner, Chief Abiola, in a "detention" that would last until his death.[93] In response to this military suppression of democracy, however, most States did not sever diplomatic relations with the Nigerian government or refuse to recognize the Abacha government. The United States terminated most economic and military aid to Nigeria, but other than withdrawing its military attaché from the US Embassy in Abuja, it took no steps to downgrade diplomatic relations with the new government.[94] In 1995, Nigeria was suspended from the

[91] David Lamb, "High Price of Coup Becomes Clear to Despairing Cambodia," *LA. Times* (Dec. 9, 1997), A1. Founded in 1967, ASEAN currently consists of Brunei, Indonesia, Laos, Malaysia, Myanmar, Philippines, Singapore, Thailand, and Vietnam.

[92] Stephen J. Morris, "Brutocracy Wins: The Travesty of Cambodia's 'Fair' Elections," *Washington Post* (Aug. 9, 1998), C1; Tina Rosenberg, "Hun Sen Stages an Election: From Cambodia, a Post-Cold-War Parable," *N.Y. Times* (Aug. 30, 1998), p. 26.

[93] Reuters, "Nigerian Opposition Leader Passes 3d Year in Detention," *Int'l Herald Trib.* (June 25, 1997), p. 6.

[94] For a description of the United States' reaction to the annulment of the 1993 elections, *see* "Assessment of U.S.–Nigeria Relations," *US Dept. of State Dispatch* 6 (July 31, 1995), 604.

fifty-four-nation British Commonwealth,[95] but was not expelled, nor did the Commonwealth impose comprehensive economic sanctions let alone threaten intervention. Why a different result than Haiti? Nigeria has a population of 100 million, is a major oil exporter globally, and has an enormous army capable not only of defending Nigeria but also of projecting considerable force throughout the region. As is the case of the treatment of China, one might say that practicalities in recognition practice at times trump principle.

In May 1997, Sierra Leone's army ousted the democratically elected President, Ahmad Tejan Kabbah. The Organization of African Unity Council of (Foreign) Ministers condemned the coup and called on all African countries, and the international community at large, to refrain from recognizing the new regime.[96] However, the primary means by which the international community assisted the ousted government was through an intervention led by none other than the non-democratic, military regime of Nigeria. Nigeria's motivation for intervening appears to lie less in its attraction to democracy, and more in either its desire for stability in Western Africa (achievable through either democratic or non-democratic governments, depending on the government) or, worse, its effort to extend Nigerian dominance throughout the region.[97]

That desire to dominate may be seen in a similar Nigerian-led intervention in Liberia in 1990. That intervention checked the forces of Charles Taylor, who had ousted the non-democratic regime of Samuel Doe and seized control of the vast majority of Liberia. While the intervention probably prevented widespread human rights atrocities by Taylor's forces in Monrovia, it could not definitively end the Liberian civil war. Seven years and 150,000 lives later, the exhausted competing factions submitted to internationally monitored elections. Ironically, with 85 percent of the people voting, Taylor was elected President with 75 percent of the vote and his party achieved a majority in Liberia's parliament.[98] In

---

[95] "Bloc Gives Nigeria a Year on Reforms," *Int'l Herald Trib.* (Oct. 28, 1997), p. 6. The United States supported the actions taken by the Commonwealth. *See, e.g.,* "Nigeria: Commonwealth Ministerial Group Recommends New Measures on Nigeria," in *US Dept. of State Dispatch* 7 (May 6, 1996), p. 235.
[96] Decision of the Organization of African Unity Council of Ministers, May 28–June 4, 1997 Meeting, OAU Document CM/DEC (LXVI) (1997).
[97] Howard W. French, "Lagos Imposes Its Will on West Africa," *Int'l Herald Trib.* (June 27, 1997), p. 1 (quoting a former Nigerian foreign minister, now in exile, that Nigeria's military ruler "would have intervened even if it had been a military regime that was overthrown" because "he cannot tolerate a coup against a government perceived to be under his protection").
[98] James Rupert, "Liberian Leader Lost the War, But May Have Won the Battle," *Int'l Herald Trib.* (July 22, 1997), p. 1; "Liberia: Farewell Guns?" *The Economist* (July 26, 1997), p. 37.

situations such as these, the international community as a whole appears to favor the maintenance or establishment of a democratic government, but the fundamental motivations of the most relevant actor(s) are far less clear.

Thus, the precedent for recognition practice in situations involving the ouster of democratic governments in Cambodia and in West Africa were far more equivocal than in Haiti. Similar precedents can be seen repeatedly in recent years with respect to *de facto* governments that usurped or annulled democratic elections. Although much criticism has been directed against the military-backed government of Myanmar (formerly Burma) for disregarding the 1990 election,[99] that government – the State Law and Order Restoration Council (SLORC) – remains the recognized government of Myanmar; its representatives are accredited to international organizations and Myanmar was admitted to ASEAN in 1997. After the Islamic Salvation Front won a resounding victory in Algeria's 1991 municipal elections, the military-backed Algerian government canceled the second round of Parliamentary elections which the Islamic Salvation Front appeared set to win and banned the Front from future elections. The action was mostly applauded by the international community, apparently on the ground that the Algerian people were not entitled to select a fundamentalist government.[100] Many States of the international community condemned Peruvian President Fujimori's 1992 "coup from above" assumption of plenary powers at the expense of the Peruvian legislature and judiciary, yet still continued to recognize his government while pressing for a return to democratic rule. Indeed, it was hard to protest too vehemently in the face of Fujimori's success in weakening the Shining Path guerilla movement, reducing inflation from some 7,500 percent to 10 percent, and bringing investment and jobs back to Peru (leading to Fujimori's overwhelming reelection in 1995). In 1997, forces loyal to the former dictator of the Republic of Congo, Denis Sassou-Nguesso, succeeded in sweeping from power the government of Pascal Lissouba, who had been democratically elected in 1993.[101]

---

[99] *See, e.g.,* United Nations General Assembly Resolution 49/197, *United Nations General Assembly Official Records,* 49th Sess., 94th plenary meeting at 217, United Nations Document A/49/197 (1994); "US Policy Toward Burma," *U.S. Dept. of State Dispatch* 6 (July 24, 1995), p. 584.
[100] Milton Viorst, "Algeria's Long Night," *Foreign Aff.* 76 (Nov.–Dec. 1997), p. 86. For a discussion of why Western democracies should consider some democratically elected governments as the "wrong" kind of democracy (i.e., democracy but without the rule of law and basic human rights), *see* Fareed Zakaria, "The Rise of Illiberal Democracy," *Foreign Aff.* 76 (Nov.-Dec. 1997), 22.
[101] Howard W. French, "Former Dictator Sweeps Back into Control of Congo Republic," *Int'l Herald Trib.* (Oct. 16, 1997), 1.

However, the international community maintained diplomatic relations with the new government.

The failure of the international community to deny recognition to authoritarian governments that suppress democracy is particularly significant given that the international community can act when it so chooses. In this sense, Haiti helps disprove the existence of an emerging norm of non-recognition of non-democratic governments, for similar action could be repeated elsewhere but is not. At the same time, the international community has denied recognition to advance values other than democracy, most notably to punish transnational uses of force, whether or not the victim State is democratic. To that end, the Security Council called upon States not to recognize any regime set up by Iraq, which invaded and *de facto* controlled non-democratic Kuwait from August 1990 through January 1991.[102] Similarly, to punish Serbian aggression against Croatia and Bosnia, the Security Council ordered States to reduce the level of their staff at diplomatic missions and consular posts in Serbia and Montenegro, to prevent persons of those States from participating in international sporting events, and to suspend scientific and technical cooperation and cultural exchanges and visits with those States.[103] These instances of non-recognition (or at least diplomatic isolation) were triggered by an effort to suppress armed conflict; similar non-recognition by the Security Council or by regional organizations apparently is not uniformly triggered by the simple ouster of a democratic government by a non-democratic one, notwithstanding the reaction with respect to Haiti.

III CONCLUSION

One need look to no other authority than Thomas Franck himself for the proposition that international rules can only command compliance when they are true and coherent. In accordance with this proposition, an international rule on the recognition of States and governments must turn on effective control, not democratic control.

Franck has expounded a detailed theory on why States comply with rules of international law. That theory argues that the "legitimacy" of rules and institutions (such as States and governments) exerts a

---

[102] Security Council Resolution 661, *United Nations Security Council Official Records*, 45th Sess., 2933d meeting at p. 13, UN Doc. S/Res/661 (1990).

[103] Security Council Resolution 757, *United Nations Security Council Official Records*, 47th Sess., 3082d meeting at p. 13, UN Doc. S/Res/757 (1992).

"compliance pull" on those addressed. States comply with rules and institutions that have been "symbolically validated" by the international community, which occurs when a signal is used as a cue to elicit compliance with a command.[104] For Franck, the validation of a State or government is "symbolically cued" by the rite of recognition; however, the cue used succeeds only when those addressed perceive it as symbolic of truth.[105] Realistic cuing in the field of recognition remains tied to effective governance, and, if this were to change, the cue would lose its effectiveness.[106] With respect to membership in the United Nations, Franck writes:

> A self-proclaimed regime may be denied validation only if it does not exercise effective control. A new State should be denied membership only if its existence is still precarious or if it does not want to, or cannot assume the duties of membership. . . . For example, it is not permissible to vote to deny membership on the ground . . . that the government has come to power in a coup.[107]

Further, Franck appears to believe that efforts to depart from this approach are destined to lead to "incoherence" in the application of the rule, thereby undercutting its legitimacy. By occasionally refusing to accredit representatives of governments that were in effective control, the United Nations has impugned its membership process, and if continued the "very notion of a community of States becomes one of doubtful validity."[108]

Notions of democratic legitimacy have existed to varying degrees in the practice of recognizing States and governments since the advent of democracy. The traditional criteria for recognizing States and governments have often been mixed with other factors. One of those factors is that democratic States, driven by deep-seated beliefs within their populace, tend to want to promote democracy in other States. With the considerable increase in the number of democratic States worldwide, there is little doubt that the trend is toward greater use of democratic legitimacy as a factor in recognition practice, and leads to certain tentative[109] conclusions:

---

[104] Thomas M. Franck, *The Power of Legitimacy Among Nations* (Oxford University Press, 1990), p. 92.
[105] *Ibid.* at pp. 111–12.   [106] *Ibid.* at pp. 118, 127–28.   [107] *Ibid.* at pp. 122–23.
[108] *Ibid.* at pp. 136–37, 140–42.
[109] These conclusions are necessarily tentative for various reasons. First, while sometimes it is clear when a State is granting or denying recognition, in fact it often is not clear and must be surmised from the maintenance of diplomatic relations or other forms of contact between governments. Second, assessing the emergence of a norm of democratic legitimacy is especially difficult in the field of recognition practice. Granting or denying recognition to a State or government is an extremely blunt diplomatic tool, in many ways ill-suited to the varying degrees

* There is no international norm obligating States not to recognize an emerging State simply because its political community is not democratic in nature. Were there such a norm, it might be accompanied by a norm permitting intervention so as to establish a democratic government.[110]
* When a political community seeks recognition as a State, the existence of a democratic referendum whereby the people of the community proclaim themselves in favor of independence will be one important, but not decisive, element in the international community's decision to recognize it as a State. However, other elements will be equally important, including the international community's adherence to the modern version of the principle of *uti possidetis* and other means for maintaining peace and stability.
* When a non-democratic regime usurps a democratically elected government, the international community may react by refusing to recognize the new *de facto* government and imposing comprehensive economic sanctions, in an effort to cajole the new government into transitioning back to democratic rule.
* However, while the international community is increasingly interested in democratic legitimacy as a factor in its recognition practice, there is an enduring desire to promote economic development, international peace, and stability as well. These values – legitimacy, development, and stability – do not always go hand-in-hand. Depending on the situation, one or the other value may dominate the decision within the international community regarding whether to recognize the State or government.

Regarding the role of democratic legitimacy as just another policy element in the practice of recognizing States and governments may be regarded as an unattractive conclusion. Rather than resorting to a ready-made legal framework on recognition, policy-makers are left

---

of democracy that exist in the world and the speed with which democracies can come and go. Third, there appear to be certain necessary legal conditions that must be met before a political community can possibly qualify as a State and there further appears to be an acceptance that, once the community meets these conditions, it must be accorded certain core international rights even if denied other rights accorded to a State. Yet beyond these core conditions and rights, recognition practice regarding either States or governments is heavily policy driven. Fourth, it is conceivable that at some stage this policy may crystallize into a legal norm of recognition practice. Yet, it seems likely that this would only happen when virtually all States are democracies, including all States with significant size and power (such as China).

[110] For a discussion, *see* Jean Salmon, "Internal Aspects of the Right to Self-Determination: Towards a Democratic Legitimacy Principle?" *in* Christian Tomuschat, ed., *Modern Law of Self-Determination* (Boston, Mass.: Martinus Nijhoff, 1993), pp. 253–82.

weighing various amorphous policy elements that provide little concrete guidance.[111] Yet, finding the right solutions through the application of differing policies to different cases is what diplomacy is all about. Democratic legitimacy is an important concept and tool, but it should not serve as a straitjacket for governments and others as they seek to find solutions, on a case-by-case basis, that promote the welfare of peoples worldwide. Whether nurturing new democracies, restoring overthrown democracies, promoting the gradual transition from non-democracy to democracy, or pursuing values that do not necessarily entail "democratic" means (such as promoting regional stability, economic development), the international community has an array of diplomatic and economic tools at its disposal, of which recognition practice is merely one.

[111] Looking upon the turbulence in Africa, Michael Reisman provides a rather grim, yet perceptive analysis when he notes:

> None of the world's options are particularly attractive. Supporting the status quo in Africa probably means tolerating autocratic one-party rule, since democratic multiparty politics, even if they can be introduced, are likely to tribalize and exacerbate the tensions that split states. Supporting an orderly deconstruction and reconstruction of states, if it is possible, means accepting huge population shifts and the attendant violence. Standing aside, with arms embargoes, relief efforts, "safe areas" and other means of refugee containment, means allowing hideous conflicts to rage.

Michael Reisman, "On Africa, No Attractive Options for the World," *Int'l Herald Trib.* (Nov. 23–24, 1996), p. 8.

CHAPTER 5

Constitutionalism and democratic government in the inter-American system

Stephen J. Schnably[1]

I INTRODUCTION: THE OAS, DEMOCRACY, AND NON-INTERVENTION

Throughout its history, the Organization of American States (OAS) has grappled with a basic tension between protecting democracy and respecting the principle of non-intervention into other States' domestic affairs. Its failure to resolve this tension has generally undermined its role as a multilateral body. With the adoption of the "Santiago Commitment to Democracy and Renewal of the Inter-American System" in June 1991, the OAS took a decisive political step in favor of the protection of democracy over the principle of non-intervention. In essence, the OAS committed itself to respond to the "sudden or irregular interruption" of democracy in a member State.[2]

The OAS's affirmation of democracy and human rights was far from new. The American Declaration of the Rights and Duties of Man (1948) and the American Convention on Human Rights (1978) both proclaim a wide range of rights. The OAS Charter has always recognized "the fundamental rights of the individual without distinction as to race, nationality, creed, or sex."[3] The OAS, moreover, has long been committed to representative democracy. Article xx of the American Declaration

---

[1] I wish to thank Hugo Caminos and Bernard Oxman for constructive comments; Edgardo Rotman, Foreign and International Law Librarian, University of Miami, for his expertise in locating materials; and Jason Alderman and Guillermo Levy for research assistance. Events are current as of October 1, 1998.
[2] OAS GAOR, 21st Reg. Sess., OEA/Ser. P/AG doc. 2734/91 (June 4, 1991). *See* § II *infra*; Domingo E. Acevedo and Claudio Grossman, "The Organization of American States and the Protection of Democracy," *in* Tom Farer, ed., *Beyond Sovereignty: Collectively Defending Democracy in the Americas* (The Johns Hopkins University Press, 1996), p. 132; César Gaviria, "Las Américas: Una Comunidad de Sociedades Democráticas," *J. Lat. Am. Aff.*, 4(2) (Fall/Winter 1995), p. 4 (OAS Secretary-General's view); Heraldo Muñoz, "The OAS and Democratic Governance," *in J. Democ.* 4(3) (July 1993), p. 29 (former chair of OAS Permanent Council).
[3] OAS Charter, Art. 3(l). References to Charter provisions herein are to the fully amended version. Not all OAS members, however, have ratified all the Protocols.

guarantees the right to participate in government and take part in "honest, periodic and free" elections with a secret ballot, as does Article 23 of the American Convention. Because Article 23 rights cannot be suspended even in time of public emergency,[4] the American Convention implicitly condemns all coups. As originally promulgated, the OAS Charter declared that its purposes required "the political organization of ... [member] States on the basis of the effective exercise of representative democracy."[5] In 1985, the Protocol of Cartagena de Indias amended the Charter to state that "representative democracy is an indispensable condition for the stability, peace, and development of the region," and to provide that it was one of the "essential purposes" of the OAS to "promote and consolidate representative democracy."[6] Finally, there is a long history going back to the 1950s of OAS resolutions – most notably the 1959 Declaration of Santiago – calling for representative democracy throughout the hemisphere.[7]

Throughout its history, however, the OAS has also firmly insisted on the principle of non-intervention. The Charter states that "[n]o State or group of States has the right to intervene, directly or indirectly, for any reason whatever, in the internal or external affairs of any other State" – whether by armed force or "any other form of interference."[8] Other Charter provisions emphasize State sovereignty and independence.[9] In 1973, the General Assembly declared that the "plurality of ideologies" among States requires respect for non-intervention, without saying anything about representative democracy.[10] The Protocol of Cartagena de Indias reiterated that the OAS has no power to intervene in members' "internal jurisdiction."[11]

The principles of non-intervention and respect for human rights are not easily reconciled. Any human right intrudes on sovereignty to a fair degree, by requiring a State to refrain from taking actions it might otherwise take (*e.g.*, suppressing dissent). But protecting even civil and

---

[4] American Convention, Art. 27(2).   [5] OAS Charter, Art. 3(d).
[6] *Ibid.*, Preamble, para. 3, Art. 2(b) (added by the Protocol of Cartagena de Indias, approved Dec. 5, 1985, entry into force Nov. 16, 1988).
[7] Fifth Meeting of the Consultation of Ministers of Foreign Affairs, Final Act, OEA/Ser.C/II.5, at 4–6; *see* this chapter, § IV.A.1 (discussing Declaration). For an excellent history and analysis of the OAS and representative democracy, see Hugo Caminos, "The Role of the Organization of American States in the Promotion and Protection of Democratic Governance," *Recueil des Cours* 273 (Hague Academy of International Law, 1999), pp. 107–237. *See also* Dinah Shelton, "Representative Democracy and Human Rights in the Western Hemisphere," *Hum. Rts. L.J.*, 12 (1991), p. 353.   [8] OAS Charter, Art. 19.   [9] *Ibid.*, ch. IV.
[10] Principles Governing Relations Among the American States, AG/RES 128 (III-o/73) (April 15, 1973), para. 3.   [11] OAS Charter, Art. 1; *see* Art. 2(b).

political rights (let alone economic and social rights) also requires extensive affirmative action, if nothing else in the creation and maintenance of an independent judiciary, the subjection of the military to civilian control, and the conduct of free elections. These are difficult to achieve and go to the heart of how a state constitutes itself. Article 3(e) of the Charter refers to the *right* of "[e]very State . . . to organize itself in the way best suited to it" without "external interference"; the Inter-American Court of Human Rights indicated how potentially intrusive a human rights regime can be when it pronounced a *"duty* to organize the State in such a manner as to guarantee" human rights.[12]

The OAS has not dealt with this tension consistently over much of its history. Its proclaimed doctrine and the practice of its more apolitical organs have gradually established that human rights are not essentially internal matters. The practice of member States and the more political organs like the General Assembly and the Permanent Council, however, shows more of a tilt towards non-intervention.

On the one hand, the very existence of the American Declaration, the American Convention, and other resolutions addressing democracy and human rights tends to undermine any claim that such matters are purely domestic. Moreover, the OAS's commitment to human rights has been increasingly institutionalized in relatively apolitical bodies. In 1959, the OAS created the Inter-American Commission on Human Rights, which can hear individual petitions against any OAS member. Significantly, in 1990 the Commission affirmed that it had jurisdiction to hear complaints of election fraud, rejecting Mexico's argument that doing so would violate the principle of non-intervention.[13] The Commission's country reports have also helped expose systematic human rights violations in some countries, and it has played a constructive role in fostering democracy in others. The Inter-American Court began functioning in 1979, and has rendered important decisions in contested cases. In 1990, the General Assembly created the Unit for the Promotion of Democracy (UPD) to assist states in "preserv[ing] their political institutions and democratic procedures."[14] The UPD monitors elections and provides technical assistance to legislatures and electoral institutions.

On the other hand, the same ascendancy of human rights over

---

[12] Velásquez Rodríguez v. Honduras, Int.-Am. Ct. H.R., Judgment of July 29, 1988, Ser. C, No. 4, para. 158 (emphasis added).
[13] Resolution No. 01/90, Cases 9768, 9780, and 9828 (Mexico), May 17, 1990, in *Annual Report of the Inter-American Commission on Human Rights 1989–1990*, OEA/Ser.L/V/II.77 rev.1, Doc. 7, May 17, 1990, p. 97.   [14] AG-RES 1063 (XX-0-90).

non-intervention has been difficult to detect in political practice. The difficulty inheres in two basic facts about the OAS. It is a regional body in which one member is vastly more powerful than the others, with a fairly consistent pattern, predating the OAS's formation, of intervening in other countries' affairs. And for much of its existence the OAS has been composed of States governed by military regimes with abysmal human rights records. One would therefore expect the practice of the OAS and its member States in regard to democracy and non-intervention to be complicated.

It may be useful to draw a distinction between the practice of the US and that of other member States. The US has invoked and violated both principles. It has often intervened in dramatic ways, occupying Haiti and Nicaragua for long periods earlier this century, overthrowing the Arbenz government in Guatemala in 1954, and invading the Dominican Republic, Grenada, and Panama. Yet it has not rejected non-intervention as a principle, either citing legal grounds such as self-defense or working clandestinely in its interventions. It has also claimed at times to enforce the principle of non-intervention against other members, relying for example on Nicaragua's alleged intervention in El Salvador's guerrilla war to justify funding the *contras*. Similarly, while its domestic human rights record compares favorably with that of many other States, the US has frequently supported regimes with massive violations of human rights. Yet rather than reject human rights as an international concern, the US has made it a central part of its stated foreign policy since the Carter Administration.

In contrast, while Latin American States are not entirely lacking in their own histories of intervention into each other's affairs, before the adoption of the Santiago Commitment they tended to emphasize non-intervention at the expense of human rights. This stance was particularly attractive to repressive military regimes, because it simultaneously provided grounds for opposing US intervention and helped shield them from human rights scrutiny. Consequently, the political bodies of the OAS took few concrete actions to promote democracy and human rights. Of course, there were exceptions; the OAS called for the overthrow of Somoza in 1979[15] and criticized a coup in Bolivia in 1980.[16]

---

[15] *See* MR.E. Res. II, OAS Meeting of Consultation of Ministers of Foreign Affairs, 17th mtg., OEA/Ser.F/II.17, OAS Doc. 40/79 rev. 2 (1979).

[16] Resolution of the Permanent Council of the Organization of American States, On Solidarity with the Bolivian People, CP/RES308 (432/80), July 25, 1980; GA Res. AG/RES.484(X-0/80), OAS Doc. OEA/Ser.P, AG/Doc.1350/80, rev. 1 (December 4, 1980), p. 31.

Still, the OAS's most dramatic actions purporting to support democracy – its suspension of Cuba's membership in 1962 and willingness to give multilateral cover to the US invasion of the Dominican Republic in 1965[17] – were essentially instances of Cold War politics under US leadership, not repeated thereafter. The main work of protecting democracy and human rights fell to the Inter-American Commission.

The Santiago Commitment thus marks a potential turning point for the OAS. Its political organs are now committed to protecting democracy, at least against its overthrow, rather than leaving the matter to more apolitical bodies. Indeed, if the Inter-American Commission takes the advent of democracy throughout the region as a cue to concentrate on adjudicating individual cases, as its then-Chairman suggested in 1996,[18] the task of protecting democracy and human rights on a systematic basis may fall almost exclusively to the OAS's political organs.

In part this shift reflects an increasing recognition that the overthrow of democratic government is not a purely domestic matter. Still, it seems unlikely that it would have come about had it not been for an unusual circumstance in 1991: virtually all the member States had some kind of constitutional democracy, though of varying depth and stability. Recently emerging from military rule, many States now viewed regional support for democracy as a necessary bulwark against another coup. Their sense that democracy remained at risk soon proved correct. A coup in Haiti in September 1991 and a "self-coup," or *autogolpe*, in Peru in 1992 threatened to extinguish democracy in those countries. Venezuela suffered coup attempts in 1992 and 1993, and there may have been efforts to plan a coup in 1995.[19] Guatemala's President attempted an *autogolpe* in 1993. Paraguay nearly suffered a coup in 1996, and a military coup seemed a realistic possibility in Ecuador in 1997.

In sharp contrast to its practice throughout most of its history, the

---

[17] Exclusion of the Present Government of Cuba from Participation in the Inter-American System, MR.E. Res. VI, OAS Meeting of Consultation of Ministers of Foreign Affairs, 8th mtg., OEA/Ser.F/II.8.OAS Doc. 68, O.14(1962). *See* M. Margaret Ball, *The OAS in Transition* (Durham, N.C.: Duke University Press, 1969), pp. 458–66, 471–80.

[18] Assessment of Democracy and of the Leadership of the Secretary General of the OAS, Press Release No 7/96, *in Annual Report of the Inter-American Commission on Human Rights 1996*, OEA/Ser.L/V/II.95, Doc. 7 rev. (March 14, 1997), p. 805. For the contrary view of a former Chairman, see Tom Farer, "The Rise of the Inter-American Human Rights Regime: No Longer a Unicorn, Not Yet an Ox," *Hum. Rts. Q.* 19 (1997), 545.

[19] *See* Miriam Kornblith, "Public Sector and Private Sector: New Rules of the Game," *in* Jennifer McCoy, Andés Serbin, William C. Smith, and Andrés Stambouli eds., *Venezuelan Democracy Under Stress* (New Brunswick, N.J.: Transaction Publishers, 1995), pp. 77, 85–86; Stephen J. Schnably, "The Santiago Commitment as a Call to Democracy in the United States: Evaluating the OAS Role in Haiti, Peru, and Guatemala," *U. Miami Int.-Am. L. Rev.* 25 (1994), p. 395 n.2.

OAS responded to these coups and coup attempts with measures to counter them. The OAS might appear to have much to show for its efforts. Virtually all countries in the Western hemisphere still have elected governments functioning under written constitutions. Aristide was restored to office; the *autogolpe* in Guatemala was foiled; and Fujimori's *autogolpe* was perhaps not as successful as he had hoped. Threatened coups in other countries have not materialized.

This record might be taken as a heartening development in the recent emergence of an internationally defined right to democracy.[20] That conclusion would, however, be premature. Effective protection against coups requires firm diplomatic pressure from the outset, not the mixed signals the OAS has sometimes sent. Moreover, purely regional economic sanctions are unlikely to be effective. And the OAS's long history of emphasizing non-intervention makes it unlikely that it would ever authorize military force, if indeed it has the power to do so without Security Council approval.[21]

The OAS's actions may also have significance for constitutional law, in the sense of internationalizing it to some extent. That is, the Santiago Commitment represents a conclusion that it makes little sense to treat a coup as an internal matter and then regard the "dirty wars" that follow as an international wrong. In that sense the internationalization of human rights entails a right to democracy. But it turns out that judging whether an interruption of constitutional democracy has occurred requires far more detailed and potentially intrusive *international* interpretation of a country's constitution than one might expect. While it may seem obvious that the military overthrow of an elected president violates the rule of law, there is no easy way to confine international condemnation to such classic cases. If, for example, a president with military backing dissolves congress and shuts down the courts without any apparent textual basis, has there been a coup worthy of international condemnation? A negative answer would clear the way for *autogolpes*. An affirmative answer would require international organizations and other countries to differ with the government's interpretation of its own constitutional law; the OAS would need some way to distinguish violations of the constitutional order from political struggles between branches of government. Even where it might seem clear that there has been an interruption (as in the case of a classic military coup),

---

[20] *See* Gregory H. Fox, "The Right to Political Participation in International Law," *Yale J. Int'l L.* 17 (1992) p. 539; Thomas M. Franck, "The Emerging Right to Democratic Governance," *Am. J. Int'l L.* 86 (1992), p. 65.   [21] UN Charter, Art. 53(1).

moreover, restoring the elected government provides the occasion for similar sorts of interpretive practices.

Perhaps this phenomenon argues for a primarily regional rather than international approach to protecting democracy. Social, political, cultural, and legal traditions are more likely to vary globally than regionally. Interestingly, Latin American constitutions have often been modeled on the US constitution.

That conclusion may be too sanguine. There is less of an interpretive community within the OAS than one might think: profound differences distinguish the US and Latin American constitutional traditions.[22] Further, the vast disparity of power between the US and other members makes the OAS a peculiar kind of regional organization, one whose aims are likely to include, for the foreseeable future, "containment" of US influence. That aspect may work against the kind of closeness that would be needed to develop anything like a regional transnational constitutional law. Moreover, States tend to view the aim of protecting democracy and human rights in light of their own interests. The more the practice of asserting detailed interpretations of other countries' constitutions comes to be viewed as legitimate, the greater the risk that more powerful States will simply enjoy an added opportunity to pursue their own particular foreign policy aims under the guise of promoting democracy. Thus in 1965 the OAS justified its transformation of US invasion forces in the Dominican Republic into an "Inter-American Force" by proclaiming that it was "charged with the responsibility of interpreting the democratic will of its members."[23] There is also a danger that international or regional organizations and their member States will tend to emphasize a partial conception of democracy, one that downplays the importance of meaningful participation in politics, economics, and social life.

These considerations indicate that the Santiago Commitment and the actions taken to implement it should be carefully examined and not merely celebrated as additional steps on the road to democracy. Section II sets out and analyzes the instruments that make up the Santiago Commitment. Section III recounts the OAS record since 1991. Section IV evaluates the OAS record, concluding that while the Santiago Commitment makes a constructive contribution to the protection of

---

[22] Keith S. Rosenn, "The Success of Constitutionalism in the United States and its Failure in Latin America: an Explanation," *U. Miami Int.-Am. L. Rev.* 22 (1990), p. 1.

[23] Meeting of Foreign Ministers (Tenth), Doc. 78 Rev. 6 Corr. (July 21, 1966), pp. 3–4, in Ball, *OAS in Transition, supra* note 17, pp. 475–76.

democracy, it also carries dangers of its own. Those dangers might best be dealt with by calling on other actors to carry some of the burden – whether the UN or sub-regional groups like MERCOSUR.

II THE SANTIAGO COMMITMENT

A *The adoption of the Santiago Commitment*

In 1991 and 1992, the OAS took three steps to help make "[s]trengthening representative democracy" and "[p]romoting the observance and defense of human rights" throughout the region central aims of the organization.[24] The first was the General Assembly's adoption on June 4, 1991, of the Santiago Commitment to Democracy and Renewal of the Inter-American System. This resolution tied support for democracy and human rights to a number of other aims: alleviating extreme poverty and inequality, defending human rights, liberalizing trade, protecting the environment, and eliminating traffic in illegal drugs. It also linked these commitments to an institutional aim – making the OAS a "political forum for dialogue" within the hemisphere and an "effective voice" globally. Finally, it committed the General Assembly to "adopt efficacious, timely, and expeditious procedures to ensure the promotion and defense of representative democracy."

The General Assembly adopted Resolution 1080, "Representative Democracy," the next day. Resolution 1080 declares that one of the OAS's "basic purposes . . . is to promote and consolidate representative democracy, with due respect for the principle of non-intervention." Noting that democracy remains under threat in the region, the Resolution

instruct[s] the Secretary General to call for the immediate convocation of a meeting of the Permanent Council in the event of any occurrences giving rise to the sudden or irregular interruption of the democratic political institutional process or of the legitimate exercise of power by the democratically elected government in any of the Organization's member States, in order, within the framework of the Charter, to examine the situation, decide on and convene an

---

[24] Santiago Commitment, June 4, 1991. On earlier (rejected) proposals for a commitment to respond to coups, *see* Schnably, "Santiago Commitment," *supra* note 17, p. 400 n.18; Kathryn Sikkink, "Reconceptualizing Sovereignty in the Americas: Historical Precursors," *Hous. J. Int'l L.* 19 (1997), p. 705. For subsequent affirmations of the OAS's new position, *see* Declaration of Managua for the Promotion of Democracy and Development, June 8, 1993, *in* Thomas Buergenthal and Dinah Shelton, *Protecting Human Rights in the Americas: Cases and Materials*, 4th edn. (Kehl, Germany: N. P. Engel 1995), p. 504; Declaration of Belém do Pará, AG/DEC. 6 (XXIV-O/94).

ad hoc meeting of the Ministers of Foreign Affairs, or a special session of the General Assembly, all of which must take place within a ten-day period.[25]

It is then up to Ministers of Foreign Affairs or the General Assembly to "look into the events collectively and adopt any decisions deemed appropriate, in accordance with the Charter and international law."[26]

The third step was taken in December 1992, when the General Assembly approved the Protocol of Washington, an amendment to the OAS Charter. The Protocol, which entered into force in October 1997, provides that a State "whose democratically constituted government has been overthrown by force may be suspended" from participation in the OAS by a two-thirds vote of the member States. This sanction may be imposed only "when the diplomatic initiatives pursued by the Organization with the object of facilitating the restoration of democracy in the affected Member States have been unsuccessful." It does not relieve the member of its obligations under the Charter, nor does it preclude the OAS from undertaking further diplomacy to restore democracy. It takes a two-thirds vote of the General Assembly to reinstate a suspended member.[27]

The Protocol is the most unsettled aspect of the OAS's new stance because it has not yet been invoked. At best, its invocation could represent a considered judgment that maximum isolation would prove an effective sanction for a particular illegal regime. At worst, suspension may amount to little more than "a manifestation of despair" that all other efforts to restore democracy have failed.[28] If suspension means that a democratic government in exile is no longer allowed to participate in OAS functions, the Protocol may prove a double-edged sword.[29]

---

[25] Representative Democracy, AG Res. 1080 (XXI-0/91), OEA/Ser.P, OAS Doc. AG/RES.1080 (XXI-0/91) (1991) para. 1.   [26] *Ibid.* para. 2.

[27] *See* Texts Approved by the General Assembly at its Sixteenth Special Session in Connection with the Amendments to the Charter of the Organization, OEA/Ser.P, OAS Doc. AG/doc.11 (XVI-E/92) (1992) (Article 8 *bis*) (Article 9 of the amended Charter).

[28] Working Document Presented by Ambassador Bernardo Percias Neto, Chairman of the Special Committee on Amendments to the Charter, at the Meeting on July 22, 1992, OEA/Ser.G, CE/CARTA-2/92, July 22, 1992, p. 4, *in* Report of the Special Committee on Amendments to the Charter, OEA/Ser.G, CP/doc.2311/92 rev. 1, October 15, 1992, App. 1, p. 14 [Rep. Spec. Comm.].

[29] Article 9 states simply that "[a] Member" in which there has been a coup "may be suspended from the exercise of its right to participate" in specified OAS functions. Argentina suggested that the overthrown government could nevertheless work with the "agency responsible for monitoring the situation" in that country. Statement by the Permanent Representative of the Argentine Republic at the Meeting of the Special Committee on Amendments to the Charter on September 24, 1992, OEA/Ser.G/, CE/CARTA-19/92, Sept. 25, 1992, p. 9, *in* Rep. Spec. Comm., *supra* note 28, App. 9, p. 195. *See also* Comments on the Preliminary Draft Articles on Suspension and the Elimination of Extreme Poverty, OEA/Ser.G, CE/CARTA-21/92 rev. 2,

What does seem clear is that the Protocol was not intended to displace the two previous resolutions. Indeed, the requirement that all diplomatic efforts to restore democracy be exhausted before it is first invoked means that Resolution 1080 will continue to be central to the OAS's response.[30] Because the Protocol and the earlier resolutions are so closely related, I will refer to them all collectively as the "Santiago Commitment."

The Santiago Commitment poses two fundamental questions. First, what is "democracy" – or, in the words of Resolution 1080, the "democratic political institutional process or . . . democratically elected government"? Second, what constitutes a "sudden or irregular interruption" of that process or of the "legitimate exercise of power" by a democratic government?

B The meaning of the "democratic political institutional process"

One definition of democracy focuses on free elections and the necessary conditions thereto, including the absence of significant repression or bias in favor of government-sponsored candidates.[31] But Resolution 1080 may require more. It refers to the "democratic political *institutional* process" and to interruptions in the "*legitimate* exercise of power" by the democratic government. These words might suggest that the government must not only be elected, but constitutional, governing under legitimate procedural and substantive constraints.[32]

But even elections and constitutionalism may not exhaust the definition of democracy under the Santiago Commitment. The Santiago resolution acknowledges the importance of fighting "extreme poverty" as essential to "the promotion and consolidation of democracy in the

---

Footnote 29 (*cont.*)
    Oct. 16, 1992, p. 3, *in ibid.*, App. 10, p. 205 (OAS may invite suspended member to attend as observer); Special Committee on Amendments to the Charter, Suspension of Nondemocratic Governments from the Organization of American States: Some Preliminary Issues (Chairman's Working Paper), OEA/Ser.G,CE/CARTA 4/92, 14 Aug. 1992, pp. 2–3, *in ibid.*, App. 2, pp. 20–21; Statement by the Ambassador Permanent Representative of Uruguay at the Meeting of the Special Committee on Amendments to the Charter, held on September 3, 1992, OEA/Ser.G/, CE/CARTA 15/92, Sept. 24, 1992, p. 3, *in ibid.*, App. 6, p. 167.

[30] *See* OAS Charter Amendment (Document Prepared by the Permanent Mission of Canada), OEA/Ser.G, CE/CARTA 13/92, Sept. 23, 1992, at p. 1, *in* Rep. Spec. Comm., *supra* note 28, App. 5; Statement by the Permanent Representative of Chile, During the Meeting of the Special Committee on Amendments to the Charter, Held on September 17, 1992, OEA/Ser.G, CE/CARTA 27/92, Oct. 6, 1992, *in ibid.*, App. 13, p. 300.

[31] *E.g.*, Samuel Huntington, *The Third Wave: Democratization in the Late Twentieth Century* (University of Oklahoma Press, 1991), pp. 5–10.

[32] Brad R. Roth, "Evaluating Democratic Progress: a Normative Theoretical Perspective," *Ethics & Int'l Aff.* 9 (1995), pp. 55, 73.

region."[33] The Protocol of Washington states that the "elimination of extreme poverty is an essential part of the promotion and the consolidation of representative democracy."[34] Similarly, the General Assembly declared in 1992 that extreme poverty is "inimical to the strengthening, consolidation and defense of democracy."[35] Thus there are grounds for concluding that the Santiago Commitment affirms a more substantive conception of democracy.

The Santiago Commitment does not say why extreme poverty is inimical to democracy, but one likely reason is its effect on civil and political rights, including the right to participate in government. As the Inter-American Commission has noted:

Popular participation, which is the aim of a representative democracy, guarantees that all sectors of society have an input during the formulation, application, and review of national policies. . . . [T]he implementation [of economic, social, and cultural rights] creates the condition in which the general population is able, *i.e.* is healthy and educated, to participate actively and productively in the political decision-making process.[36]

Greater equality may also increase the ability of popular participation to have an effect – to be meaningful. Governments tend to favor the rich; the greater the degree of inequality, the more pronounced the tendency.

Of course, a concern for lessening equality might be too ambitious in this context. Our concern is not democracy in the abstract, but when and how the OAS should react to coups and other interruptions of democracy. A focus on elections may lend itself more readily to enforcement measures like selective accreditation of diplomatic missions or election monitoring;[37] when the enforcement measure is an emergency response to a coup, a complex definition of democracy may be even less useful. A narrower definition may have merit in other respects, too. One might entertain serious doubts about the democratic nature of "delegative democracies" in Latin America – in which "whoever wins election to the presidency is thereby entitled to govern as he or she sees fit, subject only by the hard facts of existing power relations and by a constitutionally limited term of office."[38] It does not follow that the OAS should do nothing after a coup in such States.

---

[33] Santiago Commitment, June 4, 1991, para. a.
[34] OAS Charter Art. 3(f); Arts. 2(g), 33, 116 (modifications by Protocol of Washington).
[35] Declaration of Nassau, AG/DEC1 (XXII-0/92) (May 19, 1992), § I[para. 8].
[36] *Annual Report of the Inter-American Commission on Human Rights 1993*, OEA/Ser.L/V/II.85, doc. 9, rev. (Feb. 11, 1994), pp. 519, 521–522.
[37] *See* Fox, "The Right to Political Participation," *supra* note 20.
[38] Guillermo O'Donnell, "Delegative Democracy," *J. Democ.* 5 (1994), pp. 55, 59.

Still, whatever the meaning of democracy for purposes of implementing the Santiago Commitment – a matter that can be explored fully only after examining the OAS's actions – it seems appropriate to resort to a broader definition in *evaluating* it. That is the only way to gauge to what extent the project is worthwhile. If the best the Santiago Commitment can do is protect formal parliamentary democracy, that is by no means meaningless, but its limitations are surely relevant to any assessment.

Consequently, I will proceed on the assumption that any judgment as to what the Santiago Commitment has accomplished or may achieve in the future should consider two aspects of democracy. The first is what I will call "constitutional design" – a set of institutional specifications that ensure that the State is accountable and governed by the rule of law. These specifications include matters such as periodic elections, some balance of power within the government, judicial independence, and enforceable rights for individuals and groups. The second is popular participation, which can take the form of a vibrant civil society, flourishing social movements, an unfettered press, autonomous trade unions, and the like, and which entails some efforts to address persistent, fundamental inequalities in land ownership or other forms of wealth.

C What constitutes an interruption of democratic government

Too narrow a reading of the notion of an interruption of democratic government might diminish the usefulness of the Santiago Commitment; too broad an interpretation might open the way for its use "to penalize a given socioeconomic system based on ideological considerations," as the Argentine delegate put it when the Protocol was being drafted.[39] The language of the instruments, however, provides no clear guidance.

Certainly both Resolution 1080 and the Protocol cover classic military coups. The Protocol refers to the "overthrow[ ] by force" of a democratic government.[40] And there is some indication in the Protocol's drafting history that the reference in Resolution 1080 to the "sudden or irregular interruption of the democratic political institutional process" was best exemplified by a military coup.[41]

---

[39] Statement by the Argentine Republic, Sept. 25, 1992, p. 5, *in* Rep. Spec. Comm., *supra* note 28, App. 9, p. 191.
[40] *Ibid.* (suspension should be invoked in narrower circumstances than Resolution 1080).
[41] Statement by Caricom during the Meeting of the Special Committee on Amendments to the Charter, Held on October 6, 1992, OEA/Ser.G, CE/CARTA 29/92, October 7, 1992, p. 6, *in ibid.*, App. 15, p. 317; Statement by the Argentine Republic, Sept. 25, 1992, pp. 4–5, *in ibid.*, App. 9, pp. 190–91.

Both Resolution 1080 and the Protocol may encompass more than coups. An *autogolpe* would also seem to constitute an "interruption" of the democratic political process under Resolution 1080. In addition, the Resolution refers to the interruption of "the legitimate exercise of the power of a democratically elected government." The Caricom delegation maintained that the event to which that phrase refers "need not be a coup, nor need it have the result of overthrowing a government."[42] One might even argue that the Protocol itself is not limited to coups. Logically, it would be possible to regard the military-backed illegal dissolution of the legislature as an "overthrow" – a subversion – of democracy by force. Further, because some measures aimed at restoring democracy (e.g., economic sanctions) are far more intrusive than simple suspension from the OAS, it would be ironic to read the Protocol more narrowly than Resolution 1080.

Other resolutions sweep even more broadly. In the Declaration of Asunción, the OAS referred to "all forms of intervention that interfere with the free expression of the popular will."[43] In the Declaration of Nassau, the OAS condemned "any attempt against the democratic institutional order" in a member State.[44]

The potential breadth of these concepts creates its own dilemmas, as an example from Peru shows. Article 112 of the 1993 constitution does not permit a second successive reelection to the presidency. That would seem to bar President Fujimori from running for a third term in 2000, because he was elected to a second term in 1995 after first winning office in 1990. On August 23, 1996, however, the Fujimori-dominated Congress enacted a "Law of the Authentic Interpretation of Article 112 of the Constitution," which provided that Fujimori's 1995 victory was not a "reelection" under Article 112 because his first election as president had taken place before a referendum approved the 1993 constitution.

In January 1997, the seven-member Constitutional Tribunal, with four judges abstaining, ruled the August 1996 law "inapplicable" to Fujimori. Congress, in turn, impeached the three judges who constituted the plurality. Critics of the three judges charged them with exceeding a law preventing the court from invalidating legislation unless six members vote to do so – a law the Inter-American Commission had earlier criticized as resulting in the upholding of laws "that are clearly

---

[42] *See* Statement by Caricom, October 7, 1992, p. 6, *in ibid.*, App. 15, p. 317.
[43] Declaration of Asunción, AG/RES 1064 (XX-0/90).
[44] Declaration of Nassau, AG/DEC1 (XXII-0/92) (May 19, 1992), para. 5; *ibid.* para. 4 (resolving to "develop OAS mechanisms to . . . complement" Resolution 1080).

unconstitutional."[45] The plurality had determined that only a simple majority of those voting was needed because the court was simply ruling the law inapplicable rather than invalidating it.[46]

Was the impeachment a "sudden or irregular interruption of the democratic political institutional process or of the legitimate exercise of power by the democratically elected government"? The action was widely seen as an unprincipled effort to ensure that nothing stand in the way of a third term for Fujimori. The president of the Tribunal resigned in protest, and the US ambassador called the impeachment a step backwards for democracy. The Inter-American Commission expressed the hope that the Tribunal "reinitiate . . . its normal function as soon as possible, while being guaranteed due respect for its independence, impartiality and autonomy."[47]

On the other hand, neither the Secretary-General nor the Permanent Council took a public stand. In response to criticism of his silence, the Secretary-General stated that he could deal only with military coups, not "real or perceived congressional coups," which, he said, posed difficult questions of domestic constitutional law. He continued: "Eventually, it could be convenient to seek an agreement between member countries to point out clearly which actions beyond military rebellions the OAS should consider a break of constitutional rule . . . But, so far, nobody has raised that issue."[48]

Whether a greater specification of this sort would be desirable or even possible is an open question. The text of the Santiago Commitment itself cannot provide a definitive answer. The beginnings of an answer must be sought in the OAS's practice.

III IMPLEMENTING THE SANTIAGO COMMITMENT

A The coup in Haiti

On September 29, 1991, the Haitian military ousted President Jean-Bertrand Aristide, who had been elected by a landslide in December

---

[45] Int-Am. Comm'n H.R., *Annual Report 1996, supra* note 18, pp. 743–44.
[46] Human Rights Watch/Americas, "Torture and Political Persecution in Peru," 9(4B) (Dec. 1997), pp. 17–19; Jo-Marie Burt, "Unsettled Accounts: Militarization and Memory in Postwar Peru," *NACLA Rep. on the Americas* 32(2) (Sept.-Oct. 1998), pp. 35, 38–39; "Peruvians Protest Fujimori's Authoritarianism," *Wash. Rep. on the Hemisphere* 17(10) (July 5, 1997), p. 5; "Peru's Democratic Turmoil," *Wash. Rep. on the Hemisphere* 18(6) (May 1, 1998), p. 1; "OAS Non-Confrontational," *Wash. Rep. on the Hemisphere* 17(11) (July 15, 1997), p. 1.
[47] Jose Puertas, "OAS Wraps Up Summit with Criticism for Peru, Debate on China," *Agence France Presse* (June 5, 1997).
[48] Andres Oppenheimer, "OAS Chief's Silence Irks Peruvians," *Miami Herald* (June 16, 1997), 8A.

1990.[49] The Permanent Council condemned the coup the next day. On October 3, 1991, the Foreign Ministers recognized Aristide's government as the only legitimate one, and recommended that member States suspend diplomatic relations with the military government, end economic and military aid to Haiti, and break all commercial ties. On October 8, 1991, the Foreign Ministers urged member States to freeze the Haitian government's assets and impose a trade embargo – a recommendation which the US and other OAS members accepted.

Until the UN imposed a world-wide embargo on oil and arms shipments to Haiti in June 1993, however, this relatively forceful start – and the OAS's subsequent diplomatic efforts – accomplished virtually nothing. From the military's point of view, there was little reason to negotiate seriously over Aristide's return. For one thing, the OAS trade embargo appears to have had very little effect. The fact that it was imposed by a regional organization limited its effectiveness; European countries continued to trade with Haiti, supplying it with oil. And the United States' own trade with Haiti actually increased between 1992 and 1993.

Moreover, the US sent mixed messages to the military. It was far from clear that it genuinely desired Aristide's return, having long feared (correctly or not) that he might press for radical reforms. Thus it signaled very public doubts about his human rights record, one far better than that of the governments that preceded him or the military regime that had overthrown him. It also consistently lent credence to an inaccurate portrayal of Aristide as having ruled by mob violence.

Equally important, the US gave the impression that its main interest was in avoiding a refugee crisis. With President Bush's "Kennebunkport Order," issued May 23, 1992, and reaffirmed when President Clinton took office, the US appeared to insulate itself from one major effect of the Haitian military's brutality. Under the Order all Haitian refugees were interdicted at sea and forcibly returned without any attempt to determine whether they were political refugees.

President Clinton's election brought a new push for a settlement. In December 1992, the OAS Foreign Ministers sought UN involvement. On June 16, 1993, after months of inconclusive negotiations with the military, the Security Council imposed an embargo effective June 23

---

[49] For a more detailed account, with citations to the relevant OAS and UN resolutions and other documentation, *see* Schnably, "Santiago Commitment," *supra* note 19, pp. 418–60. *See also* Domingo E. Acevedo, "The Haitian Crisis and the OAS Response: A Test of Effectiveness in Protecting Democracy," *in* Lori Fisler Damrosch, ed., *Enforcing Restraint: Collective Intervention in Internal Conflicts* (New York: Council on Foreign Relations Press, 1993), p. 119.

prohibiting the shipment of oil and weapons to Haiti, and requiring all States to freeze Haitian government funds in their territories.

The UN embargo appeared to bear fruit on July 3, 1993, when negotiations on Governors Island in New York culminated in an agreement to resolve the crisis. Under the Governors Island Agreement, Aristide would name a prime minister, subject to confirmation by Parliament, after which the embargo would be suspended. General Raoul Cédras, head of the army, would retire in favor of an Aristide appointee, with full amnesty granted to coup leaders and supporters. Aristide would return to Haiti on October 30, 1993. An international police force would be stationed in Haiti, and an international aid program amounting to $1 billion over five years would be instituted.

A new cabinet was confirmed on August 25, 1993, under the leadership of an Aristide appointee, after which the UN and the OAS suspended their sanctions. The new government never gained effective control. Indeed, a mob organized by the Haitian army prevented the *USS Harlan County* from docking at Port-au-Prince on October 11, 1993, as it brought UN troops to Haiti. Though the oil embargo was reinstituted on October 18, the military remained intransigent, and Aristide was unable to return on October 30.

Little progress was made until March 1994, when Aristide formally gave the US six months' notice of his cancellation of the US–Haitian agreement on which the US based the Kennebunkport Order. In the following months, the Clinton Administration modified the Order, announcing that it would now give refugees hearings on board US ships or at other sites in the Caribbean rather than summarily return them. Shortly thereafter, the number of those fleeing Haiti skyrocketed. In early July the US declared that any Haitians who qualified for asylum would be kept indefinitely in Panama or at other sites in the Caribbean. A sharp drop in the number of refugees soon eased the United States' immediate predicament, but the crisis impelled the US to approach the problem with renewed vigor.

Acting on US initiative, the Security Council imposed a full trade embargo on Haiti on May 6, 1994, effective midnight May 21, 1994. On July 31, 1994, the Security Council authorized military intervention by a multinational regional force. On September 15, 1994, President Clinton announced that the Haitian military must relinquish power or be forced out. US troops entered Haiti on September 19, following a last-minute agreement, reached under threat of imminent invasion, between the Haitian military and a delegation led by former President Jimmy Carter.

By the second week of October, 20,000 US troops had arrived and General Cédras had left for exile in Panama. President Aristide returned to Haiti on October 15, 1994, marking a real triumph for the United States, the UN, and the OAS.

Since then, Haiti's fortunes have been mixed. Aristide abolished the military and turned over his office on February 7, 1996, to an elected successor, René Preval. In December 1997, UN peacekeeping troops left Haiti, although a small number of US troops and a UN civilian police force remained. On the other hand, Haiti's political system has been paralyzed for over a year starting in 1997. Legislative elections were held on April 6, 1997; the Lavalas Family, a new party formed by Aristide, did well enough to raise the prospect of taking control of the Senate after the run-off elections. But only around 5 percent of eligible voters participated, in part because opposition parties boycotted the election. The Lavalas Political Organization (OPL), which had dominated the parliament, claimed that the April balloting was marred by fraud and threatened to boycott run-off elections scheduled for June 15. The run-offs were postponed pending the appointment of a prime minister to replace Rosny Smarth, who resigned in June 1997. The dispute over what to do about the April 1997 elections, together with the OPL's view that Preval's nominees have been too close both to Preval and to Aristide, has left the prime minister's office vacant. The impasse has held up at least $150 million in foreign aid.

B *The* autogolpes *in Peru and Guatemala*

1 *Peru*

On April 5, 1992, President Alberto Fujimori dissolved Congress, closed the courts, and suspended the constitution.[50] He also briefly instituted media censorship, arrested some journalists and opponents of his regime, and took steps to replace the members of the Supreme Court and other judges. He cited the need to fight drug trafficking, terrorism, and corruption in Congress and the courts.

---

[50] For an account of the *autogolpe*, with citations to relevant OAS resolutions and other documentation, see Schnably, "Santiago Commitment," *supra* note 19, pp. 460–69. *See also* David Scott Palmer, "Peru: Collectively Defending Democracy in the Western Hemisphere," *in* Tom Farer, ed., *Beyond Sovereignty*, *supra* note 2, p. 257; Philip Mauceri, "State Reform, Coalitions, and the Neoliberal *Autogolpe* in Peru," *Lat. Am. Res. Rev.*, 30(1) (1995), p. 7. *See generally* Cynthia McClintock, "Presidents, Messiahs, and Constitutional Breakdowns in Peru," *in* Juan J. Linz and Arturo Valenzuela, eds., *The Failure of Presidential Democracy* (Baltimore, Md.: The Johns Hopkins University Press, 1994), pp. 360, 369.

The *autogolpe* was popular domestically, because of the perceived threat from the Shining Path and because many Peruvians had lost confidence in the courts and legislature. Still, the US immediately denounced Fujimori's actions, suspended aid, and indicated that it would oppose any further loans from international financial agencies. On April 13, 1992, the OAS Foreign Ministers strongly deplored the coup and demanded that Peru show progress by the next month toward the restoration of democracy, though they did not call for sanctions.

International condemnation appeared to have some effect. Fujimori soon released some jailed opposition leaders and journalists. At the Foreign Ministers' meeting in Nassau in May 1992, he personally promised to convene an elected constituent assembly within months. In response, the Foreign Ministers again declined to impose sanctions, though they did urge the return of representative democracy to Peru as soon as possible.

The "Democratic Constitutional Congress," elected in November 1992, was not meant to be an assertive body. It had no power to nullify any of Fujimori's decrees after the *autogolpe*. The two major parties boycotted the November election; Fujimori's candidates won a majority. The constituent assembly's draft constitution, which greatly increases the power of the executive, was approved by a narrow margin in a referendum on October 31, 1993.

Fujimori's efforts quickly bore fruit internationally. In June 1992, the Foreign Ministers ended the monitoring of Peru they had begun the previous April. Aid restrictions were soon lifted as well.

Whether the OAS's conclusion that Peru had essentially returned to democracy was justified remains unclear. Fujimori depends heavily on the military, human rights violations continue on a widespread scale, the independence of the judiciary is largely compromised, and the government shows signs of political intolerance. A law passed in June 1995 gave amnesty to military and civilian officials for human rights violations committed since 1980.

2 Guatemala

Guatemala has had an elected government since 1986 (though the military remained largely free from civilian control in its fight against a long-running guerrilla insurgency). Like Fujimori, Jorge Serrano Elias – Guatemala's second elected president since 1986 – was elected as an outsider with little connection to established political parties. In May 1993, some members of Congress charged that Serrano had bribed legislators to secure approval of a controversial increase in electricity rates in anticipation of privatizing the electric utility. On May 25, 1993, Serrano suspended the constitution and dissolved Congress, the Constitutional Court, the Supreme Court, and the offices of attorney general and human rights ombudsman, instituting rule by decree.[51] He also attempted unsuccessfully to detain the ombudsman, Ramiro de León Carpio, placed other political figures under house arrest, and instituted censorship.

Serrano's actions triggered immediate domestic opposition, as demonstrators took to the streets and members of the legislature met secretly to condemn the coup. A coalition of business leaders formed a civilian movement that included some unions and popular groups, and negotiated with the military over resolution of the crisis. The media defied the government's censors. The Supreme Electoral Tribunal refused to endorse Serrano's announced plans for new elections, and the Constitutional Court refused to accept its dissolution, instead ruling Serrano's actions to be illegal.

International reaction was equally swift. The US and other countries denounced the coup, which was widely compared to Fujimori's *autogolpe*. The US suspended aid to Guatemala and threatened to withdraw certain trade preferences. The EC and its member countries also suspended or threatened suspension of aid, as did Japan – actions of particular concern to Guatemala's export business sector.

On May 25, 1993, the Permanent Council condemned the coup and called for the immediate reestablishment of democratic institutions. It sent the Secretary-General to Guatemala to prepare a report to be presented at the next meeting of the Foreign Ministers, scheduled for June 3, 1993. The Secretary-General met with the military and business leaders during his visit, explaining the adverse consequences that would follow if the *autogolpe* succeeded.

The military, which had initially supported Serrano's actions, began to distance itself from them. It negotiated an agreement to back Serrano's plan for elections and a return to constitutional rule so long as members of the Congress he had previously dissolved would endorse it.

---

[51] For an account of the crisis, with citations to relevant OAS resolutions, see Schnably, "Santiago Commitment," *supra* note 19, pp. 470–82. *See also, e.g., La Crisis Político-Constitucional de Guatemala: Del Golpe de Estado de Jorge Serrano a la Presidencia Constitucional de Ramiro de León Carpio* (Guatemala City: Instituto Centroamericano de Estudios Políticos, 1993); Francisco Villagrán de León, "Thwarting the Guatemalan Coup," *J. Democ.*, 4(4) (Oct. 1993), p. 117; Harry Beleván and Nelson Mello e Souza, *Cambio y Continuidad: Conversaciones con João Baena Soares* (Mexico: Fondo de Cultura Económica, 1995), p. 38.

This they failed to do, despite Serrano's resort to bribery.[52] On June 1, 1993, a week after Serrano seized power – and only two days before the OAS Foreign Ministers were scheduled to meet – the military forced him from office in the face of massive demonstrations.

Under the settlement originally reached, Vice-President Gustavo Espina Salguero, who had supported Serrano's *autogolpe*, was to preside until Congress met and then resign so that Congress could choose a new president. Instead, Espina announced that he would now rightfully remain as president. The US State Department was largely noncommittal over Espina's bid for power, though it maintained its suspension of aid pending resolution of the crisis.

On June 3, 1993, the OAS Foreign Ministers condemned the May 25 coup, but took no action, instead keeping the meeting open and sending the Secretary-General to Guatemala for a second report. The next day, the Constitutional Court ruled Espina ineligible for the presidency on account of his support for Serrano's coup.[53] Under heavy military pressure, Espina abandoned his bid for the presidency. On June 6, 1993, the Congress elected de León the new President.

De León's term was marked by constant political battles with Congress. In August 1993 he called upon all 116 members of the Congress to resign, together with the entire membership of the Supreme Court. His aim was not to force all members of Congress out, but to accomplish a "selective cleansing" of sixteen members considered the most corrupt by the civilian coalition that helped oust Serrano. At least forty deputies refused to cooperate, however, including the sixteen targeted members. De León then called for a non-binding referendum. After various setbacks in court, he agreed with Congress to ask the voters to approve a plan calling for new legislative elections in 1994, with a new Supreme Court selected thereafter and the President's term reduced from five years to four. De León threatened that if the referendum failed, he would take "historic actions to comply with the people's demand for a purge of Congress." In fact, the plan was approved on January 30, 1994, by 84 percent of those who voted, although nearly 80 percent of the electorate failed to turn out.

In Congressional elections held on August 14, 1994, the party led by Efraín Ríos Montt, a right-wing fundamentalist who served as military

---

[52] Maxwell A. Cameron, "Latin American *Autogolpes*: Dangerous Undertows in the Third Wave of Democratisation," *Third World Q.*, 19 (1998), 226. For a slightly different account, see "Leader Ousted in Guatemala," *L.A. Times* (June 2, 1993), A1.
[53] *See* Guat. Const. Arts. 186(a), 268, 272 (1985, amended 1993).

dictator in 1982–83, won thirty-two seats out of the eighty, making it the single largest force. Ríos Montt was elected speaker of the Congress that December. In August 1995, however, he was forced out of that post after the Supreme Court ordered him to stand trial for abusing his authority in attempting to impeach members of the Supreme Electoral Tribunal for disagreeing with him on when elections should next be held. Ríos Montt led in the polls for the 1995 presidential elections, but – as had been the case in the 1990 elections – he was blocked from running for president by a constitutional provision barring coup leaders from holding that office. Alfonso Portillo, whom Ríos Montt then backed, almost won a run-off election on January 7, 1996, gathering nearly 49 percent of the vote.

Despite his narrow electoral mandate, the new president, Alvaro Arzú Irigoyen, announced plans to purge the army of human rights violators. He also proceeded quickly with on-going negotiations aimed at bringing an end to Guatemala's long insurgency. With the help of the UN the government concluded an "Accord for a Firm and Lasting Peace" on December 29, 1996, with the Guatemalan National Revolutionary Unity (URNG).

C Constitutional crises in Paraguay and Ecuador

1 Paraguay

On April 22, 1996, President Carlos Wasmosy – elected in 1993 as the first civilian president in forty years – ordered General Lino Oviedo, head of the army, to step down. Oviedo disobeyed the order, triggering a constitutional crisis. The US embassy immediately supported "Wasmosy's constitutional right to dismiss army commander General Lino Oviedo," and called Oviedo's refusal to accept his removal "a direct challenge to the constitutional order in Paraguay," one that "runs counter to the democratic norms accepted by the countries of this hemisphere."[54] The MERCOSUR countries, speaking through the Brazilian ambassador, also condemned Oviedo's actions.

Oviedo then called on Wasmosy and the Vice-President to resign, with the President of the Senate, third in line of succession,[55] to assume the presidency in what the Brazilian ambassador called a *golpe blanco*. Oviedo's apparent intention was to rule from "under the table," as the

---

[54] Arturo Valenzuela, "Paraguay: the Coup That Didn't Happen," *J. Democ.* 8(1) (Jan. 1997), pp. 42, 48 (quoting communiqué). [55] Paraguay Const. Art. 234 (1992).

opposition leader put it.[56] Wasmosy took refuge in the US embassy, where he reportedly offered to take a "temporary leave from my post as Constitutional President of the Republic of Paraguay, leaving it in the hands of the National Congress." Oviedo rejected the offer.

On April 23, OAS Secretary-General César Gaviria telephoned Wasmosy to offer his support, and then went to Asunción. The Permanent Council met at noon the same day and expressed "full and resolute" support for Wasmosy's government, condemning "the acts that caused an abnormal disruption of the legitimate exercise of power by the democratically elected government." The Council insisted on full support for "the government legitimately established through free and popular expression."[57]

A number of countries declared support for Wasmosy as well. On April 23, the US suspended all military aid to Paraguay, and the White House expressed concern that "democratic rule [be] maintained and that constitutional norms apply."[58] The US ambassador appeared at Wasmosy's side in Asunción as Wasmosy assured the public that he remained in full control. Foreign officials contacted the navy and air force, still loyal to Wasmosy, to offer their support. Foreign ministers of the other MERCOSUR States (Argentina, Brazil, and Uruguay) went to Paraguay, threatening to expel it if there was a coup.

There was also a strong popular reaction within Paraguay. A large demonstration was held in front of the presidential palace on April 23, and congressional leaders expressed support for Oviedo's firing. Despite this strong international and popular support, however, Wasmosy announced that Oviedo had agreed to step down as chief of the military and take up the post of Minister of Defense.[59] International reaction to the arrangement was muted; reaction within Paraguay was not. An immediate public outcry in Paraguay led Wasmosy to withdraw the offer of the Defense Ministry on April 24, 1996.

Oviedo quickly turned to electoral politics, declaring his candidacy for president. In June 1996, he was charged with rebellion and insubordina-

---

[56] See Unidad para la Promoción de la Democracia, *La Crisis Institucional de 1996 en Paraguay* (Washington, D.C., Sept. 1996), p. 11. It is not clear that the Senate President himself was working with Oviedo.

[57] Organization of American States, Annual Report of the Secretary General 1996–97, OEA/Ser.D/III, § I(2) (summarizing resolution); see "OAS Condemns Paraguay Power Struggle," *Deutsche Presse-Agentur* (April 24, 1996).

[58] "OAS Permanent Council Meets on Paraguay," *Xinhua News Agency* (April 23, 1996).

[59] Wasmosy's accommodation may have stemmed from his earlier close association with Oviedo, who had supported his 1993 presidential bid.

tion, conviction for which would bar him from running for President.[60] Nevertheless, on September 8, 1997, he won the Colorado party's nomination for president, and polls showed him leading the race.[61]

In March 1998 a military tribunal sentenced Oviedo to ten years in prison for his role in the coup attempt. Ironically, the prospect that his conviction might be overturned on appeal may have come close to triggering a coup. Shortly before an expected ruling by the Supreme Court, there were widespread rumors that a reversal of his conviction would trigger a coup. Top military officers may have feared that Oviedo would replace them with his own followers if he were elected. Wasmosy himself showed possible signs of interest in an *autogolpe*, perhaps engineering a delay in presidential elections; there were also indications that the government might simply dissolve the Supreme Court and the Supreme Court of Electoral Justice if their rulings favored Oviedo. In response, the US stated that "any interruption in the constitutional order would be severely criticized by the rest of the hemisphere."[62] MERCOSUR members pointedly referred to a newly adopted commitment, undertaken in response to the previous crisis in Paraguay, under which a member may be suspended if there is a "rupture or threat of rupture in [its] democratic order."[63] On April 17, 1998, however, the Supreme Court affirmed Oviedo's conviction. The next day the Supreme Court of Electoral Justice disqualified him from running.

Oviedo's role in politics was far from over, however. His running mate Paul Cubas Grau was named the Colorado's party candidate and was elected on May 11, 1998, on a slogan of "Cubas president, Oviedo to power." Three days after taking office on August 15, 1998, Cubas commuted Oviedo's sentence, plunging Paraguay into another crisis. Cubas claimed the power of commutation under Article 238 of the Constitution and provisions of the Military Penal Code.[64] Legislators

---

[60] Paraguay Const. Art. 236 (1992) (barring coup participant from running for President for two successive terms).
[61] Oviedo's lead may well have stemmed from the Colorado Party's long dominance and the increasing popularity of military officers in politics.
[62] Carlos Montero, "Wasmosy Will Stand His Ground," *Inter Press Service* (April 14, 1998) (quoting Assistant Secretary of State). *See* Anthony Faiola, "Paraguay Faces Ghost of Its Political Past," *Wash. Post* (April 10, 1998), A16.
[63] Declaración Presidencial Sobre Compromiso Democrático en el MERCOSUR, June 25, 1996. *See* Protocolo de Ushuaia sobre Compromiso Democrático en el MERCOSUR, La República de Bolivia y La República de Chile, July 20, 1998, Art. 5 (providing for suspension in case of a break in the democratic order).
[64] "Foreign Ministry Communiqué Defends Oviedo Decree," *BBC Summary of World Broadcasts* (Aug. 21, 1998) (quoting Foreign Ministry Declaration); "President Issues Decree Releasing Gen. Lino Oviedo," *BBC Summary of World Broadcasts* (Aug. 20, 1998) (quoting Presidential Decree 117).

from all parties (including the divided Colorado party) called the action illegal, and both chambers of the National Congress condemned it. The candidate Cubas had defeated termed the commutation a "juridical *coup d'état*" and a "true legal *coup d'état*."[65] Cubas's opponents argued that the commutation power could be exercised only after the Supreme Court had first submitted a "report," and sought a ruling from the Court on the legality of Cubas' action.[66] Still, the military tribunal that had convicted Oviedo – newly staffed with Cubas appointees – vacated Oviedo's sentence. On September 23, 1998, the Supreme Court annulled the military court's order, amidst predictions that Oviedo would soon attempt a coup.

2 Ecuador

Ecuador had its own constitutional crisis in February 1997 (one of many since its return to civilian rule in 1979),[67] when Congress removed President Abdalá Bucaram Ortiz, who had been elected in 1996.[68] Bucaram's earlier history, including his time as mayor of Guayaquil from 1984 to 1985, suggested that both populism and corruption might distinguish his ascension to power. In his brief presidency, however, he cast aside the former while assiduously pursuing the latter. Like Fujimori, Bucaram soon implemented the very austerity programs that he had rejected in his campaign. Unlike Fujimori, he cultivated a theatrical image worthy of his nickname "El Loco."

A forty-eight-hour general strike was called for February 5, 1997, to demand Bucaram's ouster for his austerity policies and corruption. Participation was near universal; civic groups, labor unions, religious groups, and even the Chamber of Commerce urged support. Three of the five previous presidents elected since the return to civilian rule called

[65] "PLRA Says Oviedo's Release 'Illegal'," *BBC Summary of World Broadcasts* (Aug. 20, 1998); "Cubas Faces Impeachment for His Crony's Release," *Inter Press Service* (Aug. 19, 1998).
[66] "Oviedo Freed," *The Economist* (Aug. 22, 1998), 26; "Legislators in Paraguay Move Against President," *N.Y. Times* (Aug. 27, 1998), A11. *See* Paraguay Const. Art. 238(10) (1992)("Based on reports by the Supreme Court of Justice," president "may pardon or commute sentences"). Presidential Decree 117 asserted, to the Court's apparent surprise, that the reporting requirement had been satisfied.
[67] Catherine M. Conaghan, "Loose Parties, 'Floating' Politicians, and Institutional Stress: Presidentialism in Ecuador, 1979–88," *in* Linz and Valenzuela, eds., *The Failure of Presidential Democracy, supra* note 50, p. 328.
[68] For background, see Carlos Larrea and Liisa North, "Ecuador: Adjustment Policy Impacts on Truncated Development and Democratisation," *Third World Q.* 18 (1997), 913; Carlos de la Torre, "Populism and Democracy: Political Discourses and Cultures in Contemporary Ecuador," *Lat. Am. Persp.*, 24(3) (May 1997), p. 12.

for Bucaram's ouster. In response, the Defense Minister, a general, announced that Bucaram had declared a state of emergency. Vice President Rosalia Arteaga Serrano charged the President of Congress, Fabian Alarcón, with planning a coup, and there were rumors that he would be arrested and Congress dissolved. Bucaram later asserted that army commander General Paco Moncayo sought to make himself president, in reaction to Bucaram's opposition to arms purchases and to his efforts to negotiate a peaceful settlement of Ecuador's border dispute with Peru. At Bucaram's request, Secretary-General Gaviria flew to Quito on February 5. Noting "the language of confrontation" then being used, Gaviria voiced "fear that this . . . [would] set back democracy in Ecuador."[69]

The next day, February 6, Congress voted to remove Bucaram for "mental incapacity" under Article 100 of the Constitution, rather than impeach him under Article 82(g), which would have required the legislators to find that Bucaram had committed treason, bribery, or another grave affront to the national honor. Displaying the same thoroughness that Serrano and Fujimori had shown in their *autogolpes*, Congress also removed the attorney-general, the comptroller, and the members of the Constitutional Court.

Bucaram called the vote an attempted coup by Congress and fled to Guayaquil. A political crisis quickly engulfed Ecuador as three people laid claim to the presidency: Bucaram, Alarcón, and Arteaga. Congress voted Alarcón the interim president the evening of February 6, while Arteaga proclaimed herself Bucaram's successor in the early morning hours of February 7. Despite concerns that the military might resolve the crisis by staging a coup, however, the reaction of the OAS and the international community was relatively muted. The Permanent Council did not meet. The US (whose ambassador had openly criticized Bucaram's government for "pervasive corruption" a week before[70]) called for respect for the "country's legal and constitutional order," but did little else. One US official was quoted as explaining, "the law is ambiguous . . . It's not for us to tell the Ecuadorean people how they should interpret their constitution."[71]

---

[69] Diana Jean Schemo, "Ecuadoreans Rally in Drive to Oust President," *N.Y. Times* (Feb. 6, 1997), A10.
[70] Gabriel Escobar, "Army Backs Removal of Ecuadoran," *Wash. Post* (Feb. 9, 1997), A26.
[71] Andres Oppenheimer, "Democracies Stay Out of Ecuador Controversy," *Miami Herald* (Feb. 8, 1997), 20A.

The Ecuadorean military was less modest, and settled Bucaram's fate by announcing on February 8 that it no longer recognized him as President. Under pressure from the military, Ecuador's political leaders negotiated a solution in which Arteaga would be sworn into office, until Congress could elect an interim president, who would in turn call an election in 1998. The day after she was sworn in, however, Arteaga apparently had second thoughts, asserting that the constitution did not allow Congress to elect an interim leader. On February 11, she backed down and Congress approved Alarcón as interim president.

A referendum held on May 25, 1997, approved Bucaram's removal and Alarcón's appointment. The referendum also authorized the creation of a Constituent Assembly to undertake constitutional reform. Headed by former President Osvaldo Hurtado, the Assembly itself proved a source of constitutional instability, including an incident when some members of the Assembly were accused of developing a plan to have it dissolve Congress, dismiss President Alarcón, and replace him with Hurtado. At the end of April 1998, the Assembly decided to extend its mandate a week beyond its term, which was to end on April 30. The government declared that the Assembly had no power to do so; the Assembly responded by proclaiming its supremacy over all the other branches of government.

Bucaram's political fortunes later briefly rose again through his support of Alvaro Noboa, a wealthy businessman running for president on a populist platform. Noboa had close ties to Bucaram, and many of his supporters treated the prospect of Noboa's victory as portending a return to power on Bucaram's part. He lost a close run-off election on July 12, 1998, to Jamil Mahuad, the mayor of Quito.

IV EVALUATING THE SANTIAGO COMMITMENT

The Santiago Commitment has worked in the sense that there has been no successful classic military coup since its adoption. But claims of success must be qualified. The military still often plays an important role behind the scenes. More perplexingly, in Guatemala, Paraguay, Bolivia, and elsewhere, former military dictators have sought or attained power by amassing support within the electorate rather than massing tanks in front of the presidential palace. Is it the ultimate triumph of democracy that former dictators now accept the ballot box as the only road to office? Or is it a sign that constitutional democracy in those countries is simply the continuation of *caudillismo* by other means?[72] Signs of a trend towards election of candidates who stand in for others effectively barred from running – as happened in Paraguay, and nearly happened in Guatemala and Ecuador – suggest that personalism retains a strong grip on politics.

Further, the OAS's response has been tepid at times. While that weakness might stem from the failure in Resolution 1080 or the Protocol to mandate a response,[73] the more fundamental problem is that the OAS has never been a particularly strong organization, and other members' suspicions or fears of US domination may keep it that way. In addition, other foreign-policy aims of the US and other member States may often preclude firm action.

Finally, other factors might have produced the same outcomes without the Santiago Commitment. On the domestic level, business groups may become uneasy with the tendency of some military regimes to become corrupt or too assertive in the management of the economy. Militaries may view acceptance of constitutional democracy as a desirable way to secure international and domestic legitimacy while pinning blame for economic mismanagement on civilians.[74] Internationally, other actors have played a key role at different points – as when the Security Council authorized military force against Haiti's dictators.

If the Santiago Commitment is notable for its qualified successes, it is also remarkable for another, less obvious effect. The OAS record shows a surprising willingness on member States' part to venture into questions of constitutional design, far more so than the Secretary-General's defense of his silence over the firing of the Peruvian justices might lead one to believe.[75] To be sure, the OAS and its members have acted at times as if constitutional questions were purely internal matters. As noted, when Bucaram was removed, the US at first said that only Ecuador could interpret its constitution. When the Guatemalan Vice-President's bid for power was contested, a State Department official maintained only that "[t]he United States is not in a position to

---

[72] *See* "General Accused of Coup Bid in Paraguay Presidential Pick," *Agence France Presse* (Sept. 23, 1997) (remark by Oviedo) ("I'm also going to bring off another coup, but at the polls May 10").
[73] *See* Schnably, "Santiago Commitment," *supra* note 19, pp. 545–55 (evaluating possible reforms).
[74] Catherine M. Conaghan and James M. Malloy, "Business and the 'Boys': the Politics of Neoliberalism in the Central Andes," *Lat. Am. Res. Rev.*, 25(2) (1990), pp. 3, 5–10.
[75] *See* this chapter, § I.C. *supra* note 48.

intervene in that constitutional dispute."[76] The OAS itself took no position on those matters. Paraguay's Foreign Ministry pointedly (if self-servingly) responded to international criticisms of the commutation of Oviedo's sentence by declaring that "the president's constitutional prerogative to commute penalties . . . falls within . . . [Paraguay's] domestic jurisdiction."[77]

These statements do not reflect a general view that constitutional interpretation is an internal matter. In other cases the US or international organizations have been quite willing to engage in just such interpretation. For example, when Alarcón appeared to reconsider his pledge to hold presidential elections in Ecuador in 1998, the US embassy publicly stated that it expected "the elections to take place in 1998."[78] Reversing its earlier hands-off approach, in March 1997 the State Department called Bucaram's removal "constitutionally debatable," asserting that "[it] cannot be seen as having strengthened democracy in the Americas, or be taken as a precedent elsewhere."[79] Similarly, the US, the OAS, and MERCOSUR made it clear that they would regard any resignation by Wasmosy under military pressure as incompatible with Paraguay's constitutional order, and supported Wasmosy's "constitutional right" to dismiss Oviedo. When Aristide criticized the UN mission for failure to disarm paramilitary groups and urged people to help police disarm "the big men with heavy weapons," the head of the UN mission replied: "The Constitution and the law say that it is the police who are responsible for keeping order, and not self-declared volunteers who say they are."[80]

If the Santiago Commitment becomes the occasion for granting legitimacy to what previously would have appeared off-limits – interpreting other countries' constitutions – what effect will that have on efforts to promote democracy in the hemisphere? The question is worth investigating because, as section III makes clear, the events to which the OAS has responded are not always sharply distinguishable from ongoing con-

---

[76] Christopher Marquis, "Confusion Reigns at OAS over Guatemala," *Miami Herald* (June 4, 1993), 10A.
[77] "Foreign Ministry Communiqué Defends Oviedo Decree," *supra* note 64.
[78] Andres Oppenheimer, "Trade Rule Puts Clamp on Partners," *Miami Herald* (March 31, 1997), 6A.
[79] "White House Not Pleased by Ouster," *Miami Herald* (March 24, 1997), 10A (Assistant Secretary of State) ("An outpouring of public anger led an elected congress to remove from office, in a constitutionally debatable manner, an increasingly unpopular but also legitimately elected president").
[80] Larry Rohter, "Haitian Leader's Angry Words Unnerve Elite and Worry Allies," *N.Y. Times* (Nov. 19, 1995), A1.

stitutional struggles for power. I will approach the question in terms of the two aspects of democracy set out earlier: constitutional design and participation.

A Constitutional design

If the OAS were to take the Santiago Commitment as the basis for a regular practice of interpreting other countries' constitutions, one methodology would be to specify a transnational constitutional law – i.e., substantive principles of constitutional law that are necessary for constitutional government anywhere. A second approach would be to insist on constitutional fidelity – to let States design whatever constitutional, democratic order they wish (at least within certain broad parameters), but to insist as a matter of international law that they respect that order.

The OAS's practice over the years does not decisively favor one over the other. Consider the United States' position on Oviedo's candidacy. In September 1997, it pronounced his candidacy "non-democratic."[81] That statement appeared to rest on a view that election of coup leaders is inconsistent with democracy rather than on any particular provision of the Paraguayan constitution. Thus it might seem to reflect a tenet of some implicit transnational constitutional law: Coup leaders should be barred from taking office, even by election. Yet in April 1998 the US signaled it would respect whatever the Paraguayan courts determined as to his candidacy, an approach that more closely resembles constitutional fidelity. Since the record of implementing the Santiago Commitment does not reveal a definitive tilt in favor of either approach, it will be useful to explore both.

1 Transnational constitutional law

One might attempt to work out the substance of constitutional democracy deductively or inductively. An example of the former is the 1959 Declaration of Santiago, affirming representative democracy as the favored form of government in the hemisphere. The Declaration lists some essential attributes of democracy, including elections, the rule of law, separation of powers, fixed terms of office, a free press, individual

---

[81] "General Accused of Coup Bid in Paraguay Ruling Party Presidential Pick," *Agence France Presse* (Sept. 8, 1997). *See* Sebastian Rotella, "In Paraguay, Rough Rider or Running Roughshod?" *L.A. Times* (Oct. 8, 1997), A1 (US ambassador) ("It is practically impossible to understand how a man who tried to stage a military coup is the kind of person who is qualified to be president of a democracy.").

rights, and economic development to provide humane living conditions.[82] The Declaration appears to be the OAS's single most comprehensive resolution on representative democracy.

Many other international law sources might supplement this definition. The Document of the Copenhagen Meeting of the CSCE (now OSCE) refers to free elections at reasonable intervals, a representative government under the rule of law, a "clear separation" of parties and State, civilian control of the military, publicly adopted legislation, individual rights, and guarantees of judicial independence.[83] In May 1992 the OAS urged Peru to return to democracy "within the framework of respect for the principle of separation of powers and the rule of law."[84] Human rights treaties typically guarantee the right to vote and take part in public affairs, together with other rights arguably essential to democracy (e.g., freedom of expression, an independent judiciary, protection against arbitrary government action).[85]

Drawing on these and other instruments and practices, Morton Halperin and Kristen Lomasney argue that a global "Guarantee Clause" modeled after Article IV, section 4 of the US Constitution is emerging.[86] The framers, they point out, considered the establishment of a monarchy in any one State to be incompatible with the union. They argue that the international community has similarly come to regard violations of constitutional democracy as incompatible with the global order – so much so that there is a duty to intervene.

Unfortunately, any attempt to deduce specific features from a general requirement of constitutional democracy is likely to be reasonably contestable. The debate over whether parliamentary or presidential regimes are preferable is one example.[87] The Copenhagen Document takes no position on that debate, saying only that the executive should be

---

[82] Fifth Meeting of the Consultation of Ministers of Foreign Affairs, Final Act, OEA/Ser.C/II.5, at 4–6, *in* Buergenthal and Shelton, *Protecting Human Rights in the Americas, supra* note 24, p. 496. *See* Int.-Am. Comm'n H.R., *Ten Years of Activities 1971–1981* (Washington, D.C.: OAS, 1982), pp. 333–35 (concerning right to participate in government).

[83] Document of the Copenhagen Meeting of the Conference on the Human Dimension of the CSCE, June 29, 1990, para. 5, *in* Arie Bloed, ed., *The Conference on Security and Co-Operation in Europe: Analysis and Basic Documents, 1972–93* (Boston, Mass.: Kluwer Academic Publishers, 1993), pp. 441–44 ["*CSCE Basic Documents*"].

[84] Democratic Reinstatement in Peru, MRE Res. 2/92, OAS Ad Hoc Meeting of Ministers of Foreign Affairs, OEA/Ser.F/V.2, para. 2, OAS Doc. MRE/RES. 2/92 (1992), *in Foreign Pol'y Bull.* (July-Aug. 1992), p. 83.

[85] Int'l Cov. Civ. Pol. Rts., Art. 25; American Convention, Art. 23; Eur. Conv. Prot. Hum. Rts. & Fund. Freed., Prot. No. 1, Art. 3; Afr. Chart. Hum. Peoples" Rts., Arts. 13, 20.

[86] "Toward a Global 'Guarantee Clause,'" *J. Democ.*, 4(3) (July 1993), 60. Article IV § 4 states that the federal government will "guarantee to every State . . . a Republican Form of Government."

[87] *See, e.g.*, Linz and Valenzuela, eds., *The Failure of Presidential Democracy, supra* note 50.

"accountable to the elected legislature or the electorate."[88] Given the wide range of possibilities – Bolivia, for example, has effectively evolved into a hybrid of presidential and parliamentary systems – it is hard to imagine how any such specification could be possible.[89] Similarly, the call to define "republican government" under the Guarantee Clause must be answered either with sonorous generalities or with proposals that would require the federal government to make all sorts of detailed and controversial judgments about State governmental structure.[90]

One might instead take an inductive approach, as the Inter-American Commission on Human Rights appeared to do in ruling that Guatemala's refusal to allow Ríos Montt to run for president did not violate Article 23 of the American Convention, which guarantees the right to participate in government. There was, it found, a "customary constitutional rule with a strong tradition in Central America" that excluded coup participants from running for president. Closely examining a number of Latin American constitutions, it concluded that "any constitutional system of law possesses the right to make its operation more effective and to defend the integrity of its citizens' rights" by limiting eligibility for high office.[91]

This method might seem to allow for both specificity and regional variation. Yet the same potential for reasonable difference that plagues a deductive approach would undercut an inductive one as well. Why should a given "customary norm" of constitutional law be imposed on one State simply because many other States (even those in the same region) have adopted it? Moreover, an inductive approach can be egregiously misleading if the full context is not considered. Thus the Commission cited a 1923 treaty among Guatemala, El Salvador, Honduras, Nicaragua, and Costa Rica as evidence of a regional customary constitutional norm.[92] Article II of that treaty obligated the parties

---

[88] Copenhagen Meeting, June 29, 1990, para. 52, in Bloed, ed., *CSCE Basic Documents*, supra note 83, pp. 439, 441–44.
[89] For differing assessments, see René Antonio Mayorga, "Bolivia's Silent Revolution," *J. Democ.*, 8(1) (Jan. 1997), p. 142; Eduardo A. Gamarra, "Hybrid Presidentialism and Democratization: the Case of Bolivia," in Scott Mainwaring and Matthew Soberg Shugart, eds., *Presidentialism and Democracy in Latin America* (Cambridge University Press: 1997), p. 363.
[90] *See, e.g.*, Arthur E. Bonfield, "The Guarantee Clause of Article IV, Section 4: A Study in Constitutional Desuetude," *Minn. L. Rev.* 46 (1962), 513, p. 560; Note, "A Niche for the Guarantee Clause," *Harv. L. Rev.* 94 (1981), 681, p. 691.
[91] *Ríos Montt v. Guatemala*, Rep. No. 30/93, Case No. 10,804 (Oct. 12, 1993), paras. 29, 38, *in Annual Report of the Inter-American Commission on Human Rights 1993*, OEA/Ser.L/V/II.85, Doc. 9 rev., Feb. 11, 1994, pp. 206, 212, 214.
[92] General Treaty of Peace and Amity, Washington, D.C., Feb. 7, 1923, *in Conference on Central American Affairs: Washington, December 4, 1922–February 7, 1923* (Washington, D.C.: GPO, 1923), pp. 287–95.

to deny recognition to another government not only when it came to power by a coup, but also when the elected president had earlier been involved in a coup or was related to a coup participant, or took office despite being "expressly and unquestionably disqualified by the Constitution."

In the abstract this provision might support an international law norm barring coup leaders. But the Commission gave no real consideration to the fact that the 1923 treaty was promulgated amidst efforts to achieve a Central American federation. One might well expect such treaty obligations to be more intrusive than would otherwise be the case, making its application to States not seeking such a union problematic. Nor did the Commission consider the strong US influence in bringing about the conference that produced the treaty, or US actions that in the eyes of many Central Americans had recently compromised two of the participants' sovereignty with canal-related treaties. That might raise questions as to whether the tradition the Commission found was indeed Central American.[93] If an inductive approach were to have any chance of working, then, it would have to be carried out with careful attention to social, political, economic, and legal contexts.

2 Constitutional fidelity

An alternative would be simply to insist that States remain faithful to whatever constitutional order they design (including prescribed methods of changing that order). This approach might seem to allow for a standard that both respects legitimate variation and offers concrete guidance. To some extent the OSCE takes that approach with regard to public emergencies. Not only must specific treaty requirements be satisfied, the State's own internal restrictions must be followed as well: "A *de facto* imposition or continuation of a state of public emergency not in accordance with provisions laid down by law is not permissible."[94]

Even this more modest approach is problematic. It runs counter to the

---

[93] See Thomas L. Karnes, *The Failure of Union: Central America, 1824–1960* (University of North Carolina Press, 1961), pp. 175–228. For one contemporary view, see William F. Slade, "The Federation of Central America," Ph.D. thesis, Clark University, Worcester, Mass. (n.d.), *in J. Race Development* 8(1) (1917), pp. 79, 267 ("Rather than continue a piece-meal method of extending the provisions of the Platt Amendment over Central America . . . the United States should undertake the federation of Central America and then extend over it the same guardianship as it exercises over Cuba [which the US occupied from 1917 to 1923], Santo Domingo [1916 to 1924], Haiti [1915 to 1934], and Nicaragua [1912 to 1925]"). To be sure, Central American unity has at times engaged the vigorous support of sectors of the population, but the particular way in which it might come about remains crucial.

[94] Document of the Moscow Meeting of the Conference on the Human Dimension of the CSCE, Moscow, Oct. 3, 1991, para. 28.4, *in* Bloed, ed., *CSCE Basic Documents, supra* note 83, pp. 605, 618.

Inter-American Court's treatment of a State's adherence to constitutional norms as a domestic matter.[95] It might also appear to run counter to at least some practice by the OAS. For example, Peru now has a significantly different (and more authoritarian) governmental structure, as well as a new constitution. Neither would have happened without the suspension of Congress and the courts – an action that Fujimori himself proclaimed to be at odds with the constitution in force at the time. Yet, in contrast to Guatemala, the perpetrator of the Peruvian *autogolpe* remains in office. Having bestowed its approval on Peru in December 1992, the OAS might be hard pressed to argue for unbending adherence to constitutional requirements.

The Peruvian example points to what is the most serious problem with simply requiring that democracies adhere to their own constitutional orders. An insistence on constitutional fidelity raises practically all the same issues that would arise in an effort to develop a transnational constitutional law – particularly if one acknowledges that constitutionalism requires more than straightforward readings of, and adherence to, a constitutional text. An analysis of the OAS's experience in implementing the Santiago Commitment show how problematic an insistence on fidelity can be.

First, the conclusion that any given *autogolpe* is illegal is not inescapable. To be sure, the Peruvian constitution of 1979 appeared to deny the president the power to suspend the Senate or the judiciary, and to limit his power to suspend the Chamber of Deputies to certain specific circumstances.[96] Moreover, Fujimori and Serrano both made it clear that they were *suspending* the constitution. But not all future dictators will announce their actions in such helpful terms. And it would not be implausible for an executive to claim a power to suspend the powers of other organs consistent with the constitutional order. Serrano claimed that the constitution permitted him to suspend it, citing Article 21, which provides that the constitution "will not lose its validity and effectiveness regardless of any temporary interruptions resulting from situations involving force."[97] He had not, he insisted, abolished the constitution.[98]

To be sure, Guatemala's Supreme Court of Justice called Serrano's

---

[95] *See* Certain Attributes of the Inter-American Commission on Human Rights, Advisory Opinion OC-13/93, para. 29 (July 16, 1993).
[96] Peru Const Arts. 227, 229, 230, 306 (1979). For an example of the tendency to view the analysis as virtually open-and-shut, see *Peru: Civil Society and Democracy Under Fire* (New York: Americas Watch, 1992), p. 2 n.2.
[97] Guatemala Const. Tit. VIII, Art. 21 (1985, amended 1993). *See* "Pronunciamiento de Jorge Serrano" (25 May 1993) *in La Crisis Político-Constitucional, supra* note 51, pp. 33, 34.
[98] "Mensaje de Jorge Serrano," May 31, 1993, *in ibid.*, at pp. 131, 132.

actions a "flagrant violation of the Constitution"; the day after the *autogolpe* de León, then the human rights ombudsman, specifically rejected Serrano's reliance on Article 21.[99] But how legitimately could the OAS or its members claim to resolve the dispute, given the complexity of any particular constitutional tradition? Enormous shifts have taken place in the relations between the US President and Congress and between the federal government and the states. The constitutional text appears to require that treaties be submitted to the Senate for ratification, whereas in practice treaties and their equivalents are also entered into by the President alone, or by the President with the approval of both houses of Congress. These changes cannot be traced to some particular amendment or amendments to the constitution. Should we celebrate a living constitution or lament a "constitutional *coup d'état*"?[100] For that matter, are formal amendments even necessary? Perhaps changes can be effected by "a mobilized majority of American citizens hammer[ing] out a considered judgment on a fundamental matter of principle," self-consciously rejecting the Article v amendment procedures.[101]

Ecuador's crisis provides a second example. Did Bucaram's removal for mental incapacity violate the constitution? There was no serious suggestion that he was in fact mentally ill or disabled. Still, a former Vice-President argued that a "declaration of 'mental incapacity' for the President does not necessarily refer to craziness as such, but the spirit or letter of the Constitution refers to the loss of faculties to carry out the post."[102] His interpretation was not unprecedented. Manuel Estrada Cabrera, reconfirmed as president of Guatemala three times in rigged elections throughout a dictatorship that lasted from 1898 to 1920, was ousted when his former allies in the Guatemalan Assembly abandoned him in response to a domestic crisis and pressure from the United States. Their chosen means was to declare him mentally incompetent.[103] In February 1976, after an impeachment effort failed, some members of

---

[99] Declaración de la Corte Suprema de Justicia, May 26, 1993, para. 1, *in ibid*, p. 76; Declaración Histórica de la Procuraduría de los Derechos Humanos, May 26, 1993, *in ibid.*, p. 72.

[100] Calvin R. Massey, "The Tao of Federalism," *Harv. J.L. & Pub. Pol'y* 20 (1997), pp. 887, 904. See generally Laurence H. Tribe, *American Constitutional Law*, 2nd edn. (Mineola, N.Y.: Foundation Press, 1988), §§ 4–5, 5–20 to 5–22; Harold Koh, *The National Security Constitution: Sharing Power after the Iran-Contra Affair* (New Haven, Conn.: Yale University Press, 1990), pp. 67–72.

[101] Bruce Ackerman, *We the People: Foundations* (Cambridge, Mass: Belknap Press, 1991), vol. I, pp. 55, 34–57.

[102] "Ecuador Congress Votes to Oust President for 'Mental Incapacity'," *N.Y. Times* (Feb. 7, 1997), A5.

[103] Chester Lloyd Jones, *Guatemala: Past and Present* (New York: Russell & Russell, 1966), pp. 64–68; Rafael Montúfar, *Caída de una Tiranía: Páginas de la Historia de Centro América (Segunda Parte)* (Guatemala: Sánchez & de Guise, 1923), pp. 32–35.

Argentina's congress considered attempting to remove President Isabel Perón on grounds of incapacity.[104] Representative Gerald Ford once offered a sweeping approach to the US Constitution's reference to "high Crimes and Misdemeanors": it means, he said, "whatever a majority of the House of Representatives considers it to be at a given moment in history."[105]

A key question in such cases is how independent other branches will be of the legislature. That the Ecuadorean Congress would prefer a broad interpretation of its powers should not have come as a surprise. In 1995 alone, Congress had impeached three members of the Supreme Court over their decision in a case involving the social security system; removed the Finance Minister for alleged corruption; and forced the resignation of the Vice President. There may be reasons for criticizing Congress's removal of Bucaram, but anything resembling a textual approach will provide only limited help in articulating them.

The succession of crises in Paraguay provides a third example, one that shows the difficulty of distinguishing between easy textual cases and others. It might be tempting, for example, to view the scope of the president's constitutional power to commute a sentence as largely a matter of domestic interpretation – it would not after all be automatically clear to an outsider what exactly Article 238(10) requires by way of prior "reports" from the Supreme Court – while taking it as obvious that the president has the power to remove the head of the military. Indeed, Article 238(9) gives the president the power to "appoint and remove" military officers.[106] This reading may well be the most reasonable and democratic-spirited, but it does not follow inevitably from the text. For example, the same article makes the grant of rank above colonel subject to Senate approval. Might that imply a necessity of Senate concurrence in the removal of generals, an act which necessarily deprives them of their rank?[107]

Similarly, it was widely assumed that if Wasmosy had acceded to Oviedo's call that he resign, constitutional democracy would have been disrupted. Suppose, however, that Oviedo's real aim had indeed been a

---

[104] Juan J. Linz, "Presidential or Parliamentary Democracy: Does It Make a Difference?," in Linz and Valenzuela, *The Failure of Presidential Democracy*, supra note 50, pp. 3, 78 n. 21; "Impeachment Bill Fails in Argentina," *N.Y. Times* (Feb. 26, 1976), 10. *See* James W. McGuire, *Peronism Without Perón: Unions, Parties, and Democracy in Argentina* (Stanford University Press, 1997), p. 168.
[105] US Const. Art. II, § 4. *See* 116 Cong. Rec. H3113–14 (daily edn. Apr. 15, 1970).
[106] Paraguay Const. Art. 238(9) (1992); Art. 173 (subordination of army to State).
[107] The US president's power to appoint cabinet officials is subject to Senate approval. US Const. Art. II, §2 cl. 2. Whether the Senate could thereby restrict the president's removal of cabinet officers was not resolved (in the negative) until Myers v. United States, 272 US 52 (1926).

golpe blanco – using military power to force out the President and replace him with the President of the Senate. It may seem obvious that for the military to decide which elected official will be president (even an official third in line for the presidency) violates the constitutional order. Indeed, at the suggestion of the Brazilian ambassador, Congress approved a resolution that it would not recognize any resignation of Wasmosy or his Vice-President on the ground that a forced resignation was invalid.[108] But then why is it not equally obvious that the constitutional order was breached by the military's role in the succession crises in Guatemala and Ecuador? De León became President of Guatemala because the military, in the face of broad opposition to the *autogolpe*, forced Serrano from office and quashed Vice-President Espina's bid for the presidency. The only real question in Ecuador's succession crisis was whether the military's role would take the form of a coup or behind-the-scenes influence and intermediation. We might distinguish the cases by the degree of influence, or judge whether that influence was brought to bear in ways that might contribute to democratic government in the long run; but nothing like a textual approach will draw that distinction for us.

Fourth, the powers and term of the Haitian presidency are far from evident simply from the text. For example, it was often taken as obvious that President Aristide's term would expire five years after he took office in February 1991, because the Haitian constitution provides for a five year term.[109] Indeed, the US required Aristide to promise not to extend his term beyond February 1996.[110] Yet Haiti's constitution does not provide for the military to force the President into exile and prevent him from carrying out his electoral mandate. The failure to extend Aristide's term beyond February 1996 effectively rewarded the military and the elite that supported it for the coup, and deprived the vast majority of Haitians of the effective leadership of the one individual they most supported. In fact, there was significant support within Haiti for Aristide to extend his term by the amount of time he spent in exile.[111] Similarly, when the impossibility of holding parliamentary elections in December 1994 – soon after Aristide's return – resulted in their being delayed until June 1995, Aristide was left to rule without any parliament for a time. Would it have been a greater violation to extend the terms of the legislators?

---

[108] *La Crisis Institucional de 1996 en Paraguay*, *supra* note 56, p. 11. The account of the Brazilian ambassador's role is somewhat different in Valenzuela, "Paraguay," *supra* note 54.
[109] *See* Haiti Const. Art. 134–1 (1987).
[110] Douglas Jehl, "Clinton Addresses Nation on Threat to Invade Haiti," *N.Y. Times* (Sept. 16, 1994), pp. 1A, 5A; Douglas Farrah, "Aristide Willing to Quit, But Many Want Him to Stay," *Wash. Post* (Oct. 1, 1995), A32.   [111] Farah, "Aristide Willing to Quit," *supra* note 110, A32.

One might reply that Haiti's history creates real concern that a leader might win an election and then find one way or another to stay in office indefinitely. Further, with the abolition of the military, there was no need to deter future generals from staging coups. Finally, one might argue, it was important to have a transition from one elected president to another to consolidate democracy.

Resolving these questions requires a careful weighing of the harm to democracy from eviscerating Aristide's presidency against the dangers of extending his term. The need to make such judgments cannot be avoided by broad admonitions to respect the text without considering the context, including violations as blatant as a coup. The unavoidability of such judgments undermines any claim that Haiti's constitutional order was simply "restored."

The long political impasse that has deprived Haiti of a prime minister since June 1997 provides a final example. Parliament has repeatedly declined to ratify nominees submitted by President Préval. Some Haitians have argued that so long as a presidential nominee meets basic requirements of eligibility (e.g., citizenship, residence, age), parliament is constitutionally required to confirm the candidate. That is one possible reading of the constitutional requirement that "the President's choice must be ratified by the Parliament." Another is that whomever the president nominates must secure parliament's consent before taking office. The underlying issue, of course, is the relative power of the president and the legislature.[112]

The inability of a straightforward textualism to tell us when a constitutional order has been breached does not make constitutional interpretation a meaningless exercise. The problem is that it is too meaningful. To decide whether a State has adhered to its own internal order requires venturing into fundamental – and contested – questions about the kind of order it *should* have. Interpretation, in short, is a form of constitutional design.

3 Discretion in constitutional design
Not surprisingly, then, the OAS and its members have not made any definitive choice in favor of either transnational constitutional law or constitutional fidelity. Whatever approach comes to predominate, it seems clear that States will tend to accord each other significant discretion: there

---

[112] Haiti Const. Art. 137 (1987); Art. 157 (eligibility requirements). *See* "Political Paralysis Persists in Haiti," *Wash. Rep. on the Hemisphere* 18(17) (Sept. 25, 1998), 7. *Cf.* Powell v. McCormack, 395 US 486 (1969).

can be no *a priori* specification of constitutional design for all States at all times. In turn that implies that the OAS and its members will have the opportunity to exercise discretion as they protect or restore constitutional governments elsewhere. What that opportunity portends for the participatory aspect of democracy is the remaining question.

B Participation and constitutional design

Constitutional structures can be designed to foster or discourage popular participation in varying degrees. In part, there may need to be limits on the majority in order to protect individual rights. There is almost always likely to be more at stake in the design of constitutions, however. The US experience is instructive. Jennifer Nedelsky has argued that, although genuinely committed to democracy, the framers assumed that there would always be a propertyless majority. That majority, they believed, would constantly threaten the security of the propertied elite even though, in the framers' view, any significant redistribution of property (e.g., through debtor relief laws) would harm everyone over time by undermining the development of a national economy. The belief that it was impossible to rely indefinitely on persuading the majority to refrain from undermining the security of property profoundly influenced their design of government. The framers sought at every turn to minimize the effect of popular participation, creating multiple layers of government, large election districts, and indirect, staggered elections. "The message," Nedelsky writes, "would be that ordinary people were not the sort to understand the issues of politics. They were competent only to grant or withhold their consent, approve or reject the actions of an elite."[113]

One might see a similar dynamic at work in regard to current questions of constitutional design. As the framers had a vision of commerce and manufacturing over agriculture as the main engine of growth, so today civilian elites and the military within Latin America have their own prescription for development. Along with decisionmakers in the US and international financial institutions, they are typically committed to the structural adjustment programs promoted by Western donor countries and international financial institutions. In their view these programs, with features like privatization, eliminating price controls and supports, cutting welfare spending, decreasing tariffs and barriers to

---

[113] Jennifer Nedelsky, *Private Property and the Limits of American Constitutionalism: The Madisonian Framework and Its Legacy* (University of Chicago Press, 1990), p. 205.

international capital flows, and reducing labor rights, will produce the conditions for long-term economic growth.[114] These elites, moreover, appear equally committed to representative democracy both as a matter of ideology and self-interest; the rule of law is important both to business investment and to human rights.[115] Reconciling these two commitments is not a simple matter for elites that assume that an impoverished majority would, if given the opportunity, reject structural adjustment programs because of their harsh effects or undermine them by failing to support them consistently. The result is a conception and practice of politics that downplays popular participation.[116]

The intersection between participation and constitutional design can take many forms, some of which seem more amenable to democracy than others. Take the general question of the role of the state in economic life. Privatizing enterprises and reducing regulations may reduce the ability of a democracy to respond to popular mandates; thus neo-liberal restructuring may limit sharply the significance of popular participation. One sign of those limits is that while the range of candidates for high office now spans conventional politicians, former dictators, self-styled populists, erstwhile theoreticians of the left, and even former guerrillas, policies implemented by elected governments in Latin America typically have strong similarities in their acceptance of some variation on the standard package of neo-liberal reforms – even when, as in Ecuador and Peru, the candidates were elected on a platform rejecting such policies. A politics in which very little is up for grabs is not the strongest basis for consolidating democracy.

A second intersection can be found in the question of executive powers and term limits. Term limits may undercut an executive's power by precluding an indefinite stay in office. Yet in the context of broad decree powers (as in the case of Ecuador), their consequences can be quite different. Osvaldo Hurtado, president from 1981–84, saw little need to consult Congress or persuade the people in implementing an

---

[114] See John Williamson, ed., *Latin American Adjustment: How Much Has Happened?* (Washington, D.C.: Institute for International Economics, 1990); Susanne Jonas, *The Battle for Guatemala: Rebels, Death Squads, and US Power* (Boulder, Colo.: Westview Press, 1991), pp. 83–84, 226–33.
[115] See The World Bank, *From Plan to Market: World Development Report 1996* (Oxford University Press 1996), pp. 87–97.
[116] For critical expositions of this phenomenon, see Guillermo O'Donnell, "Do Economists Know Best?" in Larry Diamond and Marc F. Plattner, eds., *The Global Resurgence of Democracy*, 2d edn. (Baltimore, Md.: The Johns Hopkins University Press, 1996), p. 336; Laurence Whitehead, "International Aspects of Democratization," in Guillermo O'Donnell et al., eds., *Transitions from Authoritarian Rule: Comparative Perspectives* (Baltimore, Md.: The Johns Hopkins University Press 1986), pp. 313–18; see also Beleván and Souza, *Cambio y Continuidad*, supra note 51, pp. 76–78, 94–95.

austerity program, hoping only that the people would come to see the benefits of his policies over the long run:

> You can imagine what would happen if I would have subjected economic policy to debates within the party! No political party would have ever approved of the kind of economic policy I undertook... I did not want economic policy in the hands of people who would politicize it. Economic policy is so difficult, complex, and costly (in political terms) that I did not want an opposition to form to the policy because it was directed by party people.[117]

Thus term limits are deeply ambiguous. One would expect this ambiguity to affect the reaction of other member States to "*continuismo*" – evidenced in the (sometimes unsatisfied) desire of the presidents of Brazil, Peru, Panama and possibly Argentina to overcome constitutional limits on reelection. Their response is likely to be influenced as much by concerns over what enhanced participation would mean for the ability of a president to carry out structural adjustment programs as by a desire to limit *continuismo*.

Haiti shows that questions of constitutional design and participation could not be avoided by confining the Santiago Commitment to classic military coups. Consider two ideas that one might take deductively to be essential elements of a constitutional democracy: a balance of power and the rule of law. It would be hard to dispute these general principles. In seeking to restore Haiti's elected government, however, the US unavoidably went well beyond them. Interestingly, viewed as a matter of constitutional design, its actions appear contradictory; taken as an example of a tendency to resolve questions of constitutional design in ways that minimize the perceived threat that popular participation might pose to the economic policies the US would like to see implemented, its actions appear more consistent.

Thus during Aristide's exile and after his return, the US often pressured him to agree to work more closely with the legislature. It urged him to adopt policies more in line with what the legislature would want, and draw members of the government more broadly than from his own party. It also urged him to prevent or discourage his supporters from mobilizing to pressure the parliament. In effect, the US sought to make Aristide's return to power dependent upon a particular balance of power between the executive branch and the legislature, one that would limit Aristide's scope of action.

The US, however, has not shown any general preference for strength-

---

[117] Conaghan, "Loose Parties," *supra* note 67, pp. 349–50 (quoting 1986 interview with Hurtado).

ening legislatures at the expense of executives. While it has tended to do so in certain contexts,[118] it has been quick to discard the preference in others. When de León used a demand for the mass resignation of the Guatemalan legislature and Supreme Court as a way of forcing out sixteen legislators, the US and the OAS did not condemn him. Nor did they do so when, as a January 1994 referendum neared, he publicly hinted that he would carry out his own congressional purge if the voters rejected his proposed constitutional reforms. Even de León's threat to bring the Guatemalan people to the streets to force the "cleansing" of the legislature evoked no condemnation from the US government. And there was no condemnation from the US when, shortly thereafter, he threatened to "appeal to the people" if the Guatemalan Congress proceeded with charges against him of ignoring judicial orders.

Indeed, if "disputes in parliament are the lifeblood of democracy," as Secretary of State Albright remarked,[119] the US has seemed most content with a particularly anemic version of parliamentary democracy since democracy was restored. One result – and perhaps one of the causes – of the parliamentary paralysis that currently plagues Haiti has been the absence of serious debate over privatization. Aristide did little to promote such a debate after his return, and his governments took the necessity of implementing neo-liberal reforms as a given.[120] Whether he could have chosen differently is unclear. He was under great pressure from the US and other lenders and donors to implement such a program. In October 1995, for example, when Aristide was still president, hints that the government was less than fully committed to privatization led the US to withhold aid to Haiti, provoking a run on the Haitian gourde and a political crisis that resulted in the resignation of Prime Minister Smarck Michel.[121]

In any event, it would be pointless to criticize the US for failing to have the same policy on struggles between legislatures and executives everywhere. No one balance of power between the executive and the legislature can be labeled the only democratic one. In fact, even now there is

---

[118] Thomas Carothers, "Democracy Assistance: The Question of Strategy," *Democratization* 4(3) (1997), pp. 109, 113–14.
[119] Stanley Meisler, "On Rush Visit, Albright Calls for Compromise in Haiti," *L.A. Times* (Oct. 18, 1997), A6.
[120] Michel-Rolph Trouillot, "A Social Contract for Whom? Haitian History and Haiti's Future," *in* Robert I. Rotberg, ed., *Haiti Renewed: Political and Economic Prospects* (Washington, D.C.: Brookings, 1997), pp. 47, 54.
[121] Larry Rohter, "Haitian Leader's Angry Words Unnerve Elite and Worry Allies," *N.Y. Times* (Nov. 19, 1995), p. 1; Mark Weissbrodt, "Structural Adjustment in Haiti," *Monthly Rev.* (Jan. 1997), pp. 25, 32–33.

no "presidency" or "legislature" in Haiti in the meaningful sense of long-established institutions with particular histories and relationships between them. De León's continuing struggles with the Guatemalan legislature equally demonstrate the institutional fluidity that marks the early stages of any effort to establish a constitutional government. Ecuador's continuing fights between the executive and the legislature show that even in their most extreme form – e.g., impeachment – the conflict can be endemic. Similarly, the obvious need to ensure the physical safety of members of parliament cannot translate into a general ban on popular mobilization to pressure it. Demonstrations are as much a part of democracy as are parliamentary debates and contests between the president and the legislature.

Particularly viewed in light of its insistence that Aristide step down in February 1996, the United States' actions are best understood as a preference for a constitutional design that minimized the dangers that popular participation might pose to privatization and other reforms. The US viewed Aristide as a radical with little desire to carry out such reforms. The legislature during Aristide's term was widely perceived to be more conservative, having been elected with much less of a popular mandate than Aristide himself received.[122]

In context, then, there was no contradiction between forcing Aristide to agree to work more closely with the legislature while simultaneously attempting to head off a serious legislative debate over economic policy: They were two means to the same end. Or, in Nedelsky's terms, they reflected a view that treated ordinary people "formally as the foundation [of] and, in practice, as a problem" for democracy.[123] By creating a sense that it makes little difference who is elected, the implementation of this view has likely made no small contribution to the near collapse of interest in voting for parliamentary seats in Haiti.

V CONCLUSION

In adopting the Santiago Commitment, the OAS determined that no military should ever displace a constitutional government. In those terms it has so far succeeded. Equally interesting, member States, particularly the US, appear to have taken the Santiago Commitment as the basis for offering their own interpretations of other members' constitutions.

[122] Schnably, "Santiago Commitment," *supra* note 19, p. 542 n.580.
[123] Nedelsky, *Private Property*, *supra* note 113, p. 205.

Of course, the question of what in fact motivates State actions is complex. When the US insisted that Aristide leave office in February 1996, it may have done so simply because it wanted him out of power sooner rather than later, and believed that framing its position in terms of the Haitian constitution would be the most diplomatic approach. When the US cast doubt on the validity of Bucaram's removal, its assertion may have simply represented a calculation, phrased in terms of Ecuadorean constitutional law, as to what best promotes stability in Latin America. Still, whatever States' motivations may be, the practice itself can have an impact. The willingness of the Inter-American Commission to pronounce on constitutional matters in Guatemala and Peru might reflect in part the legitimacy granted the practice by the Santiago Commitment.

Whether this development is to be welcomed remains to be seen. The history of anti-democratic intervention by the US in Latin America and the Caribbean gives reason for concern. Further, while it would be premature to draw firm conclusions about how States will behave, the prevailing wisdom about both structural adjustment and majorities' willingness to approve it at the polls may tend to push States towards interpretations that minimize the participatory aspect of democracy, though of course the actions of the OAS and its members are only one factor in the design of a given State's constitutional order.

Still, the dilemma is unavoidable. To reject entirely the legitimacy of international interpretation of other countries' constitutions is to reject the Santiago Commitment itself. As Haiti shows, *any* implementation of the Santiago Commitment, even in response to military coups, inevitably entails some willingness to tell a State how to interpret its own basic law. The question is one of degree. The more undemocratic a domestic act appears to be, as in the case of a coup, the easier it may be to condemn it, because we may assume that the international community is protecting the popular will (though majorities may sometimes choose authoritarian rulers). Conversely, the more the break appears to be a colorably interpretive act by an official or body with some electoral legitimacy, the greater will be the perception of intrusiveness if the international community responds.

If anything is clear, it is that OAS members are not likely to answer the Secretary-General's musings about the scope of the Santiago Commitment with "an agreement between member countries to point out clearly which actions beyond military rebellions the OAS should consider a break of constitutional rule." From States' perspective, the danger is that any such undertaking would provide a standard by which to criticize them as they interpret other countries' constitutions. This concern might suggest that human rights NGOs and less political intergovernmental actors like the Inter-American Commission should set out to create such detailed guidelines on their own.

That would be a mistake. Constitutional design is too fluid, too tied to each country's own history, culture, politics, and economics, to make such a venture successful, at least beyond broad generalities that would provide little guidance. A more varied approach would be preferable. Substantively, it might be useful to push the OAS to extend the Santiago Commitment beyond coups and *autogolpes* to a few selected problems that pose threats to constitutional democracy on a recurrent basis. For example, given that more than a few elected presidents have transformed themselves into dictators, it might not be desirable to deem all questions relating to eligibility for the presidency beyond the scope of the Santiago Commitment. That is not to say that human rights advocates should adopt a simple position on the matter – e.g., in favor of term limits. Suppose, however, that Fujimori had simply proclaimed that Article 112 of the Peruvian Constitution did not bar him from running for a third term, without involving Congress. The lack of any involvement by the legislative branch might bolster the case that the Santiago Commitment had been violated.

Institutionally, the danger of greater US intervention into other countries' affairs may make it preferable not to place the entire burden of regional efforts to protect democracy on the OAS. Thus, while not without their own flaws, sub-regional groups that do not include the US may prove a useful counterweight; MERCOSUR's role in Paraguay in 1996, and its subsequent adoption of its own version of the Protocol of Washington, provide a good example. The UN and the European Union (particularly with regard to trade preferences) also have a role to play.

In the end, the Santiago Commitment forces us to consider basic questions about the nature of international efforts to protect democracy. That the future will provide new occasions for working out its meaning is, unfortunately, a fairly safe prediction. Paradoxically, the more the Santiago Commitment succeeds – the more it helps keep the military in the barracks – the more subtle and difficult will be the questions it poses.

CHAPTER 6

Government networks: the heart of the liberal democratic order

Anne-Marie Slaughter

The new world order proclaimed by George Bush proved notable primarily for its absence. It was proclaimed, rhetorically at least, as the promise of 1945 fulfilled, a world in which international peace and security were guaranteed by international institutions, led by the United Nations, with the active support of the world's major powers. It was a liberal internationalist prototype of a world government, cast in the image of domestic political order. Such an order requires a governmental monopoly on force, a centralized rule-making authority, a clear hierarchy of institutions, and universal membership.

That world order is a chimera. Even as an ideal, it is unfeasible at best and dangerous at worst. Many international institutions have a vital role to play in regulating world politics, but they are destined to remain servants of their member States more than masters. The United Nations cannot function effectively independently of the will of the major powers that comprise it; those powers, in turn, will not cede their power and sovereignty to an international institution. Efforts to expand independent supranational authority, from the UN Secretary General's office to the Commission of the European Union to the World Trade Organization, have been carefully circumscribed and have produced a backlash and a determined reassertion of power by member States.

The leading alternative to liberal internationalism is "the new medievalism," a "back to the future" model of the twenty-first century. Where liberal internationalists see States as the primary subjects of international rules and institutions, the new medievalists proclaim "the end of the nation-state."[1] Less hyperbolically, Jessica Mathews describes a power shift away from the State – up, down, and sideways to supra-State,

[1] Jean-Marie Guehenno, *The End of the Nation-State* (Minneapolis, Minn.: London University of Minnesota Press, 1995); Kenichi Ohmae, *The End of the Nation State: The Rise of Regional Economies* (New York: The Free Press, 1995).

sub-State, and, above all, non-State actors.[2] These actors have multiple allegiances and global reach.

This power shift is in turn part of a larger paradigm shift in optimal organizational form: from hierarchy to network, centralized compulsion to decentralized voluntary association. Both shifts are rooted in the information-technology revolution, in technology that simultaneously empowers individuals and groups and decenters and diminishes traditional authority. The result is not world government, but "global governance." If government denotes the formal exercise of power by identifiable and discrete institutions, governance denotes cooperative problem-solving by a changing and often uncertain cast of concerned actors. The result is a world order in which global governance networks link Microsoft, the Catholic Church, and Amnesty International to the European Union, the United Nations, the Catalonians, and the Quebecois.

What has been largely overlooked by both sides in this debate is the emergence of a transgovernmental order: a dense web of relations among domestic government institutions − courts, regulatory agencies, executives, and even legislatures.[3] A new generation of international problems − terrorism, organized crime, environmental degradation, money laundering, bank failure and securities fraud − provide the incentives for such relations. In response, government institutions have created networks of their own, ranging from the Basle Committee of Central Bankers to informal links among law enforcement agencies to cross-fertilization of judicial decisions. They have institutionalized transgovernmentalism as a mode of international governance.

From this perspective, the State is not disappearing; it is disaggregating. Government officials and institutions participating in transnational government networks represent the interests of their respective nations, but as distinct judicial, regulatory, executive, and legislative interests. They respond to and interact with the growing host of non-State actors; they can link up with their sub-State and supranational counterparts. Disaggregation provides flexibility and networking capacity, while preserving the fundamental attributes of Statehood − links to a defined ter-

---

[2] Jessica T. Mathews, "Power Shift," *Foreign Aff.* 76 (1997), p. 50.
[3] Mathews argues that whereas "[b]usinesses, citizens organizations, ethnic groups, and crime cartels have all readily adopted the network model," governments "are quintessential hierarchies, wedded to an organizational form incompatible with all that the new technologies make possible." *Ibid.* at p. 52. Not so. Disaggregating the state into its component government institutions makes it possible to create functional networks of institutions engaged in a common enterprise even while they represent distinct national interests.

ritory and population and a monopoly on the legitimate use of force. That is the core of State power, power that remains indispensable for effective government at any level.

So what has all this to do with democracy and international law? This emerging transgovernmental order is concentrated among liberal democracies. It is thus a fundamental dimension of what John Ikenberry and others have described as the "liberal democratic order" – the set of relationships among predominantly Western industrialized nations.[4] The strongest link between transgovernmentalism and liberal democracy is the capacity for quasi-autonomous activity on the part of different government institutions. The norm of separation of powers that is a basic bulwark of individual liberty in these systems encourages the development of relatively strong and independent domestic institutions. Courts, regulatory agencies, executives, and legislatures all have distinct interests and the means to pursue them, although the balance of relative power and distinct identity differs in parliamentary and presidential systems. Further, the presumption of peace among liberal democracies – not the absence of conflict but the certainty that it will not escalate into a military confrontation – removes the security threat that has traditionally been the major incentive for adopting a unified foreign policy stance.

More fundamentally, for members of the liberal democratic order and for many States linked to it, the disaggregated State *is* the State. Different government institutions performing their functions at home and abroad are not simply different faces or facets of some mythical unitary State; they are the government, both domestically and – increasingly – globally. To enter into treaties requires action by the executive and the legislature, at least in most countries; ideally the courts will also be involved in interpreting and applying the resulting treaty obligations. Customary international law, on the other hand, may involve only the executive. But disaggregated institutions acting quasi-autonomously with their counterparts abroad are generating a growing body of rules and understandings that stand outside traditional international law but that nevertheless constitute a dense web of obligations recognized as binding in fact. The result is a new generation of international law – transgovernmental law – that is a critical component of the liberal democratic order and an important element in strategies for expanding that order.

The liberal democratic order is the core of the Clinton

---

[4] G. John Ikenberry, "The Myth of Post-Cold War Chaos," *Foreign Aff.* 75 (1996), pp. 79–80.

Administration's revision of liberal internationalism, returning it in part to its Wilsonian roots. The substitution of "enlargement" for "containment" as the leitmotif of American grand strategy envisions a steadily expanding community of liberal democracies. To achieve this vision, as this volume demonstrates, will require reliance on international institutions as well as many non-governmental organizations best encompassed by the new medievalist vision. Moving from the realm of heuristic models to the far more practical exigencies of policy recommendations, it is immediately apparent that traditional liberal internationalism, new medievalism, and transgovernmentalism are ultimately complementary: three paradigms focusing on different parts of the same elephant.

Nevertheless, transgovernmentalism constitutes a critical dimension of the liberal democratic order that can ameliorate and compensate for deficiencies in both old and new strategies. For instance, "enlargement" through embracing specific institutions in transgovernmental networks can sidestep the often thorny problem of labeling countries wholesale as democracies or non-democracies. A transgovernmental approach focuses instead on the nature and quality of specific judicial, administrative, and legislative institutions, whether or not the governments of which they are a part can be labeled a liberal democracy. Regular interaction between these institutions and their foreign counterparts offers less public and potentially more effective channels for the transmission of norms of democratic accountability, governmental integrity, and the rule of law. It may ultimately be possible to disaggregate the many complex elements of democratic legitimacy in ways that permit more nuanced and contextual strategies for democratization.

Similarly, the process of interaction among government institutions from nations around the world helps mediate some of the culture clashes that seem inevitably to attend a direct focus on defining and promoting democratic governance. Contrary to Samuel Huntington's gloomy predictions,[5] existing government networks include courts from Zimbabwe to India to Argentina and financial regulators of various kinds from Japan to Saudi Arabia. The functions these institutions perform offer a vital bridge across cultural boundaries while simultaneously allowing for broader input into the development of genuinely international standards.

More generally, transgovernmental mechanisms of liberal democratic norm diffusion are simultaneously more specific and more inductive

---

[5] Samuel Huntington, "The West: Unique, Not Universal," *Foreign Aff.* 75 (1996), p. 44.

than the top-down methods of international law. While efforts to define and legislate "democratic procedures" in various areas will gradually embed themselves in national consciousnesses over the long term, they also afford easy targets for nationalist and cultural opposition. A simultaneously and equally active effort to strengthen government networks as a critical horizontal structure of order can complement vertical efforts and arguably provide a more effective means to the same end.

The challenge, however, is to ensure that government networks are themselves legitimate modes of global governance. In theory, transgovernmentalism offers a model of world order that is potentially more accountable and more effective than either of the current alternatives. But it is a theory that is likely to prove very challenging to translate into practice.

On the one hand, traditional liberal internationalism poses the prospect of a supranational bureaucracy, answerable to no one. The new medievalist vision, on the other hand, depicts individuals answering to multiple overlapping authorities both above and below current State governments. It is thus attractive to a wide range of constituencies, appealing equally to States' rights enthusiasts and supranationalists. But it could easily reflect the worst of both worlds. Supranational authorities may well be too far from the individual to be properly accountable, while local or even regional authorities are likely to be too close to be properly neutral.

Transgovernmentalism, by contrast, assumes that the primary actors in the international system continue to be State actors – the same institutions that perform domestic government functions. These institutions exercise the same power as they do at home – the power that makes government so much more effective than "governance." Yet transnational and ultimately global government networks offer the same advantages of flexibility and decentralization that NGO and corporate networks do. Government institutions participating in these networks interact constantly with these non-State actors, both as regulators and as targets of lobbying and litigation efforts. They can also forge links with their supranational and subnational counterparts, creating the potential for truly global government networks.

But critical questions remain. In practice, are the decisions and decision-making processes in government networks consistent with basic liberal democratic values? This question is typically posed as one of accountability, but courts and regulatory agencies operating at home are not directly accountable. However, they are subject to a host of constraints designed to ensure their actual and perceived legitimacy: reporting requirements, internal professional norms, carefully specified decision-making procedures, and opportunities for external review. Do those constraints operate equally on transgovernmental activity?

These questions can only be posed and answered once actual government networks have been mapped and fully understood. In the end, however, government networks can only be the heart of a liberal democratic order if they themselves constitute liberal democratic government.

I GOVERNMENT NETWORKS

A transgovernmental order is actually emerging, readily visible to those whose eyes are not blinkered by traditional "billiard ball" models of State interactions. Judges, regulators, heads of State, and even legislatures are forging links with their foreign counterparts, links designed to produce more than cosmetic cooperation. In some instances these government actors have formed their own institutions, sidestepping lengthy negotiations and formal treaty ratification procedures in favor of flexible charters and working rules that permit both selectivity and speed. Bilateral and plurilateral arrangements also coexist, resulting in overlapping regulatory networks, negotiating fora, and patterns of judicial and legislative cooperation that encompass different countries in different issue areas.

A Transnational judicial networks

National and international judges are networking. They are becoming increasingly aware both of one another and of their engagement in a common enterprise. Global relations among these judges fall into three principal categories: cross-fertilization of judicial decisions; active cooperation among courts of different countries and between national and supranational courts in the solution of disputes; and direct communication on problems of common concern under the auspices of emerging regional judicial organizations.

1 Cross-fertilization of judicial decisions
The most informal and passive level of transnational judicial interaction is the cross-fertilization of ideas through increased knowledge of both foreign and international judicial decisions and a corresponding willing-

ness actually to cite those decisions as persuasive authority. The Israeli Supreme Court, the German Constitutional Court, and the Canadian Constitutional Court have long researched US Supreme Court precedents in reaching their own conclusions on constitutional issues such as freedom of speech, privacy rights or fair process. Young constitutional courts in Eastern and Central Europe and the former Soviet Union are now eagerly following suit. The paradigm case in this regard is a recent decision by the South African Supreme Court.[6] In finding the death penalty unconstitutional under the South African Constitution, the Court cited decisions from national and supranational courts all over the world, including Hungary, India, Tanzania, Canada, Germany, and the European Court of Human Rights.

Why should a court in Israel, India, South Africa, or Zimbabwe cite a decision by the United States Supreme Court or the Canadian Supreme Court or the European Court of Human Rights as a consideration in reaching its own conclusion? Decisions rendered by courts outside a particular national judicial system can have no actual precedential or authoritative value. They can have weight only due to their intrinsic logical power or because the court invoking them seeks to gain legitimacy by linking itself to a larger community of courts considering similar issues.[7] In fact, national courts have become increasingly aware that they and their foreign counterparts are often engaged in a common constitutional enterprise, attempting to delimit the boundaries of individual rights in the face of an apparently overriding public interest and the boundaries of State power in the face of the conflicting interests of other States. To take only one example, the British House of Lords recently delivered a direct rebuke to the US Supreme Court regarding its decision upholding the kidnapping of a Mexican doctor by US officials determined to bring him to trial in the United States.[8]

Nor is such cross-fertilization limited to Commonwealth countries, though it is perhaps most concentrated there. The South African Supreme Court looked to both civil and common law systems. The European Court of Justice (ECJ), which is composed of civil and common law judges, frequently looks to US Supreme Court decisions,

---

[6] *See* S. v. Makwanyane, 1995 (3) SA 391 (CC). *See also* Lawrence R. Helfer and Anne-Marie Slaughter, "Toward a Theory of Effective Supranational Adjudication," *Yale L.J.* 10 (1997), p. 371.
[7] *See* Anne-Marie Slaughter, "A Typology of Transjudicial Communication," *U. Rich. L. Rev.* 29 (1994), pp. 122–29.
[8] R. v. Horseferry Road Magistrates for the Court Ex. P. Bennett (Number 2); R. v. Horseferry Road Magistrates for the Court Ex P. Bennett, reported in *Bulletin of Legal Developments* (April 11, 1994), pp. 83–84.

as do the German and the Italian Constitutional Courts. Further afield, the Argentinean Supreme Court has long cited US Supreme Court decisions, for a wide range of propositions. Of particular interest is the way in which the Argentinean judges have invoked Supreme Court precedents to bolster the legitimacy of their own stand against abuse of State power.[9] In short, the common bond of constitutional adjudication and the core questions of individual rights versus State power, or individual responsibilities to one another as members of a constitutional polity, appear to transcend the borders of very different legal systems.

In the late 1980s, commentators such as Lord Lester and Mary Ann Glendon remarked on the spread of US constitutional decisions around the world.[10] At the time, this stream of decisions seemed to flow in only one direction, with the US Supreme Court sharply resisting any consultation, must less citation, of foreign precedents. Indeed, as Justice Scalia (in)famously declared when presented with evidence of global public opinion regarding the death penalty, "it is a Constitution for the United States of America that we are expounding."[11]

However, in the late 1990s, the tide is beginning to turn. Justice Breyer recently challenged Justice Scalia's position in his dissent in *Printz v. United States*, noting that the experience of foreign courts and legal systems "may nonetheless cast an empirical light on the consequences of different solutions to a common legal problem."[12] More generally, Justice Sandra Day O'Connor has been exhorting US lawyers around the country to pay more attention to foreign law[13] and has led several delegations of US Supreme Court Justices to meet their foreign counterparts, first from the French Conseil d'Etat, the Conseil Constitutionnel, and the Cour de Cassation and most recently from the ECJ, the

---

[9] *See* Carlos Ignacio Suarez Anzorena, "Transnational Precedents: The Argentinian Case," LL.M. Thesis, Harvard Law School 1998 (on file with author).

[10] Mary Ann Glendon, *Rights Talk* (New York: The Free Press, 1991), p. 158; Anthony Lester, "The Overseas Trade in the American Bill of Rights," *Colum. L. Rev.* 88 (1988) 537, 541.

[11] Thompson v. Oklahoma, 487 US 815, 869 (1988), n. 4 (Scalia, J., dissenting).

[12] 138 L.Ed 2d 914, 977 (1997) Breyer, J., dissenting. Writing for the majority in the *Printz* case, Justice Scalia again rejected Justice Breyer's invitation to comparative analysis with the assertion that "such comparative analysis [is] inappropriate to the task of interpreting a constitution, though it was of course quite relevant to the task of writing one." *Ibid.* at p. 935 n. 11. On the other hand, in a 1997 case brought by several Members of Congress challenging the line-item veto, Chief Justice Rehnquist, pointed out that "[t]here would be nothing irrational about a system which granted standing [to legislators] in these cases; some European constitutional courts operate under one or another variant of such a regime . . . [although] it is obviously not the regime that has obtained under our Constitution to date." Raines v. Byrd, 138 L.Ed. 2d 849, 863 (1997).

[13] Sandra Day O'Connor, "Broadening Our Horizons: Why American Judges and Lawyers Must Learn About Foreign Law," *Int'l Judicial Observer* 4 (June 1997) 2 (article adapted from a speech given by Justice O'Connor at the 1997 spring meeting of the American College of Trial Lawyers).

European Court of Human Rights, and the German Constitutional Court. Following a day-long exchange of views with ECJ members and the opportunity to attend a hearing, both Justice O'Connor and Justice Breyer noted their willingness to consult ECJ decisions "and perhaps use them and cite them in future decisions."[14]

Judge Calabresi of the Second Circuit has been even more direct, urging his US colleagues to join a global trend and pay more attention to foreign decisions, not only decisions in the same dispute but more general precedents on point for the simple purpose of learning and cross-fertilization. In a concurring opinion in *United States v. Then*, he argued that US courts should follow the lead of the German and the Italian constitutional courts in finding ways to signal the legislature that a particular statute is "heading toward unconstitutionality," rather than striking it down immediately or declaring it constitutional.[15] In conclusion, he observed that the United States no longer holds a "monopoly on constitutional judicial review," having helped spawn a new generation of constitutional courts around the world.[16] "Wise parents," he added, "do not hesitate to learn from their children."

As American lawyers find judges more receptive to foreign law, they will search out foreign decisions that support their arguments; judges will then have these citations ready to hand for inclusion in their opinions. It is the beginning of a virtuous circle that may finally open the US judiciary and legal profession to the rich wealth of learning and experience in other legal systems.

2 Cooperation in dispute resolution

Judges not only share ideas; they also cooperate in the resolution of transnational or international disputes. The most advanced form of judicial cooperation involves a partnership between national courts and a supranational tribunal. In the European Union the ECJ works directly

---

[14] "Justices See Joint Issues with the EU," *The Washington Post* (July 8, 1998), p. A24. The quote is from Justice O'Connor; Justice Breyer added the following comment: "Lawyers in America may cite an EU ruling to our court to further a point, and this increases the cross-fertilization of US–EU legal ideas."
  The US Supreme Court delegation was also scheduled to meet with judges on the European Court of Human Rights and members of both the German Constitutional Court and various French courts. Other members of the delegation included Chief Judge Richard Arnold of the 8th Circuit and Texas Chief Justice Tom Philips. "US Justices Compare US–EU Judicial Systems," Press Briefing in Brussels, July 8, 1998, *available at* <http://www.usia.gov/current/news/geog/eu/98070808.wwe.html?/products/washfile/newsitem.shtml>. Justice Anthony Kennedy was also present for the meeting with the members of the ECJ.
[15] United States v. Then, 56 F.3d 464, 468–69 (2d Cir. 1995). [16] *Ibid.* at 469.

with national courts to resolve cases presenting questions of European as well as national law.[17] National courts refer cases presenting issues of European law up to the ECJ, which issues an opinion regarding those particular issues and sends the case back to national courts. The national courts then render their own decision based on the ECJ opinion. The process transforms the judgments of a supranational tribunal into judgments issued by national courts, with the same weight and impact as decisions rendered under national law. The Treaty of Rome provides for this reference procedure, but it is the courts themselves, at both the national and supranational level, that have developed a cooperative relationship.[18] Their interaction not only facilitates the resolution of disputes involving questions of national and European law, but also serves to safeguard the rule of law in the European Union in those cases where legal obligations may diverge from the interests of the legislative and executive branches of various national governments.

Cooperation among courts in the European community is relatively structured, authorized by a provision in the Treaty of Rome and engaged in by courts from the same geographic region and broadly similar legal systems. But judicial cooperation is not limited to such structures, nor to interactions between domestic and international tribunals. In cases involving nationals from two different States, or nationals from the same State in which some part of the activity at issue in the case has taken place abroad, the courts in the nations involved have long been willing to acknowledge each other's potential interest and to defer to one another when such deference is not too costly. Much of these relations can be captured by the concept of "judicial comity," which US courts have been invoking in various guises over the past several decades.

Justice Scalia distinguished between "the comity of courts" and legislative comity in his dissent in the *Hartford Fire* decision, describing judicial comity as the decision by a court in one country to decline

---

[17] For a classic account of the construction of the European Community's legal system, see J. H. H. Weiler, "The Transformation of Europe," *Yale L.J.* 100 (1991), p. 2403. *See also* Eric Stein, "Lawyers, Judges and the Making of a Transnational Constitution," *Am. J. Int'l L.* 75 (1981), p. 1, which first alerted international lawyers of the potential significance of the ECJ's achievements. For an influential account by a member of the ECJ, see G. Federico Mancini, "The Making of a Constitution for Europe," *Common Mkt. L. Rev.* 26 (1989), 595. Two more general accounts, the first written from a legal realist perspective highlighting the motives of ECJ judges in developing a teleological interpretation of the Treaty of Rome and the second seeking to integrate legal accounts with political science theory, are Hjalte Rosmussen, *On Law and Policy in the European Court of Justice: a Comparative Study in Judicial Policymaking* (Dordrecht and Boston, Mass.: Martinus Nijhoff Publishers, 1986); and Anne-Marie Burley and Walter Mattli, "Europe Before the Court: a Political Theory of Legal Integration," *Int'l Org.* 47 (1993), p. 421.

[18] Helfer and Slaughter, "Supranational Adjudication," *supra* note 6, pp. 291–92.

jurisdiction "over matters more appropriately adjudged elsewhere."[19] By contrast, legislative or "prescriptive comity" is "the respect sovereign nations afford each other by limiting the reach of their laws."[20] Viewed through the lens of recent American case law, judicial comity comes into play when courts face questions often prior to the question of which law to apply: where the case shall be heard in the first instance, under what procedures, with what opportunities for discovery. In the words of Judge, now Justice, Stephen Breyer, these questions are all variants of a larger question: how to "help the world's legal systems work together, in harmony, rather than at cross purposes."[21] A growing number of US courts are grappling with the answer in a wide variety of contexts.

According to the 2nd Circuit, reviewing Supreme Court precedents on the enforcement of forum selection clauses, "international comity dictates that American courts enforce these sorts of clauses out of respect for the integrity and competence of foreign tribunals."[22] The court subsequently enforced a forum selection clause specifying an English forum in a securities fraud case brought by a US plaintiff – in which it was clear that neither an English court nor an English arbitrator would apply US securities law. In a similar case arising under federal trademark legislation, Judge Easterbrook of the 7th Circuit argued that foreign courts could interpret such statutes as well as US courts, noting that the entire *Mitsubishi* line of Supreme Court precedents "depend on the belief that foreign tribunals will interpret US law honestly, just as the federal courts of the United States routinely interpret the laws of the States and other nations."[23]

Other fertile sources of doctrinal developments regarding judicial comity are cases involving *forum non conveniens* dismissals, *lis alibi pendens* motions, and requests for anti-suit injunctions. In *Ingersoll Milling Machine Co. v. Granger*, the 7th Circuit affirmed the stay of an action pending before an Illinois district court following the issuance of a judgment in parallel suit by a Belgian court, noting: "International judicial comity is an interest not only of Belgium but also of the United States."[24] In the *forum non conveniens* context, courts have referred to nineteenth century admiralty decisions dismissing cases to avoid interfering with foreign

---

[19] Hartford Fire Insurance Co v. California, 509 US 764, 817 (1993).   [20] *Ibid.*
[21] Howe v. Goldcorp Investments, Ltd., 946 F.2d 944, 950 (1st Cir. 1991).
[22] Roby v. Corporation of Lloyds, 996 F.2d 1353, 1363 (2d Cir. 1993) (citing Mitsubishi Motors Corp. v. Soler Chrysler-Plymouth, Inc., 473 US 614 (1985)).
[23] Omron Healthcare Inc. v. MacLaren Exports Ltd., 28 F.3d 600, 604 (7th Cir. 1994).
[24] 833 F.2d 680, 685 (7th Cir. 1987).

regulatory regimes, a debate that has recently been rekindled in Texas.[25]

Many of these decisions still intertwine very general and amorphous notions of comity between nations with a more specific concept of judicial comity (though one can certainly be understood as a subset of the other). But even at this stage, it is possible to identify several distinct strands of judicial comity. First is a respect for foreign courts *qua* courts, rather than simply as the face of a foreign government, and hence for their ability to resolve disputes and interpret and apply the law honestly and competently. Second is the corollary recognition that courts in different nations are entitled to their fair share of disputes – both as co-equals in the global task of judging and as the instruments of a strong "local interest in having localized controversies decided at home."[26] The *Ingersoll* court made this link, declining to criticize the district court for rejecting the "parochial concept that all disputes must be resolved under our laws and in our courts."[27] The quote is from the Supreme Court's seminal decision in *Bremen v. Zapata*, in which it agreed that American litigants could be forced to litigate abroad where they had negotiated a forum clause choosing a foreign forum.[28]

Respect for foreign courts need not mean deference. But it must mean at least awareness of the presence and potential interest of a foreign court, and at best direct interaction with that court in a cooperative effort to resolve the dispute at hand. In deciding whether to allow French litigants to use US discovery procedures against an American litigant litigating in a French court (as provided for in 28 USC § 1782), Judge Calabresi of the 2nd Circuit concluded that US courts should grant such assistance in the absence of a clear objection from the foreign tribunal. The US statute "contemplates international cooperation," he wrote, "and such cooperation presupposes an on-going dialogue between the adjudicative bodies of the world community . . .".[29] As an example of the dialogue sought to be fostered, he cited a case in which two English

---

[25] *Compare* Dow Chemical Company v. Castro Alfaro, 786 S.W.2d 674, 687 (Supreme Court of Texas 1990) (Doggett, J., concurring). ("Comity – deference shown to the interests of the foreign forum – . . . is best achieved by avoiding the possibility of incurring the wrath and the distrust of the Third World as it increasingly recognizes that it is being used as the industrial world's garbage can") (internal quotations marks and citations omitted) *with* Sequihua v. Texaco, Inc., 847 F.Supp. 61, 63 (S.D. Tex. 1994) ("exercise of jurisdiction by this Court would interfere with Ecuador's sovereign right to control its own environment and resources"; case should thus be dismissed on comity grounds).

[26] Gulf Oil Corp v. Gilbert, 330 US 501, 509 (1947) (applying the *forum non conveniens* doctrine to dismiss a New York case in favor of a Virginia forum), quoted in Piper Aircraft v. Reyno, 454 US 235, 241 (1981) (dismissing a case brought in the United States in favor of a Scottish forum).

[27] 833 F.2d at 685.   [28] The Bremen v. Zapata Off-Shore Co., 407 US 1, 9 (1972).

[29] In the Matter of the Application of Euromep, *SA*, 51 F.3d 1095, 1101 (2d Cir. 1995).

courts had directly enjoined a litigant from using §1782, on the ground that "the English court should retain control of its own proceedings and the proceedings that are before it."[30] The House of Lords subsequently vacated the injunction on the ground that the discovery sought was not unfair to the opposing litigant and did not interfere with "the due process of the [English] court."[31]

As this example illustrates, judicial cooperation is not necessarily harmonious. A recent squabble between a US judge and a Hong Kong judge over an insider trading case reveals the potential for more heated discussion. The US judge refused to decline jurisdiction in favor of the Hong Kong court on the grounds that "in Hong Kong they practically give you a medal for doing this sort of thing [insider trading]." In response, the Hong Kong judge stiffly defended the adequacy of Hong Kong law to address the conduct in question and asserted his willingness to apply that law. He also chided the US judge, pointing out that any conflict "should be approached in the spirit of judicial comity rather than judicial competitiveness."[32] Such a conflict is to be expected among diplomats, but what is striking is the way in which the two courts perceive themselves as two quasi-autonomous foreign policy actors trying to combat international securities fraud.

3 Judicial organizations

Finally, judges are talking face to face. The judges of the Supreme Courts of Western Europe began meeting on a triennial basis early in the 1980s. They have become more aware of one another's decisions since they began meeting, particularly with regard to each other's willingness to accept the decisions handed down by the ECJ.[33] In addition to official meetings of US Supreme Court Justices with their European, French, English, German, and Indian counterparts,[34] a number of meetings between US Supreme Court Justices and their foreign counterparts have also been sponsored by private groups, as have meetings of judges of the supreme courts of Central and Eastern Europe and the

---

[30] South Carolina Ins. Co. v. Assurantie Maatschappij *"De Zeven Provincien" NV*, 3 W.L.R. 398 (Eng. 1986), discussed and quoted in *Euromep*, 51 F.3d at 1100 n. 3.   [31] 51 F.3d at 1100 n. 3.
[32] Naumus Asia Co. v. The Standard Chartered Bank, 1 HKLR 396 (H.P.K. High Court cp 1990).
[33] *See VI Conferencia de Tribunales Constitucionales Europeos*, Tribunales Constitucionales Europeos y Autonomias Territoriales (1985).
[34] Several official US Supreme Court visits to Europe, both to the European Court of Justice and the European Court of Human Rights and to France and Germany are described above. *See also* "India–US Legal Exchange Includes Supreme Court Justices, Lawyers," *Int'l Jud. Observer* (Sept. 1995), 1; James G. Apple, "British, US Judges and Lawyers Meet, Discuss Shared Judicial, Legal Concerns," *Int'l Jud. Observer* (Jan. 1996), 1.

former Soviet Union with US judges.[35] Law schools have also played an important role. For example, N.Y.U. Law School's Center for International Studies and Institute of Judicial Administration hosted a major conference of judges from both national and international tribunals from around the world in February 1995 under the auspices of N.Y.U.'s Global Law School Program.[36] Similarly, Harvard Law School hosted part of the Anglo-American Exchange.[37] For its part, Yale Law School has established a seminar for members of constitutional courts from around the globe to meet anually as a means of promoting "intellectual exchange" among the judges.[38] Another contribution of academic institutions to the international exchange of judicial ideas is through compilations of websites for courts to access information through the internet of the activities of national and supranational courts and tribunals from around the world.[39]

Finally, non-profit legal associations are convening transnational judicial conferences. For example, the Law Association for Asia and the Pacific (LAWASIA) with its Secretariat in Australia fosters judicial exchange through annual meetings of its Judicial Section.[40] Another way in which the American Bar Association encourages transnational judicial interaction is through sponsoring US judges to take trips abroad. The ABA Central and Eastern European Law Initiative (CEELI) periodically sends American judges to various Central and Eastern European countries to assist with law reform, codification efforts, and judicial training.[41]

The most formal initiative aimed at increasing direct judicial communication is the recently created Organization of the Supreme Courts of the Americas (OCSA). Twenty-five supreme court justices or their

[35] "European Justices Meet in Washington to Discuss Common Issues, Problems," *Int'l Jud. Observer* (Jan. 1996), 3. *See also* CEELI Update, ABA Int'l L. News (ABA, Washington, D.C.), (Summer 1991), 7; Helfer and Slaughter, "Supranational Adjudication," *supra* note 6, p. 372.

[36] Papers from the conference have subsequently been published *in* Thomas M. Franck and Gregory H. Fox, eds., *International Law Decisions in National Courts* (Transnational, 1996). *See also*, Thomas M. Franck, "N.Y.U. Conference Discusses Impact of International Tribunals," *Int'l Judicial Observer* 1 (1995), 3.

[37] See James G. Apple, "British, US Judges and Lawyers Meet," *supra* note 34, p. 1.

[38] "Yale Law School Establishes Seminar on Global Constitutional Issues," *Int'l Jud. Observer* 4 (1997), 2.

[39] *See e.g.*, the Center for Global Change and Governance at Rutgers University's website called the "Global Courts Network" <http.://andromeda.rutgers.edu/~lipscher/globo.html>.

[40] *See* <http://wwwlawasia.asn.au/lawasia/Assoc.htm>. LAWASIA member countries are: Afghanistan; Australia; Bangladesh; China; Fiji; Hong Kong, China; India; Iran; Japan; DPR of Korea; Korea; Macao; Malaysia; Nepal; New Zealand; Pakistan; Papua New Guinea; Philippines; Russian Federation; Singapore; Sri Lanka; Thailand; Western Samoa.

[41] *See* "CEELI Update," *ABA Int'l Law News*, Summer, 1991, p. 7.

designees attended a conference in Washington in October 1995 and drafted the OCSA charter, dedicated to "promot[ing] and strengthen[ing] judicial independence and the rule of law among the members, as well as the proper constitutional treatment of the judiciary as a fundamental branch of the State."[42] The Charter required ratification by fifteen supreme courts, which was achieved in spring 1996. It provides for triennial meetings and envisages a permanent secretariat. Among other activities, OCSA members plan to conduct a number of studies on procedural and substantive issues such as the relative merits of adversarial versus inquisitorial systems and the relationship of the press to the judiciary.[43]

OCSA is an initiative by judges and for judges. It has been strongly supported by the international relations committee of the Federal Judicial Conference. It is not a stretch to say that it is the product of judicial foreign policy, advancing values and interests of particular concern to a particular group of judges.

4 Toward a global community of law

Participants in judicial networks are constructing a global community of law. The members of this community share common values and interests, based on the recognition of the law as distinct but not divorced from politics. This conception of the law in turn supports a shared conception of their own role and identity as judges – as actors who must be insulated from direct political influence. At its best, this global community assures each participant that his or her professional performance is being both monitored and supported by a larger audience.

Champions of the ideal of a global rule of law have most frequently envisioned one rule for all, a unified legal system topped by a world court. A fully developed global community of law would instead encompass a plurality of rules of law achieved in different States and regions. No high court would hand down definitive global rules, although such a system could coexist perfectly comfortably with an international court of justice issuing judgments about public international law. Indeed, supranational tribunals may play a vital unifying and coordinating role, but their ultimate effectiveness will depend on their relationship with national government institutions exercising direct enforcement power. Overall, national courts would interact with one another and with

---

[42] Charter of the Organization of the Supreme Courts of the Americas, Article II, § 21.
[43] "Justices, Judges from Across Western Hemisphere Assemble, Create Charter for New Organization of Supreme Courts," *Int'l Jud. Observer* (Jan. 1996), 1–2.

supranational tribunals in ways that would accommodate national and regional differences, but that would acknowledge and reinforce a core of common values.

B *Transnational regulatory cooperation*

Perhaps the densest area of transgovernmental activity is among national regulators. National government officials charged with the administration of anti-trust policy, securities regulation, environmental policy, criminal law enforcement, banking and insurance supervision – in short, all the agents of the modern regulatory State – interact regularly and increasingly systematically with their foreign counterparts. They come together to extend their combined regulatory reach, tracking the increasingly mobile subjects of national regulation and figuring out cooperative strategies for the regulation of global markets and global problems such as air and water pollution and international *mafiosi*. The result is the creation of horizontal governance networks that both substitute for and complement international institutions. Indeed, in some cases the national regulators involved have created their own international institutions.

Domestic institutions that are autonomous and motivated enough to form transnational government networks can also interact with their supranational counterparts to create global government networks. As in the European example, the supranational institutions may play a vital unifying and coordinating role, but their ultimate effectiveness will depend on their relationship with national government institutions exercising direct enforcement power.

1 Networks of national regulators

It is hardly surprising that the globalization of financial and commercial markets, criminal enterprise, and environmental problems has led to the creation of transnational regulatory networks. National regulators have sought to keep up with their quarry by cooperating with one another. Such cooperation can arise on an *ad hoc* basis, but increasingly gives rise to bilateral and plurilateral agreements designed to cement and support such cooperation. The most formal of these agreements are Mutual Legal Assistance Treaties (MLATs), whereby two States set forth a protocol governing cooperation between their law enforcement agencies and courts. Increasingly, however, the preferred instrument of cooperation is the much less formal Memorandum of Understanding, whereby two or more regulatory agencies set forth and initial the terms of an ongoing relationship. MOUs are not treaties; they do not engage the executive or the legislature in negotiations, deliberation, or signature. They affirm existing links among regulatory agencies based on their common functions and commitment to the solution of problems.[44]

The changing nature of transnational relations among regulatory agencies is perhaps best captured by a concept developed by the US Department of Justice called "positive comity."[45] Comity of nations, an archaic and notoriously vague term beloved of diplomats and international lawyers, has traditionally signified a kind of deference granted one nation by another in recognition of their mutual sovereignty. It betokens negative cooperation, in the sense of non-interference or waiver of powers that a sovereign is clearly entitled to exercise but chooses not to. For instance, a State will recognize another State's laws or judicial judgments based on comity. Positive comity, on the other hand, requires a much more active cooperation. As developed between the Anti-trust Division of the Department of Justice and the Commission of the European Community, the regulatory authorities of both States undertake to alert one another to regulatory violations within their jurisdiction, with the understanding that the alerted authority will then take action.[46] Comity thus becomes a principle of affirmative and enduring cooperation among counterpart government institutions.

2 Transgovernmental regulatory organizations

In 1988 the central bankers of the world's major financial powers adopted capital adequacy requirements for all the banks under their supervision. The result was a major reform of the international banking system, to which some commentators attribute a major and unnecessary credit squeeze in many of the participating nations. The decision to impose these capital adequacy requirements did not take place under the auspices of the World Bank, the International Monetary Fund, or even the meeting of the G7. The forum of decision was the Basle

---

[44] *See generally* Caroline A. A. Greene, Note, "International Securities Law Enforcement: Recent Advances in Assistance and Cooperation," *Vand. J. Transnat'l L.* 27 (1994), p. 635. *See also* Charles Vaughn Baltic III, Note, "The Next Step in Insider Trading Regulation: Internal Cooperative Efforts in the Global Securities Market," *Law & Pol'y Int'l Bus.* 23 (1991/92), pp. 191–92.

[45] *See generally* Robert D. Shank, Note, "The Justice Department's Recent Antitrust Enforcement Policy: Toward a 'Positive Comity' Solution to International Competition Problems?" *Vand. J. Transnat'l L.* 29 (1996), 176.

[46] *See* Joseph P. Griffin, "EC and US Extraterritoriality: Activism and Cooperation," *Fordham Int'l L. J.* 17 (1994), pp. 367–69.

Committee on Banking Supervision, an organization composed of twelve central bank governors. The Basle Committee was created not by a treaty, but by a simple agreement reached by the bank governors themselves and announced in a press communiqué. Its members meet four times a year and follow rules of their own devising. Decisions are taken by consensus and are not formally binding; however, members agree to implement accords reached within their own domestic systems. Back home, the authority of the Basle Committee is then often cited as an argument for taking domestic action.[47]

The Basle Committee's example has been followed by national securities commissioners and insurance regulators. IOSCO, the International Organization of Securities Commissioners, has no formal charter or founding treaty; it was incorporated by a private bill of the Quebec National Assembly. Its primary purpose is to find solutions to problems affecting international securities markets and to generate sufficient consensus among its members to implement those solutions through national legislation. Its members have also entered information-sharing agreements on their own initiative. IOSCO decision-making processes are very flexible; further, although its membership is large and open, the most powerful members of the organization dominate the principal rule-making committees.[48] The International Association of Insurance Supervisors[49] follows a similar model, as does the newly created Tripartite Group – an international coalition of banking, insurance, and securities regulators created by the Basle Committee to consider methods of improving the supervision of financial conglomerates.[50]

Pat Buchanan would have had a field day with the Tripartite Group, denouncing it as a prime example of an international bureaucracy bent on taking the power out of the hands of American voters.[51] In fact, transgovernmental regulatory organizations have no direct power; on paper, at least, their functions are primarily consultative. They have no formal basis in treaties or even executive agreements; they are founded by and function for the benefit of specific groups of national regulators;

---

[47] *See* David Zaring, "International Law by Other Means: the Twilight Existence of International Financial Regulatory Organizations," *Texas Int'l L. J.* 33 (1998), 281.

[48] *See* Paul Guy, "Regulatory Harmonization to Achieve Effective International Competition," *in* F. R. Edwards and H. T. Patrick, eds., *Regulating International Financial Markets: Issues and Policies* (Boston, Mass.: Kluwer Academic Publishers, 1992), p. 291.

[49] *See* IAIS, 1994 Annual Report.

[50] *See* US Objections Prompt Limited Global Pact on Financial Services, 14 no. 16 *Banking Pol'y Rep.* 2 (1995).

[51] Patrick J. Buchanan, *The Great Betrayal: How American Sovereignty and Social Justice are Sacrificed to the Gods of the Global Economy* (Boston, Mass.: Little, Brown, 1998).

they have flexible decision-making procedures and can control their membership and governance structures; their operations are largely hidden from public view. Above all, unlike the international bogeymen of demagogic fancies, these organizations do not aspire to, nor are they likely to, exercise power in the international system independently of their members. They are vehicles to help national regulators solve transnational problems.

3 The nationalization of international law

Perhaps the most distinctive attribute of the transgovernmental regulatory networks is that their primary purpose is not to promulgate international rules but to enhance the enforcement of national law. Traditional international law requires States to implement the international obligations they incur through national law where necessary, either through legislation or regulation. Thus, for instance, if States agree to a twelve-mile territorial sea, they must change their domestic legislation concerning the interdiction of vessels in territorial waters accordingly. However, the subject of such legislation would be international, in the sense that only in a world with multiple nations would there be any need to devise rules governing spaces outside their collective borders. Similarly, only in a world with multiple nations would we need rules regulating war or commerce between them. Global commons issues and inter-State relations, whether peaceful or conflictual, have thus been the stuff of traditional international law.

Transgovernmental regulatory networks, by contrast, produce rules governing subjects that each nation must and does already regulate within its borders: crime, monopoly, securities fraud, pollution, tax evasion. The same advances in technology and transportation that have fueled globalization have made it increasingly difficult to enforce national law effectively. Regulators thus benefit from coordinating their enforcement efforts with their foreign counterparts or from ensuring that all nations adopt a common enforcement approach.

The result is the nationalization of international law. Bilateral and plurilateral regulatory cooperation does not seek to create obligations between nations enforceable at international law. Rather, the agreements reached are pledges of good faith that are essentially self-enforcing, in the sense that each nation will be better able to enforce its national law by implementing the agreement reached if all other nations do likewise. The binding or coercive dimension of law emerges only at the national level. Uniformity of result and diversity of means go hand in hand. And both the rule-makers and rule-enforcers are accountable at the national level.

C Executives and Parliaments

In the traditional conception of the international system, heads of State act as representatives of the unitary State, voicing and promoting the national interest. Legislatures, by contrast, are presumed to have no direct role in foreign affairs. They can approve or disapprove, or sometimes amend, agreements negotiated and concluded by the executives; they can also decide whether and how to implement such agreements through domestic legislation. However, their very number and decentralization is assumed to preclude direct interaction with other nations. The traditional account remains accurate as a stylized representation of legislative–executive interaction in foreign affairs, particularly in parliamentary systems. But even here, there are growing signs of independent interests and action on both sides.

Over the past decade political scientists have increasingly tracked the ways in which heads of State use international fora to promote their specific interests in the face of competing domestic actors. This is the "two-level game," whereby a head of State enhances his leverage over the national legislature by arguing that the nation's international credibility is at stake. The suspect scenario runs as follows: the President seeks to liberalize the economy. He is too weak to push through liberalizing legislation on his own. He thus meets with like-minded heads of State and negotiates an international trade agreement that will require the liberalization measures he seeks.[52] The only premise on which this scenario makes sense is that the executive has an interest distinct from the legislature and the ability to implement that interest through international interaction.

National legislatures are developing their own repertoire of responses to such games. They can and increasingly do meet directly with members of foreign delegations in international trade negotiations. In theory, they could also meet with their foreign counterparts to develop a counter-strategy. In practice, we have little evidence of such contact. However, national legislators do meet together on issues of common

---

[52] *See* Robert D. Putnam, "Diplomacy and Domestic Politics: the Logic of Two-Level Games," *Int'l Org.* 42 (1988), pp. 433–35. *See also* Peter B. Evans, Harold K. Jacobson, and Robert D. Putnam, eds., *Double-edged Diplomacy: International Bargaining and Domestic Politics* (Berkeley, Calif.: University of California Press, 1993).

interest under the auspices of international organizations such as NATO and the Organization for Security and Cooperation in Europe.[53] Many members of the US Congress also maintain home pages on the Internet that can be visited by their counterparts in other nations.

Another source of legislative networks is the spontaneous organization and mobilization of national legislators on international issues such as arms control, human rights, and democratic government. The leading organizations in this regard are Parliamentarians for Global Action and the Interparliamentary Union. While such groups can have an influence on domestic legislative initiatives and certainly promote communication and cross-fertilization of policy ideas and approaches among national legislators, they still reflect more of an effort to give legislators a voice on more traditional foreign policy issues than the development of transgovernmental networks on issues of more domestic concern. Increasingly, these parliamentary networks have become a means of asserting regional viewpoints on matters of international concern. More generally, they have provided legislators with an opportunity to meet with one another informally, providing an increasingly effective forum for the resolution of international problems.

Of particular interest regarding the issues discussed in this volume is the IPU's involvement in promulgating both information about electoral systems around the world and international law standards on free and fair elections.[54] It has been joined in this endeavor by specific regional organizations such as the Association of African Election Authorities, founded in 1997 and composed both of government officials and leaders of NGOs directly involved in monitoring and assisting elections. The Association Charter sets forth a long list of purposes, including "the promotion of free and fair elections in Africa; the promotion of independent and impartial election organizations and administrators; and the development of professional election officials with high integrity, a strong sense of public service and a commitment to democracy."[55] Here is a transgovernmental entity that includes non-governmental actors, all

---

[53] For a discussion of the North Atlantic Assembly, the NATO parliamentary organ, see Christian Brumter, *The North Atlantic Assembly* (Dordrecht and Boston, Mass.: Martinus Nijhoff Publishers, 1996). Similarly, for an overview of the OSCE's parliamentary assembly see Alexis Heraclides, *Helsinki-II and its Aftermath: The Making of the CSCE Into an International Organization* (London and New York: Pinter Publishers, 1993), p. 15.

[54] Inter-Parliamentary Union, *Electoral Systems: A World-Wide Comparative Study* (Geneva: Inter-Parliamentary Union, 1993); Guy S. Goodwin-Gill, *Free and Fair Elections: International Law and Practice* (Geneva: Inter-Parliamentary Union, 1994).

[55] AAEA, "Report on the Founding Meeting of the Association of African Election Authorities," United Nations Electoral Assistance Division (UN/EAD) (1997).

united by the desire to preserve and transmit a particular set of professional goals on an issue of crucial importance to democratic governance.

II TRANSGOVERNMENTALISM AND THE LIBERAL DEMOCRATIC ORDER

The transgovernmental networks and institutions described above coexist and interact with traditional international organizations. The hallmark of transgovernmentalism, however, is a system in which the principal actors are State units rather than unitary States, interacting horizontally with their foreign counterparts rather than ceding power to their international or supranational equivalents. Transgovernmentalism thus requires the "disaggregation" of the State into its component government institutions – institutions who will continue to recognize and represent the national interest relative to other nations, but who will also have distinct institutional interests.

Disaggregated State activity, in turn, is most concentrated among liberal democracies, defined as States providing some form of representative government secured by the separation of powers, constitutional guarantees of civil and political rights, juridical equality, the rule of law, and a market economy that protects private property rights.[56] Government networks are particularly dense and institutionalized in the EU,[57] and, more broadly, among OECD countries.[58] The members of the Basle Committee[59] and the principal rule-makers in IOSCO are all liberal democracies.[60] Government networks are equally a hallmark of relations among Commonwealth countries.[61] Even in the security realm,

---

[56] This is the definition of liberal democracy used by Michael Doyle in his pioneering work on the "democratic peace." *See* Michael W. Doyle, "Kant, Liberal Legacies, and Foreign Affairs," *Phil. & Pub. Aff.* 12 (1986), pp. 206–09. Note that the definition is quite broad: market economies that protect private property rights range from Sweden to the United States.

[57] Renaud Dehousse, "Regulation by Networks in the European Community: the Role of European Agencies," *J. Eu. Pub. Pol.* 4 (1997), 246; David Cameron, "Transnational Relations and the Development of the European Economic and Monetary Union," *in* Thomas Risse-Kappen, ed., *Bringing Transnational Relations Back In: Non-State Actors, Domestic Structures, and International Institutions* (New York: Cambridge University Press, 1995).

[58] Scott H. Jacobs, "Regulatory Co-operation for an Interdependent World: Issues for Government," *in Regulatory Co-operation for an Interdependent World* (OECD 1994), p. 15.

[59] Belgium, Canada, France, Germany, Italy, Japan, Luxembourg, the Netherlands, Sweden, Switzerland, the United Kingdom, and the United States.

[60] The IOSCO Technical Committee is composed of Australia, France, Germany, Hong Kong, Italy, Japan, Mexico, the Netherlands, Ontario, Quebec, Spain, Sweden, Switzerland, the United Kingdom, and the United States.

[61] David Howell, "The Place of the Commonwealth in the International Order," *The Round Table* 345 (1988), p. 29.

Thomas Risse-Kappen argues that they are a distinctive feature of relations within NATO and in the US–Japanese security relationship.[62] Finally, both vertical and horizontal judicial networks are most developed in Europe and among common law courts in the Commonwealth.[63] It is also noteworthy that the formation of OCSA followed the re-democratization of much of Latin America.

Although the empirical correlation between government networks and liberal democracies is easy to establish, the precise causal connections remain unproved. A number of possible explanations present themselves, however. First is the existence of the "(liberal) democratic peace," the now well-established proposition that liberal democracies are very unlikely to use military conflict to resolve their disputes.[64] As early as 1977, when identifying the features of the emerging phenomenon of "complex interdependence," Keohane and Nye listed both transgovernmental relations and a reluctance to use military force, a reluctance that was particularly observable "among industrialized, pluralist countries."[65] Writing in 1995, Risse-Kappen concurs, listing the democratic peace and transgovernmental relations as two important characteristics of "cooperation among democracies."[66] The connection between the two seems straightforward. Government institutions are likely to be far more willing to formulate and implement their own separate conceptions of the national interest if they are certain that potential conflict with other nations cannot escalate into a genuine security threat. Conversely, the prospect of war is the fastest way to ensure that all branches of a government will in fact cohere into a "unitary State."

A second factor contributing to the distinctive patterns of transgovernmental activity among liberal democracies is undoubtedly the

---

[62] Thomas Risse-Kappen, *Cooperation among Democracies: the European Influence on US Foreign Policy* (Princeton University Press, 1995), p.209. On the US–Japan security relationship, *see* Peter Katzenstein and Yutaka Tsujinaka, "'Bullying,' 'Buying,' and 'Binding,'": US–Japanese Transnational Relations and Domestic Structures," *in* Risse-Kappen, ed., *Bringing Transnational Relations Back In, supra* note 57.

[63] Helfer and Slaughter, "Supranational Adjudication," *supra* note 6, pp. 290–97, 370–73.

[64] Doyle, "Kant, Liberal Legacies, and Foreign Affairs", *supra* note 56; Bruce Russett, *Grasping the Democratic Peace: Principles for a Post-Cold War World* (Princeton University Press, 1993). Critics of this research routinely point to conflict among liberal democracies – Greece and Turkey, India and Pakistan – as contrary evidence. However, the claim is emphatically not that liberal democracies will not experience conflict, even sharp and heated conflict that threatens to escalate militarily. It is rather that such escalation can either be prevented at the outset or stepped back down, due to a wide variety of forces in both countries that ultimately work against military resolution.

[65] Robert O. Keohane, Joseph S. Nye, and Stanley Hoffmann, eds., *After the Cold War: International Institutions and State Strategies in Europe 1891–1991* (Cambridge, Mass.: Harvard University Press, 1993), p. 27.   [66] Risse-Kappen, *Cooperation among Democracies, supra* note 62, pp. 27, 38.

relatively high level of economic development among mature liberal democracies and the accompanying intensity of globalization, defined not simply as macroeconomic interdependence, but microeconomic integration of individual corporations.[67] Close transnational links between economic actors give rise to regulatory conflict and the accompanying need for repeated interaction and ultimately a framework for cooperation among national regulatory authorities. Similarly, disputes between transnational economic actors lead to conflicts between courts over judicial jurisdiction, ultimately requiring courts to devise ways to cooperate with or at least take account of one another. Another link between economic development and government networks is the level of economic development necessary for membership in the OECD, an organization that explicitly fosters government networks.

However, to say that mature liberal democracies enjoy a high level of economic development and that the economic interdependence frequently accompanying such levels of development creates a demand for government networks is not to say either that a liberal democracy will automatically prosper, or that economic development necessarily requires liberal democracy. Empirical studies have shown only that rising income levels correlate positively with the prospects for stable democracy; it is far less evident that stable democracy raises incomes.[68] Moreover, although post-Cold War conventional wisdom dictates that democracy must go hand in hand with a private-property market economy, the phenomenal growth rates in China and the experience of the Asian "tigers" prior to their democratization, not to mention the historical experience of many prosperous but non-democratic States, all suggest that the conventional wisdom is ripe for revision. Thus it may be true only that high levels of economic development are a central feature of contemporary relations among liberal democracies.

A third link between liberal democracy and transgovernmentalism is the relative strength and autonomy of the institutions participating in government networks. Fareed Zakaria has recently rekindled debate over whether "liberalism" and "democracy" automatically go together,

---

[67] Wolfgang Reinicke, "Global Public Policy," *Foreign Aff.* 76 (1997), p. 127. Consistent with the argument advanced here, Reinicke notes that most of the economic integration that has been associated with globalization has taken place among OECD countries. He cites the institutions charged with regulating this process, referred to above as transgovernmental regulatory organizations, as the "institutions of globalization," as opposed to the more traditional "institutions of interdependence" such as the IMF and the World Bank.

[68] John F. Helliwell, "Empirical Linkages Between Democracy and Economic Growth," *Brit. J. of Pol. Sci.* 24 (1994), p. 225.

arguing that "constitutional liberalism," defined as the Western tradition "that seeks to protect an individual's autonomy and dignity against coercion," rests on a set of political commitments that do not necessarily accompany free and fair elections.[69] Many scholars and practitioners sharply disagree, noting that the list of "liberal autocracies" is short, anomalous, and largely historical.[70] Nevertheless, even Zakaria's critics agree that the "liberal" and "democratic" elements of liberal democracy are distinguishable and that the preservation of individual liberty depends in part on mechanisms for curtailing the power of separate branches of government (loosely and often inaccurately defined as "the separation of powers"). Americans readily recognize this mechanism under the Madisonian rubric of "checks and balances," but important differences exist between presidential and parliamentary systems in this regard. Even in parliamentary systems, however, which typically do not recognize a formal separation of executive and legislative powers in the same way that many presidential systems do, the administrative bureaucracy enjoys substantial autonomy from shifting legislative majorities and the resulting cast of ministers. Overall, different branches of government in liberal States are nevertheless more powerful and autonomous on their home turf than their counterparts in illiberal States, whether democratic or not.

The relative power and autonomy of domestic government institutions bears on the formation of governmental networks in two ways. First, either formal or informal norms regarding separation of powers free government institutions to concentrate on their specific tasks of regulation, legislation, law enforcement and dispute resolution, leading them to take responsibility for specific government functions and thus to make common cause more easily with their counterparts in other nations performing similar functions. Second, in those systems such as the United States in which vigorous competition among domestic government institutions is encouraged, regulatory agencies, legislative committees, the executive branch, and even courts are likely to be skilled political players, accustomed to coalition-building in support of a particular institutional or policy position within.

Institutions thus empowered on their home turf are better equipped to seek out and cooperate with their foreign counterparts and indeed may be spurred to do so by competition with their fellow domestic

---

[69] Fareed Zakaria, "The Rise of Illiberal Democracy," *Foreign Aff.* 76 (1997), pp. 25–26.
[70] *See, e.g.*, John Shattuck and J. Brian Atwood, "Defending Democracy," *Foreign Aff.* 77 (1998), pp. 167–70; Marc F. Plattner, "Liberalism and Democracy," *Foreign Aff.* 77 (1998), pp. 171–80.

branches. For instance, a US court has made common cause with a British court to circumvent a Justice Department position in an anti-trust case that the US court hesitated to override on its own.[71] Examples of executives seeking to outflank their legislatures are also well documented.[72] By contrast, institutions subject to the political whims of a dictator or oligarchy, or else primarily pursuing their own material interests, are less likely to be fit interlocutors.

Here too, however, it is important not to overstate the argument. Autocracies of various stripes and illiberal democracies can and do operate specialized ministries or agencies that are committed to and carry out regulatory functions such as securities, banking, or even environmental regulation. Such entities may well have sufficient domestic power and autonomy to participate in government networks, as is evident from their membership in many of the networks described above. This aspect of government networks will be discussed further below. Alternatively, illiberal States may seek to promote independent judiciaries, primarily to attract foreign investment, or may have a tradition of independent judges who now often find themselves in opposition against the current government.

Functionalism and professionalization can thus provide a measure of common ground linking government officials from widely disparate political systems. Based on current empirical evidence, however, these broader government networks are likely to engage principally in information exchange and policy coordination. More active cooperation, collaboration, and conflict resolution require a high degree of trust, which in turn appears to depend on a sense of shared identity or "we-feeling."[73] Shared identity, however, can be derived from a common religion,

---

[71] *See* Laker Airways v. Sabena, 731 F.2d 909 (D.C. Cir. 1984). The Laker litigation began in the District of Columbia District Court as an antitrust action against a number of transatlantic airlines. The defendants obtained a preliminary injunction in the British High Court of Justice forbidding Laker from prosecuting its American antitrust action. The British Court of Appeal subsequently issued a permanent injunction requiring Laker to dismiss its suit against the British defendants, and characterized the American action as "wholly untriable." British Airways Board v. Laker Airways, [1983] 3 W.L.R. 545, 573 (C.A. 1983). For an account of the back-and-forth court decisions in the Laker litigation, see Daryl A. Libow, Note, "The Laker Antitrust Litigation: The Jurisdictional 'Rule of Reason' Applied to Transnational Injunctive Relief," *Cornell L. Rev.* 71 (1986), 655–661.   [72] *See* Putnam, "Diplomacy and Domestic Politics," *supra* note 52.
[73] Karl W Deutsch, et al., *Political Community and the North Atlantic Area: international organization in light of historical experience* (Princeton University Press, 1957), p.129. Deutsch developed the concept of a "pluralistic security community," based on a community of values that promotes "mutual sympathy and loyalties; of 'we-feeling,' trust, and consideration; of at least partial identification in terms of self-images and interests; of the ability to predict each other's behavior and ability to act in accordance with that prediction."

culture, ethnicity, or political ideology; geographic contiguity or shared historical experience; solidarity in the face of a common threat. Liberal democracies may identify with one another as members of an in-group confronted with non-democracies, but such identification or awareness of commonality does not necessarily promote government networks.[74]

The fourth link between government networks and liberal democracy is thus shared political values of a kind fostering the mode of governance that government networks represent. Liberal democratic norms of pluralism and tolerance enshrine principles of "legitimate difference" that help bridge cultural and political differences among entities seeking common ends but often through quite different means;[75] norms of equality translate into procedural requirements of consensus and consultation that help equalize power disparities among participants in governmental networks.[76] The guarantee of peaceful dispute resolution that is a concomitant of the liberal democratic peace also ensures that governmental networks will not be suddenly and violently disrupted, even if they may be stalemated by particularly intractable disputes. Making an analogous point, Risse-Kappen argues that such norms temper the "[f]ierce economic competition" that is a concomitant of shared capitalist values among liberal democracies.[77]

Chroniclers and proponents of the liberal democratic order as the principal US achievement after 1945 have focused far more on international institutions than transgovernmental relations. John Ikenberry notes that the "decentralized and open character of domestic institutions" in Western liberal democracies facilitates transnational politics, but his description of the Western "constitutional vision" emphasizes the creation of the United Nations, NATO, and the multilateral financial institutions.[78] Similarly, the Clinton Administration's foreign policy, dedicated to securing and expanding the liberal democratic order, has focused on democracy, free trade, and international institutions.

---

[74] The argument here roughly parallels the reasoning in Risse-Kappen, ed., *Bringing Transnational Relations Back In*, supra note 57, pp. 27–29 (arguing that explaining the democratic peace does not explain regular cooperation among liberal democracies within democratic international institutions).

[75] Anne-Marie Burley, "Law among Liberal States: Liberal Internationalism and the Act of State Doctrine," *Columbia L. Rev.* 92 (1992), p. 1907.

[76] Risse-Kappen, *Cooperation among Democracies*, supra note 62, p. 39.   [77] *Ibid.* at 31.

[78] Ikenberry, "The Myth of Post-War Chaos," supra note 4, pp. 88–89. As noted above, Keohane and Nye pointed to the significance of transgovernmental relations in their analysis of "complex interdependence" in the 1970s and simultaneously argued that complex interdependence was most likely to obtain among liberal democracies. However, they did not see themselves as describing a liberal democratic order.

Transgovernmental relations tend to be an afterthought, invariably described as addressing "technical" or "functional" issues.

In fact, transgovernmentalism should be understood as a central component of the liberal democratic order. As an empirical phenomenon, networks of government institutions are the primary channels of communication and cooperation among liberal democracies. As argued in this section, they are particularly likely to flourish in conditions of peace, prosperity, strong and autonomous domestic institutions, and liberal democratic norms of decision-making and dispute-resolution. But they are more than a by-product of the liberal internationalist "constitutional vision" that Ikenberry describes. Transgovernmentalism comprises its own constitutional vision of international order.

The Kantian vision of international order among liberal democracies in *Perpetual Peace* was far more horizontal than vertical, envisaging a "pacific union" bound by the loosest possible ties and cemented primarily by the convergence of domestic values and political structures. Hierarchical institutions that would recreate domestic government on a global scale were to be avoided at all costs. The transgovernmental elements of the current liberal democratic order come closest to achieving this vision. In practice, governmental networks are likely to coexist with and complement liberal internationalist institutions. But they play a critical role in creating and cementing a community of liberal democracies. Moreover, they will play an increasingly important role in expanding that community.

III GOVERNMENT NETWORKS AND (LIBERAL) DEMOCRATIZATION

A pillar of US foreign policy under the Clinton Administration has been the substitution of "enlargement" for "containment": seeking to expand the liberal democratic order.[79] The critical question is how? Labeling States "democratic" or "non-democratic," "liberal" or "illiberal," is difficult and often disingenuous. Monitoring elections is at best a first

---

[79] Policy-makers and scholars use a wide variety of terms to describe the state of relations among advanced industrial democracies, stable but less developed democracies, and emerging democracies. The Clinton Administration often refers to the "community of democracies." *See* "From Containment to Enlargement," speech by Anthony Lake, Assistant to the President for National Security Affairs (Sept. 27, 1993); Text of President Clinton's Statement on NATO Summit (Dec. 10, 1996). John Ikenberry refers to the liberal democratic order; Fareed Zakaria emphasizes the "liberal order," as does Timothy Garton Ash. *See* Ikenberry, "The Myth of Post-War Chaos," *supra* note 4; Zakaria, "Illiberal Democracy," *supra* note 69; and Timothy Garton Ash, "Europe's Endangered Liberal Order," *Foreign Aff.* 77 (1998).

step even toward democratization, much less toward building the liberal institutions that safeguard individual rights against majority whim and protect against the usurpation of political power by a particular faction.[80] Long-term, patient efforts are needed to strengthen these institutions and establish the values of transparency, honesty, and professionalism throughout government that promote genuine democratic accountability and control. In the meantime, it is also increasingly possible for citizens of one country to "borrow" the liberal democratic institutions of another – at least for limited purposes and for a limited time.

A Piercing the shell of sovereignty

Governmental networks can function as important transmission belts for these values. They can also help build and even establish specific government institutions, as well as strengthening and occasionally legitimating their existing members. The value of a transgovernmental network approach is that it sidesteps strategies that require identifying a core "liberal democratic order" that must be "enlarged," an approach that often seems above all to reinforce perceptions of an exclusive democratic – for which many would read "Western" – club. Focusing on individual government institutions instead of the governments of which they are a part acknowledges the complexity and often the contingency of any political engineering project, seeking at best to build liberal democracy one institution at a time.

As noted above, government networks are concentrated among liberal democracies. But they are not limited to them. Non-democratic States may still have institutions capable of participating fully in these networks, such as committed and effective regulatory agencies or a relatively independent judiciary. Indeed, Zakaria distinguishes not only between liberal and illiberal democracies, but also between illiberal democracies and "liberal autocracies," States without popularly elected government but with constitutional protections of individual rights and independent judiciaries.[81] Similarly, States such as China that seek to liberalize their economies without relinquishing centralized political power are finding the need to create more autonomous financial and commercial institutions and to strengthen their courts.

Governmental networks may be a particularly effective way of

---

[80] Zakaria, "Illiberal Democracy," *supra* note 69, pp. 30–32.
[81] *Ibid.*, 28–9. He cites only Hong Kong as a recent example, but notes that a number of countries have achieved this status in the past, such as the Austro–Hungarian empire.

strengthening and improving participating government institutions through a variety of mechanisms. First is simple information exchange, providing developing and/or democratizing countries with a range of institutional models by which to achieve specific policy goals. Through the Federation Internationale de Bourses des Valeurs, for instance, southern African countries such as Mauritius can quickly and easily inform themselves about various ways of regulating a stock market. Such knowledge may readily translate into power not only in the obvious sense of enhanced ability to undertake a particular regulatory project, but also into increased authority in domestic political debates.

Equally important, however, is the possibility that some of the regulatory models on display through the network will not be purely "Western" or "developed." Sovereign sensitivities, particularly against the backdrop of an imperialist past, may be much less likely to be inflamed by recommendations to follow a regulatory model borrowed from Kenya or South Korea than France or Japan. Thus substantive principles and professional values prevalent among contemporary industrialized democracies may be "laundered" through government networks to diminish their "Western" provenance and make them more palatable to States with strong historical and cultural reasons to wish to forge their own governance models. Moreover, many of the adaptations of original Western models by other countries around the world are likely to improve effectiveness of these models in particular developing countries.

A second way in which government networks can help strengthen government institutions outside the core community of industrialized liberal democracies is to provide leverage for the creation of new institutions. Many of the Memoranda of Understanding concluded between the US Securities and Exchange Commission (SEC) and foreign securities regulators, for instance, explicitly require that the foreign counterpart be delegated a certain degree of power and autonomy by its national legislature. SEC technical assistance to its foreign counterpart to build regulatory capacity and expertise is often conditioned on such legislative delegation. Environmental enforcement networks between Canada, the United States, and Mexico, developing under NAFTA auspices, similarly operate to strengthen domestic capacity for effective environmental regulation, largely in Mexico.[82] Under the global mantra

---

[82] Scott C. Fulton and Sperling I. Lawrence, "The Network of Environmental Enforcement and Compliance Cooperation in North America and the Western Hemisphere," *Int'l L.* 30 (1996), p. 111.

of "capacity-building," government networks operating institution to institution can help to reshape the domestic political landscape by creating and empowering new regulatory institutions.

Third, participation in government networks can socialize and strengthen domestic judicial and regulatory institutions in ways that will help them resist political domination, corruption, or simple incompetence back home. For many specific government institutions seeking to carve out a new role and mandate for themselves in domestic politics, participation in government networks can be a valuable source of support. The Organization of Supreme Courts of the Americas, for instance, actively seeks to strengthen norms of judicial independence among its members, many of whom must fend off powerful political forces. Heinz Klug has also described the ways in which the South African Supreme Court uses references to foreign and international law to bolster and legitimate itself while simultaneously developing a distinctively South African jurisprudence.[83] On the regulatory side, a domestic agency can justify a reform agenda by stressing the need to comply with codes of general principles adopted by like agencies around the world through a government network. Examples include principles of sound banking adopted by the Basle Committee, after extensive consultation with central banks in many developing economies, or the new IOSCO principles of securities regulation adopted through the Technical Committee.

Exchanging information, wresting a measure of autonomy from a national legislature, offering transnational moral support and such legitimation as can be afforded by pointing to a global consensus – these may seem an unlikely blueprint for building liberal democracy. But if in fact the success of liberal democratization rests not only on returning power to the people but also on preventing the abuse or usurpation of that power through the rule of law and honest and effective government, then governmental networks are the channels through which successful liberal democratic institutions can transmit their knowledge and experience and sometimes even replicate themselves.

B *"Borrowing" liberal democracy*

Individuals and groups who do not have access to liberal democratic or simply well-functioning government institutions at home may also

---

[83] Heinz Klug, "Bounded Alternatives: the Reception of Constitutional Paradigms and the Civilizing of Unnegotiable Conflicts in South Africa," *Washington Post* (July 9, 1998), A24.

"borrow" them from abroad to achieve a form of representation or a measure of justice that they cannot obtain in their own countries. The clearest example of this phenomenon arises in the human rights context, where victims of human rights violations in countries such as Paraguay, Argentina, Haiti, Nicaragua and the Philippines have sued for redress in the courts of the United States.[84] US courts essentially accepted these cases, even in the face of periodic opposition from the executive branch, by adopting a broad interpretation of a virtually moribund statute dating from 1789.[85] Under this interpretation, aliens may sue in US courts to seek damages from foreign government officials accused of torture and other human rights violations, even where the acts allegedly took place entirely within the foreign country. More generally, human rights NGOs seeking to publicize and prevent human rights violations can often circumvent non-functioning government institutions in their own States – corrupt or terrorized legislatures and politicized courts – by publicizing the plight of victims abroad and mobilizing a foreign court, legislature, or executive to take action against their own government.

Less dramatically, the Russian government has chosen to "borrow" the services of the US Food and Drug Agency, accepting any pharmaceutical licensed by the FDA for distribution in the United States as valid for Russia as well.[86] This decision would be a form of "mutual recognition," popular as a strategy for regulatory cooperation, except that it is not mutual. It is rather the wholesale adoption of the functions, standards, and results of a foreign regulatory agency – a kind of regulatory "out-sourcing." Two securities specialists have recently proposed a regime of "portable reciprocity" for global securities regulation,

---

[84] *See, e.g.*, Filartiga v. Pena-Irala 630, F.2 d 876 (2d Cir. 1980); Tel-Oren v. Libyan Arab Republic, 726 F.2d 774 (D.C. Cir. 1984); Lafontant v. Aristide, 844 F.Supp. 128 (E.D.N.Y. 1994); Fernandez v. Wilkinson, 505 F. Supp. 787 (D. Kan. 1980), aff'd 654 F.2d 1382 (10th Cir. 1981); Von Dardel v. USSR, 623 F. Supp. 246 (D.D.C. 1985); Sanchez-Espinoza v. Reagan, 568 F. Supp. 596 (D.D.C. 1983); Trajano v. Marcos, No. 86–0207 (D. Ha. July 18, 1987); Guinto v. Marcos, 654 F. Supp. 276 (S.D. Cal. 1986); Siderman v. Republic of Argentina, 965 F.2d 699 (9th Cir. 1992). *See* Richard Lillich, "Invoking Human Rights Law in Domestic Courts," *Cinn. L. Rev.* 54 (1985), p. 367.

[85] Judiciary Act of 1789, ch. 20 §9(b), 1 Stat. 73, 77, *codified at* 28 USC §1350 (1982). ("the district courts shall have original jurisdiction of any civil action by an alien for a tort only, committed in violation of the law of nations or a treaty of the United States"). Although the Carter Administration originally supported an expansive interpretation of the Alien Tort Statute to cover human rights claims in Filartiga, *supra* note 84, the Reagan Administration took the opposite position in a number of the cases litigated during its tenure, such as Tel-Oren and Argentine Republic v. Amerada Hess Shipping Corp., 488 US 810 (1988).

[86] *See* Bryan L. Walser, "Shared Technical Decision-making: The Multinational Pharmaceutical Industry, Expert Communities, and a Contextual Approach to Theories of International Relations" (May 15, 1996) (unpublished ms. on file with author).

whereby individual securities issuers would choose one country's laws to govern their activities anywhere in the world, backed up by that country's enforcement capacities.[87] And a Harvard Law professor consulting for the World Bank on financial reform in Nepal has recommended that Nepal "selectively incorporate" US financial regulation, not as the basis for new Nepalese law, but as an ongoing link to the US legal system.[88]

Borrowing foreign government institutions would hardly seem to contribute to democratic self-government. On the other hand, if the choice to go abroad is made not as an alternative to developing regulatory or judicial capacity at home but rather as a temporary expedient or even a long-term complement to strengthened and improved domestic institutions, "borrowing" can help make the fruits of liberal democracy, as well as economic development, more widely available to individuals around the world. The choice to borrow another nation's regulatory scheme may itself be made by democratically elected leaders. In the human rights cases, by contrast, the choice to borrow foreign courts is a more desperate move, but one that can nevertheless provide citizens denied the protection of their rights and government officials responsible for or at least complicit in trampling those rights a taste of what strong courts in their own system could mean.

Disaggregating the State shifts the focus away from reductionist labels of "democratic" versus "non-democratic" and toward the performance of specific government institutions. Expanding transgovernmental networks to include selected institutions from illiberal and/or non-democratic States offers opportunities to strengthen them where possible and to supplant them where necessary. The result is strategies of enlargement that are both realistic and effective.

IV TRANSGOVERNMENTALISM AND THE CHALLENGE OF GLOBAL ACCOUNTABILITY

If government networks are the heart of the liberal democratic order and the best hope of expanding that order, how can we ensure that they themselves are faithful to core liberal democratic principles? Specifically,

---

[87] Stephen J. Choi and Andrew T. Guzman, "Portable Reciprocity: Rethinking the International Reach of Securities Regulation," *S. Cal. L. Rev.* 71 (1998), 903.
[88] Howell Jackson, "A Concept Paper on the Selective Incorporation of Foreign Legal Systems to Promote Nepal as An International Financial Services Center," Professor of Law, Harvard Law School (unpublished).

how can they be held accountable? Any form of global governance faces a potential democratic deficit, this time on a global scale. But a transgovernmental order poses particular challenges and holds out particular opportunities for establishing accountable government.

Transgovernmentalism harnesses the full power of the nation-State in the effort to find and implement solutions to transnational problems. Global governance is often referred to as "governance without government." Governance without government is governance without power. And government without power rarely works. On the contrary, many of the most pressing international and domestic problems result from an absence of government – from insufficient State power – to establish order, build infrastructure, and provide at least a minimum of social services. Private actors may be taking up the slack, but cannot ultimately substitute for the State.

With the exercise of power come the responsibilities of power, but here the many advantages of networks as an organizational form threaten to become liabilities. Networks allow governments to capitalize on the virtues of flexibility and decentralization that new medievalists celebrate with regard to networks of non-State actors. Yet networks have particular deficits as mechanisms for delivering accountable government, as any feminist who has battled "the old boy network" will quickly recognize. Their flexibility and decentralization means that it is very difficult to establish precisely who is acting and when. Influence is subtle and hard to track; important decisions may be made in very informal settings.

Developing mechanisms for holding networks accountable, both in the public and the private realms, is thus a deep and important challenge. In devising strategies to meet this challenge, however, it is important to place the accountability of transgovernmental actors in perspective. Liberal internationalism poses the dangers of an unelected supranational bureaucracy; the new medievalism envisions free-form networks of public and private actors, together with the devolution of power above and below the State, that would make it difficult even to discern the lines of political authority. The accountability of government networks must be weighed and assessed against these alternatives. In this context, government networks have a number of potential advantages.

First, transgovernmentalism assumes the same conception of the State in international relations as in domestic politics: a set of competing and cooperating government institutions with both distinct and overlapping functions. In theory, at least those institutions should be as accountable in their international activities as they are in their domestic affairs. For many, however, the prospect of transnational government by judges and administrative agencies looks more like technocracy than democracy – government by specialized functionaries with little accountability to national legislatures. Government institutions engaged in policy-making with their foreign counterparts will be barely visible, much less accountable, to voters still largely tied to national territory.

These arguments have force, but many prospects for asserting democratic control remain to be explored. As national legislators become increasingly aware of transgovernmental networks, they can expand their oversight capacities and develop networks of their own. Moreover, transnational NGO networks are already capable of monitoring transgovernmental activity. The problem here, however, as many "new medievalists" recognize, is one of NGO accountability, suggesting the need to develop a transgovernmental capacity to monitor and potentially regulate the exercise of non-governmental power.

Second, transgovernmental networks will actually strengthen the State as the primary actor in the international system. The defining attribute of the State has traditionally been the possession of sovereignty – ideally conceived as absolute power in domestic affairs and autonomy in relations with other States. But as Abram and Antonia Chayes observe, sovereignty is actually "status – the vindication of the State's existence in the international system."[89] More important, they demonstrate that in contemporary international relations, sovereignty has been redefined to mean "membership in the regimes that make up the substance of international life."[90]

Disaggregating the State makes it possible to disaggregate sovereignty as well, helping specific State institutions derive strength and status from participation in a transgovernmental order. Lack of accountability is as likely to flow from a weak or failing government as an excessively strong one; liberal democracy is as threatened by anarchy as by autocracy. Thus in many cases, strengthening the State to help create effective government is the necessary first step toward creating accountable government.

Third, government networks can quite easily link up with their subnational and supranational counterparts, as well as with private actors performing the same functions as government officials. If in fact

---

[89] Abram Chayes and Antonia Handler Chayes, *The New Sovereignty: Compliance with International Regulatory Regimes* (Cambridge, Mass.: Harvard University Press, 1995), p. 27.   [90] *Ibid.*

sub- and supra-national actors prove more accountable than government institutions in a world "going global" and "going local" simultaneously, then these actors can be brought into transgovernmental networks. The EU has pioneered this type of multilevel governance through multilayered networks, particularly in areas such as regional policy and urban environmental policy. Contact with their subnational and supranational counterparts has strengthened the ability and effectiveness of national level officials. The question remains open, however, whether the constituents of these officials feel equally empowered, or whether government networks at all levels are equally alienating.

Concerns about accountability are critical to the success of transgovernmentalism as a distinctive feature of the liberal democratic order. If governmental networks cannot be made and seen to be responsive to voters at least to the same extent as national government officials, they will be deemed illegitimate. On the other hand, legitimacy may be conferred or attained independent of mechanisms of direct accountability – performance may be measured by outcomes as much as process. Courts, and even central banks, can earn the trust and respect of voters without being "accountable" in any direct sense. Accountability is a rein running to the electorate; insulated institutions are designed to counter the voters' changing will and whim. More broadly, changing forms of government may require changing criteria of what makes government good.

V CONCLUSION

The post-Cold-War order is taking shape faster than the capacities of pundits to pin it down. At its core, however, the distinctive set of institutions and practices governing relationships among liberal democracies has proved remarkably robust. Among those practices, although largely overlooked, is an increasingly dense web of relations among distinct government institutions: courts, regulatory agencies, executives, and legislators. These relations are becoming increasingly structured, creating transgovernmental networks that are well equipped to address the regulatory problems posed by a global economy and an increasingly global society.

Transgovernmentalism offers answers to the most important challenges facing US foreign policy: the loss of regulatory power attributable to economic globalization and the concomitant need for fast, flexible, and effective decision-making on a global scale. It also provides the possibility of penetrating the fast hardening divisions of the post-Cold-War world. The "first," "second," and "third" worlds have given way to liberal democracies versus everyone else; transgovernmentalism looks beyond such labels to the nature and quality of specific government institutions. Expanding government networks can thus help expand the liberal democratic order, albeit slowly and undramatically. Government networks can also help address perceptions of a global "democracy deficit" by substituting national for supranational bureaucrats. On the other hand, offshore networks of any kind – whether public or private – create their own accountability and potential legitimacy problems.

Transgovernmentalism also provides a powerful conceptual and normative alternative to a liberal internationalism that is reaching its limits and a new medievalism that, like the old Marxism, sees the State simply fading away. In practice, however, transgovernmental strategies to achieve a wide range of policy *desiderata*, including the spread of liberal democracy, will coexist with and complement the efforts both of international institutions, non-governmental organizations, and private actors of all kinds. Governments alone, even disaggregated ones, must recognize the limits of their power and find new ways to use their power most effectively. That will often mean harnessing the energies of actors both above and below the traditional State in ways that can permanently change the political identity and organization of that State. The other chapters in this volume detail many of those efforts; the plea here is primarily to count the State back in.

The new medievalists are right to emphasize the dawn of a new era, in which information technology will transform the world. Government networks are a response to that technology, creating the possibility of a genuinely new conception of world order in which networked institutions perform the functions of a world government – legislation, execution, administration, and adjudication – without the form. The challenge is to ensure not only that it is an order anchored by liberal democracies, but that it is a genuinely liberal democratic order.

PART III
Democracy and the use of force

CHAPTER 7

Sovereignty and human rights in contemporary international law

W. Michael Reisman

> anachronism . . . 1: an error in chronology; esp: a chronological misplacing of persons, events, objects, or customs in regard to each other . . . 2: a person or a thing that is chronologically out of place; esp: one that belongs to a former age and is incongruous if found in the present . . . .
>
> Webster's Third International Dictionary

I

Since Aristotle, the term "sovereignty" has had a long and varied history during which it has been given different meanings, hues and tones, depending on the context and the objectives of those using the word.[1] Bodin and Hobbes shaped the term to serve their perception of an urgent need for internal order. Their conception influenced several centuries of international politics and law[2] and also became a convenient supplementary secular slogan for the various absolute monarchies of the time. Sovereignty often came to be an attribute of a powerful individual, whose legitimacy over territory (which was often described as his domain and even identified with him) rested on a purportedly direct or delegated divine or historic authority but certainly not, Hobbes's covenant of the multitude[3] notwithstanding, on the consent of the people.

The public law of Europe, the system of international law established by the assorted monarchs of the continent to serve their common purposes, reflected and reinforced this conception by insulating from legal scrutiny and competence a broad category of events that were

---

[1] *See Encyclopedia of Public International Law* 10, R. Bernhardt, ed., (New York: North-Holland Pub. Co., 1989), pp. 397, 399 (discussion of historical evolution of term "sovereignty" from Aristotle to present).   [2] *Ibid.* at 401–02.
[3] T. Hobbes, *Leviathan*, M. Oakeshott, ed., (Oxford: B. Blackwell, 1946).

later enshrined as "matters solely within the domestic jurisdiction."[4] If another political power entered the territory of the sovereign (whatever the reason) without his permission, his sovereignty was violated. In such matters, the sovereign's will was the only one that was legally relevant.

With the words "We the People,"[5] the American Revolution inaugurated the concept of the popular will as the theoretical and operational source of political authority. On its heels, the French Revolution and the advent of subsequent democratic governments confirmed the concept. Political legitimacy henceforth was to derive from popular support; governmental authority was based on the consent of the people in the territory in which a government purported to exercise power. At first only for those States in the vanguard of modern politics, later for more and more States, the sovereignty of the sovereign became the sovereignty of the people: popular sovereignty.

It took the formal international legal system time to register these profound changes. Another century beset by imperialism, colonialism, and fascism was to pass, but by the end of the Second World War, popular sovereignty was firmly rooted as one of the fundamental postulates of political legitimacy. Article 1 of the UN Charter established as one of the purposes of the United Nations, to develop friendly relations between States, not on any terms, but "based on respect for the principles of equal rights and self-determination of peoples."

Any lingering doubt that use of the term "self-determination" might have amounted to a mechanical, or at best a deferential, carry-over from Wilsonian diplomacy, and not a radical decision that henceforth the internal authority of governments would be appraised internationally, was dispelled three years later. In the Universal Declaration of Human Rights, a document then describing itself as "a common standard of achievement" but now accepted as declaratory of customary international law, Article 21(3) provided that "[t]he will of the people shall be the basis of the authority of government; this will shall be expressed in periodic and genuine elections which shall be by universal and equal suffrage and shall be held by secret vote or by equivalent free voting procedures."[6] Of course, there had been regional pacts based upon

---

[4] Under Article 15(8) of the Covenant of the League of Nations, if the Council found a dispute between any two parties "to arise out of a matter which by international law is solely within the domestic jurisdiction of that party," the Council would refrain from making any recommendation as to its settlement. *See League of Nations Covenant* Art. 15, para. 8, *reprinted in Am. J. Int'l L.* 13, (Supp. 1919), pp. 128, 134.   [5] US Const., Preamble.

[6] Universal Declaration of Human Rights, GA Res. 217A (III), UN Doc. A/810, at 71 (1948) [hereafter UDHR].

similar notions,[7] much as there had been holy alliances based on their antithesis. The significance of this statement in the Universal Declaration was that it was now expressed in a fundamental international constitutive legal document. In international law, the sovereign had finally been dethroned.

Unlike certain other grand statements of international law, the concept of popular sovereignty was not to remain mere pious aspiration. The international law-making system proceeded to prescribe criteria for appraising the conformity of internal governance with international standards of democracy.[8] Thanks to a happy historical conjunction, modern communications technology has made it possible to verify that conformity rapidly and economically and to broadcast it widely.[9] International and regional organizational monitors now use the new technology in critical national elections so as to ensure that they are free and fair.[10] The

---

[7] *See, e.g.*, Central American Treaty of Peace (Treaty of Washington), Additional Convention to the General Treaty, Art. I, 2 Foreign Relations of the United States 1907, pp. 696ff., at p. 696, *reprinted in Am. J. Int'l L.* 2 (Supp. 1908), pp. 229ff, at pp. 229–30:

> The Governments of the High Contracting Parties shall not recognize any other Government which may come into power in any of the five Republics as a consequence of a coup d'etat, or of a revolution against the recognized Government, so long as the freely elected representatives of the people thereof have not constitutionally reorganized the country.

[8] *See, e.g.*, United Nations Declaration on the Elimination of All Forms of Racial Discrimination, GA Res. 1904 (XVIII) (Nov. 20, 1963); International Convention on the Elimination of All Forms of Racial Discrimination, opened for signature Mar. 7, 1966, 660 UNTS 195; International Convention on the Suppression and Punishment of the Crime of Apartheid, GA Res. 3068 (XXVIII) (Nov. 30, 1973); Convention against Discrimination in Education, Dec. 14, 1960, 429 UNTS 32; Convention concerning Equal Remuneration for Men and Women Workers for Work of Equal Value, June 29, 1951, 165 UNTS 303; Convention on the Elimination of All Forms of Discrimination against Women, GA Res. 34/180 (Dec. 18, 1979); Declaration on the Elimination of All Forms of Intolerance and of Discrimination Based on Religion or Belief, GA Res. 36/55 (Nov. 25, 1981); Convention concerning Forced or Compulsory Labour, June 28, 1930, 39 UNTS 55; Declaration on the Protection of All Persons from Being Subjected to Torture and Other Cruel, Inhuman or Degrading Treatment or Punishment, GA Res. 3452 (XXX) (Dec. 9, 1975); Convention against Torture and Other Cruel, Inhuman or Degrading Treatment or Punishment, GA Res. 39/46 (Dec. 10, 1984); Code of Conduct for Law Enforcement Officials, GA Res. 34/169 (Dec. 17, 1979); and Declaration of Basic Principles of Justice for Victims of Crime and Abuse of Power, GA Res. 40/34 (Nov. 29, 1985); as well as the numerous conventions on social welfare, marriage and the family and cultural rights. *See also* Resolutions Adopted by the General Assembly During its Twentieth Session, 20 UN GAOR Supp. (No. 14) at 53–65, UN Doc. A/6014 (1965) (series of resolutions adopted on non-self-governing territories).

[9] For a discussion of international election monitoring, *see generally*, W. Michael Reisman, "International Election Observation," *Pace Y.B. Int'l L.* 4 (1992), p. 1.

[10] For example, in the Namibia elections, the ballot counting and tabulation were overseen by 1,700 electoral supervisors, part of a United Nations Transition Assistance Group (UNTAG). *See* UN Chron., March 1990, p. 42. Similarly, a UN observation mission for the verification of elections in Nicaragua (ONUVEN) was set up there in December 1989 to observe and monitor the 1990 elections. *Ibid.* at 64.

results of such elections serve as evidence of popular sovereignty and become the basis for international endorsement of the elected government.[11] Indeed, in recent years the United Nations has repeatedly emphasized that genuine democratic elections serve to legitimize the nascent political institutions emerging from States undergoing periods of crisis and transformation.[12] In functional terms, this process constitutes a new type of inclusive international recognition. Decisions to withhold recognition where the will of the people has been demonstrably ignored or suppressed have increasingly led to the next stage, the institution of international programs designed to permit or facilitate the realization of the popular will.[13]

---

[11] After the November 1989 elections in Namibia, the UN Security Council congratulated the people of Namibia and affirmed the election results; the Special Committee on Decolonization declared on December 4 that the Namibian elections had been held "in conformity with established UN standards of decolonization"; and Special Representative Ahtisaari declared that the electoral process had "at each stage been free and fair." *See ibid.* at pp. 41–43.

[12] *See* Gregory H. Fox, "Self-Determination in the Post-Cold War Era: A New Internal Focus?," *Mich. J. Int'l L.* 16 (1995), pp. 733, 753 n.98 (reviewing Yves Beigbeder, *International Monitoring of Plebiscites, Referenda and National Elections: Self-Determination and Transition to Democracy* [1994]) (surveying UN resolutions passed between 1992 and 1994 that underscore the critical importance of democratic processes and, in particular, equitable elections to the reconstitution of States grappling with periods of civil unrest and transition). This trend continues presently. *See, e.g.,* SC Res. 1201, UN SCOR, 52nd Sess., UN Doc. S/Res/1201 (1998) (supporting efforts in the Central African Republic "to consolidate the process of national reconciliation and to help sustain a secure and stable environment conducive to the holding of free and fair elections"); SC Res. 1132, UN SCOR, 52nd Sess., at 1, UN Doc. S/Res/1132 (1997) (demanding that the military junta that overthrew Sierra Leone's democratically elected president on May 25, 1997 "relinquish power in Sierra Leone and make way for the restoration of the democratically-elected Government and a return to constitutional order"); SC Res. 948, 48th Sess., UN Doc. S/Res/948 (1994) (welcoming the return of President Aristide and expressing support "for efforts by [him], democratic leaders in Haiti, and the legitimate organs of the restored government to bring Haiti out of crisis and return it to the democratic community of nations"); GA Res. 117, UN GAOR 3d Comm., 51st Sess., at 8, UN Doc. A/Res/51/117 (1997) (urging Myanmar to comply with "its assurances . . . to take all necessary steps towards the restoration of democracy in accordance with the will of the people as expressed in the democratic elections held in 1990").

In his 1996 report on the human rights circumstances in Myanmar, Judge Rajsoomer Lallah, Special Rapporteur of the Commission on Human Rights, observed that the continuing exercise of all governmental powers by the State Law and Order Restoration Council (SLORC) – a totalitarian political body allegedly established as an "emergency measure" by the armed forces in 1988 – violates the international norm embodied in Articles 21(1) and 21(3) of the UDHR, which establishes the people's will, as reflected in periodic free elections, as the sole legitimate basis of governmental authority. *See Interim Report of the Special Rapporteur of the Commission on Human Rights for Myanmar Pursuant to Hum. Rts. Comm'n Res. 1996/80,* UN GAOR, 51st Sess., Agenda Item 110(c), at 30–34, UN Doc. A/51/466 (1996). Judge Lallah also noted that, although SLORC's initial exercise of power arguably constituted a temporary measure justified by "a state of public emergency," its maintenance of power for over five years subsequent to Myanmar's 1990 general elections deprived it of "any juridical legitimacy. . . ." *Ibid.* at 31.

[13] After Rhodesia's unilateral declaration of independence in 1965, the international community overwhelmingly denounced the action and refused to recognize Rhodesia as one independent State. *See generally* "The Situation in Southern Rhodesia: Resolutions Adopted by the General Assembly and the Security Council of the United Nations," *reprinted in Am. J. Int'l L.* 60

II

Although the venerable term "sovereignty" continues to be used in international legal practice, its referent in modern international law is quite different. International law still protects sovereignty, but – not surprisingly – it is the people's sovereignty rather than the sovereign's sovereignty. Under the old concept, even scrutiny of international human rights without the permission of the sovereign could arguably constitute a violation of sovereignty by its "invasion" of the sovereign's *domaine réservé*. The UN Charter replicates the "domestic jurisdiction–international concern" dichotomy, but no serious scholar still supports the contention that internal human rights are "essentially within the domestic jurisdiction of any State" and hence insulated from international law.

This contemporary change in content of the term "sovereignty" also changes the cast of characters who can violate that sovereignty. Of course, popular sovereignty is violated when an outside force invades and imposes its will on the people. One thinks of the invasion of Afghanistan in 1979 or of Kuwait in 1990.[14] But what happens to sovereignty, in its modern sense, when it is not an outsider but some home-grown specialist in violence who seizes and purports to wield the authority of the government against the wishes of the people, by naked power, by putsch or by coup, by the usurpation of an election or by those systematic corruptions of the electoral process in which almost 100 percent of the electorate purportedly votes for the incumbent's list (often the only choice)? Is such a seizer of power entitled to invoke the international legal term "national sovereignty" to establish or reinforce his own position in international politics?

(1966), p. 921. For commentary, *see* Myres S. McDougal and W. Michael Reisman, "Rhodesia and the United Nations: The Lawfulness of International Concern," *Am. J. Int'l L.* 62 (1968), p. 1.

With respect to Namibia, the United Nations consistently refused to recognize South Africa's occupation of Namibia. *See, e.g.,* Miguel Marin-Bosch, "How Nations Vote in the General Assembly of the United Nations," *Int'l Org.* 41 (1987), pp. 705ff., at pp. 705–06 (pointing out that Namibia was the subject of more resolutions than all other past decolonization issues combined). Indeed, by Resolution 2145 (XXI) of October 27, 1966, the General Assembly placed Namibia under the direct responsibility of the United Nations so as to enable Namibians to exercise their right of self-determination. It also established the UN Council for Namibia (by Resolution 2248 (S-V) of May 19, 1967) with the objective, *inter alia*, of obtaining the withdrawal of South Africa from Namibia. *See Report of the United Nations Council for Namibia*, 39 UN GAOR Supp. (No. 24) at 1, UN Doc. A/39/24 (1984). Other international programs eventually led to the independence of Namibia on March 21, 1990.

[14] On the invasion of Afghanistan by the Soviet Union and the applicable norms of armed conflict, see generally W. Michael Reisman and James Silk, "Which Law Applies to the Afghan Conflict?," *Am J. Int'l. L.* 82 (1988), p. 459.

Under the old international law, the internal usurper was so entitled, for the standard was *de facto* control: the only test was the effective power of the claimant. In the *Tinoco* case,[15] Costa Rica sought to defend itself by claiming a violation of its popular sovereignty. Tinoco, the erstwhile Minister of War, had seized power in violation of the Constitution. Therefore, the subsequent restorationist Costa Rican Government contended, his actions could not be deemed to have bound Costa Rica. But Chief Justice Taft decided that by virtue of his effective control, Tinoco had represented the legitimate government as long as he enjoyed that control.

The *Tinoco* decision was consistent with the law of its time. Were it applied strictly now, it would be anachronistic, for it stands in stark contradiction to the new constitutive, human rights-based conception of popular sovereignty. To be sure, there were policy reasons for *Tinoco*, which may still have some cogency, but the important point is that there was then no countervailing constitutive policy of international human rights and its conception of popular sovereignty.

Caudillos and their like appear to be susceptible to a megalomania that identifies their corporeal selves with the symbols of the nation and the State. They invoke a "'sovereignty' so grandiose and capricious . . . it might be supposed to be a deliberate caricature, save for the intensity of the sentiments that are mobilized around the symbol itself."[16] Happily, the international legal system in which declamations such as "l'etat, c'est moi" were coherent has long since been consigned to history's scrap heap. In our era, such pronouncements become, at least for audiences at a safe remove, the stuff of refined comedy. They would be occasions for general hilarity, even in the countries where they are still staged, were it not for the endless misery that the dictators who grant themselves sovereignty always inflict upon the human beings trapped within the boundaries of the territory the dictators have confused with themselves.

III

In many countries, the internal political situation is murky and constitutional procedures for the orderly transfer of power are nonexistent or ineffective. In a flurry of coups and putsches, both outsiders and insiders

---

[15] Tinoco Case (Great Brit. v. Costa Rica), R. Int'l Arb. Awards 1 (1923), p. 369, *reprinted in Am. J. Int'l L.* 18 (1924), p. 147.
[16] Myres S. McDougal, Harold D. Lasswell and W. Michael Reisman, "The World Constitutive Process of Authoritative Decision," *in* M. S. McDougal and W. M. Reisman, *International Law Essays* (Mineola, N.Y.: Foundation Press, 1981), p. 197.

Sovereignty and human rights

may be unable to ascertain the popular will, especially if the disorder or tyranny has prevented it from being consulted or expressed. Even in the absence of elections – indeed, even when there are "supervised" elections – it is often clear that the vast majority of the people detest those who have assumed power and characterize themselves as the government. It is more difficult, however, to say who the people would wish in their stead. They may not know, which is one of the reasons that international legal supervision of elections is designed to include an adequate period for candidacies to be developed and to allow campaigning, so that voters can make the informed choice that is at the center of free and fair elections.

But in circumstances in which free elections are internationally supervised and the results are internationally endorsed as free and fair and the people's choice is clear, the world community does not need to speculate on what constitutes popular sovereignty in that country. When those confirmed wishes are ignored by a local caudillo who either takes power himself or assigns it to a subordinate he controls, a jurist rooted in the late twentieth century can hardly say that an invasion by outside forces to remove the caudillo and install the elected government is a violation of national sovereignty.

Tanganyika, which gained its independence in 1961,[17] provides one of the earliest examples of an intervention that affirmed the modern human-rights-based conception of sovereignty. In January 1964, one week after a revolution in neighboring Zanzibar,[18] Tanganyika's small army mutinied. President Julius Nyerere turned to Britain for aid, and a small contingent of Royal Marines flew in and suppressed the mutiny in one day. The death toll amounted to three mutinous soldiers. No civilians were injured, and Britain's marines sustained no casualties. After it ended, President Nyerere promptly broadcast a message to his people, proclaiming that "an army which did not obey the people's government was not an army of that country and was a danger to the whole nation." On the following day, he sent a letter to the House of Commons, thanking "with deep gratitude . . . the help which has been given by Britain to Tanganyika." Evidently, this was politically incorrect. The next day President Nyerere apologized publicly to his people for asking Britain to restore order.[19] Tanzania, as it is now known, may not be a political paradise. But there have been no more coups, and subsequent transfers of power have been constitutional. Unfortunately, Tanzania failed to establish a firm precedent.

---

[17] "Tanzania," in *The Statesman's Year-Book 1994–95*, Brian Hunter, ed., 131ˢᵗ ed. (New York: St. Martin's Press, 1994), pp. 1268ff., at p. 1268.   [18] *Ibid.*
[19] East Africa, *Keesing's Contemporary Archives* (Mar 21–28, 1964), pp. 19, 963.

Consider, for instance, the comparatively recent failure of the international community to intervene after the 1994 military coup in the Gambia: After Sir Dawda Jawara won the presidency in 1970, the Gambia had been for over two decades one of Africa's few successful multiparty democracies. Despite persistent difficulties with national poverty, a series of Jawara governments had managed to compile a commendable record of freedom of the press, independence of the judiciary, and respect for human rights.[20] But on July 23, 1994, a small contingent of disgruntled officers in the Gambia's national army of some 800 people ousted the elected government in a bloodless coup that had been planned and mounted in less than twenty-four hours.[21] The self-proclaimed – and in multiple ways, oxymoronic – "provisional military president," a twenty-nine-year-old recent graduate of a military-police training course in the United States, promised that this would be a "coup with a difference."[22] But predictably, the new military dictatorship reneged on its pledge to announce a timetable for a return to democracy by the end of September.[23] Instead, it barred all political activity, arrested dissenting journalists, and confined ministers of the former government to house arrest.[24]

President Jawara, like Nyerere three decades before, requested military aid to restore democracy. But international response to the destruction of the Gambia's democracy diverged sharply from Britain's prompt and effective action in Tanzania thirty years earlier. Although a US warship was positioned off the coast of the Gambia on the day of the coup, Washington refused to intervene, despite the US Ambassador's

[20] *See, e.g.,* US Dep't of State, *The Gambian Rights Practices 1993* (1994), available in LEXIS, News Library, CURNWS File; James Roberts, "Soldiers Take Over in Gambia; 2000 UK Tourists Trapped," *Independent* (July 24, 1994), p. 12. *But see* Peter da Costa, "Gambia Politics: Multiparty Advocate's Tolerance Was His Undoing," *Inter Press Service* (July 25, 1994), *available in,* LEXIS, Nexis Library, INPRES File (noting institutionalized corruption of Jawara's regime, in addition to outstanding human rights record).
[21] Pap Saine, "Gambia's Capital Calm After Coup," *Reuters World Service* (July 24, 1994), *available in* LEXIS, Nexis Library, REUTER File; "Soldiers Take Power in Bloodless Coup"; Other Developments, Facts on File, *World News Dig.* (Sept. 8, 1994), p. 644, A2, *available in* LEXIS, Nexis Library, FACTS File.
[22] Howard W. French, "Waiting for the 'Difference' in Gambia's Military Coup," *Int'l Herald Trib.,* Aug. 30, 1994, *available in* LEXIS, Nexis Library, IHT File.
[23] Justice Fofanneh, "Gambia–European Union: Further Sanctions Imposed on Junta," *Inter Press Service* (Oct. 13, 1994), *available in* LEXIS, Nexis Library, INPRES File. The junta then delayed the restoration of democracy to December 1998. *See* "US-Gambia: U.S. Cuts All Aid to Gambia," *Inter Press Service* (Oct. 28, 1994), *available in* LEXIS, Nexis Library, INPRES File [hereafter "US Cuts All Aid"].
[24] Howard W. French, "In Gambia, New Coup Follows Old Pattern," *N.Y. Times* (Aug. 28, 1994), 1, p. 4.

contention that the seventy marines on board could suppress the coup.[25] In fact, for ten days, the United States failed even to condemn the coup officially. Finally, it announced that it would review security and development assistance to the Gambia in light of the coup,[26] and on October 28, the United States cut off all but humanitarian aid.[27] Europe's response was scarcely less tepid. Within three weeks, Britain, Germany, and the European Union were praising the officers for the peaceful nature of the coup and threatening to cut off aid only if democracy were shunted aside.[28] Ultimately, these States decided to suspend development aid to the Gambia.[29] But this expression of displeasure, though clearly indicative of an *opinio juris* in favor of human rights, did not restore democracy. To the contrary, it effectively punished the population at large, whose members were already victims of a violation of their fundamental political rights.

Contrast this failure to intervene in the Gambia with the international community's response to the analogous, and relatively contemporaneous, circumstances that developed in Haiti: in December 1990, after decades of dictatorship, the Haitian people overwhelmingly elected Jean-Bertrand Aristide as President. Every aspect of the election was monitored by international organizations and confirmed as "free and fair."[30] Within months, the army, an ill-trained force of some five thousand men led by General Raoul Cédras, seized power, expelled Aristide,

---

[25] Richard Dowden, "Deposed President Calls for Help; Gambia's Sir Dawda Jawara Breaks His Silence to Describe to Richard Dowden, Africa Editor, the Military Coup Which Overthrew a Model Multiparty Democracy with a Unique Human Rights Record," *Independent* (Sept. 26, 1994), p. 11.
[26] "US Condemns Coup," *Xinhua News Agency* (Aug. 2, 1994), *available in* LEXIS, Nexis Library, XINHUA File. The United States initially offered only to mediate between Jawara and the military junta that ousted him. "US Steps in as Gambia Coup Mediator," *Agence Fr. Presse* (July 24, 1994), *available in* LEXIS, Nexis Library, AFP File.   [27] "US Cuts All Aid," *supra* note 23.
[28] Pap Saine, "Long Civil Rule Handover Worries Gambians," *Reuters World Service* (Oct. 25, 1994), *available in* LEXIS, Nexis Library, REUTER File.
[29] "EU Suspends Aid to Gambia in Reaction to Continued Military Rule," *Eur. Rpt.* (Nov. 11, 1994), *available in* LEXIS, Nexis Library, EURRPT File. The World Bank, which initially had cut off aid to the Gambia, later restored some funds. "Gambia's Leader Links Ex-Finance Ministers to Plot," *Reuters World Service* (Nov. 15, 1994), *available in* LEXIS, Nexis Library, REUTER File.
[30] On international monitoring of the Haitian election of December 16, 1990, *see* Georges A. Fauriol, "Inventing Democracy: The Elections of 1990," *in* Georges A. Fauriol, ed., *The Haitian Challenge: US Foreign Policy Considerations* (Washington, D.C.: Center for Strategic and International Studies, 1993), pp. 53, 57; Inter-American Commission on Human Rights, Annual Report, 1990–91, p. 468, OEA/Ser.L/V/II.79, rev.1 (1992). For US reaction and assessment, see Howard W. French, "Haitians Overwhelmingly Elect Populist Priest to the Presidency," *N.Y. Times* (Dec. 17, 1990), A1; "Haiti's Choice, and Father Aristide's," *N.Y. Times* (Dec. 18, 1990), A24; "Haiti's First Freely Elected Leader," *Wash. Post* (Dec. 20, 1991), A23. On international election monitoring in general, see W. Michael Reisman, *supra* note 9.

and brutally suppressed popular protest. Once again, the Nyerere strategy of prompt military intervention was neglected. Instead, the Organization of American States and the UN Security Council condemned the coup and its aftermath and ordered economic sanctions to dislodge the military.

Not surprisingly, these sanctions failed. Economic sanctions are effective when the target is a rational economic maximizer. The Haitian military elite may have been rational, but no evidence suggests that the economy was its principal concern. All the sanctions accomplished was to reduce the Haitian economy – already the poorest in the hemisphere – to rubble while creating economic opportunities for the ruling military elite, which promptly added contraband to its already thriving narco-traffic business. Here again, economic sanctions, far from ousting the military insurgents, contributed to the suffering of the very individuals whose political rights they were intended to vindicate. But critically, unlike in the Gambia, the international community did ultimately determine to intervene militarily on behalf of Aristide and Haiti's democratically legitimate government. On July 31, 1994, the Security Council, acknowledging the gravity of the situation and recognizing that an "exceptional response" was required, passed Resolution 940, authorizing multinational military action.[31] This marked the first occasion on which the Security Council, acting under Chapter VII, authorized the use of military force to reinstate a democratically elected government.[32]

Cross-border military actions should certainly never be extolled, for they are necessarily brutal and destructive of life and property. They may well be unlawful for a variety of other reasons. But if they displace the usurper and emplace the people who were freely elected, they can be characterized, in this particular regard, as a violation of sovereignty only if one uses the term anachronistically to mean the violation of some mystical survival of a monarchical right that supposedly devolves *jure gentium* on whichever warlord seizes and holds the presidential palace, or if the term is used in the jurisprudentially bizarre sense to mean that inanimate territory has political rights that preempt those of its inhabitants.[33]

---

[31] SC Res. 940, 48th Sess., UN Doc. S/Res/940 (1994).
[32] *See* Morton H. Halperin and Kristen Lomasney, "Guaranteeing Democracy: A Review of the Record," *J. Democracy* (April 1998) pp. 134, 138.
[33] *See* Christopher Stone, "Should Trees Have Standing? – Toward Legal Rights for Natural Objects," *S.Cal. L. Rev.* 45 (1927), 450; Laurence Tribe, "Ways Not to Think about Plastic Trees: New Foundations for Environmental Law," *Yale L.J.* 83 (1974), 1315. For a cogent critique on this point, *cf.* Schwartz, "The Rights of Nature and the Death of God," *Pub. Interest*, 97 (1989), p. 3.

This is not to say that every externally motivated action to remove an unpopular government is now permitted, or that officer corps that feel obsolescence hard upon them can claim a new *raison d'etre* and start scouring the globe for opportunities for "democratizing" interventions. Authoritative conclusions about the lawfulness of the unilateral use of force, no less than about any other unilateral action, turn on many contextual factors: e.g., the contingencies allegedly justifying the unilateral use, the availability of feasible persuasive alternatives, the means of coercion selected, the level of coercion used (the classic test of necessity and proportionality), whether the objectives of the intervener include internationally illicit aims, the aggregate consequences of inaction, and the aggregate consequences of action.[34] But it is to say that the suppression of popular sovereignty may be a justifying factor, not a justification *per se* but a *conditio sine qua non*. And it is to say that the word "sovereignty" can no longer be used to shield the actual suppression of popular sovereignty from external rebuke and remedy.

International law is still concerned with the protection of sovereignty, but, in its modern sense, the object of protection is not the power base of the tyrant who rules directly by naked power or through the apparatus of a totalitarian political order, but the continuing capacity of a population freely to express and effect choices about the identities and policies of its governors. In modern international law, the "unilateral declaration of independence" by the Smith Government in Rhodesia was not an exercise of national sovereignty but a violation of the sovereignty of the people of Zimbabwe.[35] The Chinese Government's massacre in Tiananmen Square to maintain an oligarchy against the wishes of the people was a violation of Chinese sovereignty. The Ceausescu dictatorship was a violation of Romanian sovereignty. President Marcos violated Philippine sovereignty, General Noriega violated Panamanian sovereignty, and the Soviet blockade of Lithuania violated its sovereignty. Fidel Castro violates Cuban sovereignty by mock elections that insult the people whose fundamental human rights are being denied, no less than the intelligence of the rest of the human race. In each case, the violators often brazenly characterize the international community's condemnation as itself a violation of their sovereignty. Sadly, some organizations and some scholars, falling victim to anachronism, have given them comfort.

---

[34] *See* M. S. McDougal and F. Feliciano, *Law and Minimum World Public Order* (New Haven, Conn.: Yale University Press, 1961), ch. 3.   [35] *See supra* note 13.

In modern international law, sovereignty can be violated as effectively and ruthlessly by an indigenous as by an outside force, in much the same way that the wealth and natural resources of a country can be spoliated as thoroughly and efficiently by a native as by a foreigner.[36] Sovereignty can be liberated as much by an indigenous as by an outside force. As in the interpretation of any other event in terms of policy, context and consequence must be considered.

IV

The international human rights program is more than a piecemeal addition to the traditional corpus of international law, more than another chapter sandwiched into traditional textbooks of international law. By shifting the fulcrum of the system from the protection of sovereigns to the protection of people, it works qualitative changes in virtually every component. Many of the old terms survive, but in using them in a modern context, one should bear in mind Holmes's lapidary dictum: "A word is not a crystal, transparent and unchanged; it is the skin of a living thought and may vary greatly in color and content according to the circumstances and the time in which it is used."[37]

When constitutive changes such as these are introduced into a legal system while many other struts of the system are left in place, appliers and interpreters of current cases cannot proceed in a piecemeal and mechanical fashion. Precisely because the human rights norms are constitutive, other norms must be reinterpreted in their light, lest anachronisms be produced. This process of "updating" or "contemporization" or *actualisation*, as French scholars call it, is not unknown to international law. In the *South-West Africa* opinion,[38] the International Court indicated the absurdity of mechanically applying an old norm without reference to fundamental constitutive changes, and national courts have often expressed the need and authority to actualize.[39] The same style of actualization is required with regard to the assessment of the lawfulness of human rights actions. When this is not done, legal arguments and judgments will be marked by anachronism.

In the debate over the US action in Panama in the United Nations,

---

[36] *See* W. Michael Reisman, "Harnessing International Law to Restrain and Recapture Indigenous Spoliations," *Am J. Int'l L.* 83 (1989), 56.   [37] Towne v. Eisner, 245 US 372, 376 (1918).
[38] South-West Africa – Voting Procedure, 67 ICJ (1955) 77 (Advisory Opinion of June 7).
[39] M. S. McDougal, H. Lasswell and J. Miller, *The Interpretation of Agreements and World Public Order* (New Haven, Conn.: Yale University Press, 1967), ch. 4.

the Nicaraguan Permanent Representative, whose Government had requested the meeting, opened it by proclaiming: "Once again an offence has been committed against our peoples. Once again an attempt is being made to make brute force appear to be law. Once again the principles which are the foundation of international relations have been violated."[40] The Permanent Representative proceeded to cite, chapter and verse, the United Nations Charter and the OAS Charter to establish "[t]his flagrant violation of Panama's sovereignty and territorial integrity."[41] No reference whatsoever was made to Manuel Antonio Noriega's suppression of popular sovereignty, or to the fact that both the internationally supervised election before the military action and the opinion polls after it indicated overwhelming support for the change that was realized.[42] These issues were swept away by indirection, when the Permanent Representative said that "no argument can possibly justify intervention against a sovereign State."[43]

This is what Professor D'Amato, in his remarkable article, has called "the rhetoric of statism."[44] The anachronism here is effected by the selective use of the language of international law, carefully screening out everything that has been introduced by the human rights movement. It may be contrasted with the remark of Thomas Pickering, the US Permanent Representative, that "the people, not governments, are sovereign."[45] That formulation, in turn, oversimplifies the decision calculus now required, for, as expressed, it could make that single variable determinative of lawfulness in all future cases. But at least it expresses the critical new constitutive policy in international law, which is completely absent from the Nicaraguan formula.

When the Security Council passed Resolution 940, authorizing armed intervention against the Haitian military regime that had deposed President Aristide, critics charged that UN military action

---

[40] UN Doc. S/PV.2899, (Dec. 20, 1989), pp. 3–5. I treat this statement as made in good faith. It is not inappropriate to note, however, that those who invoke this argument frequently reserve for their governments a right of intervention for various revolutionary purposes, e.g., wars of national liberation. See, in this regard, W. Michael Reisman, "Old Wine in New Bottles: the Reagan and Brezhnev Doctrines in Contemporary International Law and Practice," *Yale J. Int'l L.* 13 (1988), 171.   [41] UN Doc. S/PV.2899, *supra* note 40, p. 4.

[42] One of the more ironic aspects of the Panama affair was that all indications before and after the US invasion were that while the vast majority of the Panamanian people viewed it as a liberation, the other governments of the region voted in the OAS to condemn it as a violation of Panamanian sovereignty. According to most news reports, the US military action in Panama was met with overwhelming approval by the Panamanian people. *See, e.g.,* "After Noriega," *Economist* (Jan. 16, 1990), p. 37.   [43] UN Doc. S/PV.2902, at p. 7 (Dec. 23, 1989).

[44] A. D'Amato, "The Invasion of Panama Was a Lawful Response to Tyranny," *Am. J. Int'l L.* 84 (1990), pp. 516, 518.   [45] UN Doc. S/PV.2902, *supra* note 43, p. 8.

against Haiti would violate its sovereignty. But whose sovereignty? In modern international law, what counts is the sovereignty of the people and not a metaphysical abstraction called the State.[46] If the *de jure* government, which was elected by the people, wants military assistance, how is its sovereignty violated? And if the purpose of the coercion is to reinstate a *de jure* government elected in a free and fair election after it was ousted by a renegade military, whose sovereignty is being violated? The military's? Multilateral intervention in Haiti, in short, did not violate but in fact vindicated Haitian sovereignty – a term appropriately identified with the wishes of Haiti's *people*.

Analogous circumstances in Sierra Leone recently led to a similar multilateral intervention. On May 25, 1997, a military coup orchestrated by Major Johnny Paul Koromah, deposed Sierra Leone's first elected president, Ahmad Tejan Kabbah. Both the United Nations and the Organization of African Unity (OAU) shortly issued statements condemning the coup, calling for the reinstatement of the democratically elected government and demanding the restoration of constitutional order.[47] Indeed, the OAU Council of Ministers, affirming the strong link between genuine popular sovereignty and international political legitimacy, called upon "all African countries, and the International Community at large, to refrain from recognizing the new regime and lending support in any form whatsoever to the perpetrators of the *coup d'etat*."[48]

Koromah remained recalcitrant, and in July 1997, the Economic Organization of West African States (ECOWAS) imposed a complete embargo on Sierra Leone. In October, the Security Council, again acting under Chapter VII of the UN Charter, reinforced this embargo with additional sanctions, and "*demand[ed]* that the military junta take immediate steps to relinquish power in Sierra Leone and make way for the restoration of the democratically elected Government . . . "[49]

---

[46] *See generally*, W. Michael Reisman, "Coercion and Self-Determination: Construing Article 2(4)," *Am. J. Int'l L.* 78 (1984), p. 642; Panel, "The United Nations Charter and the Use of Force: Is Article 2(4) Still Workable?," *Am. Soc. Int'l L. Proc.* 78 (1984), p. 68.

[47] *Statement by the President of the Security Council Regarding the Situation in Sierra Leone*, UN. SCOR, 51st Sess., 3781st mtg., UN Doc. S/PRST/1997/29 (1997); OAU Council of Ministers Res. CM/Dec.356 (LXVI), Sierra Leone, Doc. CM/2004 (LXVI), *reprinted in* UN Doc. A/52/465, Agenda Item 42, Annex.   [48] OAU Council of Ministers, *supra* note 47.

[49] SC Res. 1132, UN SCOR, 51st Sess., UN Doc. S/RES/1132 (1997). As it had with respect to Haiti's situation several years earlier, the Security Council determined that a military coup displacing a democratically elected regime – a matter conventionally regarded as "solely within the domestic jurisdiction" of a sovereign state – had created circumstances constitutive of a "threat to international peace and security," and consequently, invoked Chapter VII enforcement measures.

Although these economic pressures compelled Koromah to negotiate a peace agreement, his subsequent breach of the October 1997 cease-fire led to military intervention. On February 13, 1998, Nigerian troops authorized by ECOWAS displaced Koromah's military government and reinstated President Kabbah.[50] Critically, the military effort was in this instance spearheaded by a regional African force (and not, as in Haiti, by a force comprised largely of US troops), a fact that tends to weaken the criticism that democratic intervention will invariably constitute a mere political subterfuge for self-interested interference by the Western superpowers. Here again, the United Nations endorsed the use of a cross-border military action to restore a democratically elected regime that had been toppled by a military coup. And here again, it was the coup, not the global community's intervention, that violated national sovereignty, properly understood.[51]

Under the version espoused by Nicaragua's representative in the debate over Panama, sovereignty is not international protection of the will of the people, but international protection for a group that calls itself the government against the wishes of the people. There is no international test of the legitimacy of a self-proclaimed government. The only test is internal naked power. Under this theory, Panama's sovereignty is violated by the removal of the usurper and the establishment of conditions for the assumption of power by the legitimate government. That is an anachronism.

Anachronism can only be avoided in legal decision by systematic actualization, which considers inherited norms in the context of changed constitutive normative systems and makes sensitive assessments of the relative weight each is to be given and the various intensities with which each is demanded.

[50] *See* Halperin and Lomasney, *supra* note 32, p. 142.
[51] "At stake," wrote Secretary-General Kofi Annan on the day preceding the adoption of Security Council Resolution 1132, "is a great issue of principle, namely, that the efforts of the international community for democratic governance, grounded in the rule of law and respect for human rights, shall not be thwarted through illegal coups." *Letter from the Secretary-General to the President of the Security Council dated October 7, 1997*, UN Doc. S/1997/776 (1997). At the time of this writing, circumstances in Sierra Leone have deteriorated again, and it continues to suffer from a brutal civil war. *See, e.g.*, "The Darkest Corner of Africa," *Economist* (Jan. 9, 1999), p. 41. Yet the current situation, while deplorable, would have occurred regardless of regional African intervention; "many of its elements predate Sierra Leone's independence in 1961." *Ibid*. Indeed, its persistence is facilitated by the lack of greater political will to support the West African alliance led by Nigeria. The Nigerians "with economic troubles of their own and a continuing democratization process that will lead to pressures to withdraw troops from foreign entanglements . . . cannot possibly do the job without sustained financial, logistical and political support from the United States." Editorial, "The Horror in Sierra Leone," *Washington Post* (Jan. 28, 1999), A26.

V

The consequences of these changes are far-reaching. Some are clearly beneficial to the new values of the international system. Some hold the potential for destabilizing the system. On the credit side, international human rights puts current and erstwhile tyrants on notice that monarchical and elitist conceptions of national sovereignty cannot be invoked to immunize them from the writ of international law. The princes may not like this, but for peoples languishing under despotism and dictatorship, the development promises, at least, the condemnation by international law of the violation of their sovereignty and the possibility, uncertain as it may be, of a remedy.

On the debit side, while the bite of human rights norms is extended, so, too, is systemic instability. In decentralized systems whose members themselves perforce make the decisions, the more the number of constitutive appraisal norms, the more the number of cross-border appraisals and the greater the possibility of cross-border meddling by various actors. The problem is contained, to an extent, when internationally supervised "free and fair" elections credibly and unequivocally indicate the wishes of a majority of the people. It is also contained when other non-electoral indicators show the popular will, though without the clarity and freedom vouchsafed by secret ballot. When popular wishes are usurped violently, the confirmed expression of popular sovereignty tells everyone who the real usurper is and who should rightfully constitute the government, no matter how convincing the newspeak of the dictator's apparatus may be.

Unambiguous situations, however, may be exceptions. Restoring democracies is not always that simple. Sometimes it is messy, unpleasant, costly, and susceptible to abuse even when the intentions of the intervener are relatively pure; and sometimes it is susceptible to denunciation even when the intentions of the denouncer are not. When internationally supervised elections result in an absence of consensus on who should govern, or the integrity of the elections is doubtful, or there have been no elections, or a civil insurrection has left diverse groups vying for power, no one can be sure that the unilateral intervener from the outside is implementing popular wishes. To varying extents, the intervener will be shaping them.

In some circumstances, the banner of popular sovereignty can become a fig leaf for its suppression by foreign intervention, especially when governments bent on intervention maintain stables of alternative local leaders who can be brought forward to authorize an invasion at the appropriate time.[52] In other circumstances, as in Algeria, it may become difficult to determine the right action to take when the government about to be brought to power through a democratic election espouses a manifest program to violate fundamental human rights. But even when the right course of action is clear, external intervention may simply not be feasible.[53]

In practice, therefore, there may be a factual "gray" area between unequivocal expressions of popular will through internationally supervised, observed, or validated elections, on the one hand, and the atrocities that warrant humanitarian intervention, on the other. Situations falling into the gray area will simply not lend themselves to unilateral action.

The most satisfactory solution to this problem is the creation of centralized institutions, equipped with decision-making authority and the capacity to make it effective. But in the immediate future, that solution remains unlikely, and to make it a condition of lawful decision now only evades addressing the policies that the notion of popular sovereignty encapsulates. The given of contemporary international decision-making is the absence of such institutions and the need to focus on regulating unilateral decision-making. Because rights without remedies are not rights at all, prohibiting the unilateral vindication of clear violations of rights when multilateral possibilities do not obtain (as they did, for instance, in Haiti and Sierra Leone) is virtually to terminate those rights.

Some scholars nonetheless remain skeptical towards the notion that unilateral force may properly be employed to restore democratic governance. Professor Ruth Wedgwood, for instance, argues that "[t]he

---

[52] *See, e.g.*, Reisman and Silk, *supra* note 14, pp. 466–79 (discussion of factual situation in Afghanistan leading to "invitation" of Soviet armed forces by Afghan "government"). This danger – that the restoration of democratic government will become a subterfuge for self-interested intervention by larger, more powerful States – can be minimized when the government that has been usurped was elected in internationally monitored, free, and fair elections. That is why no one protested in December 1990, when the United States put the Panamanian police who tried to overthrow the Endara Government back in their barracks, or in November and December 1989, when US planes boxed in the Philippine air force and helped quell an incipient coup against Mrs. Aquino.

[53] Moreover, even when the issues are clear and the mission is feasible, the results do not always seem stellar. As Panama, Grenada, and the Philippines indicate, reinstating a government chosen in an internationally supervised free and fair election does not, *ipso facto*, solve all national problems. But it bears emphasis that this is not the objective of this type of humanitarian intervention. Internationally authorized military action is not a panacea for the ills of society. Its only objective is to reinstate an elected civilian government – to enable the people to have the government they selected in a free and fair election – when nothing else works. That it does not simultaneously reconstruct an economy and solve all the other ills of society does not mean that it has failed. Would Grenada be better off of it were still under the renegades who murdered Maurice Bishop and seized power? Would Panama be better off if Noriega were still dictator?

emerging norms of the United Nations, the Organization of American States, and the Conference on Security and Cooperation in Europe have not ratified the use of unilateral military intervention."[54] The basic issue at stake here is customary international law, which all international actors maintain a role in shaping. Whether Professor Wedgwood's assertion proves correct, consequently, depends upon what customary law is made. Thomas Franck, in an important, indeed indispensable, article on the emerging right to democratic governance, similarly writes, "[As a policy matter,] entitlement to democracy can only be expected to flourish if it is coupled with a reiterated prohibition on . . . unilateral initiatives."[55] But, in fact, exactly the opposite is the case.

A commitment to democracy, coupled with an unwillingness to allow for its unilateral enforcement (if that is the only feasible option), has led to uses of economic sanctions that might appropriately be dubbed "trigger-happy." On the positive side, economic sanctions confirm that the international community views the right to constitutional government as a basic human right and its violation as a threat to peace. Indeed, economic sanctions, no less than military sanctions, require such a characterization as a prerequisite to their application – and with good reason, for they are as destructive as military sanctions and far more indiscriminate. They do not distinguish between combatants and non-combatants. Thus, on the negative side, responding to these violations with economic sanctions, more often than not, severely punishes the victims while enriching the villains.

The results are anomalous: the international commitment to the democratic rights of peoples, coupled with a disposition to authorize only economic sanctions to vindicate these rights, creates sanctions programs that harm the innocent. At the same time, they serve neither to deter nor to remove the thugs responsible for these human rights violations. Nor do economic sanctions help to restore popular government. On the contrary, this misguided approach permits the persistence of violations of the democratic aspirations of peoples by military thugs and bandits, who

---

[54] Committee on International Arms Control and Security Affairs and Committee on International Law, "The Use of Armed Force in International Affairs: The Case of Panama," *Rec. Ass'n B. City N.Y.* 47 (1992), pp. 604, 688 (citation omitted) (text by Ruth Wedgwood). Professor Wedgwood restates her analysis in Ruth Wedgwood, "The Use of Armed Force in International Affairs: Self-Defense and the Panama Invasion," *Colum. J. Transnat'l L.* 29 (1991), p. 609. *But cf.*, Malvina Halberstam, "The Copenhagen Document: Intervention in Support of Democracy," *Harv. Int'l L.J.* 35 (1993), p. 163 (discussing Copenhagen Document, which supports States' action in defending democratically elected governments from overthrow).

[55] Thomas M. Franck, "The Emerging Right to Democratic Governance," *Am. J. Int'l L.* 86 (1992), pp. 46, 84–85.

will continue to find shelter in the anachronistic conceptions of "territorial integrity" and "sovereignty."

Obviously, in the long run, we must work to develop an organized and genuinely international method for maintaining democratic processes in new States. But in the meantime, in many cases, some members of the Security Council will undoubtedly refuse to authorize international action in support of internal democracy. In the short run, then, effective international protection of fledgling democracies will depend on decisive action by the great industrial democracies.

It is no longer politically feasible or morally acceptable to suspend the operation of human rights norms until every constitutive problem is solved. In the interim, new criteria for unilateral human rights actions must be established. In addition, more refined techniques for their legal appraisal and more effective means for their condemnation when such actions are themselves unlawful must be developed.[56] One contribution of our profession should be to develop methods for assessing popular will and making judgments about divergences.

The violation of sovereignty has heretofore largely been treated with a passive strategy: absorbing those who have been obliged to flee their own countries. With the increasing refinement of transportation, domestic human rights pathologies now generate larger and larger numbers of refugees. But the welfare democracies of the world, which are the preferred refuge of those fleeing human rights violations in their own countries, have begun to reach the limits of their absorptive capacities. The passive strategy of dealing with violations of sovereignty will no longer work. An active strategy that addresses the pathology itself is required, both pragmatically and by the very conception of modern sovereignty.

Unfortunately, the tendency among some diplomats – and even human rights lawyers – has been to view violations of the right to democratic governance expressed in Article 21 of the Universal Declaration as lamentable, of course, but somehow less urgent than other human rights violations. This is a serious error: when men with guns evict the elected government, dismiss the law, kill, destroy wantonly, and control the population by intimidation and terror, not only does this constitute an awful violation of the integrity of the self, but all other human rights that depend on the lawful institutions of government become matters for the discretion of the dictator. Military coups constitute terrible violations

---

[56] *See* Dino Kristsiotis, "Reappraising Policy Objections to Humanitarian Intervention," *Mich. J. Int'l L.* 19 (1998), p. 1005.

of the political rights of the collectivity, and they invariably bring in their wake serious violations of all other human rights.

Violations of the right to popular government are not, therefore, secondary or somehow less important. To the contrary, democracy is the condition *sine qua non* for the realization of many other internationally prescribed human rights. Democracy may also be the condition *sine qua non* of international peace, for a growing body of evidence indicates that democratic countries do not attack each other.[57] But democracy will not take root in many new States if outsiders fail to take steps necessary to sustain it. The doctrine of humanitarian intervention allows such action.

VI

Because human rights considerations introduce so many more variables into the determination of lawfulness, an even heavier burden of deliberation devolves upon international lawyers in assessing the lawfulness of actions. Matters become more complex and uncertain than they were in an international legal system that was composed of a few binary rules applied to a checkerboard of monarchical States and, most particularly, that lacked an international code of human rights. One can no longer simply condemn externally motivated actions aimed at removing an unpopular government and permitting the consultation or implementation of the popular will as *per se* violations of sovereignty without inquiring whether and under what conditions that will was being suppressed, and how the external action will affect the expression and implementation of popular sovereignty. The identification of what is clearly "externally motivated action" is itself an increasingly difficult task.

No one is entitled to complain that things are getting too complicated. If complexity of decision is the price for increased human dignity on the planet, it is worth it. Those who yearn for "the good old days" and continue to trumpet terms like "sovereignty" without relating them to the human rights conditions within the States under discussion do more than commit an anachronism. They undermine human rights.

---

[57] *See generally* Bruce Russett, "Politics and Alternative Security: Toward a More Democratic, Therefore More Peaceful, World," *in* Burns H. Weston, ed., *Alternative Security: Living Without Nuclear Deterrence* (1990), p. 107 (setting forth and explaining empirical data that demonstrates that democracies do not fight one another).

CHAPTER 8

"You, the People": pro-democratic intervention in international law

Michael Byers and Simon Chesterman*

What difference does it make to the dead, the orphans and the homeless, whether the mad destruction is wrought under the name of totalitarianism or the holy name of liberty or democracy? I assert in all humility, but with all the strength at my command, that liberty and democracy become unholy when their hands are dyed red with innocent blood.

M. K. Gandhi[1]

I INTRODUCTION

There is now a considerable literature on "the emerging right to democratic governance,"[2] arguing in essence that the democratic entitlements spelt out in human rights treaties are at last achieving more than hortatory status.[3] For the greater part of the twentieth century, the relatively small number of actual democracies and uncertainty as to the precise content of such a right precluded general endorsement of a principle of democracy.[4] Moreover, as James Crawford argues, the manner in which classical international law conceptualized sovereignty and the State was deeply *un*democratic, or at least capable of operating in deeply undemocratic ways.[5]

In the course of the 1980s, however, democracy came to assume far

---

* The authors would like to express their thanks to Sven Koopmans and Georg Nolte for their critical comments on an earlier draft.
[1] M. K. Gandhi, *Non-Violence in Peace and War*, 2 vols. (Ahmedabad: Navajivan Publishing House, 1942) vol. I, p. 357.
[2] Thomas M. Franck, "The Emerging Right to Democratic Governance," *Am J. Int'l L.* 86 (1992), p. 46.
[3] *See especially* Universal Declaration of Human Rights, Art. 21 ("the will of the people shall be the basis of the authority of government"); International Covenant on Civil and Political Rights, Art. 25; European Convention for the Protection of Human Rights and Fundamental Freedoms, Protocol 1, Art. 3; American Convention on Human Rights, Art. 23
[4] James Crawford, "Democracy and International Law," *Brit Y.B. Int'l L.* 44 (1993), pp. 113–16.
[5] *Ibid.* at pp. 117–19; *see also* chapter 3 of this volume.

greater importance: the number of States legally committed to open, multiparty, secret-ballot elections with universal franchise grew from about one-third in the mid-1980s[6] to as many as two-thirds in 1991;[7] new discourses in international law and international relations stressing democracy as a value emerged;[8] and the international community showed a greater willingness to encourage or apply pressure upon a State to hold or recognize the results of elections, or take part in election-monitoring.[9] Although the "right" to democratic governance remains, at best, inchoate, the crucial questions that will be addressed in this chapter are *whether* and *how* any such right may be enforced. In particular, we address the claim that the denial of a right to democracy gives rise to a right of armed intervention on the part of third States and/or the United Nations. And for this purpose we adopt the definition of intervention advanced by Hersch Lauterpacht in 1955, namely "dictatorial interference by a State in the affairs of another State for the purpose of maintaining or altering the actual condition of things."[10] To be even more specific, our focus here is neither intervention by invitation nor collective or individual self-defense, but rather uninvited intervention involving the use of force and justified on the basis of supporting or restoring democracy.

We begin by considering arguments that one State (or a coalition of States) may lawfully intervene unilaterally to promote democracy in another, absent authorization from the UN Security Council. Such arguments commonly depend upon a restrictive interpretation of the prohibition on the use of force in Article 2(4) of the UN Charter.[11] Sometimes they also seek to redefine sovereignty as "defeasible" where

---

[6] Crawford, "Democracy and International Law," *supra* note 4, p. 116.

[7] Franck, "Democratic Governance," *supra* note 2, p. 47, puts the number at 110 States, citing the US Department of State's Country Reports on Human Rights Practices for 1990 and reports in the *N.Y. Times*.

[8] *See* Crawford, "Democracy and International Law," *supra* note 4, p. 122 n.39 and sources cited therein; as well as the other chapters in this book.

[9] *See* Secretary-General of the United Nations, *Agenda for Democratization*, UN Doc. A/51/761 (1996); Secretary-General of the United Nations, *Support by the United Nations System of the Efforts of Governments to Promote and Consolidate New or Restored Democracies*, UN Doc. A/50/332 and Corr 1 (1995). *See also* Gregory H. Fox, "The Right to Political Participation in International Law," *Yale J. Int'l L.* 17 (1992), pp. 539–607; Crawford, "Democracy and International Law," *supra* note 4, pp. 123–26; Karl J. Irving, "The United Nations and Democratic Intervention: Is 'Swords Into Ballot Boxes' Enough?," *Denver J. Int'l L. & Pol'y* 25 (1996), 41–70.

[10] Lassa Francis Lawrence Oppenheim, *International Law*, 8th ed., Hersch Lauterpacht, ed. (London: Longmans, 1955), p. 305.

[11] Article 2(4) reads: "All Members shall refrain in their international relations from the threat or use of force against the territorial integrity or political independence of any State, or in any other manner inconsistent with the Purposes of the United Nations."

it is not exercised in accordance with the "will of the people." We conclude that this approach is, on either basis, neither legally accurate nor politically desirable – both conclusions being borne out by the two major examples of unilateral intervention sometimes characterized as "pro-democratic": the United States' invasions of Grenada in 1983 and of Panama in 1989.

We then turn to collective intervention under Security Council authorization. Resolution 940 – which in 1994 authorized a US-led multinational force "to use all necessary means to facilitate the departure from Haiti of the military leadership" and restore the Aristide government-in-exile[12] – is considered by some to have set an important precedent. But it is far from clear how a non-democratic regime, even one established by a violent *coup d'etat*, could in itself constitute a threat to international peace and security sufficient to invoke Chapter VII of the UN Charter. Although the legal and political checks imposed by the requirement of Security Council authorization constitute important safeguards against the abuses which may result from a unilateral right of armed intervention, they in no way avoid more basic concerns about the legitimacy of imposing democracy from the outside. This is borne out by the more recent but equally ambiguous example of the Security Council's support for the Economic Community of West African States (ECOWAS) action in Sierra Leone.

We take the position that to discuss the "democratic entitlement" in terms of external enforcement is fundamentally to misconceive its nature. "Popular sovereignty" may well represent the converging aspirations of many peoples around the globe, but the only vehicle in which this particular human right may find meaningful expression remains – in all but the most exceptional of situations – sovereignty of a more traditional kind.

II UNILATERAL INTERVENTION TO PROMOTE DEMOCRACY

Michael Reisman set this debate off in 1984 in an editorial comment in the *American Journal of International Law*. He called for a radical reinterpretation of Article 2(4) that would allow one State unilaterally to depose a despotic government in another.[13] Noting that the absence of an effective international security system required the preservation of a right to

---

[12] SC Res. 940 (1994), para. 4.
[13] W. Michael Reisman, "Coercion and Self-Determination: Construing Charter Art. 2(4)," *Am J. Int'l L.* 78 (1984), p. 642.

self-defense, he used simple premises and forceful rhetoric to argue further that the failure of the United Nations to achieve peace and order not only legitimated but also *required* individual States to resort to self-help.[14] The question, he asserted, was no longer whether but *when* self-help was lawful, which meant that the overthrow of despotic governments became a legitimate goal of States seeking to enhance order and further human rights in an essentially anarchic world.[15]

In a further editorial comment published in 1990, Reisman went on to argue that the term "sovereignty" constituted an anachronism when applied to undemocratic governments or leaders, and that traditional concepts of sovereignty were being replaced by a "popular sovereignty" vested in the individual citizens of a State.[16] This meant that unilateral armed intervention to support or restore democracy did not violate sovereignty – and therefore international law – but instead upheld and vindicated it.

These two arguments, rereading Article 2(4) and redefining sovereignty, are dealt with in turn below.

A Unilateral pro-democratic intervention in theory

As explained above, in 1984 Reisman argued that the failure of the United Nations to achieve peace and order both legitimated and required individual States to resort to self-help, and that the unilateral overthrow of despotic governments was therefore permitted under international law.[17] However, his rhetorical blurring of the line between self-defense and non-defensive uses of force served only to beg the question of the legitimacy of such action, as Oscar Schachter pointed out in his response to Reisman.[18] And, ironically, it did not achieve a significant degree of academic support until the early 1990s – at a time when the Security Council was much more active than ever before and arguments

---

[14] *Cf* Myers S. McDougal, "Authority to Use Force on the High Seas," *Naval War College Rev.* 20(5) (1967), 19, *reprinted in Inter'l L. Stud.* 61 (1980), p. 559.
[15] Reisman, "Coercion and Self-Determination," *supra* note 13, p. 643.
[16] W. Michael Reisman, "Sovereignty and Human Rights in Contemporary International Law," *Am. J. Int'l. L.* 84 (1990), p. 866. *See* chapter 7 of this volume.
[17] By seeking to justify the unilateral imposition of one State's view of the ideal political order, Reisman provided a legal basis for the so-called "Reagan Doctrine." Nicholas O. Berry, "The Conflict Between United States Intervention and Promoting Democracy in the Third World," *Temple L. Q.* 60 (1987), p. 1017. *See generally* Christopher C. DeMuth, *The Reagan Doctrine and Beyond* (Washington, D.C.: American Enterprise Institute for Public Policy Research, 1988).
[18] *See* Oscar Schachter, "The Legality of Pro-Democratic Invasion," *Am J. Int'l. L.* 78 (1984), p. 646.

in favor of unilateralism were, as a consequence, significantly weakened.[19]

1 Rereading Article 2(4) of the UN Charter

Reisman proposed to avoid the legal problems attendant to his doctrine of self-help by rereading Article 2(4) as imposing a two-stage test for legitimacy in the use of force: will a particular use of force enhance world order? And, if so, will it enhance "the ongoing right of peoples to determine their own political destinies"?[20] Although this test bears little relation to the text of Article 2(4), Anthony D'Amato adopted a similar position when he argued that the invasion of Panama complied with Article 2(4) because "the United States did not intend to, and has not, colonialized, annexed or incorporated Panama."[21] With respect, we disagree.[22] Leaving aside the arguments of consent and self-defense that are usually invoked by States acting in circumstances that might be seen to constitute pro-democratic intervention,[23] the approach taken by Reisman and D'Amato demands an interpretation of Article 2(4) that allows an exception for certain "legitimate" uses of force. Such an exception may be based either on the language of Article 2(4) itself, or on a teleological reading of the Charter.

Article 2(4) prohibits "the threat or use of force against the territorial integrity or political independence of any State, or in any other manner inconsistent with the Purposes of the United Nations." The only exceptions to this prohibition in the text of the Charter are the

---

[19] See infra, section III.   [20] Reisman, "Coercion and Self-Determination," supra note 13, p. 643.
[21] Anthony D'Amato, "The Invasion of Panama was a Lawful Response to Tyranny," Am J. Int'l. L. 84 (1990), p. 520.
[22] Such debates are, of course, not new, but echo earlier arguments over the precise limits on the use of force provided for in the UN Charter. See Derek Bowett, Self-Defence in International Law (Manchester University Press, 1958); Ian Brownlie, International Law and the Use of Force by States (Oxford University Press, 1963); Thomas M. Franck, "Who Killed Article 2(4)?," Am. J. Int'l L. 64 (1970), p. 809; Louis Henkin, "The Reports of the Death of Article 2(4) are Greatly Exaggerated," Am. J. Int'l L. 65 (1971), p. 549.
[23] Such arguments include "intervention by invitation" and the "right" to rescue nationals. On intervention by invitation, see Brownlie, Use of Force, supra note 22, pp. 317–27; Georg Nolte, Eingreifen auf Einladung – Zur völkerrechtlichen Zulässigkeit des Einsatzes fremder Truppen im internen Konflikt auf Einladung der Regierung (Intervention upon Invitation – Use of Force by Foreign Troops in Internal Conflicts at the Invitation of a Government under International Law [English Summary]) (Berlin: Springer Verlag, 1999). On the right to rescue, see Brownlie, Use of Force, supra note 22, pp. 289–98; Natalino Ronzitti, Rescuing Nationals Abroad Through Military Coercion and Intervention on Grounds of Humanity (Oxford University Press, 1985); Derek Bowett, "The Use of Force for the Protection of Nationals Abroad," in A. Cassese, ed., The Current Legal Regulation of the Use of Force (Oxford University Press, 1986), p. 3.

"inherent right of individual or collective self defense" in Article 51, and Security Council authorized enforcement actions under Chapters VII and VIII. It is occasionally argued that pro-democratic intervention and humanitarian intervention are legitimate because they are not directed against the "territorial integrity or political independence" of the target State, and are not inconsistent with the "Purposes of the United Nations."[24] But as Oscar Schachter rightly observed, the idea that wars waged in a good cause violate neither the territory nor the polity demands an "Orwellian construction" of those terms.[25] In other words, the argument runs *directly* contrary to the clear intentions behind Article 2(4), which were to prohibit unilateral determinations of the just war by vesting sole authority for the non-defensive use of force in the Security Council. Not surprisingly, the argument also runs contrary to numerous statements by the General Assembly[26] and the International Court of Justice.[27]

Reisman also argued that the failure to do more than condemn violations of Article 2(4) meant that they were "to all intents and purposes validated."[28] This argument, however, conflated the problem of the enforcement of international law with the utility of a normative system in any form, as became more clear in Reisman's 1990 editorial comment:

Because rights without remedies are not rights at all, prohibiting the unilateral vindication of clear violations of rights when multilateral possibilities do not obtain is virtually to terminate those rights.[29]

---

[24] In addition to D'Amato, *supra* note 21, *see* Fernando R. Tesón, *Humanitarian Intervention: An Inquiry into Law and Morality*, 2nd edition (Irvington-on-Hudson, N.Y.: Transnational Publishers, 1997), p. 151 and sources cited therein. For a concise expression of an opposing view, *see* Rudolf Bernhardt, *Encyclopedia of Public International Law* (Amsterdam: Elsevier, 1992), vol. II, p. 927.

[25] Schachter, "Pro-Democratic Invasion," *supra* note 18, 649.

[26] *See, e.g.*, Declaration on Friendly Relations, GA Res. 2625 (XXV) (1970) (unanimous): "No State or group of States has the right to intervene, directly or indirectly, *for any reason whatever*, in the internal or external affairs or any other State"; "Every State has an inalienable right to choose its political, economic, social and cultural systems, *without interference in any form by another State*." (Emphasis added.) *Cf* GA Res. 45/150 (1990) (adopted 128–8–9): "the efforts of the international community to enhance the effectiveness of the principle of periodic and genuine elections should not call into question each State's sovereign right freely to choose and develop its political, social, economic and cultural systems, *whether or not they conform to the preferences of other States*." (Emphasis added.)

[27] *See* Corfu Channel Case, 1949 ICJ 4, p. 35: "The Court can only regard the alleged right of intervention as the manifestation of a policy of force, such as has, in the past, given rise to the most serious abuses and such as cannot, whatever be the present defects in international organization, find a place in international law." Military and Paramilitary Activities in and Against Nicaragua (Nicaragua v. United States) (Merits) 1986 ICJ 14, p. 133. *See also* below note 109 and accompanying text.   [28] Reisman, "Coercion and Self-Determination," *supra* note 13, p. 643.

[29] Reisman, "Sovereignty and Human Rights," *supra* note 16, p. 875.

It is not clear whether this was intended as a legal argument. As for its strength as a political argument, while we accept that vigilante justice may be needed in some lawless situations, this is a far cry from the claim that sheriff's badges should be handed out to any right-minded person with a gun.

Yet notwithstanding the radical nature of this claim, we accept that it is at least *conceivable* that repeated assertions of a right of self-help by certain States (most notably the United States) could now provide the basis for a new rule of customary international law running parallel to, and supplementing, the UN Charter.[30] This new rule could operate either in respect of self-help generally, or in respect of unilateral pro-democratic intervention more specifically.

In addition to the allegedly pro-democratic interventions in Grenada in 1983 and Panama in 1989, recent possible examples of self-help include: the June 1993 US missile strikes on Iraq in response to an alleged assassination attempt on former President George Bush; the August 1998 US missile strikes on Sudan and Afghanistan in response to terrorist attacks on its embassies in Nairobi and Dar es Salaam; NATO threats to bomb Serbian forces in and around Kosovo in late 1998 and early 1999; the December 1998 strikes on Iraq by the United States and UK and the continuing enforcement by those two States of their "no fly zones." It is possible to characterize each of these four examples as the assertion of a right that was neither specifically provided for in the UN Charter, nor roundly condemned by the international community as a whole.

Although many States chose not to protest these particular actions, there are a number of reasons why it cannot be accepted that they – and the general absence of protest – have been sufficient to change the international law on the use of force in general and thus (perhaps) to

---

[30] *See* Nicaragua, 1986 ICJ 14, p. 100, para. 188: "The effect of consent to the text of such resolutions cannot be understood as merely that of a 'reiteration or elucidation' of the treaty commitment undertaken in the Charter. On the contrary, it may be understood as an acceptance of the validity of the rule or set of rules declared by the resolution by themselves... It would therefore seem apparent that the attitude referred to expresses an *opinio juris* respecting such rule (or set of rules), to be thenceforth treated separately from the provisions, especially those of an institutional kind, to which it is subject on the treaty-law plane of the Charter." On the formation of customary international law and its relationship to treaties, *see generally*, Michael Byers, *Custom, Power and the Power of Rules: International Relations and Customary International Law* (Cambridge University Press, 1999), *especially* pp. 166–80; Nancy Kontou, *The Termination and Revision of Treaties in the Light of New Customary International Law* (Oxford: Clarendon, 1994); Hugh Thirlway, *International Customary Law and Codification* (Leiden: Sijthoff, 1972).

strengthen the argument in favor of a specific right of unilateral pro-democratic intervention. First, in a situation where an almost universally ratified treaty provides rules that prohibit the unilateral use of force except in self-defense, the amount of State practice and evidence of *opinio juris* necessary to change any rule of customary international law existing parallel to those treaty rules – and thus, arguably, the treaty rules themselves – would have to be substantial, widespread, and more or less consistent, so as to overcome the resistance to change inherent in the treaty (as a set of established, legally binding obligations backed up by the principle of *pacta sunt servanda*) and in its ratifications (as individual instances of State practice and evidence of *opinio juris* for the purposes of customary international law).[31]

The State practice and *opinio juris* in favor of even a limited right of self-help is neither substantial, widespread, nor consistent. The four possible examples of self-help referred to above were not conducted with the felt and expressed purpose of developing a right of this kind. Rather than asserting an independent right of action, the acting States relied on the traditional exceptions to Article 2(4), namely self-defense and/or Security Council authorization – and even the *bona fides* of these justifications be questioned (the United States actions in "self-defense" may be more properly characterized as reprisals[32] while authorization to use force against Serbia and Iraq can only be found through a tortured reading of a number of Security Council resolutions[33]). It is also difficult to see how such practice could ever provide the evidence of *opinio juris* necessary to create a rule of customary international law when the putative rule in question is not expressly and centrally relied upon, and especially where it would have such a high threshold of contrary treaty rules, State practice, and *opinio juris* to overcome. By not asserting self-help as a principal justification, these States have in fact demonstrated that they do not believe that such a right is part of customary international law. The argument that there has been a change in favor of a more

---

[31] When, in the 1969 *North Sea Continental Shelf Cases*, the International Court of Justice addressed the issue of whether treaty provisions may generate customary international law, it stated: "There is no doubt that this process is a perfectly plausible one and does from time to time occur: it constitutes one of the recognized methods by which new rules of customary international law may be formed. At the same time this result is not lightly to be regarded as having been attained." 1969 ICJ 3, p. 41, para. 71. *See generally* Byers, *Custom*, *supra* note 30, pp. 166–80.

[32] On reprisals generally, *see* Brownlie, *Use of Force*, *supra* note 22, pp. 219–24; Derek Bowett, "Reprisals Including Recourse to Armed Force," *Am. J. Int'l L.* 66 (1972), 1; R.W. Tucker, "Reprisals and Self-Defense: The Customary Law," *Am. J. Int'l L.* 66 (1972), 581.

[33] *See* Christian Tomuschat, "Use of Force Against Iraq," *Die Friedens-Warte* 73(1) (1998), 75–81.

specific right of pro-democratic intervention has thus become even more difficult to sustain.

Even if they had been conducted with the felt and expressed purpose of developing a right of self-help, a total of six (or ten or twelve) interventions of this kind in a half-century of State practice and *opinio juris* in support of non-intervention would not a new rule of international law make. In fact, in the latter half of the twentieth century the international community has in general responded to unilateral interventions in a resoundingly negative way, no matter how morally just the cause (and with the notable exceptions of interventions by advance invitation – of which there have been many, especially in francophone Africa[34] – and interventions to protect nationals in danger[35]). The responses to the Soviet Union's interventions in Hungary, Czechoslovakia, and Afghanistan, to the US interventions in Vietnam, Grenada, and Panama, to Indonesia's invasion of East Timor, China's annexation of Tibet, and Israel's bombing of an Iraqi nuclear reactor are but a few examples of how the preponderance of State practice operates against the creation of additional exceptions to Article 2(4). Even if one argued that the *opinio juris* was not sufficiently clear in the direct responses to these actions, the many resolutions and declarations of the UN General Assembly on this point are equally decisive.

However, D'Amato and some other (principally American) international lawyers take the view that only physical acts and not statements constitute State practice for the purposes of customary international law.[36] This view has aptly been referred to by Ian Brownlie as "'Rambo' superpositivism,"[37] for in so far as it concerns the change of customary rules it would seem to require violations of customary international law. As far as the law governing the use of force is concerned, this view

---

[34] Recent examples include: Liberia (1992–99) (arguably), Lesotho (1998), Sierra Leone (1997–99) (arguably). *See generally*, Nolte, *Eingreifen auf Einladung*, *supra* note 23.

[35] Examples include: Belgian and US nationals in the Congo (1964), US nationals in Cambodia (1975), Israeli nationals at Entebbe, Uganda (1976).

[36] *See, e.g.*, Anthony D'Amato, *The Concept of Custom* (Ithaca, N.Y.: Cornell University Press, 1971), p. 88, Anthony D'Amato, "Trashing Customary International Law," *Am. J. Int'l L.* 81 (1987), 101; Fredric Kirgis, "Custom on a Sliding Scale," *Am. J. Int'l L.* 81 (1987), 146; Arthur Weisburd, "Customary International Law: The Problem of Treaties," *Vand. J. Transnat'l. L.* 21 (1988), p. 1; Karol Wolfke, *Custom in Present International Law*, 2nd rev. ed. (Dordrecht: Martinus Nijhoff, 1993), p. 42; Karol Wolfke, "Some Persistent Controversies Regarding Customary International Law," *Neth. Y.B. Int'l L.* (1993), pp. 3–4.

[37] Ian Brownlie, "The United Nations Charter and the Use of Force, 1945–1985," *in* Cassese, ed., *Use of Force*, *supra* note 23, p. 156. Rambo was a film character of the 1980s who only knew one way in which to relate to other people – through the use of force.

accords great weight to acts of intervention and no weight at all to protests, resolutions and declarations condemning them. It is therefore, in Michael Akehurst's words, "hardly one to be recommended by anyone who wishes to strengthen the rule of law in international relations."[38] It leaves little room for diplomacy and peaceful persuasion and, perhaps most importantly, marginalizes less powerful States within the international legal system. It is a view which has repeatedly been rejected by the International Court of Justice, by the vast majority of States, and by most scholars – including many from within the United States.[39]

2 Rereading sovereignty

An alternative approach that is claimed to legitimize unilateral armed intervention to promote democracy (or other noble ends) depends on a reconceptualization of sovereignty. Much has been written on the decline of sovereignty as the defining concept of international law and international relations;[40] indeed, the very idea of a "right to democracy" itself is testimony to this change. At its most extreme, "popular sovereignty" is said to have displaced the traditional notion of sovereignty as the "critical new constitutive policy" of international law.[41] On this view, the Austinian conception of the sovereign as (by definition) the repository of legal authority has been supplanted by the State authorized to represent and protect the individuals from whom it derives its *raison d'être*.[42]

Reisman, writing in 1990, used this rationale to argue that:

> The Chinese Government's massacre in Tiananmen Square to maintain an oligarchy against the wishes of the people was a violation of Chinese sovereignty. The Ceausescu dictatorship was a violation of Romanian sovereignty. President Marcos violated Philippine sovereignty, General Noriega violated Panamanian sovereignty . . .[43]

Pursuing the argument yet further, Reisman concluded that it is "anachronistic" to say that the United States violated Panama's sovereignty in

---

[38] Michael Akehurst, "Custom as a Source of International Law," *Brit Y.B. Int'l L.* 47 (1974–75), p. 8.
[39] *See* Byers, *Custom, supra* note 30, pp. 134–36 and citations therein.
[40] *See, e.g.,* Simon Chesterman, "Law, Subject and Subjectivity in International Relations: International Law and the Postcolony," *Melbourne U. L. Rev.* 20 (1996), p. 979, and citations therein.
[41] Reisman, "Sovereignty and Human Rights," *supra* note 16, p. 874. *See also* J. G. Starke, "Human Rights and International Law" *in* Eugene Kamenka and Alice Erh-Soon Tay, eds., *Human Rights* (New York: St. Martin's, 1978), pp. 113–31.
[42] *See, e.g.,* L. J. Macfarlane, *The Theory and Practice of Human Rights* (London: M. T. Smith, 1985) p. 7.
[43] Reisman, "Sovereignty and Human Rights," *supra* note 16, p. 872.

launching an invasion to capture its (allegedly) illegitimate head of State.[44]

In our view, this conclusion involved a *non sequitur* of serious proportions. Although we agree that the concept of popular sovereignty plays an important role in modern international law, it simply does not follow that the illegitimacy of one regime authorizes a foreign state – *any* foreign State (though one can guess *which* foreign State) – to use force to install a new and "legitimate" regime. Although similar positions are adopted by D'Amato and Fernando Tesón, who dismiss any defense of the principle of non-intervention as examples of "the rhetoric of statism"[45] and "the Hegelian myth"[46] respectively, what they and Reisman do not appear to consider is the possibility that *both* Noriega's voiding of the 1989 election *and* the US invasion violated Panamanian sovereignty, albeit in different ways.

The basic problem here is the failure to recognize that, within any normative system, rights will inevitably conflict. It is not enough to assert that the rights of Panamanians are being violated and that this must trump any conflicting right that prohibits the unilateral use of force in international relations. Despite the fact that sovereignty has to some degree been transformed since the adoption of the UN Charter, it is far from clear that democracy has displaced peace as the principal concern of that instrument, and of the international legal system more generally. A comparison may be made with the right to self-determination: enshrined in the major human rights instruments and numerous resolutions of the General Assembly, it is nevertheless commonly accepted to be limited – as a result, in part, of Articles 2(4) and 2(7) of the Charter – to the colonial context and by the principle of *uti possidetis*.[47]

There is also a certain question of consistency here. If one accepts that non-democratic States are international legal persons capable of acting as such (for example, in their capacity to conclude binding

---

[44] *Ibid.* at p. 874.
[45] D'Amato, "The Invasion of Panama," *supra* note 21, p. 518; *see also* Reisman, "Sovereignty and Human Rights," *supra* note 16, p. 874.
[46] Tesón, *Humanitarian Intervention*, *supra* note 24, pp. 55–61. Interestingly, in the second edition of his book-length defense of a right of humanitarian intervention, Tesón does not mention the US invasion of Panama.
[47] *See generally* Clyde Eagleton, "Self-Determination in the United Nations," *Am J. Int'l L.* 47 (1953), p. 88; U. O. Umozurike, *Self-Determination in International Law* (Hamden, Conn.: Shoe String Press, 1972); Eyassu Gayim, *The Principle of Self-Determination* (Oslo: Norwegian Institute of Human Rights, 1990), *Reference Re: Secession of Quebec*, Supreme Court of Canada (August 20, 1998), available at <http://www.scc-csc.gc.ca>. On *uti possidetis*, *see* Steven Ratner, "Drawing a Better Line: *Uti Possidetis Juris* Today," *Am. J. Int'l L.* 90 (1996), p. 590; Malcolm Shaw, "The Heritage of States: The Principle of *Uti Possidetis Juris* Today," *Brit. Y.B. Int'l L.* 67 (1996), p. 75.

treaties), it seems odd to argue that their international legal rights do not extend to the basic principle prohibiting the use of force. This inconsistency is exacerbated by the fact that the prohibition of force is widely regarded as having achieved the status of a peremptory, *jus cogens* rule. A treaty condoning the use of force would thus be void under Article 53 or 64 of the 1969 Vienna Convention on the Law of Treaties (VCLT).[48] In contrast, even the most ardent supporters of the "right to democratic governance" do not claim that this specific right has achieved *jus cogens* status. In this context it is important to note that the "right to democratic governance" is not coterminous with the right to self-determination, which is regarded by some as a *jus cogens* rule and does not require the operation of democratic processes. How a non-peremptory rule could trump a peremptory rule remains unexplained.

The point may also be made that there are distinct practical advantages associated with the international legal system's designation of the State as the autonomous holder of most rights and obligations at the international level. Among other things, this designation enables the principle of sovereign equality to reduce the distortions in law-making influence that result from the severe social inequalities that exist among States.[49] It also facilitates the smooth operation of diplomatic relations – for example, by eliminating the need to enquire whether a government accurately represents the wishes of "the people" when ratifying treaties and entering into contracts. Reisman's proposal, if accepted, would dramatically increase the uncertainty and subjectivity associated with international and transnational legal relations, to no one's advantage except, perhaps, those very few States capable of applying it in practice.[50]

---

[48] *See* Nicaragua 1986 ICJ 14, p. 100, para. 190 (citing Report of the International Law Commission, 18th Session *I.L.C. YB.* 2 (1966), pp. 172, 247). VCLT, Art. 53 provides that a treaty is void "if, at the time of its conclusion, it conflicts with a peremptory norm of general international law." Vienna Convention on the Law of Treaties, Art. 64 reads: "If a new peremptory norm of general international law emerges, any existing treaty which is in conflict with that norm becomes void and terminates." The archetypal example of such a treaty is a pact of aggression, though Dinstein argues that a treaty between two States purporting to absolve each other from the prohibition of the use of force in order to decide to settle a dispute by war will also be void *ab initio*. Yoram Dinstein, *War, Aggression and Self-Defense*, 2nd edn. (Cambridge University Press, 1994), pp. 103–04. On *jus cogens* rules generally, *see* Byers, *Custom, supra* note 30, pp. 183–95; Stefan Kadelbach, *Zwingendes Völkerrecht* (Berlin: Duncker and Humblot, 1992); Lauri Hannikainen, *Peremptory Norms "Jus Cogens" in International Law* (Helsinki: Lakimiesliiton Kustannus, 1988).

[49] *See* Byers, *Custom, supra* note 30, *especially* pp. 35–40, 75–6.

[50] An interesting comparison may be made with the approach taken by the ICJ in the *Gabčíkovo–Nagymaros Case*, where the Court rejected Hungary's submission that "profound changes of a political nature" constituted a fundamental change of circumstances for the purposes of Article 62 of the Vienna Convention on the Law of Treaties. *See* Case Concerning the Gabčíkovo- Nagymaros Project (Hungary/Slovakia), 37 ILM (1998), pp. 162, 195 (para. 104).

B *Unilateral pro-democratic intervention in practice*

Having considered the arguments advanced by academics in favor of a unilateral right of pro-democratic armed intervention, we turn now to a more detailed consideration of the two major examples of unilateral intervention sometimes characterized as "pro-democratic": the US invasions of Grenada in 1983 and of Panama in 1989. As will become clear, both examples actually prove the opposite point, that unilateral armed intervention to support or restore democracy remains prohibited by international law.

1 Grenada, 1983

On October 25, 1983, a force of about 400 US Marines and 1,500 paratroops, together with 300 soldiers from neighboring Caribbean States, landed in Grenada, where a violent *coup d'état* had been staged by radical Marxist opponents of the leftist Maurice Bishop regime. The newly self-appointed Revolutionary Military Council was deposed after three days of fighting. US troops withdrew by December 15, leaving only a small number of US and Caribbean support personnel on the island.[51] Casualties numbered just over one hundred: eighteen Americans, forty-five Grenadians (including twenty-one civilians killed in the accidental bombing of a hospital) and thirty-four Cuban soldiers.[52]

The Reagan Administration provided three justifications for the intervention.[53] First, it cited an invitation from the Governor-General of Grenada, received on October 24, 1983. According to Deputy Secretary of State Kenneth Dam, the "legal authorities of the Governor-General remained the sole source of governmental legitimacy on the island in the wake of the tragic events."[54] As a point of constitutional law, this is open to question.[55] Moreover, the invasion was

---

[51] *Keesing's Contemporary Archives* (1984), 32614–18. Edward Gordon, *et al.*, "International Law and the United States Action in Grenada: A Report," *Int'l Law.* 18 (1984), p. 334.

[52] *Ibid.* These figures were later disputed.

[53] *See* Deputy Secretary of State Kenneth W. Dam, "Statement Before the House Committee on Foreign Affairs" (November 2, 1983), *reprinted in Am J. Int'l. L.* 78 (1984), 200, p. 203; Legal Adviser of the Department of State, Davis R. Robinson, Letter dated February 10, 1984, addressed to Professor Edward Gordon, Chairman of the Committee on Grenada of the American Bar Association's Section on International Law and Practice, *reprinted in Am. J. Int'l L.* 78 (1984), 661.

[54] Dam, "Statement," *supra* note 53, 203.

[55] Under the 1973 Constitution, the Governor-General apparently had such power as part of his unenumerated reserve powers. It is unlikely that these were in effect in 1983, however, after the promulgation of the People's Laws in 1979 following the revolution: *see* Michael J. Levitin, "The Law of Force and the Force of Law: Grenada, the Falklands, and Humanitarian Intervention," *Harv. Int'l L.J.* 27 (1986).

already in an advanced stage of implementation by the time the request was supposedly received – just one day before the troops landed. Although the proximity of the request to the invasion does not go to the question of its legality, it does indicate clearly that even the United States did not regard it as decisive.[56] In any event, as *The Economist* (which strongly supported the action) concluded, the "request was almost certainly a fabrication concocted between the OECS [Organization of Eastern Caribbean States] and Washington to calm the post-invasion diplomatic storm."[57]

Second, the United States cited a request to intervene from the OECS. On November 2, 1983, Dam referred to Articles 3, 4 and 8 of the OECS Treaty, which, he stated, "deal with local as well as external threats to peace and security."[58] This reference was misleading – they do, but not in terms that could possibly justify the use of force against a member State. Three months later, the State Department's Legal Adviser, Davis Robinson, presented a modified position, relying instead on Article 6 which grants plenary authority to the heads of government of the OECS States.[59] He then referred to Article 3(2) which, he stated, "expressly empowers the heads of government to pursue joint policies in the field of mutual defense and security, and 'such other activities calculated to further the purposes of the Organisation as the member States may from time to time decide.'"[60] However, he omitted to mention that Article 3(2) merely states the fields in which member States will endeavor to coordinate, harmonize, and pursue joint policies. Moreover, the "Major Purposes" listed in Article 3(1) include the defense of member States' "sovereignty, territorial integrity and independence."[61] And on both occasions, Chapter VIII of the UN Charter, which concerns regional security arrangements, was relied upon in a manner that conflated "pacific means of dispute settlement" under Article 52 with enforcement measures under Article 53 – enforcement measures that require Security Council authorization. Only the former Article was invoked by the

---

[56] Robert J. Beck, "International Law and the Decision to Invade Grenada: A Ten-Year Retrospective," *Virginia J. Int'l L.* 33 (1993), pp. 789–90.
[57] "Britain's Grenada Shut-Out," *Economist* (March 10, 1984), 31, 34. It further stated that the decision to invade "had been 75% made on Saturday," the day before the alleged request: *ibid.*, 32. *Cf* Nolte, *Eingreifen auf Einladung*, *supra* note 23, pp. 286 ff.
[58] Dam, "Statement," *supra* note 53, p. 203.
[59] Robinson, Letter to American Bar Association, *supra* note 53, p. 663.
[60] *Ibid.* (citing Treaty Establishing the Organization of Eastern Caribbean States, June 18, 1981, done at Basseterre, St. Kitts/Nevis, 20 ILM, p. 1166, Art. 3(2)(r)).
[61] OECS Treaty, Art. 3(1)(b).

United States to justify an action that was clearly *not* "pacific" (and therefore could only have fallen within the scope of the latter).[62]

Third, the United States invoked the protection of nationals as a legal justification. The facts supporting this thesis have been contested – in particular, the United States asserted that Grenadian officials refused to let its citizens leave the island, although Canada claimed to have flown a chartered plane to and from the island on the day of the intervention.[63] In any case, it was acknowledged that the scale of the operation went beyond the limits of this "well-established, narrowly drawn ground for the use of force."[64]

A Security Council resolution protesting the intervention was vetoed by the United States.[65] The General Assembly, free of such constraints, passed a resolution that "deeply deplore[d]" the US-led intervention as a flagrant violation of international law.[66]

Subsequent events also undermined the US legal position. None of the Eastern Caribbean States involved referred to the humanitarian motives initially stressed by the US. Instead, they said that the action was "to help stabilize the country," "to restore law and order," but above all "to block the Russians and the Cubans," "to prevent another Angola," and "to prevent Marxist revolution from spreading to all the islands." They described the landing as "a pre-emptive defensive action."[67]

In the attempt to find support for a unilateral right of pro-democratic intervention, even a regional one, Grenada is a strained example. The United States itself did not seek to invoke this justification, nor any justification that could be seen to imply a right of pro-democratic intervention. In one of its most sophisticated legal explanations of the invasion, it even went so far as to stress the grounds on which it did *not* rely: an expanded view of self-defense, "new interpretations" of Article 2(4), or "a broad doctrine of 'humanitarian intervention.'"[68] Even if it had

---

[62] *See* Dam, "Statement," *supra* note 53, p. 203; Robinson, Letter to American Bar Association, *supra* note 53, p. 663. It therefore seems disingenuous of the Legal Adviser to have stated that "We are not aware of any serious contention that actions falling within the scope of Article 52 could violate Article 2(4) of the Charter." Robinson, Letter to American Bar Association, *supra* note 53, p. 663. [63] Levitin, "The Law of Force," *supra* note 55, p. 649.
[64] Robinson, Letter to American Bar Association, *supra* note 62, p. 664.
[65] *UNYB* (1983), p. 211. The draft resolution was voted down 11–1–3 (US against; Togo, UK and Zaïre abstaining). [66] GA Res. 38/7 (1983) (adopted 108–9–27).
[67] *See* Wil D. Verwey, "Humanitarian Intervention," *in* Cassese, ed., *Use of Force, supra* note 23, p. 65 (and sources cited therein).
[68] Robinson, Letter to American Bar Association, *supra* note 53, p. 664. This is cheerfully dismissed by Tesón, who marshals it as evidence of precisely such a right: Tesón, *Humanitarian Intervention, supra* note 24, pp. 216–17.

invoked the restoration of democracy as a justification, the preponderance of State practice and *opinio juris* in this instance is to be found in the negative reaction of other States, and thus supports the *contrary* rule. In light of this evidence, reference to the invasion of Grenada by supporters of a right to unilateral pro-democratic intervention does their argument more harm than good.

2 Panama, 1989[69]

Supporters of a unilateral right of pro-democratic intervention rely most heavily on the US invasion of Panama in 1989 as a paradigmatic example of their theory at work. A close analysis, however, confirms that the case of Panama supports precisely the opposite conclusion.

On December 20, 1989, 24,000 US troops began an operation to overthrow the government of Panama and capture its head of State, General Manuel Noriega. President Bush explained and justified the action on four grounds: "to safeguard the lives of Americans, to defend democracy in Panama, to combat drug trafficking, and to protect the integrity of the Panama Canal Treaty."[70] Having rendered Noriega a fugitive, the US now recognized the "rightful leadership" of the likely victors of elections held earlier that year; diplomatic relations would resume immediately and steps would be taken to lift economic sanctions imposed against the Noriega regime.[71] The US forces would be withdrawn "as quickly as possible." With no apparent irony, Bush added that he would "continue to seek solutions to the problems of this region through dialogue and multilateral diplomacy."[72]

Analysis of the legal basis for the action – somewhat hopefully codenamed "Just Cause" – is made difficult by the conflation of policy and legal reasoning in statements such as these. Of the four grounds outlined above, the exercise of an "inherent right of self defense" protected under Article 51 of the UN Charter and extending to the protection of nationals abroad most closely resembled a legal argument.[73]

---

[69] For a more detailed exposition of events, see Simon Chesterman, "Rethinking Panama: International Law and the US Invasion of Panama, 1989," *in* Guy S. Goodwin-Gill and Stefan A. Talmon, eds., *The Reality of International Law: Essays in Honor of Ian Brownlie* (Oxford University Press, 1999), p. 57.

[70] President George Bush, "Address to the Nation Announcing United States Military Action in Panama," *in Public Papers of the Presidents of the United States: George Bush 1989*, 2 vols (Washington, D.C.: US Govt. Printing Office, 1990) (December 20, 1989, 7:20AM EST) vol. II, pp. 1722–24, para. 2.

[71] *See* Memorandum Terminating Economic Sanctions Against Panama (December 20, 1989) in *Public Papers, supra* note 70, vol. II, p. 1726 (lifting economic sanctions imposed by Executive Order No. 12635). [72] Bush, "Address to the Nation," *supra* note 70, para. 10.

[73] *See generally* Chesterman, "Rethinking Panama," *supra* note 69.

But if self-defense was the primary legal justification put forward by the Bush Administration, it was the claim that intervention may be justified in support of democracy that won the most vocal support from legal academics.[74] D'Amato described US actions in Panama and, previously, Grenada as "milestones along the path to a new nonstatist conception of international law."[75] Reisman similarly heralded a new era in which "the people, not governments, are sovereign."[76] In a remarkably isolationist conception of customary international law, each regarded the invasion as a significant and positive development[77] – ignoring or discounting as irrelevant the broad condemnation of the intervention by the international community. Once again a Security Council resolution was blocked by the US veto;[78] once again the General Assembly condemned the unilateral action.[79] And to our knowledge, only one non-American international lawyer – Elihu Lauterpacht – voiced written support for the invasion, claiming that the only justification offered by the United States which had any merit was that it had "acted in support of the democratic process – a concept of internationally recognized relevance."[80]

There were two ways that the Bush Administration invoked democracy in support of the invasion: as the exercise of a right to act unilaterally to promote democracy in another State, and as legitimate assistance to a democratically elected head of State, Guillermo Endara, who had consented to that action. According to Abraham Sofaer, Legal Adviser to the State Department at the time of the invasion, when Endara was informed of the impending arrival of US troops on December 19, 1989,

> he decided to be sworn in as president. He welcomed the US action, presented his views as to the proper objectives of US efforts and immediately began to cooperate fully in their implementation. He appealed to the Panamanian forces

---

[74] *See, e.g.*, D'Amato, "The Invasion of Panama," *supra* note 21; Reisman, "Sovereignty and Human Rights," *supra* note 16; Panel Discussion, "The Panamanian Revolution: Diplomacy, War and Self-Determination in Panama: Self-Determination and Intervention in Panama," *ASIL Proc.* 84 (1990), 192 (remarks of Fernando Tesón).
[75] D'Amato, "The Invasion of Panama," *supra* note 21, p. 517.
[76] Reisman, "Sovereignty and Human Rights," *supra* note 16, p. 874, quoting 44 UN SCOR (2899th mtg), UN Doc. S/PV.2899 (December 20, 1989), pp. 31–37.
[77] *See* D'Amato, "The Invasion of Panama," *supra* note 21, p. 523; Reisman, "Sovereignty and Human Rights," *supra* note 16, pp. 874–76; W. Michael Reisman, "Humanitarian Intervention and Fledgling Democracies," *Fordham Int'l L. J.* 18 (1995), p. 803.
[78] [1989] *UNYB* 175. The draft resolution was voted down 10–4–1 (Canada, France, UK and United States against; Finland abstaining).   [79] GA Res. 44/240 (1989) (adopted 75–20–40).
[80] Elihu Lauterpacht, "Letter to the Editor: Legal Aspects of Panama Invasion," *The Times* (London) (December 23, 1989), p. 11.

"not to resist" the US action, which he said was unavoidable and "seeks to end the Noriega dictatorship and reestablish democracy, justice and freedom." He also began exercising the functions of his office, appointing officials to assume direction over components of the Panamanian government and progressively asserting control over all Panamanian territory.[81]

Even if one accepts the legitimacy of Endara and his colleagues, the United States never claimed that he actually requested the invasion. Although Bush stated that Endara "welcomed the assistance" of the United States,[82] and there was some reference to his being "consulted,"[83] he was informed of the plans for a military intervention only when troops were already in the air.[84] Bob Woodward reported that Bush had decided that this was the point of no return – if Endara refused to "play ball," Secretary of Defense Dick Cheney and General Colin Powell, who were overseeing the operation, were to check with Bush personally.[85] Endara was sworn in at Fort Clayton, a US military base in the Canal Zone, less than an hour before the invasion began.[86]

There is, in fact, some evidence that Endara was not entirely happy about the invasion, which he later described as a "kick in the head," stating that he "would have been happier without it."[87] In a profile on him written in January 1990, he explained his reaction to the news from US officials that an invasion was imminent and that they wanted him to take the oath as President:

---

[81] Abraham D. Sofaer, "The Legality of the United States Action in Panama," *Colum J. Transnat'l L.* 29 (1991), p. 289. In a press briefing, Gen. Colin Powell stated that Endara was sworn in "shortly before the operation. He was sworn in by a Panamanian justice of some kind . . ." "Fighting in Panama: The Pentagon; Excerpts From Briefings on US Military Action in Panama," *N.Y. Times* (December 21, 1989), p. A20.

[82] Letter from President Bush to Speaker of the House Thomas Foley in *Public Papers, supra* note 70, vol. 2, (December 21, 1989), p. 1734, para. 5.

[83] Letter from Mr. Pickering, Permanent Representative of the United States to the United Nations, to the President of the Security Council (December 20, 1989), UN Doc. S/21035, para. 2: "The United States undertook this action after consultation with the democratically-elected leaders of Panama." *See also* "Fighting in Panama: the State Dept.; Excerpts From Statement by Baker on US Policy," *N.Y. Times* (December 21, 1989), A19.

[84] Association of the Bar of the City of New York, *The Use of Armed Force in International Affairs: The Case of Panama* (Report of The Committee on International Arms Control and Security Affairs and The Committee on International Law, 1992), p. 66 n.282.

[85] Bob Woodward, *The Commanders* (London: Simon & Schuster, 1991), p. 182.

[86] The swearing appears to have taken place at 12:39 AM on the morning of the invasion: *Ibid.* at 182. In a press statement that was later discredited, Endara said that he had been sworn in at 2:00 AM "Panamanians in Secret Pact on Oath-Taking," *L.A. Times* (December 27, 1989), p. 2.

[87] Philip Geyelin, "Noriega Was Only Part of the Problem," *Washington Post* (January 1, 1990), A19; Michael L. Conniff, *Panama and the United States: the Forced Alliance* (Athens, Ga.: University of Georgia Press, 1991), p. 167.

It would have been very easy for me to say, "I'm not going to take this job under occupation by American forces"... But I knew that I couldn't do that. I had to assume the responsibility of Government – the people chose me to be President. I couldn't simply tell the US: "You pick the Government. You are the occupying power and you do what you want."[88]

This squarely raises the question of what might have happened had he refused to "play ball."

Sofaer explained that one reason Endara's consent was not secured prior to the invasion was that it would have exposed him to unjustifiable political and physical risk.[89] But as the New York City Bar Association has observed, the claim that unilateral force is justified in support of democratic choice is weakened when elected leaders are unable to ask openly for such intervention for fear of popular disapproval.[90] It may have been such concerns that led Endara to claim initially that he was sworn in on Panamanian territory – an assertion contradicted by witnesses and uniformly disregarded by the press.[91]

After noting that Endara's consent would have been sufficient to justify the invasion had he controlled the territory of Panama and been able to exercise governmental powers prior to December 19, 1989,[92] Sofaer asserted that the fact that he lacked such control "does not deprive his consent of legal significance."[93] It is not clear what Sofaer intended by this, but it may indicate an argument that a new government may retrospectively validate the action that brought it to power. This appears to be the import of Lauterpacht's comment that:

> What matters in law is not the technical propriety of the United States action at its inception but whether the Government of Panama itself now regards that action as lawful.[94]

The implication is that a newly installed regime may pardon violations of international law committed against its predecessor. This may be generally correct in respect of obligations *inter se* (i.e., as between particular

---

[88] David E. Pitt, "To Many in Panama, the New President is an Enigma Wrapped in a Smile," *N.Y. Times* (January 28, 1990), A6.
[89] Sofaer, "Legality of the US Action in Panama," *supra* note 81, p. 290.
[90] NY. City Bar Assoc, *Panama, supra* note 84, p. 67.
[91] "Panamanians in Secret Pact on Oath-Taking," *L.A. Times* (Dec. 27, 1989), 2; Mark A. Uhlig, "After Noriega, Change Comes Slowly and Panama's President is Frustrated," *N.Y. Times* (Nov. 3, 1990), A1.
[92] Sofaer, "Legality of the US Action in Panama," *supra* note 81, p. 290 (*citing* Oppenheim, *International Law*, 8th edn., p. 305).   [93] *Ibid.*, p. 290.
[94] Lauterpacht, "Letter to the Editor," *supra* note 80, p. 11.

States) under the rules of State responsibility – though it is difficult to see how any such an *ex post facto* waiver could be effective if the rule in question were one of *jus cogens*.[95]

Even if it were effective, third States and international tribunals are not bound to accept such a waiver.[96] In the *Barcelona Traction* case, the International Court of Justice held that certain rules of international law entail obligations *erga omnes*, where all States have a legal interest in the protection of the rights involved. And it is significant that the Court, for illustrative purposes, referred to those obligations which outlaw acts of aggression.[97] If an act of intervention is considered to violate such an obligation, all other States may be considered individually as "injured" parties.[98] Moreover, allowing the target State to authorize such an invasion retrospectively would raise concerns that this doctrine is open to abuse precisely because it may result in the imposition of regimes which are sympathetic to the acting State.

In the event, most Latin American States withdrew their ambassadors from Panama after the invasion and refused to recognize the Endara government, stating that diplomatic relations would be normalized only when US troop numbers returned to pre-invasion levels and some form of plebiscite demonstrated popular support for the new regime.[99] The Permanent Council of the Organization of American States initially

---

[95] *See* Natalino Ronzitti, "Use of Force, *Jus Cogens* and State Consent," *in* Cassese, ed., *Use of Force*, *supra* note 23, pp. 160–61. On *jus cogens* rules, see *supra*, note 48. There is now considerable support for the view that the prohibition on the use of force is just such a rule and general acceptance that *jus cogens* rules have important effects outside the law of treaties (although Articles 53 and 64 of the 1969 Vienna Convention on the Law of Treaties themselves only apply to written agreements). *See* Byers, *Custom*, *supra* note 30, pp. 184–86 (and citations therein).

[96] *See* Brownlie, *Use of Force*, *supra* note 22, pp. 317–18 and citations therein; Ronzitti, *Rescuing Nationals*, *supra* note 23, pp. 161–63.

[97] Barcelona Traction, Light and Power Co. Case (Belgium v. Spain), 1970 ICJ 31, p. 32. On obligations *erga omnes*, see Byers, *Custom*, *supra* note 30, pp. 195–203 and citations therein.

[98] The concept of "international crimes" – which is similar to that of obligations *erga omnes* – would likely be applied. *See* Article 19 of the ILC Draft Articles on State Responsibility (Part One), *in Report of the ILC on the Work of its 25th Session, Yearbook of the International Law Commission* 2, (1973), p. 32; M. Mohr, "The ILC's Distinction Between 'International Crimes' and 'International Delicts' and Its Implications" *in* Marina Spinedi and Bruno Simma, eds., *United Nations Codification of State Responsibility* (New York: Oceana, 1987), p. 115; Joseph Weiler *et al.*, eds., *International Crimes of State: a Critical Analysis of the ILC's Draft Article 19 on State Responsibility* (Berlin: de Gruyter, 1989); Dinstein, *War, Aggression and Self-Defense*, *supra* note 48, p. 112. Although the ILC has now decided not to deal with international crimes in its Draft Articles, there has been no suggestion that they do not remain an important part of international law.

[99] Robert Pear, "US Says Latin American Nations are Resuming Ties with Panama," *N.Y. Times*, (March 9, 1990), A11. Developed Western States were among the first to recognize the new regime: Don Shannon, "Panama's New Government Slowly Gains in World Acceptance Envoys: President Endara's Diplomatic Corps Has Re-Established Ties with 17 Nations," *L.A. Times* (January 6, 1990), A20.

refused to accept the credentials of the ambassador dispatched by Endara to represent Panama there, with Noriega's ambassador remaining and participating in the vote criticizing the invasion.[100] Some months passed before most governments decided to recognize the Endara regime.[101] Widespread reluctance to recognize the new government, strong objections voiced by many States in the Security Council and a condemnatory resolution adopted by the General Assembly,[102] as well as the fact that the restoration of democracy was only one of four justifications advanced by the United States for the intervention – all this evidence confirms that unilateral pro-democratic armed intervention remains prohibited by international law, and hardly supports the opposite proposition.[103]

C Concluding thoughts on "kind-hearted gunmen"

The immediate obstacle to adopting the arguments advanced in favor of a unilateral right of pro-democratic intervention is that they are simply not accepted by even a significant minority of States. Although there is some evidence of support on the part of the United States and perhaps the UK,[104] upholding or restoring democracy has not previously been asserted as an independent basis for intervention. It was not raised by Tanzania when it deposed Idi Amin in Uganda in 1979,[105] by Vietnam when it overthrew the genocidal regime of Pol Pot in

---

[100] Tom J. Farer, "Panama: Beyond the Charter Paradigm," *Am J. Int'l. L.* 84 (1990), p. 510.

[101] In Latin America, El Salvador, Guatemala, Costa Rica, and Honduras were among the first to recognize the Endara government. Colombia, Argentina, Ecuador, Venezuela, and Peru joined them in March 1990: Robert Pear "US Says Latin American Nations are Resuming Ties with Panama," *N.Y. Times* (March 9, 1990), A11.

[102] See supra notes 78–79.

[103] In May 1994, Panama held its first effective democratic elections in over twenty-five years. Ironically, the victor was Ernesto Perez Balladares of the Revolutionary Democratic Party – the party formerly controlled by Noriega. See Eric Schmitt, "Washington Talk: a Panama Enemy Becomes an Ally," *N.Y. Times* (July 21, 1994), A4. Five years earlier, Perez Balladares had managed the campaign of Carlos Duque, Noriega's hand-picked presidential candidate.

[104] In a statement on the subject of the US armed intervention in Panama, the Secretary of State for Foreign and Commonwealth Affairs, Mr. Douglas Hurd, observed in part:

> We fully support the American action to remove General Noriega, which was undertaken with the agreement of the leaders who clearly won the elections held last May. Noriega's arbitrary rule was maintained by force. We and many others have repeatedly condemned Noriega and called for the election result to be respected. Every peaceful means of trying to see the results of the democratic elections respected has failed. (*Hansard*, HC (Series 6), vol. CLXIV, col. 357 (December 20, 1989), *reprinted in Brit. Y.B. Int'l L.* 40 (1989), p. 692.)

[105] See James Crawford, "Self-Determination Outside the Colonial Context," in W. J. A. Macartney, ed., *Self-Determination in the Commonwealth* (Aberdeen University Press, 1988), p. 10.

1978–79,[106] nor by France when it helped overthrow "Emperor" Bokassa in the Central African "Empire" in 1979.[107] On those occasions when it has been invoked by the United States to justify its actions in Grenada, Nicaragua, and Panama, the action has been condemned by the international community and – when the issue came before it – by the International Court of Justice.[108]

Aside from the normative problems such an argument faces, it is also highly questionable that such a doctrine would be desirable. In the *Nicaragua* case, the Court refused "to contemplate the creation of a new rule opening up a right of intervention by one State against another on the ground that the latter has opted for some particular ideology or political system."[109] Such a rule would, *ex hypothesi*, be exercised arbitrarily. In his landmark paper on the right to democratic governance, Thomas Franck argued that for such a right to be meaningful, precisely the opposite approach was necessary:

> [S]teps should be taken to meet the fear of some smaller states that election monitoring will lead to more Panama-style unilateral military interventions by the powerful, perhaps even for reasons less convincing than those which provoked the 1989 US military strike against the Noriega dictatorship. That a new rule might authorize actions to enforce democracy still conjures up just such chilling images to weaker states, which see themselves as the potential objects of enforcement of dubious democratic norms under circumstances of doubtful probity.[110]

There are other ways for one State to manifest its concern at the undemocratic behavior of another. The most common manner of doing so is simply to refuse to recognize a regime's representative authority, or at least refuse to deal with it in certain – particularly economic – ways. However, isolation is a blunt instrument and may in fact cause harm to those whom the acting State desires to protect.[111] Another possibility may be to require third parties dealing with a grossly unrepresentative

---

[106] *See* G. Klintworth, *Vietnam's Intervention in Cambodia in International Law* (Canberra: AGPS, 1989). Indeed, in Security Council debate, the French delegate declared: "The notion that because a régime is detestable foreign intervention is justified and forcible overthrow is legitimate is extremely dangerous. That could ultimately jeopardize the very maintenance of international law and order and make the continued existence of various régimes dependent on the judgement of their neighbors." 34 UN SCOR (2109th mtg), UN Doc. S/PV 2109 (1979) para. 36.
[107] Michael Akehurst, "Humanitarian Intervention," *in* Hedley Bull, ed., *Intervention in World Politics* (Oxford: Clarendon, 1984), p. 99. Deitrich Schindler, "Völkerrecht und Demokratie," *in* Gerhard Hafner *et al.*, *Liber Amicorum Professor Ignaz Seidl-Hohenveldern* (The Hague: Kluwer, 1998), p. 626 makes the same point. [108] *See* text accompanying note 27.
[109] Nicaragua, 1986 ICJ 14, p. 133. [110] Franck, "Democratic Governance," *supra* note 2, p. 84.
[111] *See* Crawford, "Democracy and International Law," *supra* note 4, pp. 128–29.

regime to assume the risks which may be involved – for example, the risk that a subsequent government will refuse to honor the commitments of its predecessor – by modifying the applicable rules of State responsibility.[112] And in exceptional circumstances where there is broad consensus that some form of enforcement action to support or restore democracy is required, collective action through the Security Council provides the only appropriate – and legal – alternative.

III COLLECTIVE PRO-DEMOCRATIC INTERVENTION UNDER THE UNITED NATIONS

It is now trite to observe that the Security Council has assumed a far more pro-active role in international relations since the end of the Cold War. The past decade has seen a dramatic increase in its involvement in almost all areas where it has responsibilities and powers. Of particular interest for our purposes is the increased willingness of the Security Council to invoke its coercive authority under Chapter VII of the Charter in situations not traditionally regarded as threats to "international peace and security."[113] In the absence of a Chapter VII resolution, the UN is constrained by the domestic jurisdiction provision of Article 2(7).[114] Although human rights treaties, the expanded range of activities engaged in by the UN, and customary international law have all reduced the scope of that exclusive jurisdiction, arguments which seek to fit forcible pro-democratic intervention within such a revised reading do not succeed – for all the same reasons as those discussed above in the context of unilateral, unauthorized intervention.

A Disruption of democracy as a "threat to international peace and security"

There are three ways in which a disruption of democracy might be considered sufficient to justify a Chapter VII resolution.

First, and most obviously, the act of disruption *itself* may threaten international peace and security. This was arguably the case in two

---

[112] *Ibid.*, pp.129–30. This suggestion runs against the finding in the *Tinoco* arbitration, *R.I.A.A.* 1 (1923), p. 369. An obvious problem would be that the spectre of sovereign risk would dissuade investment and much useful intercourse with the State.   [113] UN Charter, Art. 39.
[114] Article 2(7) reads: "Nothing contained in the present Charter shall authorize the United Nations to intervene in matters which are essentially within the domestic jurisdiction of any State or shall require the Members to submit such matters to settlement under the present Charter; but this principle shall not prejudice the application of enforcement measures under Chapter VII."

incidents that are sometimes identified as early precedents for Security Council intervention in support of democracy.[115] The Security Council responded to the 1966 declaration of independence by the white minority government in Southern Rhodesia by imposing mandatory economic sanctions[116] and authorizing a limited use of force (by the UK) to stop oil tankers from violating the embargo.[117] The Southern Rhodesian question is perhaps unique in that the Council explicitly recognized the legitimacy of the Zimbabwean people's struggle against a colonial regime, specifically invoking the Declaration on the Granting of Independence to Colonial Territories and Peoples.[118] Subsequent resolutions referred to allegations of armed aggression on the part of the Ian Smith regime against neighboring States.[119] Similarly, the Chapter VII resolution imposing an arms embargo on South Africa strongly condemned the racist regime, but ultimately located a threat to international peace and security in the prospect of South Africa acquiring nuclear weapons.[120] Whether any given situation lends itself to being characterized as a threat to international peace and security will depend on the specific circumstances, including the consequences for neighboring States, such as (arguably) refugee flows. It is possible, though difficult, to fit the Security Council resolutions on Haiti and Sierra Leone within such a framework.

Second, at a different level of analysis, some scholars argue that the absence of democracy may itself constitute a threat to international peace and security. This is an extreme form of the "democratic peace" thesis that authentic democracies do not fight each other, or – depending on the definition of "democracy" or "fighting" – that such conflicts are exceptional.[121] (The gunboat diplomacy between Spain and Canada over fishing rights in 1995 may be such an exception,[122] as might the involvement of the United States in the 1973 overthrow of the democratically

---

[115] *See, e.g.,* W. Michael Reisman, "Haiti and the Validity of International Action," *Am. J. Int'l L.* 89 (1995), p. 83.   [116] SC Res. 232 (1966); SC Res. 253 (1968); SC Res. 277 (1970).
[117] SC Res. 221 (1966), para. 5.
[118] SC Res. 232 (1966) para. 4 (referring to GA Res. 1514 (XV) (1960)). *See also,* SC Res. 253 (1968) preamble; SC Res. 277 (1970) preamble.
[119] *See* SC Res. 386 (1976); SC Res. 403 (1977); SC Res. 411 (1977); SC Res. 423 (1978); SC Res. 445 (1979).   [120] SC Res. 418 (1977).
[121] Tom J. Farer, "Collectively Defending Democracy in a World of Sovereign States: the Western Hemisphere's Prospect," *Hum Rts. Q.* 15 (1993), pp. 724–26 and sources cited therein.
[122] *See,* Peter Davies, "The EC/Canadian Dispute in the Northwest Atlantic," *Int'l & Comp. L.Q.* 44 (1995), p. 927; Peter Davies and Catherine Redgwell, "The International Legal Regulation of Straddling Fish Stocks," *Brit. Y.B. Int'l L.* 67 (1996), 199; Byers, *Custom, supra* note 30, pp. 97–101.

elected government in Chile.) As a general principle this clearly cannot stand, as it would deprive about one-third of the world's States of the protection of Article 2(7).

Third, what might be called the Humpty-Dumpty school of interpretation[123] considers that the Security Council has an absolute license to determine what constitutes a "threat to international peace and security." This approach has the attraction of justifying all such determinations, but at the cost of any normative framework within which to situate them. Although decisions of the Security Council are in practice not subject to review (judicial or otherwise), the International Court of Justice's 1998 decision on preliminary objections in the *Lockerbie* case at least affirms that they are subject to the Charter, Article 24 of which provides that in fulfilling its "primary responsibility" for the maintenance of international peace and security, "the Security Council shall act in accordance with the Purposes and Principles of the United Nations."[124]

We take the position that the Security Council may legitimately consider the threat to or removal of a democratically elected government by a force internal to the State in question as a factor which could, together with other factors such as mass killings or refugee flows, in some circumstances *contribute* to a threat to international peace and security under recently expanded conceptions of that term.[125] The presence of more traditional factors, such as cross-boundary incursions by the new regime or foreign intervention in its support, will make such a determination easier and more credible. But a determination that a disruption of democracy in itself meets the Chapter VII threshold would allow far too much room for arbitrariness, notwithstanding the clear need for a degree of discretion here.

Having identified that there are instances where a disruption of democracy might contribute to a situation which justifies collective intervention under Security Council authorization, it is time to consider whether developments in Haiti and in Sierra Leone amounted to such situations, and thus provide any support for the argument that a right of pro-democratic intervention has become part of international law.

---

[123] "When *I* use a word," Humpty Dumpty said in a rather scornful tone, "it means just what I choose it to mean – neither more nor less." Lewis Carroll, *Through the Looking-Glass* (1872), ch. 6.
[124] *See* Questions of Interpretation and Application of the 1971 Montreal Convention Arising from the Aerial Incident at Lockerbie (Libyan Arab Jamahiriya v. USA), 37 *ILM* (1998) pp. 587, 604–05 (paras. 39–44). [125] *See* Schindler, "Völkerrecht und Demokratie," *supra* note 107, p. 624.

B Collective pro-democratic intervention in practice

1 Haiti, 1994[126]

In 1990, after some years of OAS urging to resume democratic elections, Jean-Bertrand Aristide was elected President of Haiti with 67 percent of the popular vote. The election was certified by international monitors. Aristide was removed from office by a *coup d'état* on September 30, 1991. The OAS formally condemned the coup and recommended the imposition of economic and diplomatic sanctions by its members. The Security Council failed to adopt a resolution on the issue, reportedly because China and certain non-aligned States were concerned about increased Security Council involvement in areas traditionally considered to be within the sphere of domestic jurisdiction.[127] The General Assembly, by contrast, strongly condemned the "illegal replacement of the constitutional President of Haiti," affirming that "any entity resulting from that illegal situation" was unacceptable.[128]

The refusal of Haiti's military dictators to reinstate the Aristide government, combined with the continued persecution of Aristide supporters, eventually led the Security Council to impose a mandatory economic embargo in June 1993. The resolution was adopted explicitly under Chapter VII and listed a variety of factors that had led the Council to determine "that, in these unique and exceptional circumstances, the continuation of this situation threatens international peace and security in the region."[129] These included "the incidence of humanitarian crises, including mass displacements of population," and the "climate of fear of persecution and economic dislocation which could increase the number of Haitians seeking refuge in neighboring Member States."[130]

This is clearly an atypical conception of a threat to international peace and security. (Interestingly, subsequent resolutions referred to "a threat to the peace and security in the *region*."[131]) Various commentators have questioned whether the situation actually constituted a threat to peace,[132] and there is evidence that some Council members placed more reliance on the request for assistance from the Aristide government-in-

---

[126] For a book-length exposition of the Haitian crisis and the Security Council's response, see David Malone, *Decision-Making in the UN Security Council: the Case of Haiti, 1990–97* (Oxford: Clarendon Press, 1998). [127] Tesón, *Humanitarian Intervention*, *supra* note 24, p. 250.
[128] GA Res. 46/7 (1991). [129] SC Res. 841 (1993), preamble. [130] *Ibid.*
[131] *See, e.g.*, SC Res. 917 (1994); SC Res. 933 (1994); SC Res. 940 (1994).
[132] *See* Douglas Lee Donoho, "Evolution or Expediency: the United Nations Response to the Disruption of Democracy," *Cornell Int'l L.J.* 29 (1996), 359 n.160 (and sources cited therein).

exile.[133] Confirmation of this may be found in Resolution 841, which explicitly linked the request from Haiti's Permanent Representative with actions taken by the OAS and the General Assembly in defining a "unique and exceptional situation warranting extraordinary measures."[134] In any event, this line of reasoning does not help justify enforcement measures under Chapter VII.

A credible argument can be made that refugee flows may, in some circumstances, constitute a threat to international peace and security. In previous resolutions, the Council has justified Chapter VII actions to protect Iraqi Kurds[135] and to create safe havens in the Balkans[136] and Rwanda[137] at least in part on the external effects of refugee flows. This argument is less persuasive in the case of Haiti where the number of refugees was small compared to the millions displaced in the three other conflicts.[138] Moreover, the United States was already acting to reduce the number of refugees to pre-coup levels by pursuing an interdiction programme that was as aggressive as it was illegal.[139]

The Security Council's determination that the situation in Somalia in 1992 constituted a threat to international peace and security is to some degree comparable.[140] Although there were limited refugee flows, to Kenya in particular, it was clearly the widespread humanitarian crisis within Somalia that provoked the Security Council into taking Chapter VII action.[141]

It seems that it was the embargo imposed in June 1993 which led the Haitian military junta to accept the Governors Island Agreement whereby President Aristide was to be returned to power. Sanctions were lifted in August 1993, but the agreement collapsed when violence against

---

[133] *See ibid.* pp. 347, 372 n.233 (and sources cited therein).   [134] SC Res. 841 (1993) preamble.
[135] Or so SC Res. 688 (1991) was interpreted. *See* Donoho, "Evolution or Expediency," *supra* note 132, p. 361 n. 169 (and sources cited therein).
[136] SC Res. 819 (1993); SC Res. 824 (1993); SC Res. 836 (1993).
[137] SC Res. 918 (1994); SC Res. 929 (1994).
[138] *See* Donoho, "Evolution or Expediency," *supra* note 132, pp. 362–3. *Compare* Olivier Corten, "La résolution 940 du Conseil de sécurité autorisant une intervention militaire en Haïti: l'émergence d'un principe de légitimité démocratique en droit international?" *Eur. J. Int'l L.* 6 (1995), p. 166.
[139] The US Supreme Court upheld the validity of the programme as a matter of US law in Sale v. Haitian Centers Council 509 US 155 (1993), but it has been sharply criticized by, *inter alia*, the UN High Commissioner for Refugees on the basis that the obligation of non-refoulement in Article 33 of the 1951 Geneva Convention relating to the Status of Refugees applies everywhere, including on the high seas. *See* Statement of the High Commissioner, June 22, 1993, 32 ILM (1993) p. 1215. *See also* Guy Goodwin-Gill, "Case and Comment: the Haitian *Refoulement* Case," *Int'l J. Ref. L.* 6 (1994), p. 69.   [140] SC Res. 733 (1992).
[141] *See, e.g.*, Mary Ellen O'Connell, "Regulating the Use of Force In the 21st Century: the Continuing Importance of State Autonomy," *Colum. J. Transnat'l L.* 36 (1997), p. 487 (and sources cited therein).

Aristide supporters resumed in September and October of that same year. The Security Council responded by imposing sanctions[142] and authorizing a naval blockade.[143]

On 29 July 1994, nearly three years after the coup, the Aristide government-in-exile requested "prompt and decisive action" by the UN.[144] Two days later, the Security Council, acting under Chapter VII, passed Resolution 940, which

> authorized Member States to form a multinational force under unified command and control and, in this framework, to use all necessary means to facilitate the departure from Haiti of the military leadership, consistent with the Governors Island Agreement, the prompt return of the legitimately elected President and the restoration of the legitimate authorities of the Government of Haiti, and to establish and maintain a secure and stable environment that will permit implementation of the Governors Island Agreement.[145]

Six weeks later, the United States responded to this invitation with plans for an "international" force (largely comprising US military units). A violent invasion was avoided at the eleventh hour when former President Jimmy Carter secured an agreement with the Haitian military to return Aristide to power.[146] By the end of September over 17,000 US troops were peacefully deployed in Haiti, with Aristide himself returning to Port-au-Prince on October 15, 1994.[147] There were no casualties. International reaction to the events was generally positive, with only a few States expressing serious reservations.[148]

Tesón has cited the US action in Haiti as "the most important precedent supporting the legitimacy both of an international principle of democratic rule and of collective humanitarian intervention."[149] Dismissing the argument that this might more properly be characterized as an enforcement measure under Chapter VII (read broadly), he argued that "[n]o one can seriously argue that the Haitian situation posed a threat to international peace and security in the region" and that in Resolution 940, the Security Council "sensibly abandoned the reference to the language of article 39."[150] Tesón, however, ignored the preambular determination that "the situation in Haiti continues to constitute a

---

[142] SC Res. 873 (1993).   [143] SC Res. 875 (1993). *See also* SC Res. 917 (1994).
[144] Letter dated July 29, 1994 from the Permanent Representative of Haiti to the United Nations Addressed to the Secretary-General, UN Doc. S/1994/905 (1994); Letter dated July 29, 1994 from the Permanent Representative of Haiti to the United Nations Addressed to the President of the Security Council, UN Doc. S/1994/910 (1994).   [145] SC Res. 940 (1994) para. 4.
[146] Elaine Sciolino, "On the Brink of War, a Tense Battle of Wills," *N.Y. Times* (September 20, 1994), A1.   [147] Donoho, "Evolution or Expediency," *supra* note 132, p. 348.
[148] Tesón, *Humanitarian Intervention, supra* note 24, p. 252.   [149] *Ibid.* at 249.   [150] *Ibid.* at 254.

threat to peace and security in the region,"[151] and not even Reisman supports his analysis.[152]

A more interesting question concerns whether, and to what degree, the disruption of democracy in Haiti actually constituted the basis for Resolution 940. The preamble to the resolution states that the Security Council was "*gravely concerned* by the significant further deterioration of the humanitarian situation in Haiti, in particular the continuing escalation by the illegal *de facto* regime of systematic violations of civil liberties, the desperate plight of Haitian refugees and the recent expulsion of the staff of the International Civilian Mission . . ." Democracy is not mentioned until later in the preamble, in a passage which states: "*Reaffirming* that the goal of the international community remains the restoration of democracy in Haiti and the prompt return of the legitimately elected President, Jean-Bertrand Aristide, within the framework of the Governors Island Agreement." The disruption of democracy is thus only one of several factors identified by the Security Council as contributing to a threat to international peace and security. Moreover, given the order and language of the two passages – and despite the fact than the coup was preceded by internationally monitored elections – the democracy factor appears to have been considered less important than the humanitarian situation giving rise to "grave concern." The subsidiary character of the democracy factor is confirmed by Resolution 841 of 1993 which, as has already been mentioned, identified "the incidence of humanitarian crises . . . including mass displacement of population" as the threat to international peace and security arising out of the situation in Haiti at that time.

But the aspect of Resolution 940 which most diminishes its value as a precedent in respect of any right of pro-democratic armed intervention is the emphasis placed therein on the request for UN action made by the Aristide government-in-exile in July 1994, and the fact that Resolution 940 was clearly adopted in response to that request, coming as it did only two days later. Although the Security Council does not require an invitation from the government of a State in order to authorize an intervention within that State's territory, an invitation of this kind is widely acknowledged to legitimate unilateral or collective invitation in the absence of Security Council authorization.[153] It is therefore arguable that the United States did not require Resolution 940 in order to inter-

---

[151] SC Res. 940 (1994).   [152] *See, e.g.*, Reisman, "Haiti," *supra* note 115, p. 83.
[153] *See* text accompanying note 34.

vene in Haiti as it did, and if the resolution was indeed unnecessary, its precedential effect in terms of radically redefining the international law on the use of force must again be called into question.

That said, we acknowledge that the international legal system is undergoing rapid change, especially in the areas of human rights and environmental protection. It is therefore proper for the Security Council cautiously and gradually to adapt its conception of international peace and security over time. However, it remains to be seen whether the Chapter VII actions in Haiti and Somalia demonstrate a new preparedness on its part to find that internal strife constitutes an international threat. The situation is complicated by the fact that some States – especially the US and UK – are clearly prepared to interpret Security Council mandates in a very liberal way, as developments in respect of Kosovo and Iraq indicate. Whether stretching the language of the Charter like this will benefit democratic principles is still less clear.

2 *Sierra Leone, 1997–98*

A final example goes some way to proving our thesis: that there is no right of unilateral or collective pro-democratic intervention absent Security Council authorization, and that the restoration of democracy is not yet – and should not in the future be – considered a sufficient basis for such authorization. In May 1997 the elected government of Sierra Leone was overthrown by the Armed Forces Revolutionary Committee (AFRC). Sierra Leone had been in a state of civil war since unrest in Liberia spilled across the border in 1991. The coup met with a hostile reaction throughout the region and internationally. ECOWAS, which already had troops in a peacekeeping role in Sierra Leone, made clear its determination to reverse the coup. A week later, the OAU unanimously condemned the coup and authorized ECOWAS to take military action to restore the elected government.[154]

On October 8, 1997, the Security Council unanimously adopted Resolution 1132. Determining that "the situation" constituted a threat to international peace and security, the Council *demanded* that the military junta relinquish power to make way for the restoration of the democratically elected government. To enforce this objective, it expressly authorized ECOWAS under Chapter VIII of the Charter to cut the AFRC off from foreign supplies of war *matériel*. South Korea's representative on the

---

[154] Brad R. Roth, *Governmental Illegitimacy in International Law* (Oxford: Clarendon Press, 1999), pp. 405–06.

Council gave the remarkable explanation that the "*coup* had had a destabilizing effect on the whole region by reversing a new wave of democracy which was spreading across the African continent."[155]

As with the intervention in Liberia, this was in reality a case of the Council purporting to give retrospective validation to acts that had already taken place. Despite the reference to Chapter VIII, ECOWAS continued to operate in advance of its Council mandate – Nigerian ECOMOG forces launched a major military assault in February 1998, action subsequently welcomed in a Security Council Presidential Statement[156] and later a resolution.[157]

Following the return of the democratically elected president on March 10, 1998, the Council terminated the embargo.[158] Fighting between government and rebel forces continued, however, and the Council established UNOMSIL to monitor the security situation, disarmament, and observance of international humanitarian law.[159] Brad Roth has suggested that the action in Sierra Leone is

> the best evidence yet of a fundamental change in international legal norms pertaining to "pro-democratic" intervention. The Security Council in this case took authorization of action against the "illegitimate" regime beyond the context of United Nations peacemaking *cum* electoral "arbitration," not even bothering to take refuge in assertions of "extraordinary," "exceptional," or "unique" circumstances in invoking Chapter VII. Moreover, its *post hoc* ratification of the regional organization's forcible acts neither comported with a literal interpretation of Chapter VIII nor could be rationalized by a threat of imminent humanitarian disaster. The argument can be made, with at least a modicum of plausibility, that coups against elected governments are now, *per se*, violations of international law, and that regional organizations are now licensed to use force to reverse such coups in member states.[160]

Cautious as this statement is, the two conclusions, which Roth ultimately disavows, simply do not follow. If the argument is that customary international law has changed to the point where the nature of regime-change attracts international legal consequences (though implicitly restricted to violent overthrows of elected regimes), more evidence than a Security Council determination that such a coup constitutes a threat

---

[155] UN Press Release SC/6425 (October 8, 1997) 10, *cited in* Roth, *Governmental Illegitimacy, supra* note 154, p. 407.   [156] UN Doc. S/PRST/1998/5.
[157] SC Res. 1162 (1998) (commending ECOMOG on its role in restoring peace and security).
[158] SC Res. 1156 (1998); SC Res. 1171 (1998). The resolution provided that arms were allowed to be sold only to the government, however.
[159] SC Res. 1181 (1998); SC Res. 1220 (1999), January 12, 1999 (extending UNOMSIL until March 13, 1999).   [160] Roth, *Governmental Illegitimacy, supra* note 154, p. 407.

to peace and security must be established. Similarly, the retrospective validation of acts by the Council can hardly be equated with the granting of a license to perform such acts in future.

A more cynical view is, in our view, that the ECOWAS intervention was, for all intents and purposes, a Nigerian intervention, and that Nigeria was (at the time at least) a profoundly undemocratic State with apparent aspirations to regional hegemony.[161] One could just as easily conclude that the Security Council adopted a Chapter VII resolution in order to "absorb" any contributing effect that the intervention might otherwise have had as State practice and evidence of *opinio juris* in support of a new right of unauthorized intervention,[162] and/or to impose certain legal and political constraints on the Nigerian *junta's* adventures abroad – which in our view constituted the actual threat to international peace and security here.

IV CONCLUSION

Twenty years ago, Michael Walzer proposed a thought experiment concerning what might be considered an ideal case of pro-democratic intervention. He posited a country named Algeria in which a nominally democratic revolution has evolved into a theocratic military dictatorship that suppresses civil liberties and brutally represses its citizens. The new elite allows no challenge to its authority; women are returned to their traditional religious subordination to patriarchal authority. Nevertheless, the regime has deep roots in Algeria's history, as well as its political and religious culture (a questionable claim for the regime the revolutionaries had in mind). Walzer further posited that the Swedish government has in its possession a "wondrous chemical" which, if introduced into the water supply, would turn all Algerians into Swedish-style social democrats. They would have no memory of their former views and experience no loss; they would be empowered to create a new regime in which civil liberties would be respected and women treated as equals. Should Sweden use the chemical?[163]

Although this thought experiment raises issues which go far beyond the scope of this chapter, we refer to it here because it makes an

---

[161] Roth acknowledges the relevance of this point. *Ibid.* at p. 408.
[162] *See* Georg Nolte, "The Limits of the Security Council's Powers and its Functions in the International Legal System – Some Reflections," *in* Michael Byers, ed., *The Role of Law in International Politics* (Oxford University Press, 2000), pp. 315–26.
[163] Michael Walzer, "The Moral Standing of States," *Philosophy & Public Affairs* 9 (1978–79), pp. 226–27.

important point: that how one answers the question depends on whether one accepts that the "right to democratic governance" is more complex than a simple assertion that sovereignty must be popular. We have argued that it is, and that this is reflected in tensions between different principles of international law commonly invoked in support of such a right: hence the contradiction between rights to self-determination and limits on intervention to bring it about; hence the paradox that the UN exists to promote human rights but not to interfere in the domestic jurisdiction of States. To assert that these tensions mean something at the end of the twentieth century is neither anachronistic nor, indeed, simply evidence of a "statist" approach to international law. Rather, it reflects the fact that there may often be differences between what a political community is, what it can be, and what it should be.[164]

We take the view that pro-democratic intervention may – in all but the most exceptional of circumstances – actually be inimical to human rights. As Walzer notes, it may seem paradoxical to assert a people's right to a State within which their rights are violated, but such a State is the only one that they, as a political community, are likely to call their own.[165] It could be said that the argument is a straw one: altering a people's culture through despotic control is more intrusive than "surgical" military strikes aimed at removing an undemocratic government. But the important point is that the right of self-determination that is at the heart of the democratic entitlement vests in none other than the people, and that it is they – and not some foreign power that they have similarly *not* elected – who must determine their own destiny.

Clearly there are limits to such a principle. These, we would submit, are those presently recognized by international law. Governments are no longer completely shielded by principles of sovereignty and domestic jurisdiction when they engage in egregious violations of human rights or otherwise expose their populations to widespread and serious harm. However, those who seek to intervene are also subject to constraints of a legal character. States may not use force other than in self-defense (within the strict limits of the law governing that principle), or pursuant to a legitimate request from the authorities (or, in some circumstances, from a separatist movement fighting a war of liberation from colonial domination) in advance of the intervention, or where the Security Council has authorized the use of force pursuant to a finding (which is

---

[164] *See also* Simon Chesterman, "Human Rights as Subjectivity: the Age of Rights and the Politics of Culture," *Millennium: J. Int'l Stud.* 27 (1998), p. 97.
[165] Walzer, "Moral Standing of States," *supra* note 163, p. 226.

credible and not contrary to the purposes of the Charter) that a situation is a threat to international peace and security. The constraints on forcible means do not demand that a concerned international community sit on its hands in the face of great human suffering – only that its response must be limited to peaceful means unless one of these situations applies.

The attempt by Reisman, D'Amato, and Tesón to justify US actions in the Western Hemisphere as evidence of a new right of unilateral pro-democratic intervention poses a dangerous threat to the prohibition on the use of force and, therefore, to that embattled organization – the United Nations – which is charged with principal responsibility for issues of peace and security in our increasingly interdependent world. It may also be disingenuous: Grenada could equally be explained as one of the last Cold-War battlefields, Panama as an embarrassed George Bush dealing with a US ally turned drug smuggler, and Haiti as a refugee crisis remarkable only as the first time the United States has sought Security Council authorization to intervene in the Western Hemisphere. To hold these three instances up as models of a new era of selfless intervention is to ignore the history of invasions that has characterized the relationship between the US and its southern neighbors. To use them as the foundation of a new international legal order is to drape the arbitrary exercise of power by the sole remaining superpower in the robes of dubious legality.

With history stubbornly refusing to end, there will always be a conflict between what is possible and what is right. But if the right to democratic governance means anything, it is that its content *and the manner of its expression* must be determined by the people in whom it vests.

CHAPTER 9

Pro-democratic intervention by invitation

David Wippman

I INTRODUCTION

In 1989, both the UN General Assembly and the OAS voted overwhelmingly to condemn the US invasion of Panama,[1] even though it was common knowledge that the advent of democracy in Panama had been frustrated by General Manuel Noriega's refusal to seat the government of President-elect Guillermo Endara, and even though Endara and most other Panamanians appeared to welcome the invasion.[2] Most States rejected the notion that foreign actors could legitimately employ armed force or other measures of coercion to seat a democratically elected government against the will of an indigenous political elite in effective control of the State. Indeed, many States questioned the propriety of any attempt by foreign States to influence domestic political processes.

But much has changed since 1989. A variety of developments, chronicled in detail elsewhere in this volume, make the idea of an international legal right to democratic governance much closer to reality than it was when Thomas Franck first heralded the notion of a "democratic entitlement" in 1992.[3] Perhaps most significant, for purposes of this chapter, is the international reaction to recent military coups in Haiti and Sierra Leone. In both cases, virtually the entire international community not only condemned the coups and demanded the immediate reinstatement of the elected governments, but also accepted the use of

---

[1] The General Assembly voted 75-20 to condemn the invasion; the vote in the OAS was 20-1, with only the United States dissenting. GA Res. 240, UN GAOR, 44th Sess., at 1, UN Doc. A/Res/44/240 (1989); CP/Res. 534, OAS Permanent Council, OEA/ser. G/P/Res. 534 (800/89) corr. 1 (1989).
[2] *See* Abraham D. Sofaer, "The Legality of the United States Action in Panama," *Col. J. Transnat'l L.* 29 (1991), pp. 281, 289–90.
[3] *See generally* Thomas Franck, "The Emerging Right to Democratic Governance," *Am J. Int'l L.* 86 (1992), p. 46.

force as a legitimate means to restore democracy at the request of those ousted governments.

In opposing the coup in Haiti, the United States and several of its allies managed to obtain Security Council authorization before initiating military action to dislodge the junta and to restore President Aristide to office. By contrast, in Sierra Leone, Nigeria and its allies in the Economic Community of West African States (ECOWAS) acted without the blessing of the Security Council when at the request of the ousted President Ahmad Tejan Kabbah they launched a major military offensive to drive Sierra Leone's self-styled military government from the capital city and lay the groundwork for the return of the democratically elected government.

The actions of Nigeria and its allies bring into sharp relief the issues only suggested at the time of the US invasion of Panama. Two questions in particular stand out. First, can the consent of an elected government by itself provide the legal justification for an external military intervention to restore that government to power in the event of a military coup or other unconstitutional seizure of power? Second, if so, can the necessary consent be provided in advance, by treaty? This chapter articulates a legal rationale for answering both questions with a qualified yes, but also acknowledges that recent State practice provides at most equivocal support for such an answer.

II THE LEGAL EFFECT OF CONSENT TO INTERVENTION

Notwithstanding the categorical terminology often employed in connection with the legal principles governing forcible intervention, it is widely recognized that one State may lawfully use force in the territory of another State – for example, to suppress a local disturbance – provided that the first State acts with the consent or, at least, the acquiescence of the other State.[4] When a government is both widely recognized and in effective control of most of the State, consent affords a clear alternative

---

[4] *See, e.g.*, Oscar Schachter, "The Right of States to Use Armed Force," *Mich. L. Rev.* 82 (1984), pp. 1620, 1644–45 ("in the absence of a civil war, recognized governments have a right to receive external military assistance and outside states are free to furnish such aid"); Case Concerning Military and Paramilitary Activities in and against Nicaragua (Nicaragua v. United States), 1 *ICJ* (1986), p. 126 (intervention "is allowable at the request of the government of a State..."); SC Res. 387 (1976) (recognizing "the inherent and lawful right of every State, in the exercise of its sovereignty, to request assistance from any other state or group of states"). *See also* International Law Commission, Draft Articles on State Responsibility, Art. 29(1), *reprinted in* 37 ILM (1998), pp. 440, 450 (consent "precludes the wrongfulness" of an otherwise illicit act).

to Security Council authorization as a basis for justifying external intervention, whether by States acting unilaterally or by States acting under the auspices of the UN or a regional organization.

The theoretical basis for the rule that consent may validate an otherwise wrongful intervention is not entirely clear. The International Law Commission, in a study of State responsibility for wrongful conduct, concluded that consent to intervention acts as a form of bilateral agreement between the consenting and intervening States that suspends the normal operation of the legal rules that would otherwise govern their relationship.[5] It seems more plausible, however, to conclude simply that consent or its absence is central to the definition of wrongful intervention in the first place. In other words, prohibited intervention (whether or not it rises to the level of a use of force in violation of Article 2(4) of the UN Charter) should be understood as intervention against the will of the State; in Oppenheim's formulation, it is "dictatorial interference" in a State's internal affairs that is impermissible, not external involvement *per se*.[6]

In keeping with this understanding, many States have attempted to justify military intervention in other States on the basis of consent. In some cases, the justification was relatively persuasive and the interventions met with general acquiescence. During the Cold War, both France and (to a lesser extent) the United Kingdom relied on consent to justify periodic interventions in former colonies to support friendly governments against small-scale rebellions or palace coups.[7] Most States accepted such interventions, even when the invitations at issue arguably came after the inviting officials had already lost their hold on power.[8]

---

[5] *See* Roberto Ago, Eighth Report on State Responsibility, Document A/CN4/318 and Add. 1–4, *Y.B. Int'l L. Comm'n* 2 (1979), pp. 3, 31–32.

[6] L. Oppenheim, *International Law*, H. Lauterpacht, ed., (8th edn., New York: D. McKay, 1955) (defining prohibited intervention as "dictatorial interference . . . in the affairs of another State for the purpose of maintaining or altering the actual condition of things").

[7] In 1964, Britain intervened in Tanganyika, Uganda, and Kenya to help incumbent governments quell local disturbances and mutinies in the armed forces. *See* Louise Doswald-Beck, "The Legal Validity of Military Intervention by Invitation of the Government," 1985 *Brit.Y.B. Int'l L.* p. 189 n.4 (1986). France intervened more than a dozen times in its African colonies, usually (though not always) to assist beleaguered governments to retain or to resume control in the face of attempted military coups. *See* John Darnton, "The World: Intervening with Elan and No Regrets," *N.Y. Times* (June 26, 1994), D3.

[8] When France intervened *against* an incumbent government, however, it met with more international criticism than approbation. In 1979, when French troops forcibly deposed the head of State of the Central African Republic, various countries criticized the French action as a violation of the non-intervention principle, despite Bokassa's atrocious human rights record. *See* W. Michael Reisman, "Humanitarian Intervention and Fledgling Democracies," *Fordham Int'l L.J.* 18 (1995), pp. 794, 800.

Similarly, the 1982 deployment of US, French, Italian, and British forces to assist the Lebanese government in restoring order met with little international opposition, at least at the outset.[9]

In other cases, reliance on consent proved unpersuasive. When the Soviet Union, for example, invoked the principle of State consent to justify the invasions of Hungary in 1956, Czechoslovakia in 1968, and Afghanistan in 1979, it met with widespread criticism on the ground that the invitations at issue were either manufactured or coerced.[10] Similarly, when the US sent troops to the Dominican Republic in 1965, and to Grenada in 1983, it was condemned by many States, which questioned the legal authority of the officials who issued the invitations to intervene.[11] Still, in these cases, as in the cases described above, the principle that voluntary consent from proper State authorities can validate intervention was not in dispute.

There are, of course, substantive limits on the kinds of intervention to which States can consent. Simply put, a State cannot authorize, by treaty or otherwise, conduct within its territory that it lacks legal authority to engage in by itself.[12] Put another way, there are international legal norms independent of State consent, in particular, norms that protect individuals against State power. Thus, a State cannot, for example, authorize another State to commit human rights abuses or "any act criminal under international law," such as "trade in slaves, piracy or genocide."[13] Consent can, however, validate an external military intervention taken in furtherance of aims valid under international law.

Of course, as suggested above, the consent at issue must be

---

[9] *See* Doswald-Beck, *supra* note 7, pp. 241–42. Not long after arrival, however, US (and to some extent French) forces were drawn into the conflict in a way that exceeded their status as peacekeepers. As a result, the intervention eventually attracted considerable criticism from other States. *Ibid.*

[10] *See* UN SCOR, 746th mtg 4, UN Doc. S/PV.746 (1956) (Hungary); UN SCOR, 23d yr, 1441st mtg 1, UN Doc. S/PV.1441 (1968) (Czechoslovakia); UN SCOR, 35th yr, 2185th mtg 2, UN Doc. S/PV.2185 (1980) (Afghanistan). The interventions were generally deemed invalid. Rein Mullerson, "Intervention by Invitation," *in* L. Damrosch and D. Scheffer, eds., *Law and Force in the New World Order* (Boulder, Co.: Westview Press, 1991), pp. 127, 128–29.

[11] *See* Doswald-Beck, *supra* note 7, pp. 228, 237 (noting that "diplomatic reaction" to the US intervention in the Dominican Republic "was generally unfavourable," and that "the vast majority of States, including the traditional allies of the US, characterized the intervention [in Grenada] as illegal").

[12] *See* John Lawrence Hargrove, "Intervention by Invitation and the Politics of the New World Order," *in* Damrosch and Scheffer, eds., *Law and Force, supra* note 10, pp.113, 116–17.

[13] Andreas Jacovides, *Treaties Conflicting with Peremptory Norms of International Law and the Zurich–London Agreements* (Nicosia, 1966), p. 10.

voluntary,[14] and the individual purporting to give consent must possess the legal authority to do so.[15] But these issues, although they may prove difficult to resolve in particular cases, are usually at least nominally susceptible to resolution under generally accepted principles of treaty law dealing with coercion and the representation of States.[16]

More difficult problems arise when the authority of a particular government purporting to consent to intervention on behalf of the State is subject to challenge, either because the government has lost control of a substantial portion of the State, or because more than one entity claims the title of government and with it the right to speak for the State. In such cases, the real issue is who is entitled to express the will of the State concerning intervention?

A *The effective control standard*

Although it is the consent of the State itself that is ultimately at issue, States are abstract entities, and cannot by themselves give or withhold consent to intervention.[17] In general, international law presumes that when a government exercises effective control over the territory and people of the State, the government – and more particularly, the authorized officials of that government – possess the exclusive authority to express the will of the State in its international affairs.[18] This presump-

---

[14] As Judge (then Special Rapporteur) Roberto Ago observed in his report to the International Law Commission on state responsibility, consent may be "*expressed* or *tacit*, *explicit* or *implicit*, provided however that it is *clearly established*," and is not "vitiated by 'defects' such as error, fraud, corruption or violence." Eighth Report on State Responsibility, *supra* note 5, pp. 35–36 (italics in original).

[15] To be valid, "consent must be *internationally attributable to the State*; in other words, it must issue from a person whose will is considered, at the international level, to be the will of the State and, in addition, the person in question must be competent to manifest that will in the particular case involved." *Ibid.* at p. 36 (italics in original).

[16] *Ibid.* ("The principles which apply to the determination of the validity of treaties also apply with respect to the validity of consent to an action which would, in the absence of such consent, be internationally wrongful."); Hargrove, *supra* note 12, p. 119 (legal issues regarding the genuineness of invitations to intervene "are resolvable on the basis of familiar concepts drawn straightforwardly from other areas of the law than those having to do directly with restraints on the exercise of force – for example, the law of treaties"). *See also* Vienna Convention on the Law of Treaties, UN Doc. A/CONF. 39/27 (1969), Art. 51 (rejecting the validity of consent based on coercion of a State's representative); Art. 52 (rejecting the validity of consent based on coercion of the State itself); Art. 7 (identifying individuals presumptively capable of expressing a State's consent to be bound to a treaty).

[17] Quincy Wright, "United States Intervention in the Lebanon," *Am J. Int'l L.* 53 (1959), pp. 112, 120.

[18] *See, e.g.*, Tom J. Farer, "Panama: Beyond the Charter Paradigm," *Am. J. Int'l L.* 84 (1990), pp. 503, 510 (noting "the virtually uniform practice in international relations of treating any group of nationals in effective control of their state as constituting its legitimate government"); Restatement (Third) of Foreign Relations Law of the United States § 210 cmt. d (1985) (same).

tion derives from a mix of practical and theoretical considerations. As a practical matter, States cannot ignore an effective government, whatever its origin or political leanings. Moreover, reliance on effective control as the test for a government's capacity to represent the State offers a reasonably objective and externally verifiable basis for determining governmental authority, thus "inhibiting intervention" by outside States.[19] As a theoretical matter, effective control serves as a rough proxy for the existence of some degree of congruity between the government and the larger political community of the State, which supports the government's claim to represent the State as a whole. To the extent that the government is unrepresentative, this assumed congruity may be largely fictitious.[20] But it is nonetheless widely accepted as the only viable basis on which States can conduct international relations in a decentralized system.

As a general matter, therefore, neither States nor international organizations may lawfully intervene against the will of an effective, incumbent government, even if the goal of the intervention is to replace a dictatorship with a democracy. In *Nicaragua v. United States*, the International Court of Justice had no trouble concluding that intervention at the request of opposition forces, even those characterizing themselves as "freedom fighters," violated the non-intervention principle.[21] For the same reason, the US invasion of Panama was widely condemned, even though the invasion ousted a dictatorial regime and replaced it with a democratically elected one.[22] In short, an effective government's right to seek or oppose external intervention does not ordinarily depend on the manner in which the government acquired power or on the manner in which the government exercises power.

In some cases, however, the presumption that the government speaks for the State may break down.[23] In particular, when the government's

---

[19] Farer, *supra* note 18, p. 511.
[20] *See* Fernando Tesón, "Collective Humanitarian Intervention," *Mich. J. Int'l L.* 17 (1996), pp. 323, 332 (arguing that "a rule requiring democratic legitimacy in the form of free adult universal suffrage seems the best approximation to actual political consent and true representativeness").
[21] Nicaragua v. United States, *supra* note 4, p. 126.
[22] A large majority of the UN General Assembly criticized the US invasion as "a flagrant violation of international law and of the independence, sovereignty and territorial integrity of States." GA Res. 44/240 (Dec. 29, 1989). *See generally* Ved Nanda, "The Validity of United States Intervention in Panama Under International Law," *Am. J. Int'l L.* 84 (1990), p. 494; Louis Henkin, "The Invasion of Panama Under International Law: A Gross Violation," *Colum. J. Transnat'l L.* 29 (1991), p. 293.
[23] When a government is imposed as the direct result of foreign military intervention, the dissociation between government, State, and political community is complete, so much so that international law prohibits recognition of the imposed regime. *See* Restatement (Third) of the Foreign

control over the State is effectively challenged by an internal, armed opposition, the presumption that the government represents the State may become untenable.[24] Indeed, it is precisely the authority of a particular government to speak for the State as a whole that is called into question by an internal conflict. Accordingly, in a full-scale civil war, international law is generally understood to prohibit aid to either government or rebel forces, since aid to one side might disrupt the internal play of forces and thereby violate the political independence of the State and the right of its people to determine their own political future.[25]

In the case of a full-scale civil war, however, it is reasonable to presume that both sides in the conflict are supported by a substantial share of the people of the State. It follows that an external intervention on behalf of the "democratic" forces in such a conflict, assuming that one side can be so identified, may reasonably be treated as an improper interference with the right of the State's people to determine its own future. That view is much less persuasive when a small, repressive military clique overthrows a popular and democratically elected government. In such cases, as argued below, legitimacy matters.

B *Democracy, legitimacy, and consent*

Under existing law, it is at best unclear whether a *de jure* government overthrown in violation of domestic constitutional law may authorize external intervention to reestablish its authority.[26] But recent State practice suggests an increasing willingness to accept the authority of an ousted democratic regime to invite external intervention to restore it to

---

Relations Law of the United States § 203(2) (1985) ("A state has an obligation not to recognize or treat a regime as the government of another state if its control has been effected by the threat or use of armed force in violation of the United Nations Charter.") In cases of belligerent occupation, a deposed government may establish itself on the territory of a friendly State, and may be treated as a government-in-exile if recognized as such by other States and if engaged in forcible efforts to reestablish control over its home State. *See Oppenheim's International Law* 1, Robert Jennings and Arthur Watts, eds. (Harlow: Longmans, 1992), pp. 146–47; Marjorie Whiteman, *Digest of Int'l L.* 2 (1963), pp. 467–86.

[24] *See generally* David Wippman, "Legal Justifications for Military Intervention in Internal Conflicts," *Colum. Hum. Rts. L. Rev.* 27 (1996), p. 435.

[25] *See, e.g.*, Oscar Schachter, "International Law: the Right of States to Use Armed Force," *Mich. L. Rev.* 82 (1984), pp. 1620, 1641; John Norton Moore, "Legal Standards for Intervention in Internal Conflicts," *Ga. J. Int'l & Comp. L.* 13 (1983), pp. 141, 196.

[26] *See* Domingo Acevedo, "The Haitian Crisis and the OAS Response: a Test of Effectiveness in Protecting Democracy," *in* L. F. Damrosch, ed., *Enforcing Restraint: Collective Intervention in Internal Conflicts* (New York: Council on Foreign Relations, 1993), pp. 119, 139 ("It is unclear . . . whether a de jure government that has only *formal* but not actual power may invite foreign 'military intervention' for the purpose of removing the *de facto* regime") (italics in original).

power, at least when a broad international consensus exists with respect to the legitimacy of the inviting regime and the illegitimacy of the *de facto* authorities.

On its face, external military intervention to reinstate an ejected incumbent would seem to constitute impermissible interference in a State's internal affairs. Nonetheless, a number of countries periodically send troops to help ousted leaders get back into the presidential palace. In 1964, for example, the United Kingdom came to the aid of President Julius Nyerere of Tanganyika.[27] Nyerere headed an elected government that lost control of the capital to mutinous army troops. At Nyerere's request, British troops intervened to restore order. The British action went largely unremarked in the United Nations. Similarly, France has frequently intervened militarily in its former colonies to restore *de jure* governments to power following internal military coups, without attracting much adverse comment from other States.[28]

Several factors appear to account for the apparent acquiescence of most States in actions of this nature. So long as the interventions at issue are swift and small in scale, most States seem willing to ignore the brief discontinuity in the *de jure* government's effective control of the State. In effect, States treat the coup makers as temporary usurpers whose actions do not fundamentally alter the *de jure* government's power to speak for the State. That attitude may be attributable in part to a general understanding that political constraints usually preclude the United Nations Security Council from authorizing intervention in such cases (or from doing so in a timely fashion), and in part to a sense that the former colonial powers should have some leeway to assist their former colonies in maintaining order, even at the cost of some inconsistency with international legal principles.

For the purposes of this chapter, the critical question is whether the legitimacy conferred by an electoral mandate suffices to permit the ejected government to invite military intervention on its behalf, even when the *de facto* authorities can claim effective control of the State over a significant period of time and have a strong prospect of remaining in

---

[27] *See* Reisman, *supra* note 8, p. 796.
[28] *See* Darnton, *supra* note 7, p. 3. In 1996, French paratroopers helped the democratically elected but corrupt government of the Central African Republic force mutinous army troops back into their barracks. Although the French intervention was highly unpopular within the Central African Republic itself, most other States paid little attention. *See* Jim Hoagland, "Does Anyone Care About Africa?" *The Denver Post* (June 2, 1996), F4. Some States even commended the French action. A US official praised the French intervention as "very efficient," and described France as a "force for stability in Africa." Gus Constantine, "France Keeps a Hand in Ex-Colonies: Bangui Mutiny Latest Example of Intervention," *The Washington Times* (June 6, 1996), A12.

1 Haiti

Jean Bertrand Aristide became President of Haiti in 1990, following his clear victory in an internationally monitored and supervised election.[29] Some months later, the Haitian military, alarmed by Aristide's populist rhetoric and reformist policies, staged a military coup and forced Aristide to flee the country.[30] If Aristide had immediately invited external military intervention, the military coup and its reversal might conceivably have been treated as an anomaly and largely ignored. But Aristide was extremely reluctant to invite foreign military forces into Haiti. He did so, grudgingly and obliquely, only after it became clear that months of economic sanctions and diplomatic pressure would fail to dislodge the military junta.[31] In any event, Aristide's ouster was not the typical palace coup. The officers in charge had substantial support throughout the military, and also in a significant, although clearly a minority, segment of Haitian society.[32] Accordingly, the usurpers could not be summarily dismissed as transient occupants of the Presidential palace, whose ouster would have little impact on the right of Haiti's people to self-determination.

The argument in favor of permitting intervention on the basis of an invitation from Aristide was simple. As the elected head of State, Aristide represented the people of Haiti as a whole. Following the coup, both the United Nations and the OAS continued to recognize Aristide as the legitimate head of State, and both repeatedly demanded his reinstatement.[33] Accordingly, Aristide had a strong claim that he alone was entitled to speak for the State on questions of intervention.[34] By contrast, the military junta achieved its position by force, and maintained that

---

[29] See Acevedo, *supra* note 26, pp. 129–30.   [30] *Ibid.*

[31] See Melita Marie Garza, "Aristide Can Only Hint He'd Like Armed Help," *Chi. Trib.* (June 1, 1994), § 1, p. 12. *See also* Deborah Zabarenko, "Aristide Thanks US, Gets Assurances on Haiti," *Reuter* (Sept. 21, 1994) (describing Aristide's ambivalent and shifting views on inviting foreign intervention).

[32] See Acevedo, *supra* note 26, p. 131 (noting that "traditionally entrenched groups that had always represented the power of wealth, privilege, and violence in Haiti – particularly the upper classes and the army – viewed Aristide's popular approach as a threat"); Brad R. Roth, "Governmental Illegitimacy Revisited: 'Pro-Democratic' Armed Intervention in the Post-Bipolar World," *Transnat'l L. & Contemp. Prob.* 3 (1993), pp. 481, 511–12 (noting that the "coup leadership ha[d] support in the elected legislature").

[33] See, e.g., William M. Berenson, "Joint Venture for the Restoration of Democracy in Haiti: the Organization of American States and United Nations Experience: 1991–1995" (copy on file with author).   [34] *See* Roth, *supra* note 32, pp. 511–12.

position by terrorizing much of the country. It had no legitimacy, domestic or international, and therefore should have no authority to speak for the State, or to oppose an intervention directed at restoring democracy.[35] Intervention in this context, goes the argument, would further Haitian self-determination and fulfill the much-heralded (but still emerging) right to democratic governance.[36]

The argument is a powerful one. But when the United Nations Security Council finally authorized military intervention to restore Aristide to power, it relied primarily on its authority to maintain international peace and security through coercive measures under Chapter VII of the Charter.[37] The authorizing resolution implicitly took note of Aristide's consent to intervention,[38] but the Security Council was evidently unwilling to treat that consent as sufficient in and of itself to permit military action.[39]

The Council's reluctance may reflect, at least in part, the fact that international law continues to place considerable importance on effective control as an indicator of a government's authority to act in the name of the State.[40] From this perspective, the legal authority to consent

---

[35] *See ibid.* (noting that Aristide's elected status and the military's "violent conduct and unsavory history" combined to create a situation in which there was "no contest over the mandate to articulate the will of the 'legitimate government'").

[36] As Brad Roth observed prior to the UN authorization of military intervention in Haiti, "in all likelihood, fulfillment of requests for armed assistance would not in this case be deemed a violation of international law," *ibid.* at p. 511.

[37] *See* SC Res. 940, UN SCOR, 49th Sess., 3413th mtg., UN Doc. S/Res/875 (1993) ("determining that the situation in Haiti continues to constitute a threat to peace and security in the region," and, "acting under Chapter VII of the Charter," authorizing "Member States . . . to use all necessary means to facilitate" the restoration of the Aristide government).

[38] The resolution cited two letters, one from Aristide (S/1994/905, annex) and another from Haiti's Permanent Representative to the UN (S/1994/910). Both letters implicitly supported UN-authorized military intervention.

[39] In adopting Resolution 940, the Security Council considered the options outlined in the Report of the Secretary-General on the United Nations Mission in Haiti, S/1994/828 (July 15, 1994). In that report, the Secretary-General states that an expanded UN force should operate with the consent of the legitimate authorities in Haiti, but also notes that such a force "would have to use coercive means in order to fulfill its mandate," and that it would therefore "be necessary for the Security Council to act under Chapter VII of the Charter in authorizing its mandate," *ibid.* para. 8. During the debate on Resolution 940, several States' representatives noted that Aristide's consent to intervention was an important factor supporting the decision to intervene, but no one identified it as either a necessary or a sufficient legal basis for intervention. *See* UN SC Provisional Verbatim Record, 3413th Meeting, S/PV.3413, July 31, 1994, at 17, 19, 23, 24 (statements of the representatives of Argentina, Spain, the Russian Federation, and the Czech Republic).

[40] Thus, when the United States invoked the support of Panama's President-elect, Guillermo Endara, as one of several grounds allegedly justifying US military intervention in Panama, *see* Abraham D. Sofaer, "Remarks," Panel on "The Panamanian Revolution: Diplomacy, War and Self-Determination in Panama," *ASIL Proceedings* 84 (1990) p. 182, few States considered Endara's consent legally significant.

to foreign intervention should be regarded as divided in cases such as that posed by Haiti. The military's exercise of effective control over the territory and people of the State for a period of three years supported a claim to speak for the State that the Security Council felt it could not entirely ignore, just as Aristide's democratic legitimacy, universally acknowledged by the recognition of other States and international organizations, supported an alternative and opposing basis on which to claim authority to speak for the State.

The Security Council favored Aristide's claim, but the existence of a sufficient consensus on the acceptability of authorizing military intervention rendered it unnecessary for the Council to rely exclusively on Aristide's consent as a legal basis for military intervention. Instead, the Council asserted, not entirely convincingly, that the refusal of the junta to reinstate Aristide constituted a threat to international peace and security warranting the authorization of the use of force under Chapter VII of the UN Charter. As a result, the Haitian precedent is an ambiguous one. The extent to which States would have accepted a military intervention to restore Aristide's government absent Security Council authorization remains unclear. But recent events in Sierra Leone suggest an answer.

2 Sierra Leone

In February 1996, after years of military rule, internal conflict, and general instability, Ahmad Tejan Kabbah was elected President of Sierra Leone in internationally monitored elections that were generally accepted as free and fair. Less than a year after taking office, Kabbah managed to conclude a peace agreement with the Revolutionary United Front (RUF), a rebel group that had been fighting against the government for some years.

But six months later, a group of low-level military officers overthrew Kabbah's government, suspended the Constitution, banned political parties, and outlawed all demonstrations.[41] Violence, looting, and widespread unrest followed the coup. Law and order largely collapsed, and thousands sought refuge in neighboring countries. From the outset, internal opposition to the coup was near universal, encompassing "[a]lmost all sectors of Sierra Leonean society, including trade unions, religious groups, lawyers, women's groups, teachers, students and jour-

---

[41] Amnesty International Country Report, *Sierra Leone: a Disastrous Set-back for Human Rights* (1997), pp. 4–5.

nalists . . ."[42] Ironically, the junta's principal source of support came from the RUF, the rebel forces that had previously fought against the government. The junta, known as the Armed Forces Revolutionary Council (AFRC), proved unable, however, to exercise much control over RUF forces, or even over government soldiers, both of which routinely committed gross human rights violations.

International opposition to the coup was prompt and universal. The UN, OAU, ECOWAS, Commonwealth and EU all condemned the coup and demanded the immediate and unconditional reinstatement of Kabbah's government.[43] No government recognized the AFRC.

The strongest opposition to the coup came from Sierra Leone's neighbors. Immediately following the coup, Nigeria strengthened the forces it already had in place in Sierra Leone under a pre-existing mutual defense treaty.[44] Nigeria also sought to intimidate the coup leaders by bombarding military targets in the capital of Freetown.[45]

In June 1997, at its 33rd Meeting of Heads of State and Government, the OAU declared that the coup was "unacceptable" and implicitly endorsed the use of force to reverse it, urging Sierra Leone's neighbors "to take all necessary measures" to restore President Kabbah to office.[46] Later that month, ECOWAS convened a special meeting of its foreign ministers to consider its response to the coup. The ministers "reaffirmed" the OAU's position on Sierra Leone, "urged that no State recognize the regime installed following the coup," and expressly endorsed the use of force as a legitimate response to the coup.[47] Two months later, the ECOWAS heads of State, declaring the coup a threat to international peace and security in the sub-region, announced the imposition of a total embargo on petroleum products, arms, and military supplies to Sierra Leone and stated that "sub-regional forces shall employ all necessary means to impose the implementation of this decision."[48] In the following months, ECOWAS forces engaged in sporadic attacks designed to enforce the embargo and to put pressure on the junta.

---

[42] Ibid. at p. 2.   [43] Ibid.
[44] See Sierra Leone: Military Coup, 34 Africa Research Bull. 12694 (May 1–31, 1997).
[45] Ibid. at pp. 6–7.
[46] Decision of the 33rd Summit of the Organization of African Unity (June 2–4, 1997).
[47] Final Communique, ECOWAS Special Meeting of Foreign Ministers, June 26, 1997 (stating that "every effort" should "be made to restore the lawful government by a combination of three measures, ie., the use of dialogue; the application of sanctions, including an embargo; and the use of force").
[48] Economic Community of West African States Twentieth Session of the Authority of Heads of State and Government, Decision on Sanctions Against the Junta in Sierra Leone, August 28–29, 1997.

ECOWAS's response to the coup received broad support around the world. In July 1997, the Commonwealth Ministerial Action Group welcomed the efforts of ECOWAS to restore President Kabbah's government, urged all States to continue to refuse to recognize the AFRC, and decided to suspend Sierra Leone's participation in Commonwealth meetings.[49] Similarly, the European Union praised ECOWAS's efforts to restore democracy and decided to discontinue aid to Sierra Leone until the Kabbah government was returned to power. Many individual states made similar declarations.[50]

Immediately after the coup, the UN Security Council "strongly deplore[d] this attempt to overthrow the democratically elected government and call[ed] for an immediate restoration of constitutional order."[51] On July 11, the Security Council declared the coup "unacceptable" and a threat to international peace and security. Aware that ECOWAS had already authorized (and used) force to oppose the coup,[52] the Council nonetheless "strongly support[ed]" the OAU's decision to appeal to ECOWAS to help restore constitutional order. At the same time, however, the Council signaled its preference for peaceful measures by explicitly welcoming "the mediation efforts initiated by ECOWAS," and by stating its intent "to follow closely the progress of efforts aimed at the peaceful resolution of the crisis. . . ."[53]

Two months later, aware of escalating tensions and the continued but sporadic attacks by ECOWAS against AFRC forces, the Security Council reiterated its condemnation of the coup and its demand for the "unconditional restoration" of Kabbah's government. The Council also warned that it would, "in the absence of a satisfactory response from the military junta, be ready to take appropriate measures with the objective

[49] Amnesty International, *supra* note 41, p. 8.
[50] *See, e.g.*, Statement by James B. Foley, Deputy Spokesman, US Department of State, "Sierra Leone: United States" Policy, October 3, 1997 ("We appreciate and support the efforts of the Economic Community of West African States (ECOWAS) to restore Kabbah . . .").
[51] Statement by the President of the Security Council, S/PRST/1997/29 (May 27, 1997).
[52] The communiqué expressing ECOWAS's determination to use force to restore constitutional order to Sierra Leone was circulated to the Security Council as an annex to a letter to the Council from Nigeria's Permanent Representative, S/1997/499 (June 27, 1997). Moreover, the Council's statement in support of ECOWAS came immediately after an informal briefing in which Nigeria's foreign minister explained the basis for ECOWAS's decision to use force (notwithstanding the reservations of some ECOWAS members), and in which Zimbabwe's permanent representative requested the Council's unconditional support for ECOWAS and OAU efforts to obtain the "non-recognition and demise" of the AFRC and the restoration of President Kabbah's government. "ECOWAS Asks Security Council to Send 'Unequivocal Message' to Sierra Leone Regime to Return Legitimate Government of President Kabbah to Power," *Press Release* SC/6393 (July 11, 1997).
[53] Statement by the President of the Security Council, S/PRST/1997/36 (July 11, 1997).

of restoring the democratically elected government of President Kabbah."⁵⁴ The Council did not mention the use of force by ECOWAS, but did again applaud ECOWAS's efforts to obtain a "peaceful resolution" of the crisis.

On October 1, 1997, President Kabbah appeared before the General Assembly, where he requested the Security Council to follow through on its August warning of sterner measures and to assist ECOMOG in its efforts to restore his government. He accused the junta of a "reign of terror," and expressed reservations about efforts to negotiate with the coup leaders.⁵⁵ Shortly thereafter, UN Secretary-General Kofi Annan sent a letter to the Security Council expressing support for "efforts for the peaceful resolution of the situation" and stating that "[a]t stake is a great issue of principle, namely, that the efforts of the international community for democratic governance . . . shall not be thwarted through illegal coups."⁵⁶

The Council responded promptly with a unanimous decision to impose mandatory economic sanctions aimed at undermining the coup leaders. In doing so, the Council for the first time in the conflict relied expressly on its powers under Chapter VII of the UN Charter. In addition, acting under Chapter VIII of the Charter, the Council "authorize[d] ECOWAS, cooperating with the democratically-elected Government of Sierra Leone, to ensure strict implementation of the provisions" of the resolution.⁵⁷

Although ECOWAS "had wanted additional and stronger measures included" in the resolution, it took comfort in the "message of international resolve to restore constitutional order in Sierra Leone."⁵⁸ Statements by Council members during the debate preceding adoption of the resolution expressed strong and uniform opposition to "the arbitrary overthrow of a democratically elected Government,"⁵⁹ but many also indicated a preference for a peaceful resolution of the problem. Only the Russian Federation ventured a public (though indirect) criticism of ECOWAS's previous (and possible future) use of force, stating

---

⁵⁴ Statement by the President of the Security Council, S/PRST/1997/42 (August 6, 1997).
⁵⁵ "Security Council Should Take Steps to Restore Sierra Leone's Government, President of Sierra Leone Tells General Assembly," *Press Release* GA/9318 (October 1, 1997).
⁵⁶ Letter Dated October 7, 1997 from the Secretary-General Addressed to the President of the Security Council, S/1997/776.   ⁵⁷ SC Res. 1132 (1997).
⁵⁸ Statement of Nigerian representative Ibrahim Gambari, Press Release SC/6425 (October 8, 1997).
⁵⁹ The phrase is that of the British representative SC Press Release 6425 (October 8, 1997).

that "enforcement measures should not be taken by regional organizations without Security Council authorization."[60]

The following month, the ECOWAS negotiating committee and junta leaders signed a peace plan calling for reinstatement of the Kabbah government within six months.[61] President Kabbah expressed his acceptance of the agreement,[62] as did the Security Council.[63] But the agreement soon fell apart, as junta leaders criticized key aspects of it.

After further diplomatic efforts proved ineffective, Nigeria decided to take stronger measures, perhaps to avoid the kind of protracted stalemate that occurred when ECOMOG forces attempted to restore order to Liberia. In February 1998, Nigerian-led ECOMOG forces seized Freetown after a week of sometimes intense fighting against the AFRC and RUF, forcing the leaders of the junta to flee the country.

In defense of its actions, the Nigerian government claimed that ECOMOG troops had been persistently attacked by AFRC and RUF forces, and that ECOMOG troops had responded in self-defense and then pursued their retreating adversaries into the capital.[64] Sierra Leone's permanent representative to the UN, James Jonah, defended ECOMOG's actions on the ground that the Security Council had failed to take adequate measures to oppose the AFRC's illegal seizure of power, and that therefore Sierra Leone had a right in self-defense to seek regional military assistance.[65] Jonah also suggested that the war in Sierra Leone had been instigated by Liberians in 1991, and that Liberians had also assisted the coup leaders in their efforts to control Sierra Leone, although he was unwilling to state publicly whether he thought the Liberian government was directly responsible.

Nigeria's proffered justification for taking control of Freetown seems implausible at best. Although peacekeeping forces do have a right to self-defense, and can within limits use force against those who obstruct the peacekeepers' mission, the right cannot be stretched so far as to justify a week of bombardments and a full-scale military assault designed to capture and control territory, particularly when occupation of the territory at issue is not part of the peacekeepers' mission. Such action

---

[60] *Ibid.*
[61] The peace plan is contained in a letter to the Security Council, UN Doc. S/1997/824, Annex II.
[62] S/1997/886 (November 5, 1997).   [63] *See* Press Release SC/6444 (November 14, 1997).
[64] *See* "ECOMOG May Stay in Sierra Leone for Six Months," *Xinhua News Agency*, Feb. 18, 1998.
[65] "Press Conference By Permanent Representative of Sierra Leone," *Africa News Service*, Feb. 19, 1998.

exceeds the bounds of permissible self-defense and requires a different legal justification.

Jonah's explanation contains the kernel of two different legal justifications. One is counterintervention. Assistance from Liberia to the Sierra Leone military in its fight to retain control of the State against efforts by forces loyal to President Kabbah to unseat the military regime could arguably justify Nigerian efforts to level the playing field. News reports suggest that Liberia provided both weapons and militia to aid the junta in retaining control of Sierra Leone. But the Nigerian-led assault on Freetown seems to reflect a preconceived determination to restore the Kabbah government to power whatever the level of outside support for the junta.

The second, and for purposes of this chapter more interesting, justification suggested by Jonah's explanation is that the invitation of the legitimate government constituted adequate authority for intervention in the absence of Security Council action. Jonah's attempt to invoke the principle of self-defense makes sense only if one assumes that the ousted government holds the exclusive right to speak for the State, and can therefore in the name of the State oppose external intervention (from Liberia) in support of the military and invite external assistance (from Nigeria) in opposition to the military and its Liberian supporters.

The argument in favor of accepting Kabbah's invitation as an adequate justification for a regional military intervention is much the same as the argument set forth above with respect to Aristide's authority to invite foreign military intervention in Haiti. Kabbah was the elected head of State, and the international community continued to recognize his government and demand its reinstatement following the coup. By contrast, the military junta could achieve and hold power only by violence. It had little popular support and no international legitimacy. When ECOMOG troops seized the capital, the populace celebrated (and attacked any members of the junta they could find).[66] By paving the way for the restoration of the elected and popularly supported government, the intervention arguably helped Sierra Leone's people exercise their right to self-determination.

The principal problem with reliance on consent as a legal justification is also the same as in the Haitian case: the consenting government did not have effective control of the State when it welcomed external inter-

---

[66] *See* Howard French, "Nigerians Take capital of Sierra Leone as Junta Flees," *N.Y. Times* (Feb. 14, 1998), A3; "Sierra Leone: Putting a Country Together Again," *The Economist* (US edition, Feb. 21, 1998), p. 44.

vention. The issue that the Security Council avoided in Haiti must therefore be squarely addressed: can a democratically elected and popularly supported government consent to military intervention against the wishes of *de facto* authorities more or less in control of the State?

As noted earlier, under a conventional reading of international law, effective control is an essential (perhaps the only) component of a government's authority to represent a State in international affairs. From this perspective, legitimacy (whether in the form of international acceptance or domestic popular support) is irrelevant, or perhaps more accurately, legitimacy is presumed on the basis of the population's acquiescence to its government, however that acquiescence is achieved. In the ordinary case, reliance on effective control serves important purposes in the international legal order. It precludes States from too readily ignoring the autonomy of other States, and from too easily justifying interventions that are self-interested or likely to result in counterinterventions and the internationalization of an internal dispute. Control therefore ordinarily affords *de facto* rulers a partial, if not exclusive, claim to speak in the name of the State.

In some cases, however, mechanical reliance on effective control as a proxy for authority to represent the State seems to serve no useful purpose other than helping to preserve the rule. In Sierra Leone, acquiescence to military rule was only partial (the junta did not control significant portions of the country), and did not reflect significant popular support. Moreover, the regional decision-making framework (even if dominated by Nigeria), coupled with Security Council oversight, largely eliminated any risk that intervention to reinstate Kabbah's government would convert an internal conflict into an international one and helped to lessen (though not eliminate) the danger that Nigeria would exploit the situation for its own ends. In addition, Kabbah's consent makes it difficult to accept the argument that the intervention unduly infringed Sierra Leone's autonomy. More specifically, it is hard to construe a proportionate and targeted use of force designed to restore Kabbah's government as a violation of Sierra Leone's territorial integrity or political independence, unless one is prepared to ignore entirely the preferences of the people of Sierra Leone in making that assessment.

It does not follow that any use of force that on balance is welcomed by a majority of a State's population should be treated as acceptable under international law. Such a principle is too subjective and too subject to abuse, and would largely eviscerate the general rule against using force in international relations. At the same time, however, the legitimacy of the inviting authority should – and now apparently does – carry some weight. In an extreme case such as that presented by Sierra Leone, when States unanimously continue to recognize an ousted government, and when that government carries the mantle of legitimacy conferred by elections and confirmed by popular support, it seems unduly formalistic to insist that effective control is a necessary component of the government's right to speak for the State. More specifically, in such cases, it seems reasonable to rely on the consent of the ousted government as the principal voice of the State, even when that means ignoring the competing claim of the *de facto* authorities. This approach is not without its problems and its risks, but reliance on effective control in such circumstances carries its own problems, most notably, that of failing to pay adequate heed to the will of the people of the State.

Perhaps the most problematic aspect of the ECOMOG intervention is that it short-circuited the Security Council's efforts to restore Kabbah's government through peaceful means. Any use of force in international affairs that is not authorized by the Security Council or taken in self-defense raises systemic concerns, which are not fully resolved by the consent of an elected but ousted government. Those concerns are accentuated when the Security Council is seized of a matter and has taken action that it thinks is appropriate in a particular case. When ECOMOG launched its offensive to capture Freetown, the Security Council was not deadlocked, and time constraints did not preclude ECOWAS from seeking Security Council authorization.

The failure to obtain or even to seek authorization may account for the muted international reaction to the intervention.[67] The Security Council itself, evidently troubled by the offensive but unwilling to condemn it or even criticize it directly, called for the combatants to avoid harm to the civilian population.[68] In private, at least some members of the Council apparently expressed chagrin at the fact that ECOWAS foreign ministers had briefed Council members the week before the offensive but had failed to mention that any such action was contemplated. In addition, many commentators expressed concern that Nigeria, itself a military dictatorship, would use the intervention as a

---

[67] *See* Ed O'Loughlin, "Now That One African Dictatorship Has Booted Another, Many Ask Why?" *The Christian Science Monitor* (Feb. 24, 1998), 7.

[68] *See* French, *supra* note 66, p. A3 (noting that "[a]fter the final assault began, Nigeria came under mounting criticism from many in the immediate region, particularly French-speaking countries," and that "[t]he United Nations Security Council lent force to the complaints with a call on Wednesday for an immediate cease-fire"); *see also* Press Release SG/SM/6462 AFR/38 (Feb. 11, 1998).

tool for solidifying its influence over Sierra Leone and perhaps for exploiting some of its mineral wealth.[69]

Nonetheless, a few weeks after the ECOWAS invasion, the Security Council "welcome[d] the fact that the rule of the military junta has been brought to an end . . . "[70] The Council made no mention of the use of force, but instead "commend[ed] the important role that the Economic Community of West African States has continued to play towards the peaceful resolution of this crisis."[71] The Council also encouraged ECOMOG "to proceed in its efforts to foster peace and stability in Sierra Leone, in accordance with the relevant provisions of the Charter."[72] The emphasis on a "peaceful resolution" and the reference to the Charter might be read as a veiled criticism of the ECOWAS approach. On balance, however, the Council appears to have been sufficiently pleased with the outcome that it was willing to accept the use of force to achieve it.

To some extent, the jury of international opinion may still be out on the intervention in Sierra Leone. Most States appear to have accepted or at least withheld judgment on the intervention. That might change if Nigeria is seen as exercising undue influence over Sierra Leone, or if the Kabbah government proves unable to deal effectively with the problems it now faces. If the intervention continues to be generally accepted, however, it will mark an important precedent for those who support pro-democratic intervention.

III TREATY-BASED PRO-DEMOCRATIC INTERVENTION

In justifying its intervention in Sierra Leone, Nigeria noted the existence of a mutual defense treaty between the two countries. The treaty at issue is designed to require each country to assist the other in the event of an external attack on either one,[73] and so (putting aside the question of Liberian aid to the AFRC) it adds little to Nigeria's legal case for intervention in Sierra Leone.

It is not hard, however, to imagine a case in which States enter into explicit treaty arrangements designed to permit foreign military intervention to establish or maintain democracy in a particular State or States. The validity of relying on treaties as legal justification for external military intervention has long been contested. Critics contend that

---

[69] See O'Loughlin, *supra* note 67. [70] S/PRST/1998/5 (February 26, 1998). [71] *Ibid.*
[72] *Ibid.* [73] Protocol Relating to Mutual Assistance on Defense, A/SP3/5/81 (1981).

such treaties invariably run afoul of peremptory norms of international law restricting the use of force in international affairs. Such criticisms are considered below in the context of several different situations in which treaty-based intervention might be used.

Section A, which follows, discusses in general terms the validity of treaties as a source of legal authorization for military intervention absent contemporaneous consent by a government in effective control of the State. Section B considers the validity of treaties guaranteeing intercommunal power sharing arrangements. Section C considers whether opposing centers of authority within a State may reach a binding agreement concerning the establishment or restoration of democracy and accept external guarantees concerning the implementation of that agreement. Finally, section D discusses whether a group of States with democratic governments may enter into a treaty authorizing the group to use force to restore democracy in the event of a coup in any member of the group.

A *Treaties as a source of legal authority for military intervention*

The legitimacy of treaty-based intervention has been debated for many years. Supporters of treaty-based intervention usually begin with the generally accepted proposition that "the right of entering into international engagements is an attribute of sovereignty."[74] From this starting point, the theoretical argument for the validity of treaty-based intervention is simple. States have the power to consent to limitations on their independence. Indeed, States may surrender their independence altogether, by merging with another State. Accordingly, States must be free to yield any lesser measure of their independence, in the form of a license to intervene.[75]

But the argument that the greater includes the lesser cannot automatically justify a treaty provision authorizing external military intervention. States can and do merge with other States, and thereby surrender

---

[74] "The Wimbledon," *PC.I.J.*, (1923) Ser. A., No. 1, p. 25.
[75] *See* P. H. Winfield, "The Grounds of Intervention in International Law," *Brit. Y.B. Int'l L.* 5 (1924), 149, 156; Ann Van Wynen Thomas and A. J. Thomas, Jr., *Non-Intervention: the Law and Its Import in the Americas* 92 (Dallas, Tx.: Southern Methodist University Press, 1956). *See also* Tom J. Farer, "The United States as Guarantor of Democracy in the Caribbean Basin: is There a Legal Way?" *Hum. Rts. Q.* 10 (1988), pp. 157, 168 (the validity of agreements to protect democratic governments "may follow *a fortiori* from the conceded power of a government to obliterate sovereignty altogether by merging with another state").

their international legal personality.[76] But at the moment of the merger, the first State ceases to be a State. Until that point, and so long as it remains a State, the first State retains its political independence and the other rights associated with sovereignty. Thus, the fact that international law permits States to relinquish some measure of future decision-making authority does not mean that international law places no limits on a State's present ability to sign away decision-making authority essential to the State's future independence and therefore to its continuing existence as a State. Indeed, the very existence of peremptory norms, which by definition are norms that a State cannot modify by agreement, demonstrates that international law does place some limits on States' freedom to contract. The question is whether these peremptory norms preclude States from entering into treaties authorizing future military intervention in the absence of consent from the State's then-existing government.

Critics of treaty-based intervention contend that treaties authorizing forcible intervention in another State without its contemporaneous consent necessarily conflict with a variety of *jus cogens* norms designed to protect the independence and autonomy of States, including the principles of non-use of force, sovereign equality, self-determination, and non-intervention. As discussed earlier, however, State consent can validate an otherwise wrongful military intervention. In other words, it is only intervention against the will of the State that violates the applicable *jus cogens* norms. This leaves several critical questions: Who may express the will of the State with respect to intervention at the moment of treaty formation? Can the will of the State at the time the treaty is signed override the will of the State as expressed in the treaty, and if so, who may express the will of the State at the moment intervention under the treaty is contemplated?

1 Who may express the will of the State at the moment of treaty formation?
In general, when a government signs a treaty or takes some other act in the international arena, the government is deemed to act on behalf of the State, whether or not the government has taken office by democratic means, and whether or not the particular act at issue has the support of the majority of the population. But in cases of significant internal

---

[76] The German Democratic Republic, for example, lost its identity when it was absorbed into the Federal Republic of Germany on October 3, 1990, in accordance with the Basic Law of the Federal Republic. *See* "Treaty on the Final Settlement," September 12, 1990, *reprinted in* 29 ILM (1990), p. 1187.

conflict, it is precisely the authority of the government to speak for the State as a whole that is at issue. In recognition of this problem, international law accepts that at some stage of a civil conflict, the government must share the power to speak for the State with its opposition. In the pre-Charter era, international law recognized, at least formally, that in situations of civil war amounting to belligerency, authority to represent the State in international relations had to be divided between the incumbent government and its adversaries.[77] Although the traditional conventions regarding recognition of belligerency have long since faded into disuse,[78] current State practice recognizes implicitly that authority to represent the State must sometimes be divided between or among warring sub-national communities. Thus, when an incumbent government disappears, as in Liberia or Somalia, or is deemed internationally illegitimate, as in Cambodia, the consent of all of the principal internal factions is treated in the aggregate as the consent of the State for purposes of internationally brokered peace accords. Even when the incumbent government continues in office and is widely recognized as the lawful government by other States, the international community now insists with increasing frequency, at least in cases of secessionist or ethnic conflict, on acceptance by all parties of internationally brokered settlements that effectively recognize the right of each of the contending sub-national communities to share in decisions concerning the future of the State.

I have argued elsewhere that the authority to enter into or to revoke treaties authorizing future intervention in internal strife *should* be divided when the political community of the State is clearly split.[79] A government's claim to represent the State rests in significant part on the presumption that the government has been formed by the political community of the State as a whole. If the State is openly divided into more than one political community, then that presumption becomes

---

[77] Traditional international law recognized three stages of internal conflict, on an ascending level of intensity: rebellion, insurgency, and belligerency. *See, e.g.*, Weston, Falk, and D'Amato, *International Law and World Order*, 2nd edn. (St. Paul, Minn.: West, 1990), pp. 857–58. When the conflict reached the belligerency stage, "foreign states which did not wish to be treated as active participants in a war were obliged to assume the legal posture of 'neutrality,' and to treat the two competitive authority structures as equals, each sovereign within a given geographic area." Tom Farer, "Harnessing Rogue Elephants: a Short Discourse on Foreign Intervention in Civil Strife," *Harv. L. Rev.* 82 (1969), pp. 511ff., at pp. 511–12.

[78] *See, e.g.*, Robert W. Gomulkiewicz, "International Law Governing Aid to Opposition Groups in Civil War: Resurrecting the Standards of Belligerency," *Wash. L. Rev.* 63 (1988), p. 43.

[79] David Wippman, "Treaty-Based Intervention: Who Can Say No?" *Univ. Chi. L. Rev.* 62 (1995), p. 607.

untenable. In such cases, and particularly in cases of violent ethnic or secessionist conflict, the usual deference given to incumbent governments will not further national autonomy. Instead, it will further the autonomy of one sub-national political community at the expense of another. Accordingly, when a State clearly consists of two or more distinct political communities, consent to a treaty authorizing external intervention should reflect the concurrent will of each of those communities.

2 Who speaks for the State at the moment of intervention?
Can a State withdraw consent to a treaty authorizing external intervention, and if so, under what circumstances? The issue comes to a head only at the moment the target State wishes to rescind its earlier consent to the treaty at issue. Unless and until the affected State seeks to revoke its consent to a treaty authorizing intervention, any intervention carried out pursuant to the treaty is effectively undertaken with the contemporaneous consent of the target State. But when the target State's government opposes intervention, the question arises whether the State's earlier consent remains binding.

In general, States cannot unilaterally renounce their agreements unless the agreement itself permits renunciation or such a right can be inferred from the agreement as a whole. But agreements authorizing military intervention differ from other agreements. While all international agreements place some limits on State independence, military intervention agreements go directly to the heart of State independence and the other central values associated with State sovereignty. Moreover, such agreements usually implicate concerns about the maintenance of international order, since any use of force by one State that is opposed by another threatens international peace and security.

Accordingly, it seems appropriate to conclude that the will of the State at the moment of intervention should prevail over the will of the State at the moment of treaty formation. In other words, a State's grant of authority to intervene should be deemed to be impressed with an implicit but limited right of revocation. It does not follow, however, that agreements authorizing military intervention in the absence of a State's contemporaneous consent are void. To the contrary, such agreements should be considered valid unless and until the affected State exercises its right of revocation.

In keeping with the analysis above regarding treaty formation, if the government at the moment of intervention represents the State as a whole, its decision with respect to revocation may be deemed an adequate expression of the will of the State. But if the State is openly fractured along communal lines, then the concurrent will of each of the relevant communities should be deemed necessary to rescind the treaty. The sections that follow attempt to apply this approach to analyzing treaty-based intervention to three different situations in which such treaties might be used to promote democracy.

B Intercommunal power-sharing agreements

Two cases, the 1960 Cyprus accords and the 1995 Dayton agreement, may help illustrate the possible uses and potential problems of treaty-based intervention. In each case, the agreements at issue authorized outside States to intervene militarily to preserve intercommunal power-sharing arrangements adopted in an attempt to end a protracted ethnic conflict. Although the primary aim of the agreements in both cases was to end the fighting in Cyprus and Bosnia respectively, the agreements attempted to do so through promotion of a specific form of democratic governance known as consociationalism, a system in which major decisions are made by consensus among the principal ethnic groups in a divided country.

In 1960, Greece, Turkey, and the United Kingdom entered into a set of treaties designed to create an independent Cyprus in which the interests of both Greek and Turkish Cypriots would be protected. One of those treaties, the Treaty of Guarantee, authorized both Turkey and the United Kingdom to "take action" if necessary to maintain the detailed arrangements to share power between Greek and Turkish Cypriots contained in the contemporaneously adopted Cypriot Constitution.[80] Unfortunately, within two and one-half years, the Constitution's internal political balance turned to political stalemate, and then to open conflict between the two Cypriot communities. The fighting prompted Turkey to invoke its rights as a guarantor power on several occasions. Finally, in 1974, Turkey invaded Cyprus, and assisted the Turkish Cypriots in establishing their own autonomous "State" in northern Cyprus.[81]

---

[80] Treaty of Guarantee, Art. 4, 382 UNTS 3 (1960), *reprinted in* Abram Chayes, Thomas Ehrlich, and Andreas Lowenfeld, *International Legal Process: Materials for an Introductory Course, Documents Supplement* (Boston, Mass.: Little, Brown, 1969), p. 564.

[81] A more complete historical account can be found in David Wippman, "International Law and Ethnic Conflict on Cyprus," *Tex. Int'l L.J.* 31 (1996), p. 141. The discussion that follows is based on that article.

Turkish reliance on the Treaty of Guarantee to justify its uses of force in Cyprus provoked heated and polemical debates, which have never been fully resolved. Among other things, the government of Cyprus argues that the consent of Cyprus to the Treaty was coerced, and that Turkey's reliance on the treaty runs counter to *jus cogens* norms prohibiting forcible interference in the internal affairs of sovereign States.

Both arguments have some merit. Cypriot representatives played only a minor role in the drafting of the treaties, and Cyprus had little choice but to accept the treaties if it wished to obtain independence from the United Kingdom. Moreover, the Accords did not reflect the will of most Cypriots. From the Government's perspective, decolonization in Cyprus should have enabled the island's inhabitants to choose union with Greece or any other political status that reflected the will of the majority, in keeping with the principle of self-determination. But this argument assumes, however, that self-determination can be satisfied by a simple head-count, even in a society as politically divided as Cyprus. The international community effectively rejected that proposition when it accepted Cyprus as a UN member subject to a constitutional structure that recognized two distinct political communities within one State. Moreover, the international community properly continues to reject simple majoritarianism in Cyprus, as evidenced by the UN's longstanding call for a settlement based on the political equality of the Greek and Turkish Cypriot communities.

If one regards Cyprus as a single State made up of two separate political communities, each entitled to share in decisions concerning the future of the State, then any assessment of Cypriot consent to the 1960 accords must take into account the preferences of both Cypriot communities. Greek Cypriots, of course, preferred independence, to be followed by union with Greece;[82] Turkish Cypriots preferred partition, with an option for the Turkish portion of Cyprus to merge with Turkey. Neither community's preference could be fully accommodated without sacrificing entirely the preference of the other community. The 1960 accords attempted to solve this dilemma by mandating independence and power sharing, and by prohibiting union with either Greece or Turkey. In this way, the accords attempted to approximate the joint will of the two communities by giving partial effect to the preferences of each. From this perspective, the 1960 Accords adequately represented

---

[82] In a 1949 plebiscite, 96 percent of Greek-Cypriot voters favored union with Greece. Alastos, *Cyprus in History* (London: Zeno, 1955), pp. 379–81.

the will of both Cypriot communities, and therefore the will of Cyprus as a whole. Accordingly, Cypriot consent to the 1960 treaties was not compelled (much less coerced in the Vienna Convention sense). For the same reasons, if in the future the two Cypriot communities accept a bi-communal constitutional framework along the lines envisioned in recent UN-brokered proposals, their joint consent should be deemed the consent of the State of Cyprus.

Following this line of reasoning, the Government of Cyprus could not unilaterally revoke the State's consent to the 1960 Treaty of Guarantee. Instead, only both communities acting jointly had the right of revocation. From this perspective, a use of force by Turkey consistent with the terms of the 1960 Treaty would have been in keeping with the previously expressed consent of the State of Cyprus. When Turkey invaded Cyprus in 1974, however, it did not use force in accordance with the Treaty, which authorized the guarantor powers to intervene "with the sole aim of re-establishing the state of affairs created by the present Treaty." Instead, Turkey used force to create a radically different state of affairs, involving the partition of Cyprus, an outcome expressly prohibited by the Treaty. Accordingly, Turkey's actual use of force cannot be justified under the Treaty of Guarantee.

Despite the dangers inherent in attempts to create and guarantee power-sharing arrangements as a solution to ethnic conflicts, as illustrated by the unfortunate outcome of events in Cyprus, such solutions may sometimes represent a least-worst alternative to the continuance of large-scale intercommunal warfare. In 1995, no other approach seemed to offer a viable option for ending the conflict in Bosnia. Accordingly, the United States hammered out an agreement in Dayton, Ohio designed to end the war in Bosnia through adoption of a complex set of arrangements under which Bosnian Serbs would retain substantial regional autonomy and also share power with Bosnian Muslims and Croats in the central government.[83] In Annex 1–A, the Agreement on the Military

---

[83] The Dayton agreement consists of a single General Framework Agreement among the Republic of Bosnia and Herzegovina, the Republic of Croatia, and the Federal Republic of Yugoslavia (Serbia and Montenegro), followed by twelve annexes containing agreements among the Republic of Bosnia and Herzegovina, the Federation of Bosnia and Herzegovina, and the Republika Srpska. The agreement and its annexes are reprinted in 35 ILM (1996), p. 75. The legal status of the relevant annexes is open to question. They do not constitute treaties in the usual sense, since they are not agreements between States, but rather agreements between a State and political entities within that State. Nonetheless, sub-State entities, such as belligerent communities, are generally regarded as capable of possessing a limited international personality sufficient to enter into binding international agreements. *See, e.g.*, Ian Brownlie, *Principles of Public International Law*, 4th edn. (New York: Basic Books, 1990), pp. 64–65; *Oppenheim's International*

Aspects of the Peace Settlement, the State of Bosnia, the Federation of Bosnia (a political entity created by a prior agreement between Bosnian Muslims and Croats), and the Republika Srpska, a self-declared Bosnian Serb entity within Bosnia, all agreed (with the endorsement of Croatia and the Federal Republic of Yugoslavia) to authorize outside States to enforce certain key aspects of the parties' overall settlement by whatever means necessary, "including the use of necessary force."[84]

Unlike the 1960 Cyprus Treaty of Guarantee, however, the parties to Annex 1–A expressly "invited" the UN Security Council "to adopt a resolution by which it will authorize Member States or regional organizations and arrangements to establish" the required implementation force (IFOR). Because the Security Council promptly issued the necessary authorizing resolution,[85] the periodic subsequent uses of force by IFOR in support of the Dayton settlement can be treated as lawful simply by virtue of the Security Council's authorizing resolutions, without need to rely on the consent of the parties as expressed in Annex 1–A.

Even so, the Dayton agreement might be seen as problematic for critics of treaty-based intervention. If agreements that authorize outside military intervention in the absence of the contemporaneous consent of an incumbent government are to be deemed void *ab initio*, then one might conclude that the Agreement on the Military Aspects of the Peace Settlement, the linchpin of the Dayton settlement, is void. To avoid this conclusion, one would have to read the authorization to use force as contingent on the adoption of an appropriate Security Council resolution, which is a reasonable but not the only way of reading the agreement. The argument then would be that treaties consenting to a Security Council authorized use of force are not void because the use of force at issue is expressly permitted under international law, by virtue of the Security Council's enforcement powers.

If the Security Council had refused to issue the requested authorizing resolution, or if one reads the invitation as only an invitation and not a condition precedent to the use of force by IFOR, then the legality of treaty-based intervention would be directly at issue. If such arrange-

---

Law, Jennings and Watts, eds., *supra* note 23, pp. 116–18. In the case of the Dayton annexes, the endorsement of external guarantors militates in favor of treating the agreements as treaties governed by international law. *See* John Quigley, "The Israeli–PLO Agreements: are They Treaties?" *Cornell Int'l L.J.* 30 (1997), pp. 717, 717–18. Moreover, the repeated insistence by the UN and other international organizations and States that all of the parties to the Dayton settlement comply with their agreements manifests a broad consensus that the agreements should be treated as binding under international law. [84] Annex 1–A, Art. 2(b).
[85] *See* SC Res. 1031 (1995).

ments are deemed impermissible, then the parties to the Bosnian conflict would have had little option but to keep fighting, since no party would have trusted the others to abide by its commitments in the absence of an enforceable external guarantee. On the other hand, if one treats the concurrent will of the signatories to the Dayton annexes as in the aggregate the will of the State of Bosnia, both for purposes of the formation and revocation of an intervention treaty, then IFOR could proceed as it has for the past several years simply on the basis of Bosnia's advance consent to the use of force to hold the parties to their agreements.

C Intra-State pro-democratic intervention agreements

Under heavy international pressure, the military junta that ousted popularly elected President Jean-Bertrand Aristide signed an agreement with Aristide providing for the near-term restoration of his government.[86] ECOWAS reached a similar agreement with the AFRC to return President Kabbah to power in Sierra Leone.[87] Although neither agreement expressly provided for external enforcement, it is not hard to imagine inclusion of such an enforcement provision in a future agreement somewhere else.

Would such an agreement be valid? This scenario is both different from but still similar to the intercommunal conflict typology mentioned above. Neither Haiti nor Sierra Leone presents a case of two ethnolinguistic political communities occupying the same State, each with aspirations for political self-determination that are at least in part incompatible with the equally legitimate aspirations of the other. In both cases, the struggle for power was not fundamentally between separate political communities but between political elites seeking control over the single political community of the State. Even so, both cases presented situations of conflict between competing centers of internal authority. In each case, the claim of the military junta to express the will of the State with respect to intervention rested on effective control; conversely, the claim of the ousted government in each country rested on its political legitimacy.

In some cases, as in Sierra Leone, political legitimacy may so strongly

---

[86] *See* Report of the Secretary-General on the Situation of Democracy and Human Rights in Haiti, A/47/975, S/26063, July 12, 1993 (describing the background to and reprinting the text of the July 3, 1993 Governors Island Agreement between President Jean-Bertrand Aristide and General Raoul Cedras).   [87] Conakry Agreement, UN Doc. S/1997/824, Annexes I and II.

favor the *de jure* authorities as to overwhelm any claim by the *de facto* authorities to object to intervention in the name of the State. Even in such cases, however, an agreement between the *de jure* and *de facto* authorities to restore the ousted government to power, with authority granted to outside actors to use force to ensure that the agreement is kept, may be preferable both legally and politically to reliance on an intervention premised solely on the consent of the ousted government. However weak politically a usurping junta's claim to speak for the State may be, its control of the State makes it a dangerous claim to ignore as a practical matter. In part for that reason, it is likely to be a relatively rare case in which outside States are prepared to use force to restore an ousted democratic government in the face of determined opposition by a military junta. In addition, even when violent political division within a State takes the form of a military coup, as opposed to a broad-based insurgency, it is often difficult to assess the extent to which the ousted government actually represents the will of the majority on questions of intervention. In Haiti and Sierra Leone, there was little doubt that most people strongly preferred the elected governments' prompt return to office.[88] But in many cases, it may be unclear whether the people of a State are willing to incur the costs associated with the forcible restoration of an elected government. As Tom Farer has observed in another context, if intervention against an "indigenous military establishment" is likely to "cause serious human and material damage in the target state," the majority "might prefer continued military rule."[89] Moreover, even if foreign military intervention is not likely to encounter substantial direct resistance,[90] it may still prove highly unpopular simply because it is foreign intervention.[91] In Haiti, at least, the history of previous US occupation apparently created a surprisingly broad consensus among the population against external intervention.[92]

---

[88] Aristide's support should not be exaggerated, however. Although Aristide received approximately 67 percent of the vote in 1990, his populist politics alienated a substantial segment of the population, *i.e.*, the "upper classes and the army." Acevedo, *supra* note 26, p. 131.
[89] *See* Farer, *supra* note 75, p. 164.
[90] US intelligence officials suggested that US forces would easily overwhelm any military opposition in Haiti. *See* Michael Gordon and Eric Schmitt, "Weighing Options: US Aides Assess Invasion of Haiti," *N.Y. Times* (May 30, 1994), A1.
[91] *See, e.g.*, Michael Doyle, "Sovereignty and Intervention: the United Nations, the New Globalism, and an Internationalist Alternative," 14 (1994) (unpublished conference paper) (arguing with reference to Somalia that "the very act of intervention, even by the UN, can mobilize nationalist opposition against the foreign forces").
[92] *See* Erwin Knoll, *St Petersburg Times* (May 22, 1994) (citing a National Public Radio poll of a broad cross-section of Haitian citizens).

Finally, the durability of an imposed solution is open to serious question.[93] In many cases, absent an extended period of externally supervised reform, another coup might quickly follow the departure of an external intervention force.[94] On balance, a negotiated settlement between the competing political forces in countries such as Haiti and Sierra Leone may offer the best hope for the long-term establishment of democracy.

As a legal matter, an agreement between the *de facto* and *de jure* authorities is also likely to constitute the closest possible approximation to the will of the State as a whole. Though the juntas in Haiti and Sierra Leone had relatively little popular support, particularly in Sierra Leone, they still represented a segment of the societies of those two countries. Under these circumstances, it seems reasonable to treat an agreement reached between the *de facto* and *de jure* authorities as in the aggregate representing the will of the State. Although it might be argued that any agreement requiring the democratic government to compromise with a tiny elite whose claim to power rests solely on brute force should be voidable at the will of the former, on the theory that the democratic government holds the exclusive right to speak for the State, such a principle would effectively preclude the use of such agreements as a means to restore an ousted government. *De facto* authorities would know that they could not rely on such agreements, and so would have little incentive for entering into them. It seems preferable to permit an ousted *de jure* government the flexibility to enter into a binding agreement with the leaders of a coup, even in those cases in which the ousted government's internal and international standing is sufficient to warrant treating the government as the exclusive representative of the State.

In short, in the case of an intra-State agreement providing for the restoration of democracy, both parties should be treated as bound, even if the agreement authorizes outside States to use force to reinstate the ousted government in the event that the terms of the agreement are not kept. At the time the agreement is entered into, the concurrent will of both the *de jure* and the *de facto* authorities can reasonably be treated as the will of the State. Accordingly, the *de jure* government and the *de facto* government acting together have the legal capacity to consent to exter-

---

[93] *See* Michael Walzer, *Just and Unjust Wars: A Moral Argument with Historical Illustrations* (New York: Basic Books, 1977) pp. 87–88 (discussing John Stuart Mill's argument that political liberty must be achieved through internal struggle); Doyle, *supra* note 91, p. 14 (same).
[94] *See* Thomas Carothers, "Heading Towards A Haitian Fiasco," *The Plain Dealer* (May 14, 1994).

nal military enforcement of whatever political settlement they might reach. Because the revocation of State consent is as much an act of State will as the formation of consent, neither party acting alone may revoke the agreement or its provisions relating to enforcement, except in accordance with the agreement's terms or a fundamental change in circumstances justifying renunciation of the agreement. Such an agreement would be compatible with international norms governing the use of force, because the treaty embodies the consent of the State to the use of force applied in accordance with the treaty's terms.

D Inter-State pro-democratic intervention agreements

Under the alternative scenario noted above, a group of democratic States might agree to protect each other against an unconstitutional seizure of power in any one of them. Although this scenario represents a logical extension of principles advocated by OAS members and to some extent by other multilateral groups,[95] only one scholar has analyzed the possibility in any detail. Tom Farer urges us to consider the hypothetical case of a group of Caribbean countries entering into a treaty with interested NATO members to safeguard democracy in the signatory States.[96] In the event of a coup, parties to the pact would intervene, by force if necessary, to restore constitutional government in the affected State either at the request of the ousted elected officials, or, if those officials are unable to communicate with pact members, at the initiative of two thirds of the pact's signatories.[97] Farer concludes that such a treaty would permit forcible intervention to safeguard democracy even in the absence of Security Council authorization, "since such an action is carried out with the previously expressed consent of the target State . . . "[98]

The type of treaty Farer suggests differs somewhat from the kind of agreements discussed above, that is, agreements entered into between

---

[95] In a 1991 plenary meeting, the OAS mandated prompt consideration of collective measures to restore democracy following a coup in any member country. *See* Santiago Commitment to Democracy and the Renewal of the Inter-American System, OEA/Ser.P/XXI.O.2 (1991). Similarly, the Organization on Security and Cooperation in Europe declared its intent "to make democratic advances irreversible" and to "support vigorously" any democratic government threatened by or subject to an unconstitutional overthrow. Document of the "Moscow Meeting of the Conference on the Human Dimension of the CSCE," 30 ILM (1991), pp. 1670, 1677.
[96] Farer, *supra* note 75, p. 332.   [97] *Ibid.*
[98] Tom J. Farer, "A Paradigm of Legitimate Intervention," *in* Damrosch, ed., *Enforcing Restraint, supra* note 26, pp. 316, 332.

competing centers of authority coexisting within a single State. In the case of an inter-State pro-democracy pact, intervention takes place in reliance on an agreement that does not embody the consent of both of the relevant internal sources of authority, and that is expressly designed to ensure that the will of one source of authority (the signatory government) overrides the will of the other (the successor government), even if the signatory government is no longer in existence. Of course, at the time it enters into the intervention pact, the signatory government speaks for the State as the only source of internal legal authority. Accordingly, there is no problem with the pact at the formation of consent stage.

But as Professor Farer observes, the difficult question "is whether, despite ceding to others a right to intervene under stated circumstances, the state retains, by virtue of its continuing existence as a sovereign entity, an absolute right to revoke the ceded authority."[99] One could attempt to answer this question by focusing on the legitimacy of the authority each government claims to exercise. Under that approach, since political participation is an internationally recognized human right, only the democratic signatory government is "legitimate" and therefore only its will should count as the will of the State.[100] In extreme cases, such as that presented by Sierra Leone, the claim of the ousted government to speak for the State may be strong enough to override the competing claim of the *de facto* authorities.

In other cases, however, the relative strength of the competing claims may be less evident, either because the *de facto* authorities can demonstrate significant popular and international support, or because the ousted government no longer exists. In such cases, the question is whether the new government possesses sufficient authority to revoke, in the name of the State, the consent of its predecessor to intervention. Earlier it was suggested that if the *de facto* and *de jure* governments of a State consent to pro-democratic intervention, their joint consent should be treated in the aggregate as the will of the State. Thereafter, neither government should be able to revoke that consent unilaterally; instead, a decision to revoke consent should require the concurrent will of both

---

[99] *Ibid.*
[100] *Cf.* Farer, *supra* note 75, p. 168 (arguing that a treaty with the objective of "maintaining representative government" is legitimate because that objective "has the status of an internationally recognized human right" and is therefore "beneficial to all the contracting parties and to their respective peoples").

governments. Following that line of analysis, the consent of a State to a treaty permitting pro-democratic intervention could be revoked only by a government representing the unified will of the State. If the ousted government continues to exist, and if, by reason of its continued internal and international support it possesses a reasonable claim to speak for the State, then its consent would be needed to rescind the authority to intervene previously given to pact members.

The situation is more difficult if the ousted head of State has been killed or otherwise incapacitated, and the surviving officials of the *de jure* government are divided or for some other reason cannot credibly speak for the former government. In such cases, one of the two competing centers of authority effectively no longer exists. Is the *de facto* government – the remaining party claiming the authority to speak for the State – entitled to revoke, on its own, the State's previously expressed consent to intervention? An affirmative answer would give coup makers a legal incentive to eliminate all senior officials of the prior government. It would also ignore the fact that the *de facto* government may have little or no popular support or international standing.

As noted earlier, coups may occasionally be consistent with the popular will.[101] In general, however, it seems fair to assume that absent some pressing emergency, forces that seize power unconstitutionally do so because they could not achieve power in any other way.[102] Accordingly, it may be appropriate to adopt a presumption that the unconstitutional overthrow of an elected government represents, at least temporarily, a break in the political unity of the State sufficient to preclude the new government from unilaterally revoking the consent of its democratic predecessor to a treaty permitting intervention to restore democracy, even if no official survives to express the views of the predecessor government. Such a presumption might be confirmed or rebutted depending on internal reaction to the coup and on whether the international community insists on the unconditional restoration of

---

[101] As Farer notes, "[i]n cases where a democratically elected government was unable to maintain public order or to introduce badly needed economic or social reforms, or where it launched reforms repugnant to many social groups, the coup itself may be received enthusiastically by a not trivial part of the population." *Ibid.* at p. 164. *See also* Thomas Carothers, "Empirical Perspectives on the Emerging Norm of Democracy in International Law," *ASIL Proc.* 84 (1992), pp. 261, 265 (arguing that in at least some countries in Latin America, "the departure of an elected civilian government and its replacement by some nondemocratic form of government will be supported at least initially by a majority of the population of that country").

[102] This assumption seems particularly credible when the coup makers have just lost an election to the ousted legitimate regime.

democracy, as it did in Haiti and Sierra Leone, or comes to accept the new government, as it has, for example, in Georgia.[103]

Does this analysis suggest that an authoritarian government might enter into an anti-democratic pact with like-minded countries, which might similarly be enforced against the will of a new, democratic government? It has been suggested that the Mutual Defense Pact entered into by members of the Economic Community of West African States constitutes precisely such a pact. Under the terms of the Defense Pact, the Community is entitled to intervene militarily to suppress internal strife if it is "actively engineered or supported" from "outside."[104] At least one author has described the goal of the pact as "regime survival," that is, protection of authoritarian regimes in West Africa against the threat of internal overthrow.[105] But unlike intervention to promote democracy, intervention to prevent democracy (or revolution) cannot be deemed consistent with self-determination, whether conceived of as a right to democratic governance or as a right to permit the people of a State to form a government exclusively through internal political processes. Under either view, outside intervention to suppress democracy based solely on a pre-existing treaty would impermissibly obstruct the political development of the affected State.

IV CONCLUSION

Intervention by invitation, like most other existing and proposed justifications for the trans-boundary use of force in international relations, carries many potential risks, which must be considered along with the potential benefits. As with any other justification for the use of force, the greatest risk is the potential for abuse. Intervention might take place at the behest of an inviting authority that does not adequately represent

---

[103] The elected President of Georgia, Zviad Gamsakhurdia, was ousted in a bloody civil war in 1992. Shortly thereafter, Eduard Shevardnadze became the head of State, at the invitation of the Georgian Parliament and the warlords who had ousted Gamsakhurdia. See, e.g., Misha Glenny, "The Bear in the Caucasus: from Georgian Chaos, Russian Order," Harper's Magazine, March 1994. Notwithstanding the irregular manner in which Shevardnadze obtained office, the international community has accepted him as the legitimate head of State. See, e.g., Report of the Secretary-General in Pursuance of Security Council Resolution 849, S/26250 (August 6, 1993).

[104] Protocol Relating to Mutual Assistance on Defence, A/SP3/5/81, reprinted in Official Journal of ECOWAS 9 (June 1981).

[105] John Inegbedion, "The ECOWAS Intervention in Liberia: Toward Regional Conflict Management in Post-Cold War Africa" (1993), p. 9 (unpublished manuscript on file with author).

the will of the State; intervention may entail a disproportionate use of force that causes more harm than good to the people of the affected State; intervention may result in exploitation of a State's people or resources by a self-interested intervenor.

But these risks can be minimized. An insistence on multilateral decision making and oversight is perhaps the best way to avoid abuse and to screen out any improperly self-interested decisions to intervene. Where the Security Council is seized of a matter and is not paralyzed by the veto or otherwise precluded from acting in a timely fashion, an exceptionally strong justification should be required before accepting a decision to bypass the Council's authority. Nigeria's failure to await Security Council authorization in expelling the military junta from Sierra Leone largely accounts for the muted reaction accorded to that intervention.

Similarly, unilateral assessments of the democratic legitimacy of an inviting regime will almost automatically be suspect. Conversely, broad acceptance of an inviting authority's legitimacy should go far toward resolving fears of overriding the will of the people of the affected State. The virtually universal refusal to recognize the *de facto* authorities in Haiti and Sierra Leone, and the continued recognition of the ousted governments in both countries, provided compelling evidence of the legitimacy of the inviting authorities in both cases.

Finally, the risks of inaction should be borne in mind as well as the risks of action. While we should be skeptical of a legal regime that permits too easy intervention in the internal affairs of other States, we should also be wary of a regime that too readily confers the shield of non-intervention on an unrepresentative military clique or an ethnic sub-group bent on the political exclusion and subordination of non-members.

CHAPTER 10

The illegality of "pro-democratic" invasion pacts
Brad R. Roth

I INTRODUCTION

Few of the leading scholars who now proclaim "an emerging right to democratic governance" in international law have asserted that right as a general legal justification for military action against non-democratic regimes.[1] A general license to impose democracy at gunpoint fits poorly, most concede, with the scheme of international peace and security embodied in the United Nations Charter. Redress of a human rights violation – if that is what a denial of democracy is – is seldom propounded *per se* as an exception to the peremptory obligation of States "to refrain . . . from the threat or use of force against the territorial integrity and political independence of any state, or in any other manner inconsistent with the Purposes of the United Nations."[2]

Yet if the edifice of established peace and security norms is impervious to frontal assault, it remains vulnerable to the Trojan Horse. That is because there is a basis in international law for the proposition that "the lawful governmental authorities of a State may invite the assistance in the territory of military forces of other states or collective organizations in dealing with internal disorder as well as external threats."[3] Given the

---

[1] Even Thomas Franck, who coined the expression, has denied that the "democratic entitlement" licenses unilateral efforts at forcible implementation. Thomas M. Franck, "The Emerging Right to Democratic Governance," *Am. J. Int'l L.* 86 (1992), 46, pp. 84–85; but *see* W. Michael Reisman, "Humanitarian Intervention and Fledgling Democracies," *Fordham Int'l L. J.* 18 (1995), p. 794 (favoring unilateral armed efforts).
[2] United Nations Charter, Art. 2(4), *see also* Art. 103 ("In the event of a conflict [with] any other international agreement, [States'] obligations under the present Charter shall prevail"). The International Court of Justice has held that the norm exists as well in customary international law, and that it has the status of *jus cogens*. Military and Paramilitary Activities (Nicaragua v. United States), Merits, 1986 ICJ 14 (June 27, 1986).
[3] Statement of the US State Department Legal Advisor in defense of the 1983 invasion of Grenada, *quoted in* Rein Mullerson, "Intervention by Invitation" *in* Lori Fisler Damrosch and David J. Scheffer, eds., *Law and Force in the New International Order* (San Francisco, Calif.: Westview Press, 1991) pp. 127, 132. Of course, the proposition is often inappropriately invoked.

principle that a State may consent to foreign uses of force in its territory, adherents of the democratic entitlement thesis may seek to open the door to pro-democratic intervention in two ways: (1) by designating a government that enjoys an electoral mandate (or other "democratic" credentials), but not effective control, as bearer of the legal capacity to render contemporaneous consent on behalf of the State; (2) by validating the effort of an elected government to render the State's consent in advance, by treaty, to forcible restoration of the constitutional government upon the occurrence of a revolution or *coup d'état*. This chapter will address the latter strategy.[4]

Notwithstanding the superficial appeal of such a device, a "treaty of guarantee" (or, less euphemistically, "invasion pact") meant to "lock" one or more parties into a particular mode of governance, if ever enacted, should be regarded as void *ab initio*, on grounds of conflict with the UN Charter[5] and with customary norms having the status of *jus cogens*.[6] The self-determination of a people – the fundamental principle underlying the sovereignty of the State – cannot be reconciled with an alienation to foreign powers of control over its political destiny. That this is so is most apparent where the "treaty of guarantee" serves an arbitrary political end. It is less apparent, but no less true, where the treaty is tailored to putatively democratic purposes.

II THE ILLEGALITY OF GENERIC INVASION PACTS

As noted by the UN General Assembly in the unanimous 1970 "Declaration on Principles of International Law Concerning Friendly Relations and Co-operation among States in Accordance with the Charter of the United Nations" (the "Friendly Relations Declaration"), and reiterated consistently since:

Every State has an *inalienable* right to choose its political, economic, social and cultural systems, without interference in any form by another State. . .[7]

---

[4] The argument for pro-democratic "treaties of guarantee" is stated in the greatest detail in David Wippman, "Treaty-Based Intervention: Who Can Say No?" *U. Chi. L. Rev.* 62 (1995), pp. 607, 674–78 (1995); *see also* Tom J. Farer, "A Paradigm of Legitimate Intervention," *in* Lori Fisler Damrosch, ed., *Enforcing Restraint: Collective Intervention in Internal Conflicts* (New York: Council on Foreign Relations 1993), pp. 316, 332.

[5] Article 103 of the Charter holds that "[i]n the event of a conflict between the obligations of the Members of the United Nations under the present Charter and their obligations under any other international agreement, their obligations under the present Charter shall prevail."

[6] Article 53 of the Vienna Convention on the Law of Treaties makes clear that "[a] treaty is void if, at the time of its conclusion, it conflicts with a peremptory norm of general international law," Vienna Convention on the Law of Treaties, 8 ILM (1969), p. 679.

[7] GA Res. 2625 (XXV) (1970) (emphasis added).

Inherent in the very nature of sovereignty is the ongoing prerogative of the sovereign entity to determine the shape of its governing institutions through internal processes, without the coercive intervention of outsiders.

There is, of course, no doubt that sovereignty entails not only rights against intervention, but also the legal capacity to waive sovereign rights and to consent to some forms of intervention. Article 2(7) of the UN Charter bars intervention "in matters which are essentially within the domestic jurisdiction," but it in no way requires States to insist that their internal affairs are matters of exclusive domestic jurisdiction. States may, and frequently do, enter into treaties that provide for international adjudication of affairs ordinarily regarded as domestic, and that even may impose coercive sanctions for non-compliance with international judgments.

Furthermore, a State government, if uncoerced, has the legal capacity to extinguish its State's sovereignty altogether by merging with another State (*e.g.*, the German Democratic Republic with the Federal Republic of Germany). After that fateful decision, no one – including the local government of the administrative department encompassing the former State – will ordinarily be allowed to reassert the sovereign rights of the lapsed State.[8] Incorporation into another State is, of course, a far greater alienation of sovereignty than entry into a pact that forcibly guarantees the maintenance of a particular form of government.

It is ordinary to conclude with respect to legal capacities that "the greater includes the lesser." It might thus be argued that the government's capacity to waive the whole of the State's rights in the international system entails the capacity to waive any part of them. Advanced as a purely syllogistic formulation, this argument would be applicable to a legitimist alliance of any type, such as among monarchist, fascist, Stalinist, or Islamist States, not merely to an alliance among certifiably democratic States.

The syllogistic argument for the validity of invasion pacts does not, however, hold up. Although it might appear a truism that "the greater power includes the lesser," this is hardly an "iron law of powers."[9]

---

[8] Instructive is the recent unhappy experience of Southern Yemen, which first merged with its northern neighbor and then sought to secede. The secession effort was militarily crushed, and the use of force was widely regarded as an internal affair.

[9] Consider, for example, US jurisprudence on procedural due process (*e.g.*, Goldberg v. Kelly, 397 US 254 (1970), holding that states, while not required to sustain any welfare programs whatsoever, cannot terminate benefits to individual welfare recipients without a prior hearing comporting with constitutional standards of due process) or discrimination (employers have the prerogative to act on a frivolous basis or on no basis at all, but not on a discriminatory basis).

Sovereignty is not a continuum; if it were, the international system would inevitably come to recognize poor, dependent States as legally less sovereign than powerful States, rather than as legal equals. (This may yet come to pass, but it would not be the international legal system we know.)

Although there are sovereign rights that can be waived, there is an irreducible core without which the concept of sovereignty loses its meaning. That core can be extinguished, but it cannot be incrementally diminished. The international system does not, for example, recognize conditional States, susceptible of losing their status upon non-fulfillment of a commitment to the States from which they successfully seceded; there is only one class of sovereign Statehood. So, too, a sovereign State cannot exist which privileges foreign States to use force within it to impose a will other than that of the political community as manifest at that time. A sovereign political community can either relinquish its political independence and forfeit its standing in the international system, or it can maintain its political independence, and with it its right in the future to resist any uses of force to which it does not contemporaneously consent.

To be sure, there is nothing inherently irreducible about the standing of the ruling apparatus to assert the rights of the political community. But given the traditional prevalence of the effective control doctrine over competing bases for the recognition of governments, that standing is widely understood to rest on the factual situation manifest in the present, not on arrangements carrying over from the past. Popular "acceptance" of a regime – demonstrated, however imperfectly, by widespread acquiescence – has generally been, and remains, the essential criterion of that regime's perceived legal capacity to assert rights of the State in the international system.

The long and disreputable history of legitimist intervention pacts demonstrates the incompatibility of such devices with the present international system. In 1815, in the aftermath of the upheavals occasioned by the French Revolution, Austria, Prussia and Russia initiated the "Holy Alliance," declaring as follows:

> Any state forming part of the European Alliance which may change its form of interior government through revolutionary means, and which might thus become a menace to other states, will automatically cease to form a part of the Alliance, and will remain excluded from its councils until its situation gives every guarantee of order and stability . . .
> . . . In the case of States where such changes have already taken place and such action has thereby given cause for apprehension to neighbouring states (if it lies within the ability of the powers to take such useful and beneficent action) they

will employ every means to bring the offenders once more within the sphere of the Alliance. Friendly negotiations will be the first means resorted to, and if this fails, coercions will be employed, should this be necessary.[10]

The Alliance was intended to legitimate aggressive interference in the internal processes of foreign states for the purpose of stamping out a destabilizing example of incipient republicanism and restoring "rightful" monarchy.

Though repudiated later in the nineteenth century, treaties seeking to internationalize the basis of domestic authority resurfaced early in the twentieth century, this time as the ostensible friend rather than the declared enemy of popular sovereignty. The resuscitation of this device was predicated on a doctrine of constitutional legitimism enunciated in 1907 by Carlos R. Tobar, a former Ecuadorean foreign minister. Tobar proposed that

> The American republics, for the good name and credit of all of them, if not for other humanitarian and "altruistic" considerations, should intervene, at least mediately and indirectly, in the internal dissensions of the republics of the continent. This intervention might be, at least, by denying recognition to governments *de facto* born of revolutions against the constitutional order.[11]

The Tobar Doctrine was embodied in a 1907 treaty executed by the five Central American republics (Guatemala, El Salvador, Honduras, Nicaragua, and Costa Rica), which declared "every disposition or measure which may tend to alter the constitutional organization in any of them" to be "a menace to the peace" of all.[12] The parties thus undertook to deny recognition to any government that might come to power "as a consequence of a *coup d'état* or revolution against the recognized Government, so long as the freely elected representatives of the people thereof have not constitutionally reorganized the Country."[13] As *de facto* regimes have little difficulty in effecting such "constitutional reorganization," a 1923 accord among the parties followed up by extending the refusal of recognition to elected post-revolutionary governments headed by revolutionary leaders or their close relatives.[14]

The United States, though not a party to the treaties, observed their

---

[10] Sir Hersch Lauterpacht, *Recognition in International Law* (Cambridge University Press, 1947), p. 103 and n.4, quoting Cresson, *The Holy Alliance* (1922), p. 99.
[11] P. K. Menon, *The Law of Recognition in International Law* (Lewiston, N.Y.: The Edwin Mellon Press, 1994), pp. 74–75, *quoting* J. Irizarry y Puente, "The Doctrines of Recognition and Intervention in Latin America," *Tulane L. Rev.* 28 (1954), pp. 313, 317.
[12] *Am. J. Int'l L.* 2 (1908), Supp. at p. 219.   [13] *Ibid.* at p. 229.
[14] *Am. J. Int'l L.* 17 (1923), Supp. at p. 117.

terms, and remarkably had occasion to deny recognition to a government of every one of the signatory States between 1917 and 1931.[15] Although the treaties did not expressly authorize any interferences in internal affairs beyond the denial of recognition, the governments to which the US denied recognition had an uncanny tendency to fall.[16]

The Tobar Doctrine's constitutional legitimism suffered from a logical incoherence. After all, "every constitution has an extra-legal origin";[17] every governmental system is traceable to a usurpation, i.e., a revolutionary seizure of power that violated the previously existing constitutional order. Moreover, constitutional arrangements are inherently a function of the balance of interest-group and ideological forces extant in a political community at a given time. There is no conceptual basis for according them independent weight when they cease to reflect that reality.

Sovereignty resides in the political community, not in the constitutional system that has gained acceptance at any particular time. Even if one dismisses the traditional effective control doctrine as rank apologism for tyranny, constitutional legitimism seems a poor substitute. Whatever question there might be about a new regime's legal capacity to represent the political community, no backward-looking inquiry is appropriate to the ascertainment of popular will, except for what light it sheds on the present.

The Tobar Doctrine's constitutional legitimism eventually went much the same way as the dynastic legitimism of the Holy Alliance, for many of the same reasons. Latin Americans came broadly to view constitutional legitimism as a means by which the United States and allied local elites sought to thwart, not vindicate, popular will. Tobar-type treaties came to be seen as a legal foundation for intervention to restore a tyrannical "constitutional" order in the face of the contrary democratic will of a popular uprising. The hemispheric 1933 Montevideo Convention

---

[15] Menon, *supra* note 11, p. 76.
[16] A 1927 State Department memorandum made the point as follows:

> Our ministers accredited to the five little republics . . . have been advisers whose advice has been accepted virtually as law. . . . We do control the destinies of Central America and we do so for the simple reason that the national interest absolutely dictates such a course. . . . Until now Central America has always understood that governments which we recognize and support stay in power, while those we do not recognize and support fall.

Robert Armstrong and Janet Shenk, *El Salvador: The Face of Revolution* (Boston, Mass.: South End Press, 1982), pp. 225–26, citing Under Secretary of State Robert Olds, State Department Memorandum, *quoted in* Richard Millet, "Central American Paralysis," *Foreign Policy* (Summer 1980), p. 101.

[17] Glanville Williams, *Salmond on Jurisprudence* (11th edn. 1957), *quoted in* Mokotso v. King Moshoeshoe II, *Int'l L. Rpts.* 90 (1990), pp. 427, 477 (decision of the Lesotho High Court, 1988).

on the Rights and Duties of States,[18] stressing non-intervention in internal affairs, implicitly repudiated all Tobar-style arrangements.

A further disreputable effort to invoke treaty relations as a basis for intervention in a State's internal affairs was the so-called "Brezhnev Doctrine," articulated by the Soviet leader in defense of the 1968 invasion of Czechoslovakia. Albeit an independent State, Czechoslovkia, reasoned Brezhnev, had joined the community of socialist States, and so had bound itself to the governmental norms of that community:

> Just as . . . a man living in a society cannot be free from the society, a particular socialist state, staying in a system of other states composing the socialist community, cannot be free from the common interests of that community. The sovereignty of each socialist country cannot be opposed to the interests of the world of socialism, of the world revolutionary movement . . .[19]

Although one might question the voluntariness of Czechoslovakia's initial decision to join this community, and might note that nothing in the Warsaw Pact or other treaty commitments undertaken by Czechoslovakia directly authorized military intervention in its internal affairs, elimination of these flaws would scarcely have salvaged Brezhnev's rationale as a legal argument. The decisive objection to Brezhnev's reasoning lay elsewhere, in its heedlessness of the continuing and inalienable right of the Czechoslovak people to determine their own political destiny.

In sum, for both analytical and normative reasons, generic invasion pacts are manifestly unable to pass muster in an international legal system predicated on the sovereign equality of States and the self-determination of their peoples. Indeed, most scholars would scarcely question that coercive intervention in internal affairs, justified on the basis of treaty terms reminiscent of the Holy Alliance, the Tobar Doctrine, and the Brezhnev Doctrine, runs afoul of both Article 103 of the UN Charter and the *jus cogens* provision of the Vienna Convention of the Law of Treaties. The only serious question, then, is whether the invasion pact device, void generically, can serve as a bootstrap to validate intervention where the pact purports to be of a special kind.

III   PRO-DEMOCRATIC INVASION PACTS

Current-day advocates of treaty-based intervention do not, of course, propose indiscriminate admissibility of invasion pacts. They wish to

[18] LNTS 165 (1933), p. 19.
[19] 'Pravda Article Justifying Intervention in Czechoslovakia," 7 ILM (1968), pp. 1323–25.

allow for the use of force to perpetuate only *democratic* constitutional orders. They doubtless believe that democratic invasion pacts – as distinct from anything reminiscent of the Brezhnev Doctrine – are an exception to the logic sketched out above on the ground that the overthrow of a democratic constitutional order can be conclusively presumed not to be an embodiment of the contemporaneous popular will.[20]

Such a contention, though appealing on its face, does not withstand close scrutiny. Even if one could posit a generally held, determinate conception of democracy, and even if that conception could be identified permanently with the outcomes arising out of a particular constitutional or treaty-based procedural order, the proposed presumption would seem illegitimate, for it would impose on a political community once and for all a form of government that it may decide (however much to its misfortune) to repudiate. It would replace the principle of sovereign equality of peoples – the principle that underlies a legal system designed to mediate the conflicts of peoples who may disagree fundamentally as to how communal life ought to be structured – with a principle of dominance for a single world-view. In any event, democratic norms lack the requisite determinacy to sanctify particular constitutional orders,[21] and to allow treaties to render a particular order sacrosanct would, even from an unabashedly pro-democratic standpoint, pose great potential for the very mischief that non-intervention norms were designed to preclude.

Elections properly reflect, not transcendent principles of natural law, but historically contingent agreements among diverse political actors about how power may legitimately be exercised. Elections presuppose resolution of antecedent questions, not only about the configuration of the relevant voting constituency (the "majority of whom?" question), but also about the categories of issues to be left open to resolution by majority (or plurality) vote. Where an ethnic, ideological, or interest-group faction finds the stakes of electoral competition unacceptably high, it

---

[20] Even invasion pact proponents, however, concede that coups against "democratic" processes frequently accord with popular will. *See* Wippman, *supra* note 4, p. 676; Tom J. Farer, "The United States as Guarantor of Democracy in the Caribbean Basin: Is There a Legal Way?," *Hum. Rts. Q.* 10 (1988), pp. 157, 164 ("[i]n cases where a democratically-elected government was unable to maintain public order or to introduce badly-needed economic or social reforms, or where it launched reforms repugnant to many social groups, the coup itself may be received enthusiastically by a not trivial part of the population"). Of course, the problem can be solved by making the link between "democratic" constitutional processes and "genuine" popular will tautological, but that is a troubling (not to say "Brezhnevite") solution.

[21] I have elsewhere stated my contention that the content of the democratic norm is deeply contested and that none of the contesting views can ultimately be reduced to a procedural formula. *See* Brad R. Roth, "Evaluating Democratic Progress," chapter 17 of this volume.

can be expected to resist the process, and there is no mechanistic means of assessing the "democratic" merits of its cause.

"Free and fair elections" frequently yield outcomes that can be characterized as undemocratic. An uncontroversial example is predatory majoritarianism, where elections empower a majority faction to oppress an ethnic minority: instead of conferring on all citizens equal influence over the collective decisions that affect their lives, the elections leave members of the minority group totally without influence on those decisions – a potentially fatal circumstance. The more controversial examples are endless. (Of course, a test of "equal influence on the collective decisions that affect citizens' lives," even if it could be agreed on as the democratic criterion, and even if its terms were not subject to radically differing interpretations in principle,[22] would altogether defy procedural implementation.) Democrats of all stripes place reservations on their acceptance of electoral outcomes, in the name of such plausibly "democratic" values as liberty, equality, community, and so on. Thus, a test for democratic legitimacy that focused exclusively on electoral procedures would yield arbitrary results.

Although support for competitive electoral processes worldwide is far greater now than at any time in history, significant sources of resistance remain, and some plausibly draw on democratic values. Ugandan leader Yoweri Museveni has argued with some force, for example, that multiparty electoral competition systematically fails to produce democratic outcomes in societies where political polarization results, not from clashing conceptions of the common good, but from ethnic and religious cleavages.[23] A democratic outcome may require either that these cleavages be denied political expression (Museveni's solution), or that identity politics be accommodated within a "consociational" scheme (such as championed in Arend Lijphart's famous 1969 article) that drastically restricts the range of issues that elections actually decide.[24] Either approach may furnish a "democratic" rationale, not only for restricting electoral competition, but, in times of crisis, for overthrowing a "freely and fairly" elected government.

Moreover, in many contexts, open electoral processes have accom-

---

[22] Consider the following questions, among others. Does not the differential access of elites to the mass media count as "influence"? Are not the effects of market forces ultimately attributable to "collective decisions"? Does not the licensing of "private" acts that arguably undermine the moral fabric of the community "affect citizens' lives"?
[23] Interview (Yoweri Museveni), *Africa Report*, vol. XXXVIII, No. 4 (July–August 1993), pp. 23–25.
[24] Arend Lijphart, "Consociational Democracy," *World Politics* 21 (1969), pp. 207, 215.

plished little more than to allow voters to select from among parties dominated by economic and social elites – with no guarantee of governmental responsiveness to popular needs, let alone initiatives or input. It is not clear that democratic values hallow the rule of the highest vote-getter among choices that happen to have been presented to an electorate at a given moment.

In short, notwithstanding any presumptive preference for a given set of procedures, the meaning of democracy remains inherently contestable, and never more so than in moments of actual crisis, where consensus on the legitimacy of governmental authority has broken down. In seeking to place the most fundamental political question beyond the reach of domestic contestants and into the hands of external actors, invasion pacts assail the very essence of self-determination.

Since democratic invasion pacts are at present only hypothetical, there is little by way of State practice or *opinio juris* against which to test the thesis that they would be void *ab initio*. Nonetheless, some hint can be taken from the decision of the International Court of Justice in the *Nicaragua* case, which identified as *jus cogens* the norm barring the use of force against the territorial integrity or political independence of any State.[25] The Court there addressed the argument, advanced not in the defendant's pleadings but in political pronouncements that the Court found worthy of mention, that the use of force was justified in response to alleged Nicaraguan violations of a pledge to the Organization of American States regarding democracy and human rights, in return for which pledge the OAS had recognized the revolutionary government nearly a month before it seized the capital and won the civil war.[26] The Court held that even if the pledge had amounted to a legal undertaking (the Court held that it had not) and even if the pledge had been violated (as to which the Court made no finding), it would have provided no justification for the use of force. "Of its nature, a commitment like this is one of a category which, if violated, cannot justify the use of force against a sovereign State."[27]

One can, of course, only speculate about the Court's response to a pledge – not coercively extracted but part of a voluntary mutual arrangement – that expressly purports to license forcible measures. What the *Nicaragua* decision establishes beyond cavil is that a pact that does not unambiguously provide for forcible measures cannot provide

---

[25] Military and Paramilitary Activities in and against Nicaragua (Nicaragua v. United States), 1986 ICJ 14, para. 190.   [26] *Ibid.*, paras. 257–68.   [27] *Ibid.*, para. 262.

post hoc justification of such measures. General pronouncements, such as the 1991 OAS "Santiago Commitment" to address in unspecified fashion "any occurrences giving rise to the sudden or irregular interruption of the democratic political institutional process" in any member State,[28] cannot be read to license uses of force otherwise at odds with the UN Charter and customary law.

Concededly, international law does allow the use of force within the territory of sovereign States against their will where such use is necessary to vindicate the very purposes for which the system of sovereign equality exists. Those purposes most obviously include common protection against aggression, giving rise to UN Charter provisions for individual and collective self-defense (Article 51) and for Security Council measures (Articles 39 and 42). Arguably, in an international system concerned with States as the political expressions of peoples rather than as mere apparatuses of control, these purposes further include the suppression of crimes against humanity within sovereign States. Article 53 of the Vienna Convention points out that a peremptory norm (such as the norm against the use of force) "can be modified . . . by a subsequent norm of general international law having the same character."[29] Norms against genocide, slavery, and the like thus plausibly qualify the strict prohibition against military intervention.

Whatever legal norms pertain to general methods of internal governance, however, quite clearly cannot be said to rise to this level. In addition to the implausibility, at the conceptual level, of regarding a particular interpretation of democracy as a peremptory norm, the considerable diversity of governmental systems that remains in the international community argues against it, as does the continued adherence to the principle of non-intervention that permeates those UN General Assembly resolutions addressing democratic processes within States.[30]

IV CONSOCIATIONAL PACTS: AN EXCEPTION TO THE RULE?

Although we have yet to see invasion pacts embodying a principle of democratic entitlement, we have seen at least one treaty of guarantee,

---

[28] Representative Democracy, OEA/Ser. P/AG/RES. 1080 (XXI-o/91), para. 1 (June 5, 1991). The "Commitment" on the one hand arguably links interruptions of democratic processes to the mechanisms for enforcing collective security, but on the other hand gives "due respect to the principle of non-intervention." Warrant for the use of force to restore such processes can only be inferred by extensive (and rather one-sided) extrapolation.

[29] Vienna Convention, *supra* note 6, Art. 53.

[30] *See, e.g.*, GA Res. 45/150; GA Res. 45/151 (1990); GA Res. 49/180 (1994).

and one treaty-based intervention, in a different context. This is the case of Cyprus, where external guarantors were reserved "the right to take action" to preserve a constitutional arrangement providing for power-sharing between the two ethnic groups that together comprised the Cypriot political community. In 1974, Turkey invoked the treaty as a justification (or pretext) for invading Cyprus, a move that, although plausibly provoked by predatory designs of the extra-constitutional Cypriot leadership in collusion with Greece, led to a partition of the country accompanied by measures now known as "ethnic cleansing."

The debate over the legality of the Cyprus treaty itself – as distinct from the debate over the legality of the actions that Turkey sought to justify by reference to it – was inconclusive.[31] It is not clear whether any of the actions condemned by the international community could properly be characterized as within the treaty, but some statements, such as that of the Indian representative, cast aspersions on the treaty's validity:

> It is a dangerous concept to sanction external intervention in an independent State on the grounds of ethnic or religious affinities. The future of Cyprus, its constitutional arrangements and so forth are, in our opinion, for the people of Cyprus themselves to determine, in conditions of peace, freedom, and democracy.[32]

In 1963, Cyprus had argued before the Security Council that the treaty violated *jus cogens*, but the Council had expressed no opinion at that time.[33]

Although the Cypriot experience was an unhappy one, the recent rash of ethnic civil wars has given rise to proposals that seek to resuscitate the concept of treaties of guarantee.[34] It must thus be asked whether such proposals run afoul of the *jus cogens* argument set forth above, and if so, whether the practical need for such treaties demands a rethinking of that argument.

Where the invasion pact seeks to enforce not simply a democratic but a consociational formula, the principle of self-determination of peoples

---

[31] *See* Louise Doswald-Beck, "The Legal Validity of Military Intervention by Invitation of the Government," *Brit Y.B. Int'l. L.* 56 (1985), pp. 189, 246–50.

[32] *Ibid.*, quoting Security Council debate, UN Doc. S/PV.1785 (July 27, 1974).

[33] *Ibid.* at p. 247, citing Schwelb, "Some Aspects of International *Jus Cogens* as formulated by the International Law Commission," *Am. J. Int'l L.* 61 (1967), p. 53.

[34] Wippman, *supra* note 4, pp. 607–08, citing efforts for Liberia, Bosnia, Georgia, Somalia, and the Palestinian territories as well as a concluded agreement in Cambodia. *See* Agreement on a Comprehensive Political Settlement of the Cambodia Conflict, (Oct. 30, 1991), Letter dated October 30, 1991 from the Permanent Representatives of France and Indonesia to the United Nations addressed to the Secretary-General 10, UN Doc. A/46/608, S/23177 (1991), *reprinted in* 31 ILM (1992), p. 180.

potentially informs the issue. The international system has never satisfactorily reconciled self-determination and non-fragmentation norms, and the question of what constitutes a "people" has always been plagued by the danger that an almost infinite number of minorities might claim a right to Statehood. The system's post World War II approach to minorities (other than "indigenous" groups) has been to accord their members rights as individuals under human rights instruments, but otherwise to leave unqualified the sovereignty of the larger political communities within which they find themselves. Some States, however, have adopted constitutional structures expressly recognizing political sub-communities in their midst and according those sub-communities a quota of political power to shield them from the potential harm that majoritarianism might pose to their interests.[35]

The classic conceptions of monarchical and popular sovereignty, as embodied in the works of Bodin and Rousseau, attribute to the political community a unitary will. International law, though not unduly dependent on such conceptions in other respects, perpetuates this attribution.

But this attribution arguably needs to be qualified where representatives of the political sub-communities within a State have jointly acknowledged that the inherent conflict of group interests is such that no unitary will can be found within the State, except as embodied in the power-sharing arrangements to which the factions have agreed. If those arrangements are later overthrown by the unilateral will of one of the sub-communities, the government that assumes effective control may be said to lack the unilateral authority to exercise the sovereign rights of the political community.

On the basis of this line of reasoning, one might make the following contention: a treaty of guarantee operates not to impose an outdated or foreign will on the community but to preserve the relative positions within which each of the sub-communities is free to form its own will. By implication, the sub-communities are recognized as essentially sovereign, and therefore capable of concluding enforceable agreements with one another regarding intercommunal relations. Accordingly, the treaty should be enforced because no sovereign will is violated thereby.

An alternative argument might run as follows: the single sovereign will of the State is recognized only when exercised jointly by the sub-communities, in accordance either with the pact or with some other consociational framework that does not negate any group's fundamental

---

[35] For the pioneering examination of such structures, *see* Arend Lijphart, "Consociational Democracy," *World Politics* 21 (Jan. 1969), p. 207.

interests. Accordingly, although the treaty cannot be enforced and no foreign intervention can be sanctioned without the contemporaneous consent of all of the factions, no government that does not secure the consent of the sub-communities – manifested in a manner somehow specified – ought to be accorded *de jure* recognition.

Consociational arrangements are often miserably unjust, if not at the outset, then down the road. They are frequently agreed to in a violent context, and therefore reflect not so much considerations of justice as the balance of armed force at a given moment. As demographics change, power relations fluctuate or new groups develop a group consciousness, crisis often becomes endemic to consociational structures. Moreover, such structures might needlessly essentialize and reify group identities. To freeze factional relations with a treaty of guarantee – especially one with no expiration date – presents questions both of popular sovereignty and of sheer prudence.

Issues of this nature are at the frontier of the system of sovereign equality. Pressing problems of civil war in much of the world bespeak the need for innovative solutions. Whether the sovereign equality system as we know it can accommodate solutions such as treaties of guarantee – and if not, whether it is the system that will be forced to give way – remains unclear. What can be said with greater confidence is that outside this special context, consent in advance to armed intervention in internal affairs cannot be deemed legally effective.

V CONCLUSION

Even if treaties of guarantee can be justified to address the special circumstance of consociational arrangements between ethnically based political sub-communities, it does not follow that they are legitimate devices to "lock in" a choice of governmental system, however putatively "democratic," on the part of political communities in the ordinary course. Indeed, in the latter context, the treaty rationale is little more than a sleight of hand that allows adherents of the democratic entitlement to avoid facing up to the implications of a liberal–democratic *jihad*.

Whatever the merits of the purportedly emergent democratic entitlement as a norm of the international legal system, the case for that norm ought to be advanced directly and not through the artificial device of "treaties of guarantee." As I have argued at length elsewhere,[36] popular

---

[36] Brad R. Roth, *Governmental Illegitimacy in International Law* (Oxford: Clarendon Press, 1999).

sovereignty, albeit at a high level of abstraction, is the foundation of the international system, and a government that can be said, notwithstanding its exercise of effective control, to have been manifestly repudiated by its populace – in the judgment of an international community that reflects the full range of cultural and ideological perspectives – may lose its legal capacity to assert the State's right against intervention. Such events are far rarer than the democratic entitlement's adherents would prefer, but even if one sees fit to adopt a more determinate – that is to say, more partisan – reading of popular sovereignty, the focus needs to be on interpretation of a people's present will, not on prior treaty commitments.

To the extent that constitutionally established modes of political participation identified with "democracy" provide evidence of contemporaneous popular will at odds with effective control, that evidence argues against the *de jure* recognition of the *de facto* government, and perhaps even for the legality of an invitation of intervention by the deposed government, without any need for reference to a special treaty. Treaties bind the *State*, regardless of its present will, whereas the issue at hand in such circumstances is that of which *government* represents the State's present will. The past may be relevant to establishing present consent to the use of force, but where a peremptory norm is at stake, past consent is no consent.

CHAPTER 11

International law and the "liberal peace"
John M. Owen, IV*

History may not be over yet, but the United Nations and other international organizations are doing their best to end it. If all viable alternatives to liberal democracy have gone the way of the divine right of kings,[1] it is in part because of pressure from international society. Most States now want to participate in the world economy, and are thus complying with international rules requiring that they liberalize their domestic economies. Relatedly, as other contributors to this volume show, international law is moving from its traditional neutrality on States' domestic institutions to a decided preference for liberal democracy. One grounding for this new international–societal pressure is the proposition that liberalism brings peace – more precisely, that *liberal States*, generally defined as States that limit governmental power via civil rights and competitive elections, *do not fight wars against one another*. Such States generally engage in war with normal frequency, but their enemies are virtually never fellow liberal States. If the "liberal peace"[2] proposition is true, then international actors charged with making and keeping peace, such as the United Nations, can simplify their tasks by spreading and consolidating liberal government.

The liberal peace proposition is widely accepted as a law-like generalization among political scientists who study international relations.[3]

---

* The author wishes to thank the Olin Institute for Strategic Studies for its generous support, and Robert Art, Michael Desch, Gil Merom, Daniel Philpott, Randall Schweller, David Spiro, and two anonymous reviewers for comments.
[1] Francis Fukuyama, *The End of History and the Last Man* (New York: Avon, 1993).
[2] The term *democratic peace* is also used in the scholarly literature, and in everyday discourse *democracy* is more common than *liberal State*. I prefer to use liberal rather than democratic because, as I explain below, I hold the set of ideas that compose liberalism responsible for the peace.
[3] The literature on liberal peace is enormous and still growing. Among those works establishing that the peace is significant even after controlling for other potential causes are Stuart Bremer, "Democracy and Militarized Interstate Conflict, 1816–1965," *Int'l Interactions* 18 (1993), pp. 231–49; and Zeev Maoz and Bruce Russett, "Alliances, Contiguity, Wealth, and Political Stability: is the Lack of Conflict between Democracies a Statistical Artifact?" *Int'l Interactions* 17 (1992), pp. 245–67.

Whether it is actually liberalism that causes the peace is more controversial. Lacking has been a satisfactory account of the causal mechanism linking liberal democracy and peace. In this chapter I delineate and empirically test such an account, and thus attempt to provide a scientific grounding for the liberal peace proposition.[4]

My argument is that liberalism, a set of ideas about the good society, produces liberal peace via two pathways, ideology and institutions, working in tandem. First, liberalism generates a foreign policy ideology that prods liberal States toward good relations with States they consider fellow liberals, and conversely toward confrontation with States they consider illiberal. Second, liberalism generates domestic political institutions that allow this ideology to shape foreign policy.

Liberal *ideology* holds that individuals everywhere are fundamentally the same, and are best off pursuing self-preservation and material well-being. Freedom is required for these pursuits, and peace is required for freedom; coercion and violence are counterproductive. Thus all individuals share an interest in peace, and should want war only as an instrument to bring about peace. Liberals believe that liberal States seek their citizens' true interests and that thus by definition they are pacific and trustworthy. Illiberal States may be dangerous because they seek other ends, such as conquest or plunder. Liberals thus believe that their nation's interest calls for accommodation of fellow liberal States, but for confrontation and sometimes war with illiberal States.

Liberal *institutions* translate this ideology into policy. The liberals who hold the ideology are societal elites, or what some call "opinion leaders." During ordinary times they may have little effect on foreign policy. In times of crisis, however, when war is possible, they begin to agitate for their preferred policies. Two institutions allow this agitation to affect policy: freedom of discussion exposes the public and members of government to liberal arguments, which many of them find persuasive; and the regular, competitive elections that all liberal States feature provide the same public with leverage over the government. That is, should the government of a liberal State be tempted to go to war against a fellow liberal State, or appease an illiberal State, the possibility of punishment at the next election persuades it to resist that temptation.

My description of a causal mechanism linking liberalism and peace lends credibility to the liberal peace proposition. It thus generally supports the notion that, insofar as the UN and other international organizations value peace, they should have as an end a world with more

---

[4] For a fuller account, *see* John M. Owen, IV, *Liberal Peace, Liberal War: American Politics and International Security* (Ithaca, N.Y.: Cornell University Press, 1997).

Table 1

Year	Winner	Country
1964	Martin Luther King, Jr.	US
1974	Seán MacBride	Ireland
1975	Andrei Sakharov	USSR
1977	Amnesty International	UK
1980	Adolfo Pérez Esquivel	Argentina
1983	Lech Walesa	Poland
1984	Desmond Tutu	South Africa
1989	The Dalai Lama	India*
1991	Aung San Suu Kyi	Burma
1992	Rigoberta Menchú	Guatemala
1996	Carlos Filipe Ximines Belo	E. Timor**
1996	José Ramos-Horta	E. Timor**

Note:
* The Dalai Lama resides in India but claims to be leader of Tibet, which is part of China.
** E. Timor was under the control of Indonesia.

liberal States. It does not imply, however, that peace outweighs other ends, such as international stability or State sovereignty, or that international regimes can ignore questions regarding means and unintended consequences in trying to reach that end. I discuss these complications in my concluding section.

I INTERNATIONAL–SOCIETAL PRESSURE TO LIBERALIZE

The notion that liberal States ought to spread liberalism has been with us at least since the French Revolution, and it gained the rhetorical adherence of a majority of States after the First World War. Liberals of course typically believe that liberal democracy is self-justifying, that self-government is a good thing *per se*. In recent years, however, the proposition that liberal democracy is also good because it brings peace – a proposition that has been argued for since the high point of the Enlightenment in the eighteenth century[5] – has been increasingly recruited to support the spread of liberalism. Indeed, self-government and peace are thought by many to be virtually identical. Consider for example the recent Nobel Peace laureates listed in Table 1.

---

[5] *See* for example Thomas Paine, *The Rights of Man* (Harmondsworth, Penguin, 1987); Immanuel Kant, "To Perpetual Peace, a Philosophical Sketch," *in* Ted Humphrey, ed., *Perpetual Peace and Other Essays* (Indianapolis, Ind.: Hackett, 1983).

Each of these laureates worked first and foremost not on behalf of peace, but of liberalism, e.g., civil or human rights, or self-government. For each, peace was a means to the end of justice. That the Norwegian Nobel Committee considers liberal activists synonymous with peace activists demonstrates the power of the belief that liberalism and peace are closely linked, if not identical.

The power of this identification of liberalism and peace has not been lost on those entities with the largest stakes in regional and global peace, international organizations (IOs) such as the United Nations (UN), European Union (EU), and Organization for Security and Cooperation in Europe (OSCE). These and other IOs have lately supported the development of liberal institutions and civil society in various collapsed States and States abandoning authoritarianism. To be sure, there are reasons for supporting liberal government other than international peace: political liberalism may also be supportive of if not necessary for economic liberalism; and as mentioned above it may be self-justifying. But the notion that liberalization brings peace is compelling to the UN in particular because it touches on one of that organization's central tasks: "to take effective collective measures for the prevention and removal of threats to the peace."[6] Put bluntly, in supporting liberalism, the UN may be making this primary task easier.

II THE UNITED NATIONS[7]

Although it claims to be impartial regarding States' internal institutions, the UN is now explicitly pro-liberal. In 1992, the Under-Secretary General for Political Affairs established an Electoral Assistance Division to aid States that request it in holding free and fair elections. The division coordinates international election monitors and provides "technical assistance," which includes the very non-technical category of "voter and civic education." The UN, that is, is now in the business of promoting liberal culture. At least eighty States have requested help from the division (some have been refused due to insufficient lead time or lack of safety guaranteed). Examples have been Angola in 1992, Cambodia in May 1993, El Salvador in 1994, and Haiti in 1990–91, 1995, and 1997.[8]

More obviously, the Security Council has passed resolutions in a

[6] UN Charter, Art. 1(1).
[7] I am grateful to Gregory Fox and Brad Roth for their suggestions on this section.
[8] See <http://wwwun.org/Depts/dpa/docs/websit13.htm>.

number of cases condemning the overthrow of democratically elected governments.[9] In the famous 1994 Haitian case, the Council authorized a US-led invasion to overthrow a military junta and restore Jean-Bertrand Aristide to the presidency.[10] What makes these resolutions curious is that the Security Council's mandate is to maintain international peace and security,[11] not domestic liberalism; that is, its concern is relations *among* sovereign States, not *within* them. Recognizing this mandate, the Security Council never fails to stipulate that the situation in the illiberal country in question is a "threat to peace and security in the region." How might illiberal government in one State threaten an entire region? Arguably, refugee flows from such States may destabilize neighboring regimes; an estimated 500,000 Liberians, for example, fled that country during its civil war.[12] In areas with strong transnational ethnic groups, such as sub-Saharan Africa, persecution of one group may invite intervention by a foreign State dominated by that same group.[13]

Yet, recent Secretaries-General who (formally) bring the Security Council's attention to these cases have had another rationale in mind. A statement of Boutros Boutros-Ghali to the General Assembly on democracy bears quoting at length:

> Democratic institutions and processes within States may likewise be conducive to peace among States. The accountability and transparency of democratic Governments to their own citizens, who understandably may be highly cautious about war, as it is they who will have to bear its risks and burdens, may help to restrain recourse to military conflict with other States. The legitimacy conferred upon democratically elected Governments commands the respect of the peoples of other democratic States and fosters expectations of negotiation, compromise and the rule of law in international relations. When States sharing a culture of democracy are involved in a dispute, the transparency of their regimes may help to prevent accidents, avoid reactions based on emotion or fear and reduce the likelihood of surprise attack.[14]

In short, liberalization has become a "practical necessity."[15] Here Boutros-Ghali borrows language from two influential academic writers

---

[9] Examples include Liberia (SC Res. 1100, March 27, 1997) and Sierra Leone (SC Res. 1132, October 8, 1997). [10] SC Res. 940, July 31, 1994. [11] UN Charter, Art. 24.
[12] Mary Fitzpatrick, "Liberia's Tenuous Election," *Christian Science Monitor* (August 1, 1997), p. 20.
[13] For a social–scientific treatment of this problem, *see* David R. Davis, Keith Jaggers, and Will H. Moore, "Ethnicity, Minorities, and International Conflict," *in* David Carment and Patrick James, eds., *Wars in the Midst of Peace: the International Politics of Ethnic Conflict* (University of Pittsburgh Press, 1997), pp. 148–63. [14] UN Doc. A/51/761, December 20, 1996, at § II, para. 18. [15] *Ibid.*, II 25.

on the democratic peace: Immanuel Kant, the eighteenth-century Prussian philosopher, and Michael W. Doyle, the political scientist at Princeton who first applied Kant to the liberal peace phenomenon.[16]

American policy-makers too make overt references to the liberal peace. "Democracies don't attack each other," President Clinton declared in his 1994 State of the Union address, meaning that "ultimately the best strategy to insure our security and to build a durable peace is to support the advance of democracy elsewhere." Clinton has called democratization the "third pillar" of his foreign policy.[17]

Clearly, then, the notion that liberal States do not fight one another is one foundation undergirding the UN's newfound mission of spreading and supporting political liberalism. But the question must arise: are Boutros-Ghali and Clinton right? Does liberal government deliver on its promise as a force for peace? Can we be confident that the liberal peace is genuinely caused by liberalism, and not something else? The answer, I argue, is yes.

I begin by briefly reviewing previous theories of liberal peace and attempts to test them. I then summarize the foundations of liberalism and the foreign-policy ideology it produces. In so doing, I explore the perceptual aspect of the causal mechanism. Next I describe how liberal institutions make it likely that liberal ideology will influence policy during a war-threatening crisis. I then illustrate the argument in four historical cases: the Franco–American crisis of 1796–98, and the Anglo–American crises of 1803–12, 1861–63, and 1895–96. I answer realist critics of the liberal peace proposition, and suggest possible ways to synthesize the two dominant international relations theories of realism and liberalism. I conclude by considering how far the liberal peace proposition ought to alter the goals and methods of the UN and other international bodies concerned with peace and stability.

---

[16] Kant writes: "If . . . the consent of the citizenry is required in order to determine whether or not there will be war, it is natural that they consider all its calamities before committing themselves to so risky a game. (Among these are doing the fighting themselves, paying the costs of war from their own resources, having to repair at great sacrifice the war's devastation, and, finally, the ultimate evil that would make peace itself better, never being able – because of new and constant wars – to expunge the burden of debt.)" Kant, "Perpetual Peace," *supra* note 5, §351, p. 113. Doyle writes: "[D]omestically just republics, which rest on consent, presume foreign republics to be also consensual, just, and therefore deserving of accommodation." Doyle, "Kant, Liberal Legacies, and Foreign Affairs, Part 1," *Philosophy and Public Aff.* 12 (1983), p. 230.

[17] "Excerpts from President Clinton's State of the Union Message," *N.Y. Times* (January 26, 1994), A17; "The Clinton Administration Begins," *Foreign Pol'y Bull.* 3, nos. 4/5 (January–April 1993), p. 5.

III PREVIOUS ATTEMPTS TO EXPLAIN LIBERAL PEACE

Typically, theories of the liberal peace are divided into *structural* and *normative* theories. Structural accounts attribute the peace to the institutional constraints within liberal States. Chief executives must gain approval for war from cabinet members or legislatures, and ultimately from the electorate. Normative theory locates the cause of the liberal peace in the ideas or norms held by liberal States. These States believe it would be unjust or imprudent to fight one another. They practice the norm of compromise with each other that works so well within their own borders.[18]

On balance, statistical tests of these two theories have yielded no clear winner.[19] Moreover, although quantitative studies provide a necessary part of our evaluation of these theories by identifying correlations, by their nature they cannot tell us the full story. First, they often must use crude proxy variables that are several steps removed from the phenomena being measured.[20] Second, they infer processes from statistical relationships between these variables, but do not examine those processes directly. Overcoming these limitations requires looking at the actual processes in historical cases, or "process tracing."[21] Joseph Nye writes that liberal peace "need[s] exploration via detailed case studies to look at what actually happened in particular instances."[22] One way to carry out

---

[18] Some explanations, including those of Kant, "Perpetual Peace" *supra* note 5; Doyle, "Kant, Part I" *supra* note 16; and R. J. Rummel, *Understanding Conflict and War*, 5 vols. (Beverly Hills, Calif.: Sage, 1974), vol. IV, contain both structural and normative elements. However, these writers disagree as to what constitutes a democracy and why they forgo wars against one another; they do not take perceptions into account; and they underspecify how democratic structures work.

[19] Studies favoring some form of structural theory include Bruce Bueno de Mesquita and David Lalman, *War and Reason: Domestic and International Imperatives* (New Haven, Conn.: Yale University Press, 1993); and T. Clifton Morgan and Sally Howard Campbell, "Domestic Structure, Decisional Constraints, and War: So Why Kant Democracies Fight?" *J. Conflict Resolution* 35 (1991), pp. 187–211. Favoring normative theory are Zeev Maoz and Bruce Russett, "Normative and Structural Causes of Democratic Peace, 1946–86," *Amer. Pol. Sci. Rev.* 87 (1993), pp. 624–38; and William J. Dixon, "Democracy and the Peaceful Settlement of Conflict," *Amer. Pol. Sci. Rev.* 88 (1994), pp. 14–32.

[20] For example, Maoz and Russett infer democratic norms from regime stability and from levels of internal social and political violence. Maoz and Russett, "Normative and Structural Causes," *supra* note 19, p. 630.

[21] Alexander L. George and Timothy J. McKeown, "Case Studies and Theories of Organizational Decision Making," in *Advances in Information Processing in Organizations*, 2 vols. (Greenwich, Conn.: JAI Press, 1985), vol. II; *see also* David Dessler, "Beyond Correlations: Toward a Causal Theory of War," *Int'l Stud. Q.* 35 (1991), pp. 337–45; James Lee Ray, *Democracy and International Conflict: An Evaluation of the Democratic Peace Proposition* (Columbia, S.C.: University of South Carolina Press, 1995), ch. 4.

[22] Joseph S. Nye, Jr., *Understanding International Conflicts* (New York: HarperCollins, 1993), p. 40.

such tests is to ask: If the theory is true, then what else should we expect to observe happening?[23]

In carrying out such process tracing on a dozen cases, I uncovered problems in both structural and normative accounts. I found that liberal institutions were nearly as likely to drive States to war as to restrain them from it. Cabinets, legislatures, and publics were often more belligerent than the government heads they were supposed to constrain. I found that the normative theory neglected to take perceptions into account. Often States which today's researchers consider liberal did not consider each other liberal. Thus the anticipated normative check on war was frequently absent.[24]

These findings do not kill the liberal peace thesis. That neither structures nor norms by themselves explain the liberal peace does not imply that the two in tandem cannot do so. The structure/norms typology used by the literature is used merely for analytic convenience. If in trying to determine whether an automobile will run I separate its gasoline from its engine, then find that neither component by itself suffices to run the automobile, I cannot then conclude that the car will not run. It could still be that liberal ideology motivates some citizens against war with a fellow liberal State, and liberal institutions allow this ideology to affect foreign policy.

Some of the cases suggest such a synergy, I found, but only when the actors' perceptions are taken into account. For example, most Americans in the nineteenth century thought in terms of *republics and monarchies* rather *than democracies and non-democracies*. When in 1873 the United States nearly went to war with Spain during the *Virginius* affair, many Americans, including the Secretary of State, explicitly argued for peace precisely because Spain was at the time a republic.[25] Again in 1892, when President Benjamin Harrison asked Congress to declare war on Chile after the *Baltimore* affair, many Americans expressed opposition based on the fact that Chile was a republic.[26] These considerations

---

[23] *See* Gary King, Robert O. Keohane, and Sidney Verba, *Designing Social Inquiry: Scientific Inference in Qualitative Research* (Princeton University Press, 1994).
[24] *See* John M. Owen, "Is the Democratic Peace a Matter of Luck?" (paper presented at the annual meeting of the American Political Science Association, Washington, D.C., September 1993).
[25] *See especially* the attitude of Hamilton Fish, the US Secretary of State, *in* Allan Nevins, *Hamilton Fish: the Inner History of the Grant Administration* (New York: Dodd, Mead, 1936), pp. 668–74. The fullest treatment of the crisis is in Richard H. Bradford, *The "Virginius" Affair* (Boulder, Colo.: Associated University Press, 1980).
[26] *E.g.*, in opposing Harrison, Representative William Breckinridge of Kentucky told Congress: "War . . . is only the last resort, especially so when the war must be with a republic like our own,

combine with quantitative evidence to suggest that liberal peace is a genuine phenomenon that simply needs a better explanation. Multivariate analysis indicates that it is not the product of some omitted variable. In separate studies, Bremer and Maoz and Russett found that liberalism as an independent variable still had explanatory power after controlling for an impressive array of competitors. Variables suggested by realism such as relative power, alliance status, and the presence of a hegemon did not erase the effects of liberalism.[27]

As explained at the end of this chapter, however, I do not argue that power politics has no force in determining the foreign policies of liberal democracies. Rather, I describe a second force – liberalism – which prods democracies toward peace with each other, and toward war with non-democracies. Looking within the State, I suggest domestic foundations for those studies that have explored the international systemic aspects of the liberal peace.[28]

IV LIBERALISM AS THE CAUSE OF LIBERAL PEACE

Liberal ideas are the source – the independent variable – behind the distinctive foreign policies of liberal States. These ideas give rise to intervening variables – liberal ideology and domestic liberal institutions – which shape foreign policy. Liberal ideology prohibits war against liberal democracies, but sometimes calls for war against illiberal States. Liberal institutions allow these drives to affect foreign policy and international relations.[29]

anxious for liberty, desiring to maintain constitutional freedom, seeking progress by means of that freedom." 52d Congress, 1st sess., *Congressional Record*, vol. XXIII (January 26, 1892), p. 550. See also Joyce S. Goldberg, *The "Baltimore" Affair* (Lincoln, Nebr.: University of Nebraska Press, 1986).

[27] Bremer, "Democracy and Militarized Interstate Conflict," *supra* note 3; Maoz and Russett, "Alliances, Contiguity, Wealth, and Political Stability," *supra* note 3.

[28] On the level of the international system, this model is compatible with others that essentially present democracies as constrained (for various reasons) to prevent disputes among themselves from turning into wars. For Bruce Bueno de Mesquita and David Lalman, for example, democracies know each other to be prevented by domestic checks and balances from initiating war. This knowledge makes cooperation the rational choice in the "international interactions game." At the same time, democracies know that non-democracies, which are unconstrained, have the same knowledge and are prone to exploit them for that reason. Democracies thus may find it rational to attack non-democracies preemptively for fear of being exploited. See Bueno de Mesquita and Lalman, *War and Reason*, chap. 5, *supra* note 19; *see also* Dixon, "Democracy and the Peaceful Settlement," *supra* note 19; and D. Marc Kilgour, "Domestic Political Structure and War Behavior: a Game-Theoretic Approach," *J. Conflict Resolution* 35 (1991), pp. 266–84.

[29] *See* Judith Goldstein and Robert O. Keohane, eds., *Ideas and Foreign Policy: Beliefs, Institutions, and Political Change* (Ithaca, N.Y.: Cornell University Press, 1993), pp. 13–17.

Liberalism is universalistic and tolerant. Liberal political theory, such as that of Hobbes, Locke, Rousseau, and Kant, typically begins with abstract man in a state of nature in which he is equal to all other men. Although beliefs and cultures may differ, liberalism says, *all* persons share a fundamental interest in self-preservation and material well-being.[30] There is thus a harmony of interests among all individuals. To realize this harmony, each individual must be allowed to follow his or her own preferences as long as they do not detract from another's freedom. People thus need to cooperate by tolerating one another and forgoing coercion and violence.[31] Since true interests harmonize, the more people are free, the better off all are. Liberalism is cosmopolitan, positing that all persons, not just certain subjects of one's own State, should be free. The spread of liberalism need not be motivated by altruism. It is entirely in the individual's self-interest to cooperate.[32] In sum, liberalism's ends are life and property, and its means are liberty and toleration.

Liberals believe that not all persons or nations are free, however. Two conditions are necessary for freedom. First, persons or nations must be themselves enlightened, aware of their interests and how they should be secured.[33] Second, people must live under enlightened political institutions which allow their true interests to shape politics.[34] Liberals disagree over which political institutions are enlightened. Kant stressed a strict

---

[30] John Locke, for example, writes: "The great and *chief end* therefore, of Mens uniting into Commonwealths, and putting themselves under Government, *is the Preservation of their Property.*" Locke, *Second Treatise of Government*, chap. 9, para. 124. For Locke, "property" includes "Life, Liberty, and Estate," *ibid.*, chap. 7, para. 87, *in* Locke, *Two Treatises of Government*, in Peter Laslett, ed. (Cambridge University Press, 1988), pp. 350–1, 323.

[31] Kant argues that over time, the devastation of conflict teaches them that it is best to cooperate with others so as to realize their full capacities. *See* for example Kant, "Idea for a Universal History with a Cosmopolitan Intent," *in* Humphrey, ed., *Perpetual Peace, supra* note 5, pp. 31–4. *See also* Locke, *Second Treatise, supra* note 30, chap. 2, para. 5, p. 270. In referring to "harmony," I do not imply that uncoordinated selfish action by each automatically results in all being better off (a "natural" harmony). All individuals are interested in peace, but enlightenment, the right institutions, and cooperation are necessary to bring peace about. On the distinction between uncoordinated harmony and cooperation, *see* Robert O. Keohane, *After Hegemony: Cooperation and Discord in the World Political Economy* (Princeton University Press, 1984), pp. 49–64.

[32] Kant says a republic is possible "even for a people comprised of devils (if only they possess understanding)," *in* Humphrey, ed., *Perpetual Peace, supra* note 5, p. 124. *See also* Alexis de Tocqueville, "How the Americans Combat Individualism by the Doctrine of Self-Interest Properly Understood," *in* J. P. Mayer, ed., George Lawrence, trans., *Democracy in America* (New York: Harper and Row, 1988), part 2, chap. 8, pp. 525–28.

[33] *See* Kant, "An Answer to the Question: What Is Enlightenment?" *in* Humphrey, ed., *Perpetual Peace, supra* note 5, pp. 41–48.

[34] For a brief history of the view that selfish rulers rather than ordinary people are responsible for war, *see* Michael Howard, *War and the Liberal Conscience* (New Brunswick, N.J.: Rutgers University Press, 1978), pp. 14–18.

separation of the executive from the legislative power.[35] For most Americans in the nineteenth century, only republics (non-monarchies) were "democracies" or "free countries."[36] Today, Westerners tend to trust States that allow meaningful political competition. Central to all these criteria is the requirement that the people have some leverage over their rulers. That is, nineteenth-century republics and today's liberal democracies share the essential liberal goal of preventing tyranny over individual freedom.

These ideas give rise to a foreign-policy ideology and a set of domestic institutions that together produce liberal peace. The next two sections explore these two intervening variables in turn.

V LIBERAL FOREIGN-POLICY IDEOLOGY

Liberalism gives rise to an ideology that distinguishes States primarily according to regime type: in assessing a State, liberalism first asks whether it is liberal or not.[37] This is in contrast to neo-realism, which distinguishes States according to capabilities. Liberalism, in looking to characteristics other than power, is similar to most other systems of international thought, including Communism, Fascism, and Monarchism.[38]

Liberalism is, however, more tolerant of its own kind than these other systems. Once liberals accept a foreign State as liberal, they adamantly oppose war against that State. The rationale follows from liberal premises. *Ceteris paribus*, people are better off without war, because it is costly and dangerous. War is called for only when it would serve liberal ends, i.e., when it would most likely enhance self-preservation and well-being. This can only be the case when the adversary is not liberal. Liberal

---

[35] Kant, in Humphrey, ed., *Perpetual Peace*, *supra* note 5, pp. 112–15. Kant calls such States "republics," but by his definition monarchies may be republics.
[36] *See* for example David M. Fitzsimons, "Tom Paine's New World Order: Idealistic Internationalism in the Ideology of Early American Foreign Relations," *Diplomatic Hist.* 19 (1995), pp. 569–82.
[37] I have benefited from conversations with Sean Lynn-Jones on many of these points. For an attempt to reformulate liberal international relations theory based on distinctions among domestic political orders, *see* Andrew Moravcsik, "Taking Preferences Seriously: a Liberal Theory of International Politics" *Int'l Organization* 51:4 (Autumn 1997), pp. 513–53.
[38] Modern realists, ancient Greeks, medieval Muslims, and communists all see State-level distinctions as important. *See* E. H. Carr, *The Twenty Years' Crisis* (London, Macmillan, 1946), p. 236; Hans J. Morgenthau, *Politics among Nations*, 3rd edn. (New York: Alfred A. Knopf, 1965), p. 131; Sohail Hashmi, "Islamic Ethics in International Society," *in* Terry Nardin and David Mapel, eds., *The Constitution of International Society* (Princeton University Press, 1997); Robert Jervis, "Hypotheses on Misperception," *World Pol.* 20 (1968), p. 467.

States are believed reasonable, predictable, and trustworthy, because they are governed by their citizens' true interests, which harmonize with all individuals' true interests around the world. Liberals believe that they understand the intentions of foreign liberal States, and that those intentions are always pacific toward fellow liberal States. Again, it is not necessary that liberals be motivated by justice, only by self-interest.[39]

Illiberal States, on the other hand, are viewed *prima facie* as unreasonable, unpredictable, and potentially dangerous. These are States either ruled by despots, or with unenlightened citizenries. Illiberal States may seek ends such as conquest, intolerance, or impoverishment of others. Liberal States do not automatically fight all illiberal States in an endless crusade to spread freedom, however. Usually, they estimate that the costs of liberalizing another State are too high, often because the illiberal State is too powerful.[40] Liberal States do not fully escape the imperatives of power politics.

A The importance of perceptions

That a State has enlightened citizens and liberal institutions, however, is not sufficient for it to belong to the liberal peace: if its peer States do not believe it is liberal, they will not treat it as such. History shows many cases where perceptions foiled liberal peace. For example, as Christopher Layne demonstrates, the French after World War I did not consider Germany a fellow liberal State, even though Germans were governed under the liberal Weimar constitution. The salient fact about Germany, in the French view of 1923, was not that it had liberal institutions, but that it was peopled by Germans, who had recently proven themselves most unenlightened and were now reneging on reparations agreements.[41]

Thus, for the liberal mechanism to prevent a liberal State from going

---

[39] Here my argument differs from that of Doyle, who writes that "domestically just republics, which rest on consent, presume foreign republics to be also consensual, just, and therefore deserving of accommodation." Doyle, "Kant, Part 1," *supra* note 16, p. 230.

[40] Compare this with the Union's attitude toward Britain in the Civil War, described below. For explanations that see democratic prudence as more central to the democratic peace, *see* Randall L. Schweller, "Domestic Structure and Preventive War: Are Democracies More Pacific?" *World Politics* 44 (1992), pp. 235–69; and David A. Lake, "Powerful Pacifists: Democratic States and War," *Amer. Pol. Sci. Rev.* 86 (1992), pp. 24–37.

[41] *See* Christopher Layne, "Kant or Cant: The Myth of the Democratic Peace," *in* Michael Brown, Sean Lynn-Jones, and Steven Miller, eds., *Debating the Democratic Peace* (Cambridge, Mass.: The MIT Press, 1996), pp. 157–201. For an exploration of how a State comes to be regarded by its peers as liberal, *see* Owen, *Liberal Peace*, *supra* note 4.

to war against a foreign State, liberals must consider the foreign State liberal. Most explanations of liberal peace posit that liberal States recognize one another and refuse to fight on that basis; but the researchers never test this assumption.[42] In fact, often it does not hold. The refusal to take this into account keeps the liberal peace literature from understanding apparent exceptions to the peace, such as the War of 1812, the American Civil War, and the Spanish–American War.[43] My argument explains these apparent exceptions. As shown below, most Americans did not consider England liberal in 1812 because England was a monarchy. In 1861, Southern slavery prevented liberals in the Union from considering the Confederacy a liberal polity.[44] Almost no Americans considered Spain liberal in 1898. To determine which States belong to the pacific union, we must do more than simply examine their constitutions. We must examine how the liberals themselves define a free State.

Skeptics would immediately counter that the subjectivity inherent in terms such as "liberal," "democracy," and "despotism" means that these concepts have no independent causal force. When leaders want war, they simply define the rival State as despotic; when they want peace, they define the friend as liberal. Thus Joseph Stalin became "Uncle Joe" when Americans needed to justify fighting alongside the Soviet Union against Germany in World War II.

In fact, however, liberalism and despotism are not wholly subjective. Liberals have relatively stable conceptions of what a free State looks like. In the nineteenth century, most Americans applauded when other States became republican, and anticipated friendly relations with those States.

---

[42] For example, Bueno de Mesquita and Lalman assert: "The presence of the constraint is not alone sufficient to ensure cooperation or harmony. However, it is common knowledge whether a given state is a liberal democracy," *in War and Reason, supra* note 19, pp. 156. The same assumption is used (less explicitly) by Doyle, "Kant, Part I," *supra* note 16; Bruce M. Russett, *Grasping the Democratic Peace: Principles for a Post-Cold War World* (Princeton University Press, 1992); James Lee Ray, *Democracy and International Conflict: An Evaluation of the Democratic Peace Proposition* (Columbia, S.C.: University of South Carolina Press, 1995), ch. 3; Lake, "Powerful Pacifists" *supra* note 40; Schweller, "Domestic Structure and Preventive War," *supra* note 40; and Rummel, *Understanding Conflict and War, supra* note 18.

[43] Kenneth Waltz asserts that the War of 1812 and the Civil War were fought between democracies; Waltz, "The Emerging Structure of International Politics," *Int'l Security* 18 (Fall 1993) p. 78. David Lake, who argues for the democratic peace proposition, calls the Spanish–American War a war between democracies. Lake, "Powerful Pacifists," *supra* note 40, p. 33.

[44] As the nineteenth century reached its midpoint, slavery came to be seen by such Southern figures as John C. Calhoun as "the most safe and stable basis for free institutions in the world." It mattered a great deal to Northerners that the South was illiberal. Thus the *New York Tribune* in 1855 could write: "We are not one people. We are two peoples. We are a people for Freedom and a people for Slavery. Between the two, conflict is inevitable." *See* Eric Foner, *Politics and Ideology in the Age of the Civil War* (Oxford University Press, 1980), pp. 40–1, 52–3.

More recently, the attitude of the Western democracies toward Russia shows the independent power that liberalization has on expectations of hostility. The failed August 1991 coup and subsequent breakup of the Soviet Union did not cause the vast Soviet nuclear arsenal to disappear. Yet James Baker, then US Secretary of State, announced on February 5, 1992:

> The Cold War has ended, and we now have a chance to forge a democratic peace, an enduring peace built on shared values: democracy and political and economic freedom. The strength of these values in Russia and the other new independent states will be the surest foundation for peace – and the strongest guarantee of our national security – for decades to come.[45]

VI LIBERAL INSTITUTIONS

The domestic structures that translate liberal preferences into foreign policy are likewise a product of liberal ideas. Liberalism seeks to actualize the harmony of interests among individuals by insuring that the freedom of each is compatible with the freedom of all. It thus calls for structures that protect the right of each citizen to self-government. Most important for our purposes are those giving citizens leverage over governmental decision makers. Freedom of speech is necessary because it allows citizens to evaluate alternative foreign policies. Regular, competitive elections are necessary because they provide citizens with the possibility of punishing officials who violate their rights. Liberalism says that the people who fight and fund war have the right to be consulted, through representatives they elect, before entering it.[46]

When all citizens of a country are liberal, and all liberals agree on a foreign policy, then the constraints provided by liberal institutions are unnecessary to explain liberal peace. In practice, however, liberals, whom I define as those individuals who favor liberal institutions in their own State, are not always the only ideological group in a country. Moreover, often liberals will hold diverse criteria concerning what makes a foreign State liberal. Finally, many liberals with direct material interests at stake will allow those interests to trump the directives of liberal foreign-policy ideology (as defined above). For example, liberals in State

---

[45] On April 21, 1992, Baker declared, "Real democracies do not go to war with each other." Quoted in Russett, *Grasping the Democratic Peace*, supra note 42, pp. 128–29.

[46] "If the consent of the citizenry is required in order to determine whether or not there will be war, it is natural that they consider all its calamities before committing themselves to so risky a game." Kant, *Perpetual Peace*, ed. Humphrey, supra note 5, p. 113.

A who consider State B illiberal may still favor good relations with B if they have money invested in that State. Under such conditions, two liberal States may fall into crises with one another. They can do so because the general public pays little attention to everyday foreign policy.

A Elites and everyday foreign policy

Day-to-day foreign policy is mostly the province of elites. Ordinary citizens have good reason for ignoring relations with other nations. Since relations with most nations have little perceptible impact on the individual citizen, the expected payoff to each is not worth the time investment.[47] This collective-action problem means that normal foreign policy is delegated to representatives.

In making everyday foreign policy, the main domestic influences on these representatives are elites. Together, representatives and elites form what James Rosenau calls *opinion leaders:* people "who occupy positions which enable them regularly to transmit, either locally or nationally, opinions about any issue to unknown persons outside of their occupational field or about more than one class of issues to unknown professional colleagues." They include "government officials, prominent businessmen, civil servants, journalists, scholars, heads of professional associations, and interest groups."[48] In liberal democracies, these include staunch liberals who always desire to see good relations with fellow liberal democracies, and often desire confrontation with those States they consider illiberal. Without the leverage provided by public attention, the liberal elite has no special advantage over other elites, such as special interests.[49] The State may thereby fall into a crisis with a fellow liberal State.

B When war is threatened: liberal elites and the public

At the point where war is threatened, however, it becomes in the interest of each citizen to pay attention. War costs blood and treasure, and these high costs are felt throughout society. It also requires public mobil-

---

[47] This reasoning follows that of Anthony Downs, *An Economic Theory of Democracy* (New York: Harper and Row, 1957), pp. 207–76.

[48] James Rosenau, *Public Opinion and Foreign Policy: An Operational Formulation* (New York: Random House, 1961), pp. 35–9; Michael Leigh, *Mobilizing Consent: Public Opinion and American Foreign Policy, 1937–47* (Westport, Conn.: Greenwood Press, 1976), pp. 4–5.

[49] For a theory of how special interests can "hijack" foreign policy, *see* Jack Snyder, *Myths of Empire: Domestic Politics and International Ambition* (Ithaca, N.Y.: Cornell University Press, 1991), pp. 31–55.

ization. Those statesmen and elites who want war must persuade public opinion that war is necessary. In liberal States, this persuasion typically includes arguments that the adversary State is not liberal. When the prior liberal consensus is that the adversary *is* a liberal State, however, bellicose actors find that they cannot mobilize the public.

This is in part because they face strong opposition from liberal opinion leaders. Using the tools allowed them by domestic institutions – the media, public speeches, rallies, and so on – liberal elites agitate against war with fellow liberal States. They prevent competing actors from persuading the public that war is necessary.[50] Statesmen find that war with a liberal State would be extremely unpopular. Moreover, they begin to fear electoral ouster if they go to war against a fellow liberal State. Even statesmen who disagree with the liberal consensus are then compelled to act as liberals and resolve the crisis peacefully.[51] Alternatively, there may be times when liberals desire war with an illiberal State, yet other elites oppose such a war. Using the same institutions of free discussion and the threat of electoral punishment, liberals may force their leaders into war. Such was the case in the Spanish–American War.[52]

Recent research on public opinion and foreign policy indicates just this sort of dialectic among elites, the general public, and policy-makers. A number of studies indicate that opinion changes precede policy changes, suggesting that the former cause the latter rather than vice versa.[53] Moreover, a recent work finds that in the 1970s and 1980s the greatest influences on aggregate shifts in US public opinion were television news commentators and experts. For example, television commentators' statements on crises in Vietnam in 1969 and the Middle East in 1974–75 and 1977–78 evidently swayed public opinion. Often these media commentators opposed official governmental policy.[54] Together, these findings suggest that, at least in the United States, an opinion elite

---

[50] On the importance of free speech to liberal peace, *see* Stephen Van Evera, "Primed for Peace: Europe after the Cold War," *Int'l Security* 15 (1990/91), p. 27.

[51] Works that have used the assumption that elected officials value reelection above all else include Downs, *Economic Theory, supra* note 47; and David R. Mayhew, *Congress: the Electoral Connection* (New Haven, Conn.: Yale University Press, 1974).

[52] *See* John L. Offner, *An Unwanted War: The Diplomacy of the United States and Spain over Cuba, 1895–98* (Chapel Hill, N.C.: University of North Carolina Press, 1992).

[53] For a summary, *see* Lawrence R. Jacobs and Robert Y. Shapiro, "Studying Substantive Democracy," *PS: Pol. Sci. and Pol.* 27 (1994), pp. 9–10.

[54] Popular presidents had strong effects, while unpopular ones had little effect. Interestingly, special interest groups usually caused public opinion to move in a *contrary* direction. Benjamin I. Page, Robert Y. Shapiro, and Glenn R. Dempsey, "What Moves Public Opinion," *Am. Pol. Sci. Rev.* 81 (1987), pp. 23–43.

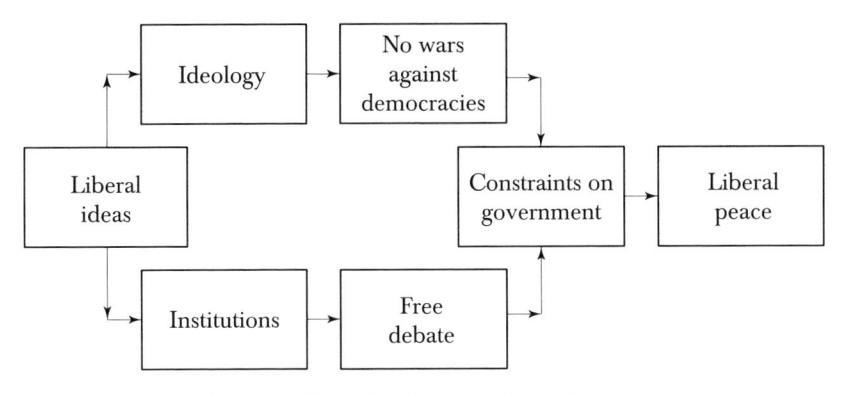

```
          ┌──────────┐    ┌──────────┐
      ┌──▶│ Ideology │───▶│ No wars  │──┐
      │   └──────────┘    │ against  │  │
      │                   │democracies│  │
      │                   └──────────┘  │
┌──────────┐                            ▼
│ Liberal  │              ┌──────────────┐   ┌─────────┐
│  ideas   │              │ Constraints on│──▶│ Liberal │
└──────────┘              │  government  │   │  peace  │
      │                   └──────────────┘   └─────────┘
      │                           ▲
      │   ┌──────────┐    ┌──────────┐
      └──▶│Institutions│──▶│  Free   │──┘
          └──────────┘    │ debate  │
                          └──────────┘
```

Figure 1 Causal pathways of liberal peace

at times shapes public positions on issues, thus constraining foreign policy.

Fig. 1 illustrates the argument. Liberal ideas form the independent variable. These ideas produce the ideology which prohibits war with fellow liberal States and sometimes calls for war with illiberal States. The ideas also give rise to liberal institutions. Working in tandem, the ideology and institutions push liberal States toward liberal peace.

C *Liberalism, not democracy*

I refer to *liberal States* rather than *democracies* for two reasons. First, democracy is the more ambiguous term, having been applied, rightly or not, to States as different as classical Athens, the United States, and North Korea (the "Democratic People's Republic of Korea"). Second, its own ambiguity aside, liberalism better captures the causal mechanisms described above. Because democracy literally means the rule of the *demos* or people, it is empty of content, and may thus be illiberal. As the German example of 1933 shows, a majority of the people may want an end to regular competitive elections and free discussion. An ancient illiberal democracy was the Athens of Thucydides, which did not contain the electoral safeguards of modern liberal States (or, relatedly, the modern liberal conception of individual liberty).[55] A current example is

---

[55] Classical Greek democracies fought wars against one another, I would argue, precisely because they were not liberal. On Athenian illiberalism, *see* Charles Taylor, *Sources of the Self: the Making of the Modern Identity* (Cambridge, Mass.: Harvard University Press, 1987), pp. 115–18. For an exploration of democracy and peace in classical Greece, *see* Bruce Russett and William Antholis, "The Imperfect Democratic Peace of Ancient Athens," *in* Russett, *Grasping the Democratic Peace*, *supra* note 42, pp. 43–71.

the Islamic Republic of Iran, which features universal adult suffrage and vigorous parliamentary debate but also a minister of culture who censors out ideas believed erroneous.

At the same time, liberal States as I define them may not be very democratic. They need not feature universal adult suffrage, and may even allow slavery, as the United States did prior to 1865. All that is necessary is that an electorate, however small, have real leverage over foreign policy – i.e., be able to discuss foreign policy freely and have the potential to oust leaders who enact policies it dislikes. Today, most liberal States are also democratic, and vice versa, but it is liberalism that keeps liberal democracies at peace with one another.

VII HYPOTHESES ON LIBERAL PEACE

A causal mechanism such as I describe may be logically coherent yet empirically false. I now turn to the search for clues that this liberal mechanism really exists and works. As I did with previous theories of liberal peace, I ask: if this argument were valid, what would we expect to observe in the foreign policy processes in liberal States? I check these expectations or hypotheses against real historical cases. If the hypotheses are falsified – if history does not bear out my expectations – then my argument is like it predecessors inadequate.[56] The hypotheses are:

Liberals will trust States they consider liberal and mistrust those they consider illiberal. I argue that liberal ideology divides the world's States into liberal and illiberal States. Because they share the enlightened ends of self-preservation, material well-being, and liberty, liberal States are seen as trustworthy and pacific. States ruled by despots and those populated by unenlightened citizens seek illiberal ends, and are believed potentially dangerous.

When liberals observe a foreign State becoming liberal by their own standards, they will expect pacific relations with it. Although definitions of "liberal State" vary across time and space, these definitions are relatively stable rather than arbitrary. If a State once thought despotic adopts the right institutions, or comes to be dominated by liberals, liberals in other States will begin to trust it more.

Liberals will claim that fellow liberal States share their ends, and that illiberal States do not. Specifically, liberals will say that liberal States seek the preservation and well-being of their citizens, that they love peace and

---

[56] *See* King, Keohane, and Verba, *Designing Social Inquiry, supra* note 23.

freedom, and that they are cooperative. They will say of illiberal States that they seek conquest to the detriment of their citizens' true interests, disdain peace, and are treacherous.

Liberals will not change their assessments of foreign States during crises with those States unless those States change their institutions. When a liberal State is embroiled in a dispute with a State it considers a fellow liberal its liberals will not switch to viewing the State as illiberal. Similarly, when a liberal State is in a dispute with a State it considers illiberal, its liberals will not suddenly decide that the State is liberal after all, unless its domestic institutions change. (If this hypothesis is not borne out, the liberal peace is illusory, because power politics or some other force would actually be determining what label liberals attached to foreign States.)

Liberal elites will agitate for their policies during war-threatening crises. In a crisis with a fellow liberal State, liberals will use the news media and other fora to persuade leaders and the public to resolve the crisis peacefully. In crisis with an illiberal State, liberals may agitate in favor of war if they believe it would serve liberal ends.

During crises, statesmen will be constrained to follow liberal policy. When officials are themselves liberal, they will simply find a way to defuse crises with liberal States, or they may escalate them if the other State is illiberal. When officials are not liberal, they will still be pressured by public opinion, which has been aroused by a liberal elite, to forgo war with a liberal State; or, if the foreign State is illiberal, they may be spurred into war.

VIII FOUR CASES

Four historical cases illustrate the argument: Franco–American relations in 1796–98, and Anglo–American relations during 1803–12, 1861–63, and 1895–96. These are four of the twelve cases from which I derived the argument.[57] I chose the twelve original cases because, first, they hold the identity of one State, the United States, constant. The United States has throughout its history been liberal. Second, the cases allow the perceptions and governmental systems of the other State in each crisis to vary. In some crises, liberal Americans had previously considered the

---

[57] The original cases are: United States–Britain 1794–96; United States–France 1796–98; United States–Britain 1803–12; United States–Britain 1845–46; United States–Mexico 1845–46; United States–Britain 1861–63; United States–Spain 1873; United States–Chile 1891–92; United States–Britain 1895–96; United States–Spain 1895–98; United States–Mexico 1914–16; and United States–Germany 1916–17.

foreign State liberal; in others, they had not; in still others, opinion was divided. Moreover, in some of the cases the other State was dominated by liberalism and had free elections, and in others it did not. Third, choosing cases from before 1945 allows me to rule out the effects of bipolarity and nuclear weapons, two powerful confounding factors.

I chose these four cases because they have been written about extensively, and my claims are easily tested. The causal factors in my argument also vary across the four. France in 1796–98 was not liberal; Britain in 1803–12 was only semi-liberal; and Britain in 1861–63 and 1895–96 was fully liberal. These cases also point up the importance of perceptions to liberal peace. Many Americans did not consider Britain liberal in either 1803–12 or 1861–63; and many British did not consider the Union liberal in 1861, but they changed their minds in the fall of 1862. In addition, the three Anglo–American cases have all been cited as evidence *against* liberal peace.[58]

A Franco–American relations, 1796–98

In 1798 the United States initiated what became known as the Quasi-War with France in which the two nations fought a series of naval battles in the Caribbean Sea. The American action was in response to French seizures of US merchant vessels on the high seas, and to the "XYZ Affair," in which the French government attempted to extort thousands of dollars from three US envoys in Paris. The French, then at war with England, had taken these actions in retaliation for the Jay Treaty, in which the Americans promised the British not to trade with France.[59] Here I argue that liberal ideology in the form of anti-monarchical solidarity prevented France and the United States from engaging in full-scale war.

The United States in the late 1790s qualifies as a liberal State. Although suffrage in most states was limited to white males who owned property, regular elections were mandated by law, and Republican oppo-

[58] On the War of 1812, *see* Waltz, "Emerging Structure," *supra* note 43, pp. 1861, 1895–96; *see* Layne, "Kant or Cant," *supra* note 41.
[59] Accounts of the origins of the conflict may be found *in* Alexander DeConde, *The Quasi-War; The Politics and Diplomacy of the Undeclared War with France 1797–1801* (New York: Charles Scribner's Sons, 1966); Albert Hall Bowman, *The Struggle for Neutrality: Franco–American Diplomacy During the Federalist Era* (Knoxville, Tenn.: University of Tennessee Press, 1974); William C. Stinchcombe, *The XYZ Affair* (Westport, Conn.: Greenwood Press, 1980); E. Wilson Lyon, "The Directory and the United States," *Am. His. Rev.* 43 (1938), pp. 514–32; and James A. James, "French Opinion as a Factor in Preventing War between France and the United States, 1795–1800," *Am. His. Rev.* 30 (1924), pp. 44–55.

sition to the Federalist government was lively. Republicans held to liberal tenets. They considered only republics – non-monarchies – to be liberal States, and they viewed France as a sister republic.[60]

They did so even though France was by my definition illiberal. The Constitution of the Year III (1795) mandated regular elections, and the French press was free, but the Executive in effect destroyed any institutional claim France had to liberalism. In September 1797 and again in March 1798, radicals in the Directory ordered *coups d'état* expelling members of the executive and legislature who opposed them.[61] French foreign policy making is therefore not of direct interest here. Instead, I only show that processes in the United States conform to the hypotheses derived from my argument.

1 US Republicans trusted France and mistrusted Great Britain
Even after the French maritime depredations and the XYZ Affair, the Republicans forgave the French even as they excoriated the British. Their rationale was that France remained a sister republic, and England remained a monarchy. One Republican newspaper averred: "There is at present as much danger of an invasion from the French, as from the inhabitants of Saturn."[62] Thomas Jefferson, vice president and leader of the Republicans, applauded rumors of a pending French invasion of Britain, because it would "republicanize that country" so that "all will be safe with us."[63]

2 Republicans had cheered the French Revolution and expected pacific relations with their sister republic
In 1789, American support for the French Revolution had been nearly unanimous. With the execution of Louis XVI and establishment of the First Republic in 1793, Federalists turned against the French, but most Republicans remained staunch supporters. One historian writes:

Democratic papers commenced a calculated program of justifying those in power in Paris. This practice was consciously pursued throughout the remainder of the decade and must be acknowledged in order to assess the part of foreign relations in the political propaganda of the period. A defense was found

---

[60] *See* for example Bowman, *Struggle for Neutrality*, *supra* note 59, pp. 25–30.
[61] Georges Lefebvre, *The Thermidoreans and the Directory*, trans. Robert Baldick (New York: Random House, 1964), pp. 176–79; R. R. Palmer, *The Age of the Democratic Revolution* (Princeton University Press, 1964), pp. 214–17, 255–59.
[62] *Independent Chronicle* (Boston), March 4, 1798, *quoted in* Donald H. Stewart, *The Opposition Press of the Federalist Period* (Albany, N.Y.: State University of New York Press, 1969), pp. 442–43.
[63] Stinchcombe, *XYZ Affair*, *supra* note 59, p. 118.

for every French action, from Robespierre's Feast of the Supreme Being to the seizures of American ships.[64]

Republicans did not simply decide in 1798 to oppose war with France and invent an ideological justification for that position; they had been well disposed toward France since 1789.

3 Republicans claimed that the French shared their ends, and that the British did not
The Republicans saw the Anglo–French struggle as one between the principles of monarchy and republicanism more than between two European powers, and thus as part and parcel of the same struggle they had themselves fought only a decade before.[65] During the debate over the Jay Treaty in 1796, one Virginian told his fellow Congressmen: "As it has not been in the power of the United States to assist their Republican allies, *when fighting in fact their battles,* the least they can do ... must be, that they will not put the enemies [the British] of those allies into a better condition than they were."[66]

4 Republicans did not change their favorable assessment of France during the crisis, despite Federalist efforts
Much American public opinion of France had soured after the XYZ Affair, but Republican elites stood by France against England. One newspaper declared that "'our Pharaohs' still wishfully looked for the downfall of the Republic and were ready to 'lend a hand to effect it.'" Another said of the Federalists: "The tory faction will endeavour to torture fact, in order to excite our feelings against the cause of liberty and the revolution. . . . Let us be calm."[67]

5 Republicans agitated against war with France
In Congress, the party of Jefferson used all its energy to stave off a war declaration. Accusing President Adams of trying to declare war by himself, they introduced resolutions stating that "it is not expedient for the United States to resort to war against the French Republic."[68] The

---

[64] Stewart, *Opposition Press, supra* note 62, p. 120.
[65] *See* Jerald Combs, *The Jay Treaty* (Berkeley, Calif.: University of California Press, 1970), pp. 110–11; Samuel Flagg Bemis, *Jay's Treaty: a Study in Commerce and Diplomacy* (New York: Macmillan, 1923; repr. edn., Westport, Conn.: Greenwood Press, 1975), pp. 95–6.
[66] 4th Cong, 1st sess., *Annals of Congress* (April 20, 1796), vol. V, p. 1099. Emphasis added.
[67] Stewart, *Opposition Press, supra* note 62, p. 286.
[68] 5th Cong, 2d sess., *Annals of Congress* (March 27, 1798), vol. II, p. 1329.

Republican press shrieked in protest against the possibility of a Franco–American war.[69]

6 The president and the congressional Federalists were constrained by the Republicans from declaring war on France

In the spring of 1798, Adams wanted war with France. In March he drafted a war message to Congress saying, "All men will think it more honorable and glorious to the national character when its existence as an independent nation is at stake that hostilities should be avowed in a formal Declaration of War."[70] Yet the president never presented the message to Congress. He could not do so, because he knew he did not have the votes to obtain a war declaration. Not everyone in Congress opposed Adams: the "high Federalists" had wanted war long before he had. It was the Republicans and the moderate Federalists who would not vote for war.

The Republican motivation is already clear. The moderate Federalists opposed war in part because the nation was so divided – i.e., because Republican opposition was so adamant. Believing only a united effort would enable the nation to fight France effectively, the moderates were in effect constrained by a liberal ideology they did not even hold. As one moderate put it after the defeat of a test vote in the House of Representatives in July 1798, "we should have war; but he did not wish to go on faster to this state of things than the people of this country, and the opinion of the world would justify."[71]

B Anglo–American relations, 1803–12

Another Anglo-French war, begun in 1803, likewise entangled the US merchant marine. Both the British and French were again humiliating the United States by seizing US cargoes, and the British were impressing American sailors into service as well. Ultimately, under the presidency of James Madison, the United States went to war.[72] The War of 1812 is often cited by critics of the liberal-peace proposition as an example of two liberal States at war.[73] By my definition, however, Britain can only be considered semi-liberal, and the war only a partial

---

[69] Stewart, *Opposition Press, supra* note 62, pp. 289–90.
[70] DeConde, *Quasi-War, supra* note 59, pp. 66–68.   [71] *Ibid.*, p. 106.
[72] *See* Reginald Horsman, *The Causes of the War of 1812* (Philadelphia, Penn.: University of Pennsylvania Press, 1962); Roger H. Brown, *The Republic in Peril: 1812* (New York: W. W. Norton, 1971); Bradford Perkins, *Prologue to War* (Berkeley, Calif.: University of California Press, 1961).
[73] *See* for example Waltz, "Emerging Structure," *supra* note 43, p. 78.

exception.[74] Moreover, even a cursory examination of the events leading up to the war shows that very few Americans, and virtually no British, considered Great Britain a liberal State at the time. Here again, Republicans in the United States act as my argument would predict.

1 Republicans mistrusted England, and some still trusted Napoleonic France
Thomas Jefferson, president from 1801 to 1809, wrote privately to a friend in 1810 that the nature of the British government rendered England unfit "for the observation of moral duties," and that it would betray any agreement with the United States. Napoleon, on the other hand, was safe: "A *republican* Emperor, from his affection to republics, independent of motives of expediency, must grant to ours the Cyclops' boon of being the last devoured."[75]

2 Republicans claimed that England did not share their ends
With few exceptions, Republicans blasted England for opposing the cause of liberty.[76] One Congressman exclaimed that "the standard of freedom had never been raised in any country without [England's] attempting to pull it down."[77] Republicans believed England was trying to wipe republicanism from the face of the earth. One newspaper asserted:

Not only the rights of the nation, but the character of the government, are involved in the issue . . . The deliberations of Congress "at this momentous era," will perhaps, do more to stamp the character of genuine republican governments, than has been effected in this respect since the creation of the world.[78]

Republicans feared that continued foreign humiliation would lead to a Federalist government which would align the United States with England and set up a monarchy.[79]

---

[74] Elections in pre-reform Britain were noncompetitive. Many seats in the House of Commons represented tiny boroughs where one patron determined who was elected; other towns were entirely disenfranchised. Votes in the Commons were effectively bought and sold in an open market. The House of Lords, an unelected body, could veto legislation. Moreover, the cabinet, which possessed war powers, was responsible to the king rather than to parliament. *See* E. L. Woodward, *The Age of Reform 1815–70* (Oxford: Clarendon Press, 1938), pp. 18–28.

[75] Robert W. Tucker and David C. Hendrickson, *Empire of Liberty: the Statecraft of Thomas Jefferson* (Oxford University Press, 1990), pp. 329–30.

[76] One prominent exception was John Randolph of Virginia, who agreed with Federalists that England rather than France was fighting for the liberties of the world. *See* Brown, *Republic in Peril*, *supra* note 72, pp. 151–55.

[77] 12th Cong, 1st sess., *Annals of Congress*, vol. XXIII (January 6, 1812), p. 688.

[78] *Quoted in* Brown, *Republic in Peril*, *supra* note 72, pp. 76–77.   [79] *Ibid.*, pp. 74–84.

3 Republicans defined England as illiberal before and during the crisis

Far from changing their views of the British to suit the moment, Jeffersonians had consistently hated the mother country since before the American Revolution. In 1806 one Congressman rhetorically asked if his colleagues could tolerate "that same monarch [George III] . . . who, instead of diminishing, has added to the long and black catalogue of crimes set forth in our Declaration of Independence."[80]

4 Republicans agitated for war

Both Jefferson and James Madison, Republican president from 1809 to 1817, preferred economic sanctions to war. But the 1811 War Hawk Congress decided with Madison that force had to be used to punish the British. Henry Clay, John C. Calhoun, and other young Republican Congressmen demanded war, as did the Republican press.[81]

5 Statesmen followed Republican ideology

Since Republicans controlled the executive and Congress, they did not need to be forced by liberal institutions to initiate war. Public support for war was certainly not unanimous; New England in particular was vehemently opposed. But Madison and the War Hawks declared war anyway. One biographer writes of Madison:

> To have submitted to [Britain's] unilateral decrees, her discriminatory trade regulations, or her naval outrages would have . . . ratified unjust principles in international law and emboldened antirepublican forces in Britain and the United States, thus threatening, in Madison's opinion, the survival of free government anywhere in the world.[82]

Realists at the time opposed the War of 1812, and in fact realists ever since have had difficulty accounting for it. Morgenthau calls it "the sole exception" to the rule that the United States has followed realist tenets in dealing with Europe.[83] In their 1990 book, Robert Tucker and David Hendrickson chide Jefferson for throwing America's lot in with France rather than Britain during the Napoleonic Wars. The United States would have avoided trouble, had it

> publicly recognized that England was in truth engaged in a contest for public liberty and international order, and that by virtue of its own stance against

---

[80] 9th Cong, 1st sess., *Annals of Congress*, vol. xv (March 7, 1806), pp. 609–10.
[81] Horsman, *Causes of the War of 1812*, supra note 72, ch. 13.
[82] Ralph Ketcham, *James Madison* (New York: Macmillan, 1971), p. 530.
[83] Hans J. Morgenthau, *In Defense of the National Interest* (New York: Knopf, 1951), p. 5.

Napoleon Britain protected the United States from the peculiar menace that Bonaparte embodied . . . Jefferson would not say this because he did not believe it.[84]

That is, the Republican conception of the national interest ultimately required war because Britain was a monarchy.

C Anglo–American relations, 1861–63

Fifty years later, most Americans still saw the world as divided between republics and monarchies.[85] For these Americans, Britain remained a monarchy and therefore a despotism. At several points during the American Civil War, Britain and the Union teetered on the brink of war. In none of these crises did liberal affinity for England play much of a role in keeping the Union from attacking Britain. And in the first, the *Trent* affair,[86] British liberal affinity for the Union was rather weak as well, which in turn fed Union hostility toward England. The resolution of the *Trent* crisis can be explained without reference to liberal-peace theory: the administration of Abraham Lincoln backed down to a British ultimatum because it could not afford war with such a powerful foe over such an issue.[87] With the Union fighting for its life against the Confederacy, Lincoln and his cabinet prudently decided that no liberal purpose would be served by an Anglo–American war.

By my definition, Britain in the 1860s *was* a liberal State. The 1832 Reform Act had made elections fairer, and had made the cabinet responsible to parliament rather than to the Crown. This meant the executive was ultimately responsible to the electors, giving the public leverage over war decisions.[88]

---

[84] Tucker and Hendrickson, *Empire of Liberty*, supra note 75, pp. 226–27.
[85] Sources on this case include Ephraim Douglass Adams, *Great Britain and the American Civil War*, 2 vols. (New York: Longmans, Green and Co., 1925); Brian Jenkins, *Britain and the War for the Union*, 2 vols. (Montreal: McGill-Queen's University Press, 1974 and 1980); Howard Jones, *Union in Peril: the Crisis over British Intervention in the American Civil War* (Chapel Hill, N.C.: University of North Carolina Press, 1992); Norman B. Ferris, *The "Trent" Affair: a Diplomatic Crisis* (Knoxville, Tenn.: University of Tennessee Press, 1977); Martin P. Claussen, "Peace Factors in Anglo–American Relations, 1861–65," *Mississippi Valley His. Rev.*, 26 (1940), pp. 511–22.
[86] The crisis occurred when a Union ship seized the British mail packet *Trent* as it carried two Southern emissaries to London to try to negotiate formal recognition of the Confederacy. The British were almost unanimously outraged, and clearly would have declared war had Lincoln not apologized and returned the emissaries. See Ferris, *"Trent" Affair*, supra note 85.
[87] *See* Layne, "Kant or Cant," *supra* note 41. Again, I do not argue that liberals will continually seek war against states they consider illiberal. Liberalism determines the ends, but power politics may circumscribe the means.
[88] The shift in cabinet responsibility was *de facto* rather than *de jure*; since 1832, no monarch has ever dismissed a ministry. *See* Robert Livingston Schuyler and Corinne Comstock Weston, *British Constitutional History Since 1832* (Princeton, N.J.: D. Van Nostrand, 1957), pp. 26–44.

British liberal sympathy for the Union was weak during *Trent* because most British took Lincoln at his word that the Civil War was about restoring the Union – a cause uninspiring to the British – rather than abolition.[89] Britons of all classes had supported the abolition of slavery since the 1830s. Then in September 1862, Lincoln issued the preliminary Emancipation Proclamation, declaring that as of January 1, 1863, all slaves in the rebellious states would be free. Although it was condemned by pro-Confederates as likely to provoke a slave insurrection, the Proclamation caused British opinion to shift to the Union side. This shift helped prevent Britain from intervening in the Civil War.[90]

1 British liberals trusted the Union
Even before the Emancipation Proclamation, the Union had its staunch supporters among the Philosophical Radicals, notably John Bright and Richard Cobden. Bright told Parliament in early 1862, "there probably never has been a great nation in which what is familiarly termed mob law is less known or has had less influence . . . Understand, I confine my observations always to the free States of the North."[91] Bright's view gained wide acceptance after the Proclamation, because abolitionists viewed slave-holding states as aggressive by nature.[92]

2 After the Emancipation Proclamation, liberals wanted better relations with the Union, and believed the Union shared liberal ends
Britain's Radical *Morning Star* newspaper summarized the change in October: "the inevitable has come at last. Negro emancipation is formally and definitively adopted as the policy in war and peace of the United States."[93] The *Daily News* predicted that now "the most audacious Secessionists" in England would shy away from proposing recognition of the "confederated Slave States." All through the war the Union had blockaded the Confederacy, preventing cotton from reaching England and causing extreme distress in the Lancashire textile region. Yet after the Proclamation, most of England's working class newspapers shifted over to the Union's side, proclaiming that the Union's cause, liberation of the masses, was their cause. One paper said the most

---

[89] In his first inaugural address, Lincoln said: "I have no purpose, directly or indirectly to interfere with the institution of slavery in the States where it exists. I believe I have no lawful right to do so, and I have no inclination to do so." *Quoted in* Adams, *Great Britain and the Civil War*, *supra* note 85, vol. I, p. 50.
[90] Christopher Layne's account of Anglo–American relations in this time ("Kant or Cant," *supra* note 41) misses this crucial point because he only looks at the *Trent* affair.
[91] *Hansard's Parliamentary Debates* (Commons), 3d ser, vol. CLXV (February 17, 1862), col. 382.
[92] *See, e.g.*, the remarks of Goldwin Smith in the Venezuelan crisis, below.
[93] Jenkins, *Britain and the War*, *supra* note 85 vol. II, p. 152.

dangerous problem facing Britain was now "the recognition of the slave-holding Confederate States, and, as an almost necessary consequence, an alliance with them against the Federal States of America."[94]

3 Liberals agitated against intervention after the Proclamation
As the Proclamation energized evangelical Christian and other emancipation groups in Britain, Bright stated that the "anti-slavery sentiment" of his country was finally being "called forth."[95] One historian writes that "there took place meeting after meeting at which strong resolutions were passed enthusiastically endorsing the issue of the emancipation proclamation and pledging sympathy to the cause of the North."[96] In Manchester, a rally at the end of 1862 approved a missive to Lincoln congratulating him for the "humane and righteous course" he had taken in furthering America's founding concept that "all men are created equal." In London during the spring of 1863, a rally of 2,500 or more workers pledged themselves "to use their 'utmost efforts' to prevent the recognition of any government 'founded on human slavery.'"[97]

4 The British Cabinet was constrained by Liberalism from intervening in the Civil War
Shortly after the Proclamation, the cabinet was considering a French proposal to offer joint mediation to end the Civil War. All knew that the Union would almost certainly refuse, and armed intervention would have to follow to enforce mediation. Advocates of intervention, including Lord John Russell and William Gladstone, wanted to end the Union blockade of the South. They were also sickened at the brutality of the war, and supported the Southerners' right to self-determination.[98] Other advocates also argued that a permanently divided and weakened America was in long-term British interests.[99] Viscount Palmerston, the prime minister, had at times supported intervention as well.[100] But in late October, he soured on the prospect.

Palmerston gave many reasons, but significantly, his main obstacle seems to have been the shift in public opinion caused by the Emancipation Proclamation. In October, Palmerston wrote privately to

---

[94] *Ibid.* at p. 216; Philip Foner, *British Labor and the American Civil War* (New York: Holmes and Meier, 1981), p. 69. [95] Jenkins, *Britain and the War*, supra note 85, vol. II, pp. 209–11.
[96] Adams, *Great Britain and the Civil War*, supra note 85, vol. II, p. 107.
[97] Foner, *British Labor*, supra note 94, pp. 41, 61.
[98] Jones, *Union in Peril*, supra note 85, pp. 178–9, 184–5, 203; Adams, *Great Britain and the Civil War*, vol. I, pp. 212–15; Jenkins, *Britain and the War*, vol. II, pp. 168–69.
[99] For example, William Lindsay, a member of Parliament, said he desired intervention because he "desired the disruption of the American Union, as every honest Englishman did, because it was too great a Power and England sh'd not let such a power exist on the American continent." Jones, *Union in Peril*, supra note 85, p. 134. [100] *Ibid.* pp. 150–51.

Russell that slavery was now England's "great difficulty" in trying to put together peace terms. Could the cabinet, he asked, "without offence to many People here recommend to the North to sanction Slavery and to undertake to give back Runaways, and yet would not the South insist upon some such Conditions after Lincoln's Emancipation Decree?" The French were more willing to intervene, he wrote, because they were freer from the "Shackles of Principle and of Right & Wrong on these Matters, as on all others than we are."[101]

To be sure, Palmerston heard other arguments against intervention. His Secretary for War, George Cornewall Lewis, was primarily concerned that British recognition of the Confederacy would set a bad international legal precedent. Lewis also argued that the European powers would have difficulty forcing the Union to accept terms. Also on Palmerston's mind was the progress of the war itself, which had recently not gone well for the South.[102] But as Palmerston had said to the Russian ambassador to London in 1861, there were "two Powers in this Country, the government & public opinion, and that both must concur for any great important steps."[103]

After the autumn of 1862, public opinion rendered British intervention impossible. Russell himself stopped Britain from selling ironclad warships to the Confederacy in the spring of 1863, writing privately to a colleague: "If we have taken part in interventions, it has been in behalf of the independence, freedom and welfare of a great portion of mankind. I should be sorry, indeed, if there should be any intervention on the part of this country which could bear another character."[104] Even Gladstone argued against intervention during the summer: "A war with the United States . . . ought to be unpopular on far higher grounds, because it would be a war with our own kinsmen for slavery."[105]

D Anglo–American relations, 1895–96

Just over thirty years later, Britain and the United States were again close to war.[106] President Grover Cleveland and Richard Olney, his Secretary

---

[101] *Ibid.* at pp. 191, 206.   [102] *Ibid.* at pp. 210–17.   [103] Ferris, *"Trent" Affair, supra* note 85, p. 158.
[104] Jenkins, *Britain and the War, supra* note 85, vol. II, p. 241.
[105] *Hansard's Parliamentary Debates* (Commons), 3d ser, vol. CLXXI (June 30, 1863), cols. 1805–06.
[106] Accounts of this crisis are found in Ernest R. May, *Imperial Democracy: the Emergence of America as a Great Power* (Chicago, Ill.: Imprint Publications, 1991); H. C. Allen, *Great Britain and the United States* (London: Odhams Press, 1954); Dexter Perkins, *The Monroe Doctrine 1867–1907* (Baltimore, Md.: The Johns Hopkins University Press, 1937); A. E. Campbell, *Great Britain and the United States 1895–1903* (Westport, Conn.: Greenwood Press, 1960); and Marshall Bertram, *The Birth of Anglo–American Friendship: the Prime Facet of the Venezuelan Boundary Dispute* (Lanham, Md.: University Press of America, 1992).

of State, saw a boundary dispute between British Guiana and Venezuela as an opportunity to assert US power in the New World. Cleveland and Olney demanded US arbitration in the dispute, arguing that England was violating the Monroe Doctrine by trying to expand its territory in the Americas. After Lord Salisbury, British prime minister and foreign minister, told Cleveland that it was no affair of the United States, Congress voted unanimously in December 1895 to fund an American commission to decide the boundary, with its recommendations to be enforced by whatever means necessary. War fever was loose for a few days in America. But the crisis was resolved peacefully over the next few months, and never again would these two nations seriously consider war with each other.

1 Americans had observed Britain liberalizing in the 1880s and had begun to expect better relations

Many Americans in the 1890s still viewed Britain mainly as a monarchy and thus not liberal. But others had begun to challenge this old view after the Third Reform Act in 1884 enormously expanded the franchise in Britain. The Scottish emigre and staunch republican Andrew Carnegie then proclaimed, "Henceforth England is democratic," and predicted that "British democracy is to be pacific, and that the American doctrine of non-intervention will commend itself to it."[107] On the eve of the Venezuelan crisis, Joseph Pulitzer, publisher of the *New York World*, decried a senator's proposal that the United States align with Russia and wage war against England:

> Russia represents the worst despotism that civilization has permitted to survive, except possibly that of Turkey. England represents Anglo–Saxon liberty and progress only in less degree than does our own government. We have much in common with the English. We have nothing whatever in common with Russia.[108]

A liberal elite desired good relations with England precisely because the nation had liberalized.

2 Most Britons now saw the United States as trustworthy

One reason was the end of slavery. The scholar Goldwin Smith wrote during the crisis, "I am firmly convinced that since the abolition of

---

[107] Andrew Carnegie, "Democracy in England," *No. Am. Rev.* 142 (1886), p. 74.
[108] *Public Opinion* (November 21, 1895), 21. One publicist called England "the Crowned Republic," Moncure D. Conway, "The Queen of England," *No. Am. Rev.*, 145 (1887), p. 121.

slavery there prevails among them no desire for territorial aggrandizement."[109] Another was liberalization in Britain itself. A historian writes, "anti-Americanism, traditionally associated with a disappearing social order, had long been on the wane . . . Thus in all the tensions of the period, and particularly in the Venezuela dispute, the most important influence for amity and peace was the new English democracy."[110] Fear of Russia and Germany influenced this desire for American friendship, but the point is that the new Britain was more inclined than the old to choose America as friend. William Vernon Harcourt, Liberal leader in the House of Commons, often referred to "we semi-Americans" when writing to his friend Joseph Chamberlain, the Liberal colonial secretary.[111] On both sides of the Atlantic, Anglo-Saxon chauvinism played a strong role in this affinity.[112]

3 American liberals continued to see England as liberal during the crisis
Neither Cleveland nor Olney was part of the liberal pro-British elite in the United States, and much of the American public wanted war at the beginning of the crisis. But the US ambassador to London, Thomas F. Bayard, was a pro-British liberal who viewed the United States and Great Britain as the "two guardians of civilization." During the crisis, Bayard stressed his well-known views that England was to be trusted because, unlike Venezuela, it was governed by law.[113] In Congress, Senator Edward O. Wolcott of Colorado declared Venezuela one of South America's "so-called republics" in which the "rulers are despots and suffrage a farce." He hoped the Venezuelan mines would be governed by "English common law" with its "certainty of enforcement."[114]

Most pro-British liberals were found outside government, however. Prominent among these was Pulitzer, whose *New York World* said on December 21:

There is not a hothead among the jingoes who does not know that England is more likely to become a republic than the United States are to revert to monarchism. The entire trend of government for the past fifty years has been toward democracy . . . Observe the working of the leaven of democracy in England.[115]

---

[109] *N.Y. Times*, December 25, 1895, p. 3.
[110] Allen, *Great Britain and the United States*, supra note 106, p. 525.
[111] *The Life of Sir William Vernon Harcourt* (London: Constable, 1923), vol. II, pp. 396–97.
[112] Campbell, *Great Britain and the United States*, supra note 106, pp. 9–10.
[113] Charles Callan Tansill, *The Foreign Policy of Thomas F. Bayard* (New York: Fordham University Press, 1940), p. 716.
[114] 4th Cong, 1st sess., *Congressional Record* (December 20, 1895), vol. XXVIII, pt. 1, pp. 859–60.
[115] John L. Heaton, *The Story of a Page* (New York: Harper and Bros., 1913), p. 114.

"In a word," commented the *Nation*, "the American Secretary of State's references to Venezuelan republicanism and friendship and English monarchy and hostility have no more to do with the facts than with the planet Jupiter."[116]

4 British liberals continued to see the United States as liberal through the crisis
The British press expressed general revulsion at the prospect of war with the United States. The *Standard* gave a typical opinion:

> We feel confident that a vast majority of the Americans will soon be profoundly sorry for what Mr. Cleveland has done. He has travestied and damaged a principle that they hold dear, and has made the Republic which we have all honored on account of its supposed attachment to peace and non-intervention, figure in the eyes of Europe as a gratuitously aggressive and reckless champion of war.[117]

The *Daily Telegraph* calmly stated, "we are perfectly satisfied to rely upon the straightforward, high-bred simplicity of Lord Salisbury's diplomacy and the good sense, widespread honesty, intelligence, and kindliness of the American people."[118]

5 American liberals agitated for peace
Pulitzer led the peace movement, sending cablegrams to influential British asking their opinions on the crisis. On Christmas Day the *World*'s front page featured a selection of responses under the headline "PEACE AND GOOD WILL," expressing alarm at the thought of an Anglo–American war.[119] There was, moreover, an interactive effect as Americans observed this British good will. In January 1896 the

---

[116] *The Nation*, January 2, 1896, p. 5.
[117] *Quoted in* the *N.Y. Times* (December 21, 1895), p. 6. It is also interesting to note that the London *Review of Reviews* took great pains to counter those Americans who claimed England was not democratic. "The superstition that the United States is in a peculiar sense Republican, whereas we are Monarchical, is being utilized for all it is worth in order to bolster up the case for intervention in Venezuela. If British subjects in Guiana would but repudiate their allegiance to the British Empire, and set up in business as a British republic, no American citizen would object to them eating their way into the heart of Venezuela. All the difficulty arises from the prejudice against the monarchy – a prejudice that is as old as George III, and ought to have been buried with him." *Review of Reviews* (London) (December 14, 1895), pp. 484–85.
[118] *N.Y. Times* (December 19, 1895), p. 3.
[119] Heaton, *Story of a Page*, *supra* note 115; W. A. Swanberg, *Pulitzer* (New York: Charles Scribner's Sons, 1967), p. 199. This is in stark contrast to Pulitzer's behavior two years later in the crisis with Spain, a country few if any Americans considered democratic. In agitating for war, the *World* declared, "War waged on behalf of freedom, of self-government, of law and order, of humanity, to end oppression, misrule, plunder, and savagery, is a holy war in itself." Heaton, *Story of a Page*, *supra* note 115, p. 162.

Philadelphia Press asserted, "Nothing in the succession for a month past of discussion, declaration and feeling, personal and public, private and National, has so moved the American Nation as a whole as the sudden revelation which has been Made of English Horror of War with this Country."[120]

6 British liberals agitated for peace

Not only the British press, but also Joseph Chamberlain, the colonial secretary who had originally agreed with Salisbury to rebuff Cleveland and Olney, "determined to move heaven and earth to avert conflict between the two English-speaking peoples," one biographer writes.[121] In a speech in Birmingham, Chamberlain proclaimed:

> War between the two nations would be an absurdity as well as a crime ... The two nations are allied more closely in sentiment and in interest than any other nations on the face of the earth ... I should look forward with pleasure to the possibility of the Stars and Stripes and the Union Jack floating together in defence of a common cause sanctioned by humanity and justice.[122]

His friend Harcourt made it clear that he would make the crisis a major issue in the upcoming session of Parliament. He urged Chamberlain to grant the Americans all they wanted.[123]

7 Resolution of the crisis

Especially in the United States, liberals had a difficult task. Not only were Cleveland and Olney unimpressed by British liberalization, but much of the American public, especially Irish-Americans, roared its approval at this "tweaking of the lion's tail." One cannot prove what drove officials on either side of the Atlantic to defuse the crisis. What can be said is that on January 2, 1896, Cleveland appointed a distinguished commission to adjudicate the Venezuelan–British Guianan border, with only one member who could be construed as anglophobic. Since the president could have appointed a much more inflammatory commission, this must be seen as a conciliatory step.

The British cabinet voted on January 11, over the objections of Salisbury, to accept the US commission's jurisdiction. It was the liberals

---

[120] *Public Opinion* 20 (January 23, 1896), p. 107.
[121] J. L. Garvin, *The Life of Joseph Chamberlain*, 3 vols. (London: Macmillan, 1934), vol. III, p. 67.
[122] May, *Imperial Democracy*, supra note 106, pp. 44–45, 53–54.
[123] *Ibid.* at p. 49; Gardiner, *Life of Harcourt*, supra note 111, pp. 396–97; Garvin, *Chamberlain*, supra note 121, p. 161; Bertram, *Anglo–American Friendship*, supra note 106, p. 83. Harcourt had always admired the United States, and argued vigorously against British intervention in the US Civil War.

in the cabinet, led by the pro-American Chamberlain, who favored the settlement. Salisbury, a realist with no affinity for American democracy, would have accepted war, and he nearly resigned in protest when the cabinet outvoted him.

The resolution of the Venezuelan border crisis was the beginning of the apparently permanent Anglo–American friendship. Today, realists argue that Britain appeased the Americans here and elsewhere because it could no longer sustain its "splendid isolation" in the face of rising threats from Germany and Russia.[124] That argument begs the question of why the British aligned with the United States rather than with Germany. Germany threatened British interests in Africa, but the United States threatened British interests in the New World. Liberalism offers an answer: British liberals trusted the democratic United States *more* than imperial Germany. During the Venezuelan crisis, the German emperor sent the infamous Kruger telegram congratulating the Boers in southern Africa for repelling the British Jameson raid. In a striking contrast to its calm reaction to the Cleveland–Olney provocations, the British public was outraged. One historian writes, "when 'Yankee Doodle' was cheered and 'Die Wacht am Rhein' hissed in London, it demonstrated clearly how utterly different was popular feeling towards the two countries."[125]

Appeasement of the United States was no arbitrary choice. Now that Britain was more liberal than ever, its government and people trusted liberal America more than ever.[126]

IX LIBERAL PEACE AND THE REALIST CHALLENGE

Many realists have declared liberal peace a fantasy. Stable, long-term peace between mutually recognized liberal States, they argue, is not possible. Liberal States, like all others, must base foreign policy on the imperatives of power politics. Some realists argue that there is no theoretically compelling causal mechanism that could explain liberal peace. Others claim that even if there were, the foreign-policy processes of

---

[124] Layne, "Kant or Cant," *supra* note 41.
[125] Allen, *Great Britain and the United States*, *supra* note 106, p. 354.
[126] Stephen Rock writes: "Englishmen, who could agree on practically nothing else, were in fact almost unanimous in their distaste for the German political system, its ideology, and its methods ... Both [Germany and the United States] were rising imperial powers with growing navies. Yet Britons, while they detested and feared Germany, almost universally admired the United States and felt minimal apprehension at her ambitions." Stephen Rock, *Why Peace Breaks Out: Great Power Rapprochement in Historical Perspective* (Chapel Hill, N.C.: University of North Carolina Press, 1989), pp. 86–87.

liberal States show that such a mechanism is empirically impotent.[127] Realist skeptics make a number of claims.

They claim that if neither liberal structures nor norms alone can explain the liberal peace, then there is no liberal peace.[128] I have already pointed out the logical fallacy behind this claim. The structural/normative distinction is epistemological, not ontological. Structure and norms work in tandem: liberal ideas proscribe wars among liberal States, and liberal institutions ensure that this proscription is followed.

Realists claim that if there were a liberal peace, then liberal States would never make threats against one another. The claim is that the "logic" of the liberal-peace proposition implies that liberal States will never try to coerce one another.[129] But of course, logic does not inhere in the mere proposition that liberal States do not fight one another; rather, it would inhere in a theory purporting to explain that proposition. My theory answers realism in two ways. First, liberal States do not always consider each other liberal. What a scholar in 1998 considers liberal is not always what a statesman in 1898 considered liberal. Second, everyday foreign policy in liberal States is sometimes dominated by elites whose direct material interests contradict the directives of liberal ideology. Such leaders may make threats; they are simply unable to mobilize the nation for war, due to the constraints of liberal institutions.

Realists claim that if there were liberal peace, then public opinion in liberal States would never want war with a fellow liberal State.[130] Like the previous claim, this one makes two assumptions: that all citizens of liberal States allow liberal ideology to trump all other concerns, and that they agree on which foreign States are also liberal. Neither assumption is true, and neither is necessary for liberal peace to occur. All that is necessary for statesmen to be constrained is that they believe war would be too unpopular.

Realists claim that when power politics requires war with a liberal State, liberals will redefine that State as a despotism; when power politics requires peace with an illiberal State, they will redefine that State as liberal.[131] Ideological labels are sugar-coating to make otherwise bitter

---

[127] See John J. Mearsheimer, "Back to the Future: Instability in Europe after the Cold War," *Int'l Security* 15 (Summer 1990), pp. 5–56; Waltz, "Emerging Structure," *supra* note 43; Layne, "Kant or Cant," *supra* note 41; Henry Farber and Joanne Gowa, "Polities and Peace," in Brown, Lynn-Jones, and Miller, eds., *Debating the Democratic Peace, supra* note 41, pp. 157–201.

[128] Layne, "Kant or Cant," *supra* note 41.   [129] *Ibid.*   [130] *Ibid.*

[131] This is implied in Hans Morgenthau's argument that Woodrow Wilson led the United States into World War I "not to make the world safe for democracy," but because "Germany threatened the balance of power . . . Wilson pursued the right policy, but he pursued it for the wrong reason." Morgenthau, *National Interest, supra* note 83, pp. 25–26.

policies easier to swallow. Statesmen's public rationales for foreign policy are solely rhetorical; one must look at their confidential statements to understand their true motives. In this chapter, however, I have shown that in crises liberals hang fast to the ideological labels they previously gave foreign States. Republicans stood by France after the XYZ Affair. They mistrusted England from the time of the American Revolution up to the end of the War of 1812 (and beyond). Many Americans began to see England as liberal in the 1880s, and continued to do so during the Venezuelan crisis. Britons began admiring the United States well before the rise of Germany "forced" them to make friends in the late 1890s. The one case where liberals changed their opinion of a foreign State during a crisis was in the Civil War. There, British opinion shifted to the Union side after the Emancipation Proclamation. The cause of this shift was not power politics, but the Emancipation Proclamation, which signified that the Union was fighting for abolition, a liberal cause the British had long supported.

Realists claim that "strategic concerns and the relative distribution of military capabilities ... should crucially – perhaps decisively" affect the outcomes of crises between liberal States, and moreover that "broader geopolitical considerations pertaining to a State's position in international politics should, if implicated, account significantly for the crisis's outcome."[132] I do not contest the relevance of power politics to the foreign policies of liberal democracies. These realist hypotheses, however, imply that during a crisis, statesmen will be able either to ignore liberals or to persuade them to change their minds. But liberal ideology and institutions clearly had independent power in 1798, when John Adams could not ask Congress for war against France due to staunch Republican opposition. In 1862, Palmerston privately admitted to being constrained by pro-Union opinion from intervening in the Civil War. Realism would and did counsel the British to work to keep the United States divided and weak, but they passed up the opportunity. In 1895–96, war would clearly have been highly unpopular, especially in England, and Salisbury was thwarted by Liberals in his own cabinet from confronting the United States.

Realists claim that States that view each other as liberal will still balance against each other.[133] Realists who posit that States balance solely against capabilities must explain why Britain conciliated the

---

[132] Layne, "Kant or Cant," *supra* note 41.
[133] Waltz, "Emerging Structure," *supra* note 43, pp. 66–67, predicts that Japan and Germany will acquire nuclear capabilities to balance against the United States.

United States rather than Germany. As explained below, a more nuanced realism, such as balance-of-threat theory, could account for this outcome. In assessing whether a foreign State is a threat, liberals such as Chamberlain look at, among other things, the State's regime type.

Realists claim that Wilhelmine Germany was a democracy, and therefore liberal States fought one another in World War I.[134] There is not the space to address this claim fully, but two things may briefly be said. First, even before the war, most British and Americans saw Germany as illiberal. The British abhorred German ideology, and although many Americans admired Germany's progressive social policies,[135] most viewed the country as politically backward. "Germany is mediæval," said one magazine in 1912. "'Divine Rights' is written on the brow of the Kaiser . . . This is the trinity that rules Germany: a mediæval king, a feudal aristocracy, and the pushing parvenus of coal dust and iron filings."[136] Second, the chancellor was responsible to the Emperor William rather than the legislature. The electorate had little leverage over war decisions. The press was not wholly free, as illustrated when William suppressed an antiwar book in 1913. The emperor also controlled the upper chamber of the legislature, the Bundesrat, which had veto power over the legislation of the lower house.[137] Thus, by neither the standards of its time nor those of this study can Germany be called a liberal State in 1914.

X IS A REALIST–LIBERAL SYNTHESIS POSSIBLE?

Both realists and liberals who have written about liberal peace have been loath to cede any ground to the opposing side. Yet my argument and evidence suggest that both camps are describing real forces in international politics, namely, power politics and liberal ideas. It is conceivable that these two forces sometimes push in different directions in a particular case, yielding a weak effect in favor of one or the other. Jon Elster discusses such dynamics in a very different context: suppose a weak

---

[134] Layne, "Kant or Cant," *supra* note 41.
[135] For a strong challenge to the liberal-peace thesis based upon the admiration American political scientists had for Imperial Germany, *see* Ido Oren, "The Subjectivity of the 'Democratic' Peace: Changing US Perceptions of Imperial Germany," *in* Brown, Lynn-Jones, and Miller, eds., *Debating the Democratic Peace*, *supra* note 41, pp. 263–300.   [136] *World's Work* (June 1912), p. 146.
[137] John L. Snell, *The Democratic Movement in Germany, 1789–1914* (Chapel Hill, N.C.: University of North Carolina Press, 1976), pp. 165, 212–19, 237–38, 343, 366; *Literary Digest*, June 14, 1913, pp. 1332–3. For an argument that the German political system contributed to the coming of war, *see* Paul Kennedy, "The Kaiser and German *Weltpolitik*," *in* J. Rohl and N. Sombert, eds., *Kaiser Wilhelm II: New Interpretations* (Cambridge University Press, 1982), pp. 143–68.

aggregate tendency were discovered for people to donate more to charity when others do so. The weak tendency may well be due to the existence of two different types of people with opposite tendencies: one, slightly dominant, that gives much more when observing others give (following a norm of reciprocity), and one that gives less (following a utilitarian norm). The combined effect conceals two strong mechanisms working at cross purposes.[138] Similarly, it could be that *Realpolitik* pushes policy in one direction and liberalism in another, and that the combined effect weakly favors one or the other.

A key to synthesizing the two theories would seem to be that liberals define national interest in such a way that cooperation with fellow liberal democracies is required. Given this premise, two synthetic approaches seem promising. First, Stephen Walt's balance-of-threat theory could incorporate States' estimates of regime type. Walt writes that a State's alliance decisions are based not only on the aggregate and offensive power and geographic proximity of foreign States, but also on how aggressive the intentions are. He cites the Eyre Crowe memorandum of 1907, which states that the British welcomed the growth of German power *per se*, but were concerned about German intentions.[139] My argument holds that liberals judge foreign States' intentions in part based on whether those States are liberal democracies. Had Eyre Crowe considered Germany liberal, he would not have been so worried.

A second approach would use the ideational framework of Alexander Wendt, David Lumsdaine, and others. Essentially, this approach postulates that international anarchy does not necessarily lead to self-help and power politics. Rather, these features are derivative of States' identities, which in turn are constructed by their practices, in particular the quality of their interactions. That is, even absent a world sovereign, States must hold certain beliefs about each other before they fear each other.[140] Neo-realism posits that these beliefs are always product of power factors and thus not an independent variable. But the evidence that there is liberal peace and that it is a product of liberal ideas suggests neo-realism is wrong. Power would not drop out of a framework that claims ideational

---

[138] Jon Elster, *Political Psychology* (Cambridge University Press, 1993), pp. 2–7. I thank David Dessler for bringing this source to my attention.
[139] Stephen M. Walt, *The Origins of Alliances* (Ithaca, N.J.: Cornell University Press, 1987), pp. 21–25.
[140] *See* Alexander Wendt, "Anarchy Is what States Make of It: the Social Construction of Power Politics," *International Organization* 46 (1992), pp. 391–425; and David Halloran Lumsdaine, *Moral Vision in International Politics: the Foreign Aid Regime, 1949–89* (Princeton University Press, 1993), pp. 3–29.

sources of national interest. It would simply be one of several forces, filtered through an ideational lens.

XI CONCLUSION

A *The UN and perpetual peace?*

I have described and shown at work a causal mechanism linking liberal government and international peace. In so doing, I have attempted to lend credibility to the proposition that liberal States tend not to fight wars against one another. The liberal ideas undergirding liberal democracies constitute the mechanism linking liberal States and peace. Liberalism says that all persons are best off pursuing self-preservation and material well-being, and that freedom and toleration are the best means to these ends. The liberal commitment to individual freedom gives rise to foreign policy ideology and governmental institutions that work together to produce liberal peace.

Ideologically, liberals trust those States they consider fellow liberal States and see no reason to fight them. They view those States they consider illiberal with suspicion, and sometimes believe that the national interest requires war with them. In different countries at different times, liberals have differed on question of form, but the essential ideology is the same. Institutionally, liberalism brings about institutions that give citizens leverage over governmental decisions. Sometimes liberals run the government and simply implement their view of the national interest. Even when they do not, the institutions of free speech and regular, competitive elections allow liberal elites to force even illiberal leaders to follow liberal ideology. When a liberal State is in a war-threatening crisis with a State it considers liberal, its liberal elites agitate against war. Illiberal leaders find they cannot persuade the public to go to war, and moreover fear they will lose the next election if they do go to war. By the same process, they may be goaded into war with States that liberals believe to be illiberal.

In strengthening the case for liberal peace, my argument implies that, insofar as the UN and other international organizations value peace, they should aim for a world with more liberal States. It does not imply, however, that IOs ought to attempt to liberalize indiscriminately. Endeavors to spread and support liberal government will often produce unintended, deleterious consequences, and may even be self-defeating.

Furthermore, other ends, such as international stability and state sovereignty, continue to have value. Liberal government is not the final solution to the problem of war. In this final section I address some of these issues.

B Unintended consequences

One short-term unintended consequence may be more rather than less war. This could happen in two ways. First, Edward Mansfield and Jack Snyder argue that democratizing (as distinguished from mature democratic) States can actually be more belligerent than stable authoritarian States. When an authoritarian regime collapses, old and new elites typically compete for domestic influence by means of nationalistic appeals which in turn may bring on conflict and war with neighboring States.[141] Although the Mansfield–Snyder thesis has been attacked on theoretical and empirical grounds by a number of scholars,[142] it does draw a helpful distinction between established liberal States and States lurching in a liberal direction. As citizens of Cambodia, Liberia, and Bosnia–Herzegovina can attest, simply holding one "free and fair" election under UN or OSCE observation does not make a State liberal. Liberalization is a long and complex process that requires *inter alia* the development of a liberal culture.[143]

A second path toward more rather than less war could be an exponential growth in the number of forcible UN interventions. If the liberal peace exists, one inference is that illiberal government anywhere is a threat to peace. The language of the Security Council resolutions on Haiti and Sierra Leone already suggests that that body has drawn just that inference. Is a norm arising calling for the extirpation of illiberal government wherever it is found? Such a norm, of course, would lead to continuous interventions around the world. But so long as China remains illiberal, the Security Council will not adopt that norm. Instead, it seems to have adopted a more limited norm opposing the forcible overthrow of liberal government. The Council is leaving established authoritarian States alone, but acting to restore liberal government where it has

---

[141] Edward D. Mansfield and Jack Snyder, "Democratization and the Danger of War," *International Security* 20 (1995), pp. 5–38.
[142] *See, e.g.,* critical responses by Reinhard Wolf, Erich Weede, and Andrew Enterline in *Int'l Security* 20 (1996), pp. 176–79; and William R. Thompson and Richard Tucker, "A Tale of Two Democratic Peace Critiques," *J. of Conflict Res.* 41 (1997), 428–54.
[143] Boutros-Ghali acknowledges this point. *See* Boutros-Ghali, *supra* note 14, IV., pp. 41–43.

been illegally removed. Even these cases, however, are numerous enough that the UN ought to be wary of applying this norm in rote fashion.

The probability of exponentially multiplying interventions is even higher than may first appear, because the Security Council typically does not intervene itself, but rather authorizes third parties to intervene. This practice leads to yet another unintended consequence: shifts in regional balances of power. In the case of Sierra Leone, the only actor willing to send in troops to restore President Ahmad Tejan Kabbah, overthrown by his own military in May 1997, was Nigeria, West Africa's most powerful State and itself a military dictatorship.[144] Although Sierra Leoneans were on the whole better off after the Nigerian intervention, that intervention enhanced the power of a heavily armed illiberal regime by making the survival of a neighboring government dependent on it. In fact, insofar as individual States, including the United States, do the liberalizing, one can be sure that those States are seeking to expand their influence at least as much as to expand the number of liberal States.[145] Spheres of influence are not necessarily antithetical to peace, but rapid expansions of such spheres can be, because neighboring States may begin to fear for their own security. The UN needs to remember that States generally do not do charity work: they always want power or wealth in return for intervening.

Another unintended consequence of IO-sponsored liberalization might be failure. The problem of liberalization from without was raised in the nineteenth century by John Stuart Mill, who argued that freedom not won by a people for itself would be ephemeral. Such "freedom" would be self-contradictory, in that it would be dependent on foreigners.[146] Americans learned in the Vietnam War that even an actor with vast resources cannot make a country into a prosperous liberal democracy where the conditions are wrong. With their much smaller resources, IOs must be wary of similar failures. Still, the point must not be pushed too far. Americans are notorious for forgetting that their own country was helped toward freedom and independence by France and other enemies of England. Today's Germany and Japan owe their

[144] Ed O'Laughlin, "First Africa-Wide Effort to Restore a Democracy: So Far, So Good," *Christian Science Monitor* (March 11, 1998), p. 7.
[145] For an analysis of this phenomenon, *see* John M. Owen, IV, "Why do States Impose Domestic Regimes?" presented at the annual meeting of the American Political Science Association, Washington, D.C. (August 28–31, 1997).
[146] J. S. Mill, "A Few Words on Non-intervention," *in his Dissertations and Discussions: Political, Philosophical, and Historical* (New York: Henry Holt, 1874), vol. III, pp. 238–63.

liberal–democratic status at least as much to external (chiefly American) coercion as to home-grown liberalism.[147] Those who like Mill draw a sharp distinction between organic and artificial liberal States ignore the histories of the "organic" ones. The real lesson of the history of liberalization from without is that it may entail more costs than the Security Council is willing to bear.

C The question of sovereignty

Even if all unintended consequences of liberalization from without could be eliminated, there would remain objectives other than peace that the UN is bound to uphold. The most nettlesome of these, state sovereignty, is implied in most of the unintended consequences adduced above. The UN Charter recognizes the juridical equality of States, and prohibits "intervention in matters which are essentially within the domestic jurisdiction of any State."[148] Since the birth of the modern States system in the seventeenth century, a State's internal institutions have been considered as belonging within its domestic jurisdiction. Thus, the traditional notion of State sovereignty directly contradicts the evident UN bias toward liberal government: if a State has supreme authority over its territory, then no external body has a right to alter its internal institutions and practices. Of course, sovereignty has never been absolute in practice,[149] and the UN Charter explicitly states that the non-intervention principle does "not prejudice the application of the enforcement measures under Chapter VII," *i.e.*, pertaining to the preservation of peace.[150]

The question of how to balance peace and State sovereignty is a moral one, and I shall not attempt to answer it here. There is however a large normative literature on international intervention. Apart from extreme cosmopolitans who ascribe no moral weight to sovereignty, most writers see some value in granting a "default" position to non-intervention.[151] For the majority of writers, then, even liberal peace would not necessarily open the door to boundless UN interventions on behalf of liberal government. The UN's claim that it does not impose liberal-

[147] For an exploration of the German and Japanese democratizations, and other successes, *see* Tony Smith, *America's Mission: the United States and the Worldwide Struggle for Democracy in the Twentieth Century* (Princeton University Press, 1994).   [148] Art. 2(1); Art. 2(7).
[149] Stephen D. Krasner, "Compromising Westphalia," *Int'l Security* 20 (1995), pp. 115–51.
[150] UN Charter, Art. 2(7).
[151] *See* the discussion in Michael W. Doyle, *Ways of War and Peace: Realism, Liberalism, Socialism* (New York: Norton, 1997), ch. 11.

ism, but only facilitates it when asked, suggests that it still takes State sovereignty seriously.[152] Highly problematic is the question of whether the party making the request of the UN may legitimately do so. Who, after all, speaks for "the nation" when by definition no liberal mechanisms are in place by which the people may voice their will? The potential for abuse by the UN and other external actors is obvious.

D *No liberal crusades*

Liberal peace is real, and thus IOs that value peace ought to aim for a world of more liberal States. But IOs must lose sight of neither the self-defeating potential of many interventions on behalf of liberalism, nor of other goods, especially State sovereignty. The international legal community would do well to heed the example of Kant, the prophet of liberal peace. In his later years, Kant emphatically rejected the notion of a world sovereign in favor of a league of sovereign republics. Relatedly, he envisaged progress *toward* perpetual peace via a federation of republics, but explicitly stated that permanent peace is "an unachievable ideal." The league of liberal States would become unwieldy as it grew, and would finally be "ungovernable"; and a world with two or more such leagues would simply reenter the original state of war.[153] In other words, unlike many of his modern interpreters, Kant did not regard liberal government as a magic bullet, but only as a limited means to make war less frequent. Since liberalism is no final solution to the problem of war, it must not be allowed to efface all other values in international life. Should we ignore Kant's own caution, we may find ourselves fighting perpetual war for the sake of perpetual peace.

---

[152] Boutros Boutros-Ghali maintains that the UN only offers assistance in democratization when requested to do so, and thus remains "impartial." *See supra* note 14, I. 11–13. Of course, since the UN would not help a country set up authoritarian rule if asked, it is not impartial at all.

[153] Immanuel Kant, *The Metaphysics of Morals*, §54, §61, Mary Gregor, ed. (Cambridge University Press, 1996), pp. 114–15, 119.

PART IV

Democratization and conflicting imperatives

CHAPTER 12

Intolerant democracies

Gregory H. Fox and Georg Nolte

If there be any among us who wish to dissolve this union, or to change its republican form, let them stand undisturbed, as monuments of the safety with which error of opinion may be tolerated where reason is left free to combat it.

Thomas Jefferson[1]

This will always remain one of the best jokes of democracy, that it gave its deadly enemies the means by which it was destroyed.

Joseph Goebbels[2]

I INTRODUCTION

How should a democracy react to the presence of anti-democratic actors in its midst? Debate over this question could hardly involve a broader set of issues. Looking to history, the twentieth century provides examples of totalitarian parties attaining power through democratic elections, and thereafter dismantling their countries' democratic institutions. Yet there are also societies in which toleration of anti-democratic actors appears to have diminished their popular appeal. Turning to political theory, some scholars conceive of democracy as an essentially procedural idea, one in which open debate and electoral competition among all ideological factions serves as the touchstone of democratic legitimacy. Others posit a substantive conception of democracy holding, in Rawls's terminology, that democratic societies need not tolerate the intolerant.[3] And in the discipline of comparative politics, scholars debate whether democracy in some societies is so

---
[1] Thomas Jefferson, "First Draft of the Inaugural Address (Mar 4, 1801)," *in* Paul Leicester Ford, ed., *The Writings of Thomas Jefferson* (G.P. Putnam's Sons: New York, 1897), vol. VIII, pp. 1ff, at p. 3.
[2] "Das wird immer einer der besten Witze der Demokratie bleiben, dass sie ihren Todfeinden die Mittel selber stellte, durch die sie vernichtet wurde," *quoted in* Karl Dietrich Bracher *et al.*, eds., *Nationalsozialistische Diktatur* (Düsseldorf: Drosle Verlag, 1983), p. 16.
[3] John Rawls, *A Theory of Justice* (1971), p. 214.

fragile that it cannot withstand vigorous popular appeals by its committed opponents.[4]

These questions are difficult enough. For international lawyers, an added layer of complexity exists. Since the end of the Cold War the international community has devoted substantial resources to fostering national transitions to democracy. As the other chapters in this volume attest, however, a robust debate continues over the normative status of a "democratic entitlement." Given the unsettled state of international law on the requirement of (or the right to) democratic governance, can international lawyers nonetheless take up the question of whether "democracy" should be protected by action against its opponents? Can human rights law, for example, countenance the banning of a neo-Fascist political party on the grounds that it might dismantle a State's democratic institutions? If it is true that international law now regards certain political institutions as part of an essential democratic minimum – in particular, the holding of periodic elections[5] – might not such a State have a legal *obligation* to ensure that the Fascist party does not attain power and implement its anti-democratic agenda? If so, would not international law effectively resolve the definitional problems of democratic government at the remedial stage without having done so at the normative stage? What, in other words, is international law attempting to protect? And even if agreement on a minimal legal conception of democracy is possible, must an anti-democratic party with a substantial following among voters be sacrificed in order for a State to abide by its obligation to ensure that democratic government continues?

Then there are tactical questions. Whether or not an anti-democratic party enjoys broad appeal in a State would seem to be an intrinsically local question. Democracy in the United States managed to survive Huey Long, Father Caughlin, and David Duke; democracy in Weimar Germany obviously did not survive the Nazi Party. Finding normative lessons in these respective histories, German and American law now take opposite approaches to the advocacy of extremist ideologies. How can international law hope to create uniform standards in the face of such diverse national experience? Would the promotion of democracy truly be furthered if, for example, Germany were obligated as a matter of

---

[4] *See* Andres Schedler, "What is Democratic Consolidation?" *J. Democ.* 9 (1998), 91.
[5] As the UN Secretary-General stated bluntly in his 1998 annual report on the work of the organization, "[c]redible elections are a core ingredient of good governance and the process of democratization." Annual Report of the Secretary-General on the Work of the Organization, UN Doc. A/53/1 (1998), para. 120.

international law to permit the formation of new neo-Nazi parties? Or if the United States were required to suppress symbols of racial, ethnic, or religious hatred? Would not both societies be better served by a focus on the social ills that allow extremist ideologies to flourish?

Not long ago these would have been unthinkable questions for international lawyers. But as issues of domestic governance move from the exclusive realm of national constitutional law and enter the purview of international human rights law, these have become challenges addressed to the international community at large. The answers are of interest to both opponents and proponents of a normative democratic entitlement. Proponents would regard norms clarifying the status of anti-democratic actors as an essential next step in elaborating an international conception of democratic government. Given the fragility of many new democracies, it is argued, elected leaders in those States are entitled to know whether international law will move beyond encouraging an initial transition to democratic rule and countenance legal measures designed to protect the new system from those who would dismantle it using its own electoral regime as the vehicle. Opponents, on the other hand, have pointed to the persistent appeal of anti-democratic ideologies as evidencing the folly of multilateral efforts to consolidate democratic institutions.[6] That international law must devise ways to prevent voters from making the "wrong" choice simply underlines their skepticism. That both sides now debate this issue as a question of how *international actors* should proceed, however, suggests that few still regard the success or failure of democracy in any State as a purely local matter.

This chapter asks whether nascent international standards on anti-democratic actors have begun to form. In section II we examine the nature of the problem by reference to two cases in which the institutions of electoral democracy were challenged by anti-democratic actors: the rise of the German Nazi party in the early 1930s and the experience of the Islamic Salvation Front in the 1991 Algerian elections. In section III we describe two paradigms of democratic theory that frame opposing solutions to the problem of anti-democratic actors. In section IV, drawing on the "procedural" and "substantive" approaches outlined in section III, we review national experience in a select group of democratic States. In section V we review the practice of global and regional human rights regimes. Finally, we conclude in section VI, based on the national and international practice examined, that States are under no

---

[6] *See* Fareed Zakaria, "The Rise of Illiberal Democracy," *For. Aff.*, (Nov./Dec. 1997), p. 22.

legal obligation to tolerate anti-democratic actors and may, according to a set of well-defined procedures, act to exclude them from electoral processes.

II THE NATURE OF THE PROBLEM

What is the nature of the conflict between "democratic" regimes and their opponents? Two historical examples provide an essential framework to begin answering this question.

A *The rise of the German Nazi party*

A central historical example of the anti-democratic phenomenon is Hitler's rise to power in Weimar Germany. The Weimar example is an important starting point not only because it involved such a pointed clash between liberal and authoritarian ideologies, but also because the Nazi experience weighed heavily on the minds of UN delegates who drafted the post-war human rights instruments.[7]

The Weimar constitution, like most modern democratic systems, provided for proportional representation in the German parliament (*Reichstag*). While the Nazi Party won an increasing number of seats in the *Reichstag* in the early 1930s, it never actually won a majority of seats.[8] In January 1933, when Hitler was appointed Chancellor (head of government), the party held slightly less than one-third of the seats in the *Reichstag*, where it was nevertheless the largest party. Despite the Nazis' lack of a governing majority, they succeeded in eroding support for the Republic by working within established democratic institutions. Beginning with elections in the summer of 1932, the Nazis held, together with the Communist party, a "negative" majority in the *Reichstag*. This allowed them to block the formation of any government with parliamentary support.[9] Under these circumstances, President Hindenburg first tried to derail Hitler's rise to power by appointing minority Chancellors

---

[7] Richard B. Lillich, "Civil Rights," *in* Theodor Meron, ed., *Human Rights in International Law* 115 (1984), pp. 115ff, at p. 122; Moses Moskowitz, *International Concern with Human Rights* (Leiden: Oceana, 1974), p. 8.

[8] Before Hitler's appointment as Chancellor in January 1933, the Nazi high-water mark occurred in the elections of July 31, 1932 when the party received 37.4 percent of the popular vote. A. J. Nicholls, *Weimar and the Rise of Hitler* (Basingstoke: Macmillan, 3rd edn. 1991), p. 136.

[9] The results of all *Reichstag* elections under the Weimar Constitution are contained in E. R. Huber, ed., 3rd edn., *Ergebnisse der Wahlen im Reich 1919 bis 1933, reprinted* as Doc. No. 533 in IV *Dokumente Zur Deutschen Verfassungsgeschichte* 668 (Stuttgart: Kohlhammer, 1991).

and allowing them to rule by presidential emergency legislation. After two Chancellors failed, however, Hindenburg was persuaded to appoint Hitler as Chancellor of a coalition government on the understanding that Hitler's ultra-conservative coalition partners would contain him and prevent the implementation of his then all-too-clear agenda.[10]

Not surprisingly, Hitler abused his power over the few key ministries held by his party to arrest and intimidate opponents before calling for new elections.[11] Despite rampant intimidation of other parties and their candidates by the now unchecked Nazi storm troopers, the elections of March 1933 still did not yield an absolute majority for the Nazis.[12] But Hitler's position was now strong enough to pressure *Reichstag* deputies to vote for the *Ermaechtigungsgesetz*, a statute temporarily suspending most aspects of constitutional rule and permitting the government to legislate by decree.[13] By vesting near absolute authority in the government, the *Ermaechtigungsgesetz* effectively nullified the principle of separation of powers. A dictatorship, in the eyes of most contemporaries, had been legalized. Although it is possible to raise technical objections to the constitutional validity of the *Ermaechtigungsgesetz*,[14] the requisite two-thirds majority of deputies in the First Chamber had clearly consented to its passage.[15] A totalitarian regime thus came to power in Germany without clearly violating the strictures of a democratic constitution.[16]

B *The 1991 Algerian elections*

The second example involves Algeria. On December 26, 1991, Algeria held its first multiparty election in thirty years. The Islamic Salvation Front (FIS) won 189 of the 231 parliamentary seats distributed in the first round of the elections. This margin of victory virtually assured the FIS

[10] Details may be found in E. R. Huber, ed., VII *Dokumente Zur Deutschen Verfassungsgeschichte* (Stuttgart: Kohlhammer, 1984), pp. 1052–1265. [11] Nicholls, *supra* note 8, pp. 138–39.
[12] *Ibid.* at 139–40.
[13] *Gesetz zur Behebung der Not von Volk und Reich*, RGBl I 141 (1933), reprinted in Huber, *supra* note 10, p. 665 (Doc. No. 532).
[14] Hans Schneider, "Das Ermaechtigungsgesetz vom 24 Marz 1933," in Gotthard Jasper, ed., *Von Weimar zu Hitler* (Köln: Kiepenheuer and Witsch, 1968), pp. 1930–33, 405, 430.
[15] *See* Ernst Friesenhahn, "Zur Legitimation und zum Scheitern der Weimarer Reichsverfassung," in K. D. Erdmann and H. Schulze, eds., *Weimar, Selbstpreisgabe einer Demokratie* (Düsseldorf: Droste, 1980), pp. 91, 94.
[16] At the time, Germany was not the only country facing a threat from totalitarian parties. Throughout the inter-war years, Fascist and other far-right political parties competed in elections in European states, a number of which attempted to ban or restrict their activities. Karl Loewenstein, "Militant Democracy and Fundamental Rights," *Am. Pol. Sci. Rev.* 31 (1937), pp. 417ff, at pp. 420–24.

of winning sufficient additional seats in the second round to attain the two-thirds parliamentary majority necessary to ratify constitutional amendments.[17] The elections were generally thought to be free from serious irregularities.[18] The FIS, founded in 1989, made clear during the election that if victorious it intended to remake Algeria into an Islamic State. While FIS leaders issued contradictory statements as to whether their plans included holding future elections, several expressed open hostility toward multiparty democracy.[19]

Before the second round of voting could occur, however, President Chadli Benjedid resigned and the Algerian army took effective control of the country. A "High Security Council" announced itself to be in charge and immediately canceled the second phase of the elections.[20] Shortly thereafter, security forces carried out mass arrests of FIS members, restricted political activities at mosques, and effectively shut down several pro-FIS newspapers.[21] A state of emergency was declared on February 9, 1992, and remains in effect to this day.[22]

The government's Minister for Human Rights, Ali Haroun, explained the crack-down as follows:

The FIS, which has at least shown some honesty and frankness in this area, said that it is not democratic, that it is against democracy, that it does not want democracy. It has said that when it takes power there will be no more elections;

---

[17] "Human Rights in Algeria Since the Halt of the Electoral Process," *Middle E. Watch* (Feb. 1992), p. 3.   [18] *Ibid.*
[19] *See generally* Peter A. Samuelson, "Pluralism Betrayed: the Battle Between Secularism and Islam in Algeria's Quest for Democracy," *Yale J. Int'l L.* 20 (1995), 309. For example, in early January FIS leader Imam Abdelkader Moghni told an audience at a mosque, "Islam is light. Why do you fear it? It is in democracy that darkness lies. Those who refuse the light want to create injustice in society," "Human Rights in Algeria," *supra* note 17, 13. FIS deputy chief Ali Belhadj reacted to the prospect of a pluralist Algeria by declaring: "If the Berber activist expresses himself, the communist expresses himself, along with everyone else, then our country will become a battleground of diverse ideologies in contradiction with the hopes of our people." *Ibid.* Other more theoretical, but no less aggressive attacks on democracy by Ali Belhadj are compiled *in* Mustafa Al-Ahnaf *et al.*, eds., *L'Algérie par ses islamistes* (Paris: Karthala, 1991), pp. 87–100. According to one commentator:

> Few were convinced that the FIS, once in power, would respect the multi-party system. Statements by the party such as "democracy is blasphemy" and "no charter, constitution, just the word of Allah" did little to reassure Algerians that the country would be safe in fundamentalist hands. (Alfred Hermida, "Democracy Derailed," *Africa Report*, Mar.–Apr. 1992, p. 14.)

See also II *Weltgeschehen* (Neckar-Verl: Villingen-Schwenningen, 1993), p. 107.
[20] Hermida, *supra* note 19, pp. 14–16.   [21] "Human Rights in Algeria," *supra* note 17, pp. 5–11.
[22] "Algeria Presents Timetable for a Return to Democracy," *N.Y. Times* (June 22, 1993), A9; "Algeria: First Round to the Assassins," *Africa Confidential* (July 3, 1992), p. 7.

there will be the Shura, the religious men who meet together and decide on your behalf ... As a minister of human rights, my question is: who is there to defend the notion of human rights? Am I going to allow a situation where, in a month or two, people will no longer have any rights? I cannot do that. There are currently men in Algeria who are assuming their responsibilities. There is a great part of the population that feels reassured. We are going to take the time to set up real institutions to lead this country toward real democracy – not some pretext of using a democratic process that ends up killing democracy.[23]

C Perspectives on anti-democratic challenges

Both the German and Algerian examples involved elections in which a challenger to the incumbent regime threatened to put an end to free elections once in office. In Germany the challenger succeeded in doing so. In both cases the anti-democratic parties attracted substantial popular support. Germany and Algeria thus present the dilemma of anti-democratic actors in its purest form: a system of free public choice is used by a citizenry to put an end to the possibility of choice in the future. This is not the "tyranny of the majority" problem normally described as the principal threat to human rights in majoritarian systems; in such cases, majorities use their superior numbers to deprive minorities of protected liberties. Here, the majority or plurality chooses to deny *itself* the opportunity of meaningful electoral choice in the future, as well as numerous other associated rights. Counter-majoritarian protections have little relevance to such episodes. While one may point to the rights of those voting *against* anti-democratic parties as minority rights worthy of protection, such rights cannot be defended on the grounds that majority choice must be preserved. For choice has been exercised in such a case, and the majority that is presumptively the holder of such a right has, in effect, chosen not to choose.

The stark alternatives presented to voters in cases such as Germany and Algeria require clear arguments to be made about the essential purpose of an electoral process.[24] Those who would oppose restrictions on participation by extremist parties must explain why the principle of popular sovereignty may permit one generation of voters to ensure that future generations of voters never have the opportunity to select their leaders, save through violent revolution. In blunt terms, opponents of restrictions must explain why an electoral system should be permitted to

[23] "Human Rights in Algeria," *supra* note 17, p. 5.
[24] In Weimar, the Nazis succeeded in mobilizing civil society organizations on their behalf. *See* Sheri Berman, "Civil Society and the Collapse of the Weimar Republic," *World Pol.* 49 (1997), p. 401.

commit suicide. Alternatively, those favoring party restrictions must explain how a commitment to electoral choice requires annulling the choice made by a majority or plurality of voters. If the exercise of popular sovereignty is taken to be an essential legitimating factor for any system of government – in the words of the Universal Declaration, "the will of the people shall be the basis of the authority of government"[25] – then what notion of governmental legitimacy can be invoked to trump "the will of the people" to support an anti-democratic party? Again in blunt terms, it must be explained why rejecting a particular public choice is essential to preserving the process of public choice.[26]

It is the centrality of elections to these two examples that compels such stark questions. Only elections both embody the idea of popular sovereignty and create the potential for its negation. Opposition to elections is thus the paradigmatic form of "anti-democratic" action to be examined in this chapter. But what of actors who favor "anti-democratic" acts of other kinds within a democratic State? Do parties threatening to end elections exhaust the universe of actors threatening democratic institutions? As noted, opposition to the holding of elections is clearly the paradigmatic case; a negation of the process of choice through exercise of the right of choice. But opposition parties may also oppose other human rights or the institutionalized rule of law – two features included in most definitions of liberal democracy. A party may, for example, call for restrictions on the rights of women or an end to judicial independence. As we will see, even where the survival of electoral institutions is not at stake, international law has developed a rather flexible set of standards that assesses not only the threat posed by the opposition party but also the record of the incumbent regime itself. That record must be deemed worthy of protection when weighed against the threat to human rights posed by an opponent. But the core concern has been preserving a system of electoral choice. Most definitions of democracy are substantially broader than the mere holding of elections, as are the claims of many States describing themselves as democratic. But this does not render a focus on elections inappropriate for this analysis, and, more importantly, does not entail adopting an unnecessarily narrow conception of democracy. This is true for three reasons.

The first reason is normative: there is now broadening support for the view that whatever its other attributes, a regime must attain power

---

[25] Universal Declaration of Human Rights, Art. 21(3).
[26] Or, as some would have it, why is it necessary to destroy democracy in order to save it?

through periodic and fair elections to be considered democratic.[27] This view regards elections as the essential procedural connection between individuals (the subjects of all human rights norms) and the political institutions that govern their daily lives. While the principle of popular sovereignty embodied in elections is analytically distinct from the notions of personal dignity and moral autonomy undergirding the protection of individual rights, in practice (according to this view) an elected regime has substantially greater incentives to respect the rights of citizen voters than a regime that need not seek a popular mandate.[28] International organizations have widely adopted this view.[29] Empirically the connection appears correct: States with the worst human rights records are disproportionately governed by unelected regimes.[30]

The second reason is terminological: beginning with Cold-War divisions over the necessity of elections to legitimate governance, the term "democracy" came to be used in human rights law to refer only to majoritarian elections. Other protections of individual liberty, while normally associated with democratic governance, are treated separately as questions of "human rights." Prior to 1989 this division allowed

---

[27] *See*, for example, the comment of the Human Rights Committee that the electoral rights set out in Article 25 of the International Covenant on Civil and Political Rights lie "at the core of democratic government based on the consent of the people and in conformity with the principles of the Covenant." Human Rights Committee, General Comment 25, adopted at the 1510th Mtg (July 12, 1996). Or the observation of the Inter-American Commission on Human Rights that "the concept of representative democracy is based on the principle that it is the people who are the nominal holders of political sovereignty and that, in the exercise of that sovereignty, elects its representatives – in indirect democracies – so that they may exercise political power." Report No. 14/93, Case 10.956 (Mexico) (Oct. 7, 1993), *in Annual Report of the Inter-American Commission on Human Rights 1993* (1994), p. 269. Or the holding of the European Court of Human Rights that freedom to form political parties seeking elected office for their candidates plays "an essential role in ensuring pluralism and the proper functioning of democracy." Case of the Socialist Party and Others v. Turkey, Case 20/1997/804/1007, para. 41 (May 25, 1998).

[28] In the case of women, for example, the Committee on the Elimination of Discrimination Against Women has noted: "The examination of states parties reports show that where there is full and equal participation of women in public life and decision-making, the implementation of their rights and compliance with the [women's] convention improves." General Recommendation 22 (1995), para. 14, reprinted in *Int'l Hum. Rts. Rep.* 5 (1998), p. 6.

[29] The Inter-American Commission's views are representative:

the concept of representative democracy is founded upon the principle that it is the people who have political sovereignty; exercising that sovereignty, they elect their representatives – in indirect democracies – to exercise political power. These representatives, moreover, are elected by the citizens to apply certain policy measures, which in turn means that the nature of the policies to be applied has been widely debated – freedom of thought – among organized political groups – freedom of association – that have had an opportunity to voice their opinions and assemble publicly – right of assembly. (*Annual Report of the Inter-American Commission on Human Rights 1990–91*, OEA/Ser. L/V/II.79, rev. 1, doc. 12 (1991), p. 5.)

[30] *See* Freedom House, *Freedom in the World 1997–98* (New York: Freedom House, 1998).

eastern-bloc countries and some countries of the south to voice support for human rights without jeopardizing incumbent leadership through the holding of elections. Yet the division continues today and international legal texts are still replete with disjunctive references to democracy *and* human rights.[31] The distinction is not, one should add, without intellectual content. It is familiar to American constitutional theorists as the distinction between majoritarian and counter-majoritarian rights.[32] Others, writing in a broader context, refer to the "democratic" and "liberal" aspects of governance.[33] Whatever terminology is employed, it is important to note that the persistence of this distinction in human rights law does not have the effect of diminishing the total quantum of protected individual rights. Related rights have simply been redeployed in analytically distinct categories.

Third, a focus on opposition to elections is appropriate for reasons of political dynamics. An election is a defining moment in a country's political life. During a campaign, all manner of ideological, personal, ethnic, and other conflicts come to a head. Long-time incumbents may be forced from power, as in the 1986 Philippine elections, or familiar figures may be returned to office, as in the reelection of former Communists in Poland.[34] Claims of authenticity and legitimacy are tested against the empirical data of electoral results. At election time, in short, societies are faced with unique moments of introspection and choice. By opposing elections anti-democratic actors deny societies recourse to this important exercise.

---

[31] Examples could be cited *ad infinitum*. *See* Final Declaration and Action Plan on Human Rights and Democracy of the Council of Europe's Second Summit Meeting of Heads of State and Governments 1997, *reprinted in Int'l Hum. Rts. Rep.* 5 (1998), 581 (reaffirming commitment to "pluralist democracy, respect for human rights, the rule of law"); Treaty on European Union, Art. 130(u)(2) (Community policy in the sphere of development cooperation "shall contribute to the general objective of developing and consolidating democracy and the rule of law, and to that of respecting human rights and fundamental freedoms"); European Commission for Democracy through Law, "Opinion on the Constitutional Situation in Bosnia and Herzegovina with Particular Regard to Human Rights Protection Mechanisms," *reprinted in Human Rts. L.J.* 18 (1997), pp. 297, 298 ("[h]uman rights – along with the right to free elections and freedom of movement of person, goods, services and capital throughout the country ... are at the centre of the Dayton Agreement"); Organization of American States, *Santiago Commitment to Democracy and the Renewal of the Inter-American System* (June 4, 1991) (declaring commitment "to the defense and promotion of representative democracy and human rights in the region"); World Conference on Human Rights, *Vienna Declaration and Programme of Action*, UN Doc. A/Conf.157/23, Part I, para. 8 (1993) ("[d]emocracy, development and respect for human rights and fundamental freedoms are interdependent and mutually reinforcing.")

[32] *See* John Hart Ely, *Democracy and Distrust* (Cambridge, Mass.: Harvard University Press, 1980).

[33] Zakaria, *supra* note 6, p. 24–26.

[34] *National Democratic Institute for International Affairs, Forming the Philippine Electoral Process: Developments 1986–88* (NDI 1991); Alexander Smolar, "Poland's Emerging Party System" *J. Dem.* 9 (April 1998), p. 122.

Such a focus on elections does not tie our conclusions to a single political model or dynamic. The demise of the Weimer Republic suggests that threats to liberal regimes may arise not only, as in Algeria, when a single radical party wins or threatens to win an absolute majority of seats in parliament, but also in a variety of circumstances when democrats become demoralized[35] or are caught between competing extremist forces.[36] Moreover, our own survey of State practice covers a broad cross-section of States describing themselves as democratic. As will be seen, these data reveal not only a diversity of political settings in which threats arise but a wide divergence in the way evidence of a potential threat is received. In a widely noted statement, for example, Hitler swore under oath in court that he would seek power only by constitutional means.[37] Even the *Ermaechtigungsgesetz* provided that elections would be held after the expiration of the current electoral period. On paper, at least, the events of 1933 did not put an end to democracy in Germany.[38]

III THEORIES OF DEMOCRATIC TOLERANCE

The rise of totalitarian movements after World War I spurred many democratic theorists to address the question of whether or not to tolerate anti-democratic actors. This is perhaps the central paradox of democratic regimes: to suppress anti-democratic movements infringes notions of tolerance at the heart of the democratic ideal, but to allow them endangers the survival of the very system institutionalizing

---

[35] Friesenhahn, *supra* note 15, p. 108.
[36] Kurt Sontheimer, *Antidemokratisches Denken in der Weimarer Republik* (Munich: Nymphenburger Verlagsbuchhandlung, 1962), pp. 391–400.
[37] In September 1930 Hitler was called to testify at the trial of three army officers accused of high treason for infiltrating the army with Nazi propaganda. He stated:

> The national-socialist movement will try to attain its aims in this state by constitutional means. The constitution only prescribes the methods but not the goal. We will try to obtain the necessary majorities in the legislative bodies by constitutional means in order to mold the state, once we have succeeded, into the form which conforms to our ideas.

Herbert Michaelis, "Ursachen und Folgen – vom deutschen Zusammenbruch 1918 und 1945 bis zur staatlichen Neuordnung Deutschlands," *in Die Gegenwart* (Berlin: Wendler, 1962), p. 532. As to Hitler's "legality tactics" generally, *see* Karl Dietrich Bracher, *Die Aufloesung Der Weimarer Republik* (Villingen: Ring-Verlag, 5th edn., 1971), pp. 110–15.
[38] Dissenting in the Dennis case, Justice Douglas took an explicitly comparativist (though today, rather condescending) view of the issue:

> Some nations less resilient than the United States, where illiteracy is high and where democratic traditions are only budding, might have to take drastic steps and jail these men merely for speaking their creed. But in America they are miserable merchants of unwanted ideas; their wares remain unsold. The fact that their ideas are abhorrent does not make them powerful. Dennis v. United States, 341 US 494, 588–89 (1951) (Douglas, J., dissenting).

principles of tolerance.[39] On this fundamental question democratic theory has broken into two broad camps.

A Procedural democracy

The first model defines democracy as fundamentally a set of procedures. In Joseph Schumpeter's classic formulation, democracy is that "institutional arrangement for arriving at political decisions in which individuals acquire the power to decide by means of a competitive struggle for the people's vote."[40] Its rather formal character derives from its Enlightenment roots as a reaction against societies based on religious orthodoxy and the authority of a single moral order. In their place, theorists of the seventeenth and eighteenth centuries invoked "the figure of reasoning man who might achieve total knowledge, total autonomy, and total power; whose use of reason would enable him to see himself, not God, as the origin of language, the maker of history, and the source of meaning in the world."[41] A legitimate political society embodied the triumph of such rational discourse among citizens on a national scale.

According to the procedural view, because an individual's capacity to reason was sufficient to "enable movement along the path of political enlightenment and progress,"[42] there was little need for government to protect citizens from the influence of anti-rationalist ideas. When rational citizens agree to create a political society, they do not delegate to their government the power to select among the various points of view present in their midst. In giving up its claim to truth, the modern secular political order takes no position when a plurality of truths is asserted.[43]

The procedural model acknowledges that for many citizens such an enforced heterogeneity can become disconcerting. Central organizing truths provide a sense of comfort that a constitutional "agreement to disagree" cannot.[44] In any pluralistic society, therefore, certain groups will continue to agitate for a return to orthodoxy of one form or another, whether political, ethnic, religious, or based on a cult of personality. In order to combat this tendency and remain vital, the procedural view

---

[39] *See generally* Benjamin E. Lippincott, *Democracy's Dilemma: the Totalitarian Party in a Free Society* (New York: Ronald Press, 1965).

[40] Joseph A. Schumpeter, *Capitalism, Socialism and Democracy* (New York: Harper, 2d ed. 1947), p. 269.

[41] Kate Manzo, "Modernist Discourse and the Crisis of Development Theory," *Stud. Comp. Int'l Dev.* 26 (1991), pp. 3, 7.   [42] *Ibid*.

[43] Of course, this begs the question of whether the ethic of tolerance is itself an asserted truth. Democratic States have certainly acted as if this were the case. Few such States take the position that their ideology is no better or worse than any other. *See* W. J. Stankiewicz, *Approaches to Democracy* (London: Edward Arnold, 1980), 100.   [44] Loewenstein, *supra* note 16, 428.

holds that a democratic system must subject itself to continued self-criticism by exploring the value of tolerance.[45] Electoral politics, in the procedural view, is the primary vehicle for this self-examination to occur. Opponents of democracy will be among the likely participants.

By opening the electoral process to its critics, democracy necessarily retains the possibility of failure. This is implicit even in the cherished central image of democratic theory – the social contract – which suggests that pluralistic systems are not somehow ordained *a priori*, but rather arise from a decision of the people. If a popular majority may create a democratic system, it would seem to follow that it should also have the power to disband it.[46] The process itself cannot guarantee that supporters of democracy will always emerge victorious; that is a question of political will.[47] But the procedural view holds that the political will of committed democrats can be considerably strengthened if the alternatives to democracy are debated and, ultimately, better understood.

B *Substantive democracy*

The second view is substantive, defining democracy as not merely the process of ascertaining the preferences of political majorities but a society in which majority rule is made meaningful.[48] The substantive view begins with the proposition that majorities are fluid. In order for citizens to move in and out of the majority as issues change, they must at all times enjoy a core of political rights that ensures effective participation. In this view, democratic procedure is not an end in itself but a means of creating a society in which citizens enjoy certain essential rights, primary among them the right to vote for their leaders.[49]

---

[45] As Thomas Emerson writes: "Even if we consider freedom of expression an absolute value . . . nevertheless it is important that it remain open to challenge. Otherwise it becomes a 'dead dogma,' ill-understood, lacking in vitality, and vulnerable to erosion or full-scale attack." Thomas I. Emerson, *The System of Freedom of Expression* (New York: Random House, 1971), p. 51.
[46] *See* Hans Kelsen, *Vom Wesen und Wert der Demokratie* (Tübingen: Mohr, 2d edn., 1929), pp. 94, 98, 102–03; Emerson, *supra* note 45, pp. 49–50.
[47] *See* Carl Cohen, *Democracy* (Athens, Ga.: University of Georgia Press, 1971), p. 202; Ernst Wolfgang Bœckenfœrde, "Demokratie als Verfassungsprinzip," *in* Josef Isensee and Paul Kirchhof eds., *Handbuch des Staatsrechts der Bundesrepublik Deutschland* (Heidelberg: C.F. Müller Verlag 1987), pp. 1, 912–14.
[48] Ralph Gilbert Ross, "Democracy, Party and Politics," *Ethics* 64 (1953), pp. 100, 120–21.
[49] In the words of the Canadian Supreme Court, "Democracy is not simply concerned with the process of government. On the contrary . . . democracy is fundamentally connected to substantive goals, most importantly, the promotion of self-government . . . Put another way, a sovereign people exercises its right to self-government through democratic procedures." In the Matter of Section 53 of the Supreme Court Act, R.S.C., 1985, C.S-26; and in the Matter of a Reference by the Governor in Council Concerning Certain Questions Relating to the Secession of Quebec from Canada, as set out in Order in Council P.C. 1996–97, dated September 30, 1996 (1998), para. 63.

None of these rights, however, is absolute in the sense that it may be used to abolish the right itself or other basic rights. Thus, an authoritarian party does not achieve legitimacy simply because it enjoys support among the electorate at a given moment. This is true because the principles of justice undergirding a democratic society, while tolerant of virtually all forms of dissent, cannot be understood as permitting their own alienation.[50] Otherwise the principles would become meaningless: they would describe as fundamental a social condition that no longer exists once a totalitarian party takes power. One cannot, it is argued, simultaneously postulate tolerance as the fundamental organizing principle of government and accept the possibility that a group preaching mass intolerance may one day gain control of that government.

Substantive theories of democracy find perhaps their clearest articulation in the writings of John Rawls and Carl Schmitt. Rawls proceeds from an Anglo–American tradition that holds equal liberty of conscience among citizens to be an essential touchstone of any legitimate political order.[51] Tolerance of divergent viewpoints is, of course, the necessary concomitant to preserving equality of conscience among a heterogenous citizenry. As a social contractarian, Rawls holds that citizens simply would not invest a State with authority to choose among particular viewpoints, a power that could work to the detriment of some, most, or all of them.[52] On the other hand, when acceptance of particular views could act to jeopardize the very institution of tolerance itself, then the value of tolerance in such circumstances must be reconsidered.[53]

Under this framework, Rawls examines the problem of "toleration of the intolerant." He asks two central questions. First, does an intolerant group "(have) any title to complain if it is not tolerated"? Rawls answers no: "[a] person's right to complain is limited to violations of principles

---

[50] This argument is commonly phrased as saying that freedom can permit skepticism about all viewpoints save the value of freedom itself. As Carl Auerbach writes:

> (I)f the theory that there are no political orthodoxies is taken to mean that we must also be skeptical about the value of freedom and therefore tolerate freedom's enemies, it will tend to produce, in practice, the very absolutism it was designed to avoid – as experience with modern totalitarianism demonstrates. (Carl A. Auerbach, "The Communist Control Act of 1954: a Proposed Legal–Political Theory of Free Speech," *U. Chi. L. Rev.* 23 (1956), pp. 173, 188.)

[51] Rawls, *supra* note 3.

[52] *Ibid.* at p. 212 ("The government has no authority to render associations either legitimate or illegitimate any more than it has this authority in regard to art or science. These matters are simply not within its competence as defined by a just constitution.")

[53] John Locke gave early expression to this view in his writings on religious tolerance. John Locke, *A Letter Concerning Toleration* (2d edn., Indianapolis, Ind.: Bobbs-Merrill 1955), pp. 14–18, 51 (1689).

he acknowledges himself."[54] Rawls's position can be restated in terms more directly relevant to our problem: if a party announces its intention to suppress minorities once it attains power, claiming justification in an electoral mandate, then that party may be subject to suppression while it is itself in the minority. Such an act would be appropriate because, as Rawls says, it is justified by a principle that both sides accept.

Second, Rawls asks under what conditions a tolerant group has the right not to tolerate those who are intolerant. Rawls answers that intolerance is permissible only where there are "some considerable risks to our own legitimate interests."[55] Short of such a dire threat, tolerant citizens must have faith in the remedial powers of their democratic institutions:

> (T)he natural strength of free institutions must not be forgotten . . . Knowing the inherent stability of a just constitution, members of a well-ordered society have the confidence to limit the freedom of the intolerant only in the special cases when it is necessary for preserving equal liberty itself. [56]

Rawls is willing to invest much time and faith in this "psychological principle" on the assumption that in most cases an intolerant group whose liberties are protected "will tend to lose its intolerance and accept liberty of conscience."[57] But should such tolerant proceduralism fail, Rawls approves of repressive measures against the intolerant not as a suspension of principle but as an application of principles of justice agreed to even by the intolerant in the original position. "What is essential is that when persons with different convictions make conflicting demands on the basic structure as a matter of political principle, they are to judge these claims by the principles of justice."[58] Thus, despite the denial of liberty to a group of citizens, the fundamental organizing principles of justice according to Rawls are, in the end, well-served.

In continental Europe, the most influential critique of a purely procedural understanding of democracy is that of Carl Schmitt. Drawing on writings of the French constitutional theorist Maurice Hauriou,[59] Schmitt suggested an alternative to the procedural positivism and relativism that prevailed in Germany during the Weimar era.[60] In his famous 1932 article *"Legalitaet und Legitimitaet"* ("Legality and Legitimacy"),[61]

---

[54] Rawls, *supra* note 3, p. 217.   [55] *Ibid.* at p. 219.   [56] *Ibid.*   [57] *Ibid.*
[58] *Ibid.* at p. 221.   [59] *See* Maurice Hauriou, *Précis de droit constitutionnel* (Paris: Tenin, 1923), p. 297.
[60] *See* Helmut Steinberger, *Konzeption und Grenzen freiheitlicher Demokratie* (Berlin: Springer, 1974), pp. 208–09.
[61] *See* Carl Schmitt, "Legalität und Legitimæt," *reprinted in* Carl Schmitt, *Verfassungsrechtliche Aufsætze* (Berlin: Duncker and Humblot, 1958), p. 263.

Schmitt made a distinction between the procedural rules in a constitution and its substantive principles. Schmitt claimed that basic substantive principles such as the democratic character of the state were the result of a fundamental decision of the "pouvoir constituant" (the people) and therefore could not be simply swept aside by the "pouvoir constitué" (the elected representatives), even if the procedures for constitutional amendment were followed.[62] Because procedural rules cannot function to abolish the essence of that which they were designed to effectuate, Schmitt maintained, they contain implied limitations. Consequently, in 1933 Schmitt interpreted Hitler's rise to power not as a legal appointment under the Weimar constitution but as a successful revolution.[63]

The idea of constitutions containing an unalterable core received widespread support in Germany after the Second World War.[64] Article 79(3) of the Basic Law (*Grundgesetz*) explicitly provides that articles guaranteeing the dignity of man and the basic principles of government (democracy, rule of law, separation of powers, federalism, social state) cannot be changed by constitutional amendment. The idea of the unalterable core also serves the function of legitimizing legal institutions designed to prevent a democratic constitution from being turned against itself. Thus, Schmitt's views find expression in those provisions of the *Grundgesetz* setting out a procedure for banning anti-democratic parties (Art. 21), for stripping extremist individuals of certain civil rights (Art. 18), and giving every citizen, when no other means are available, the right of resistance against attempts to overturn the constitutional order (Art. 20 (4)).

Schmitt's theory is not limited to democratic constitutions, however, and should therefore be regarded as morally relative.[65] This was borne out by Schmitt's own life. Although he served as a counsel to President Hindenburg until 1932, and supported his efforts to preserve the demo-

---

[62] *See ibid.* at p. 311; *see also* Carl Schmitt, *Verfassungslehre* (Munich: Duncker and Humblot, 1928), pp. 102–12; Carl Schmitt, *Der Hueter der Verfassung* (Tübinger: Mohr, 1931), p. 16.

[63] Carl Schmitt, "Das Gesetz zur Behebung der Not von Volk und Reich," 38 *Deutsche Juristenzeitung* (Heymann: Berlin, 1933), pp. 455–58; Carl Schmitt, *Das Reichsstatthaltergesetz* (Berlin: Heymann, 1933), p. 9.

[64] More recent constitutions embody this idea as well. For example, the Constitution of Bosnia-Herzegovina, drafted as part of the 1995 Dayton Accords, provides in Article X(2): "No amendment to this Constitution may eliminate or diminish any of the rights and freedoms referred to in Article II of this Constitution or alter the present paragraph." Constitution of Bosnia and Herzegovina, 35 ILM 75, p. 125 (1996). Article II contains an extensive list of protected rights and provides that Bosnia shall be a party to the European Convention on Human Rights, which "shall have priority over all other law." *Ibid.* at p. 119.

[65] Steinberger, *supra* note 60, p. 191.

cratic constitution against totalitarian movements,[66] Schmitt became the best-known legal defender of the Nazi regime once Hitler assumed power.[67] While this switch cost Schmitt his position as a university teacher after the Second World War,[68] the influence of his theory of the unalterable core and his parentage of Article 79(3) of the German Basic Law is widely, although sometimes not explicitly, recognized.[69]

C Democratic theory and international norms

What is the value of these two theoretical models – the procedural and substantive conceptions of democracy – to an understanding of international law? Theoretical conceptions of democracy do not possess normative value as such, and in particular, as models of domestic constitutionalism, they have no necessary international normative value. However, discussions of democratic theory do not take place in a political or normative vacuum. Often, by drawing upon ideas expressed in nascent legal rules and political institutions, theoretical discussions serve to crystallize a new conception of democracy arising in a state. The discussion among constitutionalists in Weimar Germany – with its main protagonists Hans Kelsen and Carl Schmitt – was closely followed by an interested public and profoundly influenced popular opinion on the subject.[70] In this sense theoretical discussions often reflect the very practical need of democratic societies to reassess and redefine their identities in times of crisis. In so doing, they generate a practice to which the international lawyer may turn for normative guidance.

In addition, theoretical debate aids the pedagogical task of meaningful classification. The range of possible responses to the problem of democratic intolerance is necessarily limited, even taking into account the many differences among the world's democratic societies. Any thorough discussion of the issue, therefore, will inevitably revert to the level of abstraction represented by the substantive and procedural models, and eventually to those models themselves. This will become apparent

---

[66] J. W. Bendersky, *Carl Schmitt: Theorist for the Reich* (Princeton University Press, 1983), pp. 172–91.
[67] *See ibid.* at pp. 195–218; Paul Hirst, *Representative Democracy and its Limits* (Oxford: Polity, 1990), pp. 128–37; David A. J. Richards, "Comparative Revolutionary Constitutionalism: a Research Agenda for Comparative Law," *N.Y.U. J. Int'l L. & Pol.* 26 (1993), pp. 1, 53–59.
[68] Bendersky, *supra* note 66, p. 274.
[69] *See* Guenter Dürig and Theodor Maunz, *Grundgesetz Kommentar*, (Münich: Beck, 1963) Art. 79 nos. 21–25; Friedrich Karl Fromme, *Von der Weimarer Verfassung zum Bonner Grundgesetz* (Tübingen: Mohr, 1960), pp. 179–80; Friesenhahn, *supra* note 15, p. 92; Bendersky, *supra* note 66, pp. 283–84.
[70] Kurt Sontheimer, *Antidemokratisches Denken in der Weimarer Republik* (Munich: Nymphenburger Verlagsbuchhandlung, 1962), pp. 82–84, 94–98, 105–12.

in the next section where we use these two models of democracy as a framework to classify and analyze State practice.

IV THE PRACTICE OF REPRESENTATIVE DEMOCRATIC STATES

In this section we examine national practice among a group of States generally considered democratic, but which at a minimum hold regular elections comporting with international standards of fairness. There is a straightforward reason for limiting our analysis to these States. The general question we address is whether anti-democratic actors (political parties, other groups, or individuals) may be excluded from the political process and, if so, whether such exclusions compromise a State's "democratic" character. The question of whether a State remains democratic after such an act necessarily presupposes that it is already democratic beforehand. Surveying States not considered democratic – specifically, those not holding periodic and fair elections – is simply not helpful in answering this question.

We have classified the States examined according to the substantive and procedural models of democracy outlined in section III. This theoretical typology is only a rough approximation of actual State practice. In an attempt to bring the classification closer to meaningful ideal types, we have further subdivided these two broad categories into "tolerant" (passive) and "militant" (active) categories. These designations allow us to take account not only of a State's formal constitutional framework but also of how its norms regarding anti-democratic actors have been interpreted and implemented over time. Thus, we divide State practice into the following four categories: (1) tolerant procedural democracy; (2) militant procedural democracy; (3) tolerant substantive democracy; and (4) militant substantive democracy.

A Tolerant procedural democracy in the United Kingdom, Botswana, and Japan

1 Procedural democracy in the United Kingdom

The unwritten British constitution rests on the concept of the sovereignty of Parliament.[71] Traditionally, the British Parliament is not bound by any substantive limitations and every Act of Parliament is

---
[71] J. Alder, *Constitutional and Administrative Law* (Munich: Buchhandlung, 1989), pp. 63–67; *see* Manuel v. Attorney-General (1983) 1 ch. 77, p. 89 (appeal taken from Canada).

valid if enacted according to proper procedures.[72] Such legislative supremacy is a formidable obstacle to introducing an anti-majoritarian bill of rights into British law. While an absolutist view of the sovereignty of Parliament is increasingly questioned today, "short of an extreme situation," it is still "very unlikely that the courts would of their volition begin to exercise power derived solely from common law to review the validity of Acts of Parliament."[73] Therefore, the United Kingdom still appears to adhere to a purely procedural model of democracy.

This lack of written substantive principles, on the other hand, allows the British government substantial latitude in confronting anti-democratic actors. In practice, though, the British Parliament has only enacted laws empowering the government to dissolve certain groups – including political parties – if they pose a threat of violent behavior. Section 2(1)(b) of the Public Order Act of 1936,[74] for example, criminalizes membership in any association "organized and trained or organized and equipped either for the purpose of enabling them to be employed for the use or display of physical force in promoting any political object." And according to Section 28(2) of the Northern Ireland (Emergency Provisions) Act of 1991,[75] the Secretary of State may proscribe "any organization that appears to him to be concerned in terrorism or in promoting or encouraging it."[76]

In the scheme of possible restrictions on political actors these provisions are fairly benign.[77] Not only do they require that the groups engage in or support actual physical violence, but the application of these laws has been measured and restrained. Although the British government would clearly have had the power to dissolve Sinn Fein – a party which openly sided with the outlawed Irish Republican Army – it has refrained from doing so.[78] The threat posed by anti-democratic actors is perhaps minimized by Britain's "first past the post" electoral system, based on single-member electoral districts, which acts as an efficient barrier to extremist parties becoming serious contenders for political power.

---

[72] E. C. S. Wade and A. W. Bradley, *Constitutional and Administrative Law* (New York: Longman, 11th edn. 1993), pp. 68–81. This remains true even after Britain's adoption of the ECHR as the British Bill of Rights.   [73] *Ibid.* at p. 75.   [74] Public Order Act, 1 Edw. 8 & 1 Geo. 6, ch. 6, § 2 (1936) (Eng.).
[75] Northern Ireland Act (Emergency Provisions Act), 1991, ch. 24 (Eng.).
[76] *Ibid.* A number of organizations are already proscribed by the Act. See § 28(2) and sched. 2. *Ibid.* These rules were first embodied in the 1974 Prevention of Terrorism Act.
[77] Compare the legal restrictions in Britain with the more militant restrictions described *infra* section IV (D).
[78] Gordon Smith, "Die Institution der politischen Partei in Grossbritannien," *in* Dimitris Tsatsos *et al.*, eds., *Parteienrecht im Europäischen Vergleich* (Baden-Baden: Nomos-Verlagsgesellschaft, 1990), pp. 304, 329.

2 Procedural democracy in Botswana

Like the United Kingdom, the Republic of Botswana has maintained a democratic system which has remained officially tolerant with respect to anti-democratic actors since its independence in 1966. Botswana's constitutional provisions on freedom of expression and association provide that those rights may be restricted if "reasonably justifiable in a democratic society."[79] These clauses have not, however, been invoked to suppress anti-democratic parties.[80] The remarkable atmosphere of relative cooperation and mutual trust that has marked Botswanan politics is no doubt responsible for the absence of extremist groups and any laws designed to restrict their activities.[81] The procedural character of Botswanan democracy is further evidenced by a lack of restrictions on the scope of constitutional amendments.[82]

3 Procedural democracy in Japan[83]

The procedural character of the Japanese system is evident in two clauses of the Japanese constitution that might conceivably justify party restrictions. The first provides that the people "shall refrain from any abuse" of constitutional freedoms and rights.[84] The second, which renounces war as a sovereign right of the nation,[85] has been interpreted as "excluding antidemocratic militarism from national politics and governmental power."[86] Most Japanese constitutional scholars agree, however, that the lack of a clause explicitly permitting restrictions and the presence of a guarantee of freedom of association would likely render legislation authorizing a ban on a party unconstitutional.[87] In addition, the Japanese Political Finance Control Law does not contain a procedure for excluding political parties from participating in the electo-

---

[79] Bots Const. ch. II, §§ 12, 13.
[80] *See* John D. Holm, "Botswana: One African Success Story," *Current Hist.* 93 (1994), pp. 198, 200–01; John Holm and Patrick Molutsi, eds., *Democracy in Botswana* (Athens, Ohio: Ohio University Press, 1989), p. 167; National Democratic Institute for International Affairs, Democracies in Regions of Crisis: Botswana, Costa Rica, Israel (Washington, D.C.: NDI, 1990), pp. 89–120.
[81] *See* National Democratic Institute for International Affairs, *supra* note 80, p. 109; James J. Zaffiro, "The Press and Political Opposition in an African Democracy: The Case of Botswana," *J. Commonwealth & Comp. Pol.* 27 (1989), pp. 51–73.   [82] Bots Const. ch. V, pt. IV, § 89.
[83] We would like to thank Akiho Shibata, former Senior Fellow of the Center for International Studies at New York University Law School, for his assistance in providing information for this section.   [84] Kenpo (Constitution) ch. III, Art. 12 (Japan).   [85] *Ibid.* at ch. II, § 9.
[86] Lawrence W. Beer, "Constitutionalism and Rights in Japan and Korea," *in* Louis Henkin and Albert J. Rosenthal, eds., *Constitutionalism and Rights* (New York: Columbia University Press, 1990), pp. 225, 235.   [87] Koji Sato, *The Constitution* (Tokyo: Seirin Shoin, 1981), pp. 96–97.

ral process.[88] Despite constitutional provisions to the contrary, the Japanese system operates as a procedural democracy.

B Militant procedural democracy in the United States

Like the United Kingdom, Botswana, and Japan, the United States practices a procedural form of democracy. One clear line of demarcation between "militant" and "tolerant" systems is whether the national constitution can be amended to alter or eliminate democratic institutions. As we will see, a number of constitutions contain seemingly paradoxical clauses which provide that certain basic structures cannot be altered, even by amendment. In the United States, however, no rule precludes the remote possibility of amending the Constitution to abolish the republican form of government.[89] In *The Federalist*, Alexander Hamilton declared that it is a "fundamental principle of republican government" to allow "the people to alter or abolish the established Constitution, whenever they find it inconsistent with their happiness."[90]

Yet despite a professed commitment to open political competition regarded by some as the primary justification for judicial review,[91] the United States has enacted qualitatively more restrictive anti-subversion legislation than the United Kingdom. Three major statutes, all products of hot and cold wars, have been designed to frustrate the activities of allegedly subversive parties.[92] The Smith Act of 1940 parallels British

---

[88] Martin E. Weinstein, "Japan," *in* George E. Dulry, ed., *World Encyclopedia of Political Systems and Parties*, (New York: Facts on File, 2nd edn., 1987), p. 608.

[89] Two areas of the United States Constitution are explicitly unamendable, though neither preserves representative government *in toto*. Article v prohibits amendments concerning certain slavery issues and the equality of state representation in the Senate. US Const., Art. v. Article IV, section 4 of the Constitution, which provides that "(t)he United States shall guarantee to every State in this Union a Republican Form of Government," addresses only the federal government's obligation to states, but not its obligation to itself or the alteration of that obligation by amendment. (US Const. art. IV, § 4). Moreover, any claim that the "guarantee clause" does make the form of state government immutable would almost certainly be dismissed by the federal courts as a non-justiciable political question. *See* Pac. States Tel. & Tel. Co. v. Oregon, 223 US 118 (1912); Luther v. Borden, 48 US (7 How.) 1 (1849). For a discussion of possible implied limitations on the amending power, especially where the Bill of Rights is concerned, *see* John R. Vile, *Contemporary Questions Surrounding the Constitutional Amending Process* (1993), pp. 127–46.

[90] Alexander Hamilton, *in* Benjamin Fletcher Wright, ed., *The Federalist* 78 (Cambridge, Mass.: Harvard University Press, 1961) p. 494.   [91] *See* Ely, *supra* note 32, p. 106.

[92] A fourth, the Espionage Act of 1917, was used to prosecute Eugene V. Debs, the Socialist party candidate for President in 1920. *See* Debs v. United States, 249 US 211 (1919). The Debs case and other prosecutions under the Espionage Act, however, were limited by the terms of the statute to times of war. *See* Espionage Act, ch. 30, § 3, 40 Stat. 217, 219 (1917), codified as 18 US.C. § 2388 (1988).

legislation by criminalizing membership in groups dedicated to overthrowing the United States government by force.[93] Ten years later, the Internal Security Act of 1950 abandoned the requirement of showing an actual or imminent threat to the democratic system by establishing a registration system for parties designated as "subversive" by the Subversive Activities Control Board.[94] And finally, the Communist Control Act of 1954 divested the Communist party of the United States (CPUSA), and any of its successors, of all rights and privileges under state and federal law.[95] Although these statutes have not been invalidated, they have not been the basis for any reported prosecutions since the early 1960s.[96]

Because the United States Constitution does not explicitly guarantee freedom of association, these statutes have been challenged under the First Amendment as violations of free speech. In reviewing convictions under these statutes, the United States Supreme Court has generally distinguished protected speech about anti-democratic activity from unprotected incitement to action against democratic institutions.[97] In early cases involving the CPUSA, the Court declined to consider whether the party was by its nature dedicated to overthrowing the government. Instead, the Court chose to take judicial notice of the party's goals[98] or to give deference to congressional findings.[99] Later, the Court began to require specific evidence that individual defendants were active members of the CPUSA and had knowledge of its illegal activity.[100]

Nevertheless, the Court has consistently upheld the core of these statutes as legitimate acts of preemptive self-defense by a democratic society[101] under an evolving standard.[102] This judicial confirmation of

---

[93] 18 US.C. § 2385 (1982).   [94] 50 US.C. §§ 781–835 (1991).   [95] 50 US.C. §§ 841–44 (1991).
[96] *See, e.g.*, United States v. Robel, 389 US 258 (1967); Communist Party of United States v. United States, 384 F.2d 957 (D.C. Cir.1967).
[97] *See* Laurence H. Tribe, *American Constitutional Law* (Mineola: Foundation Press, N.Y., 2d edn. 1988), p. 841.   [98] Dennis v. United States, 341 US 494, 510–11 (1950).
[99] Communist Party of the United States v. Subversive Activities Control Board, 367 US 1, 93–94 (1960). Congress had declared that "a world Communist movement" existed, whose goal was "to establish a Communist totalitarian dictatorship in the countries throughout the world" and that in the United States members of the Communist party "in effect transfer their allegiance to the foreign country in which is vested the direction and control of the world Communist movement." (50 USC. §§ 781(1) & (9) (1991)).
[100] Robel, 389 US p. 262 (1967); Aptheker v. Secretary of State, 378 US 500, 511 n.9 (1964); Scales v. United States, 367 US 203, 229 (1961); Yates v. United States, 354 US 298, 318–27 (1957).
[101] Dennis, 341 US, p. 509.
[102] The standard used early in the century to uphold convictions under the 1917 Espionage Act was the existence of a clear and present danger. Schenck v. United States, 249 US 47, 52 (1919). The standard was later modified in Dennis to require the courts to "ask whether the gravity of the 'evil,' discounted by its improbability, justifies such invasion of free speech as is necessary to avoid the danger." (Dennis, 341 US, p. 510).

anti-subversive legislation makes it possible to speak of the United States as a militant procedural democracy, although it has become progressively less so since the 1950s. In its more recent jurisprudence, the Court has heightened its scrutiny, returning to its original "clear and present danger" standard. For example, the Court has held that lawful advocacy becomes unlawful incitement only "where such advocacy is directed to inciting or producing imminent lawlessness and is likely to incite or produce such action."[103] This significantly enhanced standard of proof has made successful prosecutions extremely difficult.[104]

C Tolerant substantive democracy in France, Canada, and India

1 Substantive democracy in France

In contrast to the American system, Article 89 of the 1958 French constitution explicitly provides that "the republican form of government shall not be subject to amendment."[105] Article 4 of the constitution provides that all political parties must respect the principles of national sovereignty and of democracy.[106] While a number of French scholars have questioned the legal force of these articles,[107] it is nevertheless clear that French law manifests several elements of a substantive model of democracy.

None of the various French constitutions have explicitly guaranteed the right of association, though the legislature proclaimed this right and circumscribed its limitations by statute in 1901.[108] It was only in 1971 that the *Conseil Constitutionnel* declared in a landmark decision that certain core principles ("*principes fondamentaux*") of civil rights, including the right of association, may not be infringed by parliament.[109] The precise impact of this judgment is not entirely clear. Nevertheless, because political parties owe a constitutional duty to respect the principle of

---

[103] Brandenburg v. Ohio, 395 US 444, 447 (1968).
[104] The Supreme Court has reinforced the procedural nature of First Amendment theory by striking down a "hate speech" ordinance as impermissible content regulation. R.A.V. v. St. Paul, 112 S.Ct. 2538 (1992). [105] La Constitution de la France (Oct. 4, 1958) *titre* XIV, Art. 89.
[106] *Ibid.* at Art. 4, p. 53 ("Les partis et groupements politiques . . . doivent respecter les principes de la souveraineté nationale et de la démocratie.")
[107] *See e.g.*, Dimitri Georges Lavroff, *Le droit constitutionnel de la Ve République*, p. 379 (Paris: Dalloz, 2nd edn., 1997); Charles Debbasch *et al.*, *Droit constitutionnel et institutions politiques* (Paris: Economica, 3rd edn., 1990), p. 93; Jean-Louis Seurin, Art. 4 *in* Francois Luchaire and Gérard Conac, *La constitution de la République Francaise* (Paris: Economica, 2nd edn., 1987), pp. 213, 215–16.
[108] Law of July 1, 1901 (J.O. July 2, 1901) 4025–27; *see* Jacques Robert, *Libertés publics et droits de l'homme*, Paris (Paris: Montchrestien, 4th edn. 1988), pp. 94, 584–604.
[109] Judgment of July 16, 1971, Conseil Constitutionnel, 29.

democracy (Article 4), it appears that behavior threatening the democratic process would not be protected by the *Conseil Constitutionnel* as a core element of the right of association.

Article 3 of the 1901 law provides that any association that intends "to infringe on the republican form of government is null and void," as pronounced *ex officio* by a civil court.[110] In practice, a prohibition under the law of 1901 has never taken place. The same is not true of a 1936 law that gives the President of the Republic the power to dissolve groups that: (1) provoke armed demonstrations, (2) are of a paramilitary nature, or (3) have as their goal the dismemberment of the territorial State, the forceful overthrow of the republican form of government, the instigation of racial or other group discrimination, or the dissemination of propaganda promoting such discrimination.[111] This rather imprecisely worded statute[112] has frequently[113] been invoked by French Presidents against small groups on the political fringe,[114] though it is clear the statute could also be applied against major political parties.[115] The highest French administrative court, the *Conseil d'Etat*, is empowered to review the President's action. The court has interpreted the 1936 law rather broadly. For instance, the court has held that a group need not pose a threat of violent behavior to come within the law's purview if, for example, its platform or published views question the integrity of the national territory. Accordingly, the *Conseil d'Etat* has affirmed the dissolution of parties and groups based solely on their secessionist goals.[116]

2 Substantive democracy in Canada

Canada can also be labeled a tolerant substantive democracy. A new Charter on Rights and Freedoms for Canada came into force by act of the British Parliament in 1982. While section 2 of the Charter guarantees both freedom of expression and of association, section 1 provides that those rights are subject to "such reasonable limits prescribed by law

---

[110] *See ibid.* at 588.   [111] Law of Jan. 10, 1936 (J.O. Jan. 13, 1936, p. 522) Art. 1.
[112] *See* Jean-Jacques Israel, Art. 4, *in* Luchaire and Conac, *supra* note 107, p. 218.
[113] The *Conseil d'Etat* reviewed nineteen dissolution decisions between 1955 and 1995. *See* (1955–64) Conseil D'Etat, Tables Décennales, (1965–1974). *See* Conseil D'Etat, Tables Decennales, *passim*.
[114] *See* Michel Fromont, "Die Institution der politischen Partei in Frankreich," *in* D. Tsatsos, D. Schefold and H.-P. Schneider, eds., *Parteienrecht im europäischen Vergleich*, (Baden-Baden: Nomos Verlagsgesellschaft, 1990), p. 219.   [115] *See* Israel, *in* Luchaire and Conac, *supra* note 107, p. 218.
[116] Judgment of Oct. 16, 1992 (Battesti) Conseil d'Etat, Lebon 371 (Fr.) (self-determination for the Corsican people); Judgment of Oct. 8, 1975 (Association Enbata), Conseil d'Etat, Lebon 494 (Fr.) (seeking to "liberate" the French part of the basque country from the "domination" of the French State); Judgment of Jan. 9, 1959 (Sieurs Huang-Xuan Man), Conseil d'Etat, Lebon 25 (disseminating propaganda hostile to French sovereignty over Indochina); Judgment of July 15, 164 (Dame Tapua et autres), Conseil d'Etat, Lebon 407 (Fr.) (political party in Tahiti seeking to found an independent Polynesian republic).

as can be demonstrably justified in a free and democratic society." In the *Oakes case*, the Canadian Supreme Court analyzed section 1 restrictions through a two-pronged test: (1) the objective served must be of sufficient importance to warrant overriding a protected right or freedom; and (2) the means chosen must be reasonable and demonstrably justified.[117]

Section 1 has never been invoked to justify restrictions on political parties, although prior to the enactment of the Charter Canada had placed severe restrictions on communist party activities, and in 1970 it declared the *Front de Liberation de Quebec* an illegal organization.[118] During the Charter era, the controversy most relevant to party restrictions has been the attempted regulation of so-called "hate speech." In 1990 the Canadian Supreme Court heard three cases challenging the constitutionality of statutory provisions criminalizing speech which fosters hatred against persons based on their group status.[119] Following the *Oakes* test, the Court first found an overriding societal interest in combating the sense of inequality fostered by hate speech, which, it held "erod(es) the tolerance and open-mindedness that must flourish in a multicultural society which is committed to the idea of equality."[120] Second, the Court found the legislative restrictions both reasonable and justifiable, primarily on the grounds that the hate speech targeted was "only tenuously connected to the values underlying the freedom of speech" and its suppression engendered minimal cost to Canadian democracy.[121]

The hate-speech decisions would seem clear precedent for the constitutionality of self-protection legislation in Canada. The Supreme Court has opted for a strongly substantive model of democracy, viewing free speech as a contingent value which may, at certain crucial moments, erode rather than enhance fundamental democratic principles.[122] Some

---

[117] Regina v. Oakes, 19 C.R.R. 308, 311 (1986).
[118] *See* J. Patrick Boyer, *Election Law in Canada* 1 (Toronto: Butterworths, 1987), pp. 19–24; Thomas R. Berger, *Fragile Freedoms: Human Rights and Dissent in Canada* (Toronto: Clarke, Irwin, 1981), pp. 127–62.
[119] *See* Criminal Code § 319(2) (targeting those "who, by communicating statements, other than in private conversation, wilfully promote hatred against any identifiable group"); Canadian Human Rights Act § 13(1) (concerning telephone communications) (1976–77).
[120] Taylor and W Guard Party v. Canadian Human Rights Comm'n, 3 C.R.R. (2d) (1990), pp. 116, 134; *see also* Regina v. Keegstra, 3 C.R.R. (2d), pp. 226–29; Regina v. Andrews, 3 C.R.R. (2d) (1990), pp. 176, 188. The emphasis on equality over absolutist notions of liberty pervades Canadian constitutional law. *See* section 27 of the Charter.   [121] Keegstra, 3 C.R.R. (2d), pp. 256–57.
[122] *See ibid.* at p. 237 (while dissent must be allowed to flourish "it is equally destructive of free expression values, as well as the other values which underlie a free and democratic society, to treat all expression as equally crucial to those principles" embodied in the Charter); *ibid.* at p. 240 ("(e)xpression can work to undermine our commitment to democracy where employed to propagate ideas anathemic to democratic values.")

Canadian commentators have argued that suppressing anti-democratic parties will only increase their allure.[123] But this is a question of tactics. Doctrinally, self-protection legislation in Canada would appear to have a firm constitutional footing.

3 Substantive democracy in India

The Indian Supreme Court is granted the power of judicial review under Article 132(1) of the Indian Constitution, thereby enabling it to protect the fundamental rights set out in Articles 12–35. One of these rights is the freedom of all citizens "to form associations or unions,"[124] subject to "reasonable restrictions" which are enacted by law "in the interests of the sovereignty and integrity of India or public order or morality."[125] As in Canada, the right of association in India is formulated in general terms and applies to political parties as well as to all other associations. Unlike Canada, however, in India the Supreme Court has rendered an important decision concerning the prohibition of political parties.

At issue in the 1952 case, *State of Madras v. V.G. Row*,[126] was an order issued by the state government of Madras declaring the "Peoples Education Society" unlawful. The government relied on a 1908 law which gave it the power, after obtaining the consent of an advisory board, to declare an association unlawful if in the opinion of a provincial government, it: (1) interferes or has for its object interfering with the administration of the law, (2) does so with regard to the public order, or (3) constitutes a danger to the public peace.[127] The government argued that it had obtained information indicating the Society was actively engaged in helping the banned Communist party.[128] The question for the Court was whether these restrictions met the constitutional requirement of reasonableness.

The Indian Court observed that "reasonableness" could not be defined in the abstract, but must be gleaned from the circumstances surrounding enactment of each restriction. The Court expressed considerable reluctance to challenge the judgment of the legislature, since the people's elected representatives had clearly found the restrictions reasonable.[129] Nevertheless, the Court struck down the statute because the legislature had failed to provide for sufficient procedural safeguards in the application of a ban:

---

[123] Boyer, *supra* note 118, p. 20.   [124] India Const., Art. 19, § 1 (c).   [125] *Ibid.* at Art. 19, § 4.
[126] State of Madras v. V.G. Row, 1952 S.C.R. 597 (1952).   [127] Madras, 1952 SC.R., p. 601.
[128] *Ibid.*   [129] *Ibid.*

The formula of subjective satisfaction of the Government or of its officers, with an Advisory Board thrown in to review the materials on which the Government seeks to override a basic freedom guaranteed to the citizen, may be viewed as reasonable only in very exceptional circumstances and within the narrowest limits, and cannot receive judicial approval as a general pattern of reasonable restrictions on fundamental rights.[130]

Despite its ultimate holding, the Madras opinion seems to allow for a wide range of party prohibitions. The Indian Court's main concern was ensuring the possibility of judicial review of the factual basis for a ban; it had little to say about the actual deprivation of rights. Indeed, the Court's emphasis on the need for judicial review of the factual basis for bans is clearly incompatible with holding bans to be unconstitutional in themselves. In the end, the Indian Court's approach was a substantive one. This is confirmed by other decisions of the Court holding that Parliament's power to amend the Indian Constitution does not extend to dismantling fundamental features of the government, such as the separation of powers or its republican form.[131]

D Militant substantive democracy: Germany, Israel, and Costa Rica

1 Militant substantive democracy in Germany

When the West German *Grundgesetz* (the "Basic Law," which is now the constitution of unified Germany) was drafted in 1948–49, two overarching factors influenced its content: the fresh memory of the Nazi-regime and the knowledge that an authoritarian regime was rapidly consolidating power in the East. These factors are widely seen as having led to the *Grundgesetz* containing several provisions described by the Federal Constitutional Court (*Bundesverfassungsgericht*) as expressing the principle of "militant democracy."[132] These include Article 79(3), according to which several core principles (including that of representative democracy) are unalterable even by constitutional amendment, and Article 9(2), according to which all associations whose purposes or activities violate criminal law or are directed against the constitutional order may be prohibited.

---

[130] *Ibid.* at p. 607–08.
[131] *See* Kesavananda v. State of Charily, 1973 A.I.R. (S.C.) 1461, 1535 (1973); Sunder Roman, *Constitutional Amendments in India* (Calcutta: Eastern Law House, 1989), pp. 1–18.
[132] *See* Communist Party Case, 5 BVerfGE 85, 139 (1956), *translated in* Donald Kommers, *The Constitutional Jurisprudence of the Federal Republic of Germany* (Durham: Duke University Press, 1989), p. 228.

A group to which a dissolution order is addressed must challenge the order in court. If, however, the group is a political party, the dissolution order is initiated by the federal government filing an application with the *Bundesverfassungsgericht*.[133] The Court will order dissolution upon a finding that parties "by reason of their aims or the behavior of their adherents, seek to impair or abolish the free democratic basic order or to endanger the existence of the Federal Republic of Germany..."[134] A similar procedure appears in Article 18, according to which individuals may forfeit certain fundamental rights if they have used those rights to combat the "free democratic basic order."

The most important differences between the French and the German systems lie not in the written law, but in their interpretation and application. In post-war France, no association or political party has been dissolved without a showing that it either posed a threat of violent behavior or pursued secessionist goals. In Germany, by contrast, two prominent and non-violent political parties were declared unconstitutional by the *Bundesverfassungsgericht*: the neo-Nazi *Sozialistische Reichspartei* in 1952,[135] and the German Communist party in 1956.[136] In the first case, the *Bundesverfassungsgericht* reached its conclusion based exclusively on the party's platform.[137] In the second, the Court adopted a higher standard of proof, requiring that the party adopt "a fixed purpose constantly and resolutely to combat the free democratic basic order" and that it manifest this purpose "in political action according to a fixed plan of action."[138] This seemingly objective standard, though formulated in terms of actual danger to the democratic system, does not require evidence of imminent harm. The focus is on a party's attitude as revealed by its conduct. Proof of a concrete undertaking to that end, or evidence of an actual danger to the democratic system, is not necessary.[139]

The instruments of "militant democracy" continued to play a role in Germany after the prohibition of the Communist party. In the 1960s, the federal government brought applications for the forfeiture of fundamental rights against two individuals.[140] In the 1970s, the principle of

---

[133] *Ibid.* Art. 21, § 2; *see* generally Paul Franz, "Unconstitutional and Outlawed Political Parties: a German–American Comparison," *B.C. Int'l & Comp. L. Rev.* 5 (1982), p. 51.

[134] Sozialistische Reichspartei Case, 2 BVerfGE 1 (1952), *translated in* Kommers, *supra* note 132, p. 509.   [135] *Ibid.*   [136] Communist Party Case, *supra* note 132.   [137] *Ibid.* at 244.

[138] Communist Party Case, 5 BVerfGE 85, p. 141, *translated in* Kommers, *supra* note 132, p. 228.

[139] In the Communist Party Case the Court relied on the party's program, its official declarations, the statements of its leaders, and its educational materials. *See ibid.*

[140] 11 BVerfGE 282 (1960); 38 BVerfGE 23 (1974). The government later chose not to pursue the cases and the applications were eventually dismissed.

militant democracy played an important role in a debate over disloyal public servants.[141] In the early 1990s, the rise of right-wing violence following reunification prompted the federal government to dissolve several organizations under Article 9(2) of the *Grundgesetz*.[142] Applications by the federal government to have several small neo-Nazi organizations dissolved under the party prohibition clause, however, were rejected by *Bundesverfassungsgericht*. Because these organizations had not made serious efforts to seek elected office, the Court held, they were too insignificant to qualify as political parties.[143] However, the Court did not preclude the possibility that these groups might be dissolved under Article 9(2) of the *Grundgesetz*.

2 Militant substantive democracy in Israel

Like the United Kingdom, Israel does not possess a formal constitution. However, the Israeli Knesset has passed several so-called Basic Laws which do not rank higher than ordinary laws but nonetheless possess some constitutional significance. According to Section 7A of the Basic Law on the Knesset, a party "shall not participate in elections to the Knesset if its objectives or actions entail, explicitly or implicitly, one of the following: (1) a denial of the existence of the State of Israel as the State of the Jewish nation, (2) a denial of the democratic character of the state, (3) incitement to racism."[144]

This basic law only excludes political parties from elections and not from political life altogether. Its essential feature is a loosely phrased test focusing on the goals or organizing principles of a party. This attitude-based standard thus mirrors Article 21(2) of the German *Grundgesetz*. Section 7A was enacted in response to a 1984 decision of the Israeli Supreme Court which had found no legal basis for the Israeli Election Commission having barred two political parties from participating in the Knesset elections that year.[145] When the Election Commission, this time acting under the new section 7A, decided to exclude the same two political parties from the next elections, the Israeli Court affirmed its

---

[141] *See* K. H. F. Dyson, "Anti-Communism in the Federal Republic of Germany," *Parl. Aff.* 27 (1975), pp. 51–67.   [142] *See* Philip Kunig, *Vereinsverbot, Parteiverbot Jura* (1995), pp. 384–87.
[143] 91 BVerfGE 262 (1994) and 276 (1994); Wiebke Wietschel, "Unzulässige Parteiverbotsanträge wegen Nichtvorliegens der Parteieigenschaft," *ZRP* 28 (1996), pp. 208–11.
[144] This is an unofficial translation of Basic Law: the Knesset, § 7A, in Dan Gordon, "Limits on Extremist Political Parties: a Comparison of Israeli Jurisprudence with that of the United States and West Germany," *Hastings Int'l & Comp. L. Rev.* 10 (1987), pp. 347, 364 n.117. We would like to thank Judge Itzak Zamir of the Supreme Court of Israel for providing information for this section.   [145] *See* Gordon, *supra* note 144, pp. 35–64.

actions.[146] Not unlike the German *Bundesverfassungsgericht* in the *Communist Party case*, the Israeli court focused on party goals as manifested in concrete actions: it held that in order to meet its burden, the government must prove beyond any doubt, and by clear and unequivocal evidence, that (1) a party has as its dominant and central objective one of the proscribed goals set out in the statute; and (2) that it intends to implement this goal in a concrete manner.[147]

This standard was held to be satisfied by the right-wing Kach party, whose objectives and activities were found to be clearly racist in the sense contemplated by the statute.[148] The test was not satisfied by the other party, which advocated a form of Palestinian nationalism.[149] Thus, the Court seems to have tightened the requirements of the statute by rejecting exclusion of a party solely on the basis of its platform.

3 Militant substantive democracy in Costa Rica

Costa Rica is an example of a militant democracy which has become more tolerant over the years. Originally, Article 98 of its constitution prohibited "the founding or the activity of political parties which for their ideological stance, means of action or international connections try to destroy the foundations of the democratic organization of Costa Rica, or which act against the sovereignty of the country."[150] The Costa Rican Parliament, acting on the basis of this rule, outlawed the Communist party in 1950 by the required two-thirds majority vote.[151] In 1975, however, the formal party-prohibition procedure was abolished by constitutional amendment. Today, Article 98 of the constitution grants citizens "the right to join parties in order to participate in national politics," subject to the restriction "that such parties are committed in their platforms to respect the constitutional order of the republic."

4 Militant substantive democracies in other countries

The laws of several other established democracies also permit restrictions on anti-democratic actors. Both the Italian and Spanish constitutions contain clauses prohibiting the reestablishment of the Fascist

---

[146] Election Appeal 1/88, Naiman v. Chairman of the Central Appeal Committee of the Twelfth Knesset, 42(4) P.D. 177 (1988). [147] Naiman, *supra* note 152.
[148] Jacqueline Gatti-Domenach, "Le Systeme Electoral Israelien," *Revue du Droit Public et de la Science Politique en France et à l'étranger* (1990), pp. 989, 1031–32. [149] *Ibid*.
[150] Quoted in Oscar Aguilar Bulgarelli, *Democracia y Partidos Politicos En Costa Rica* (1950–62), p. 80 (San José, Costa Rica: 1977) (authors' translation). [151] *Ibid*. at 84.

Intolerant democracies 419

party.[152] The Portuguese constitution prohibits all paramilitary associations which adhere to a Fascist ideology.[153] In Finland, a group can only register as a political party if it demonstrates, by its actions, a respect for democratic principles.[154] Austria makes it a criminal offense to found an association dedicated to endangering national independence or the constitutionally mandated form of government.[155] And the Greek constitution prohibits the abusive exercise of fundamental rights.[156]

In addition, the model provided by the German *Grundgesetz* has been adopted by several of the new and nascent Central and Eastern European democracies, including Croatia,[157] Lithuania,[158] Poland,[159] Romania[160] and Slovenia.[161] In Russia the former Constitutional Court affirmed President Yeltsin's dissolution of the Communist party.[162] However, in Bulgaria the Constitutional Court refused to declare

---

[152] La Costituzione della Repubblica Italiana (Constitution) Art. XII(1) (Italy); Constitucion de Espana (Constitution) Art. 6 (Spain).
[153] Constituicao Da Republica Portuguesa (Constitution) Art. 46(4) (Portugal).
[154] Rainer Hofmann, "Die rechtliche Stellung der Minderheiten in Finnland," *in* Jochen Abr. Frowein *et al.*, eds., *Das Minderheitenrecht Europaischer Staaten* (Berlin: Springer, 1993), p. 118. For a discussion of prohibitions on irredentist groups in Finland, *see* Klaus Tornudd, *Finland and the International Norms of Human Rights* (Nijhoff: Dordrecht, 1986), p. 171.
[155] Thilo Marauhn, "Die rechtliche Stellung der Minderheiten in Osterreich," *in Minderheitenrecht*, *supra* note 154, p. 254.
[156] Sintagma Tis Ellathas (Constitution) Art. 25(3) (Greece); *see* Prodromos Dagtoglou, "Der Missbrauch von Grundrechten in der Griechischen Theorie und Praxis," *in* Julia Ilioupoulos-Strangas, ed., *Der Missbrauch von Grundrechten in der Demokratie* (Baden-Baden: Nomos Verlagsgesellschaft, 1990), pp. 103–16.
[157] Ustav Republike Hrvatske (Constitution) Arts. 6 and 43 (Croatia) (setting out prohibition procedure for all organizations that endanger the democratic constitutional order, independence, unity, or territorial integrity of the State).
[158] Lietuvos Respublikos Konstitucija (Constitution) Art. 2(3) (Lithuania) (declaring "strictly forbidden" the establishment and activities of political parties "whose programme documents propagate and whose activities practice racial, religious, social class inequality and hatred, methods of authoritarian or totalitarian rule, methods of violent seizure of power, war and violent propaganda, violation of human rights and freedoms, or other ideas or actions which are incompatible with universally recognized norms of international law").
[159] Konstytucja Rzeczypospolitej Polskiej (Constitution) Art. 84(3) (Poland) (granting the right of association subject to the condition that "(i)t shall be prohibited to set up and to participate in associations whose objective or activities threaten the social and political system or the legal order of the Republic of Poland"). In Poland, an existing political party may be banned only if a danger of violent behavior exists. *See* Mahulena Hoskova, "Die Rechtliche Stellung der Minderheiten in Polen," *in Minderheitenrecht*, *supra* note 154, p. 299.
[160] Constitutia Romaniei (Constitution) Arts. 8(2) and 37(2) (Romania) (parties working against "political pluralism" are unconstitutional).
[161] Uradni List Republike Slovenije (Constitution) Arts. 63 and 160 (Slovenia) (prohibiting incitement "to national, racial, religious or other inequality and the encouragement of national, racial, religious or other hatred and intolerance").
[162] *Keesing's Record of World Events* 38 (1992), pp. 39, 224.

unconstitutional a party supported mainly by the Turkish minority population. This decision is surprising, given that Article 11(4) of the Bulgarian constitution expressly prohibits the formation of ethnically or religiously based political parties.[163]

Finally, in a 1993 decision the Inter-American Commission on Human Rights reviewed a Guatemalan law prohibiting groups or individuals involved in coups or other extraconstitutional changes in government from standing for election. The Commission found that the principles embodied in the law reflected "a customary constitutional rule with a strong tradition in Central America."[164]

E Conclusion

The foregoing analysis of State practice makes clear that some form of party prohibition procedure is common to most democratic systems. Even the systems manifesting a procedural view do not seem inconsistent with Rawls's observation that "(j)ustice does not require that men must stand idly by while others destroy the basis of their existence."[165] At the same time, there are substantial differences among these democratic States in their treatment of extremist political actors.

International norms, which are the subject of the next section, obviously cannot assimilate all the vast diversity of this national experience. Yet there are at least two reasons why the variety of State practice just reviewed need not frustrate the development of international law in this area. First, we have noted there exists rough consensus at a general level on the legitimacy of some form of self-protection. This provides important common ground for adjudication of individual disputes. As human rights tribunals evaluate cases in this area, they will begin to give contour and detail to the general principles already formalized in human rights instruments by drawing on aspects of various national traditions.

The second reason for hope is precedent. Creating international law on issues of local concern without reference to the historical tradition of any one national community is not a problem unique to this area of human rights: it inheres in every human rights issue with a normative dimension. The response of human rights law, by-and-large, has been to work at legitimating certain minimum standards of conduct as

---

[163] See Emilia Drumeva, "Das bulgarische Verfassungsgericht – Rechtsgrundlagen und erste Entscheidungen," ZAORV 53 (1993), pp. 112, 128–29.
[164] Report No. 30/93, Case 10.804 (Guatemala) (Oct. 12, 1993), in Annual Report of the Inter-American Commission on Human Rights 1993, p. 206, para. 29.   [165] Rawls, supra note 3, p. 218.

universal, though at the same time leaving room for local traditions not inconsistent with guarantees of basic rights. An international regime on the question of anti-democratic actors may emerge by following the same pattern.

V THE STATE OF INTERNATIONAL LAW ON THE QUESTION OF ANTI-DEMOCRATIC POLITICAL PARTIES

A *Substantive democracy in the political covenant and other human rights treaties*

Bans on anti-democratic actors find both direct and indirect support in human rights treaties. All comprehensive human rights instruments provide that certain key rights, normally deemed essential to effective political participation, may be restricted when "necessary in a democratic society."[166] Article 22 (2) of the Political Covenant, protecting freedom of association, provides a typical example of such a provision:

> No restrictions may be placed on the exercise of this right other than those which are prescribed by law and which are necessary in a democratic society in the interests of national security or public safety, public order, the protection of public health or morals or the protection of the rights and freedoms of others.

The rights to vote and to be elected are not subject to a "democratic society" clause; restrictions on these rights are measured by a different test of reasonableness.

Other provisions of the Covenant address the legitimacy of self-protection legislation more directly. Article 5 (1) of the Covenant provides a clear manifestation of substantive democratic principles:

> Nothing in the present Covenant may be interpreted as implying for any State, group or person any right to engage in any activity or perform any act aimed at the destruction of any of the rights and freedoms recognized therein or at their limitation to a greater extent than is provided for in the present Covenant.[167]

Human rights tribunals have issued a number of opinions construing Article 5 (1)-type clauses and have confirmed their role as a protection

---

[166] For close analyses of these provisions, *see* Oscar M. Garribaldi, "On the Ideological Content of Human Rights Instruments: the Clause in a Democratic Society," *in* Thomas Buergenthal, ed., *Contemporary Issues in International Law: Essays in Honor of Louis B. Sohn* (Arlington, Va.: N.P. Engel, 1984), p. 23; Susan Marks, "The European Convention on Human Rights and its Democratic Society," *Brit. Y.B. Int'l L.* 60 (1995), 209.

[167] *See also* European Convention On Human Rights, Art. 17; American Convention on Human Rights, Art. 29.

422 *Democratization and conflicting imperatives*

against erosion of democratic systems from within.[168] In a 1984 decision the UN Human Rights Committee held that organizing a Fascist party was an act "removed from the protection of the Covenant by article 5 thereof."[169] Similarly, the European Court of Human Rights has held that a virtually identical article of the European Convention was designed "to prevent totalitarian groups from exploiting in their own interest the principles enunciated in the Convention."[170] In pursuit of similar goals, Article 20 of the Covenant requires States to prohibit propaganda for war and the advocacy of national, racial, or religious hatred. These clauses suggest that the drafters of these instruments did not share the proceduralists' unwavering confidence in the power of open debate to discredit insidious ideas. Such ideas, these instruments suggest, have real power and citizens in an open society must in some circumstances bear responsibility for the potentially destructive consequences of their advocacy.

B The limits to restrictions on civil and political rights

More difficult than establishing the principle that anti-democratic actors may be excluded from the electoral process is determining where, according to human rights law, the precise limits of this power lie.

1 The applicable standard

a The abuse clause in context The Political Covenant seems not to contain any language describing the circumstances in which rights of anti-democratic actors may be restricted. Article 5 does not say when the exercise of some protected rights may be considered "aimed at the destruction of any of the [other] rights and freedoms recognized" elsewhere in the

---

[168] In its General Comment on Article 25 of the Political Covenant – guaranteeing the right to political participation – the Human Rights Committee took special note that Article 5(1) applies with equal force to Article 25 rights. General Comment 25 (1996), para. 27.
[169] M.A. v. Italy, Communication No. 117/1981, *reprinted in* 2 Selected Decisions of the Human Rights Committee under the Optional Protocol, UN Doc. CCPR/C/OP/1 (1984), pp. 31, 33 (hereinafter Selected Decisions).
[170] Lawless Case (Merits), 1961 Y.B. Eur. Conv. H.R. 438, 450 (Eur. Ct. H.R.); *see also* De Becker Case, 123 Eur. Comm'n H.R. (ser. B.) (1962), p. 137 (Article 17 of European Convention "applies only to persons who threaten the democratic system of the Contracting parties"); Glimmerveen and Hagenbeck v. Netherlands, 1979 Y.B. Eur. Conv. H.R. 366 (Eur. Comm'n H.R. (similar holding); Kommunistische Partei Deutschlands, 1957 Y.B. Eur. Conv. H.R. 219 (Eur. Comm'n H.R.).

Covenant. It is quite hard to determine, therefore, when exercising the right to organize a political party would be "aimed at the destruction" of the right to hold elections. The categorical decisions of the Human Rights Committee on the (re)establishment of a Fascist party in Italy[171] and the European Commission's decision on the German Communist party[172] would seem to suggest that restrictions of anti-democratic parties are so clearly permitted by human rights treaties that they need not be justified by any formula or threshold of proof.

But such an interpretation cannot be correct. If a government were permitted to deprive a political actor of protected rights merely by labeling him or her "anti-democratic," then these treaties would lose much of their practical effect.[173] Many of the Covenant's provisions, particularly those regarding freedom of expression and conscience, are designed specifically to prevent the uncontrolled suppression of political dissent based on spurious claims of subversion and "anti-state" activity. The legal standards set out in the two decisions cited above, therefore, should not be extended much beyond their factual settings. Both tribunals were confronted with cases of party prohibitions for the first time, and in both the outcome was never in doubt: the Italian Fascist party and the German Communist party had always belonged to a small group of obvious candidates for prohibition proceedings. Such parties were indeed the inspiration for clauses such as Article 5(1) of the Political Covenant.[174] It is not surprising, therefore, that both tribunals were concerned primarily with establishing the principle that exclusions are permissible rather than delineating its contours and possible limitations.

When confronted with more ambiguous cases, however, tribunals must move beyond such simplistic interpretations. Article 5 of the Political Covenant and its regional equivalents stand in the larger context of their entire instruments, and must not be interpreted so as to frustrate the essence of the rights guaranteed. It follows that States cannot enjoy unlimited powers to exclude political actors under abuse clauses such as Article 5. The European Court of Human Rights

---

[171] *See supra* note 169.   [172] *See supra* note 170.
[173] Frowein argues that the invocation of Article 17 of the European Convention must be carefully reviewed lest its application should itself become a danger to the democratic system. Jochen Abr. Frowein and Wolfgang Peukert, *Europäische Menschenrechtskonvention – EMRK – Kommentar* 492 (Kehl: Engel, 2nd ed. 1996).
[174] The discussion in section IV demonstrated how many Western States restricted or wholly banned Communist parties.

424 *Democratization and conflicting imperatives*

recently adopted this position in a case concerning the prohibition and dissolution of the United Communist Party of Turkey.[175] In its judgment the Court noted that "an association, including a political party, is not excluded from the protection afforded by the Convention simply because its activities are regarded by the national authorities as undermining the constitutional structures of the State and calling for the imposition of restrictions."[176] This does not mean, the Court added, that "the authorities of a State in which an association, through its activities, jeopardizes that State's institutions are deprived of the right to protect those institutions."[177] Referring to its prior jurisprudence, the Court explained that "some compromise between the requirements of defending democratic society and individual rights is inherent in the system of the Convention."[178] To achieve the correct balance between these two interests the Court insisted that an application of the abuse clause (Art. 17) could only be considered *after* an examination of whether intervention by the authorities was in accordance with the freedom of association and in particular its limitation clause.[179]

The European Court of Human Rights thus recognized that to interpret the abuse clause in isolation would be inconsistent with important broader goals of the treaty: to further free expression and association. This holding, in turn, embodies the general rule of treaty law that a provision must be interpreted in light of its context and of the treaty's object as a whole.[180] Under this analysis, the Court's view of Article 17 of the European Convention may be applied to the "reasonableness" clause limiting the Political Covenant's right to political participation (Art. 25) and the "necessity" clause limiting other associated rights. Of course such a borrowing of ordinary limitation clauses cannot itself serve to frustrate the ultimate purpose of Article 5 of the Political Covenant (or any other abuse clause), which is to prevent anti-democratic actors from using protected liberties as a vehicle to realize their goals.

b The standards of reasonableness and necessity What is the nature of these two alternative standards of review, "necessity" and "reasonableness"? The difference emerges from a distinction basic to the Covenant as a whole. As suggested by its title, the Covenant guarantees both "civil" and "political" rights. Civil rights, such as freedom of expression and association, are those which guarantee individuals or groups certain

---

[175] Case of United Communist Party of Turkey, Judgment of January 30, 1998 Case No. 133/1996/752/951. [176] *Ibid.* [177] *Ibid.* [178] *Ibid.* [179] *Ibid.*
[180] Vienna Convention on the Law of Treaties, May 23, 1969, Art. 31 (1), 1155 UNT.S. 331.

freedoms *from* State interference. Political rights, such as the right to free and fair elections, are those which facilitate participation *in* public affairs.[181] The difference is not merely semantic, since the Covenant provides for different types of restrictions in each category. While restrictions on most "civil rights" are permitted only if "necessary in a democratic society," political rights such as the right to participation in Article 25 are guaranteed "without unreasonable restrictions." The Covenant's drafting history suggests that the restrictions clause of Article 25 was intended primarily to cover issues of eligibility to vote, such as age and mental capacity.[182] But neither the legislative history nor the text precludes the use of this clause to evaluate more far-reaching restrictions on the right to be elected, such as excluding a party from taking part in elections.

According to this distinction between the "civil" right of association and the "political" right of standing for election, if a political party is prohibited only from taking part in elections, such a restriction should be measured according to the "reasonableness" standard. Strictly speaking, the freedoms of expression (Covenant Article 19) and of association (Covenant Article 22) are not at issue, and so neither is the "necessity" standard. As rights to be free *from* interference, they do not involve an affirmative right of participation. If, however, *all* activities of a political party are prohibited, both the right of the party's members to associate and their freedom of expression would be implicated. Such a measure would require additional justification under the stricter standard of "necessity in a democratic society."[183]

This distinction is embodied in the difference between German and Israeli law.[184] In Germany, certain extremist groups may be completely dissolved and their members prohibited from collectively engaging in any sort of public debate. In Israel, by contrast, such groups are excluded only from the electoral process. That both systems can be supported by rational arguments suggests that the distinction we propose represents an important value judgment – on which these two legitimate democratic regimes differ – concerning the capacity of particular democratic societies to withstand ideological assault.

---

[181] Manfred Nowak, *UN Covenant on Civil and Political Rights: a CCPR Commentary* (Arlington, Va.: N.P. Engel, 1993), p. 436.
[182] *Ibid.* at p. 445; Gregory H. Fox, "The Right to Political Participation in International Law," *Yale J. Int'l L.* 17 (1992), pp. 539, 553–54.
[183] On the distinction between "unreasonableness" and stricter standards in administrative law, *see* Itzhak Zamir, "Unreasonableness, Balance of Interests and Proportionality," *in Tel Aviv Studies in Law* (1992), 131–36. [184] *See* discussion *supra* section IV.

2 Refining "reasonable" and "necessary" restrictions

A "necessity" standard proceeds from the assumption that every restrictive measure must be shown to be necessary, while a "reasonableness" standard requires only that the decision not be clearly unjustifiable.[185] In the first case, the State carries a heavy burden of proof to justify its restrictive measure, while in the second, the party affected by the restrictive measure must be able to identify a clearly verifiable error of judgment by the State.

Two factors must be considered, however, which blur this seemingly bright line between the two standards. First, in human rights law, the necessity principle is generally mitigated by a "margin of appreciation" accorded to State parties by international supervisory organs.[186] The scope of the margin depends upon the nature of the activities involved.[187] In the past, the European Commission on Human Rights has held this margin to be particularly wide with regard to actions which domestic authorities regard as critical to the prevention of disorder or crime.[188] In its recent judgment concerning the prohibition of the United Communist Party of Turkey, the European Court seemingly departed from this approach and emphasized that the clause limiting the freedom of association, "where political parties are concerned, [is] to be construed strictly; only convincing and compelling reasons can justify restrictions on such parties' freedom of association."[189] Because this is new law for the European system, one cannot assume the Human Rights Committee would follow the Court's lead in a similar case under the Optional Protocol and narrow the margin of appreciation for its State parties.

Second, the standard of "reasonableness" may become more rigid depending on the nature of the right or the type of restriction at issue. For example, the Human Rights Committee strengthened the "reasonableness" standard of Article 25 of the Political Covenant by introducing the principle of proportionality in a case in which an individual had, for political reasons, been deprived of his right to vote and be elected for fifteen years.[190] Although these mitigating factors do not make the two standards indistinguishable, they do suggest that together they constitute

---

[185] Zamir, *supra* note 183, p. 131.
[186] *See* Handyside v. United Kingdom, 24 Eur. Ct. H.R. (ser. A) (1976), pp. 21–23.
[187] *See* Dudgeon v. United Kingdom, 45 Eur. Ct. H.R. (ser. A) (1981), pp. 21–22.
[188] X v. United Kingdom, App. No. 3898/68, (1971) 13 Y.B. Eur. Conv. on H.R. 666, 684.
[189] United Communist Party of Turkey v. Turkey, para. 46.
[190] Pietraroia v. Uruguay, Communication No. 44/1979, *reprinted in* 1 Selected Decisions, *supra* note 169, pp. 76, 79.

a sliding scale which permits certain more or less far-reaching restrictions of the rights at issue. The application of this sliding scale must take place with due regard to the usual practice of democratic States.

This analytical framework suggests the following hierarchy. The most severe and suspect restriction on the right to free elections is the establishment of a one-party system.[191] The European Court of Human Rights has recognized that "the free expression of the opinion of the people in the choice of the legislature . . . is inconceivable without the participation of a plurality of political parties"[192] and the Human Rights Committee has held that the breadth of restrictions involved in silencing all organized political opposition renders the one-party State unreasonable *per se*.[193] A less severe type of restriction would exclude from elections those parties or individuals which pose a threat to the State's democratic form of governance. Since Article 5 of the Covenant expressly legitimizes action against opponents of democracy, such exclusions are permissible under the less stringent standard of "reasonableness."[194] The total prohibition and dissolution of a political party, on the other hand, must satisfy a higher level of scrutiny since such a measure impinges not only on the right to free and fair elections but also on the freedom of association, a right which is subject to the standard of "necessity in a democratic society." The international supervisory organ applying this formula should confine itself to ascertaining whether the respondent State exercised its discretion reasonably, carefully and in good faith. It must also look at the interference complained of in the light of the case as a whole and determine whether it was "proportionate to the legitimate aim pursued" and whether the reasons adduced by the national authority to justify it are "relevant and sufficient." This includes ascertaining whether the decision was "based on an acceptable assessment of the relevant facts."[195] This test formulated by the European Court of Human Rights provides a standard of review that both allows close scrutiny of the threat posed to a democratic system *and* permits international organs a flexible approach to party prohibition procedures. Because the prohibition of parties involves both a highly nuanced assessment of local political conditions (a factor militating

---

[191] *See* Fox, *supra* note 182, pp. 556–60.
[192] United Communist Party of Turkey v. Turkey, para. 44.
[193] Bwalya v. Zambia, Commun. No. 314/1988, *reprinted in Hum. Rts. L. J.* 14 (1993) p. 408.
[194] The Human Rights Committee has described as "reasonable" restrictions on eligibility to stand for elections intended "to guarantee the democratic decision-making process." *See* Debreczeny v. The Netherlands, Communication No. 500/1992, para. 93 (Oct. 14, 1993), *reprinted in Int'l Hum. Rts. Rep.* 2 (1995), 561.   [195] *See* United Communist Party of Turkey v. Turkey, para. 47.

toward deference), *and* the potential disruption of electoral processes routinely described by human rights instruments as lying at the heart of the democratic order (militating toward stricter scrutiny), this test seems particularly well calibrated. And because it leaves room to consider the interests and values which are protected by the abuse clause it can also be applied at the universal level. Finally, because individuals typically pose less of a threat to the democratic system than organized groups, restrictions on their rights are appropriately subject to stricter scrutiny.

3 Forms of conduct prohibitable by Article 5
When does the threat posed by a political party justify the application of Article 5? Since such a measure is subject to a rather high level of scrutiny ("necessity"), it might seem appropriate to require that such groups engage in specific destructive "acts" in order to justify State action against them. Merely holding anti-democratic opinions would not appear to be sufficient under this standard. This view finds some support in the drafting history of the Universal Declaration of Human Rights and among some commentators.[196]

The problem with this view is that a number of established democracies have at times considered it necessary to prohibit political groups or parties based on far lesser showings than a demonstrable threat to the democratic system. In France, secessionist goals alone were sufficient to ban certain groups.[197] In West Germany, a neo-Nazi party was banned without the government showing that it posed an actual danger.[198] In Israel, certain parties may be excluded from elections if their goal is primarily to spread racist propaganda.[199] In the United States, the Supreme Court in the 1950s diluted its danger-oriented standard to such a degree that one can legitimately ask whether it had not become mainly fictitious.[200] On the international plane, the European Commission of Human Rights has confirmed that the abuse prohibition clause in Article 17 of the European Convention would justify the prohibition of a party merely upon evidence of anti-democratic goals,

---

[196] UN GAOR, 3d Comm., 3d Sess., 155th mtg., p. 667, UN Doc. A/C.3/SR.155 (1948) (statement of Mr. Jimenez de Aréchaga, Uruguay) ("The word 'acts' did not include opinions, but did include conspiracy and attempts, whether successful or not, to destroy any of the rights and freedoms prescribed in the declaration."). *See also* Thomas Buergenthal, "To Respect and Ensure: State Obligations and Permissible Derogations," *in* Louis Henkin, ed., *The International Bill of Rights* (New York: Columbia University Press, 1981), pp. 72, 88–89; Nehemiah Robinson, *The Universal Declaration of Human Rights* (New York: Institute of Jewish Affairs, 1958), p. 79.
[197] *See* discussion *supra* § IV (C)(1). [198] *See* discussion *supra* § IV (D)(1).
[199] *See* discussion *supra* § IV (D)(2). [200] *See* discussion *supra* § IV (B).

even if it were established that the party would limit its activities to acquiring power by legal means.[201] And the European Court of Human Rights recently limited its review of Turkey's ban on the United Communist party of Turkey to evaluating whether the party's program contained anti-democratic goals. Only after the Court found that the Party (1) was "not seeking, in spite of its name, to establish the domination of one social class over the others,"[202] (2) did not describe the Kurdish people as a "minority," (3) made no claim – other than recognition of their existence – that Kurds ought to enjoy special treatment or rights, and (4) did not call for Kurdish secession from Turkey, did it find the prohibition to violate the party's right of association.[203] The Court made no suggestion that it would only have upheld the ban upon a showing of dangerousness based on the party's deeds, as opposed to its stated goals.[204]

This practice suggests that a party may reasonably be considered a threat to democratic institutions based upon (1) its members holding anti-democratic beliefs, *and* (2) their exhibiting a manifest intent to act on those beliefs through the vehicle of the party.[205] The evidence need not include the commission of violent acts directed against the democratic infrastructure. Under this formulation, small parties as well as large movements that have made significant electoral gains may be subject to restriction. The legitimacy of this decidedly preemptive approach, applicable to large and small groups alike, traces its roots to two aspects of the Weimar experience. First was the mistaken belief on the part of the political moderates that either Hitler would not pursue his stated agenda once in power, or that his coalition partners would not

---

[201] Kommunistische Partei Deutschlands, *supra* note 175, pp. 224–25.
[202] United Communist Party of Turkey v. Turkey, *supra* note 195, para. 54. [203] *Ibid.* para. 56.
[204] In another case involving the prohibition of a mildly secessionist Turkish party, however, the Court held that States may not declare every constitutional principle to be so fundamental as to require protection by allowing the dissolution of parties seeking to change such principles by constitutional means. The Court noted "that the fact that . . . a political programme is considered incompatible with the current principles and structures of the Turkish State does not make it incompatible with the rules of democracy" and "that it is of the essence of democracy to allow diverse political programmes to be proposed and debated, even those that call into question the way a State is currently organised, provided that they do not harm democracy itself." *See* Case of the Socialist Party and Others v. Turkey, Judgment of 25 May 1998, para. 47.
[205] Article 20 of the Political Covenant, which requires prohibition of "any advocacy of a national, racial or religious hated," takes a middle ground between a focus on pure opinion and requiring concrete acts. Such advocacy may be prohibited only when it constitutes "incitement to discrimination, hostility or violence." This test is consistent with the standard set out in the text; it does not require concrete acts, but requiring "incitement" injects a formidable intent requirement.

permit him to do so. Second was the practical impossibility of restricting or banning the Nazi party after its representation in the Reichstag jumped from 12 to 107 seats in the elections of September 1930, thereby making it the second largest party in Germany.[206]

4 Procedural limitations
Unfortunately, substantive standards alone cannot ensure that governmental overreaching will not occur, particularly when the State concerned does not allow its citizens to bring individual petitions under the Covenant's First Optional Protocol. This leaves significant potential for abuse which can only be mitigated if a government follows certain procedural requirements before implementing a banning order.

That procedural steps must be followed is indicated by the practice of both States and international organs. Each democratic State we have surveyed provides for judicial review of prohibition decisions.[207] The Indian Supreme Court even declared that a law empowering the government to dissolve political organizations would be invalid if it did not provide for judicial review.[208] This requirement is particularly relevant to the formulation of a global standard, coming as it does from a court in a developing country with a multiethnic and multireligious population. On the international plane, the Human Rights Committee has already taken a first step toward exercising review powers by imposing a strict burden of proof on a State that has failed to give clear reasons for depriving an individual of his or her political rights, including the right to be elected.[209] The European Court imposed similar burdens in its two Turkish cases.[210] Both State and international practice suggest, therefore, that party prohibitions are only justifiable under the Covenant if their validity can be tested before an independent tribunal or other independent body. Such an institutional safeguard ensures that the final decision on a ban will not come from the political branches of the government, which may have a direct stake in outlawing an opponent.[211]

---

[206] Nicholls, *supra* note 8, p. 124.   [207] *See* discussion *supra* § IV.
[208] Madras, *supra* note 127, pp. 607–08.
[209] Tourón v. Uruguay, Communication No. 32/1978, *reprinted in* Selected Decisions, *supra* note 169, pp. 61, 62.
[210] United Communist Party of Turkey v. Turkey, *supra* note 195, para. 46; Case of the Socialist Party and Others v. Turkey, *supra* note 27, para. 44.
[211] *See* UN GAOR, Hum. Rts. Comm., 4th Sess., 96th mtg., p. 3, UN Doc. CCPR/C/SR.96 (1978) (West German representative explains to UN Human Rights Committee that power to ban subversive parties is vested exclusively in the Federal Constitutional Court "in order to prevent a governing party from eliminating an opposition party for political reasons").

C Potential pitfalls

While we have demonstrated that international law clearly permits party restrictions under appropriate circumstances, it is equally clear that it does not *encourage* such restrictions as the first response of a government seeking to diffuse the appeal of extremist movements. Groups such as the German Nazi party and the Algerian FIS have generally struck responsive chords in societies where citizens – for a variety of reasons – have lost faith in governing institutions.[212] It would seem that the most fruitful course of action for regimes facing such crises of legitimacy would be to address these underlying social ills, thereby demonstrating to their citizens that resort to extremism is unnecessary to achieve real social change.[213]

Yet even if an elected regime has taken these steps and the extremists' appeal persists, there are still a number of reasons for it to pause before identifying conditions of "necessity" required to permit restrictions on anti-democratic actors. First, the right to ban certain political parties carries with it an enormous potential for abuse. Virtually every democracy can point to shameful episodes in its history in which alleged "subversives" – who often espoused legitimate social grievances – were denied political rights.[214]

A second problem is determining whether a political movement constitutes a threat to democratic institutions. In a judicial-type inquiry, absent an overt breach of the peace, clear evidence of an intent to carry out anti-democratic objectives will be rare and often contradictory.[215] Few parties will call for an outright end to future elections. Others may adopt the rhetoric of committed democrats as a tactical device.[216] Justice Robert Jackson, concurring in the United States Supreme Court's upholding of restrictions on Communist party activity, acknowledged this difficulty:

[to find] that petitioner's conduct creates a 'clear and present danger' of violent overthrow, we must appraise imponderables, including international and

---

[212] For a discussion of this phenomenon in Algeria, *see* John P. Entelis, "State and Society in Transition," *in* John P. Entelis and Phillip C. Naylor, eds., *State and Society in Algeria* (Boulder, Colo.: 1992), p. 1.
[213] John L. Esposito and John O. Voll, *Islam and Democracy*, (1995), pp. 154–58; Robin Wright, "Islam, Democracy and the West," *Foreign Affairs*, Summer (1992), p. 131.
[214] *See* Emerson, *supra* note 45, pp. 51–52.
[215] *See* Carl J. Friedrich and Arthur E. Sutherland, "Defense of the Constitutional Order," *in* Robert R. Bowie and Carl J. Friedrich, eds., *Studies in Federalism* (Boston, Mass.: 1954), p. 683.
[216] *See* David Reisman, "Civil Liberties in a Period of Transition," *Pub. Pol.* 3 (1942), 33, 56.

national phenomena which baffle the best informed foreign offices and our most experienced politicians. We would have to foresee and predict the effectiveness of Communist propaganda, opportunities for infiltration, whether, and when, a time will come that they consider propitious for action, and whether and how fast our existing government will deteriorate . . . The judicial process is simply not adequate to a trial of such far-flung issues. The answers given would reflect our own political predilections and nothing more.[217]

Third, special care must be taken in the case of newly established democracies. As the Russian experience suggests, the period immediately following an emergence from authoritarian rule can be marked by extreme instability, as various factions vie to create a new political identity for the State.[218] In such situations, two equally powerful, but contradictory arguments can be made regarding the advisability of restricting anti-democratic actors. One might argue that given the fragility of newly formed democratic civil societies, and, in particular, the prevalent distrust of motives among political opponents, to legitimate bans would simply confirm their mutual suspicions and lead quickly to polarized societies. On this view, there can be no worse beginning to a democratic experiment than to allow the first regime to achieve power to begin banning other actors from the process.

However, one might well argue the opposite. From this perspective, the boundaries of legitimate political advocacy must be made clear at the very outset.[219] If one believes as a general matter that opponents of majority rule have no right to participate in the majoritarian process, then that norm is best established before anti-democratic parties gather strength. This argument can also be stated on a more theoretical level. The transition to democracy is often secured only after long struggles against authoritarian regimes, sometimes taking the form of violent revolution. A right of revolution against oppressive regimes is central to the Western democratic tradition. Given the legitimacy of revolution once such regimes have *attained* power, it would seem anomalous to hold that

---

[217] Dennis, 341 US 570 (Jackson, J., concurring). Early in its history, the Supreme Court indeed refused to decide which of two competing factions constituted the lawful government of a state, citing the absence of judicially manageable standards to guide its decision. *See* Luther v. Borden, 48 U.S. (7 How.) 1 (1849).

[218] Ted R. Gurr, *Minorities at Risk* (Washington, D.C.: United States Institute of Peace, 1993), pp. 137–38 (discussing the risks of instability and civil war in democratizing autocracies).

[219] As Sam Rainsy, the Cambodian opposition leader, has remarked: "You can be patient with a nascent democracy when it is moving in the right direction, but if it moves in the wrong direction, the more time you allow such a regime to continue, the more harm it will do to innocent people" *See* Deutsche Presse Agentor, "Cambodian Opposition Wants Stiffer Condition on Aid" (April 8, 1997).

anti-democratic parties cannot be restricted during their *ascension* to power when the possibility of their defeat is much greater. From the perspective of normative political theory, the former (anti-democratic revolution) would appear to legitimize the latter (restricting anti-democratic parties) *a fortiori*.[220]

Finally, the international community should recognize that choices of whether to ban anti-democratic parties mark important episodes in a State's democratic development.[221] Mistakes made in the short term – arguably the case in the United States with the Smith Act of 1940, the Subversive Activities Control Act of 1950, and the Communist Control Act of 1954 – may become valuable negative lessons over time. These are lessons that the international community is unlikely to impart in any meaningful fashion by fiat. This view suggests that while the international community may define a permissible range of responses to authoritarian movements, it should not dictate a choice among them.

VI CONCLUSION

The growing recognition in international law and practice of a democratic entitlement represents an emerging consensus among States regarding the nature of a "democratic" society. Given the ideological and cultural obstacles in the path of reaching such a consensus, it is not surprising that the earliest points of agreement have been on questions of procedure: what is a "free and fair" election; must more than one party participate; must ballots be secret? At first glance, the problem of dealing with anti-democratic actors might be seen as yet another procedural question. All electoral systems have rules concerning who may participate and who may not. This might simply be one more.

But the issue transcends procedure. Whether a political system elevates tolerance above all other values is a fundamental choice that defines the nature of the polity itself, not simply the rules of engagement between those who have agreed to compete within its boundaries. The choice itself generally does not occur at a singular moment in a State's history but rather emerges from the tumult of struggles, debates, wars, and the daily experiences of governing that together create the social and political identity of a society. These observations might lead one to

---

[220] *See* Auerbach, *supra* note 50, pp. 192–93; but *see* Emerson, *supra* note 45, pp. 49–50 (responding to Auerbach).
[221] Michael Walzer, *Just and Unjust Wars* (New York: Basic Book: 2d edn. 1992), pp. 86–108; Michael Walzer, "The Moral Standing of States," *Phil. & Pub. Aff.* 9 (1980), 209.

be quite pessimistic about the possibility of agreement on a global legal standard. The body of this chapter, however, has demonstrated that the international community is not hopelessly divided on the problem of anti-democratic actors. Sources of law that include human rights treaties, the decisions of human rights bodies, and the practices of representative democratic States all point overwhelmingly to a substantive theory of democracy. Even the United States – which entered reservations to the Political Covenant's articles on freedom of expression on the grounds that they would erode the First Amendment's tolerance of virtually any political opinion, however dangerous or offensive[222] – bears a legacy of debilitating restrictions on the American Communist party. The international community would seem to have adopted a substantive view of democracy as a legal norm.

The substantive view, as we have described it, holds restrictions on anti-democratic parties and individuals to be legitimate acts of self-protection. At a minimum, restrictions may be imposed on those who manifestly intend to end future elections in the State. In adopting the substantive view, the international community has evinced a collective interest in the maintenance of majoritarianism, a goal intimately connected to its broader protection of all human rights.

International law has developed various mechanisms for separating actions with normative significance from "mere" politics. Yet here is a norm that is about politics. It seeks to inject the rule of law into societies facing challenges to their fundamental institutions by well-organized extremist groups. Inevitably, even in the most optimistic scenario, the strict letter of these rules will be tempered to accommodate political exigencies. Bans on parties with substantial followings may cause unrest; bans on parties with little support may serve as instruments of repression; and bans of either sort may be enacted based on evidence that is not much more than speculation. This chapter has been filled with responses to such prudential concerns. The standards discussed are calibrated to take account of such potential pitfalls. The necessity of a procedural check, in the form of an independent review, is also essential if abuses of the power to exclude anti-democratic actors are to be curtailed.

Yet the question remains of how a norm about politics can stand apart from politics. It may be that, for the time being, the international community must recognize that a rule embodying a substantive view of

[222] 138 Cong Rec. S4781–84 (daily edn., Apr. 2, 1992).

democracy – requiring that restrictions on anti-democratic parties be "reasonable" – may be ignored, or used as convenient cover for repression. Realistically, the best that the community may hope for is that the consequences of a decision to ban a party will not result in the collapse of a State's democratic system altogether. Using institutional carrots and sticks to encourage a return to full pluralism may prevent this result. Through this minimally interventionist route, the international community may slowly bring about adherence to the letter of the norms themselves.

CHAPTER 13

Whose intolerance, which democracy?

Martti Koskenniemi

In "Intolerant Democracies,"[1] Gregory Fox and Georg Nolte discuss the classical political theory problem of democracy's self-defense. May democracies resort to "undemocratic" means to defend their existence? While I thought the chapter an important piece in the recent stream of liberal international scholarship, I found myself in a spiral of uneasiness about the authors' main theses. Despite their moderate and balanced argumentative style, something in the authors' tone of voice, in their self-positioning was disturbing and conflicted with the apparent neutrality and detachedness of their arguments.

I am troubled by the initial pairing of the notions of democratic government and undemocratic opposition on which their chapter relies. Such a pairing assumes an external view of the particular political conflict and fails to grasp the way it appears from the inside, to the participants involved. For clearly, political passions in the modern age are not enlisted for struggles for or against "democracy." If interviewed, all sides would normally argue their case in terms of democracy – a "true" or "real" democracy in contrast to the opponent's distorted view. The absence of an internal perspective from the authors' account, however, bars access to aspects of the participants' lives that inform their differing constructions of "democracy." It is not clear that any understanding of the conflict is involved – and the risk of imperialism looms large.

The authors think it useful for lawyers to underwrite governmental policies that seek to defend "democracy" against something that is not "democracy." But if both sides are able to argue their case in terms of democracy, then the conflict will automatically refer back to the contexts of life from which "democracy" takes these contrasting meanings. At that point, lawyers may no longer rely on some transparent idea of "democracy" but must articulate their view in terms of the ideals of

---

[1] Gregory H. Fox and Georg Nolte, "Intolerant Democracies," *Harv. Int'l L. J.* 36 (1995), p. 1. Some references below are to portions of the article that have not been reproduced in Chapter 12 of this volume.

the good life that inform their preferred construction, and evaluate it in relation to what it is beyond the word "democracy" that the government and the opposition seem to represent. From this perspective, the vocabulary of "democracy" appears as unhelpful to understand the struggle as it would have been to understand what went on, say, during the Huguenot wars in sixteenth- and seventeenth-century France. And it provides no more guidance than does a general commitment to the good!

This point may become clearer if one reflects upon the dynamics of political struggle appearing to oppose different conceptions of "democracy" against each other. The authors distinguish two types of democracy – procedural and substantive – from the perspective of how they are capable of justifying intolerance. But they do not discuss the effects of such a distinction to the characterization of the government/opposition relation. At least four different characterizations are opened up, each of which escapes their simple "democratic versus undemocratic" dichotomy:

(1) G procedural v. O substantive
(2) G substantive v. O procedural
(3) G procedural v. O procedural
(4) G substantive v. O substantive.

In each of these four pairs both government (G) and opposition (O) claim to be waging a democratic struggle because they interpret "true" democracy as being either procedural or substantive, (1) and (2), or because they interpret the procedural, (3), and the substantive, (4), criteria in contrasting ways. I believe that from an internal perspective, this is how the participants normally view their struggle, or at least how they formulate their claims when seeking support from the West. In that search, nobody can afford to claim to replace "democracy" by something else – making it seem as if it were all about different notions of democracy.

Neither the authors nor other concerned Western intellectuals in search of political commitment can (without circularity) privilege conceptions of democracy by further reference to "democracy," without already having become involved in the controversy as participants. They are automatically compelled to present an external ideal, or a principle, of the good life by reference to which their understanding of democracy may seem justified. The debate between "us" (international lawyers, Western liberals) and "them" (Others) turns out to be about whose democracy to prefer. Appeal to an apparently universal value of "democracy" obscures the terms of particular struggles. The committed lawyer is always called upon to step down from universal principle to a contextual assessment of the merits of what the government and the opposition represent. But represent to whom?

The procedural and the substantive conceptions that the authors do discuss do not exhaust the meaning of "democracy." Both capture democracy mainly as having to do with the realization of individual rights within a political realm (cf., their definition of the substantive conception as "a core of political rights"). Both also leave aside powerful aspirations that are neither about procedural correctness nor about political participation, but that stress the primacy of spiritual and economic well-being to political rights and the quality of communal life to individual life-choices.

For example, both government and opposition might claim that the special care they take to preserve or strengthen existing communal principles, or the extraordinary efforts they hope to make to raise the population's well-being, necessitate a temporary setting aside of electoral procedure and individual rights. And they might argue – particularly for Western audiences, obsessed with the rhetoric of democracy – that this in fact exhibits a higher form of democratic rule as it gives effect to values hierarchically superior to electoral fairness and individualism. Would such a (traditionalist, communitarian–democratic) government be allowed to be "intolerant" against a Western-minded modernist opposition? Should a modernist government limiting its own role to guaranteeing individual rights in the "public" sphere while opening the rest of society to market forces be given international support in its struggle against its (traditionalist, say) opposition?

Or imagine the opposite case. A corrupt government ruling over an uneducated population arranges "periodic elections" in which the voters in their ignorance always vote in favour of the government. The opposition calls for suspending the results of the vote and for substantive reforms in the educational and economic fields. The government refuses all reform and bans the opposition from publishing its views as "undemocratic" because it does not respect the results of the vote. It is hard to think that Professors Fox and Nolte's liberal intuitions would go far in supporting such a government. But do not these examples require an (endless) refining of the authors' original thesis so that its general applicability as a "pro-democratic" political commitment is watered down into a call for contextual management of far-away societies in reference to Western-liberal policies?

The difficulties with the word "democracy" are enhanced when the authors discuss the international aspects of the problem. When they do this, Fox and Nolte glide from a rather straightforward definition of democracy as electoral fairness[2] to a much larger and more ambiguous idea of democracy as "openness, cooperation, and non-violent resolution of disputes."[3] I have great problems with the character of the assumed link between democracy and peace. True, if one defines democracy in the latter terms, it follows tautologically (from "non-violent resolution of disputes') that such societies are not prone to make war. But the problem clearly lies in us (and them) getting there in the first place! There is an intuitively plausible argument to the effect that the West has been able to promote peaceful growth (i.e., the conditions of openness, cooperation and non-violent resolution) only at the expense of the undeveloped South/East. War has not been absent but has been externalized – wars by proxy. If so, then the causal link is not between democracy and peace but between imperialism, development, and peace – with the implication of underdevelopment and war *au delà*. But I do not find it even psychologically credible that the presence of procedural democracy is proof against war. If scarcity of resources were to make it necessary for two countries governed by electoral democracy (instead of the more substantive notion into which the authors glide in their discussion of the international aspects) to think of a pattern of dividing up the cake there would be no guarantee against a vote for war – that much seems suggested by the "Khaki election" in Britain in 1900.

I think the most fundamental problem I had with the chapter, as I have also with the writings of other liberal internationalists such as Anne-Marie Slaughter and Ferdinand Tesón, is with the initial positioning of the author him/herself, as possessing a transparent view of the essential meaning of democracy and constructing an argument to impose it on "them." Though a common posture in Western societies, not much of our history of relations with non-Western cultures supports its beneficiality. The nation-state and its democratic forms may not be for export as pure form. They may equally well constitute a specific product of Western history, culture and, especially, economy. Importing those forms imports (if at all possible) the substance as well. So the proposition that there is an international or universal norm of "democracy," "tolerance" or something of the sort that should or may be realized within existing political communities may in fact be unacceptable because over- and under-inclusive at the same time, too general to

[2] *Ibid.*, pp. 2-6. [3] *Ibid.*, p. 63.

provide political guidance and always suspect as a neocolonialist strategy. It is too easily used against revolutionary politics that aim at the roots of the existing distributionary system, and it domesticates cultural and political specificity in an overall (Western) culture of moral agnosticism and rule by the market. A generalized defence of exceptional governmental power – whatever the justification – is unacceptable because it takes too much for granted the present distribution of wealth and power in actually existing political communities and their *de facto* authorities.

This leaves me with a call not for universal democracy or indeed with anything "universal" at all. Situations are idiosyncratic and our familiar procedural and substantive principles can only be applied or negotiated with those specificities in mind. Their application does not produce identical consequences in different circumstances. Instead of applying principles (and then going home), international lawyers could perhaps develop more concrete forms of political commitment: by engaging us in actual struggles, both as observers and participants, and by bringing in a wealth of historical experience but taking the participants' self-understanding seriously. As long as international lawyers look at the conflict between secular authorities and religious fundamentalists, for instance, as a general "human rights" or "democracy" matter, we are unable to reach the historical, moral and political core of the conflict. We shall remain outsiders with a political bias couched in apparently neutral or universal language, and intervention will appear ineffective at best, imperialism at worst. The doctrines and practices of the participants to social conflict will need to be addressed directly; and when addressed, the assumption should not be that we remain unmoved by them.

CHAPTER 14

Democratic intolerance: observations on Fox and Nolte
Brad R. Roth

The authoritarian German jurist Carl Schmitt once pointed out that "a philosophy of concrete life must not withdraw from the exception and the extreme case, but must be interested in it to the highest degree. The rule proves nothing; the exception proves everything."[1] In seeking to further specify the purported "emerging international right to democratic governance," the authors of "Intolerant democracies,"[2] Gregory H. Fox and Georg Nolte, have grasped the fundamental significance of the exception: the real meaning of a democratic norm cannot be understood without examining precisely those cases in which democratic values argue for a suspension of democratic processes. The question is whether the assertion of a meaningful international consensus on the "democratic entitlement" can withstand such an examination.

Once a pejorative term in the writings of the most esteemed political philosophers, "democracy" has in recent parlance been transmogrified into a repository of political virtues: rule ratified by a manifestation of majority will (popular sovereignty); orderly mediation of political conflict through participatory mechanisms (polyarchic constitutionalism); individual freedom under the rule of law (liberalism); broad popular empowerment to affect the decisions that condition social life (democracy, properly so called); *et cetera*.[3] No term can mean so many things and continue to mean anything, for political virtues do not come in neat packages. No set of formal procedures can stand above the clash of competing priorities, nor can a cogent theory of democratic "primary goods" – things everyone wants, regardless of what else anyone wants – be crafted to avoid controversial choices that arise in the moments of crisis to which Schmitt referred.

---

[1] Carl Schmitt, *in* George Schwab, trans., *Political Theology: Four Chapters on the Concept of Sovereignty* (1922) (Cambridge, Mass.: The MIT Press, 1985), p. 15.
[2] Gregory H. Fox and Georg Nolte, "Intolerant Democracies," *Harv. Int'l L.J.* 36 (1995), p. 1.
[3] I have elsewhere attempted to disentangle these ideas. *See* Brad R. Roth, "Evaluating democratic progress," chapter 17 of this volume.

The consequence of this indeterminacy is that "democracy" becomes identified with whichever choice engages our sympathies. All too often, democracy is equated with freedom and power for those members of foreign societies who most closely resemble ourselves.

The idea of an emerging right to democratic governance transfers this problem from the realm of rhetoric to the realm of legality. Once there, the problem migrates inexorably from the area of human rights to that of peace and security; the democratic entitlement calls into question not merely a regime's conduct but also its legal capacity to assert, *inter alia*, a sovereign people's rights against foreign intervention. The ultimate danger is that ideological legitimism, seen most recently in the form of the Reagan Doctrine, will capture international law. Even a benevolent ideological legitimism will deprive international law of its indispensable role as an overlapping consensus among societies that otherwise radically differ on fundamental matters (including, but not limited to, choices among "democratic" priorities). A less benevolent ideological legitimism will make international law the plaything of interventionist powers.

Fox and Nolte deem international law to prescribe a democratic procedure that "is not an end in itself but a means of creating a society in which citizens enjoy certain essential rights."[4] They thereby acknowledge the potential for tension or even contradiction between prescribed procedures and democratic ends, an acknowledgment that leads them to sympathize with the Algerian *coup d'état*. Yet in thus purporting to take a "substantive" view of democracy, they commit themselves to very little substance, perhaps recognizing that a truly substantive view would transform the democratic entitlement into precisely the ideological battleground I fear. They instead slide back into proceduralism by positing as "primary" among citizens' essential rights "the right to vote for their leaders," the very right they support withholding from the Algerians (as long as the latter persist in wanting to vote the wrong way).

This does not hold water. If one is to say to the people, in essence, "The fundamental principle of democracy dictates that you can have any government except the one the majority of you presently think you want," there had better be a more compelling argument for democracy than that it enables the people to choose. There is nothing intrinsically valuable about choosing among undesired options. After all, Iran, too, has elections, with some range of choice. Fidel Castro also famously sub-

---

[4] Fox and Nolte, *supra* note 2, p. 16.

scribes to a theory of democratic choice: "within the revolution, everything; against the revolution, nothing." Fox and Nolte would not on this account acknowledge Castro as a democrat. Yet if, as in their quote from Rawls, "[a] person's right to complain is limited to principles he acknowledges himself,"[5] on the basis of what principles can they challenge Castro's stricture? If their "democracy" would prevent Castro's Communist party from coming to power, why cannot his "democracy" prevent them from ousting his system and foreclosing it as a future option?

The problem is not that Fox and Nolte are incapable of answering this question. The problem is that they cannot plausibly answer the question without relying on propositions about the deeper meaning of a democratic society, propositions that are both controverted and justly controvertible. Such reliance is at odds with their positivistic claim that the world community has embraced the democratic entitlement as international law. Moreover, while appeals to controverted world views are appropriate to the realm of moral persuasion, such appeals are inappropriate and dangerous where they call into question bedrock principles of international peace and security, with the prospect that those worldviews will be foisted on populaces that do not share them.

Dictatorships have frequently in human history been seen by their subjects to secure very real benefits (e.g., protection against chaos, ethnic strife, or national disintegration; resistance to foreign penetration and domination; distributive justice through the disenfranchisement of entrenched social elites) that might be irretrievably lost by tolerating organized opposition. Once we (quite appropriately) acknowledge the legitimacy of intolerance of threats to the substance of democracy as we understand it, we must concede the *prima facie* legitimacy of intolerance of threats to substantive political virtue as others understand it.

The foregoing does not mean that we must, in the name of nonintervention, stand idly by while thuggish usurpers impose themselves in the face of a contrary popular will that has been clearly and overwhelmingly manifested (as, for example, in Haiti's internationally observed elections). It does not preclude a developing international consensus about modes of rule that are definitively illegitimate (the Pol Pot regime comes to mind), nor does it preclude a legal onus on all intolerant regimes to expose their conduct to international fact-finding and to

---

[5] *Ibid.* at p. 17, *quoting* John Rawls, *A Theory of Justice* (Cambridge, Mass.: Harvard University Press, 1971), p. 214.

articulate justifications that acknowledge widely shared interpretations of international human rights instruments. But it does – in accordance with international law that, to my mind, remains fairly well settled – preclude calling "into question each State's sovereign right freely to choose and develop its political, social, economic and cultural systems, whether or not they conform to the preferences of other States."[6]

---

[6] GA Res. 45/150 (1990). It is noteworthy that the above reiteration of the traditional non-intervention norm was included in this generally pro-democratic resolution, which passed 129-8-9 with the support of the liberal-democratic States. The accompanying resolution, GA Res. 45/151 (1990), passed over the objection of liberal-democratic States, was yet more emphatic on this point. Subsequent resolutions on this topic have followed a similar pattern. *See, e.g.,* GA Res. 49/180 (1994).

CHAPTER 15

A defense of the "intolerant democracies" thesis

Gregory H. Fox and Georg Nolte

Since Koskenniemi and Roth take us to task for a number of positions we do not hold, it is important to make clear precisely the issue we address in our chapter. Our analysis centers on regimes that profess adherence to a system of "genuine periodic" elections. We ask whether these regimes may restrict the rights of political actors who represent a demonstrable threat to such a system of electoral choice. Many legal commentators, especially in the wake of the 1991 Algerian elections, answer in the negative by arguing that the essence of a fair electoral system is equal opportunity for competition among all opposition groups. Our chapter asks whether contemporary international law supports this view. After an extensive review of international jurisprudence and State practice we found – subject to important qualifications and standards of proof – that it does not. The international community has of late made a sufficient commitment to the creation and strengthening of electoral institutions for it to find value in efforts at their preservation. We found little basis for two alternative answers to our question: that international law has nothing to say to States seeking guidance on whether restrictions on opposition actors are legal or illegal, or that States are affirmatively prohibited from imposing such restrictions.

The basis for our answer is neither, as Roth suggests, commitment to a comprehensive international blueprint of democratic legitimism nor, as Koskenniemi claims, viewing national political struggles through a distorting "external" lens that either wholly fails to comprehend how the parties perceive themselves or selectively accepts the government's characterization of parties' "democratic" (or "undemocratic") nature. Rather, the basis for our conclusion is the large number of States having undertaken to hold "genuine periodic" elections by ratifying certain human rights treaties.[1] An extensive repertoire of international practice

[1] One hundred forty-four States, for example, have ratified the International Covenant on Civil and Political Rights, representing approximately 70 percent of UN membership.

now defines these terms with reasonable clarity. The force of the State's legal commitment is equally unaffected by incumbent regimes' "auto-coups" which annul the results of elections or, crucially, the sentiments of voters in electoral majorities or pluralities that they have had enough of elected government. As in other areas of human rights law, such actions constitute violations of the norm in question and not evidence of its non-existence.

Roth's warning of the dangers of a militant legitimism mistakes our use of the terms "substantive" and "procedural" democracy for comprehensive models of government. He is correct that the "substantive" view commits one to "very little substance," but that is only a problem if, in Schmittian fashion, one is looking for more. We do not seek to fill out a robust definition of "democracy." That is an ongoing process in itself and may even result in emphasis being placed on "spiritual and economic well-being" and "communal identifications" (Koskenniemi), though human rights treaties circumscribe the extent to which political rights may be minimized. The substantive view commits us only to a profound and much controverted choice as to whether an electoral system should be forced to provide the means for its own destruction. We doubt that any definition of democracy, assuming it included the holding of elections, could avoid taking a position on this issue.

It is in fact rather surprising that by raising this question we have been accused of militant legitimism. We would have rather expected a charge of unacceptable relativism – that we are excessively tolerant of exclusionary regimes claiming to be "democratic." Indeed, one of our aims was to remind those States now demanding more "democratic" governance abroad that they should not ask more of regimes in transition or of new States than they are or were prepared to accept for themselves in comparable circumstances. After all, it was these mostly Western States who were responsible for the "substantive democratic" provisions in human rights instruments. Taking this position does not represent militant legitimism but an attempt to ensure that nascent and fragile democracies are treated fairly when it comes to demonstrating their democratic *bona fides*, a procedure which, for better or worse, occurs with increasing frequency in international affairs.

Roth next offers a critique seemingly grounded in American-style proceduralism, claiming to find little intrinsic value in an electorate forced to choose "among undesired options." To this one can make the rather obvious response that there is certainly intrinsic value for future voters, who may be denied any opportunity to change their government save through extra-constitutional means. But more importantly, it is unclear why Roth's argument would compel rejection of our approach. The most likely alternative to applying international norms on this subject is that anti-democratic parties will be banned anyway. By encouraging international bodies to review the propriety of bans there will at least be an opportunity for the number of bans to be reduced. The same answer may be given to Koskenniemi's concern for the self-perceptions of political actors involved. The only way to ensure that different self-perceptions are in fact considered is to commence a dialogue about these questions above the national level. This is particularly true of the self-perceptions of opposition groups, which may be all but lost if discussion of a ban remains mired in the recriminations of national politics. And because international bodies do not generally take the initiative in such dialogues, and do not even provide the primary frame of reference for determining whether an actor is excludable (it is rather the national constitution), they are unlikely to initiate a "religious war" or to make an existing conflict more religious than it already has become. Our approach merely lends legitimacy to demonstrable efforts at safeguarding electoral choice in the terms set out in provisions such as Article 25 of the Political Covenant.

It is true, as Koskenniemi argues, that the case for democracies not fighting each other has not been definitively proven. He may even be correct that the almost complete absence of wars between democratic States has much to do with an externalization of their problems in the form of imperialist adventures or otherwise. Our point, however, is that it is at least as legitimate for international human rights treaties to assume (as they appear to do) that a connection exists between democracy and peacefulness and to devise their rules accordingly. As long as this assumption has not been shown to be invalid, it may properly be considered in the process of interpretation.

Koskenniemi posits a number of scenarios designed to engage one's sympathies for a banned opposition group – in other words, hard cases. Yet these cases are offered less to illustrate the inadequacy of the legal standards we propose than to suggest the essential futility and even dangerousness of any universal norms in this area. To this we can only respond that even if international law is "unable to reach the historical, moral, and political core of the conflict" it shares this property with almost any form of law. As we understand it, international law in this field does not prejudge most aspects of national political struggles and has the limited function of addressing only certain forms of unacceptable conduct which the international community has deemed unworthy of even the noblest political goals.

Thus, in the chapter we take care to point out that the norms applicable to evaluating restrictive measures would be largely borrowed from established human rights jurisprudence. In our view, human rights law would grant governments the "margin of appreciation" they enjoy elsewhere, though nonetheless requiring that they (1) make a demonstrable case that the excluded actor presents a danger to the continuance of regular elections, and (2) ensure that the ban is reviewable by a national court and, to the extent provided for in a human rights instrument, by an international body as well.

On the basis of these standards, we would not (to take Roth's case) accept Castro's Cuba as "democratic" in the sense contemplated by the Political Covenant as long as a multiparty system does not exist and elections are not otherwise "genuine" along the lines of relevant UN standards. On the other hand (to take Koskenniemi's case), if an elected but traditionally minded regime established a *prima facie* case that an opposition group perceiving itself as "Western-minded" would do away with the principle of genuine and periodic elections – perhaps because this party considers the voters not to be sufficiently enlightened in the short run – it could well convince an international body of the legitimacy of a ban. Even if it could not make such a case, the traditionally minded regime still retains vast legislative powers "to preserve existing communal identifications."

Despite raising these issues on the legal merits, both Roth and Koskenniemi end up as legal agnostics, denying the propriety of normative approaches to issues of "democracy." In the post-Cold-War era, we regard this view to be as extreme as self-righteous democratic legitimism. International law is no longer blind to the nature of national political systems. During the Cold War such blindness was more convincingly justified because a consensus was lacking on the minimum requirements of genuine elections. Now that such a consensus is emerging, the discussion among international lawyers must change its level of abstraction. It is still inappropriate to proclaim a universally applicable blueprint of democracy. But certain essential elements of what a "democracy" may or may not do have begun to emerge. We are now in a period of transition. Such periods are disquieting and often provoke demands for radical simplification in the form of too much or too little law. In our view, the more appropriate response to a process of gradual change is to ground any generalizations or prescriptions firmly in international practice. This was the purpose of our chapter.

CHAPTER 16

Democracy and accountability: the criss-crossing paths of two emerging norms

*Steven R. Ratner**

The blossoming of concern for human rights by a broad spectrum of States since the end of the Cold War has assumed both a proactive and reactive posture. On the one hand, governments around the world, responding to the desires of their people for a full participatory role in deciding their nation's future, have moved toward adoption of democratic forms of governance. At the same time, the resulting new regimes and their constituencies have been forced to reckon with the legacy of authoritarian systems or civil wars and to devise the proper way to hold accountable those who have violated human rights. Thus, demands for and attempts to create democracy and accountability have become central forces in our millennial era. Both developments constitute an attempt to deepen the meaning of human rights beyond the notion of protections from specific abuses, to include a system of governance that will prevent abuses in the future and that will effectively respond to those in the past.

By democracy, I mean, as do others in the volume, liberal or constitutional democracy – a political system with governments elected by popular majority, and with the rule of law enshrined to protect those not in the majority.[1] Accountability refers to a process for holding individuals personally responsible for human rights abuses they have committed. These two trends, of course, are not merely political, but profoundly normative in two senses. First, claims for both democracy and account-

---

* I appreciate comments from Sarah Cleveland, Gregory Fox, Priscilla Hayner, Samuel Issacharoff, Douglas Laycock, John Robertson, Naomi Roht-Arriaza, Brad Roth, and David Wippman. I gratefully acknowledge the excellent research assistance of James Mayor and translation assistance of Monica Jara.
[1] *See* Carl Cohen, *Democracy* (Athens, Ga.: University of Georgia Press, 1971), pp. 72–77; Carlos Santiago Nino, *The Constitution of Deliberative Democracy* (New Haven, Conn.: Yale University Press, 1996), pp. 1–4; Yash Ghai, "The Theory of the State in the Third World and the Problematics of Constitutionalism," *in* Douglas Greenberg *et al.*, eds., *Constitutionalism and Democracy: Transitions in the Contemporary World* (Oxford University Press, 1993), pp. 186–87.

ability build upon a core of conventional and customary human rights law that guarantees all persons certain basic freedoms by obligating States to respect those rights. Advocates for each thus work from a tradition stretching back to the Universal Declaration of Human Rights.[2] Second, democracy and accountability are increasingly advocated not simply as good ideas for promoting human dignity, but as human rights themselves, or, contrariwise, duties upon States. Democracy creates a duty to provide a certain form of government; and accountability imposes duties to bring individuals to some form of justice for human rights abuses.

But the normative firmness of these claims remains a subject of great debate. In the case of democracy, some international organizations and States invoking the term are increasingly viewing it as a duty and not just good policy; others disagree.[3] Actors referring to accountability share far less of a consensus regarding its normative nature.[4] International law's requirements concerning, for instance, whether to prosecute or pardon, establish a truth commission, or dismiss human rights offenders from office remain in many respects uncertain. The degree to which the law should countenance different responses to crimes of a prior regime and those of the current government is also open to debate. In this sense, both norms are inchoate, but accountability seems especially so.

The relationship between these two putative norms is now assuming great significance, though it remains analytically unexamined. In an important sense, these two norms ask a State to undertake two very different courses of action. A claimed norm of democracy asks it to make organizational, systemic change in the functioning of the polity – to end authoritarian rule and be governed by electoral results and the rule of law. Those demanding accountability, on the other hand, ask a State to focus specifically on a set of individuals, to ensure that those who have abused face the consequences of their actions. The tension between the two claims becomes most pronounced when each norm

---

[2] GA Res. 217, UN Doc. A/810 (1948), p. 71.
[3] *See, e.g.,* Santiago Commitment to Democracy and Renewal of the Inter-American System, OAS Gen. Ass., 21st Sess., Proceedings, vol. 1, p. 1, OAS Doc. OEA/Ser.P/XXI.0.2 (1991) ("representative democracy is the form of government of the region"); Charter of Paris for a New Europe, Nov. 21, 1990, 30 ILM (1991), pp. 190ff., at pp. 193–95; Europ. Parl. Res. 78/95, para. 60, 1995 O.J. 126 ("the right to political participation in the political process is a fundamental and universal human right, as is the establishment of representative democracy"); *but see* GA Res. 52/119, UN GAOR, 52nd Sess., Supp. No. 49, pp. 268–69, UN Doc. A/52/49 (1997) (calling for non-interference in States' electoral processes). *See also* Gregory H. Fox, "The Right to Political Participation in International Law," *Yale J. Int'l L.* 17 (1992), p. 539.
[4] *See infra* text at notes 99–109.

seems to pull a State in different and perhaps even opposite directions. Most notably, how are States undergoing a transition to democracy – and thus attempting to fulfill that norm – to respond to a claim that members of the prior regime, e.g., a military junta, be held to account for their atrocities if they believe that will compromise the success of that transition? If these duties are found to conflict, the potential for normative incoherence – and thus irrelevance of international law – runs high. The issue is hardly theoretical and has occupied the political consciousness of societies in Latin America, Eastern Europe, Africa, and Asia.

This chapter, then, seeks to inquire into the interaction of these two contemporary normative and political developments. After reviewing the progress of international attempts to hold individuals responsible for violations of human rights (section I), I then examine the unique nature of political transitions – contemporary laboratories in which democracy and accountability play an intertwined role in State decision-making (section II). The chapter then considers the state of international law concerning the purported duty of accountability (section III). It then ponders the interaction between the democracy and accountability in terms of potential conflicts or compatibilities (section IV). I conclude (section V) with an attempt to circumscribe accountability within a framework that renders it both normatively viable and harmonious with the growing consensus on participatory government.

I A BRIEF HISTORY OF ACCOUNTABILITY

A *The increased concern of international law*

International law had little to contribute on this issue for most of its history. As defined by the positivist school that dominated the field from the late eighteenth century, international law exclusively governed relations between States, with individuals at best the third-party beneficiaries. The notion that the law would govern behavior of governments *vis-à-vis* their own citizens, let alone prescribe accountability for individuals for violations of such norms, was anathema to the entire exercise.[5] The only areas that addressed violations of individual rights

---

[5] *See, e.g.*, Dreyfus v. von Fink, 534 F.2d 24, 31 (2d Cir.), *cert. denied*, 429 U.S. 835 (1976), *dictum overruled in* Filartiga v. Pena-Irala, 630 F.2d 876 (2d Cir. 1980). *Cf.* S.S. Lotus (Fr. v. Turk), 1927 P.C.I.J., ser. A, no. 10, p. 18. *See generally* L. Oppenheim, *International Law*, 1st edn., vol. 1, (New York: Longmans, Green, 1905), pp. 102–05; W. Michael Reisman, "Sovereignty and Human Rights in Contemporary International Law," *Am. J. Int'l L.* 84 (1990), 866.

by governments concerned actions by governments against citizens of other States, as covered by the law of State responsibility for injury to aliens, and the laws and customs of war.[6] Thus, by early this century, the Law of the Hague had placed limits on methods of warfare, while the Law of Geneva imposed duties toward enemy civilians and soldiers no longer engaged in battle.[7] But the law of war traditionally was silent as to the consequences for individuals who violated it, leaving some States to develop domestic codes punishing violations of the laws of war.[8]

The silence of international law regarding the consequences for government-sponsored abuses of human rights began to change after the First World War, and even more so after World War II. This change in the law flowed directly from the new scale of destruction brought about by these global conflagrations and manifested itself in two ways: first, the beginning of a trend suggesting that international law should prescribe some individual accountability for violations of the laws of war; and second, the evolution of international human rights to prescribe limits upon a government's conduct toward its own citizens in peace and war. These two trends would eventually marry in the Nuremberg trials and their aftermath.[9]

With respect to accountability, following World War I, the Allies created a fifteen-member commission to look into war crimes. In its report to the 1919 Preliminary Peace Conference, the majority of the commission found that the Central Powers had committed numerous acts "in violation of established laws and customs of war and the

---

[6] *See generally* Karl Josef Partsch, "Individuals in International Law," *in* Rudolph Bernhardt, ed., *Encyclopedia of Public International Law* (North-Holland, 1995), vol. II, pp. 957, 959–60.
[7] *See generally* Geoffrey Best, *War and Law since 1945* (Oxford: Clarendon Press, 1994), pp. 39–59; M. Cherif Bassiouni, "Regulation of Armed Conflicts," *in* M. Cherif Bassiouni, ed., *International Criminal Law* (Irvington-on-Hudson, N.Y.: Transnational Publishers, 1986), pp. 201ff, at pp. 201–04.
[8] Timothy L. H. McCormack, "From Sun Tzu to the Sixth Committee: the Evolution of an International Criminal Law Regime," *in* Timothy L. H. McCormack and Gerry J. Simpson, eds., *The Law of War Crimes: National and International Approaches* (Boston, Mass.: Martinus Nijhoff, 1997), pp. 31, 37–43; Yves Sandoz, "Penal Aspects of International Humanitarian Law," *in* Bassiouni, ed., *International Criminal Law*, vol. I, pp. 209, 209–213; Leo Gross, "The Punishment of War Criminals: the Nuremberg Trial," *Neth. Int'l L. Rev.* 2 (1955), pp. 356ff, at p. 358; James W. Garner, "Punishment of Offenders Against the Laws and Customs of War," *Am. J. Int'l L.* 14 (1920), p. 70.
[9] A third constitutive development in international law, toward the outlawing of war entirely, also developed during this period. *See, e.g.,* General Treaty for Renunciation of War as an Instrument of National Policy, Aug. 27, 1928, [46 Stat. 2343,] 94 LNTS 57; UN Charter Art. 2, para. 4; Charter of the International Military Tribunal, in Agreement for the Prosecution and Punishment of the Major War Criminals of the European Axis, Aug. 8, 1945, Art. 6(a), [59 Stat. 1544, 1547,] 82 UNTS 279, 288 [hereinafter IMT Charter].

elementary laws of humanity,"[10] and the Allies eventually inserted into the Treaty of Versailles three articles providing for the punishment by Allied military tribunals of persons accused of violating the laws and customs of war.[11] However, the Allies never held any trials, accepting a small number of trials by the German government, and developments in the law of war did not substantially move toward individual accountability.[12]

The watershed for the principle of individual accountability for human rights abuses was the exercise undertaken by the international community following the previously unimaginable atrocities of World War II, particularly the Holocaust. The creation of the International Military Tribunal (IMT) at Nuremberg and the related war crimes trials evinced a decision by the Allies that officials bear personal responsibility for outrageous conduct toward their own citizens and foreigners during wartime. As a result, the IMT Charter provided for individual criminal responsibility for violations of the laws and customs of war, as well as other egregious acts in connection with the war encompassed under the rubric of "crimes against humanity."[13] The IMT Charter also eliminated the defenses of superior orders, command of law, and act-of-state immunity, thereby subjecting even heads of State to liability for criminal violations. These same crimes and principles appeared in the Charter of the Tokyo Tribunal and in Control Council Law No. 10, which governed the US prosecution of many Nazis below the level of those tried by the IMT.[14]

Nuremberg had at least three jurisprudential progeny concerning the protection of individuals. First, it paved the way for the International Committee of the Red Cross to lead the effort to codify the law of armed conflict, dubbed international humanitarian law, anew in the 1949 Geneva Conventions and, later, the 1977 Protocols thereto.[15]

---

[10] Commission on the Responsibility of the Authors of the War and on Enforcement of Penalties, "Report Presented to the Preliminary Peace Conference, March 29, 1919," reprinted in Am J. Int'l L. 14 (1920), pp. 95, 115.

[11] Treaty of Peace, June 28, 1919, Arts. 228–30, 225 Consol. T. S. pp. 188, 285–86. The Treaty also indicted the Kaiser himself for starting the war and provided for his trial, but the Netherlands refused to hand him over for trial.

[12] Sandoz, "Penal Aspects," pp. 216–19; McCormack, "From Sun Tzu," pp. 47–50.

[13] It also criminalized the war itself, and indeed made the initiation of aggressive war the chief crime of the Nazis. See IMT Charter, Art. 6(a).

[14] Charter of the International Military Tribunal for the Far East, Jan. 19, 1946, amended Apr. 26, 1946, 4 Bevans 20; Allied Control Council Law. No. 10, Dec. 20, 1945, reprinted in Trials of War Criminals before the Nuernberg Military Tribunals under Control Council Law No. 10 (US GPO, 1949), vol. 1, p. xvi.

454   *Democratization and conflicting imperatives*

Second, although the IMT Charter, strictly speaking, addressed atrocities only in connection with the war, Nuremberg proved a springboard for the development of international human rights law generally, and the new United Nations took the lead in drafting an international bill of rights.[16]

Third, and most significant for our purposes, Nuremberg laid the groundwork for further formulation of international law on individual criminal responsibility for violations of international humanitarian and human rights law.[17] For violations of the law of armed conflict, the Geneva Conventions and Protocol I included provisions for individual culpability for certain war crimes and obligated States to prosecute offenders.[18] Outside of war, the first effort to criminalize human rights atrocities was the negotiation and conclusion of the Genocide Convention in 1948. Significant effort to create a comprehensive regime of individual criminality began in 1950, when the UN's International Law Commission sought to draft a Code of Offenses against the Peace

---

[15] Geneva Convention for the Amelioration of the Condition of the Wounded and Sick in Armed Forces in the Field, Aug. 12, 1949, [6 UST 3114,] 75 UNTS 31; Geneva Convention for the Amelioration of the Condition of Wounded, Sick and Shipwrecked Members of Armed Forces at Sea, Aug. 12, 1949, [6 UST 3217,] 75 UNTS 85; Geneva Convention Relative to the Treatment of Prisoners of War, Aug. 12, 1949, [6 UST 3316,] 75 UNTS 135; Geneva Convention Relative to the Protection of Civilian Persons in Time of War, Aug. 12, 1949, 6 UST 3516, 75 UNTS 287 [hereinafter Geneva Convention IV]; Protocol Additional to the Geneva Conventions of August 12, 1949, and Relating to the Protection of Victims of International Armed Conflicts, Dec. 12, 1977, 1125 UNTS 3 [hereinafter Protocol I]; Protocol Additional to the Geneva Conventions of August 12, 1949, and Relating to the Protection of Victims of Non-International Armed Conflicts, Dec. 12, 1977, 1125 UNTS 609 [hereinafter Protocol II].

[16] This would eventually include: the Universal Declaration of Human Rights; the Convention on the Prevention and Punishment of the Crime of Genocide, Dec. 9, 1948, 78 UNTS 277 [hereinafter Genocide Convention]; the International Covenants on Civil and Political Rights and on Economic, Social and Cultural Rights, Dec. 19, 1966, 999 UNTS 171 [hereinafter ICCPR]; the International Convention on the Elimination of All Forms of Racial Discrimination, Mar. 7, 1966, 660 UNTS 195; the Convention on the Elimination of All Forms of Discrimination Against Women, Dec. 18, 1979, 1249 UNTS 13; the Convention against Torture and Other Cruel, Inhuman or Degrading Treatment or Punishment, Dec. 10, 1984, 1465 UNTS 85 [hereinafter Torture Convention]; and the Convention on the Rights of the Child, Nov. 20, 1989, GA Res. 44/25, UN GAOR, 44th Sess. Supp. No. 49, p. 166, UN Doc. A/44/49 (1989).

[17] As stated by the UN War Crimes Commission in 1948, the IMT Charter:

> presupposes the existence of a system of international law under which individuals are responsible to the community of nations for violations of rules of international criminal law, and according to which attacks on the fundamental liberties and constitutional rights of peoples and individual[s]... constitute international crimes not only in time of war, but also, in certain circumstances, in time of peace.

See United Nations War Crimes Commission, *History of the United Nations War Crimes Commission and the Development of the Laws of War* (HMSO, 1948), pp. 192–93.

[18] See, e.g., Geneva Convention IV, Art. 146, [6 UST, p. 3616,] 75 UNTS, p. 386.

and Security of Mankind that would include certain egregious violations of human rights. But this process has staggered along slowly; after completing a draft in 1954,[19] the ILC suspended work until 1983 and, after thirteen more years of debate, completed a new draft code in 1996 whose future remains uncertain.[20]

Beginning in the 1980s, States concluded conventions on peacetime crimes beyond genocide, notably torture and disappearances, that held individuals responsible and required States to prosecute them.[21] And various UN- and regional-treaty bodies interpreted human rights conventions to create various duties upon States regarding accountability.[22] The 1990s marked a renewed interest in international criminal tribunals as a means of enforcing individual accountability. First, the atrocities committed in the former Yugoslavia and Rwanda goaded the UN Security Council to create two *ad hoc* tribunals to try individuals.[23] These developments, in turn, heightened attention among the UN's members to the need for a permanent international criminal court. After the ILC drafted a statute for such a court, States met to negotiate the details of it from 1995 to 1998, concluding a treaty for this purpose at a June 1998 Rome conference.[24]

Second, the transition from autocratic rule to democracy in numerous countries, beginning in South America but extending to Eastern Europe and parts of Africa, Central America, and Asia, has caused new governments to devise strategies for coming to terms with the human rights abuses of prior regimes and, in some cases, guerrilla opposition groups. In most cases in which States have decided to seek accountability, they have charted their own course under domestic law, creating mechanisms tailored to their individual circumstances. This pattern has led to criminal trials, truth commissions, purging of former officials from office, and civil suits against abusers.

---

[19] Draft Code of Offenses Against the Peace and Security of Mankind, in Report of the International Law Commission to the General Assembly UN Doc. A/2693 (1954), *reprinted in* 1954[II] *Y.B. Int'l L. Comm'n*, pp. 140, 149.
[20] Report of the International Law Commission on the Work of its Forty-Eighth Session, UN GAOR, 51st Sess., Supp. no. 10, p. 14, UN Doc. A/51/10 (1996); GA Res. 51/160, UN GAOR, 51st Sess., Supp. no. 49, p. 333–34, UN Doc. A/51/49 (1996).
[21] Torture Convention; Inter-American Convention on the Forced Disappearance of Persons, June 9, 1994, 33 ILM 1529 (1994).   [22] *See* infra text at notes 53–63.
[23] SC Res. 827, UN SCOR, 48th Year, Res. and Dec., p. 29, UN Doc. S/INF/49 (1993); SC Res. 955, UN SCOR, 49th Year, Res. and Dec., p. 15, UN Doc. S/INF/50. *See also* John M. Goshko, "US asks UN for Khmer Rouge Tribunal," *Washington Post* (May 1, 1998), A31.
[24] Rome Statute of the International Criminal Court, July 17, 1998, UN Doc. A/CONF. 183/9, 37 ILM 999 (1998).

B *Liability norms and accountability norms*

The result of this process, then, is a set of what might be termed both liability norms and accountability norms regarding human rights atrocities – what Agnes Heller has called "genuinely heinous crimes" that are "manifestations of evil."[25] The liability rules create State responsibility if a State fails to abide by treaties and customary law requiring it to respect certain basic rights in peace and war.[26] The accountability rules, on the other hand, apply directly to persons and engender individual criminal responsibility for certain especially egregious harms against human dignity. Not all liability rules correspond to accountability rules, for many violations of human rights and humanitarian law create only State and not individual responsibility.[27] Rather, in order for a breach of international law to entail such accountability, the international community must share a consensus on the gravity of these offenses and appropriate means of enforcement.[28]

For certain norms defined by treaties, the liability rules and accountability rules are quite clear. For example, the Genocide Convention creates State responsibility for a State's failure to prevent genocide on its territory and individual accountability insofar as it declares genocide to be an international crime. Its obligation on States to try persons committing genocide on their territory gives rise to both State and individual responsibility.[29] Greater disagreement obtains over the scope of customary law on these questions. Customary law recognizes certain human rights obligations on all States;[30] and it recognizes individual

[25] Agnes Heller, "The Limits to Natural Law and the Paradox of Evil," *in* Stephen Shute and Susan Hurley, eds., *On Human Rights: The Oxford Amnesty Lectures* (New York: Basic Books, 1993), pp. 149, 155.
[26] State responsibility is generally civil in nature (as opposed to criminal) in that it entails certain duties of reparation on the part of the State. See, *e.g.*, Rosalyn Higgins, *Problems and Process: International Law and how we use it* (Oxford: Clarendon Press, 1994), p. 162; Nguyen Quoc Dinh, with Patrick Daillier and Alain Pellet, eds., *Droit International Public*, 5th edn. (Paris: Librairie Générale de Droit et de Jurisprudence, 1994), p. 621.
[27] *See* Secretary-General of the United Nations, The Charter and the Judgment of the Nürnberg Tribunal (UN, 1949), pp. 45–46, UN Doc. A/CN.4/5, UN Sales No. 1949.V.7. *Cf.* United States v. Lanier, 520 US 259 (1997) (limiting scope of criminal statute permitting prosecutions for violation of any constitutional rights).
[28] M. Cherif Bassiouni, "The Proscribing Function of International Criminal Law in the Process of International Protection of Human Rights," *Yale J. World Pub. Ord.* 9 (1982), pp. 193ff, at pp. 195–96; Wright, "The Scope," pp. 562–63.
[29] Genocide Convention, Arts. I, VI, 78 UNTS, pp. 280–82.
[30] Barcelona Traction, Light and Power Co. (Second Phase) (Belg. v. Spain), 1970 ICJ 3, p. 32 (Feb. 5); *see generally* Symposium, "Customary International Human Rights Law," *Georgia J. Int'l Law* 25 (1995–96), p. 1.

accountability for certain acts – war crimes, genocide, crimes against humanity, torture, and slavery – at least insofar as it accepts the right of all States to criminalize them and prosecute anyone committing them (universal jurisdiction).[31]

But the harder question remains determining the intersection of these two norms, i.e., where does international law impose a liability rule on States to provide for individual accountability? Certainly, it does not follow that, simply because the law recognizes State responsibility for violations of human rights, that States are obligated to punish people who commit those abuses;[32] nor does an obligation to punish follow from individual accountability for certain human rights atrocities.[33] Instead, an independent search must be undertaken for the scope of these duties. In so doing, however, we must take care as to what is meant by accountability. A duty of criminal accountability would require States to prosecute offenders; a duty of non-criminal accountability would mean a lesser duty to hold abusers responsible through, for instance, civil suits by victims, naming by a truth commission, disqualification from office, and other mechanisms.[34]

The easiest starting point for this search are the treaties addressing specific international crimes, for they create what I would term specific duties of criminal accountability by explicitly requiring parties to prosecute offenders for crimes. The 1930 Forced Labor Convention and 1948 Genocide Convention require parties to punish for crimes committed on their soil;[35] the 1949 Geneva Conventions and Protocol I, the 1984 Torture Convention, and the 1994 OAS Convention on Disappearances require parties to extradite or punish offenders for crimes committed

---

[31] Steven R. Ratner and Jason S. Abrams, *Accountability for Human Rights Atrocities in International Law: Beyond the Nuremberg Legacy* (Oxford: Clarendon Press, 1997), pp. 140–41.
[32] *See, e.g.,* José Zalaquett, "Confronting Human Rights Violations Committed by Former Governments: Principles Applicable and Political Constraints," in *State Crimes: Punishment or Pardon* (Queenstown, Md.: Aspen Institute, 1989), pp. 23, 41–43; Ruti Teitel, "How are the New Democracies of the Southern Cone Dealing with the Legacy of Past Human Rights Abuses?" (paper presented to Council on Foreign Relations, May 17, 1990), *excerpted and reprinted in* Neil J. Kritz, ed., *Transitional Justice* (Washington, D.C.: United States Institute of Peace Press, 1995), vol. I, pp. 146, 147.
[33] *See* Ratner and Abrams, *Accountability, supra* note 31, p. 133. The reverse, however, would follow under a broad view of individual accountability, i.e., that a duty to punish would create individual accountability. *See ibid.* pp. 10–11 (defining individual accountability as occurring if the global community intends through a variety of strategies to hold individuals directly responsible).
[34] For an excellent compilation of the literature on these mechanisms, *see generally* Kritz, ed., *Transitional Justice, supra* note 32, vol. I, pp. 223–333, 459–591.
[35] June 28, 1930, as modified by the Final Articles Revision Convention of the International Labor Organization, Art. 25, 39 UNTS 55, 74; Genocide Convention, Art. VI, 78 UNTS, p. 282.

anywhere;[36] and the 1956 Slavery Convention and 1973 Apartheid Convention appear to take the strongest approach of requiring all parties to prosecute (not merely prosecute or extradite) for the crimes regardless of their place of commission.[37] Beyond these treaties, although there seems little doubt that customary law permits all States to prosecute for these crimes regardless of their situs or the nationality of the offender or victim, it is difficult to determine the extent to which the law obligates all States to do so.[38]

In addition to these treaties on specific crimes, it bears brief mention that certain conventions to address specific civil conflicts have included provisions regarding individual accountability. Most notable are the Dayton Accords' pledges of cooperation by the Bosnian parties with the work of the UN's criminal tribunal for the former Yugoslavia and the exclusion of indicted fugitives from positions of authority in Bosnia;[39] the Cambodia settlement Accords' requirement on Cambodia to undertake its obligations under relevant human rights instruments, which would include the Genocide Convention's duties to prosecute;[40] the El Salvador peace Accords' creation of a truth commission and somewhat watered-down pledge to end impunity;[41] and the Guatemala peace Accords' commitment upon the government to criminalize disappearances and extra-judicial executions.[42] These treaties do oblige the parties to undertake various forms of accountability, though none contains an

---

[36] Geneva Convention IV, Art. 146, [6 UST, p. 3616,] 75 UNTS, p. 386; Torture Convention, Art. 7(1), 1465 UNTS, p. 115; Inter-American Convention on the Forced Disappearance of Persons, Art. 7, 33 ILM, p. 1531.

[37] Supplementary Convention on the Abolition of Slavery, the Slave Trade, and Institutions and Practices Similar to Slavery, Sept. 7, 1956, Arts. 3, 6 [18 UST 3201, 3205–06], 266 UNTS 3, 42, 43; International Convention on the Suppression and Punishment of the Crime of Apartheid, Nov. 30, 1973, Arts. IV-V, 1015 UNTS 243, 246.

[38] Ratner and Abrams, *Accountability, supra* note 31, p. 141. *See also* Diane F. Orentlicher, "Settling Accounts: the Duty to Prosecute Human Rights Violations of a Prior Regime," *Yale L.J.* 100 (1991), pp. 2537, 2584–85, 2593–94.

[39] *See* General Framework Agreement for Peace in Bosnia and Herzegovina, Bos.–Croat.–Serb., Dec. 14, 1995, Art. IX, Annex 4 (Constitution) Art. IX(1), 35 ILM 75, 90, 125 (1996).

[40] Agreement on a Comprehensive Political Settlement of the Cambodia Conflict, Oct. 23, 1991, Art. 15(2), 31 ILM 174, 186 (1992). *See also* Steven R. Ratner, "The Cambodia Settlement Agreements," *Am. J. Int'l L.* 87 (1993), pp. 1, 26.

[41] Mexico Agreements, Commission on the Truth, *in* El Salvador Agreements: The Path to Peace (UN, 1992), p. 16, UN Pub. No. DPI/1208–92614–May 1992–5M; Peace Agreement, Jan. 13, 1992, Art. 5, *ibid.* p. 53 (referring the issue of impunity to the Commission on Truth "without prejudice to the principle ... that acts of this nature ... must be the object of exemplary action by the law courts so that the punishment prescribed by law is meted out to those found responsible").

[42] Comprehensive Agreement on Human Rights, Dec. 29, 1996, Art. III, 36 ILM 258, 276 (1997) [hereinafter Guatemala Human Rights Agreement].

explicit and unequivocal obligation on the parties to punish certain offenses.

Yet the current debates over accountability tend to be defined not so much in the narrow terms of prosecution for specific crimes recognized under international law, or even the duties in the context of certain parties to peace accords, but, rather, in terms of what I will term a generalized duty of criminal accountability for atrocities as defined above. The distinction is more than academic. For example, a summary execution or severe physical harm outside of armed conflict that is not part of a pattern constituting genocide or crimes against humanity is not, at the present time, an international crime under any treaty.[43] Yet proponents of a generalized duty would certainly regard such a duty as requiring a State to punish those committing summary executions. The debate thus concerns whether all serious human rights abuses must be prosecuted. And it has assumed special significance today in States undergoing transition to democracy – States that seem ready to embrace human rights norms but are reluctant to judge prior regimes too harshly.

II ACCOUNTABILITY AND THE GROWTH OF DEMOCRACY

Arguments about a duty of accountability resonate quite differently across the planet. We might divide the world into three groups of States with regard to their confronting accountability for human rights abuses. First are authoritarian States where governmental officials regularly order or commit serious human rights abuses. To them, the debate may seem amusing, for they have no intention of punishing abusers unless forced to do so by outside pressure. Second are States with overall good human rights records. They too are likely to ignore claims of an international duty to prosecute serious human rights abuses, but for the totally opposite reason. These governments are committed to prosecuting them in principle (though they may let abuses fester in fact);[44] serious abuses tend to be the exception rather than the rule and thus easier to address; and popular opinion, to which the government is sensitive, will

---

[43] See Steven R. Ratner, "The Schizophrenias of International Criminal Law," Texas Int'l L.J. 33 (1998), p. 237.
[44] See, e.g., Report of the United States of America to the Human Rights Committee, August 24, 1994, UN Doc. CCPR/C/81/Add.4, para. 98(i)-(j) (listing legal avenues for prosecution of officials for human rights abuses); Report of Spain to the Human Rights Committee, August 5, 1994, UN Doc. CCPR/C/95/Add.1, paras.37–38 (describing new law punishing torture by public officials); Report of Norway to the Human Rights Committee, May 26, 1997, CCPR/C/115/Add.2, paras. 21–26 (new law to punish police violence).

often not tolerate impunity.[45] The latter group of States are, to a fault, all States we would regard as liberal or constitutional democracies. For them (and for me, for that matter), democracy's emphasis on the rule of law necessarily implies punishment for serious human rights abuses. Indeed, it is part of the definition of modern democracy. They can ignore the debate because they already largely comply or are at least committed to complying with any norm that might be asserted.

It is a third group of States for whom the accountability debate has the most meaning and whose experiences also enrich the debate itself. These States are, in essence, moving from the first group to the second. Contrary to popular understanding, this third group encompasses not a narrow group of States who have announced their commitment to democracy and are only dealing with the prior regime. Rather, it comprises a broad range of States, from mildly authoritarian regimes hoping to make steps toward the rule of law, to states with democratically elected governments and a professed commitment to a future rule of law. It would also include those trying to end civil wars, as those conflicts manifest the incompleteness of democracy in that people are not settling their disputes through democratic processes.[46] For these societies, the debates over accountability assume the greatest relevance, and these arguments often become intertwined with discourses about the normative nature and desirability of democracy. They thus form the laboratory for those seeking to understand the relationships between these two phenomena of our contemporary world.

What makes these transitional situations so special for evaluating these two possibly emerging norms? First and most generally, these States have to look forward and backward at the same time. In seeking democracy – rule of the people and the rule of law – for the future, they wish to place the past behind them, but they ask legitimately whether the most extreme form of that action – impunity – will promote or detract from their vision for a better future.[47] If holding individuals accountable for human rights abuses forms part of the rule of law and thus democracy,[48]

---

[45] *See, e.g.*, Barry James, "Belgium's Confidence Crisis is Deepening," *Int'l Herald Trib.* (Sept. 12, 1996), p. 2 (public outcry over improper investigation of murders of children).
[46] *See* Joseph A. Schumpeter, *Capitalism, Socialism and Democracy* (New York: Harper and Row, 1950), p. 269 (democracy exists where "individuals acquire the power to decide by means of a competitive struggle for the people's vote").
[47] *See generally* Tina Rosenberg, *The Haunted Land: Facing Europe's Ghosts after Communism* (New York: Vintage, 1995), pp. 397–405.
[48] *Cf.* James G. March and John P. Olsen, *Democratic Governance* (The Free Press, 1995), pp. 59–60 (political accountability of officials, including subjection to sanctions, as part of democracy).

Democracy and accountability 461

these States are essentially deciding whether abstaining from accountability for the past, and thus from a fuller expression of democracy, will promote that fuller democracy in the long term.

Second, not only do those who have committed the abuses remain in a nation's midst but, in many situations, they retain some form of formal or informal power.[49] The transitional regimes may claim publicly or privately that only impunity will prevent the return of the military regime (e.g., Chile, Uruguay, or Argentina), or simply have agreed to include in their midst parties that committed abuses (e.g., Mozambique, South Africa). The linkage between democracy and accountability is not merely about a relationship between the past and the future, but one that immediately implicates the present and the status of the transition.

Third, regardless of the power of those who committed the abuses, the rule of law is not yet fully in place in such societies. This creates a question in the mind of the elites and populace of such States as to whether accountability can be achieved in a way that respects the rule of law and is not simply revenge.[50] The judicial system may lack crucial indicia of fairness and might be institutionally incapable of judging a potentially very large group of targets.[51] The trials of leading officials and lustrations of a broader group of supporters of the *ancien régime* have highlighted this issue.[52]

III THE STATE OF THE GENERALIZED ACCOUNTABILITY

A Treaty-based law

Most debate among States, NGOs, and observers over a generalized duty stems from a vacuum in treaty law – namely the absence of any specific obligations in the key universal human rights accord, the International

---

[49] *See, e.g.*, Samuel P. Huntington, *The Third Wave: Democratization in the Late Twentieth Century* (Norman, Okla.: University of Oklahoma Press, 1991), p. 114 (distinguishing between "transformations," "replacements," and "transplacements"); Zalaquett, *supra* note 32, "Confronting Human Rights Violations," pp. 45–47 (six forms of transition); Carlos Nino, *Radical Evil on Trial* (New Haven: Yale University Press, 1996), pp. 118–21. For a comparison of three cases, *see* David Pion-Berlin, "To Prosecute or Pardon? Human Rights Decision in the Latin American Southern Cone," *Hum. Rts. Q.* 16 (1994), pp. 105, 111–14; Jorge Correa S., "Dealing with Past Human Rights Violations: the Chilean Case After Dictatorship," *Notre Dame L.R.* 67 (1992), pp. 1455, 1460–63.
[50] *See* Luc Huyse, "Justice after Transition: on the Choices Successor Elites Make in Dealing with the Past," *Law and Social Inquiry* 20 (1995), pp. 51, 57–58. *See also* Ruti Teitel, "Transitional Jurisprudence," *Yale L.J.* 106 (1997), pp. 2009, 2040–41.
[51] *See* Ratner and Abrams, *Accountability, supra* note 31, p. 159 (four minimal criteria for fair judicial system); Carla J. Ferstman, "Domestic Trials for Genocide and Crimes Against Humanity: the Example of Rwanda," *Afr. J. Int'l and Comp. L.* 9 (1997), p. 857.
[52] *See* Rosenberg, *The Haunted Land, supra* note 47, pp. 402–03.

Covenant on Civil and Political Rights (ICCPR), that a State prosecute and punish abusers of human rights. Rather, the Covenant contains only less precise obligations, notably those to "respect and ensure to all individuals within its territory and subject to its jurisdiction the rights recognized [therein]," and to provide "an effective remedy," language echoed in the European and American Conventions on Human Rights.[53]

But while the treaty texts lack a generalized duty of accountability for serious abuses, the bodies charged by their parties with interpreting them have proclaimed such a norm.[54] Thus, the Human Rights Committee established under the ICCPR has repeatedly found that States have a duty to investigate and prosecute those committing disappearances, summary executions, ill-treatment, and arbitrary arrest and detention.[55] It has also, in particular, condemned amnesties (non-prosecution of a class of offenders), originally confining its concern to their effect on the right against torture[56] and more recently extending its concern to blanket amnesties generally.[57] In condemning amnesties for crimes of the prior regime, the Committee implicitly holds, as international law requires, that a State's duties under international law do not disappear by virtue of a change in government.[58] Nevertheless, the Committee has not recommended that States with amnesty laws replace

---

[53] ICCPR, Arts. 2(2)-(3), 9(5), 14(6), 999 UNTS, pp. 174, 176, 177; American Convention on Human Rights, Nov. 22, 1969, Arts. 1(1), 10, 25,1144 UNTS 123, 124, 127, 131; European Convention for the Protection of Human Rights and Fundamental Freedoms, Nov. 4, 1950, Arts. 1, 5(5), 13, 213 UNTS 221, 228, 232. *See* Robert O. Weiner, "Trying to Make Ends Meet: Reconciling the Law and Practice of Human Rights Amnesties," *St. Mary's L.J.* 26 (1995), pp. 857, 862–64.

[54] *See generally* Naomi Roht-Arriaza, "Sources in International Treaties of an Obligation to Investigate, Prosecute, and Provide Redress," in Naomi Roht-Arriaza, ed., *Impunity and Human Rights in International Law and Practice* (Oxford University Press, 1995), pp. 24, 28–32.

[55] *See, e.g.,* Comments on Nigeria, para. 284, *in* Report of the Human Rights Committee, UN GAOR 51st Sess., Supp. No. 40, p. 41, UN Doc. A/51/40 (1996); Bautista de Arellana v. Colombia, Comm. No. 563/1993, UN Doc. CCPR/C/55/D/563/1993, para. 8.6 (1995) (duty "to prosecute criminally"). In the latter case, the Committee reiterated that this duty does not stem from any individual right to force a government to prosecute someone.

[56] General Comment 20 (44) (Article 7), para. 15, *in* Report of the Human Rights Committee, UN GAOR, 47th Sess., Supp. No. 40, Annex VI, pp. 193, 195, UN Doc. A/47/49 (1992) ("[a]mnesties are generally incompatible with the duty of States to investigate such acts").

[57] *See, e.g.,* Preliminary Observations on Peru, para. 9, UN Doc. CCPR/C/79/Add.67 ("amnesty prevents appropriate investigation and punishment of perpetrators of past human rights violations, undermines efforts to establish respect for human rights, contributes to an atmosphere of impunity among perpetrators or human rights violations"); Comments on Argentina, paras., 153, 158, *in* Report of the Human Rights Committee, UN GAOR, 50th Sess., Supp. No. 40, pp. 31, 32, UN Doc. A/50/40 (1995); Hugo Rodriguez v. Uruguay, Comm. No. 322/1988, UN Doc. CCPR/C/51/D/322/1988 (1994).

[58] Robert Jennings and Arthur Watts, eds., *Oppenheim's International Law*, 9th edn. (New York: Longman, 1992), vol. 1, pp. 234–35; American Law Institute, *Restatement (Third) of the Foreign Relations Law of the United States* (ALI, 1987), § 208, cmt. a.

them with prosecutions (perhaps due to concerns about retroactive application of the law), but has, instead, requested investigations, compensation for victims, and removal of offenders from office.[59]

The potentially most sweeping call for a generalized duty of criminal accountability has come from the Inter-American Court of Human Rights in the now-famous *Velasquez-Rodriguez* decision of 1988, in which relatives of a "disappeared" Guatemalan brought a claim against the Government of Guatemala for violations of the American Convention on Human Rights (ACHR). There the Court stated that each party had a duty "to use the means at its disposal to carry out a serious investigation of [human rights] violations committed within its jurisdiction, to identify those responsible, to impose the appropriate punishment and to ensure the victim adequate compensation."[60] That case did not, however, concern an amnesty by a democratic government for acts of a prior regime, but rather ongoing conduct by a still-repressive regime that had denied responsibility and refused to cooperate with the Inter-American Commission on Human Rights;[61] and even on those facts, the Court did not specifically mention prosecution as the exclusive method of punishment and might have left open the door to administrative punishment alone.[62] Subsequent opinions of the Inter-American Commission on Human Rights have, however, pronounced general amnesties incompatible with the American Convention and emphasized prosecutions.[63] Nonetheless, the Commission has not, perhaps out of a sense of the politically delicate nature of this question, exercised its prerogative to refer any of these cases to the Court for a binding decision.

Standing beside the ICCPR and the American Convention is Protocol II to the Geneva Conventions of 1949, which calls upon States after the conclusion of civil wars to "grant the broadest possible amnesty

---

[59] *See* Preliminary Observations on Peru, para. 20; Comments on Argentina, para. 158.
[60] Velasquez-Rodriguez Case, Inter-Am. Ct. H.R. (ser. C), No. 4 (1988) (judgment), para. 174.
[61] *See* Tom Farer, "Consolidating Democracy in Latin America: Law, Legal Institutions and Constitutional Structure," *Am. U. J. Int'l L. and Pol'y* 10 (1995), pp. 1295, 1307–08.
[62] *See* Michael P. Scharf, "The Letter of the Law: The Scope of the International Legal Obligation to Prosecute Human Rights Crimes," *Law and Contemp. Probs.* 59 (1996), pp. 41, 50–51.
[63] *See* Report No. 36/96 (Chile), October 15, 1996, para. 111, 1996 Ann. Rep. Inter-Am. Comm'n on Human Rights 156, 183 (1997) (recommendation to change self-amnesty law with a view to "identifying the guilty parties, establishing their responsibilities and effectively prosecuting them"). This should be compared to earlier cases, *see, e.g.*, Report No. 29/92 (Uruguay), October 2, 1992, para. 54, 1992–93 Ann. Rep. Inter-Am. Comm'n on Human Rights 154, 165 (1993) (recommending "just compensation" and "measures necessary to clarify the facts and identify those responsible" but not prosecutions). *See also* Douglass Cassel, "Lesson from the Americas: Guidelines for the International Response to Amnesties for Atrocities," *Law and Contemp. Probs.* 59 (1996), pp. 197, 208–19; Weiner, "Trying to Make Ends Meet," *supra* note 53, pp. 868–69.

to persons who have participated in the armed conflict."[64] The International Committee of the Red Cross has stated publicly that Protocol II's encouragement of amnesty to participants in civil wars "does not aim at an amnesty for those having violated international humanitarian law."[65]

As welcome as these rulings and opinions are to those advocating a broad duty of criminal accountability, they have not been welcomed, or especially followed, by most States – transitional democracies all – to which they are directed. Thus, Argentina, Uruguay, Chile, Brazil, Peru, Guatemala, El Salvador, Honduras, Nicaragua, Haiti, Ivory Coast, Angola, and Togo have all passed broad amnesty laws in the last ten years – or honored amnesties of prior regimes – covering governmental atrocities;[66] and South Africa is immersed in a long process of judgment of the past that includes, at its centerpiece, confession to a commission of inquiry in exchange for amnesty.[67]

Indeed, this practice of States is central to interpreting these treaties,

---

[64] Protocol II, Art. 6(5), 1126 UNTS, p. 614.

[65] Naomi Roht-Arriaza, "Combatting Impunity: Some Thoughts on the Way Forward," *Law and Contemp. Probs.* 59 (1996), pp. 93, 97 (quoting letter from head of ICRC Legal Division).

[66] *See, e.g.*, Law No. 23492, Dec. 23, 1986 (Argentina), *reprinted in* Kritz, ed., *Transitional Justice, supra* note 32, vol. III, p. 505; Law No. 15,848, Dec. 22, 1986 (Uruguay), *reprinted in* Kritz, ed., *Transitional Justice, supra* note 32, vol. III, p. 598; Decreto Ley No. 2.191, Apr. 18, 1978 (Chile); Lei No. 6.683, Aug. 28, 1979, Art. 1 (Brazil); Ley No. 26479, June 14, 1995, *available at* <www.congreso.gob.pe/ccd/leyes/cronos/1995/ley26479.htm> (Peru); Ley de Reconciliation Nacional, Decree No. 145–96, Art. 5, Dec. 18, 1996 (Guatemala) [hereinafter Guatemala Amnesty Law]; Decree No. 486, March 20, 1993 (El Salvador), *reprinted in* Kritz, ed., *Transitional Justice, supra* note 32, vol. III, p. 546; Decreto Numero 87–91, July 23, 1991 (Honduras); Law No. 81 on General Amnesty and National Reconciliation, May 9, 1990 (Nicaragua), *reprinted in* Kritz, ed., *supra* note 32, *Transitional Justice*, vol. III, p. 591; Loi Relative a L'Amnistie, *published in* Le Moniteur, Journal Officiel de la Republique d'Haiti, Oct. 10, 1994 (Haiti), *reprinted and translated in* Michael P. Scharf, "Swapping Amnesties for Peace: Was There a Duty to Prosecute International Crimes in Haiti?" *Tex. Int'l L. J.* 31 (1996), 1, 15–16 [hereinafter Haiti Amnesty Law]; "Ivory Coast Parliament Passes Amnesty Law," July 29, 1992, Reuters Library Report (available on NEXIS); "Angola: National Assembly Approves Amnesty Law," BBC Summary of World Broadcasts (Televisao Popular de Angola), May 9, 1996 (available on NEXIS); Tchidah Banawe, "Togo – Politics: Trying to Heal the Wounds," Inter Press Service, March 2, 1995 (available on NEXIS). The Argentine law was repealed in Ley. No. 24.952, April 15, 1998, though the repeal is not expected to have retroactive effect. *See* Marcela Valenta, "Rights – Argentina: Dissatisfaction with Repeal of Amnesty Laws," *Inter Press Service*, March 25, 1998 (available on NEXIS); *see also infra* text at note 85 (exceptions from amnesty laws). Kai Ambos, "Impunity in International Criminal Law: a Case Study on Colombia, Peru, Bolivia, Chile, and Argentina," *Hum. Rts. L. J.* 18 (1997), p. 1; US Department of State, "State Practice Regarding Amnesties and Pardons," *available at* <gopher://gopher.igc.apc.org:70/100/orgs/ICC/natldocs/prepcom4/amnesty.us> (submitted to UN Preparatory Committee on the Establishment of a Permanent International Criminal Court).

[67] *See* Promotion of National Unity and National Reconciliation Act, Law No. 34 of 1995, July 26, 1995 (South Africa) [hereinafter South Africa Amnesty Law]; Azanian People's Organisation (AZAPO) and Others v. President of the Republic of South Africa, 1996(4) SA 671 (upholding constitutionality of Act); Timothy Garton Ash, "True Confessions," *N.Y. Rev. Books* (July 17, 1997), p. 33.

along with their plain meaning, context, subsequent agreements, and relevant rules of international law.[68] How do we reconcile this practice with the purported duty to prosecute? First, it could be argued (as a human rights NGO might) that the duties in both the ICCPR and ACHR to "respect and ensure" rights and provide a "remedy" are themselves clear from their plain meaning and thus recourse to subsequent practice is unwarranted.[69] This argument is problematic, however, in two senses: (a) the term "remedy" could be said from its plain meaning to mean only a civil recovery for victims of abuses; and the term "respect and ensure rights" is sufficiently broad and vague as to suggest the need for recourse to other aids to interpretation; and (b) perhaps more important, the Vienna Convention on the Law of Treaties does not, in fact, contain such a hard-and-fast rule, and indeed recognizes the possibility, in the words of Ian Sinclair, that "the subsequent practice of the parties may operate as a tacit or implicit modification of the terms of the treaty."[70] This suggests that amnesties might even be considered an acceptable way to respect and ensure rights in the Convention.[71]

A second argument possible from those advocating such a duty would discount the interpretive force of these amnesties because, although they represent the practice of some States under those treaties, they do not constitute the consistent practice of all or even most parties to these treaties.[72] Thus, the willingness of many States to prosecute violations of human rights counters any argument that States have agreed that amnesties are permissible. This may be true, but the failure of States to condemn amnesties suggests that it is simplistic to say that States have interpreted the treaties to forbid them.[73]

---

[68] Vienna Convention on the Law of Treaties, Art. 31, 1155 UNTS 331, 340.
[69] See Yehudah Z. Blum, *Eroding the United Nations Charter* (Norwell, Mass.: Martinus Nijhoff, 1993), pp. 243–44 (subsequent practice cannot override plain meaning).
[70] See Ian Sinclair, *The Vienna Convention on the Law of Treaties*, 2d edn. (Manchester University Press, 1984), p. 138. [71] See, e.g., Report No. 29/92 (Uruguay), paras. 22–23 (arguments of Uruguay).
[72] See Sinclair, *The Vienna Convention*, supra note 70, p. 137; Mustafa Kamil Yasseen, "L'Interpretation des traités d'après la Convention de Vienne sur le Droit des Traités," *Recueil des Cours* 151 (1976), pp. 1, 48–49.
[73] For an example of the weak international response, see GA Res. 51/197, para. 8, UN GAOR, 51st Sess., Supp. No. 49, pp. 57, 59, UN Doc. A/51/49 (1997) (General Assembly "[r]ecognizes the commitment of the Government and civil society of Guatemala to advance in the fight against impunity and toward the consolidation of the rule of law"); see also Cassel, "Lesson from the Americas," supra note 63, pp. 222–27 (noting reluctance of UN to condemn amnesties in Guatemala, El Salvador, and Haiti). For rare exceptions, see US Dep't of State, Country Reports on Human Rights Practices for 1996 (US GPO, 1997), p. 541 (noting Peru's "[a]mnesty Law demonstrates a lack of serious commitment to accountability and the protection of human rights"); Assessment of the Peace Process in El Salvador: Report of the Secretary-General, July 1, 1997, UN Doc. A/51/917, p. 7 (condemning amnesty as "clear rejection of the conclusion of the Truth Commission").

In response to these two rather unnuanced uses of treaty law, I would propose two alternatives that point in opposite directions. A first response would approach the question of subsequent practice with a finer instrument than that above. It would note that, although practice is inconsistent, it can be reconciled into a discrete pattern. Those States with stable democracies and working judiciaries are interpreting the agreement to require prosecution of human rights abusers; while those States in transition are interpreting it to allow them leeway to provide amnesties for offenses of their predecessors. One might thus say that the States parties to the ICCPR and ACHR have agreed, as a whole, to afford more leeway in implementing their duties to States in democratic transitions, perhaps out of a belief that these situations permit derogations from the duties to prosecute.[74] One could thus conclude that States accept the use of amnesties in transitional situations as a permissible gloss on the duties in the treaty to guarantee rights and provide a remedy.

Second, one could emphasize the authority of the body providing the above opinions and the views of States parties regarding this authority as opposed to the actual practice of States.[75] Thus, while the Human Rights Committee's opinions are not binding upon member States, they do command great respect.[76] The Committee has itself even asserted the right to be the authoritative interpreter of the ICCPR with respect to the consistency of States parties' reservations to the ICCPR.[77] As for the Inter-American Court, its rulings are legally binding upon the parties to a particular contentious case and generally accepted by States as

---

[74] The ICCPR permits derogations in the event of "national emergency," ICCPR, Art. 4; and the Torture Convention implicitly allows a derogation of the duty to extradite or prosecute by not classifying that duty as non-derogable. For arguments that the duty to prosecute is nonetheless non-derogable, see Naomi Roht-Arriaza, "Special Problems of a Duty to Prosecute: Derogation, Amnesties, Statutes of Limitation, and Superior Orders," in Roht-Arriaza, ed., *Impunity and Human Rights*, *supra* note 54, pp. 57, 62–63; Orentlicher, "Settling Accounts," *supra* note 38, pp. 2606–12.

[75] For excellent comparative background, see R. Andrew Painter, "Monitoring State Compliance with International Human Rights Obligations: The Role of the Human Rights Treaty Bodies," paper prepared for New York University School of Law Conference on Administrative and Expert Monitoring of International Legal Norms, Feb. 3, 1996.

[76] Sian Lewis-Anthony, "Treaty-based Procedures for Making Human Rights Complaints within the UN System," in Hurst Hannum, ed., *Guide to International Human Rights Practice*, 2d edn. (University of Pennsylvania Press, 1992), pp. 41, 48. See also "The UN Human Rights System: Is it Effective?," *ASIL Proc.* 91 (1997), p. 460.

[77] General Comment No. 24 (52), para. 20, in Report of the Human Rights Committee, UN GAOR, 50th Sess., Supp. No. 40, Vol. I, Annex v, p. 119, UN Doc. A/50/40 (1995). See also Torkel Opsahl, "The Human Rights Committee," in Philip Alston, ed., *The United Nations and Human Rights: a Critical Appraisal* (Oxford: Clarendon Press, 1992), pp. 369, 434 ("the Committee's independence and authority give this contribution [i.e., its General Comments and views] a particular weight").

authoritative interpretations of that document.[78] The opinions of the Inter-American Commission on Human Rights are, like those of the Human Rights Committee, non-binding.[79] Even if the member States do not regard a ruling by these bodies as binding on all States, their acceptance of the influential nature of their rulings would argue for interpreting these treaties as mandating the broader duties stated by these organs, notwithstanding the practice of States.[80]

The combined effect of these four approaches to treaty interpretation is, it seems, uncertainty. The parties have not all taken the same path to implement the treaties, and whether the provision of amnesty is a violation or a legitimate interpretation accepted by all States as permissible for States in transition is not clear. The views of the treaty implementation bodies are obviously important, but ultimately the contemporary meaning of a treaty depends as much, if not more, on what States do than what such bodies say.[81] In the end, it is difficult to conclude that States are prepared to interpret these two conventions to provide for a duty to prosecute all serious violations of human rights, especially those that took place in the prior regime.

B Customary law

The practice of States in addressing abuses of the past is not only relevant as subsequent conduct to various treaties; it is, of course, a core indicium of customary law.[82] As a starting point, it would seem that if

---

[78] American Convention on Human Rights, Art. 68(1), 1144 UNTS, p. 140. *See also* Scott Davidson, *The Inter-American Court of Human Rights*, 2nd ed. (Aldershot, Hants.: Dartmouth, 1992), pp. 109, 213; Christina Cerna, "International Law and the Protection of Human Rights in the Inter-American System," *Hous. J. Int'l L.* 19 (1997), pp. 731, 755.

[79] Caballero Delgado and Santana Case, Inter-Am. Ct. H.R. (Ser.C), No. 22 (1996) (judgment), para. 67. *See also* Cerna, "International Law," *supra* note 78, p. 752.

[80] The US and British responses to General Comment 24 clearly demonstrate, however, that they do not regard the Committee as the final arbiter of the ICCPR. *See* Observations on General Comment No. 24 (52), United States of America, *in* Report of the Human Rights Committee, UN GAOR, 50th Sess., Supp. No. 40, Vol. 1, Annex v, pp. 126, 126–27, UN Doc. A/50/40 (1995); Observations on General Comment No. 24 (52), United Kingdom of Great Britain and Northern Ireland, *in ibid.* pp. 130, 132–33.

[81] Myres S. McDougal and W. Michael Reisman, "The Prescribing Function in the World Constitutive Process: How International Law is Made," *in* Myres S. McDougal and W. Michael Reisman, eds., *International Law Essays* (Mineola, N.Y.: Foundation Press, 1981), pp. 355, 377 (question is whether duty "is viewed as authoritative by those to whom it is addressed and ... its audience concludes that the prescriber ... intends to and, indeed, can make it controlling"); *see also* Carlos S. Nino, "The Duty to Punish Past Abuses of Human Rights Put Into Context: the Case of Argentina," *Yale L.J.* 100 (1991) pp. 2619, 2621 ("a necessary criterion for the validity of any norm of ... positive international law is the willingness of ... states and international bodies to enforce it").

[82] Statute of the International Court of Justice, Art. 38; North Sea Continental Shelf (FRG/Den., FRG/Neth.), 1969 ICJ 3, 45 (Feb. 20).

State practice does not support reading those treaties to suggest a conventional obligation to punish, then that same State practice does not support a customary law-based duty to punish.[83] And here, the lack of consonance between the purported norm and the actual practice of States forms a very high barrier to the existence of that norm.

As noted, the number of States that have chosen to employ legal amnesties inconsistent with the idea of a duty of criminal accountability for serious governmental abuses is not insignificant.[84] On the other hand, some of the above amnesties, such as those of Guatemala, Haiti, and South Africa, do at least contemplate the possibility of prosecutions for serious crimes or have been limited by executive or judicial interpretation;[85] and some new governments (not all democracies) – Greece after the rule of the colonels, Argentina, Bolivia, Ethiopia, Romania, Hungary, and Rwanda – have successfully prosecuted key officials of the prior regime for serious human rights abuses.[86] But the practice cannot be regarded as consistent.

---

[83] It is, of course, possible for State practice not to argue in favor of a treaty having a particular meaning (in this case, a generalized duty of criminal accountability) but nonetheless to suggest the existence of a customary law norm with the same meaning. One obvious example would be the norm against prosecution of foreign diplomats in the years before the Vienna Convention on Diplomatic Relations, Apr. 18, 1961, [23 UST 3227,] 500 UNTS 95. Although State practice would not support the view that States had interpreted the UN Charter to forbid prosecution of foreign diplomats, that practice, when combined with *opinio juris*, did support the existence of the norm as a matter of custom. *See* B. Sen, *A Diplomat's Handbook of International Law and Practice*, 3d rev. edn. (Norwell, Mass.: Martinus Nijhoff, 1988), pp. 107–10.

[84] *See* sources cited in note 66. For examples of amnesties for rebel groups, *see, e.g.*, Brazil Const. (1988), Transitional Constitutional Provisions Art. 8; Ley No. 25499, May 16, 1992, Arts. II, III (Peru); "Ministry of Defence Says 5,500 Deserters have Returned Home," BBC Summary of World Broadcasts (Yemeni Republic Radio), Aug. 5, 1994 (available on NEXIS) (amnesty for members of Yemeni Socialist Party); Peace Agreement between the Government of the Republic of Sierra Leone and the Revolutionary United Front of Sierra Leone, Nov. 30, 1996, Art. 14, *in* Letter Dated 11 December 1996 from the Permanent Representative of Sierra Leone to the United Nations Addressed to the Secretary-General, Dec. 11, 1996, UN Doc. S/1996/1034, Annex, p. 6. *See also* Agreement on the Gaza Strip and the Jericho Area (Israel–PLO), May 4, 1994, Art. XX, 33 ILM pp. 622, 635–36 (1994) (Israeli non-prosecution of 5,000 Palestinians for offenses committed prior to Sept. 13, 1993).

[85] *See, e.g.*, Guatemala Amnesty Law, Art. 8 (exempting "the crime of genocide, torture, forced disappearance, as well as those [crimes] which are imprescriptible or which do not permit the extinction of penal responsibility in conformity with internal law or international treaties ratified by Guatemala"); Guatemalan Constitutional Court Opinion on Amnesty, Oct. 7, 1997 (on file with author); Haiti Amnesty Law (vague terms); South Africa Amnesty Law, Art. 20 (limited to official acts as determined by Commission).

[86] *See, e.g.*, Ratner and Abrams, *Accountability*, *supra* note 31, pp. 146–56 and sources cited therein; P. Nikforos Diamandouros, "Regime Change and the Prospects for Democracy in Greece: 1973–83," *in* Guillermo O'Donnell *et al.*, eds., *Transitions from Authoritarian Rule: Southern Europe* (Baltimore, Md.: The Johns Hopkins University Press, 1986), pp. 138, 161; William R. Long, "Bolivia Imposes 30-Year Term on Ex-Dictator," *L.A. Times* (April 22, 1993), A12.

Moreover, the reaction of the rest of the international community suggests some acceptance of this practice in the case of transitional governments dealing with past abuses. Although governments and international organizations have condemned authoritarian States for failing to punish human rights abusers,[87] they have, with the exception of those bodies responsible for interpreting treaties above, generally refrained from condemning those States for failure to prosecute past abuses once they adopt democratic government.[88]

As for the other element of custom as traditionally viewed, *opinio juris* seems difficult to glean from the existing practice of States dealing with accountability. Those States that routinely prosecute human rights abusers do not seem to claim it is an international law obligation to do so;[89] and States that do not prosecute have advanced a number of arguments that international law permits, or at least does not prohibit, forms of impunity.[90]

Some scholars have argued that in the context of deriving customary human rights norms, both State practice and *opinio juris* take on different contours. Instead of a consistent pattern of practice backed by evidence that the States regard the practice as legally required, one might focus on resolutions of international organizations, statements of governments, the content of domestic constitutions, and other professions of belief.[91] But even this method yields mixed results at best about a duty

---

[87] *See, e.g.,* GA Res. 37/185, para. 10, UN GAOR, 37th Sess., Supp. No. 51, pp. 204, 205, UN Doc. A/37/51 (1982) (El Salvador); GA Res. 36/157, para. 4(d), UN GAOR, 36th Sess., Supp. No. 51, pp. 188, 189, UN Doc. A/36/51 (1981) (Chile); *see also* Orentlicher, "Settling Accounts," *supra* note 38, p. 2584 n. 205 (citing reports of UN Special Rapporteurs).

[88] *See* sources cited in note 73.

[89] *See, e.g.,* sources cited in note 44, which do not contain any statement of obligation on the part of the parties to prosecute. The absence of *opinio juris* need not signal the absence of custom if accompanied by sufficient State practice. *See* Maurice Mendelson, "The Subjective Element of Customary International Law," *Brit. Y.B. Int'l L.* 66 (1995), pp. 177, 204–08. Yet here no such practice is evident.

[90] *See, e.g.,* Letter from President Sanguinetti to Amnesty International Regarding the Ley de Caducidad, *reprinted in* Kritz, ed., *Transitional Justice, supra* note 32, vol. III, p. 600 (Uruguay) (amnesty as acceptable method to safeguard rights while avoiding "social upheavals"); Report No. 36/96 (Chile), paras. 18–25 (noting amnesty was passed by military regime and new government cannot revoke it); AZAPO, 1996(4) SA, p. 691 (relying on Protocol II); Unconstitutionality Judgement Proceedings No. 10–93 (El Salv. Sup. Ct.), *reprinted in* Kritz, ed., *Transitional Justice, supra* note 32, vol. III, pp. 549, 555 (same).

[91] For a useful review (as well as criticism) of these views, *see* Bruno Simma and Philip Alston, "The Sources of Human Rights Law: Custom, *Jus Cogens*, and General Principles," *Austrl. Y.B. Int'l L.* 12 (1992), pp. 82, 84–102; *see also* Richard B. Lillich, "The Growing Importance of Customary Human Rights Law," *Ga. J. Int'l and Comp. L.* 25 (1995/96), p. 1; Hurst Hannum, "The Status of the Universal Declaration of Human Rights in National and International Law," *Ga. J. Int'l and Comp. L.* 25 (1995/96), p. 278.

of accountability. Undoubtedly, some resolutions of international organizations support a generalized duty of criminal accountability. The 1993 World Conference on Human Rights called on States to "abrogate legislation leading to impunity for those responsible for grave violations of human rights such as torture and prosecute such violations."[92] The Economic and Social Council, in its 1989 Principles on the Effective Prevention and Investigation of Extra-legal, Arbitrary and Summary Executions, called on governments to ensure that persons accused of such acts "are brought to justice."[93] Beyond these resolutions, the United Nations has stated officially to Human Rights Watch, in the context of the Guatemalan peace process, that it could not condone any peace accord in violation of principles of human rights and international law and that impunity of gross abusers is "the most serious problem" facing that State.[94] The General Assembly has recently noted the importance of addressing the array of crimes under international and Cambodian law committed by the Khmer Rouge.[95] The Human Rights Commission's Special Rapporteur on the question of impunity has even formulated a "right to know" and the "right to justice" for victims and interpreted it to require States to adopt measures to expose the truth and combat impunity.[96]

But when one moves beyond resolutions, statements, and special rapporteurs, one confronts the opinions of governments in transition that international law does not require them to punish prior offenders.[97] Contrast this with the statements of governments in regard to the underlying human rights norms (e.g., the ban on torture or summary executions), where States do not dispute the existence of the norm and even

[92] See Vienna Declaration and Programme of Action, June 25, 1993, para. 60, in World Conference on Human Rights: The Vienna Declaration and Programme of Action June 1993, (UN, 1993), p. 61, UN Sales No. DPI/1394-39399–August 1993–20M.
[93] ESC Res. 1989/65, Annex, UN ESCOR, 1st Sess. Supp. No. 1, p. 5 (1990). See also Declaration of Basic Principles of Justice for Victims of Crimes and Abuse of Power, Art. 4, GA Res. 40/34, Annex, UN GAOR, 40th Sess., Supp. No. 53, pp. 213, 214, UN Doc. A/40/53 (1985) (victims should have "access to the mechanisms of justice and to prompt redress, as provided for by national legislation, for the harm that they have suffered").
[94] Letter from Marrack Goulding, UN Under-Secretary-General for Political Affairs, to Jose Miguel Vivanco, Executive Director, Human Rights Watch/Americas, August 8, 1996 (on file with author). For the group's report, see UN Doc. A/53/850–5/1999/231.
[95] GA Res. 52/135, paras.15–16, UN GAOR, 52nd Sess., Supp. No. 49, pp. 288, 289, UN Doc. A/52/49 (1997) (proposing appointment of group of experts to examine options for accountability).
[96] See Question of the impunity of perpetrators of human rights violations (civil and political), Revised final report prepared by Mr Joinet pursuant to Sub-Commission decision 1996/119, Oct. 2, 1997, UN Doc. E/CN.4/Sub.2/1997/20/Rev.1, paras.16–30 [hereinafter Joinet Report].
[97] See sources cited in note 90.

the violators prefer to deny the facts rather than contest the norm.[98] At a minimum, then, this suggests a lack of sense of obligation to prosecute, at least in these cases of transition.

C Some tentative judgments

What then, is the status of the generalized duty of criminal accountability? Much depends upon the framework one uses to characterize rights and duties in international law. In the language of orthodox international law, the above analysis shows that treaties recognize specific duties of accountability, but that neither treaties nor custom support at this time a generalized duty of criminal accountability for either abuses of the current regime or abuses of the prior regime.[99] To adopt the framework of the New Haven School, one might say that States do not yet regard a generalized duty as accompanied by either an "authority signal" or a "control intention."[100] It is not authoritative in that States do not appear to regard some of the fora that have asserted it (UN conferences, ECOSOC, or Amnesty International) as capable of prescribing law, although States presumably do recognize greater law-prescribing or at least law-clarifying functions when it comes to the Inter-American Court or Commission or the Human Rights Committee. More critically, perhaps, States do not yet regard any entity proclaiming the duty as in a position to enforce it.

In the framework adopted by Thomas Franck to evaluate claims for law, the norm of general criminal accountability also does not fare well. For Franck, the critical issue is the legitimacy of the purported norm – the "pull" it exerts for voluntary compliance – as measured by four indicia: historical pedigree, determinacy, coherence, and adherence.[101]

---

[98] *See* Richard Baxter, "Multilateral Treaties as Evidence of Customary International Law," *Brit. Y.B. Int'l L.* 1965–66, pp. 275, 300 ("[t]he firm statement by the State of what it considers to be the rule is far better evidence of its position than what can be pieced together from the action of that country at different times and in a variety of contexts"); Oscar Schachter, *International Law in Theory and Practice* (Boston, Mass.: Martinus Nijhoff, 1995), p. 336; Higgins, *Problems and Process*, *supra* note 26, pp. 20–22. *See also* Military and Paramilitary Activities in and Against Nicaragua, 1986 ICJ 14, p. 98 (June 27).

[99] John Dugard, "Is the Truth and Reconciliation Process Compatible with International Law? An Unanswered Question," *S. Afr. J. Hum. Rts.* 13 (1997), pp. 258, 267; Carla Edelenbos, "Human Rights Violations: a Duty to Prosecute?" *Leiden J. Int'l L.* 7 (1994), pp. 5, 20.

[100] W. Michael Reisman, "International Lawmaking: a Process of Communication," *ASIL Proc.* 75 (1981), pp. 101, 110–11.

[101] Thomas M. Franck, "The Emerging Right to Democratic Governance," *Am. J. Int'l L.* 86 (1992), pp. 46, 51; *see generally* Thomas M. Franck, *The Power of Legitimacy Among Nations* (Oxford University Press, 1990).

As for historical pedigree, although accountability of individuals for certain atrocities goes back at least as far as Nuremberg, the duty of governments to prosecute such individuals beyond the treaty-based crimes is a fairly recent claim. As for determinacy, or the norm's ability to communicate content, criminal accountability is reasonably clear, although the extent to which individuals can be punished can provoke serious disagreement. As for coherence and adherence, or the consonance of the norm with related norms and with higher norms of the international system, one finds tremendous disagreements among States. Some governments argue that accountability furthers protection of human rights for the future and prevents future conflicts; others see it detracting from both goals by preventing the burying of the past.[102]

But the scope of non-treaty law is not as bleak as the above appraisal would suggest. First, at least one of the specific duties in treaties – the Genocide Convention's duty to punish genocide on one's territory – also now seems a duty as a matter of customary law. The core nature of the norms at issue, the invocation of the treaty in international documents, and the numerous domestic statutes criminalizing genocide, support not merely the customary nature of the ban on genocide but the duty to prosecute genocide as well.[103] Such an argument might be made with respect to other conventions, such as those on torture and disappearances, but the more recent vintage of those treaties and the amnesties issued in their wake make such a customary-law duty to prosecute more speculative.

Second, even if a generalized duty of criminal accountability is only in a very nascent stage, a generalized duty of broadly defined accountability appears to have more support behind it. The very State practice that casts doubt on the duty of prosecution does suggest that States are increasingly accepting two other forms of accountability: (1) that States should not completely bury the crimes of the past and should reveal the truth about the role of organizations – and at times, individuals – in the crimes; and (2) that at least some of those who committed such crimes should face some form of sanction. In essence, this broader form of accountability ultimately turns not on criminal punishment of perpetrators of serious human rights abuses, but on knowledge of the crimes (if

[102] *See* text at notes 118–29.
[103] Reservations to the Convention on Genocide, 1951 ICJ 15, p. 23 (May 28) ("principles underlying the Convention are . . . recognized by civilized nations as binding on States even without any conventional obligation"); Baxter, "Multilateral Treaties," *supra* note 98, p. 286; Theodor Meron, *Human Rights and Humanitarian Norms as Customary Law* (Oxford: Clarendon Press, 1989), pp. 93–94. *See also* Guatemala Amnesty Law, Art. 8 (exception for genocide).

not the names of all the criminals) by the public, acknowledgment by the State,[104] and sanction in some form against key offenders.

The willingness of many States in transition to conduct some kind of inquiry through an investigatory commission (whether those that assess blame to organizations or those that also blame individuals), to disqualify certain persons from public office, and to administratively sanction atrocious conduct may well mark the beginning of a normative trend.[105] State practice in support of such a view includes most of the South American and East European States. International bodies and NGOs have criticized these efforts as either falling short of criminal prosecutions[106] or as failing to provide guarantees for those accused of crimes.[107] But their adoption is itself evidence of those governments' willingness to embrace some form of accountability. As is typical with custom, the State practice is emerging before any clear expression of obligation under international law.[108] Nonetheless, States taking such steps have acknowledged the normative factors, rather than mere political ones.[109]

IV DEMOCRACY AND ACCOUNTABILITY: DISSECTING THE NORMATIVE CONNECTIONS

With the current state of the law considered, we now turn more explicitly to the connection between democracy and accountability. My purpose here is not to rehash all the claims made by actors in the processes of transition, let alone to resolve them (as if that were possible).

---

[104] On knowledge v. acknowledgment, *see* Lawrence Wechsler, *A Miracle, A Universe: Settling Accounts with Torturers* (Pantheon Books, 1990), p. 4 (quoting comments of Thomas Nagel).

[105] *See generally* Kritz, ed., *Transitional Justice*, *supra* note 32, vol. II, pp. 323–692 (review of practices of Argentina, Uruguay, Brazil, Chile, Uganda, Czechoslovakia, Germany, and Hungary).

[106] *See* Bautista de Arellana v. Colombia, para. 8.2 ("purely disciplinary and administrative remedies" inadequate in cases of "particularly serious violations of human rights"); Report No. 34/96 (Chile), paras. 74–75, 1996 Ann. Rep. Inter-Am. Comm'n on Human Rights 175, 176 (1997); Human Rights Watch, *Special Issue: Accountability for Past Human Rights Abuses* (New York: Human Rights Watch, 1989), no. 4, pp. 1–2.

[107] International Labor Office, Report of the Committee Set Up to Examine the Representations Made by the Trade Union of Bohemia, Moravia and Slovakia and by the Czech and Slovak Confederation (no. 111), 75 Official Bulletin, Ser. B, Supp. 1 (1992), *reprinted in* Kritz, ed., *Transitional Justice*, *supra* note 32, vol. III, p. 322.

[108] Jennings and Watts, eds., *Oppenheim's International Law*, *supra* note 58, vol. I, p. 30. *See also* Mendelson, "The Subjective Element," *supra* note 89, pp. 201–02.

[109] *See, e.g.*, Decree No. 187 (Argentina), Dec. 15, 1983, *reprinted in* Kritz, ed., *Transitional Justice*, *supra* note 32, vol. III, p. 101 (in setting up the Commission on the Disappeared, noting "the question of human rights transcends governments, it is the concern of civil society and the international community"); Supreme Decree No. 355 (Chile), Apr. 25, 1990, preamble para. 1 (in setting up Commission on Truth and Reconciliation, "the moral conscience of the nation demands that the truth . . . be brought to light").

Rather, because the focus here is upon appraising the relationships between two normative developments, I attempt to recast the debate in a framework that will advance that goal. From that instrumental perspective, the relationship between the two can be said to involve claims about causation and priority.[110] One fast and dismissive response to these claims is to reject them by simply defining democracy to include accountability for the sins of the new and of the prior regime: neither causes the other nor is more important than the other; rather, they are definitionally inseparable. Our purpose here, however, is to analyze the actual claims and responses made by State and non-State actors in the international arena in the hopes of explicating normative trends. If that is our goal, then adopting an ideal definition of democracy that does not match interactions in the international community will not move us forward.

A The causal relationship

Most of the interactions among participants addressing accountability for their States contain arguments about a causal link between democracy and accountability.

1 Claims that democracy promotes accountability
It seems rather unassailable that liberal democracy, with its inherent respect for the rule of law, promotes accountability for violations of human rights. That is, if the rule of law is entrenched in a society and the government is elected by the people, that regime is more likely than an undemocratic government not only to protect human rights, but to address and indeed punish abuses thereof.[111] Those violations and impunity for them imply a preferred place in the society for specific officials, which is antithetical to the two core notions of liberal democracy – the rule of the people and the rule of law.[112]

But is the causation any stronger? With respect to accountability for abuses of a prior regime, it appears not. Democracy is not necessary for accountability for prior abuses, as one can discern from the ability and

---

[110] For related bifurcations of the arguments, *see* Jaime Malamud-Goti, *Game Without End: State Terror and the Politics of Justice* (University of Oklahoma Press, 1996), pp. 8–17 (distinguishing between utilitarian arguments and retributivist claims, though noting latter can have a goal-oriented approach as well); Nino, *Radical Evil*, *supra* note 49, p. 134 (distinguishing between political and moral claims).   [111] *See supra* note 48.
[112] *See, e.g.*, Nino, *The Constitution*, *supra* note 1, pp. 2–7.

eagerness of non-democratic States, such as Poland, to punish Nazi war criminals after World War II.[113] Moreover, democracy is not sufficient for bringing about accountability for the sins of the prior regime. Some new democracies, such as Spain, have chosen to ignore the past completely.[114] Others have created non-criminal mechanisms for accountability, such as truth commissions, that let most offenders off without even naming them (Uruguay or Chile).[115] However, the causation does appear stronger with respect to accountability for violations by officials of the new regime. Here, the prevalence of impunity in non-democratic States suggests that democracy is a necessary factor for future accountability.[116] Without the pressure of the popular will and the commitment to the rule of law, officials of a new regime will enjoy the same impunity as those of the old for any abuses they commit. That again is not to say that democracy is sufficient for accountability, for democracies can choose to ignore ongoing abuses committed by governmental officials.[117] Thus, a tentative conclusion might be stated as follows: democracy contributes to accountability for human rights abuses, and indeed is a necessary condition for accountability for post-transitional abuses.

2 Claims that accountability promotes democracy
The effect of accountability upon democracy has generated the most disagreement among actors in the process of transitions; the disagreement, as noted above, has tended to concern criminal accountability rather than other, lesser forms. (Indeed, many States that have refrained from criminal accountability have justified non-criminal mechanisms, such as lustrations, precisely because they are said to

---

[113] *See, e.g.*, Trial of Obersturmbannfuhrer Rudolf Franz Ferdinand Hoess, 7 *Law Reports of Trials of War Criminals* 11 (Sup. Nat'l Trib. Poland 1947) (trial of Auschwitz commandant); Ratner and Abrams, *Accountability, supra* note 31, p. 268 (1979 show trials of Khmer Rouge by Vietnamese-installed regime).

[114] *See* Guillermo O'Donnell and Philippe Schmitter, *Transitions from Authoritarian Rule: Tentative Conclusions about Uncertain Democracies* (Baltimore, Md.: The Johns Hopkins University Press, 1986), pp. 28–32.

[115] *See generally* Ratner and Abrams, *Accountability, supra* note 31, pp. 193–204. As noted, the Argentine and Salvadoran truth commissions have identified perpetrators. Moreover, some States have held trials, *see* note 86; and others, such as El Salvador and Czechoslovakia, have engaged in programs to purge the military and much of the civilian bureaucracy, respectively, of those associated with the former regime. *See, e.g.*, Mark S. Ellis, "Purging the Past; the Current State of Lustration Laws in the Former Communist Bloc," *Law and Contemp. Probs.* 59 (1996), p. 181.

[116] *See generally* Amnesty International, *Amnesty International Report 1997*.

[117] *See, e.g., ibid.*, 1997, pp. 123–25 (Columbia), 173–74 (Honduras), 177–80 (India), 191–93 (Israel), 323–34 (Venezuela); Rita Maran, *Torture: the Role of Ideology in the French–Algerian War* (New York: Praeger, 1989), pp. 169–73, 191–92.

promote democracy.[118]) Moreover, the debate has concerned accountability for pre-transitional abuses, rather than accountability for ongoing or future ones; both sides seem to agree that accountability for violations by the new regime furthers (and may indeed agree that it is an inherent part of) democracy.[119] In brief, opinions are generally divided along a fault line between governments, on the one hand, and human rights NGOs, victims groups, certain international bodies, and scholars, on the other. Officials and organs in States undergoing transitions have claimed that criminal accountability for past abuses undermines democracy and thus must be either limited or eliminated. This position has been voiced by chief executives,[120] legislatures,[121] and courts.[122] For these governments, retrospective criminal accountability is not only unnecessary and insufficient for bringing about democracy, but is an affirmative obstacle to it: rather, the absence or limitation of such accountability for past abuses is necessary to consolidate democracy.

While sharing this conclusion, governmental officials and organs have held different rationales for it. A minority, typically consisting of those who committed the most serious abuses, would prefer impunity for its own sake and use the democracy argument for public consumption. This would include the Argentine generals who promulgated a self-amnesty on their way out of office[123] and those who insist that the new government promulgate an amnesty or refuse to prosecute as a condition for surrendering power.[124] The more prevalent argument, however, is one that relies on the notion of reconciliation as a *sine qua non* for democracy and insists that criminal prosecutions are an obstacle to

[118] *See* Constitutional Court Decision on the Screening Law (Czechosl.), Nov. 26, 1992, *reprinted* and translated *in* Kritz, ed., *Transitional Justice, supra* note 32, vol. III, pp. 346, 350–51 ("A democratic State has the duty to endeavour to eliminate unjustified preferences of a group of citizens . . .").
[119] *See, e.g.,* Guatemala Human Rights Agreement, Art. III (on importance for democracy of ending impunity).
[120] Letter from President Sanguinetti, p. 604 ("This law [ending future prosecutions] had and has the aim of ensuring the permanence, development and reinforcement of the democratic system").
[121] *See, e.g.,* Decree No. 486 (El Salvador), p. 546 (purpose of amnesty "to be consistent with the development of the democratic process and the reunification of the Salvadorian society").
[122] AZAPO, 1996(4) SA, p. 686 (South Africa not alone in need for "amnesty for criminal acts to be accorded for the purposes of facilitating the transition to, and consolidation of, an overtaking democratic order").
[123] Law No. 22.924 (Argentina), Sept. 22, 1983, *reprinted in* Kritz, ed., *Transitional Justice, supra* note 32, vol. III, p. 477. *See also* Decree Law 2.191, 1978 (Chile).
[124] *See* AZAPO, 1996 (4) SA, p. 685 ("If the Constitution kept alive the prospect of continuous retaliation and revenge, the agreement of those threatened by its implementation might never have been forthcoming. . . .").

reconciliation.[125] This view of trials may stem from fear about the power of the former regime, which might react to the prospect of trials of large numbers of its members (or even of its leaders alone) through a coup;[126] or it may reflect a genuine desire to bring the community together.[127]

The other side of the debate has adopted a number of different positions. Arguing that retrospective accountability is a necessary condition for (or, perhaps, inherent in) democracy, the UN Human Rights Committee, in its condemnation of Peru's blanket amnesty, declared impunity "a very serious impediment to efforts undertaken to consolidate democracy."[128] Human rights NGOs and others have similarly stressed the connection among accountability, reconciliation, peace, and democracy.[129]

Some positions straddle the fault line. Former Argentine President Alfonsin's two key advisers on human rights, Carlos Nino and Jaime Malamud-Goti, have each elaborated sophisticated positions that admit the possibility of both a positive and negative causal relationship between accountability and democracy. After noting how trials can be destabilizing, Nino concludes that the link ultimately

---

[125] *Ibid.* at 684–86; Statement by President Aylwin on the Report of the National Commission on Truth and Reconciliation, Mar. 4, 1991, *reprinted in* Kritz, ed., *Transitional Justice, supra* note 32, vol. III, pp. 169, 171 ("national unity in democracy . . . demands that each and every one make a great effort to put himself in the other person's place and try to understand him . . . to recognize his own mistakes and limitations and with generosity to pardon the other person's mistakes"); Pion-Berlin, "To Prosecute or Pardon?" *supra* note 49, p. 128 (describing Uruguay President Sanguinetti's position). *See also* Huyse, "Justice After Transition," *supra* note 50, p. 63 (on need of new democracies to incorporate administrative skills of members of prior regimes).

[126] *See* text at note 49. This would be the case with Haiti, Chile, or Argentina. Argentina's Due Obedience Law, *reprinted in* Kritz, ed., *Transitional Justice, supra* note 32, vol. III, p. 507, was passed precisely to prevent lower level officers from facing charges.

[127] *See* South Africa Const., epilogue, para. 4 (contemplation of amnesty, noting "there is a need for understanding but not for vengeance, a need for reparation but not for retaliation, a need for *ubuntu* but not for victimisation"); Rosenberg, *The Haunted Land, supra* note 47, pp. 403–04; Heller, "The Limits," *supra* note 25, 160–64.

[128] Preliminary observations on Peru, para. 9. *See also* Hugo Rodriguez v. Uruguay, para. 12.4. The danger amnesties pose for democracy, as opposed to human rights broadly, is a new development. *Cf.* General Comment 20, para. 15 (not mentioning democracy).

[129] *See, e.g.,* Juan Mendez, "Accountability for Past Abuses," *Human Rts. Q.* 19 (1997), pp. 255, 273–75; Larry Rohter, "Huge Amnesty is Dividing Guatemala as War Ends," *N.Y. Times* (Dec. 18, 1996), p. A9 ("There can be no real peace without justice" in words of Indian leader Genara Lopez); *see also* Judith Shklar, *Legalism: Law, Morals, and Political Trials* (Cambridge, Mass.: Harvard University Press, 1986), p. 158 (trials replace "private, uncontrolled vengeance with a measured process of fixing guilt in each case, and taking the power to punish out of the hands of those directly injured"). *But see* Michael Ignatieff, *The Warrior's Honor: Ethnic War and the Modern Conscience* (New York: Henry Holt and Company, 1997), p. 184 ("if trials assist the process of uncovering the truth, it is doubtful whether they assist the process of reconciliation. The purgative function of justice tends to operate on the victims' side only").

depends on what makes democracy self-sustainable. If one believes that self-interested motivations are enough, then the balance works heavily against retroactive justice. On the other hand, if one believes that impartial value judgments contribute to the consolidation of democracy, there is a compelling political case for retroactive justice.[130]

Malamud-Goti works from the same experience and, like Nino, places the primary value on democracy. Rejecting both views of causation, he argues for punishment only if it will "contribute to the making of a rights-based democracy,"[131] with the interests of the victim at the heart of this approach.

Beyond the positions that seek to cross the lines, I would identify at least three situations where the differing sides presumably share the same opinion. A first case concerns authoritarian regimes that pass self-amnesties with the hope that the future regime will not examine them.[132] This lack of accountability, insofar as it is not chosen by the new government, has led even those normally opposed to accountability for pre-transitional abuses to admit that this situation should not stand[133] – though a self-amnesty might, it could be argued, help sustain a democracy by taking a politically charged issue off the table. Second, accountability can be conducted with scant regard for the rights of targets of investigation – such as part of Czechoslovakia's lustration process, Rwanda's trial and execution of persons involved in the 1994 genocide, or, the summary trial and execution of the Ceaucescus in 1989. Here those who argue that accountability furthers democracy would admit – and indeed publicly advocate – that in such a situation accountability actually undermines it.[134] In this situation, they make strange bedfellows with those from the prior regime who fear any accountability.[135] A final case, though perhaps an uncommon one, is where abusers are so sub-

---

[130] Nino, *Radical Evil*, supra note 49, p. 134. *See also* pp. 120–30.
[131] Malamud-Goti, *Game Without End*, supra note 110, p. 15.   [132] *See* sources cited in notes 123–24.
[133] *See* Zalaquett, "Confronting Human Rights Violations," *supra* note 32, p. 43; *See also* text at notes 161–64. Of course, the two sides might differ as to the next appropriate step, i.e., whether to ratify, modify, or terminate the amnesty. *See, e.g.*, Statement by President Aylwin on the Report of the National Commission on Truth and Reconciliation, March 4, 1991, *reprinted in* Kritz, ed., *Transitional Justice*, *supra* note 32, vol. III, pp. 169, 172 (noting respect for current amnesty but interpreting it to permit investigations into certain violations).
[134] *See* Memorandum of Helsinki Watch and Others to the Constitutional Court of the Czech and Slovak Federal Republic in the Matter of the Constitutionality of Act No 451/1991 (1992), *reprinted in* Kritz, ed., *Transitional Justice*, *supra* note 32, vol. III, pp. 335, 345.
[135] *See* Rosenberg, *The Haunted Land*, supra note 47, p. 77 ("In the Czech Republic there were two kinds of people who opposed lustrace – human rights activists and old Communists"); Steven R. Ratner, "Judging the Past: State Practice and the Law of Accountability," *Eur. J. Int'l L.* 9 (1998), pp. 412, 419–20. *See also* text at note 152.

verting democracy that only trial and punishment will remove them from office and bring an end to this behavior. The clearest case of this is Bosnia, where (at this writing) indicted war criminals Radovan Karadzic and Ratko Mladic continue to subvert attempts to plant peace and the beginnings of democracy and the rule of law in that shattered State.[136] Here, as with the first case, even those who argue that retrospective accountability undermines democracy would presumably admit that this is a clear case where accountability not only furthers it, but may well be necessary.

3 Normative consequences
If democracy is indeed crystallizing as a norm of international law, and accountability is only just beginning to undergo such a normative evolution (with criminal accountability generally confined to specific treaty duties), then what effect do the claims by decision-makers about causation have on these two concepts legally? As stated above, at this point the greater consensus is on democracy's positive effect upon prospects for accountability, especially accountability for future abuses. This link to accountability provides another justification for advocates of democracy, and another argument that can be invoked by States, international organizations, individuals, and NGOs for advancing democratic forms of government. Democracy not only means rule of the people coupled with the rule of law, but also renders it increasingly likely that those who commit grievous abuses of human rights will be held accountable for their deeds. This, admittedly, is not likely to boost the pace of democratization remarkably, as accountability may not itself be an important value to various actors (see section v below). But it does lend additional "coherence," in the words of Franck, to the concept by linking it with other values such as the rule of law and protection of human rights.[137]

As for debate over the effect of accountability on democracy, the lack of consensus over the effect of prosecuting pre-transitional abuses and the numerous ways in which case studies on this issue can be interpreted[138] suggests that the normativity of accountability for those abuses

---

[136] *See* Payam Akhavan, "Justice in the Hague: Peace in the Former Yugoslavia," *Hum. Rts. Q.* 20 (1998), p. 737.   [137] Franck, *The Power of Legitimacy*, *supra* note 101, pp. 143–48.
[138] For instance, in cases where States have abstained from real accountability and now enjoy fairly successful democracies, *see* Ambos, "Impunity," *supra* note 66, p. 2 (noting improvement in human rights in Bolivia, Chile, and Argentina since return to democracy), proponents of accountability will attribute some of the country's problems to lack of accountability; while opponents will argue that the successes are due to the lack of trials. Of course, implementing of a policy of non-accountability might have no causal effect on the status of democracy in either direction.

– the extent to which States regard such accountability as a legal duty – is not considerably aided by the increased acceptance of the duty to install democratic government. That is, in the absence of an accepted causal link between such accountability and democracy, or perhaps consensus that the two are definitionally inseparable, claims in favor of the necessity of democracy are not likely to "spill over" into claims in favor of the necessity of prosecuting pre-transitional abuses.[139] On the other hand, because there does seem to be a general acceptance that accountability for post-transitional abuses fosters (and may form an essential element of) democracy, the binding nature of such accountability is liable to increase as democracy becomes more entrenched as a norm of international law. Moreover, because there appears to be consensus that in certain limited cases, impunity for past offenses is antithetical to democracy (the Karadzic and the self-amnesty examples noted above), the greater acceptance of democracy is likely to encourage States to reject these forms of impunity.

B *Democracy and accountability: the question of priority*

The second set of claims regarding these two developments does not seek to link the two, but rather asserts the importance of each value in isolation.

1 The arguments

Those parties asserting that certain forms of retrospective accountability, notably criminal methods, undermine democracy and thus should not be applied, necessarily assume that democracy has a value in and of itself and is the greater priority for society.[140] This position, like the argument of causation, has been set forth by a number of governments in transition.[141] The implications of such an argument are vast. At its extreme, it could imply that any efforts to examine the past that might hurt the chances for democracy must be rejected. This willful amnesia has characterized Spain's treatment of the past since the return of democracy in the 1970s.[142] Indeed, such an argument is only one stop

---

[139] *Cf.* McDougal and Reisman, "The Prescribing Function," *supra* note 81, pp. 372–74.
[140] Of course, some parties asserting that accountability furthers democracy may also assume that democracy is a greater priority, but they would argue that accountability will in fact further that greater goal.
[141] *See, e.g.*, Letter from President Sanguinetti, p. 604 ("If democracy ceased to exist, all human rights would disappear"). [142] *See supra* note 114.

away from a position that accountability for abuses by the new government should be avoided if it somehow threatens stability.

The opposing view appears in arguments that criminal accountability for past and future abuses is a duty of a State that cannot be sacrificed for other purposes. The argument is not typically stated in the form that accountability is more important than democracy, but rather that it has its own value irrespective of any deleterious effects on other values. This view has a normative correspondence to, and perhaps origin in, the legal instruments discussed above, such as the Genocide, Torture, and Disappearances Conventions, for those treaties require States to prosecute (or extradite or prosecute) certain abuses and do not recognize the possible effects on democratization as legitimate reasons not to prosecute.[143] Thus, for example, the Inter-American Commission on Human Rights responded to arguments of Uruguay that its Ley de Caducidad was necessary to further democracy not by saying that such measures were unnecessary, but rather by focusing exclusively on the State's legal obligations to protect human rights under the American Convention.[144]

Although it seems at first difficult to find common ground between these competing deontological arguments, one can discern some attempts among those who count democracy as most important to take accountability into consideration. Jose Zalaquett of Chile's truth commission would use democracy itself as a check on impunity and insist that any decision regarding the abuses of the past "represent the will of the people."[145] Democracy is still the priority in the sense that he insists on deferring to the will of the people, but he is willing to incur the risks accountability might create for democratic transitions if the people so choose. Carlos Nino carefully examines the advantages and disadvantages of trials for transitional societies, and ultimately concludes, with Zalaquett, that "[t]he process of public deliberation is the optimal way to forge a balance,"[146] any other position risks "moral elitism" and violation of Kant's categorical imperative.[147]

The South African Constitutional Court took a small step beyond the above positions of complete deference to democratic preferences in its opinion reviewing that nation's amnesty-for-confession law. As do most

---

[143] On derogability, see discussion in note 74.
[144] Report No. 29/92, paras.46, 49, 51, 52, 54. See also Mendez, "Accountability for Past Abuses," supra note 129, pp. 261–64.
[145] See Zalaquett, "Confronting Human Rights Violations," supra note 32, p. 34.
[146] Nino, Radical Evil, supra note 49, p. 148.
[147] Ibid. See also Shklar, Legalism, pp. 143–62, supra note 129 (on dangers of political trials).

organs of States in transition, the South African Constitutional Court suggests that democracy is the most important value;[148] yet it makes ample mention of the decision of the legislature not to provide total impunity, but to condition amnesty upon confession to the Truth and Reconciliation Commission and a determination by it as to the official nature of the crime.[149] It thus implicitly suggests the possibility of the amnesty provisions of the law being less acceptable if the legislature had opted for a regime of total impunity (although even such an amnesty might well have been found constitutional).

2 Normative consequences

The impact of this debate for the legal valence of purported norms requiring democracy and accountability depends ultimately upon the reactions of States to it. If, as appears to be the case, democracy is increasingly accepted as the sole or most legitimate form of government, the result may well be pressure to relegate criminal accountability, at least for past abuses, to second-class status, to treat it as an altogether small and deferable component of the rule of law. If States and international organizations continue to push for democracy above all, they are likely to tolerate decisions by States that those States have decided will further democracy, especially if those decisions are themselves clearly supported publicly (e.g., by a referendum). Thus, while States might scrutinize and criticize the new democratic Estonia's treatment of the Russian minority,[150] they are less likely to care if Uruguay decides not to continue prosecutions of former junta leaders, for that, unlike the Estonia case, is not regarded by States as violating anybody's fundamental human rights.[151] The only caveat seems to be that these actors might well insist that States adopting forms of accountability in order to bolster democracy do so in a way that does not itself violate human rights, as happens in the case of show trials, unfair lustration practices, or viola-

---

[148] AZAPO, 1996(4) SA, pp. 676, 687 (goal is "to develop constitutional democracy and prevent a repetition of the abuses").
[149] *Ibid.*, pp. 684–86; *see also* Promotion of National Unity and Reconciliation Act, Art. 20.
[150] *See* Recommendations on the question of the implementation of the Estonian Law on Aliens, June 14, 1994 (containing March 9, 1994 letter of OSCE High Commissioner on National Minorities to Foreign Minister of Estonia and April 4, 1994 reply); Foundation on Inter-Ethnic Relations, *The Role of the High Commissioner on National Minorities in OSCE Conflict Prevention* (Foundation on Inter-Ethnic Relations, 1997), pp. 52–56.
[151] *See* sources cited in note 55 (views of Human Rights Committee that duty to prosecute does not stem from individual right); *but see* Joinet Report, paras. 26–39 (advocating right to justice).

tions of *nullum crimen sine lege*.[152] The effect is that States can be expected to criticize accountability that violates human rights (due process) protections more than they will criticize impunity for past abuses itself.

One response to this prediction would be to assert that States will only tolerate impunity if they already believe that retrospective accountability is not an inherent part of democracy. If they believed accountability were an essential part of democracy, they would push for it as well. Human rights groups would thus argue that the key is to convince States to stop treating accountability for past abuses as a mere afterthought to democracy.[153] But as the earlier discussion has indicated, the tolerance of impunity suggests that States are perfectly willing to divorce democracy from retrospective criminal accountability and place a strong priority on the former. Here the arguments of causation and priority merge a bit. For the proponents of accountability as a non-derogable norm to advance that position, they will have to adopt – and indeed have already adopted – the more empirical, causation-centered argument that accountability for pre-transitional abuses actually furthers democracy.[154] By urging States to accept this causal link, they move themselves one step closer to having States accept that such accountability is an independent value that, in the abstract, must be advanced even if it does not further democracy as a whole (or alternatively, that accountability is simply inherent in democracy regardless of its effects on other aspects of democratic governance). Human rights activists will not make the latter, strong claim in such stark terms, for their goal is simply to ensure that accountability for past abuses is taken more seriously and not automatically assumed *ex hypothesi* to undermine democracy.[155]

The hardest problem for them arises from the many forms of amnesty adopted through democratic means, such as in Uruguay and South Africa.[156] Here opponents of amnesties essentially have to argue that (a) a democratic choice to provide an amnesty does not really advance

---

[152] *See* US Dep't of State, Country Reports on Human Rights Practices for 1992 (US GPO, 1993), pp. 753–54 (concerns about Czech and Slovak Federal Republic's lustration laws).
[153] *Cf.* Mendez, "Accountability for Past Abuses," *supra* note 129, pp. 278–79.
[154] *See* text at notes 128–29.
[155] *See* Rodriguez v. Uruguay, para. 12.4 (after condemning Uruguayan amnesty, Human Rights Committee adds that an "atmosphere of impunity . . . may undermine the democratic order"). Even Human Rights Watch does not argue that impunity should be rejected regardless of its effects on democracy, but rather than impunity that originates in a democratic process deserves no special respect. Human Rights Watch, *Special Issue*, *supra* note 106, p. 2.
[156] For a detailed account of the Uruguay case, *see* Wechsler, *A Miracle, A Universe*, *supra* note 104, pp. 83–236.

democracy; (b) a democratic choice to provide an amnesty is definitionally undemocratic; or (c) a democratic choice to provide an amnesty violates core norms of international law about a duty to provide accountability. In such situations, they are caught between a rock and a hard place. Taking the more modest position (a) forces them to say that democracies do not know how to promote democracy.[157] Taking the second position (b) forces them to attack a State's definition of democracy. Taking position (c) is, of course, both legally and morally compelling, as human rights law by its very nature rejects the notion that majorities may override core human rights.[158] But it nonetheless forces them to argue that a duty exists though States do not yet accept it.

V THROUGH THE THICKET

Despite the cleavages highlighted in this chapter, most actors in new regimes addressing issues of transitional justice recognize the value of both individual accountability and liberal democracy. Their disagreements are, rather, over causation – are the two complementary or in tension – and over priority. To date, both concepts are in a state of normative evolution, though it is fair to say that democracy is much further advanced. The challenge then is to see how States will continue to react to claims made in favor of each norm by its advocates. Is there some way that States might advance the normative development of both ideas, or are we resigned to a trade-off between the two regardless of the various arguments that one promotes the other?

A Compliance with treaty-based duties

First, the treaty obligations of States represent the most promising starting point for rules of accountability not meant to undermine democracy. States parties to the applicable treaties have clear international

---

[157] *Cf.* Robert A. Dahl, *Democracy and its Critics* (New Haven, Conn.: Yale University Press, 1989), pp. 171–73 (debate over rationality of democracies); Gregory H. Fox and Georg Nolte, "Intolerant Democracies," *Harv. Int'l L. J.* 36 (1995), pp. 1, 5–13 (on whether democracies can protect themselves from non-democratic forces that use democratic mechanisms).

[158] *See* Report No. 29/92, paras. 30–32 (approval of Uruguayan law by referendum does not prevent Commission from examining consistency with American Convention on Human Rights); Human Rights Watch, Special Issue, *supra* note 106, p. 2 ("[I]t is not the prerogative of the many to forgive the commission of crimes against the few."); *see also* Wechsler, *A Miracle, A Universe, supra* note 104, pp. 244–45 (quoting Aryeh Neier); Farer, "Consolidating Democracy," *supra* note 61, p. 1309 (calling arguments defending amnesties based on popular will "meretricious").

obligations to prosecute genocide, and must also extradite or prosecute those who commit war crimes, torture, or disappearances. These conventions are part of the core treaty law on human rights, rather than of some separate, broader corpus of law or nascent duty of accountability. As human rights treaties (as opposed to custom), they create expectations of compliance even for those transitional societies, as witnessed by even the strongest advocates of the priority of democracy having recognized their significance.[159] Following these human rights treaties ought to be portrayed by supporters of the duty of criminal accountability as a matter of a State's honoring its commitments, regardless of the State's position on criminal accountability *per se*.[160] As a substantive matter, these agreements surely place an impediment on some amnesties. As for the broader duties suggested by the treaty bodies implementing the ICCPR and the American Convention on Human Rights, these opinions will presumably have a greater influence on State behavior as those mechanisms themselves gain in acceptance among States as authoritative interpreters of those instruments.

In the meantime, democracy is likely to lead criminal accountability in its normative development. The internal and external pressures on States to democratize are substantial compared to those calling for accountability (criminal or otherwise), which most States still regard as a matter of their domestic jurisdiction. It is frankly a sterile debate to discuss whether, in fact, accountability fosters human rights observance more than do the other elements democracy; the States participating in our human rights revolution have simply decided, for the moment, that democracy is a prerequisite to accountability for future abuses (and for overall promotion of human rights), and that any attempts to promote accountability for past abuses that they perceive will undermine democracy are to be avoided.

B *Softer duties regarding criminal accountability*

The norm of criminal accountability can, however, grow beyond the specific treaty obligations in a number of senses. First, States are

---

[159] *See* Zalaquett, "Confronting Human Rights Violations," *supra* note 32, pp. 40–44.
[160] I appreciate this insight from Ambassador Tim Guldimann. *See also* Abram Chayes and Antonia Handler Chayes, *The New Sovereignty: Compliance with International Regulatory Agreements* (Cambridge, Mass.: Harvard University Press, 1995), pp. 8–9 (on propensity of States to comply with unambiguous treaty provisions).

increasingly wary of self-amnesties.[161] They raise two fundamental legal difficulties. First, they are undemocratic in that they deny the right of the new regime to choose its own path to democracy and accountability; and second, they violate a general principle of law prohibiting a person from being a judge in his own case (*nemo debet esse judex in propria causa*).[162] Of course, many new regimes have adopted limited or wholesale criminal impunity after due deliberation, so the end result for victims and perpetrators may be the same. And democracies have also passed amnesties for acts committed during their own tenure.[163] But at least one form of impunity is consistently held in great suspicion – suggesting a first step toward acceptance of a legal duty not to ratify self-amnesties.[164] Nonetheless, Chile and Brazil's decisions to respect the self-amnesties, without criticism from abroad, suggests that States will still tolerate this practice.

Second, the increased discussion of accountability suggests that the prospects for a norm against blanket amnesties for former officials is stronger than one against selective amnesties, or trials followed by pardons of those convicted. It is notable that each amnesty found illegal by a treaty-monitoring body has been a blanket amnesty; those bodies have not yet had a chance to opine about selective amnesties or pardons.[165] Such a norm could be a sort of compromise that recognizes the importance of democracy but does not dismiss criminal accountability completely.

Third, the prospect of a norm of criminal accountability alongside a norm of democracy might be more palatable to States if the former is viewed, for now, not as an obligation to actually punish past abusers, but as the obligation to seriously consider the consequences of both punishment and non-punishment, rather than assuming that only the latter will

---

[161] *See* Law No. 23.040 Dec. 27, 1983 (Argentina), *reprinted in* Kritz, ed., *Transitional Justice*, *supra* note 32, vol. III, p. 480 (nullifying military's self-amnesty); Zalaquett, "Confronting Human Rights Violations," *supra* note 32, p. 43. With the exception of Chile and Brazil, all amnesties currently in force have been passed by new regimes, rather than the military regime. *See also* discussion in note 133.

[162] *See* Ambos, "Impunity," *supra* note 66, p. 7. *See also* El Triunfo Case (US v. El Salv.) (1902), Papers Relating to Foreign Relations of the United States 1902, pp. 859, 871; Walker v. Birmingham, 388 US 307, 320–21 (1967); Wolfgang Friedmann, "The Uses of 'General Principles' in the Development of International Law," *Am. J. Int'l L.* 57 (1963), pp. 279, 290 (1963).

[163] This is the case of the Peruvian law from 1995. *See* Ley 26479; James Craig, "Peru: Congress Reaffirms Controversial Peru Amnesty," *Reuter Textline*, June 29, 1995 (available on NEXIS).

[164] *See* Weiner, "Trying to Make Ends Meet," *supra* note 53, p. 859 ("an exercise in power, not legitimacy").

[165] *See, e.g.*, Comments on Argentina, para. 153 ("pardons and *general* amnesties may promote an atmosphere of impunity") (emphasis added).

preserve democracy. Part of the impunity problem today is that States too readily err on the side of presuming trials will lead to instability and hurt the country.[166] In some case, the new regime may assert that the old regime remains powerful, or that impunity is necessary to foster reconciliation, but may actually fear the prospect of the heavy hand of criminal justice being brought to bear on its own members.[167] Even if States ultimately decide to adopt a form of impunity, pressure can be brought on them to consider carefully the costs and benefits of accountability. This seems to have been done by the South African government in its innovative confession-for-amnesty scheme. Alas, rules requiring States to base their decisions on certain factors to the exclusion of others, without constraining their final outcome, are notoriously difficult to enforce, as States may easily make up reasons to justify their reliance on impermissible factors in terms of permissible factors.[168]

Fourth, a duty of criminal accountability might be more realistic if it were limited to those in policy-making roles or those responsible for the most heinous offenses, such as leaders of extermination or torture centers.[169] This again is a partial form of criminal accountability, although one that would be harder for States to accept than the other three insofar as it risks trials of leading figures of the prior regime. Nonetheless, if the numbers are kept fairly small and the trials are undertaken expeditiously, States may begin to see them as a realistic way of bringing about accountability without endangering democracy.[170]

C Prospects for the broader version of accountability

Each of the five approaches in subsections A and B above attempts to discern the possibility of development of a duty to provide criminal accountability that can grow alongside the increased expectation of a

---

[166] See Pion-Berlin, "To Prosecute or Pardon?" supra note 49, pp. 117–18, 120–21, 127 (cautious position of Uruguayan President Sanguinetti); Ratner and Abrams, Accountability, supra note 31, p. 136.
[167] See Ash, "True Confessions," pp. 33, 37 (on confessions and applications for amnesties by ANC members to Truth and Reconciliation Commission).
[168] See, e.g., Conditions of Admission of a State to Membership in the United Nations (Article 4 of the Charter), 1948 ICJ 57, pp. 62–63 (Advisory Op. of May 28) (permissible vs. impermissible factors for voting on admission of States); Bruno Simma, ed., The Charter of the United Nations: A Commentary (Oxford University Press, 1995), p. 161 (ICJ opinion "continually disregarded").
[169] Ratner and Abrams, Accountability, supra note 31, p. 297; Orentlicher, "Settling Accounts," supra note 38, pp. 2602–03.
[170] See Ratner and Abrams, Accountability, supra note 31, p. 297; Alex Boraine, Janet Levy, and Ronel Scheffer, eds., Dealing with the Past: Truth and Reconciliation in South Africa, 2nd edn. (Cape Town: IDASA, 1997), pp. 93, 101–02 (views of Juan Méndez and Aryeh Neier).

duty of participatory government. These approaches seem more consonant in the short term with the emerging duty of democratic governance insofar as they do not demand that States punish all serious human rights abuses of the prior regime regardless of the consequences for democracy. The result, however, is not particularly encouraging for the duty to prosecute serious human rights abuses. Only partial versions – prosecution of specific treaty-based crimes, or the worst criminals – or soft, weak versions – the duty not to accept self-amnesties, not to pass full amnesties, and not to assume accountability will undermine democracy – seem possible for building normative expectations about criminal accountability in the short term.

But another set of expectations can also emerge, namely in favor of a duty of more broadly defined accountability. Expectations in this regard are not as constrained by the push for participatory government. States today see no contradiction – indeed find a positive correlation – between truth commissions or lustration, on the one hand, and democracy, on the other, as witnessed by their engaging these mechanisms as part of their democratization process.[171] If negotiators and outside actors insist that States address accountability in some legitimate form, even if not through prosecutions, then the prospects for a norm of accountability grow.

Determining the minimally acceptable degree of accountability is not easy. But it seems that an insistence upon the two criteria listed above for a norm of non-criminal accountability[172] would be reasonable to expect outside States to endorse and transitional States to accept. First, accountability must, in Nagel's words, provide both knowledge and acknowledgment.[173] This suggests the need for official investigation and apology, though not necessarily a full listing of the names of perpetrators and victims.[174] Second, accountability must provide some form of sanction against the most serious abusers. This means removal from office, demotion, naming, or some other public recognition that the

---

[171] *See, e.g.,* Constitutional Court Decision on the Screening Law (Czech and Slovak Federal Republic), Nov. 26, 1992, *reprinted in* Kritz, ed., *Transitional Justice, supra* note 32, vol. III, pp. 346, 350 ("A democratic State has the duty to endeavour to eliminate unjustified preference of a group of citizens, based on the principle of their membership in a certain political party . . ."); AZAPO, 1996 (4) SA, p. 685.   [172] *See* text at note 104.

[173] *See* note 104; *see also* Correa, "Dealing with Past Human Rights Violations," pp. 1478–81 (relying on truth and acknowledgment as starting points for reparation).

[174] *See* Cassel, "Lesson from the Americas," *supra* note 63, pp. 219–20 (results of OAS jurisprudence on duty to investigate); Weiner, "Trying to Make Ends Meet," *supra* note 53, p. 871 (suggesting parameters for investigations and amnesties).

person has not achieved impunity for his actions. This must, of course, be conducted in a manner that is respectful of the target's due process rights.

The most promising formula in accordance with this minimal standard is South Africa's, with its confession for amnesty scheme that strives for the truth and identifies perpetrators, while leaving open the option of prosecution for those who choose not to admit their misdeeds. Other States' policies seem roughly in line with such criteria as well, though a bit more awkwardly – Argentina and El Salvador with their truth commissions and removal of key offenders from the military; Czechoslovakia and Germany with their public lustration campaigns. Yet certainly in some situations – Chile and General Pinochet, to name an obvious case[175] – even that has proved impossible. And advocates of criminal accountability, including the Human Rights Committee, have stated that disciplinary measures are not a substitute for prosecutions in the case of serious human rights violations.[176]

This broader version of accountability seems to me the only way the law can provide a coherent response to the most challenging of transitional scenarios, those where norms arguing for criminal accountability ignore other important constitutive values. Suppose a ruthless military regime will turn over power to a democracy, but only if it receives a full amnesty for whatever atrocities it committed? Suppose both factions in a civil war will, in fact, only lay down their arms in exchange for a total amnesty? In these situations, we assume that one side or both has decided to insist on criminal impunity as a *sine qua non* of surrendering power or ending a struggle. In these cases, where only impunity will end the bloodshed, an unequivocal condemnation by international law seems both ill-advised and unrealistic. Rather, the non-criminal mechanisms can provide a meaningful, if less court-centered, form of assigning blame, identifying abusers, and excluding them from public life. This is not to say that international law should categorically endorse this choice. Diplomatic protest against total amnesties may well be appropriate to preserve the principle of criminal accountability, and certainly to signal the community's unwillingness to assume that, in fact, such an amnesty was necessary to end the conflict.[177] The result is, admittedly a mixed signal lacking in complete candor, one not uncommon in certain

---

[175] *See* Calvin Sims, "As Thousands Protest, Pinochet Assumes Chilean Senate Seat," *N.Y. Times* (March 12, 1998), A9.   [176] *See* note 106.
[177] *See* Jennings and Watts, eds., *Oppenheim's International Law*, supra note 58, vol. 1, pp. 1193–94.

realms of international (and domestic) law where the law's limits are reached and clear-cut rules leave us unequipped to address a problem.[178]

If States begin to accept that they must engage in these non-criminal methods – and that these will not undercut the transition to democracy – and if they can combine them with the modest steps in the area of criminal accountability discussed above, the prospects for parallel evolution of norms is promising. If, however, transitional States and outside actors continue to identify accountability only with trials of all serious abusers, then the current preference for democracy is likely to trample to death any nascent norm of accountability. It is only through tentative steps that these two partners in our contemporary human rights revolution can begin to see their common interests and work together, rather than separately, toward improving human dignity.

[178] *See, e.g.,* Guido Calabresi, *A Common Law for the Age of Statutes* (Cambridge, Mass.: Harvard University Press, 1982), pp. 173–74 (describing failure of absolute rules); Franck, *The Power of Legitimacy, supra* note 101, pp. 74–80 ("idiot rules" v. "sophist rules"); Larry Alexander and Ken Kress, "Against Legal Principles," *Iowa L. Rev.* 82 (1997), p. 739.

PART V
Critical approaches

CHAPTER 17

*Evaluating democratic progress**

Brad R. Roth

I INTRODUCTION

The post-Cold-War world has been marked by a series of astonishing changes, many of which have involved openings to popular participation in politics. These openings have occurred in the name of democracy, and have made use of familiar institutional mechanisms of electoral competition. Much recent academic literature has rushed to embrace these events. In the exuberance of the moment, issues become conflated, and differences regarding crucial principles are obscured.

Democracy – or at least something bearing that name – is now commonly asserted as a global norm. Increasingly jettisoned are long-held theories about the historical peculiarity of democracy, theories emphasizing structural prerequisites or cultural dispositions present almost exclusively in developed Western countries. Whether or not the new trend's enthusiasts are possessed of sufficient rhetorical audacity to proclaim a liberal–democratic "end of history" (in some Hegelian sense), they do appear satisfied on two crucial points: first, that a democratic reality has in fact come to pass in so much of the world as to refute claims of the norm's limited applicability; and second, that the superiority of this "actually existing democracy" over all alternatives is so firmly established that, in normative terms, nothing remains to be discussed. Some have gone so far as to assert an "emerging right to democratic governance" in international law, thereby linking the legitimacy of governments to "free and fair" competitive electoral processes.[1]

This chapter will argue that much of the current discourse on the diffusion of democratic norms is misleading. That discourse tends to

---

* The author wishes to thank David Caron, Kenneth Sharpe, and Giuseppe Di Palma for their helpful comments. The opinions and any errors herein are, of course, solely those of the author.
[1] *See, e.g.*, Thomas M. Franck, "The Emerging Right to Democratic Governance," *Am. J. Int'l L.* 86 (1992), p. 46; Gregory H. Fox, "The Right to Political Participation in International Law," *Yale J. Int'l L.* 17 (1992), p. 539.

focus narrowly on the increasingly widespread adoption of a familiar set of institutions, ascribing to that phenomenon the moral weight that comes with the use of the word "democracy," without exploring the extent to which the events in question actually serve the purposes that underlie democracy's moral significance. Mechanisms of competition among political elites for the votes of the governed are evaluated on the basis of a handful of formal criteria – the indicia of procedural democracy, or "polyarchy" – while broader issues, involving the ends of democracy and the problematic role of polyarchy in fulfilling those ends in particular social contexts, are glossed over.

We have not, alas, reached the end of history. Great ideological issues remain to be resolved, even if particular ideological positions now belong solely to the past. Democracy still admits of radically contradictory interpretations, and events that appear to embody the diffusion of a single set of norms are in fact more complex.

The prevalent approach exaggerates democratic progress, encouraging an unjustified triumphalism that is both messianic (with respect to States that have not yet achieved polyarchy) and complacent (with respect to those that have). At the same time, the prevalent approach fails to identify distinct forms of political progress that do not necessarily entail democracy, but are significant from the standpoint of democratic values. It therefore misses an opportunity to mitigate the cynicism of those who emphasize the gap between procedures touted as democratic and social realities that belie any such description.

This article distinguishes three normatively significant ends, to which the establishment of competitive electoral mechanisms may to a greater or lesser extent be relevant: (1) the furtherance of broad popular empowerment with respect to the full range of social decisions that condition life in the society ("substantive democracy"); (2) the establishment of a government to which the populace may in some manner be said to have manifested consent ("popular sovereignty"); and (3) the establishment of a broadly recognized basis for, and thereby limitation on, the legitimate exercise of power ("constitutionalism"). It is with respect to these differentiated normative ends that the promise, as well as the all-too-real precariousness, of recent progressive developments can be brought into focus.

A careful, differentiated approach to the transitions taking place in various parts of the world will reveal that progress does not occur on all fronts at once. Substantive democracy, which embodies values at the moral core of the democratic heritage, has not been greatly furthered by many of the recent developments, and in some respects is suffering a setback. Nonetheless, the norm of popular sovereignty, linking governmental legitimacy to some empirical manifestation of popular consent (obviously an important component of the scheme of democratic values), has been greatly strengthened. And the phenomenon of constitutionalism, which to an increasing extent has taken the form of institutions open to competitive political processes, is greatly on the rise, providing an alternative to unmediated, often bloody social conflict.

The goal of this differentiated approach is a realistic normative assessment of recent developments that neither exaggerates democratic progress nor disparages other kinds of progress, and that avoids the indulgences of messianism and complacency on the one hand and cynicism on the other. That polyarchy and its component institutions are significant is not to be denied. Their significance, however, can be seen only in social context, and only with an appreciation of the theoretical background to the issues at stake in the countries undergoing what are, indeed, remarkable transitions.

II POLYARCHY AND THE DEMOCRATIC *TELOS*

For all of the triumphalist rhetoric about the diffusion of democracy, the definition of democracy in much of the current literature is remarkably thin. The tendency is either to ignore historical controversies over the content of democracy, or to treat the issue as having been resolved by recent events. The result is a non-teleological definition of democracy, one that lists institutional requisites without revealing the underlying logic of ends that generates the list.[2] In the absence of that logic, it is not

---

[2] The following list of requisites is typically cited:
1 Control over governmental decisions about policy is constitutionally vested in elected officials.
2 Elected officials are chosen and peacefully removed in relatively frequent, fair and free elections in which coercion is quite limited.
3 Practically all adults have the right to vote in these elections.
4 Most adults also have the right to run for the public offices for which candidates run in these elections.
5 Citizens have an effectively enforced right to freedom of expression, particularly political expression, including criticism of the officials, the conduct of the government, the prevailing political, economic, and social system, and the dominant ideology.
6 They also have access to alternative sources of information that are not monopolized by the government or any other single group.
7 Finally they have an effectively enforced right to form and join autonomous associations, including political associations, such as political parties and interest groups, that attempt to influence the government by competing in elections and by other peaceful means. (Robert A. Dahl, *Polyarchy* 233 [New Haven, Conn.: Yale Univ. Press, 1971].)

clear how to derive the refinements and corollaries that would allow one to examine real-world complexities and shortcomings and to evaluate whether the requisites are satisfied.

Examination of the purposes underlying the supposed institutional requisites exposes radical differences where there appeared unity. These differences manifest themselves in every dispute over what counts as a democratic development, whether regarding the controversial wartime Central American elections of the 1980s, the conduct of the Aristide Government in Haiti prior to its 1991 overthrow, Boris Yeltsin's unconstitutional 1993 dispersal of the Russian Parliament, or any of the myriad of less dramatic events occurring day to day. Assessments of this type cannot be resolved by deduction from a procedural model, because whatever is deduced is ambiguous or incomplete without reference to the substantive social purposes for which one values the procedures.

Moreover, any teleological view recognizes the connection between democratic procedures and democratic goals to be imperfect. In some cases, all of the procedural requisites will be achieved, but the crucial goals will remain almost totally unfulfilled, whereas in other cases, significant imperfection in the achievement of the requisites will seem to pale in significance, given the overall success in achieving the goals. A dogmatic emphasis on procedure assumes that the path to democracy is linear, that other forms of democratic progress are realized only after polyarchy is first perfected, and that therefore any country where polyarchy is more advanced is necessarily more democratic than one where polyarchy is less advanced or absent. Yet one might reject this assumption, and consequently emphasize social realities over formal structures – even while conceding that polyarchy, other things being equal, greatly enhances the prospects for a democratic outcome and is necessary for the consolidation of such an outcome. (One might therefore, for example, take a comparatively favorable view of a one-party State that does not allow organized opposition, but that is widely popular, incorporates public input in decision-making, and responds effectively to the needs of the vast majority.) Where ends are not discussed, of course, such a controversy cannot even be engaged.

My point is not that the democratization literature that fails to focus explicitly on the democratic *telos* is uncertain of its objective, or is mistaking its means for its ends. It is rather that crucial assumptions about ends are often submerged, and that these assumptions are not universally attractive. In particular, these assumptions frequently incorporate into the conception of democracy much of nineteenth-century liberal political theory.

The relationship between this kind of liberalism and democracy, however, is both historically and conceptually problematic. Most significantly, the liberal conception of democracy posits that democracy is compatible with a sharply class-divided society, notwithstanding the contrary view of ancient and early modern democratic thinkers on the one hand and a large segment of democratic socialist opinion on the other. Liberal democracy tolerates vast disparities in the ability of social groups to marshal the resources necessary to affect political decisions, and even greater disparities in the power of social groups to affect non-governmental decisions touching fundamental aspects of their lives. These latter decisions include, most importantly, decisions about resource allocation and the organization of work that are made in a marketplace that may be dominated by formidable concentrations of economic power. Democracy in this view operates in a confined realm.

More nuanced versions of liberalism, of course, recognize some limit to the extent of socioeconomic polarization compatible with democracy, but this point is often neglected in the literature, caught up as it is in the superimposition of Western-style formal structures on non-Western social realities. The result tends to be an acquiescence in the application of the term "democracy" to socioeconomically polarized societies where the criteria of procedural democracy, or "polyarchy," are satisfied.

A democratic vision that emphasizes establishment of a relatively equal distribution of power over all social decisions, while hardly oblivious to the value of formal participatory structures in achieving the end, will contextualize the familiar criteria differently. In this view, only progress oriented toward the achievement of a "substantive" democracy is worthy of association with the term "democracy."

The issue is no mere question of semantics. The moral authority associated with the word "democracy" is formidable. The term is widely used to demarcate the moral high-ground in political struggles. It thus not only confers maximal legitimacy on those actors associated with it, but also strips of all legitimacy those who militantly oppose the actors and structures that enjoy the term's imprimatur. As the following section will argue, labels of such significance should reflect realities, not mere institutional forms.

III SUBSTANTIVE DEMOCRACY

It has to be remembered that until recently there was a strong feeling that there was an alternative out there to liberal democracy. There was a belief in a higher form of democracy, one that emphasized results, equality, that could really achieve things. (Carl Gershman, National Endowment for Democracy, 1991.)[3]

Carl Gershman's use of the past tense in the above extract speaks volumes about the conventional wisdom regarding substantive democracy in the wake of the collapse of Communism. Communism had appropriated that part of the democratic tradition left behind by liberalism, and since Communism by 1991 lay in ruins, it seemed natural to conclude that the liberal conception of democracy had the field to itself.

Indeed, although Eastern European dissident movements had largely been led by those who imagined innovative structures of participation and even the realization of long-betrayed promises of social justice, the months following the collapse saw large majorities throughout the region embrace what was presented as a tried and true solution. The most compelling slogan of 1990 was "No More Experiments!" Ironically, this was the most unrealistic slogan of all; the question, it turns out, is not whether to experiment or to select a ready-made Western-style reality, but what kind of experiment to attempt in the face of an uncharted future. The quick resurgence of barely renovated neo-Communist parties in much of the region is but one sign that the expectations of 1990 are being reassessed, and that foreign models are of limited relevance.

In Eastern Europe as in Latin America and elsewhere, democracy is best understood not as a set of importable institutions, but as a normative orientation that requires creative application to the distinct problems of individual countries. But how shall this normative orientation be specified?

Herein lies the controversy between those who, like Gershman, believe the issue to have been definitively resolved in favor of a narrow ("nineteenth-century") liberal conception of democracy's ends and those who hold out for a more expansive conception. The former regard the expansive conception as a dangerous fantasy, whereas the latter regard achievement of it (in whatever measure) as the *sine qua non* of democracy's moral authority.

---

[3] Richard Bernstein, "New Issues Born from Communism's Death Knell," *N.Y. Times* (Aug. 31, 1991), p. 1.

The liberal conception, notwithstanding its seeming emphasis on a determinate set of institutions, is no less teleological than its adversary. It is rooted in a Lockean division between civil society and the State, the latter acting as the agent of the former to solve a limited set of collective action problems. The dominant organizing principle of civil society is the market, idealized as a free and competitive interaction of autonomous individuals. The State exists to provide the legal and political requisites to the operation of the market (*i.e.*, positive law, impartial judges, enforcement) and to address exceptional instances of market failure (*e.g.*, by providing needed non-excludable public goods and by breaking up monopolies).

Market society, including even the original distribution of property, is conceptualized as logically (even if not historically) prior to the existence of the State. Market mechanisms, then, even if tampered with by the State in response to some perception of market failure, are not to be understood as mere instruments by which the State shapes social outcomes in accordance with some collective vision of the good. However much the State may cushion the impact of market processes, it is the free market, not the State, whose role it is to determine winners and losers. The State does not pursue the common good by breaking down the diverse interests of market society; rather, the common good consists precisely in making society safe for the diversity of interests.

The above description plainly does not do justice to the complexity or diversity of liberal thought, but it accurately highlights an essential element of the liberal *telos*: the limited mission of government. When liberals speak of establishing limited government, they mean it not simply in the narrow sense of institutionalizing restraints against the arbitrary exercise of power by governmental organs, but in the broad sense of limiting the reach of collective decision-making in social life. (Given the destruction that grander schemes have wrought, the current popularity of the liberal view is unsurprising.)

Since liberalism emphasizes containment rather than enhancement of collective decision-making, the role of democracy in liberalism is accordingly narrow. The popular franchise is meant to serve, not "the liberty of the ancients" (collective participation in the decisions affecting the lives of the governed), but "the liberty of the moderns" (individual freedom to pursue one's own agenda without undue interference). Political democracy's purpose is to render the State apparatus accountable to civil society, so that public power does not tread on private right, and so that no faction of civil society can capture enough of State power to disproportionately advantage itself at the expense of other interests. Formal political equality has no necessary implications for inequalities, however gross, existing within civil society itself. Liberals of different hues may quarrel over whether the furtherance of social equality is an admissible goal in the exercise of political power, but none posit this as political democracy's essential function.

Yet democracy owes much of its moral authority to a grander vision that predates the liberal conception. It is a vision of a community coming together, on terms of equality, to forge a common interest and pursue the common good.[4] This vision, dominant in democratic thought from ancient to early modern times, emphasized substantive equality among citizens (albeit often providing for classes of non-citizens). As Montesquieu summarized the prevailing notion in his classic text on governmental systems, *The Spirit of the Laws*, democracy presupposes virtuous commitment to the public good over the private, which can be nourished only by economic equality and frugality. "[I]n a democracy real equality is the soul of the state," for which reason founders of ancient republics "divided the lands equally," and to which end "[o]ne must . . . regulate . . . dowries, gifts, inheritances, in sum, all kinds of contracts." At a minimum, the laws "must make each poor citizen comfortable enough to be able to work as the others do and must bring each rich citizen to a middle level such that he needs to work in order to preserve or to acquire."[5]

The relationship between equality and democracy was specified most systematically in the work of Rousseau. A democratic polity (or republic, in Rousseau's terminology) is governed on the basis of a social contract whereby each citizen surrenders individual autonomy in return for an equal share in the collective ("general") will. An individual enjoys civil liberty by virtue of being governed only according to "general" laws, by which that individual is burdened to no greater or lesser extent than any other, and in which that individual has an equal say. Yet this will be genuinely so only where the citizens are similarly situated, so that politics does not become dominated by conflicting and unequal interest groups,

---

[4] Aristotle opined that human beings, as political animals, seek political community in the collective pursuit of excellence; "for without this end the community becomes a mere alliance . . . and law is only a convention, 'a surety to one another of justice,' . . . and has no real power to make the citizens good and just". *See* Aristotle, *The Politics*, Stephen Everson, ed. (New York: Cambridge University Press 1988) 64 (bk. III, para. 9). Alternatives to liberalism, whether democratic or not, have frequently emphasized this grander mission of politics.

[5] Montesquieu, *The Spirit of the Laws*, A. Cohler, B. Miller, and H. Stone, eds. (New York: Cambridge University Press, 1989), pp. 44–48 (bk. v. chs. 5–6).

leading to the triumph of "particular" interests over the common good. Thus, it is essential that "no citizen shall ever be wealthy enough to buy another, and none poor enough to be forced to sell himself." Laws, Rousseau wrote, "are always of use to those who possess and harmful to those who have nothing: from which it follows that the social state is advantageous to men only when all have something and none too much."[6]

The pre-liberal–democratic ideal thus went well beyond equal distribution of the franchise. It extended to a rough equality in material conditions, which translates into a rough equality of power over the socially structured decisions (especially concerning the allocation and use of material resources) that condition daily life. In part this reflected the belief that only relative equality in social conditions could provide the proper basis of effectively equal political participation. More essentially, however, it reflected the belief that the whole purpose of formal political equality was the effectively equal empowerment of citizens across the society in all realms of social activity.

As C. B. Macpherson puts it, for most ancient to early modern democratic thinkers, "democracy *was* a classless or one-class society, not merely a political mechanism to fit such a society"[7] (though the ancient view excluded from "society" classes of non-citizens). The split between public and private realms, between a political community of equal citizens acting cooperatively and a civil society of unequal individuals acting competitively, with the former relegated to the role of guaranteeing the conditions for the latter, was an innovation of liberalism.[8]

Initially hostile to the extension of the franchise beyond the propertied classes, liberal elites gradually incorporated the democratic program as the latter proved susceptible of "domestication." The advent of the universal franchise, it turned out, had less effect than anticipated on the distribution of real political influence, which continued largely to reflect the distribution of power in civil society.

This reality, in turn, increasingly drove critics of social inequality to a hostile stance toward "bourgeois democracy"; not only were its democratic properties grossly incomplete, but its mechanisms of popular

---

[6] Jean-Jacques Rousseau, "The Social Contract," *in* G. D. H. Cole, trans., *The Social Contract and Discourses*, (Toronto: J. M. Dent and Sons Ltd, 1973), p. 204 (bk. II, ch. 11), p. 181 n.1 (bk I, ch. 9).
[7] C. B. Macpherson, *The Life and Times of Liberal Democracy* (New York: Oxford University Press 1977), p. 10.
[8] For the most famous critique of liberal democracy along these lines, *see* Karl Marx, "On the Jewish Question," *in* Robert C. Tucker, ed., *The Marx–Engels Reader* (New York: W.W. Norton and Co., Inc., 1978), pp. 26, 42–43.

participation could even be seen as an *obstacle* to genuine popular empowerment. Through cultural hegemony and the multifaceted influences of money, the upper classes would ever be able to subvert working-class consciousness and undermine the unity of any electorally based challenge to the *status quo*. Moreover, there was the suspicion that the true powers-that-be would allow bourgeois democracy to operate only so long as it did not produce a revolutionary result, that the promise of fidelity to whatever outcome the process might produce veiled a secret resolution to prevent social change by all means necessary, in which case the humble classes would be caught unprepared and unarmed.

The unhappy results of this logic need not be detailed here. Suffice it to say that little has proved more lethal to popular empowerment than the imputation of popular will to a vanguard that promises to create by coercion the conditions of the popular will's authentic expression. History's refutation of that experiment, however, does not invalidate the insights that prompted so many to embrace it.

For its part, liberal democracy withstood the challenge from "people's democracy" largely because it adapted to incorporate part of the agenda of substantive democracy. This adaptation came partly as a response to the threat of the anti-liberal Left; popular enfranchisement necessitates co-optation, and co-optation has its price. The adaptation also stemmed, however, from the very logic of the fusion of liberalism and democracy: if the enfranchised lower classes are to enjoy the benefits of liberalism – the ability to autonomously pursue diverse interests – something more than guarantees of non-interference will be necessary to enable that enjoyment. Democratic legitimacy, even for liberal democracy, requires not only formal processes, but a democratic social reality. Although there is no consensus on the necessary content of this social reality, some homage must be paid to the egalitarian component of the democratic heritage.

Recognition of democracy's substantive component informs consideration of the problem of false democratization. Although the formal structures of Western liberal democracy may be packaged for export, their transplantation into societies marked by rigid social stratification and widespread economic deprivation does not thereby render those societies "democracies." The universal franchise may allow all sectors of the society to select once every four years from among pre-packaged candidates of parties controlled by social elites, but this scarcely implies the rudiments of accountability, let alone genuine popular empowerment. Popular prerogative to reject one given set of administrators of the social order in favor of another, while not a trivial development, is very far from the power to make government responsive to popular initiatives, input, or needs. Where opposition groups operate without resources in a context of widespread illiteracy, economic dependence, and entrenched habits of deference to traditional authority, meager are the prospects for making real the promises associated with the democratic label. And this is even assuming that the polyarchic processes are genuine, rather than a sham to disguise repression of real opposition and reserves of power for military or other elite institutions.

False democratization occurs where polyarchic institutions are introduced not as a component of social reform, but as a substitute for it. The purpose of false democratization is to manipulate the internationally recognized symbols of legitimacy, so as to discredit militant (often armed) opposition and deflect international criticism that has impeded the flow of foreign (often military) aid. Wartime elections in this context have served not as an opening to the resolution of civil war, but as a war strategy. Yet even where the institutions of polyarchy are implemented less manipulatively, use of the democratic label tends to vastly exaggerate the extent of progress. The formal mechanisms associated in the West with democracy may be in place, but absent the social context that in the West causes them to be normatively meaningful.

Western liberal democracy, whatever its shortcomings, has realized enough of the democratic ideal to delegitimate those critics who seek to overthrow it rather than seek change within it. The same should not automatically be assumed for the Western model's imitators in less developed countries. From the standpoint of substantive democracy, competitive electoral processes are valuable to the extent that they improve the distribution of power in society; where they are unlikely to do so significantly, the primary focus of normative inquiry must be on, not formal procedures, but social reform.

Egalitarian social policies, *i.e.*, policies oriented toward greater economic equality, material security, and access to the institutions of civil society, are essential to democracy in three ways:

(1) They *enable* democracy, by providing the material base for meaningful and effective political participation, so that less advantaged sectors can advance their self-conceived interests in the political arena on the same terms as social elites.
(2) They *reflect* democracy, for they are evidence – perhaps the only truly persuasive evidence – of the real weight of popular sectors in political decisionmaking.

(3) They *embody* the essence of democracy, in that they empower less advantaged sectors with respect to social decisions taken outside the political realm, decisions likely to have the greatest concrete effect on people's lives.

In less developed countries marked by social stratification and political polarization, especially in Latin America, polyarchy and social reform have often constituted not complementary but contradictory programs of political forces claiming the mantle of democracy. False democratization, as described above, has been to varying extents the norm. Where rare opportunities for social change have presented themselves, the agents of change have understandably been reluctant to allow the project to be derailed in the name of fidelity to procedural niceties. Ironically, among the most vociferous advocates of polyarchy have been embattled social elites subjected to populist or socialist regimes. Determining which side, if any, deserves to be identified with the cause of democracy is far from being a straightforward matter.

Meanwhile, Eastern Europe has seen the collapse of (partly foreign-imposed) regimes which had accomplished, parasitic *nomenklatura* notwithstanding, economic and social levelling and an austere material security. This accomplishment, however, came at the cost not only of the denial of authentic political participation, but the systematic eradication of civil society's autonomy, with respect not only to economics but to all aspects of social activity. "Actually existing socialism" incorporated all civic organizations into the State apparatus, not for the stated purpose of involving citizens more directly in the revolutionary process, but in order to crush any organized autonomy from the State. By no definition was this democracy. Yet "democratization" has so far sought to reverse those few features that, from the standpoint of substantive democracy, are favorable: relative social equality and the concentration of economic resources in the hands of a public sector that might potentially be held accountable to collective decision-making. Although the introduction of market mechanisms is unquestionably desirable – indeed, economically essential – the choice of marketization strategy has enormous consequences for substantive democracy.

Neo-liberal "democratization," in both Latin America and Eastern Europe, has involved social policies that calculatedly *deepen* economic inequality, material insecurity, and social stratification (albeit purportedly only in the short run) in the name of eliminating an inefficient and parasitic State apparatus and opening markets to capitalize on comparative advantage. Although arguably reflecting a mere recognition of economic realities, these policies threaten to place vital economic decisions exclusively in the hands of international markets, foreign investors, and well-positioned domestic elites, leaving them permanently beyond the reach of political decision-making. For sectors lacking market power, it is hardly clear that the promised long-run advantages will ever materialize; as ever, their destiny appears to be out of their hands. Unfortunately, the cause of substantive democracy has thus far been unable to inspire a coherent alternative economic strategy.

Gershman purported to eulogize the notion of "a higher form of democracy . . . that could really achieve things." But however badly the expansive conception of substantive democracy has lately been battered, democracy is, in the final analysis, not separable from "real achievements." What those achievements must be is a matter of intense ideological dispute, but to the extent that one claims the moral authority associated with the democratic tradition, as opposed to merely redefining democracy as nineteenth-century liberalism, one must measure democratization in terms of real, not just formal, popular empowerment. One should not, then, speak of democracy in isolation from egalitarian social policies.

IV POPULAR SOVEREIGNTY

If there is an emerging global consensus about governmental norms, it is not a consensus about democracy. However much conventional mechanisms for the election of governments may have diffused, there is no clear accompanying trend toward the substantive democratization of societies; indeed, one might argue that the trend is in certain respects to the contrary. Moreover, as the foregoing section makes clear, there is no agreed-upon method of measuring such progress. Competing conceptions of substantive democratization suggest differing criteria, often in tension and sometimes contradictory. Whatever overlapping consensus exists is primarily a consensus about what democracy *is not*; consideration of an affirmative program will immediately bring discord to the surface.

There is, however, a separate issue as to which the possibilities of consensus are more promising, and to which democratic values are relevant. This is the issue of assessing, not a governmental system's progress in realizing elusive ends nowhere achieved in full, but the system's success in producing a government that meets certain minimum requisites for international recognition as the nation's legitimate sovereign representative. This issue has taken on new significance in the last few years, moving beyond the realm of abstract moralizing and into the realm of international legal debate. At stake is a government's right to invoke in the State's name the UN Charter prohibitions against foreign intervention in matters which are "essentially" within the State's domestic jurisdiction (Art. 2(7)) and foreign threats or uses of force against a State's political independence (Art. 2(4)).

Traditionally, the internal character of a regime was irrelevant to the government's international standing. The international order was formally based on the association of equal sovereign States, the logic of which implied that whoever held effective control of the national territory and population had unquestioned authority to speak for the State in international affairs. It was hence inappropriate for the international community to grant or withhold recognition based on the method by which a government came to power or the extent of popular approval of those who spoke in the nation's name.

Recent events, however, have prompted reconsideration of the traditional view.[9] This reconsideration is perhaps a predictable eventual result of a UN Charter that, in wake of the horrors of World War II, fused the customary principles of international law with moralistic references to the "self-determination of peoples" (Art. 1(2)) and "universal respect for, and observance of, human rights and fundamental freedoms" (Art. 55(c)). Article 21(3) of the Universal Declaration of Human Rights, approved by the UN in 1948, stated that "[t]he will of the people shall be the basis of the authority of government."[10] Although international instruments purporting to specify requisites for the realization of these principles are vaguer than they might at first appear, having been drafted and approved with the participation of unrepentant one-party States,[11] they constituted a step away from the antiquated notion of national sovereignty as a right vested in a sovereign monarch. Formally, State sovereignty was now popular sovereignty, although what counted as an articulation of the popular will was still considered a matter "essentially within the domestic jurisdiction," in practice leaving beyond challenge the *de facto* ruler's claim to speak for his people.

---

[9] I have elsewhere presented an analysis of the legal ramifications of this development. Roth, *Governmental Illegitimacy in International Law* (Oxford: Clarendon Press, 1999); *see also* Roth, "Governmental Illegitimacy Revisited: 'Pro-Democratic' Armed Intervention in the Post-Bipolar World," *Transnational Law & Contemporary Problems* 3 (Fall 1993), pp. 481–513.

[10] Universal Declaration of Human Rights, GA. Res. 217(A), UN Doc. A/810, p. 71 (1948).

[11] *See, e.g.*, Henry J. Steiner, "Political Participation as a Human Right," *Harv. Hum. Rts. Y.B.* 1 (1988), pp. 77–134 (discussing Article 21 of the Universal Declaration and Article 25 of the International Covenant on Civil and Political Rights).

Whatever else may be said for the consequences of the "third wave of democratization" that has swept through old bastions of resistance to liberal–democratic political forms, it can at minimum be said that the imputation of popular will to *de facto* regimes is no longer found persuasive. True, an international community that takes the self-determination principle seriously can scarcely impose a specified method of self-government as a condition of according States the very respect and protection that international law purports in the name of national self-determination to provide. But one can no longer simply accept at face value the claims of autocratic leaders that their leadership is the expression of an unmanifested popular will or indigenous cultural norms, of which the leaders purport themselves to be the authoritative interpreters. Too often, *de facto* leaders have proved to have been tyrannical despots, reviled by their subjects for having made a cruel joke of the norms on which they predicated their right to rule. For popular sovereignty to have genuine meaning, the link between the people and sovereign power must be empirical.

John Locke, that quintessential theorist of government by consent of the governed, reasoned that individuals, by virtue of consenting unanimously to the formation of political society, bestowed upon the majority the power to select the form of government as it saw fit, whether that form be democracy, aristocracy, elective monarchy, or hereditary monarchy.[12] How this "majority" decision came to be perceived is unclear. Locke interposed no requirement of elections or plebiscites to determine the majority's will. (Indeed, for Locke, the linchpin of legitimacy was the government's conduct, not its form.) Nonetheless, where the "majority" had placed the greater part of the legislative power into the hands of Parliament, Locke deemed the usurpation of this power by the King to constitute the dissolution of the legitimate government.[13] This raises questions, since imputation of majority consent from mere acquiescence might as easily ratify a change in the form of government (as from mixed to monarchic in Locke's England) as the establishment of the original form. Perhaps the consent of the majority is to be inferred only from long-standing traditions or from developments occasioned by the participation of some substantial part of the political community.

What is clear is that the majority has the right to select, by whatever means of articulation, even hereditary monarchy, notwithstanding that once selected, this option forecloses the majority from further

---

[12] John Locke, "Second Treatise of Government," *in* P. Laslett, ed., *Two Treatises of Government* (New York: Cambridge University Press, 1988), pp. 354–55 (ch. x, paras. 132–33).
[13] *Ibid.*, pp. 407–10 (ch. xix, paras. 212–18).

participation in government. Although the government can by its behavior forfeit its legitimacy, there is no indication that its legitimacy can simply be revoked by a subsequent majority decision. After all, the point of adopting an authoritarian form of government is precisely to promote unity, stability, decisive government, and long-term planning, all of which are undermined by making governmental legitimacy the hostage of the whims of temporary future majorities.

Such a view of majoritarianism is reminiscent of a famous lamentation about elections in numerous African States at the time of independence: "one man, one vote, one time." Democratic constitutions have frequently embodied a founding pre-commitment to a "republican form of government" or "free democratic basic order" that overrules contradictory decisions taken by a subsequent majority or even supermajority. But what do democratic values have to say about a majority decision to adopt authoritarian government, whether that decision is manifested by election or plebiscite, or by some less concrete form of articulation, such as time-honored traditions or mass demonstrations?

The answer to this question is more complicated than is usually conceded by those who proclaim the advent of an "emerging right to democratic governance." The moral authority of democracy is tied to an insistence on the right of all people to participate on an equal basis in the decisions affecting their destiny, but this also implies that people be able to assign to others, on terms of their own choosing, their power of decision. Representative democracy itself requires this principle, though only on the basis of fixed terms, sometimes augmented by recall provisions. Judicial review of legislation implicates this principle to an even greater extent, subject only to provisions for constitutional amendment that may require complex combinations of supermajorities.

Do not democratic principles then imply that a community may, through a majority decision somehow manifested, delegate political decision-making to an authoritarian government in perpetuity, conditioned only on that government's fulfillment of the purposes for which the delegation was made? The initial answer, it seems, must be yes. Any other answer violates the very equality of respect that democratic principles require us to accord members of different societies with different values, goals, and traditions.

But that is only half the answer. In an authoritarian society, a mere change in majority preferences is scarcely seen or felt. The issue only arises in the context of a crisis of legitimacy, which occurs only when a substantial sector of the society manifests its view either that the delegation had not been made by a true majority in the first place, that the government has violated the terms of the delegation, or that changed circumstances have made the purposes of that delegation obsolete. And under these conditions, the judge of the truth of these contentions can, by the application of democratic principles, only be the current majority, whose views must be manifested in a manner clear enough to direct the international community's application of the principles mandating respect and protection for legitimate governments.[14]

The numerous internationally monitored elections taking place in less developed countries in the last several years should not, then, be seen as part of a democratization crusade.[15] They are better understood as an application of Lockean principles of popular sovereignty to discrete instances where there have been internal crises of governmental legitimacy. There is no movement – nor should there be – to delegitimate non-polyarchic governments generally. As for the phenomenon of "one man, one vote, one time," such a result, for all the problems it creates, remains consistent with the scheme of popular sovereignty if it be the majority will.

What do democratic values dictate where popular sovereignty generates a result grossly at odds with substantive democracy? On the one hand, egalitarian social policies enable, reflect and embody broad popular empowerment; on the other hand, majorities often willingly vote to maintain, reinforce, or even restore socioeconomic stratification. There has thus been the temptation to equate popular sovereignty with some imputed popular will that represents, not the empirical will of the populace, but a higher will, one that embodies what the populace would will if it were to recognize its true interests or achieve full social consciousness. This vanguardist temptation, of course, has led to apologism for tyranny, and not just of the Leninist variety. In the face of many real-world circumstances, however, the temptation is all but irresistible.

---

[14] Elections alone frequently fail to resolve the issue. A popular will is subject to competing articulations. Freely elected heads of State may vitiate their mandates before the end of their terms by running afoul of the constitution, generally accepted customs, or public opinion as expressed in polls, mass demonstrations, or general strikes. Contradictions may arise, as in Russia in 1993, between the elected President and the elected legislature, each asserting the authority to remove the other, with a weak high court weighing in on the basis of a poorly esteemed constitution. However great the value of established processes, popular sovereignty cannot be reduced to any mechanistic formula.

[15] For such an interpretation of these developments, *see* Fox, "Right to Political Participation in International Law," *supra* note 1, pp. 579–90. My disagreement with Fox is based not only on the above normative analysis, but on a different assessment of the actual *opinio juris* of States in these contexts. *See* Roth, "Governmental Illegitimacy Revisited," *supra* note 9, pp. 509–10, n.100.

Rousseau dealt directly with this paradox of substantive democracy. In order for the necessary institutions to be built, "the social spirit, which should be created by these institutions, would have to preside over their very foundation." The role of institutional architect falls to the Rousseauian "legislator," whose task is no less than to transform "each individual, who is by himself a complete and solitary whole, into part of a greater whole from which he in a manner receives his life and being." Yet if the legislator were to have unilateral authority to impose these institutions, "his private aims would inevitably mar the sanctity of his work." "[O]nly the general will can bind the individuals, and there can be no assurance that a particular will is in conformity with the general will, until it has been put to the free vote of the people." Rome, he added, "suffered a revival of all the crimes of tyranny, and was brought to the verge of destruction, because it put the legislative [drafting] authority and the sovereign power into the same hands."[16]

For Rousseau, legitimate governance requires that the majority will and the principle of generality (i.e., rudimentary social justice) coincide; "when they cease to do so, whatever side a man may take, liberty is no longer possible."[17] And so it may be that between deference to the majority's consent to a socioeconomic elite's self-interested "particular" will and the vanguardist impulse to drag the masses kicking and screaming to the promised land, there simply is no choice consistent with democratic values. Recent history may indicate that, other things being equal, the vanguardist approach is the worse of the two, but that may be a transitory prejudice that will be negated by future historical disasters of the opposite kind.

There are at least two types of circumstance where "other things" are not equal. The first is where "liberty is not *possible*," i.e., where *de jure* or *de facto* conditions are such as to provide no reasonable possibility for the forces of egalitarian social reform to make progress while at the same time respecting the institutions ratified by the empirical popular will. Under conditions where social hierarchy is locked in, such as non-polyarchy or sham democratization, the democratic perspective would not seem to favor legitimating the *status quo* and casting its disloyal opposition into a kind of international outlawry.

The second exceptional circumstance is where the particularism of the majority will is so great as to be predatory. This is often the

---

[16] Rousseau, "The Social Contract," *supra* note 6, pp. 194–96 (bk. II, Ch. 7).
[17] *Ibid.*, pp. 250–51 (bk. IV, ch. 2).

case in societies marked by racial, ethnic, or religious polarization. Majoritarianism is not a principle unto itself; it is an application of the principle of equal respect and empowerment. Majorities must be drawn from a collection of groups with overlapping interests capable of generating a general will, even if only on the basis that each group is too small and vulnerable to see a high-stakes grab for predatory power as an attractive option. Where there is a cohesive majority faction intent on plundering the minority, the minority's power over its affairs in a majority vote is zero. Even if there were some promise of this changing through the institutionalization of polyarchy and steps toward the de-ethnification of politics, a minority group's vital interests might be irremediably damaged before that promise could be realized.

Assuming majority will is to be deferred to, the final issue involves determining what shall count as a manifestation of that popular will. Where governments face a crisis of legitimacy, the answer of contemporary custom is to hold a "free and fair election." UN (and NGO) observer groups have made impressive progress in generating a broadly recognized set of specifications for such an election, which I will not detail here.

The critical difficulty in these elections involves "levelling the playing field," so that the majority has a fair chance to decide its will. Although recognized standards now extend beyond electoral mechanics to the conduct of electoral campaigns, additional obstacles lie a step farther back, in the social reality that provides the broader context for the election.

The problem is particularly acute where opponents of the *status quo* suffer both from socioeconomic disadvantage and from the lingering effects of a history of political exclusion and repression. Whatever compensations are attempted, the playing field cannot truly be levelled. Although the militant opposition cannot, without contradicting democratic principles, use this fact indefinitely as an excuse to evade majority judgment, it is justified in conditioning its indispensable participation in a test of governmental legitimacy on both procedural and substantive guarantees regarding the future. The playing field may be sufficiently level for holding the first of a perpetual series of periodically scheduled elections (to be held under gradually improving social conditions), but not for a "one man, one vote, one time" determination of how the country is to be run for the indefinite future. In specific cases, therefore, efforts to effectuate the principle of popular sovereignty may entail pursuing aspects of procedural and/or substantive democratization.

Popular sovereignty is conceptually distinct from democracy, even though its content may be specified through application of democratic principles. At stake is a regime's minimal legitimacy, not its democratic quality. Yet the concerns that give rise to tests of legitimacy based on majority consent also give rise to a felt need to reproduce evidence of majority consent at regular intervals. Polyarchic norms can thus contribute to a form of political progress that, while fully distinct from substantive democratization, is nonetheless normatively significant from a democratic point of view.

V CONSTITUTIONALISM

As standards for measuring political progress in developing States, substantive democracy and popular sovereignty have significant shortcomings. First, the goals they represent are the extreme ends of a spectrum. Substantive democracy is a maximal goal, relevant to normative evaluation of all regimes but susceptible only of incomplete realization in even the most highly developed polity. Popular sovereignty is a minimal goal, requisite to the bare recognition of a government's legitimacy against the claims of rival contestants. Progress beyond satisfaction of the norm of popular sovereignty, but not directly relevant to the realization of substantive democracy, remains to be considered.

Second, substantive democracy and popular sovereignty are norms imposed from without, grounded in abstract principles rather than in the thinking of political actors in the society in question. They gauge legitimacy from the perspective of the foreign observer, not the domestic participant. The focus is on whether and to what extent participatory processes serve democratic values, not on the usefulness of such processes in forging a political order that satisfies the essential purposes of the society's powerful actors. These actors may be oblivious to democratic values, but the achievement of a stable social peace among them may nonetheless constitute real progress for the nation, even as gauged from abroad by an observer animated by democratic values.

Constitutionalism represents a different gauge of progress. Constitutionalism, in the sense to be discussed herein, denotes *the establishment of a broadly recognized basis for the legitimate exercise of power, from which can be deduced procedural and substantive limitations on power's legitimate exercise.*

Where constitutionalism prevails, the constitution is not merely descriptive (reflecting the transitory configuration of the *de facto* power structure) or programmatic (reciting high-minded aspirations), but operative, effectively setting the perimeters of the permissible actions of State organs and officials. The emphasis here is not on instrumentalities (which may or may not include a founding document or a system of judicial review), but on social effects. A constitutionalist order is achieved where the politically relevant actors come to share a commitment to established principles and institutions of government; those in power recognize that they may exercise it only within the established competences of their offices, and those out of power recognize that they must obey the final decision of those officeholders duly authorized to render it. Wherever and to whatever extent constitutionalism is absent, little beyond personalistic loyalty or habits of obedience stands to prevent an unmediated clash of social forces,[18] i.e., politics as war by other means, at best.

The substantive and procedural content of the constitutional arrangement, including the existence *vel non* of competitive electoral processes and a broad franchise, will depend on the balance of forces in the political community (though it must in all cases establish legal limits to the discretionary exercise of power and independent oversight of those limits). Absent commonly recognized traditions and philosophical premises, some combination of overlapping consensus and compromise must reconcile disparate views and interests.

Constitutionalism is possible only where all of the society's essential political actors regard the cost of imperiling the constitutional arrangement as greater than the cost of being defeated on the issues immediately at stake. One way to create this condition is for the constitution to embody a completely static substantive compromise, with no significant competitive processes, and perhaps with factional vetoes, so that no essential issues are subject to a unilateral discretionary decision. An opposite approach would be to subject all issues to competitive electoral processes, guaranteeing only the perpetuation of the competitive processes with specifications that hold out to the losers the hope of increasing their influence in the next election. The greatest likelihood is an intermediate solution that combines an element of fluidity with substantive guarantees. A static compromise would freeze the legal balance of power irrespective of changes in the balance within society, resulting in great incentives to void the deal as soon as one party's societal power has

---

[18] Compare Max Weber, "Politics as a Vocation," *in* H. H. Gerth and C. Wright Mills, trans., *From Max Weber: Essays in Sociology* (Boston, Mass.: Routledge and Kegan Paul, 1958), pp. 77, 78–79 (habitual conformity, charisma, and legality as the three "legitimations of domination").

significantly improved. A solely procedural solution raises the stakes of political competition to unacceptably high levels for groups that expect to be perpetual losers, as well as for groups fearing that the decisions of the present term could irremediably damage their interests (or even destroy them *qua* interest groups) before the next election. (Of course, for them to void the deal, these groups must also believe they could do better in an unmediated power struggle.)

Competitive electoral systems do not necessarily mean full polyarchy. The deal may involve freezing out some contestants, or grossly limiting the franchise (*e.g.*, along property qualification, gender, or ethnic lines). The system need be legitimate only in the eyes of those whose judgment of illegitimacy would be seriously destabilizing; if radical parties are marginal, or if sectors of the society are effectively outside the political arena, they will not have sufficient chips to come to the table.

Nonetheless, there are strong reasons why polyarchy is an increasingly common outcome of constitutional bargains. Where militant opposition parties caused the crisis of which the constitutional process is the attempted solution, they obviously cannot be excluded. Where such parties are weak, excluding them unnecessarily clouds the claim of the constitutional arrangement to legitimacy, both internally and with respect to the international community. Where such parties are weak but feared to become strong, they are likely to be dealt with by means that, however undemocratic, are more subtle than outright exclusion.

Resistance to universal adult enfranchisement is also an unlikely result. First, the international norm of universal enfranchisement is much stronger than any norm requiring elections to be meaningful; formal disenfranchisement is simply an international public relations disaster. Second, whereas during European feudalism one could speak of the masses as being simply outside the political arena, it is difficult to say this now of significant sectors in even the least developed countries. Part of this may be owing to an international diffusion of a sense of entitlement to participate in politics, but for whatever reason, it is difficult to imagine situations where legitimacy in the eyes of the masses is not a relevant political consideration. Moreover, the lower classes have proved easier to co-opt than to exclude, and the "learning curve" on this has helped to spare less developed countries the struggles over enfranchisement that took place in the first polyarchies. Finally, even if the popular classes were not demanding a voice in politics, elites would not likely be sufficiently cohesive to resist the temptation to try to recruit the masses to help shift the elite power balance.

Constitutionalism, though it is now likely to include polyarchy as an ingredient, is not in and of itself a pursuit of democracy, and certainly does not necessarily imply the broad popular empowerment associated with substantive democracy. Polyarchy here is a means to a different end: it provides an incentive for estranged groups to accept the deal. Forces favoring substantive democratization may accept the solution for no other reason than that they have no higher cards to play. At the same time, their acceptance is evidence that the arrangement is preferable to the unmediated clash of social forces that is the alternative to constitutionalism.

In countries whose histories have been marked by a less civilized mode of politics, the establishment of a broadly recognized basis for the legitimate exercise of power is a major accomplishment, separate and apart from issues of substantive democratization and popular sovereignty. It should be appreciated and gauged in its own terms, and not conflated with a phenomenon – polyarchy – that at times is present, in whatever degree, as a subordinate component.

VI CONCLUSION

Recent academic literature on democracy in both the comparative politics and international law fields has emphasized the widespread diffusion of polyarchic procedural norms in the post-Cold-War world. Such an emphasis is potentially misleading. It courts the twin dangers of messianism and complacency, encouraging ill-conceived interventions against governmental systems that fail to embody what passes for some transcendent democratic "truth," while providing ideological cover for regimes that continue systematically to deprive their citizenries of genuine participation in the decisions that affect their lives.

At the same time, the prevalent literature fails to appreciate distinct types of political progress that do not entail democracy, but that are associated, to a greater or lesser extent, with polyarchic mechanisms. Such mechanisms have proved valuable (though not a panacea) in resolving destructive crises of governmental legitimacy. They have played a part both in the implementation of the international standards that purport to bridle foreign responses to internal conflict and in domestic solutions, grounded in local political realities, that forge an agreed-upon basis for and limitations on the exercise of governmental power. The former aspect has been treated above under the heading of "popular sovereignty," the latter under the heading of "constitutionalism." These are forms of progress that democrats should welcome, and yet they fall far short of yielding the substance that renders democracy a distinctively compelling cause.

By differentiating between substantive democracy, popular sovereignty, and constitutionalism, one can recognize certain types of progress relevant to democratic values without committing the democratic imprimatur to still-problematic regimes. A ready example is El Salvador as it appeared in the wake of its March 1994 "elections of the century." The legitimacy of its elected government for purposes of international recognition seemed clear beyond cavil; prospects for consolidating constitutional structures that could maintain social peace were hopeful but still problematic; genuine empowerment for vast deprived sectors of the society remained far off.

A realistic assessment of the progress of societies in transition will focus attention on the problems that remain to be solved. Only in this way will normative evaluation make a contribution to progress in the achievement of democratic ends.

CHAPTER 18

What kind of democracy does the "democratic entitlement" entail?

Jan Knippers Black

One of the very positive developments of the last several years in Latin America, Eastern Europe, parts of Central Asia and East Asia, and even Africa, has been the spread of democracy – or at least of elections, and the generalized requirement of elections – as the sole acceptable means of rule legitimation. It would be very dangerous, however, to view this trend as unidirectional – "the end of history"[1] – or as the best we can do toward achieving the popular ideal of democracy. It represents, rather, a change in the nature, rules, and venues of the game of power competition that offers both new opportunities and new vulnerabilities. Over the longer term, the spread of elections has by no means been an unbroken trend; it has come in fits and starts, waves and cycles, incomplete and always subject to reversal.

The development or de-development of democracy (understood as popular, as opposed to elite, rule) should not be simply equated with or tracked through national elections. Elections are a means, not an end, and means are always subject to subversion or corruption. There may well have been more democracy in "primitive" or pre-modern societies than is common in contemporary democracies. In the absence of more reliable means of recording choice in complex societies, however, it has become difficult to speak convincingly of democracy without reference to elections.

The nation-state system is itself a fairly recent social construct, and national elections did not become commonplace, even in Europe and its liberated offspring, until the mid-nineteenth century. At the turn of the twentieth century, by some assessments, there were only nine countries that could legitimately be considered democratic, and by 1960 only

---

[1] The reference is to the much-cited article by Francis Fukuyama, "The End of History?" *The National Interest* (Summer 1989).

twenty-nine. A similar survey in 1990 found sixty-five countries engaging in creditable elections.[2]

Thereafter, with the implosion of the Soviet Union and the spread of separatist fervor, there was an explosion in the number of recognized states and thus in the number of national elections. Qualitative considerations aside, there were well over one hundred States in the early 1990s having elected governments. While dubious in terms of output (i.e., accountability), the current era of electoral democracy is, in terms of input (i.e., the staging of and participation in elections), certainly the most far-reaching geographically. It is also the most firmly entrenched in international law, from the political participation provisions of the International Covenant on Civil and Political Rights, now signed by more than one hundred countries, to the spreading practice of international and non-governmental monitoring of elections.

MAKING WAVES: GRAVITATIONAL FORCES AND NEW FRONTIERS

This new era of democracy is not simply a byproduct of the end of the Cold War. Like any development so unlikely, it has been overdetermined, produced by many factors. This new wave of democratization might be traced to Western Europe in the mid 1970s. Having developed strong domestic economies and a strongly democratic vocation, having discarded the costly last throes of straightforward colonialism (as opposed to neo-colonialism) and having found economic strength in unity, the European Community exerted a strong pull on the continent's unconverted fringes. The lure of membership in the Community gave an indispensable edge particularly to democratic forces confronting authoritarian regimes in Portugal, Spain, and Greece.

The influence of Europe was felt in the Western hemisphere as well, but a climatic change in the post-Vietnam-War United States made a greater difference in Latin America. The first clear-cut reversal for Latin America's devastating era of militocracy came with President Jimmy Carter's insistence on respect for the electoral outcome in the Dominican Republic in 1978.[3]

With the end of the Cold War, the proliferation of new States – shards

---

[2] Gregory H. Fox, "The Right to Political Participation in International Law," *Yale J. Int'l L.* 17 (1992), pp. 539–607.

[3] In 1961 all but about three of the Latin American countries were generally considered democratic. By 1976 all but about three were considered authoritarian. By 1991 all but one or two were considered democratic.

of the Soviet Empire – constituted a new frontier, an irresistible challenge to seekers of power and profit as well as to those of more benign motives. But whatever the motive, whether revision of property and investment codes or the facilitation of new forms of expression and participation, the staging of elections launched the reorganization and offered the essential legitimation.

For the Third World in general, the end of the Cold War meant both liberation and resignation. For the Right it meant the loss of their cover story, for the Left the loss of their dream. First-World potentates and profiteers lost their rationale for openly propping up monsters like Mobutu on security grounds. But then, they no longer needed such monsters. In an unregulated globalized capitalist economy, there was little danger that hungry natives could compete successfully under any form of government for a share of Africa's riches. In such a context, both revolutionary and militarist–modernizer legitimation have shrinking constituencies; and the forces that had constituted at times the political extremes, at times the political options, are left with no marketable alternative to elections.

POLITICS AND MARKET POWER

Perhaps the weightiest factors in explaining the trend to democratization, or electoral legitimation, are best illustrated by reference to the exceptions to the rule: the countries that scarcely bother to put up a democratic facade. The most obvious and numerous in that category are China and its expanding sphere of influence and the oil-producing Muslim States. Yet the lack of international attention to democratic criteria in these cases is not a reflection of Western respect for cultural diversity. Muslim religion and culture have no more to do with the major powers' acceptance of dictatorship in the Persian Gulf and Brunei than has Communism, Confucianism or any other "ism" with acceptance of such in China.

In a sense, virtually all States in the now globalized economic system are vanquished States – that is, the public sector has been eaten by the private sector. China is, of course, another matter – the 500 lb. panda who sits anywhere he pleases. The disinclination of the West to challenge the legitimacy of China's government or even seriously to protest its systematic human rights abuses might be attributed to prudent caution in dealing with powerful States. But prudence in international politics is not customary; single-mindedness in profit-seeking is. The power that takes precedence now is market power. It happens that the most powerful constituents of Western governments – the money-movers – are not anxious to risk disruption in China or with China as they are busily moving their money there.

In sum, apart from players holding trumps, like China or Saudi Arabia, States, as such, hold weak hands. Elections are becoming the *modus operandi* for selection of governments in large part because economic interests are less threatened now than they were two or three decades ago by the formal processes of democracy. That is, global concentration of economic power is such that elected leaders have very little latitude in economic policy-making, anyway; and elite interests are well served by allowing elected governments to absorb the blame for policies punishing to the poor. Faced with the expense of an increasingly high-tech, media-led, professionalized game of electoral policies, and finding the vestments of office akin to a straightjacket, leaders unable to deal with the needs of the unaffluent are discredited and defeated by leaders uninterested in doing so.

REDEMOCRATIZATION IN THE SOUTHERN CONE: THE LEGACY OF ABUSE

The struggle for redemocratization, or democratic transition, in Latin America in the late 1970s and early 1980s, particularly in Brazil and the Southern Cone, was undertaken at great personal risk and sacrifice by popular leaders and movements. But it left no celebrated heroes, no monuments, no holidays, or commemorative stamps. In fact, for those most engaged the conflict never really ended; it simply moved inside and lodged in their souls.

At Córdoba's University City, one can still see the concrete and steel foundations of the military bunkers that sixteen years ago surrounded Argentina's oldest college of philosophy and letters. But the casual visitor would not notice such things. Unlike international wars, civil wars, and revolutionary wars, counter-revolutionary wars – of governments against their own citizens – leave few visible scars, but the wounds take longer to heal.

In late 1994, Brazil and South America's Southern Cone seemed caught in a time warp. One who was there thirty years earlier, as I had been, might have expected to have a sensation of *déjà vu*. When I was a Peace Corps Volunteer in Chile in the early 1960s, President Alessandri, a Conservative, was about to be replaced by a Christian Democrat named Eduardo Frei. In Argentina at that time a civilian, of the Radical Party, had just replaced a military regime, with the help of the Peronist vote. In Brazil there was a president backed by organized labor and a nationalist movement promoted by dependency theorists, like Fernando Henrique Cardoso.

In Chile thirty years later, a Christian Democratic president named Eduardo Frei had defeated a Conservative named Alessandri. (On the campaign trail, Frei-the-son quipped that he had just two things going for him: one was his last name, Frei; the other was his first name, Eduardo.) In Argentina, a Peronist had replaced a Radical who had taken over from the military. In Brazil, a popular labor leader running for the presidency on a nationalist, dependency-type platform had been overtaken and defeated by a candidate representing the Center-Right – the same Fernando Henrique Cardoso.

Does that mean that the political and economic game has come full circle in thirty years? No. The ghosts of democracies past are just that. Now, as in the early 1960s, most Latin American governments are considered democratic because elections have taken place. Now, as then, there is less to such democracy than meets the eye. But the obstacles and deceits are of a different order.

In the early 1960s, "democracy" was being discredited – in Central America and the Caribbean by fraud,[4] in the Southern Cone by vulnerability to military intervention. Now, in the 1990s, democracy is being discredited by irrelevance – by the absence of options and expectations.

The democracy of the 1960s was unstable precisely because there was hope, hope that political democracy might lead in the direction of economic democracy. The democracy of the 1990s is more nearly stable because there is little such hope (and consequently, little fear). More than ever, electoral politics is the moral equivalent of sport.

In the 1960s, the United States was promoting growth, but also social change – within limits. Not surprisingly, Latin American leaders chafed at the limits. Those who rejected the limits were labeled by the US and its Latin-American allies as subversives. Those who accepted the limits were labeled by their own people *"entreguistas"*, or sell-outs. The *entreguistas* then began to lose their political bases to the "subversives," a trend highly perturbing to those who had the most to lose.

Whereas some parties on the Left rejected liberal electoral democracy

---

[4] In Haiti, the referendum that legitimated the assumption by Baby Doc of the late Papa Doc's lifetime presidency registered two million votes for and one against. I always imagined that lonely one had been cast by Baby Doc himself.

in principle but accepted it in practice, parties of the Right did just the opposite. They embraced electoral democracy in principle but rejected it in practice. So the region suffered a decade or more of counter-revolutionary terror and another of economic disaster – of unemployment and hyperinflation, disintegration of social infrastructure and dissolution of social fabric. With the beginning of the 1990s, the region was celebrating the completion of a trend towards redemocratization and was even experiencing spurts of economic growth – major accomplishments, achieved at great social and personal costs. But what do these things mean now, in the context of the global village?

One of the problems for the analyst, as for the voter, is that of confusion between what is old and what is new in this regional and global new order. It seems to me that three old problems, closely linked then and now, have taken on new dimensions and perhaps a new order of significance. (1) *Violence*. Official violence has diminished, but has not disappeared, and few civilians want seriously to test the durability of the social truce. Meanwhile, freelance violence has exploded, deepening the tendency to anomie and social isolation. (2) *The growing gap*. Latin America is both richer and poorer than it was three decades ago – a consequence of trends both regional and global and of policy decisions, not of policy failures. The Latin American States are not in danger of disintegrating in the manner of East European and Central Asian ones, but as in the United States their societies are fragmenting nonetheless, between heavily armed ghettoes and fortified suburbs, between those inside double-bolted doors and those left out on the street. (3) *The surrender of sovereignty*. Even as elections became freer, the elected become less so. In the 1990s, the mantle of office looks evermore like a straightjacket.

PERVASIVE VIOLENCE AND THE BATTERED POPULATION SYNDROME

Brazil's observation in 1994 of the thirtieth anniversary of the military counter-revolution that so profoundly affected its political and economic course was a very low-key affair. Commenting on a newly released book in which military commanders of the 1960s and 1970s conceded for the first time that torture had been a systematically employed policy tool, an active duty general shruggingly asked why such matters should be brought up now.

Ariel Dorfman's play, "Death and the Maiden," dealing with the toxic residue of the Pinochet dictatorship, played well in London, and a movie

What kind of democracy does the "democratic entitlement" entail? 523

version played well in the United States, but in Chile it quietly bombed. Argentine and Uruguayan friends tell me that the topic of the "dirty wars" – of military repression and popular resistance – is generally avoided because the hate and fear that lie just beneath the surface of public, and even private, relationships are best left untapped.

The celebrated redemocratization of the Southern Cone – the reconciliation of the privileged and the wretched, of the armed and the unarmed, of abusers and victims leaves whole populations with something akin to the battered-wife syndrome. In the absence of punishment of the perpetrators, of open and definitive social condemnation of their deeds, victims tend to blame themselves, either for somehow causing or inviting the assault or for allowing themselves to be victimized, or both. Rather than a cause for moral outrage, the episode or epoch becomes a source of social embarrassment. As open resistance had been limited and abuse to some degree selective, victimization is unevenly experienced. Thus the national soul-searching that should be expressed in social analysis is expressed instead in individual angst and psychoanalysis.

In fact, the withdrawal of the military has not been to a safe enough distance to allow democracy free rein. Coup attempts and threats and other acts of military insubordination surfaced from time to time throughout the 1980s in Uruguay and Argentina, and in Chile there was no pretense of subordination of the armed forces to elected civilian leadership. Instead, there was talk of co-government – a recipe, the British might say, for horse and rabbit stew: equal parts, one horse, one rabbit. In July 1994, President Frei publicly declared that the commander of the *Carabineros*, or National Police, accused of responsibility for a massacre in years past, did not enjoy the confidence of the government. But under the rules of the game – the stacked deck that civilian leaders saw no choice but to accept – Frei could not remove him. Despite Chile's real progress toward redemocratization, the leader of the Communist party was arrested in 1996 for publicly criticizing Pinochet.

In general, the abusers of the era of militocracy, from the tyrants to the petty freelance torturers, continued to enjoy impunity. Attempts by civilian governments in Argentina and Uruguay in the 1980s to prosecute had met with such ominous military counter-measures that henceforth the amnesties that military conspirators had granted themselves were treated by civilians as if they had the sanctity of law. Several former members of governing juntas in Argentina who had been convicted of human rights abuses and imprisoned under the government of Raul

Alfonsin were subsequently pardoned by the government of Carlos Saul Menem. In Uruguay, in 1996, the admission of a former military officer that during the military regime detainees had been tortured and killed and buried secretly on military property caused a brief stir in the media, but it did not spill over into the political arena.

It was not until 1998 that the issue began seriously to be revisited. At that time, Argentine jurists concluded that amnesty laws protecting the murderers of mothers did not relieve them from liability for trafficking in their orphaned children. Former junta leader, General Jorge Videla, was imprisoned on such a charge early in the year, and further action was pending at year's end on a similar charge lodged against Admiral Emilio Massera.

The most dramatic breach to date in the wall of impunity was the arrest of Chile's retired dictator, General Augusto Pinochet (now, by his own rules, Senator for Life) in London on October 16, 1998, pursuant to a Spanish request for extradition on a range of human rights-related charges. In Chile, the arrest led to much rejoicing but also much concern and, in some quarters, anger. The government's defense of Pinochet, the degree of unease and polarization and the extent of hedging and evasiveness among those, even on the Left, who enjoyed a political forum, suggested that Pinochet, or Pinochetismo, still cast a long shadow across the land and that the need for exorcism remained acute. (In the US as well, the architects and enablers of Latin America's era of militocracy had been displaced only, not defeated or discredited; the conflicted response in Washington to the prospect of a trial for Pinochet suggested a need for exorcism there also.)

Even so, selective political violence, "democratized" during the years of militocracy in the sense that the affluent were also susceptible, has abated. Official violence is generally limited once again to the poor, who were always vulnerable. But, along with the poor, the middle class has fallen prey to another kind of violence – a cultural import, some say, from the United States – a sort of street-level tax collection. Throughout Latin America, locals now suggest "safe" taxis and a firm grip on wallets.

In Rio de Janeiro, the tunnels that move traffic through the mountains to connect the principal parts of the city in the early 1990s had become "toll tunnels," as heavily armed thugs blocked the entrances and systematically collected; and the nightly sounds of machine gun shoot-outs as drug lords competed for control of *favelas* had generated a siege mentality in a city so recently famed as fun-loving. Such menacing anarchy is almost as subversive of democratic prospects, as certain to sever links among races and classes and generations, as is tyranny. With the metropolitan murder rate running at twenty a day, most Cariocas seemed relieved when the federal government, in late 1994, launched Operation Rio, a series of assaults involving several thousand troops, against the *favelas* assumed to be the most heavily infested with narco-traffickers.

ECONOMIC POLARIZATION AND SOCIAL DISSOLUTION

One need not see the latest figures from the UN Economic Commission on Latin America to know that the region's income gap is widening dramatically, at a pace accelerated by the growth spurts of the 1990s. On all sides in the private sector one sees monuments to new wealth.

Cutting a swath across virgin forests in the mountains above Rio de Janeiro, the property of a Coca-Cola franchise heiress sports an incongruent modern mansion, with matching mini-mansion for the security guards and a city-pound-size kennel for guard dogs. In Uruguay's Punta del Este and Rio's Barra de Tijuca, in Santiago's Barrio Alto and La Paz's Barrio Abajo there is a flourishing of gated and guarded communities, of ghost towns of palaces used only for holidays and parties. A single Christmas party in Punta del Este (at the estate of the Scarpa family, brewers of Brazil's Brahma beer) is said to have cost a million dollars.

But *favelas* and *poblaciones populares* and *villas miserias* are growing, too. Such growth is a consequence, in part, of rural to urban migration, as shown in a recent study in Córdoba, but also, as indicated in a study of Brasilia's "satellite cities," of slippage from the middle class. Of course, the poor are the front-line victims of the new-style urban anarchy, and in the shanty-towns, too, those who can afford them are buying guard dogs.

Meanwhile, for the public sector, the new free-market order has been very expensive. Throughout the region that sector has been asset-stripped. Most who serve the public, from garbage collectors to university professors, have seen their standards of living dropping for two or three decades. Services that might pay for themselves, or even, at higher cost to consumers, bring in a profit are privatized, while local, state or national governments with no visible means of support are left to pick up the rest. For this they resort generally to regressive taxes, like Chile's 18 percent value-added tax.

In Argentina a frenzy of privatization – a governmental going-out-of-business sale – brought several years of rapid growth, but that growth in the private sector has come at the expense of deterioration of basic services in the public sector – education, health, housing. Most services, now privatized, are as bad as ever; but now they cost more. Argentina's economy grew by some 8 percent between mid-1996 and mid-1997, but representatives of the country's largest teachers' union, marching along with 30,000 others in a protest in July 1997 against unemployment, claimed that their current real wages are only 37 percent of what they were earning in 1980. Chile's "economic miracle" of the late 1980s (6–7 percent annual growth) was a catch-up in part after the disaster of the early 1980s (−13 percent). Attempts of the Christian Democratic governments in office since 1990 to deal with the social deficit are said to have lifted about a million people out of poverty, but it was not until 1996 that real wages in the formal sector climbed back to the levels attained in the early 1970s, and some 40 percent of the population remained stuck in the unprotected, hand-to-mouth, informal sector.

In Brazil, as in Argentina, exhaustion with hyperinflation has led the public to accept currency stabilization plans that mean First World prices and Third World salaries. (Brazil's minimum wage was about $70 a month in 1994 when one could spend $10 in Brasilia for a single serving of coffee and ice cream.) Like Argentina's Menem, Cardoso, whose *Plano Real* is credited with his meteoric rise in the polls and his stunning first ballot victory on October 3, 1994, gambled that consumers now buying clothes and shoes on lay-away plans would opt for currency stability above all. But unlike Argentina and Chile, Brazil cannot court the favor of international capital through a policy of de-industrialization. Though in many ways it is one of the world's least developed countries, it is also now among the world's most highly industrialized.

The price that has generally been demanded of heavily indebted countries in Latin America and elsewhere for reentry into the game of international commerce is a price that Brazil, at least until the mid-1990s, had been reluctant to pay. That price is relinquishment of economic sovereignty, the denationalization of economic decision-making. The State itself under that circumstance comes to be unemployed, except to the extent that it serves as a collection agency for creditors. The otherwise beached ship of state is then subcontracted as a receivership.

INPUT DEMOCRACY AND THE UNEMPLOYED STATE

What has come to be the operative definition of democracy in Latin America as elsewhere in the 1990s is a curiously lopsided one, one that disregards representation and accountability. This is not necessarily the fault of the elected. Taking office is not the same as taking power; the ritual of an election does not confer power if power does not reside in the electorate.

The main elements of power are material resources and force, or money and guns, and in Latin America election offers neither. Elections may offer more slack in the leash for expanding human and civil rights, but they provide no means of rewarding low-income constituencies with economic gains. In fact, any suggestion of an upward shift in burden-bearing would likely dry up credit and set off a stampede of fleeing capital. The rules set by creditors and enforced by such institutions as the International Monetary Fund ensure that those who pay the interest on the debt will be the classes who did not benefit from the loans. Otherwise the game would soon be stalemated.

Meanwhile, the kind of democracy that is compatible with the new version of free enterprise turns out to be very expensive. With campaign contributions routinely in the millions of dollars, corruption becomes institutionalized and virtually all politicians are in some degree vulnerable – the most vulnerable, often, being those who steal least and spread it around the most. In other words, to the extent that money fuels the process and all politicians are dependent, the charge of corruption becomes just another weapon in a conflict in which the side with the best-stocked armory has the advantage. British economist John Maynard Keynes once said, "in the long run we are all dead"; in Brazilian political circles, where indictments were being handed down wholesale in the early 1990s, the proverb came to be "in the long run we are all in jail." In the end, with options so narrowed, pressures so fierce, and vulnerability so great, elected leaders, especially those with the largest and most hopeful followings, are in danger of being utterly discredited, along with their parties or movements and perhaps the ideal of democracy itself.

In this context, the entire political spectrum in Latin America has shifted sharply to the Right. Programs elaborated in the 1990s – in Chile by Christian Democrats in coalition with Socialists and in Argentina by supposedly labor-oriented Peronists – might have seemed embarrassingly anti-nationalist and anti-popular even to Conservatives two decades ago. The Left has not disappeared, but now chastened and pragmatic, it has slipped over to occupy what used to be the Center. In Uruguay, the traditional Blanco and Colorado parties have become almost indistinguishable; where the Colorado party used to be, more or less, is the previously "subversive" Frente Amplio. The programmatic limb Frente Amplio is out on includes sparing from privatization those government services that are being frugally and efficiently run.

For Brazil's general elections of 1994, Lula (Luis Inácio da Silva), the fearless champion of the working class, tutored by media advisers and lectured by First World economists, clipped his beard, donned coat and tie, and tempered his rhetoric. Engaging in time travel, one might say that Lula had run as Fernando Henrique (the Fernando Henrique, that is, of the 1960s and 1970s) while Fernando Henrique had run as José Sarney (the conservative president of the mid to late 1980s). Brazilians on the Left found grounds for optimism in the fact that as a candidate Fernando Henrique had already sold out his friends in order to appeal to his enemies. They figured that as a president he could only sell out his enemies. But they were to be disappointed.

Actually Brazil's presidential contests of the 1990s point up the difficulty in sorting out illusion and reality, good news and bad news. The good news was that both of the major candidates – Fernando Henrique Cardoso, the extraordinarily sophisticated and insightful social scientist, and Lula Da Silva, the skillful community organizer and eloquent spokesman of popular interests – were a cut above the best in the political stables of most countries of North and South. The bad news was that that is no longer enough to convert participation in elections into participation for the majority in the fruits of their labor. (Privatizations of the late 1990s have attracted foreign investment on a massive scale, but such riches do not trickle down and the income gap continues to grow.) Even if these two remarkable men and their constituencies had seen fit, directly or indirectly, to cooperate or coordinate, it is not clear that they would have been able to hold off the creditors and carpetbaggers and the muggers operating in the streets and suites long enough to break that great country's slide into anarchy.

THE VANQUISHED PUBLIC DOMAIN

At this moment in the eternal struggle to determine means and ends of power distribution, the norm of elections occupies the winner's circle. But how are we to see democracy as having won while in so much of the "democratized" world, winners in both political and economic terms are the very classes, sectors, agencies, even individuals, who engaged in every imaginable maneuver to obstruct democracy?

There is a great danger in welcoming so many "ringers" into the celebration of this ritual. It is that they will succeed in redefining electoral democracy, redrawing its parameters in such a way as to trivialize it – to further marginalize governments from economic policy-making, to equate free thinking with free markets, the right to compete with the right to destroy competition, to such an extent that no matter how large a majority preferred that a function (e.g., campaign finance) be removed from the private realm or that a service (e.g., running water or health care) be offered in the public realm, such a policy would be seen as anti-democratic. The initiative for setting boundaries between public and private domains has been seized by the private; redrawn borders are rapidly being codified into national and international law, and border regions vacated by the public are being homesteaded by the private.

To say that this wave of democratization is not so meaningful as the cheerleaders would have us believe is not to say that it offers no hope. But it offers hope only if those who are serious about democracy understand the players and the game well enough to treat elections as an opening pitch rather than the final clearing of bases – i.e., "the end of history." A party or sector or movement that is able to mount a campaign and win an election, like one that mounts an effective, insurrectionary campaign, proves only that it cannot be ignored – that it is a contender, not the major wielder of power. In fact, real power almost always lies elsewhere.

Democracy understood only or mainly as elections misses the essence of politics as the action at the top of the food chain. To find the arena where the crucial decisions are made, one would do well to take the advice that Deep Throat offered to the journalists investigating the Watergate break-in: follow the money.

Democracy is more likely to be found where the money is not: in small and/or resource-poor States, or at local levels of government. If democracy breaks out at ground level, the power game merely shifts to higher ground. In the nation-state system, there has been a tendency for control over resources, including tax revenues and taxing authority to move up the system, from local levels to state or regional and national, while responsibility for social well-being, especially over the last two decades, has moved down.

As elected governments here and there, in First World and Third, in the 1960s and 1970s became accountable to broader constituencies, creditors and corporations with the greatest interests at stake on the one hand threw their weight behind anti-democratic forces within State systems and on the other sought protection for their assets and freedom from regulation beyond the reach of any nation-state. Globalization, made possible finally by the collapse of the alternate market, is the completion of that great escape. It is the ultimate centrally planned economy, in which taxes are paid in the Bahamas, and campaign contributions, paid in Washington, Tokyo, Berlin, and Beijing, along with the ever-present threat of capital flight and currency speculation, leave governments around the world working for and competing for the favors of the same banks and corporations. Meanwhile, as governments divest, disintegrate, and proliferate, the corporations they serve fold and merge, becoming fewer and larger, richer and ever more powerful.

Even if the decisions that most fundamentally affect the allocation of resources and opportunities are not made at the national level, there are still many rewards to be gleaned by stateholders, as well as by domestic and foreign private stakeholders who will be making them offers they cannot refuse. Thus, to the extent that national leadership is really to be determined through elections, it must be expected that great resources will be expended in manners legal and illegal, democratic and anti-democratic, to control the process. To the extent that determination as to which elections have been "free and fair" and thus creditable is to be made by the inter-governmental and non-governmental election monitors, and that diplomatic recognition, credit, investment, and other currency flows rest on such determination, the political end game will move into the arena of election monitoring. And while it may not be visible to the naked eye, there will be a furious struggle to control who monitors, in which countries, using what criteria, and which of the many monitoring organizations will be allotted the first word or the last word by the media.[5]

As the United Nations gains ground in the now anarchic field of election monitoring and approaches the status that by logic it should acquire – the court of last resort with respect to pass-or-fail judgments on elections and thus the credentialling of governments – we will see the end game come to be the struggle for the soul of the United Nations.

What is at issue here is not a conspiracy but a system; it is the nature

---

[5] If election monitoring is to continue to have an important role in the credentialling of governments, it is essential that the process be generalized – including extension to First World governments and democracies of long standing. That should serve to remove the stigma of being monitored, to establish comparative models and standards, and to highlight First World shortcomings, like the corruption of campaign finance.

of political competition in a globalized capitalist economy. Such a system is not devoid of room for maneuver by those who are serious about democracy as government accountable to the great majority of the people. But it requires that they understand the nature and the stakes of the contest at least as well as those who would use it to line their own pockets. And it requires that they understand that to every solution there is a problem. So long as there remain great inequities in the distribution of wealth and power, the haves will soon figure out how to turn any change in the means – the rules of the game – to their advantage so as to continue to dominate the mechanisms governing distribution. It is incumbent, then, on would-be guardians of the public interest to stay ahead of the game, to be alert always to new challenges, new pitfalls, and new opportunities.

CHAPTER 19

International law, democracy and the end of history

Susan Marks*

Democracy used to be a word that international legal commentators preferred to avoid. At least by the second half of the present century, this was not because too few governments identified themselves as democratic. It was rather because too many did so. The world's most repressive regimes joined their more representative counterparts in claiming a title that had become synonymous with praiseworthy and justified politics. In some cases modifying adjectives were used ("one-party democracy," "people's democracy," etc.); in other cases the appropriation was unmodified. Either way, observers found normative inferences difficult to draw, for democracy appeared to mean everything, and therefore nothing.

What put an end to the commentators' reticence was, of course, the demise of Communism and the turn in all regions of the world to multi-party electoral politics. For many, these events confirmed both that democracy was the foundation of political legitimacy, and that repressive regimes, whatever they chose to call themselves, lacked that legitimacy. Influential international legal scholars felt able to declare that a "right of democratic governance" was now "emerging,"[1] and that international law was, or at any rate should now be, beginning to take in the lessons of "liberal internationalism."[2]

---

* I would like to thank Professor James Crawford for his invaluable assistance and support in the writing of the Ph.D. dissertation on which my arguments draw.
[1] The leading exponent of this is Thomas Franck. *See, especially,* "United Nations Based Prospects for a New Global Order," *N.Y.U. J. Int'l L. & Pol.* 22 (1990), p. 601; "The Emerging Right to Democratic Governance," *Am. J. Int'l L.* 86 (1992), p. 46 (hereinafter Franck 1992); "Democracy as a Human Right," in Louis Henkin and John Hargrove, eds., *Human Rights: An Agenda for the Next Century* (Washington, D.C.: American Society of International Law, 1994), 73 (hereinafter Franck 1994); and *Fairness in International Law and Institutions* (Oxford: Clarendon Press, 1995) (hereinafter Franck 1995), ch. 4 (largely reproducing Franck 1992).
[2] *See especially* Anne-Marie Slaughter (Burley), "Revolution of the Spirit," *Harv. Hum. Rts. J.* 3 (1990), p. 1 (hereinafter Slaughter 1990); "Towards an Age of Liberal Nations," *Harv. Int'l L.J.* 33 (1992), p. 393 (hereinafter Slaughter 1992a); "Law Among Liberal States: Liberal Internationalism and the Act of State Doctrine," *Columbia L.R.* 92 (1992), p. 1907 (hereinafter Slaughter 1992b); "Law and the Liberal Paradigm in International Relations Theory," *Proc. ASIL* (1993), p. 180 (herein-

532

This chapter examines these claims.[3] My concern is not to affirm or deny that State practice and *opinio juris* square with an emerging right of democratic governance. I shall not present the evidence relevant to deciding that doctrinal question, and will offer no conclusion with respect to it. Nor do I seek to maintain that democracy is a Western artefact, with limited relevance outside the West. On the contrary, I believe that, *provided* it is understood to refer to a general concept or ideal of self-rule on a footing of equality among citizens,[4] rather than to particular democratic arrangements and institutions, democracy is an idea of potentially universal pertinence. Its historical roots may be localized. But the world-wide struggles being waged in democracy's name surely leave little room for doubt that democracy has today become globalized.

The previous paragraph's proviso is, however, a very large one, and points to the central enquiry of this chapter. What is the understanding of democracy that informs the claims concerning the right of democratic governance and liberal internationalism? The argument developed here is that the international legal scholars who put forward these claims precisely *do not* identify democracy with a concept or ideal of self-rule on a footing of equality among citizens. Rather, they largely elide democracy with certain liberal ideas and institutions. I shall highlight some of the ways in which this serves to attenuate the emancipatory and critical force that democracy might have, and thus to limit the contribution that international law (should it develop along the lines the scholars suggest) might make with respect to anti-authoritarian politics. At stake, I shall argue, is international law's contribution with respect to anti-

---

after Slaughter 1993); and "International Law in a World of Liberal States," *EJIL* 6 (1995), p. 503 (hereinafter Slaughter 1995). For a related theme, *see* Fernando Tesón, "The Kantian Theory of International Law," *Col. L.R.* 92 (1992), 53 (hereinafter Tesón 1992).

[3] For elaboration of these claims, *see also* Gregory H. Fox, "The Right to Political Participation in International Law," *Yale Int'l L.J.* 17 (1992), p. 539; Gregory H. Fox and Georg Nolte, "Intolerant Democracies," *Harv. Int'l L.J.* 36 (1995), p. 1; and Christine Cerna, "Universal Democracy: an International Legal Right or a Pipe Dream of the West?," *N.Y.U. J. Int'l L. & Pol.* 27 (1995), p. 289. For arguments refuting the claims, *see* Thomas Carothers, "Empirical Perspectives on the Emerging Norm of Democratic Governance," *Proc. ASIL* (1992), p. 261; Martti Koskenniemi, "'Intolerant Democracies': A Reaction," *Harv. Int'l L.J.* 37 (1996), p. 231; and Brad R. Roth, "Democratic Intolerance: Observations on Fox and Nolte," *Harv. Int'l L.J.* 37 (1996), p. 235. For discussion of the claims, *see* Panel "National Sovereignty Revisited: Perspectives on the Emerging Norm of Democracy in International Law," *Proc. ASIL* (1992), pp. 249–71.

[4] Amongst the vast literature on the subject of democracy, David Held, *Models of Democracy* (Cambridge: Polity Press, 2nd edn., 1996), and John Dunn, ed., *Democracy: The Unfinished Journey 508 BC to AD 1993* (Oxford University Press, 1992), provide exceptionally valuable overviews of the roots and vicissitudes of this ideal. In evoking the ideal, this chapter seeks not to define democracy (the contestability of which resists definition), but rather to associate itself with a venerable and powerful strand of democratic thought. For an exemplary distillation of that strand, *see* D. Beetham, "Key Principles and Indices for a Democratic Audit," *in* David Beetham, ed., *Defining and Measuring Democracy* (London: Sage Publications, 1994), p. 25.

authoritarian politics not just in countries yet to embrace democracy or newly embracing democracy, but also in countries of longstanding democratic commitment, and indeed in the innumerable other non-national settings of contemporary political life.

The elision of democracy with certain liberal ideas and institutions can be linked to a more general perspective evinced in the claims concerning the norm of democratic governance and liberal internationalism. Bringing this into focus helps to illuminate the presuppositions and implications with which this chapter is concerned. I shall refer to this general perspective as "liberal millenarianism." The first section explains how and why I use this expression (which hopefully makes up in salience for what it lacks in euphony). The second section reviews the international legal scholarship in which the claims about democracy are elaborated. The final section then relates this scholarship to the perspective I call liberal millenarianism, and seeks to show how, in replicating characteristic features of liberal millenarianism, the international legal scholarship also replicates characteristic limitations, problems, and dangers. The conclusion I propose is that, if international law is to lend its support to ongoing efforts to extend and deepen democracy's purchase, the emerging norm of democratic governance and liberal internationalism offer, at best, a partial agenda.

I LIBERAL MILLENARIANISM

Liberal millenarianism finds its most extreme, and certainly its best known, expression in the work of Francis Fukuyama in the late 1980s and early 1990s.[5] Fukuyama undoubtedly set out to provoke, and this he very effectively did. His work of this period attracted many critics and few unqualified supporters.[6] One is tempted to dismiss him as isolated, a passing gadfly not to be taken too seriously. To do that would, however,

---

[5] Fukuyama's thesis, discussed below, was first advanced in an article published in 1989, and then elaborated in a further article and in a book published three years later. See Francis Fukuyama, "The End of History?" *The National Interest* (Summer 1989), p. 16 (hereinafter Fukuyama 1989); "A Reply to my Critics," *The National Interest* (Winter, 1989/90), p. 18; and *The End of History and the Last Man* (New York: Free Press, 1992) (hereinafter Fukuyama 1992).

[6] For a sampling of critiques, see Samuel Huntington, "No Exit: The Errors of Endism," *The National Interest* (Fall, 1989), p. 3; Stephen Holmes, "The Scowl of Minerva," *New Republic* (March 23, 1992), p. 27; Jonathan R. Macey and Geoffrey P. Miller, "The End of History and the New World Order: the Triumph of Capitalism and the Competition between Liberalism and Democracy," *Cornell Int'l L.J.* 25 (1992), p. 277; and David Held, "Liberalism, Marxism and Democracy," *Theory and Society* 22 (1993), p. 249 and "Anything But A Dog's Life? Further Comments on Fukuyama, Callinicos and Giddens," *Theory and Society* 22 (1993), p. 293.

be to ignore his many qualified supporters. It would be to overlook that his premises and argument found resonance – and continue to find resonance – in the work of a broad spectrum of commentators, including many whose outlook is considerably more moderate than his. Liberal millenarianism refers to this whole spectrum. That said, precisely because he articulates in bold, telegraphic fashion, and even at times rhetorically overstates, that which others more delicately bury or hedge, Fukuyama's work offers an excellent vantage point for surveying the shared terrain.

A Fukuyama and the end of history

Fukuyama's central thesis is that the end of the Cold War confirms a world-wide consensus in favour of liberalism, including not just capitalism but liberal democracy as well. As he sees it, liberalism has conquered all rival ideologies, most recently Communism, and liberal democracy is now the sole legitimate system of government. This marks the "triumph of the West."[7] More than that, it heralds – he proposes – the "end of history."

What we may be witnessing is not just the end of the Cold War, or the passing of a particular period of postwar history, but the end of history as such; that is, the end point of mankind's ideological evolution and the universalisation of Western liberal democracy as the final form of human government.[8]

This claim obviously relies on a distinctive notion of "history." If most scholars today conceive history as without grand design, Fukuyama considers this an understandable response to the abominations of the first half of the twentieth century. But he holds that this conception now requires rethinking. In the events of the century's closing decades he finds warrant for returning to the teleological notion of history that can be found in the work of Hegel and Marx, their secular reworkings of the pre-modern deterministic understanding. According to this perspective history is purposive, directional, progressive, and oriented towards a particular goal. Fukuyama endorses the view, which he identifies especially with Hegel,[9] that the goal towards which history is oriented is rationality and freedom, and that human societies progress towards it dialecti-

---

[7] Fukuyama 1989, *supra* note 5, p. 3. [8] *Ibid.*, p. 4.
[9] A consideration of whether this is accurate is beyond the scope of this chapter. Fukuyama acknowledges, in any event, that his understanding of Hegel is strongly influenced by the interpretation of French philosopher Alexandre Kojève (himself introduced in English translation by Allan Bloom).

cally, through the clash of ideologies. The culmination – or "end" – of history is eventually reached when perfect freedom and rationality are attained, and the clash of ideologies is resolved. This is what Fukuyama argues may now have occurred. Ideological competition appears to be over. Whereas Marx thought democracy in the shape of Communism was our final destiny, it turns out – so Fukuyama holds – to be liberal democracy that has emerged from the fray, to await us at the end of history. It turns out to be liberal democracy that overcomes all the defects, irrationalities, and contradictions of earlier forms of government, and promises to bring the historical dialectic to a close.

Fukuyama recognizes, of course, that not all countries of the world have embraced liberal democracy, and that those which have done so face continuing challenges. His point, he insists, is that history may have ended in the sense that the ideology of liberal democracy represents the final stage of political evolution. By this he appears to mean that the idea of liberal democracy cannot be improved upon. Ideology (understood here as a system of ideas and beliefs) is one thing; social practice is quite another, and in this case lags far behind. Thus, the end of history does not entail that there may, or will, be no further events and no further conflict. Nationalism and religion, in particular, appear to Fukuyama likely to remain sources of violence. Many societies have not yet begun, or have scarcely begun, to realize liberal democracy, and face turbulent times before they do. In particular, he remarks, "the vast bulk of the Third World remains very much mired in history."[10] Even "post-historical," Western societies have incompletely implemented liberal democratic principles. For this reason they are likely to experience continuing internal strife. In their relations with one another, however, war has – so Fukuyama holds – become "unthinkable."[11] In this connection, he argues that the post-historical West should actively defend its gains through a "league of democratic nations," "capable of forceful action to protect its collective security from threats arising from the non-democratic part of the world," and "inclined also to expand the sphere of democracy, where possible and prudent."[12]

---

[10] Fukuyama 1989, *supra* note 5, p. 15.   [11] Fukuyama 1992, *supra* note 5, p. 283.
[12] Fukuyama links this idea with Kant and the tradition of liberal internationalism, as to which *see infra*, sections II and III. He considers that the league of democratic nations he recommends – a "Kantian liberal international order" (Fukuyama 1992, *supra* note 5, p. 283) – already exists to an extent under the umbrella of organizations such as NATO, the EC, the OECD, the Group of Seven and GATT. He contrasts such a league with other organizations and alliances, such as the UN, which are not limited to liberal democratic nations. *See* Fukuyama 1992, *supra* note 5, pp. 276–84 (quotations are at pp. 283 and 280 respectively).

Why is it that liberal democracy has achieved such a victory, at least at the level of ideas or consciousness? On what basis does Fukuyama claim that liberal democracy embodies perfect rationality and freedom? He takes the view that the main engine of progress in the modern world is what he terms the "logic of modern natural science."[13] By this he means instrumental rationality, especially calculations of economic cost and benefit. According to Fukuyama the logic of modern natural science accounts for the triumph of capitalism and the establishment of a "universal consumer culture." It also accounts for the decline of traditional forms of social organization and the profound world-wide impact of technological innovation. But of itself this logic cannot account for liberal democracy's privileged place in history. While liberal democratic countries generally fare best economically, and while economic modernization may help create the material conditions for liberal democracy, such as urbanization and education, economic efficiency may in some contexts militate in favour of authoritarian–bureaucratic government rather than liberal democracy. Economics alone cannot explain liberal democracy's consummate status. In his words, the logic of modern natural science "gets us to the gates of the Promised Land of liberal democracy, but does not quite deliver us to the other side."[14]

Fukuyama believes that liberal democracy may represent the ultimate form of government because it satisfies certain fundamental human psychological needs. These he refers to (drawing again on Hegel) as the desire for "recognition," a desire he takes to be manifested in such feelings as self-respect, self-esteem, dignity, ambition, pride, and concern for prestige. For Fukuyama "the problem of human history can be seen ... as the search for a way to satisfy the desire of both masters and slaves for recognition on a mutual and equal basis; history ends with the victory of a societal order that accomplishes that goal."[15] As he sees it, liberal democracy is that order; it offers a framework for mutual and equal recognition of all citizens.

And yet, if liberal democracy awaits us at history's end, there is another sense in which, according to Fukuyama, the human desire for recognition will be left profoundly unfulfilled, even debilitated. There is an aspect of that desire that can find fulfillment only in the context of ideological competition. Whereas those – he refers to them as the "first men" – who began struggling for liberal democracy had to exhibit

---

[13] This is explained further in Fukuyama 1992, *supra* note 5, ch. 6. [14] *Ibid.*, p. 134.
[15] *Ibid.*, p. 152.

courage, take risks, and aim high, the "last men" at the end of history will have no further need of heroism.[16] Indeed, they will be encouraged not to stand out. Fukuyama worries about the mediocrity, ignobility, and materialism of liberal democracy's "last men." Following in the tradition of Tocqueville and others,[17] his enthusiasm for liberal democracy is thus tinged with regret for the decline of aristocracy, and a belief that too much equality, rather than too little, may pose liberal democracy's greatest challenge.

B Liberal millenarianism

This thesis was widely interpreted – and Fukuyama himself confirms that it was intended – as an attempt to provide an antidote to the prevailing "declinist" mood of American political analysis in the 1980s.[18] Those "pessimists" who were continuing to assert that the power and influence of the United States were in decline had failed to notice the "good news"[19] that a "liberal revolution" was underway world-wide. Those "intellectuals who believe they grasp the world in all its complexity and tragedy"[20] had failed to see that history has a pattern, and that, posturing aside, "[t]oday . . . we have trouble imagining a world that is radically better than our own."[21]

Patently, Fukuyama's antidote was strong stuff. Though not without ambivalences, his work makes few concessions to those who do not share his outlook, and is almost ostentatious in its disdain for those he takes to be left–liberal or, perhaps, un-American. And yet, his themes are not confined to what has been called the New Right. Rather, they appear, as noted earlier, to exemplify a more widely held perspective. It is this perspective to which liberal millenarianism refers. Its key features may be summarized as follows.

In the first place there is the notion that history has a *telos*. This involves a view of historical change as directional, linear, and evolutionary, with identifiable developmental stages and an end-point that can be known, and potentially reached. Secondly, there is the supposition that

---

[16] Concerning the "last man," *see* Friedrich Nietzsche (R. Hollingdale, trans.), *Thus Spoke Zarathustra* (London: Penguin Books, 1969), pp. 45–47.
[17] *See* A. de Tocqueville *in* G. Lawrence, trans., J. Mayer, ed., *Democracy in America* (London: Fontana Press, 1994), vol. II, pp. 690–95. Fukuyama's contemporary influences are conservative–elitist thinkers, Leo Strauss and Allan Bloom.
[18] *See, e.g.*, Robert Keohane, *After Hegemony* (Princeton University Press, 1984) and Paul Kennedy, *The Rise and Fall of Great Powers* (London: Unwin Hyman, 1988).
[19] Fukuyama 1992, *supra* note 5, p. xiii.   [20] *Ibid.*, p. 69.   [21] *Ibid.*, p. 46.

history's *telos* is liberalism, or at any rate liberal democracy in association with a market-oriented economy. This is based both on an empirical assertion that all alternatives to liberalism have been eliminated, and on a normative assertion that liberalism is superior to all alternatives. A third feature is a distinctive voice, a "we" who (fine tuning aside) *have* liberal democracy and experience no serious – or, at any rate, no intractable – problems, in contradistinction to a non-liberal "they" (in the Third World and elsewhere) for whom things will necessarily remain more complicated and more unpleasant. Finally, there is a distinctive tone, a call to celebrate the present, tempered perhaps by nostalgia for the past, but nonetheless optimistic, confident and flushed with a sense of victory over the forces of regression.

Millenarianism refers in Christian doctrine to the belief that Christ will return to reign on earth for a thousand years. More generally, it is applied to premonitions of global futures of diverse kinds, but especially redemptive ones.[22] Liberal millenarianism's *millenarianism* thus consists in its perception that the world may stand on the brink of an unprecedented era of peace and good government, a perception which is millenarian also in the more literal sense that it pertains to the millennium just beginning.[23] Reinforcing the millenarian character of this vision in Fukuyama's work is the annunciatory, exalted, sometimes even ecstatic, language in which it is expressed, and the evocation of eschatological, especially evangelical,[24] themes. The *liberal* character of liberal millenarianism derives obviously from the fact that this is presented as a vision of a liberal world. But what sort of liberal world? To pursue this ques-

---

[22] Frederic Jameson contrasts this with "inverse millenarianism" – claims about "the end of this or that" – which he associates with postmodernism. See Frederic Jameson, *Postmodernism, or the Cultural Logic of Late Capitalism* (London and New York: Verso, 1991), p. 1. The difference between millenarianism and "inverse millenarianism" appears to be principally one of emphasis, however, for both look at once backwards and forwards. Liberal millenarianism, in any event, has this ambivalence.

[23] James Crawford refers to "the facile millenarianism that was an immediate product of 1989." See James Crawford, *Democracy and International Law: Inaugural Lecture* (Cambridge University Press, 1994), p. 25.

[24] Jacques Derrida finds a specifically Christian resonance in Fukuyama's work, thus buttressing the present characterization of Fukuyama as "millenarian." When Fukuyama says that economics takes us "to the gates of the promised land but does not quite deliver us to the other side," and when he finds a spiritual basis for his "good news" concerning liberal democracy in the human desire for recognition, Fukuyama is, Derrida suggests, not only choosing Hegel in preference to Marx, but is also (in so doing) choosing a Christian account in place of a Jewish one. The other great religion of the "promised land," Islam, does not feature in Fukuyama's allusive repertoire; he observes that the Islamic world falls outside the consensus he finds in favor of liberalism. See Jaques Derrida (Peggy Kamuf, trans.), *Specters of Marx* (New York and London: Routledge, 1994), pp. 59–61, 66.

tion, and also to explore further liberal millenarianism's implications for the meaning of democracy, it is helpful to draw into the discussion some of Fukuyama's critics.[25]

C Liberal millenarianism and democracy

One striking feature of Fukuyama's argument is that it largely proceeds as if there is, and can be, only one liberalism, one democracy and one liberal democracy. While recognizing a certain diversity of institutional arrangements, Fukuyama fails to consider the diversity of values and beliefs that contributes to producing divergent understandings of the meaning of liberalism and democracy, and of their interrelation. Liberal democracy cannot spell the end of ideological struggle because it is itself the subject of ideological contestation, and will continue to be so.

What, then, of Fukuyama's own understanding of liberalism, democracy, and liberal democracy? A number of critics highlight Fukuyama's failure to address the tension between liberalism and democracy. The liberal preoccupation with rights and freedom from government control, and the democratic preoccupation with equal participation in, and accountability of, public power, may point in different directions. Rights and freedoms justified by reference to liberalism may compromise the extent to which all citizens are equally enabled to participate in politics; political decisions justified by reference to democracy may compromise individuals' rights and freedoms. On this point David Held observes that Fukuyama endorses economic liberalism without examining the extent to which the "free market" constrains democratic processes by generating and sustaining systematic inequalities of wealth that involve systematic inequalities of power.[26] Thus, without addressing the implications of doing so, Fukuyama effectively resolves the tension between liberalism and democracy in favour of liberalism (especially in its neo-liberal economic aspect). This leads him, Jonathan Macey and Geoffrey Miller remark, to proclaim a victory for liberal democracy wherever he sees economic liberalism.[27]

---

[25] The following discussion draws mainly on Held, *supra* note 6; Macey and Miller, *supra* note 6; Huntington, *supra* note 6; and Derrida, *supra* note 24. These critiques proceed, it should be noted, from widely divergent standpoints and reach widely divergent conclusions from their analysis of Fukuyama.   [26] Held, *supra* note 6, pp. 257–58.
[27] Macey and Miller, *supra* note 6, p. 282. This comment finds support in Fukuyama's inclusion, in a list of countries he characterizes as liberal democratic, of Singapore, South Korea, Honduras, and Mexico. *See* Fukuyama 1992, *supra* note 5, pp. 49–50. (But see also his later discussion of, e.g., Singapore's authoritarianism, p. 241.)

International law, democracy, and the end of history 541

Also of concern is Fukuyama's "uncritical affirmation"[28] of liberal democracy. He neglects to investigate alternatives to prevailing liberal democratic practices, and gives little sign of grasping those practices' limitations. Indeed he leaves largely unexplained the basis on which an evaluation might be made. His celebration of liberal democracy, thus ungrounded, overlooks the obvious failures of liberal democracy, its omissions with respect to the historic promise of self-rule on the basis of equality among citizens. These omissions find reflection in the pervasiveness of unaccountable power and the persistence of asymmetrical life chances between sexes, ethnic groups, and classes.[29] At the same time, Fukuyama's celebration also overlooks that liberal democracy has never been under so much strain. He considers the challenges posed by nationalist and religious movements. But, as Held and others observe, he fails to address the far-reaching challenges associated with the diffusion of decision-making power and political activity in the contemporary world.[30] This arises from a wide range of developments, among them innovations in the media and communications and information technology, economic globalization, and the rising importance of social movements (the environmental and women's movements, etc.).[31] In profound and diverse ways these developments put in doubt the tenability of an account of liberal-democratic politics that focuses solely on national governments, and treats periodic elections, the rule of law and civil and political rights as not just necessary but largely sufficient. Yet this is the account that informs Fukuyama's claims.

Fukuyama's uncritical approach to liberal democracy is, moreover, accompanied by a portrayal of the world that is hard to locate in actuality. Like Voltaire's Pangloss, he insists on an account of this "best of all possible worlds" that defies, rather than attends to, contemporary realities. Jacques Derrida puts this point starkly:

---

[28] Held, *supra* note 6, p. 295.
[29] An illustrative summary of democracy's "broken promises" and "unforeseen obstacles" can be found in Norberto Bobbio (Roger Griffin, trans., Richard Bellamy, ed.), *The Future of Democracy* (Cambridge: Polity Press, 1987), pp. 27–39. (The conclusions Bobbio draws are, however, at variance with the position adopted in this chapter.)
[30] For a wide-ranging and instructive discussion of the implications of globalization for democracy, see David Held, *Democracy and the Global Order* (Cambridge: Polity Press, 1995).
[31] Amongst the many accounts of globalization and associated developments, from diverse perspectives, Malcolm Waters, *Globalization* (London and New York: Routledge, 1995), is especially instructive. A valuable corrective to over-enthusiastic accounts of globalization, especially economic globalization, can be found in Paul Hirst and Grahame Thompson, *Globalization in Question* (Cambridge: Polity Press, 1996).

[N]ever have violence, inequality, exclusion, famine, and thus economic oppression affected as many human beings in the history of the earth and humanity. Instead of singing the advent of the ideal of liberal democracy and of the capitalist market in the euphoria of the end of history . . . let us never neglect this macroscopic fact, made up of innumerable singular sites of suffering: no degree of progress allows one to ignore that never before, in absolute figures, have so many men, women and children been subjugated, starved or exterminated.[32]

These sites of suffering, of course, crosscut the distinction Fukuyama draws between "historical" and "post-historical" States, and serve to assure the continuance of ideological divergences in both categories of countries.

A further problematic element in Fukuyama's argument is his premise that a "liberal revolution" is underway. He acknowledges that the Islamic world stands outside the consensus that he takes to be forming concerning liberal democracy, but discounts the significance of resistance there and elsewhere. Commentators have countered that, while few profess to reject the basic ideas associated with democracy, and while some form of capitalism characterizes most economies, there is little evidence of support in many countries for liberal values more generally. Fukuyama exaggerates the scope of the consensus by finding liberal democracy almost – though not invariably – wherever he finds some variant of capitalism.

Fukuyama's defence is that his thesis about the end of history posits the end of ideological contestation (in the sense of contestation over ideas and beliefs), and is not an empirical claim. Thus it is not falsifed by the obvious fact that not all societies have embraced liberal democracy. But does this thesis not presuppose compelling evidence as regards aspirations, even if not as regards political practices and institutions? What precisely is Fukuyama's "good news"? Derrida calls attention to the way Fukuyama characterizes liberal democracy both as an ideal and as an occurrence, alternating between the two to suit his argument.[33] On the one hand Fukuyama refutes evidence that contradicts his thesis, insisting that he is speaking of an ideal that transcends events. On the other hand he maintains that events have occurred – the death of Communism, the establishment of liberal democracy and Capitalism as ideologies of near-universal choice, the recognition accorded by Western liberal democracies to their citizens – which represent the realization of this ideal. Fukuyama's "good news" thus intends to refer,

---

[32] Derrida, *supra* note 24, p. 85.   [33] *Ibid.*, at pp. 62–63.

Derrida shows, both to an accomplished fact and to a vision of the future.

This leads to a final observation. Inasmuch as Fukuyama's linear conception of history admits of only one future, it reduces and oversimplifies the processes of historical change. While Fukuyama acknowledges that reversals are possible, he assumes that the trends he identifies will broadly continue. In this, Samuel Huntington observes, Fukuyama overstates the predicability of history and the permanence of the moment. Current trends may continue, but experience suggests that they may well not.[34] The historical record to date offers little support for Fukuyama's notion of progress. Held too finds that Fukuyama has failed to appreciate the contingency of events and the complexity of social processes. Held highlights that Fukuyama's essentialized conception of "man" and his two master engines of modernity (instrumental rationality and the desire for recognition) cannot adequately explain such central historical phenomena as classes, gender inequalities, and the international division of labour.[35] If this is the case, then the predictive value of his conceptual framework must likewise be open to question.

To summarize, it can be argued that the thesis of the end of history – as the ideological triumph of capitalist economics and liberal democracy – attaches insufficient importance to a number of matters which render ideological divergences inescapable and, indeed, vital. These include the following points: the meaning ascribed to the terms involved is itself at least partly a matter of ideology; the enduring tension between liberalism and democracy invites continuing contestation concerning liberal democracy; liberal democracy is subject to profound – increasingly profound – challenge; at the end of the twenty-first century progress is far from obvious; the scope of support for any version of liberal democracy, even at the level of ideas and beliefs, is not clear; history follows not a single path but multiple and diverse trajectories that proceed and interact in complex and imponderable ways.

Critics draw diverse conclusions from their analyses of Fukuyama's thesis, though almost all find in it a dangerous inducement to complacency. Huntington's worry is that it may encourage Americans to underestimate the contemporary sources of political instability, and on this basis to relax their vigilance in foreign relations. Declinism, in Huntington's view, was, in contrast, a useful warning and goad to

---

[34] Huntington, *supra* note 6, p. 10.   [35] Held, *supra* note 6, pp. 296–97.

action.[36] Held has a different concern. Only fifty years after Nazism, Fascism and Stalinism almost eclipsed liberal democracy, Fukuyama prematurely pronounces liberal democracy's future secure, and glosses over the most serious challenges that currently confront it.[37] Derrida shares this anxiety that Fukuyama masks the fragility of liberal democracy, and thus reduces the possibilities for strengthening and improving it. In this regard Derrida expresses particular disquiet at the way Fukuyama seeks to deny (while himself, however, in key respects exemplifying)[38] the continuing relevance of ideas and critical practices that draw inspiration from Marx.[39] Like a number of other scholars,[40] Derrida takes the view that these ideas and practices are rendered more, not less, pertinent by liberalism's gains.

The points discussed here arise in relation to Fukuyama's writings. But most apply with equal force to liberal millenarianism generally. This is because most stem from the features of Fukuyama's work that have been characterized as, more broadly, liberal millenarian: the progressivist notion of history; the identification of liberal democracy as history's *telos*; the distinctive "post-historical" voice; the celebratory tone. Indeed, the critical perspectives just reviewed highlight the extent to which these features are interrelated and mutually reinforcing. With respect to the progressivist conception of history that is a central pillar of liberal millenarianism, Fukuyama's critics echo insights that can be found in the work of many other scholars. Among these, Michel Foucault's well-

---

[36] Huntington, *supra* note 6, p. 4.   [37] Held, *supra* note 6, p. 296.
[38] A number of commentators make this argument on the basis, e.g., of Fukuyama's teleological notion of history and his turn to "grand theory." *See, e.g.,* Huntington, *supra* note 6, pp. 9–10. Others, however, disagree. *See, e.g.,* Alex Callinicos, *Theories and Narratives* (Cambridge: Polity Press, 1995), ch. 1.
[39] Derrida, *supra* note 24, pp. 68–69 and 86–94. Derrida has an intriguing explanation for why Fukuyama does this. He proposes that, in advancing the thesis of the end of history, Fukuyama is engaging in a kind of "mourning work" following the death of "actually existing socialism." Out of fear and "bereavement" as Marx's unacknowledged heir (for, Derrida insists, we are all Marx's heirs, whether we wish it or not), Fukuyama is denying the continued relevance of socialist critique. As Derrida puts it, adapting Marx and Engels's own immortal image, Fukuyama is attempting to "conjure away" the "spectre of Marx" that has long haunted liberalism. Yet, Derrida maintains, this work of mourning cannot succeed. It can displace, but it cannot efface, the spectre of Marx, for that spectre is liberalism's necessary accompaniment. In this regard Derrida refers not only to Marx and Marxian thought. He evokes the spectre – or, as he prefers to say, spectres (for he stresses the extent to which Marx's legacy is plural and diverse) – of Marx *metonymically* to stand for *all* the forms of critique that can help to evaluate ideals, grasp realities, and reduce the gap between them. In view of the importance of these forms of critique, Derrida urges instead a "counter-conjuration," a strategy of active engagement, rather than disavowal. In this, he contends, scholars have a particular role. Quoting (at p. 176) a line in connection with another famous ghost, Derrida recalls Hamlet's injunction: "Thou art a scholar; speak to it, Horatio." *See* Derrida, *supra* note 24, pp. 61, 68–77.
[40] *See, e.g.,* the essays *in* Robin Blackburn, ed., *After the Fall* (London and New York: Verso, 1991).

known account of history and genealogy is worth briefly recalling at this point.[41] Foucault shows how progressivist history confirms rather than unsettles established power relations. It represses dissension, struggle, and domination, rather than articulating and addressing them. It presents the world comfortingly, as simple, coherent, and ordered, rather than challengingly, as complex, heterogeneous, and contingent. In seeking to hold onto things as they are, it asserts blithely, but also impotently, that things must be as they are. What this puts in relief is the sense in which liberal millenarianism, for all its professed optimism, is ultimately pessimistic, not – as Fukuyama suggests – because it envisions a world of excessive equality, but because it envisions a world of enduring and immutable inequalities.

II THE "NORM OF DEMOCRATIC GOVERNANCE" AND OTHER THESES

Insofar as the thesis of the emerging norm of democratic governance and related claims share the liberal millenarianism of Fukuyama's end of history narrative, the foregoing discussion is rich in implications. But so far I have only made very brief reference to the character of these international legal claims. Before addressing the scope and implications of their liberal millenarianism, I must set out the arguments involved. For this purpose a distinction may be drawn between two types of thesis concerning democracy's normative status. In the first place there are theses in which the primary issue is whether democracy has achieved the status of a right and, if so, what that right entails. In the second place, there are theses in which the primary issue is how international law should respond to evidence and/or theorizing to the effect that democracy is positively correlated to peace and, in particular, whether democracy should on this basis become a legal criterion of government legitimacy.

A Democracy as a right

The right-oriented theses involve the claim – first advanced by Thomas Franck,[42] but subsequently taken up and developed by others as well[43] –

---

[41] Michel Foucault, "Nietzsche, Genealogy, History," in Paul Rabinow, ed., *The Foucault Reader* (London: Penguin Books, 1984), p. 76. I am grateful to Professor Gerald Frug, Harvard Law School, for calling my attention to this text, and for an illuminating discussion of it.
[42] *See* the references cited at note 1. The thesis has earlier roots, which can be found, e.g., in Henry Steiner, "Political Participation as a Human Right," *Harv. Hum. Rts. Y. B.* 1 (1988), p. 77.
[43] *See supra* note 3.

that international law is beginning to embrace a "norm of democratic governance" or "global democratic entitlement." Such a norm or entitlement would mean three things. First, it would entail that the legitimacy of governments is judged by international – rather than purely national – rules and processes. Second, it would connote that those international rules and processes stipulate democracy; that is to say, only democratic governments are legitimate. And third, it would establish that democracy is an internationally guaranteed human right, in respect of which international procedures of monitoring and enforcement are justified and, indeed, required.

How has this norm or right come to "emerge"? Franck offers the fullest explanation. He traces the normative and customary evolution of the global democratic entitlement by reference to three overlapping phases or "generations"[44] of international rule-making and implementation. The first generation, born after the First World War (but with older antecedents), is the right of self-determination. The plebiscites, popular consultations, and commissions of inquiry that were mandated at the Versailles Peace Conference in connection with the redrawing of European boundaries gave rise to the idea that "a people organised in established territory (has the right) to determine its collective political destiny in a democratic fashion."[45] At the same time, a body of practice concerning plebiscite-holding and international supervision was initiated. This was further developed when self-determination was applied outside Europe in the context of decolonization.

The second generation, born after the Second World War, is the international legal recognition of human rights. With this the idea was established that all human beings have the right to freedoms of expression, thought, assembly, and association (among other rights). Procedures for holding governments to their obligations in this regard, and for clarifying the scope of the rights and correlative obligations, were also elaborated. The third generation, still in its infancy, is the right to free and open elections. This was effectively born with the transformations of the late 1980s. While the right to vote and stand for election had been recognised in key human rights instruments decades before, it was not until those transformations occurred that this right began to be taken seriously as a norm of universal application. It was not until those transfor-

---

[44] Franck 1992, *supra* note 1, p. 52. Franck is not referring to the three-generational scheme used (and debated) in human rights commentary, according to which civil and political rights are the first generation; economic, social, and cultural rights are the second; and peoples' rights are the third.   [45] *Ibid.*, p. 52.

mations occurred, in other words, that it became possible to consider this right an emerging norm of customary international law. That it has begun to be taken seriously is reflected in the fact that a substantial majority of States now actually practice "a reasonably credible version of electoral democracy."[46] This is also reflected in international efforts to establish and define the "principle of genuine and periodic elections"; in the increasingly common provision of "technical assistance" by the UN and other organizations and agencies to governments holding democratic elections for the first time; and in the expanding practice of international and regional election monitoring. Varying his metaphor so as to emphasize the way the right to free and open elections extends, and depends on, international legal developments with respect to self-determination and human rights, Franck sometimes refers to these as three "building stones"[47] in the edifice that is the global democratic entitlement.

Other scholars likewise hold that, while the global democratic entitlement has had a basis for decades in international human rights instruments, and before that in the principle of self-determination of peoples, it has only recently begun to be respected, monitored and enforced to a significant extent.[48] Thus, it has only recently begun to acquire the status of a norm of customary international law. In addition to the evidence of this to which Franck calls attention, Christina Cerna notes the procedures elaborated in the 1990s within the framework of the Council of Europe and the Organization of American States for conditioning admission or continued participation on democratic government.[49]

As this suggests, these scholars take free and fair elections to be the decisive criterion of democracy, though they in no way underestimate

---

[46] *Ibid.*, p. 64. [47] *Ibid.*; Franck 1995, *supra* note 1, ch. 4; and Franck 1994, *supra* note 1, *passim*.
[48] *See, e.g.*, Fox, *supra* note 3, and Cerna, *supra* note 3.
[49] Cerna, *supra* note 3. In connection with applications for membership from Central and Eastern European States, the Council of Europe has begun to require evidence of commitment to democracy. *See, e.g.*, "Report on the Legal Order of the Russian Federation," Council of Europe Doc. AS/Bur/Russia 7 (1994), *reprinted in Hum. Rts. L.J.* 15 (1994), p. 249. The Organization of American States has long had this as a formal – though, for much of the OAS's life, unenforced – requirement for OAS member States. See the Declaration of Santiago, adopted at the Fifth Meeting of Consultation of Ministers of Foreign Affairs, August 1959, *reprinted in* Thomas Buergenthal and Robert E. Norris, eds., *Human Rights: the Inter-American System* (Dobbs Ferry, N.Y.: Oceana) (hereinafter Buergenthal and Norris), Binder 1, Booklet 6, p. 134. More recently, the OAS has sanctioned the further step of engaging in collective action to secure the installation, or reinstatement, of democratic government in the event that a coup occurs. *See* OAS General Assembly Resolution 1080 (adopted June 5, 1991), *reprinted in* Buergenthal and Norris, Binder 2, Booklet 7.6, 43; and Protocol of Amendments to the Charter of the OAS ("Protocol of Washington") (adopted December 14, 1992), OAS AG/DOC.11 (XVI-E/92).

the extent to which the right to such elections presupposes other rights, especially freedoms of expression, thought, assembly, and association. Elections are in this perspective decisive because they legitimate governance. Thus, the expressions "democratic entitlement," "right to democracy," "norm of democratic governance," "entitlement to a participatory electoral process," "right to political participation," "electoral rights," and the "right to free and open elections" are employed with relative interchangeability. Franck explains:

The term "democracy," as used in international rights parlance, is intended to connote the kind of governance that is legitimated by the consent of the governed. Essential to the legitimacy of governance is evidence of *consent to the process by which a populace is consulted* by its government.[50]

Franck acknowledges that this is a limited conception of democracy. "This definition," he observes, "is not ambitious, it is not necessarily unambiguous, and it is almost certainly not the one Americans would prefer."[51] But given the diversity of polities and traditions in the world, and given the inbuilt resistance of the States system to the international regulation of national affairs, he considers that this conception or something like it "probably represents the limit of what the still frail global system of states can be expected to accept and promote as a right of peoples assertable against their own, and other, governments."[52]

Gregory Fox and Georg Nolte, while sharing the view that elections are the central issue in a norm of democratic governance, have highlighted that holding regular elections which are free and fair may not always be sufficient to protect the democratic entitlement.[53] Where candidates are opposed to liberal democracy, and are committed to the establishment in its place of, for instance, a theocratic political order, the question arises whether those candidates should be allowed to stand. Based on a survey of constitutional laws and traditions of diverse democratic states, Fox and Nolte contend that in customary international law the exclusion of such candidates is warranted, and perhaps even required. This reflects, they observe, a conception of democracy as not simply a set of procedures for ascertaining majority preferences, but rather as a means by which citizens are enabled to enjoy basic rights. Thus, Fox and Nolte find support in customary international law for an account of democracy that tolerates only the tolerant, and that in this respect insists on the value of "political liberalism."[54] More generally,

---

[50] Franck 1994, *supra* note 1, p. 75. Emphasis added.   [51] *Ibid.*, p. 75.   [52] *Ibid.*, p. 75.
[53] Fox and Nolte, *supra* note 3. They have in mind particularly the case of Algeria.
[54] *See* John Rawls, *Political Liberalism* (New York: Columbia University Press, 1993).

they find support for an account of democracy that rests on the liberal notion that government is legitimated not just procedurally but also to the extent that it fulfils its side of the social contract and protects citizens' rights.

Those who advance the thesis of the emerging norm of democratic governance give close attention to the question of how compliance might be monitored and enforced. As noted, existing election-monitoring efforts and innovations with respect to participation in regional organizations are among the developments which persuaded the scholars that the norm was emerging in the first place. They consider a number of possible ways of strengthening enforcement. Franck proposes that the "older democracies" might volunteer to have their elections monitored, so as to encourage a custom of election-observation that might eventually evolve into an obligation.[55] In the longer term, he proposes that democratic government might be made a precondition to participation in all international organizations, including the United Nations, a proposal Fox also develops.[56] Franck suggests additionally that democratic government might be made a precondition for fiscal, trade, and development benefits, and for the protection of UN and regional collective security measures. He strongly rejects as a means of enforcement unilateral intervention to install or reinstate elected governments, though he finds acceptable collective action at UN or regional level, even, in extreme cases, involving the use of force. Franck considers that, while the question of the scope and incidents of the norm of democratic governance is likely to remain on international law's agenda, the more pressing problem is the monitoring and enforcement of compliance. He urges that the future emphasis of international efforts should be laid accordingly.[57]

B *International law and the "liberal peace"*

The writers so far considered base their case for the emerging democratic entitlement on, above all, developments with respect to the holding of elections, international and regional election-monitoring, and democratic conditionality in regional organizations. Those whose work will now be reviewed are also impressed with these developments. What strikes them as even more significant, however, is the correlation between liberal democracy and peace.[58] This forms the basis of an argument that

---

[55] Concerning this and the other proposals considered here, *see* Franck 1992, *supra* note 1.
[56] Fox, *supra* note 3.   [57] Franck 1994, *supra* note 1.
[58] The scope of the correlation that is claimed to exist will be discussed below.

there should be a norm of democratic governance, and that the signs that it is emerging confirm this. The theorists of the right to democratic governance also draw support from the correlation between liberal democracy and peace to help explain and vindicate the right.[59] Thus, the difference between the two sets of theses is largely one of emphasis. Both sets are at once empirically based claims that a norm is emerging, speculations concerning its future as *lex lata*, explanations of why it is emerging, and justifications for its recognition in international law. And in both sets the so-called "liberal" or "democratic" "peace" plays a part.

Among the leading proponents of theses of this second type are Fernando Tesón[60] and Anne-Marie Slaughter.[61] In presenting the correlation between liberal democracy and peace, they take account of both speculative and empirical literature. With respect to the former the key figure is Kant. These scholars, like the international relations analysts on whose work they draw, look to Kant for the insight that liberal States are likely to maintain peaceful relations with one another. As is well known, Kant held that "perpetual peace" would depend on three things: every State having a "republican" constitution; a "pacific federation" being established among States, in the shape of an agreement to refrain from war against one another; and extensive international commerce, underpinned by "cosmopolitan law." Republican government would discourage warfare, he believed, because, if government was accountable to citizens, the fact that citizens would suffer the consequences of war – as soldiers, bereaved civilians, taxpayers, etc. – would serve to engender caution in waging it.[62]

Internationalists have long attended to the points about the pacific federation and extensive international commerce. Particularly compelling in the aftermath of the twentieth century's two World Wars, these ideas are reflected in the League of Nations, the Kellogg-Briand Pact, the United Nations, and the General Agreement on Tariffs and Trade. Indeed, they inform the whole enterprise of modern international law and institution-building. But what, according to Tesón, Slaughter, and

---

[59] *See, e.g.*, Franck 1995, *supra* note 1, pp. 134–137, and Fox and Nolte, *supra* note 3, pp. 61–63.
[60] *See esp.* Tesón 1992, *supra* note 2.
[61] See the references to Slaughter's work cited at note 2. Slaughter 1995 develops a more general "Liberal model" of international law. "Liberalism" is presented as an account of how some – liberal – States "do behave rather than how they should behave" (p. 508). But "Liberal" theory appears to be envisaged as serving a normative function as well, inasmuch Slaughter evokes the possibility that this theory might become "normatively applicable to all States even if positively descriptive of only some" (p. 538). See further *infra*, section III.
[62] *See* Immanuel Kant (H. B. Nisbet, trans.), "Perpetual Peace: A Philosophical Sketch" (1795) *in* Hans Reiss, ed., *Kant: Political Writings* (Cambridge University Press, 1991), p. 93 ff.

the international relations analysts, has *not* received sufficient attention is Kant's insight about republican government. For these scholars the sort of "republican" State Kant had in mind corresponds in contemporary terms to a liberal-democratic State.[63] The Second World War, along with the bitter ideological rivalries of the Cold War, fueled a realist outlook which got in the way of a proper appreciation of Kant's idea. Now that many countries of the world have embraced this liberal model, a fresh appraisal is called for. The notion that the prospects for peace may be greatest among liberal States should – these scholars maintain – no longer be ignored.

Slaughter and Tesón observe that international relations scholars have presented evidence which appears to back up this notion. Based on analysis of international wars since 1817, Michael Doyle, among others, has argued that a separate "zone of peace" does indeed exist among liberal States.[64] This zone has steadily expanded as the number of liberal States has increased. Doyle has reported that throughout this period liberal States, while they have engaged in wars with non-liberal States, have remained at peace with one another. From this he has drawn the inference that liberal States are likely to be more pacific than non-liberal States, not in general, but at least in their relations with other liberal States. The scope of this claim, the precise character of the link it posits, and the reasons for that link, remain the subject of debate. In its broad lines, however, the "democratic" or "liberal" "peace" is spoken of as a "fact"[65] and "as close as anything we have to an empirical law in international relations."[66] It is an empirical law that, according to Slaughter and Tesón, has profound implications for international law.

The first implication is that international law should place the question of the legitimacy of governments on its agenda. It should abandon the idea that this is an exclusively national issue. The second implication is that international law should accept as legitimate only liberal

---

[63] If Kant himself drew a sharp distinction between a republican constitution and a democratic one, this was because his conception of democracy was a pre-modern one. His frequently quoted definition of a "republican" constitution entails three principles: "firstly, the principle of *freedom* for all members of society (as men); secondly, the principle of *dependence* of everyone upon a single common legislation (as subjects); and thirdly, the principle of legal *equality* for everyone (as citizens)." He wrote that "republicanism [is] that political principle whereby the executive power . . . is separated from the legislative power," and that "republican" government is, in principle, "representative." *Ibid.*, pp. 99–102.
[64] Michael Doyle, "Kant, Liberal Legacies and Foreign Affairs," *Philosophy & Public Affairs* 12 (1983), 205 (part 1) and 323 (part 2). For a survey of relevant empirical literature, *see* Bruce Russett, *Grasping the Democratic Peace* (Princeton University Press, 1993), ch. 1.
[65] Russett, *supra* note 64 (ch.1: "The Fact of Democratic Peace").
[66] Jack Levy, "Domestic Politics and War," *J. Interdisciplinary History* 18 (1988), pp. 653, 662.

democratic governments. It should stipulate that a legitimate government – one that has a right to exercise sovereign authority – is not just any government that wields factual power; it is a liberal democratic one. Tesón calls this a "Kantian theory of international law." Slaughter employs the international relations scholars' name, "liberal internationalism."[67] *Internationalism* evokes the second and third dimensions of Kant's formula for perpetual peace noted above, those that find reflection in international cooperation; *liberal* internationalism includes also the first dimension, "republican government." Against an international law that is in thrall to realism and power politics, Slaughter counterposes a vision of an international law that takes seriously the connection between national political ideology and international relations, and in this way dedicates itself (in the phrase of one international relations scholar) to "grasping the democratic peace."[68]

In effect this is a vision of a norm of democratic governance along the lines proposed in the first category of theses considered, though without the same emphasis on the notion of democracy as a human right.[69] Slaughter thus finds signs that her vision is beginning to materialize in the developments to which Franck and others call attention. She also finds signs that the "zone of peace" is accompanied and reinforced by a "zone of law," in that transnational disputes involving only liberal States are more readily resolved through judicial procedures than is the case where non-liberal States are involved. She presents evidence that courts of liberal States cooperate with one another, and take into account each other's national interests, in a way that courts of non-liberal States do not, and in a way that courts of liberal States themselves do not where a dispute involving a non-liberal State is at issue.[70]

On the question of how this norm might be enforced, Tesón concurs with Franck and Fox that the UN and other international organizations might change their rules to admit only States with liberal democratic governments, and to allow only such governments to participate. In his

---

[67] For her general "model" of international law, developed in recent work, Slaughter prefers the term "Liberal," and distinguishes a "Liberal" theory of international relations from "Wilsonian liberal internationalism." *See* Slaughter 1995, *supra* note 2, p. 508 ff. for her definition of "Liberal" in this context.   [68] Russett, *supra* note 64.

[69] Tesón does, however, argue that international law should accord legitimacy only to liberal democratic states not just for prudential reasons but also because this is morally justified His "Kantian theory" includes the idea that governments should be required to respect liberal rights because this is the right thing to do. *See* Tesón 1992, *supra* note 2, *esp.* pp. 81–84.

[70] Slaughter 1992b, *supra* note 2. *See* Slaughter 1995, *supra* note 2, for further development of this argument. Slaughter claims, for instance, that interaction between the executive and legislative branches of government is also greater among liberal States than among non-liberal States or between liberal and non-liberal States.

view the unilateral use of force might even be justified in some circumstances, especially where violation of the norm is associated with gross abuses of human rights. Tesón also proposes that the law of treaties might be made to reflect the illegitimacy of non-liberal governments; such governments might, for instance, be deprived of the competence to create binding obligations in their own favour. Diplomatic law too might be changed so as to deny diplomatic status to representatives of non-liberal regimes.[71] Slaughter differs in rejecting the right of unilateral intervention, and generally distances herself from Tesón's professed anti-statism. Nonetheless, she shares the view that liberal democracies have a "leadership" role to play in relation to liberal internationalist international law.[72]

As this discussion indicates, these claims revolve around a distinction between "liberal" or "liberal democratic" States and "non-liberal" States. It is worth pausing at this point to note more fully how the theorists understand this distinction. Slaughter defines a liberal State as, in broad terms, a State with "juridical equality, constitutional protections of individual rights, representative republican governments, and market economies based on private property rights."[73] This uncontroversial definition corresponds closely to that used by Doyle and other international relations analysts in their work on the "liberal peace."[74] Tesón adopts a similar approach, variously referring to the legitimate state of his "Kantian theory of international law" as a "democratic State," "free State," "liberal democracy," and "form of political organisation that provides full respect for human rights."[75] For both scholars the key feature of a liberal State, which explains its irenic character (at least *vis-à-vis* other liberal States), is the fact that there are powerful checks on the exercise of public power – constraints that operate principally through the periodic recall of legislators, the separation of powers and the protection of civil and political rights.

III LIBERAL MILLENARIANISM AND INTERNATIONAL LAW

It is now possible to address the relationship between these international legal arguments and liberal millenarianism. What is the basis for my

---

[71] Tesón 1992, *supra* note 2, p. 100.
[72] Slaughter 1992a, *supra* note 2, pp. 404 and 394. Doyle for this reason expresses concern at what he takes to be the decline of the United States from hegemonic status. *See* Doyle, *supra* note 64, pp. 233–35.
[73] Slaughter, 1992b, *supra* note 2, p. 1909. This is largely reiterated, though the need for market economies based on private property rights is separately stated, in Slaughter 1995, *supra* note 2, pp. 511–12.   [74] *See, e.g.,* Doyle, *supra* note 64, p. 206.   [75] Tesón 1992, *supra* note 2, *passim*.

assertion at the beginning of this chapter that these arguments share the distinctive perspective which I have termed liberal millenarianism? And why does it matter if they do? In particular, what is entailed by the understanding of democracy that informs the theses? In broad outline at least, the answers to these questions are perhaps already clear, but in this section I illustrate and comment on the liberal millenarian character of this body of international legal scholarship. At the end I offer some reflections on the implications of hitching international law to liberal millenarianism. In assessing these implications, it will be worth recalling that, if these international legal scholars are right, democracy has, will have, or at any rate ought to have, far-reaching significance in international law, as determinant of the legitimacy of governments.

A Liberal millenarian perspectives

If asked to take up positions in relation to Fukuyama, most or perhaps even all of the international legal scholars discussed in this chapter would very likely locate themselves at some considerable distance from him on almost every issue. Certainly, none of the scholars shares the narrow, elitist outlook that pervades Fukuyama's account of the "end of history." A number explicitly dissociate themselves from that account. Franck, for instance, states that he does not consider that "[exulting] in smug satisfaction at the 'end of history'" is an appropriate response to the post-Cold War juncture, which he sees rather as an occasion for the "seizing the moment to rethink the basic structure and processes of the international system."[76] Slaughter explains that liberal internationalism promises a result that is "neither utopia nor the end of history, but holds out the hope of at least a small measure of progress toward individual rights and the global rule of law."[77] There are some grounds for believing that liberal millenarianism may, nonetheless, be built into the form and structure of these scholars' arguments. As discussed earlier, liberal millenarianism includes, but extends beyond, Fukuyama. It is characterized by a progressivist notion of history, coupled with a conceptualization of history's *telos* in terms of liberalism, and a distinctive voice and tone. On what basis, and to what extent, can it be said that the international legal theses considered here exhibit these features?

A progressivist view of historical change is evident in Franck's history of the development of the norm of democratic governance. His account

---

[76] Franck 1990, *supra* note 1, p. 601. *See also* Franck 1995, *supra* note 1, p. 141.
[77] Slaughter 1992a, *supra* note 2, p. 405.

is divided into developmental phases, beginning with the principle of self-determination and culminating in the right of free and open elections, now evolving from lip service into widely respected normative commitment. "The transformation of the democratic entitlement from moral obligation to prescription has evolved gradually," he explains, but "in the past decade the tendency has accelerated."[78] Each phase pushes further along the course to eventual prescription. The fact that the phases overlap does not detract from, but rather reinforces, the impression of progress and directionality, as do the metaphors of generations and building blocks. The norm of democratic governance appears to be growing out of, or building on, earlier developments. This evolutionary logic also informs the work of scholars who put forward liberal internationalist and Kantian theses. Slaughter, for instance, in seeking to connect international law with developments in international relations, offers an unmistakably progressivist account of the history of international relations. This account starts with Wilsonian internationalism (or idealism, in the phraseology of those who later called themselves realists), passes through the stage of realism, and reaches its conclusion with liberal internationalism, which is said to combine the strengths, but also to overcome the shortcomings, of both its forerunners. Since these forerunners are presented as the only alternatives, liberal internationalism is made naturally to appear an advance.[79] The notion of the "liberal peace," liberal internationalism's central premise, likewise posits that historical change is incremental and directional. The image is one of an expanding zone of peace among liberal States that will reach the end of its expansion when all are included within it.

The second aspect of liberal millenarianism is that history's *telos* is taken to be liberal democracy, along with a market-oriented economy. It hardly needs restating that this is indeed the goal envisaged in the international legal theses examined here. That this should be so is believed, in the liberal millenarian perspective described earlier, to be supported empirically, by the elimination of all ideological alternatives. It is also believed to be supported normatively. That is to say, these ideological alternatives have been eliminated because they were flawed, as democracy and capitalism – at least in principle, if not in current practice – are not. Both points are alluded to in a memorable passage by Franck:

---

[78] Franck 1992, *supra* note 1, p. 47.
[79] *See, e.g.*, Slaughter 1993, *supra* note 2. For a further narrowing of alternatives to "Realism" and "Liberalism," *see* Slaughter 1995, *supra* note 2.

[T]he [global democratic] entitlement now aborning is widely enough understood to be almost universally celebrated. It is welcomed from Malagache to Mongolia, in the streets, the universities and the legislatures, not only because it portends a new, global political culture supported by common rules and communitarian implementing institutions, but also because it opens the stagnant political economies of states to economic, social and cultural, as well as political, development.[80]

For Slaughter, "the geopolitical framework for the millennium is . . . liberal internationalism."[81] An eventual "world of liberal States" is the sole alternative to "[sacrificing] the values of universalism . . . to the realism of recognising that States in the international system inhabit very different worlds."[82] The choice, in her account, is either liberal universalism or realist difference, either grasping the liberal–democratic peace or living perpetually on the edge of war. The embrace of liberal democracy in every country thus appears as humanity's ultimate salvation.[83]

Liberal millenarianism involves, thirdly, a "post-historical" voice or standpoint that figures the non-liberal world, still mired in "history," as radically "other." Progress towards the full achievement of liberal democracy is taken to be more or less straightforward in liberal societies, while elsewhere the almost total transformation of prevailing realities will be required. This is, again, apparent in the thesis of the emerging norm of democratic governance. Such governance is portrayed as something some largely have, and the rest almost entirely lack. Thus, Franck writes that for the citizens of some States this norm will "merely embellish rights already protected by their existing domestic constitutional order. For others it could be the realization of a cherished dream."[84] A similar standpoint orients the liberal internationalist and neo-Kantian approaches. Slaughter envisions that her model of international law for a one-world order of liberal States might be "normatively applicable to all States even if positively descriptive of only some."[85] In practice, she

---

[80] Franck 1992, *supra* note 1, p. 90.
[81] Slaughter 1992a, *supra* note 2, p. 393 (emphasis omitted).
[82] Slaughter 1995, *supra* note 2, p. 538.
[83] It also appears as *international law's* salvation, inasmuch as liberal universalism also represents an option in favour of law, rather than politics. Liberal internationalism thus seems to rescue international law from realist irrelevance. Fukuyama suggests this too, arguing that, while "international law in general" (Fukuyama 1992, p. 281) became discredited owing to the failure of the League of Nations and the United Nations, the "states making . . . up [the 'league of democratic nations' which he proposes] would be able to live according to the rules of international law in their mutual dealings" (Fukuyama 1992, *supra* note 5, p. 283).
[84] Franck 1992, *supra* note 1, p. 50.   [85] Slaughter 1995, *supra* note 2, p. 538.

observes, the distinction between liberal and non-liberal States may be difficult to apply, especially in the context of "quasi-liberal" and "transitional States." Certainly, it cannot be treated as an "absolute divide."[86] But the point of the "liberal peace," around which her argument turns, is that, as Doyle explains, liberal States are not just relatively but "fundamentally different" from non-liberal States. Hence the "separate peace" among them.[87] If this is the reason for the "separate peace," it is, of course, also the consequence. In any event, the claim of liberal internationalism, as of the norm of democratic governance, is that this fundamental difference should, and is beginning to, be reflected in international law.

There is, finally, the issue of liberal millenarianism's distinctive tone, its momentous, celebratory, and apparently optimistic, key. Liberal millenarianism seeks to call attention to events which augur that history's destination may finally be in sight. The discussion in the previous section gave only a slight indication of the tone of these international legal arguments. The quotation from Franck above is, however, typical of the terms in which his claims, and those of some of the other international legal scholars, are expressed.[88] Thus, for instance, Franck goes on to speak of a "cosmic but unmysterious change" in which governments, "no longer blinded by the totalitarian miasma" have come to recognize the advantages of democracy.[89] Slaughter likewise writes emphatically of revolutions that "liberated millions. *Millions . . .*" and occasioned a "human rights victory on an unprecedented scale, a triumph of human dignity and the human spirit."[90] On the basis of those events she proposes liberal internationalism as a new vision of peace and good government for a new age.

If the thesis of the emerging norm of democratic governance and related claims share key features of liberal millenarianism, they also give rise to a number of the concerns raised by Fukuyama's critics. In accounts of the norm of democratic governance and the order of liberal States envisioned by the liberal internationalist and Kantian theories, liberal democracy is presented largely as an identifiable, coherent, and stable system. It is stressed that a great variety of practices and institu-

---

[86] Slaughter 1992b, *supra* note 2, pp. 1988–89.
[87] Doyle, *supra* note 64, p. 235. Slaughter takes up Doyle's phraseology, noting the "fundamental difference in the nature of relations among liberal States as compared to relations between liberal and non-liberal States." Slaughter 1995, *supra* note 2, p. 537.
[88] But not all express themselves in this way. *Cf.* the more cautious tone of, *e.g.*, Fox and Nolte, *supra* note 3.   [89] Franck 1995, *supra* note 1, p. 85–86.   [90] Slaughter 1990, *supra* note 2, p. 1.

tions is consistent with liberal democracy, but little attention is drawn to the diversity of the values, ideas and principles that might animate those practices and institutions. In particular, little attention is given to the enduring tensions within liberal democracy between liberal and democratic preoccupations, and to the implications for that tension of different models of liberal democracy. While the international legal theorists are less apt than Fukuyama to mistake capitalism for liberal democracy, their arguments nonetheless tend, like his, toward an attenuation of the democratic dimension.

The democratic component of liberal democracy comes to revolve, principally, around elections. That what is denoted is a particular method of producing governments is made particularly clear in the thesis of the emerging norm of democratic governance. Democracy's part there is adjectival; it is a procedure for securing the acquiescence of citizens in their governance by others.[91] The same holds, however, whether democracy is understood in these terms, or in terms of a social contract to protect citizens' rights (as by Fox and Nolte), a mechanism to ensure that government acts not just in its own interests but in the interests of society as a whole (as by Slaughter) or a system of government that is not just prudentially but also morally justified (as by Tesón). The shared assumption is that democracy refers to the "process by which the people choose those they entrust with the exercise of power,"[92] the right "to participate in the selection of one's own national government."[93]

Yet, according to some political theorists, democracy entails not just the right to participate in the selection of national governments, but also the right to participate directly in decision-making affecting one.[94] For other theorists, democracy involves not just the process of selecting governments but also the process of connecting people with their governments through civil society.[95] Still other theorists emphasize that democracy requires not just the right to vote and stand for election and associated civil liberties, but also the whole range of further rights that actually enable participation in public life on a footing of equality.[96] While Franck, Fox and Nolte take their position to be dictated by that

---

[91] Franck 1992, *supra* note 1, p. 51 and *passim*.   [92] *Ibid.*, p. 50.   [93] Fox, *supra* note 3, p. 542.
[94] *See, e.g.*, Benjamin Barber, *Strong Democracy* (Berkeley, Calif.: University of California Press, 1984).
[95] *See, e.g.*, Jean Cohen and Andrew Arato, *Civil Society and Political Theory* (Cambridge, Mass.: The MIT Press, 1992).
[96] Amongst the innumerable different ways and contexts in which this argument has been advanced, *see, e.g.*, Anne Phillips, *Engendering Democracy* (Cambridge: Polity Press, 1991) and *Democracy and Difference* (Cambridge: Polity Press, 1993).

International law, democracy, and the end of history 559

which customary international law will support,[97] what is being suggested here is that it is also embedded in the structure of their argument. Inasmuch as elections stand at the narrative's climax, democracy is made to appear to have nowhere further to go. Issues of citizenship, accountability, and equality, and their respective significance and relative importance – along with other issues at the heart of democratic debate – are thus removed from view.

An additional, related concern is these theses' uncritical, affirmative approach towards liberal democracy. Franck's reference, cited above, to the embellishment of rights in existing liberal States suggests a perception that such States are already satisfactory; the rest is ornament. Depicting democratic political practice as entailing a "genuine [openness] to meaningful political choice"[98] and a "free market in ideas,"[99] Franck puts to one side the many grounds for doubting the meaningfulness of political choice and the freedom of the market in ideas. Slaughter attaches much importance to what she refers to as the "paradox of liberal States." By this she intends that "as a factual rather than a legal matter, liberal States are likely to have a lesser capacity for autonomous economic and political action than non-liberal States."[100] But she too neglects to consider how well these constraints on power work, whether they work better for some social groups than others, and whether further constraints might be valuable. With liberal democracy the pinnacle of political development – and with dictatorship, Communism, and "forced march modernization" the only alternatives ever mentioned[101] – questions concerning liberal democracy's limitations can scarcely arise, let alone be addressed. It is not only issues of the kind just noted that are left out of account, however. The whole matter

---

[97] Fox also emphasizes that his position is dictated by that which is feasible, elections being the most readily monitored dimension of democratic politics. *See* Fox, concluding comments in Panel, "National Sovereignty Revisited: Perspectives on the Emerging Norm of Democracy in International Law," *Proc. ASIL* (1992), pp. 249, 270–71, and *infra* text at note 121 for discussion of this point.

[98] Franck 1995, *supra* note 1, p. 86. Franck lists 130 States which as of late 1994 were "legally committed to permit open, multiparty, secret-ballot elections with a universal franchise." Of these he remarks that "[w]hile a few may arguably be democracies in form rather than substance, most are, or are in the process of becoming, genuinely open to meaningful political choice." Franck 1995, *supra* note 1, pp. 85–6.   [99] *Ibid.*, p. 138.

[100] Slaughter 1992a, *supra* note 2, pp. 395–96 (emphasis omitted). The sense in which this is a paradox is unclear. If the thought is that the freedom associated with liberal States entails in another sense greater constraint than is the case with non-liberal States, then the paradox remains obscure, inasmuch as the freedom is that of citizens and the constraint is that of the State.   [101] *See, e.g.,* Franck 1995, *supra* note 1, p. 86.

of liberal democracy's tenability in a world of intensified globalization is largely passed over. While globalizing processes are certainly registered,[102] the ways in which they are putting democracy under strain receive limited attention.[103] These scholars evoke a liberal democracy that is triumphant, vigorous, redemptive.

They also evoke a liberal democracy that provides the key to expanded prospects for peace. In this respect too, however, limitations are glossed over. The "peace," which some international relations analysts claim is now a "fact," is a "*liberal* peace"; it is said to hold *among liberal States*. Relations between liberal and non-liberal States are not claimed to be especially pacific, and may, according to the analysts, even be especially aggressive.[104] In finding warrant in this for a norm of democratic governance, the international legal scholars give little attention to the implications of the fact that democratic governance does not appear to induce pacific relations with non-liberal States.

But there is also a much larger limitation of which these writers take insufficient cognisance. The "peace" that is postulated among liberal States is an absence of armed conflict between them. Yet the Clausewitzean paradigm of war between nation-States to which this refers today fits only a minority of violent conflicts, even large-scale ones. Mary Kaldor highlights that much contemporary conflict arises out of the break-up of States, and centers on issues of "identity politics" (ranging from religious communalism, to ethnic nationalism, to "tribalism").[105] Support frequently comes from overseas diasporas, along with foreign governments and "experts." State actors are often hard to distinguish from non-State actors. Fighting is commonly sporadic, scattered within and across borders, and focused to a large extent on civilian targets.[106] Is this peace or war? Civil war or international war? The boundaries between these categories – like those between violent crime and armed conflict, public aims and private aims, combatants and civilians – are becoming blurred. Kaldor concludes that

---

[102] *See, esp.* Slaughter 1995, *supra* note 2.
[103] A rare example of such attention can be found in the final eight pages of Franck's 484-page study of "fairness" in international law and institutions. *See* Franck 1995, *supra* note 1, pp. 477–84.
[104] *See* Doyle, *supra* note 64, pp. 323ff.
[105] Mary Kaldor, "Introduction," *in* Mary Kaldor and Basker Vashee, eds., *Restructuring the Global Military Sector*, vol. 1: *New Wars* (London: Pinter Press, 1997).
[106] For a similar account of war in the 1990s, *see* Supplement to an Agenda for Peace: Position Paper of the Secretary-General on the Occasion of the Fiftieth Anniversary of the United Nations, UN Doc. A/50/60; S/1995/1 (1995), *esp.* para. 10ff.

the prognosis is grim. The breakdown of the distinction between war and peace, the re-privatisation of violence, implies more or less continuous and geographically pervasive low-level violence, ranging from individual criminality to organised warfare.[107]

Alongside these considerations concerning the character of war are further questions concerning the character of peace. There is, for instance, the question of whether peace can be held to prevail where certain forms of non-forcible coercion are occurring, arising (*inter alia*) from the exploitation of relations of dependency. There is also the broader issue of whether systemic inequalities of power, resources, and opportunities, between and within nation-States, may in themselves constitute a type of ongoing "structural violence."[108] The identification of peace with an absence of armed conflict leaves out of account the possibility that peace may entail more than the failure to resort to arms.

It follows that the scope of the claims associated with the "liberal peace" is highly circumscribed. Even assuming those claims are justified on their own terms, they miss important contemporary sources of violence, and important questions that arise in connection with that violence.

Moreover, Derrida's "macroscopic fact, made up of innumerable singular sites of suffering" cited earlier finds scarcely greater resonance in these arguments than does Kaldor's "grim prognosis." These international lawyers are undoubtedly no Panglosses. Yet the progressivist premises of their claims, buttressed by the celebratory tone and "posthistorical" voice, do tend to shift attention away from the scale, character, and sources of deprivation, oppression, and conflict in the contemporary world. To read this international legal literature is to be filled with enthusiasm about the state of, or at any rate prospects for, human flourishing.

Also arguably overestimated is the extent to which there is evidence to support an emerging norm of democratic governance. For Franck and the other theorists of the emerging norm, this empirical issue – raised by some of Franck's critics[109] – has a different significance than it does for Fukuyama. While Fukuyama might shift between the empirical and the ideal, the international legal commentators cannot avoid con-

---

[107] Kaldor, *supra* note 105.
[108] The notion of "structural violence" is elaborated in the work of Johan Galtung. *See, e.g.*, "Violence, Peace and Peace Research," *Essays in Peace Research* 1 (1975), ch. 4.
[109] *See, e.g.*, Carothers, *supra* note 3.

fronting state practice if they are to make good their claim that the norm is emerging in international law. Or maybe Fukuyama's move, or something like it, is precisely what they intend. Perhaps characterizing the norm as "emerging" allows it to remain poised between occurrence and prediction.

Finally, the international legal arguments are inclined to overstate the significance of the present moment, as an indication of the future. While the possibility of setbacks is certainly acknowledged, the evolutionary logic of the arguments tends to signal that contemporary trends will continue in a more or less linear fashion. As Fukuyama's critics highlight, the processes of historical change appear to be far more complex and contingent than this logic allows.

The observations made by Fukuyama's critics are also worth recalling as regards the consequences of these concerns. There is a danger of inducing complacency, and of prematurely pronouncing liberal democracy's future secure. In masking the limitations of liberal democracy, the prospects that those limitations might be addressed are correspondingly reduced. Inequalities may be made to seem, and to become, unalterable. And, to the extent that Kaldor's "grim prognosis" is inadequately heeded, there is a danger of attaching insufficient importance and urgency to the medicine she prescribes. This entails re-establishing legitimate control of violence at a transnational level.[110]

To these points might be added further misgivings expressed by international legal commentators. Martti Koskenniemi emphasises the "risk of imperialism" that attends efforts to establish and refine a norm of democratic governance.[111] Such efforts tend to resolve themselves, he observes, into "a call for contextual management of far-away societies in reference to Western liberal policies."[112] Thomas Carothers likewise argues that "[a]dvocacy of a democratic norm actually highlights [the] West versus non-West division and the tension in international law concerning the fact that it is at root a Western system that Western countries are seeking to apply to the whole world."[113] Carothers worries too about the harm that might be done, via sanctions or armed intervention, in the "implementation" of such a norm. Is the way opened up for the waging of "just wars" or neo-colonial adventures? All the international legal scholars whose work is discussed here recognize the force of this

---

[110] Kaldor, *supra* note 105.   [111] Koskenniemi, *supra* note 3, p. 231.   [112] *Ibid.* at 233.
[113] Carothers, *supra* note 3, p. 264. Derrida likewise discerns the outlines of a renewed European Christian alliance. Derrida, *supra* note 24, pp. 60–61.

International law, democracy, and the end of history 563

concern.[114] With the exception of Tesón, none accepts unilateral intervention as a legitimate means of enforcing the norm, though each does appear to accept collective action by regional organizations and the United Nations.

Koskenniemi and Carothers here echo a widely shared apprehension as regards the division of the world into liberal democratic and non-liberal democratic States. This is an apprehension that cannot forget all the other notorious divisions of history: between civilized and barbarian, Christian and heathen, European and oriental, developed and underdeveloped. Given the historical record, there is a case to be answered that a norm of democratic governance, like Fukuyama's "league of democratic nations," would express a "new ideology of imperialism."[115] The thrust of this chapter's argument is that charges of neo-imperialism would indeed be difficult to resist, were international law to engage with democracy along the lines envisaged by Franck, Slaughter, Tesón, and the others. I have sought to show how these scholars' proposals operate within a liberal millenarian framework. A universal norm, developed within a liberal millenarian framework, would, in Koskenniemi's words, "always be suspect as a neocolonialist strategy."[116] Such a norm is – as he puts it – "too easily used against revolutionary politics that aim at the roots of the existing distributional system and it domesticates cultural and political specificity in an overall (Western) culture of moral agnosticism and rule by the market."[117]

But if democracy's universal relevance cannot be defended within the specific framework of liberal millenarianism, from this it does not follow that democracy's universal relevance can never be defended. As noted at the outset, I believe that democracy can be shown to have universal pertinence, though I must leave that claim and its implications for another discussion. In the present context I seek simply to recall that the vision of democracy which informs recent efforts to establish or promote democracy's international legal status is not the only one conceivable. To quote Koskenniemi again, there is no "transparent view of the essential meaning of democracy,"[118] for democracy is a contested concept and has no essential meaning. All accounts of democracy are positions in a debate that is not just *about* politics, but is itself also a site *of* politics.

---

[114] *See, e.g.*, Franck 1992, *supra* note 1, p. 84.
[115] Frank Füredi, *The New Ideology of Imperialism* (London: Pluto Press, 1994). Franck and others acknowledge the concern. *See, e.g.*, Franck 1992, *supra* note 1, pp. 80, 82.
[116] Koskenniemi, *supra* note 3, p. 234.   [117] *Ibid.*   [118] *Ibid.*

Of course, this applies as much to those who would seek to challenge liberal millenarianism as the basis of a universal democratic norm as it does to those who embrace liberal millenarianism. Neither side has privileged access to the "truth" of democracy's meaning; in the course of academic argument, each side necessarily engages in a form of political struggle. Nonetheless, the important point remains that the prospects for refuting charges of neo-imperialism are not to be judged by reference solely to the particular – liberal millenarian – approach that has predominated to date. Defenders of democracy's universal relevance have a wide range of alternative democratic possibilities upon which to draw. Amongst these possibilities are many that are substantially more congenial to redistribution and difference, and substantially less subordinate to the market and its managers, than is liberal millenarianism.

B Conclusion

The thesis of the emerging norm of democratic governance, and the liberal internationalist and neo-Kantian perspectives considered here, grapple with the international legal significance of profound transformations. They call attention to notable normative, institutional and academic developments, and relate those developments both to one another and to international law. In doing so, however, they adopt a narrow understanding of democracy, largely equating it with certain liberal ideas and institutions. Franck expresses regret that this is all customary international law will currently support.[119] Fox recognizes that democracy entails much more than periodic national elections, but considers that elections, being easier for international organizations to monitor than other facets of democratic life, are international law's most appropriate starting point. "It is much more difficult," he observes, "to stay in a country after elections, for the long haul, to monitor all institutions of government and attempt to secure key elements of democracy ... Elections ... must not end the push to a democratic society, but they are an essential first step."[120]

Yet it is not self-evident either that elections are democracy's first step or that ease of monitoring by international organizations should determine international law's priorities. Democracy involves no necessary order of events, and difficulties of monitoring have all too frequently

---

[119] This is what Franck appears to suggest, when defending a conception which, he acknowledges, is "not ambitious, not unambiguous, and ... almost certainly not the one Americans would prefer." *See* Franck 1994, *supra* note 1, p. 75.   [120] Fox, *supra* note 97, pp. 270–71.

served in international law to make chosen priorities seem unavoidable.[121] This is not to suggest that periodic elections and related institutions lack value.[122] It is just to highlight the way democracy's further dimensions may be eclipsed. This chapter has sought to show that, whatever may be the constraints of the international legal system, they are not the only constraints in operation. The scholars' liberal millenarian standpoint also plays a part in shaping the account of democracy that informs their claims.

At the same time, the theses provide powerful reasons for being concerned about this. If a norm of democratic governance indeed "emerges," this will entail – to reiterate earlier discussion – that international law lays down criteria of governmental legitimacy, and that those criteria require democracy. It may also entail that individuals can claim a human right to democracy. The international legal scholars suggest that the norm should be enforced by making admission to, and participation in, international organizations conditional on democratic government (as is currently the case with some regional organizations). Franck proposes that financial and trade benefits and development assistance, and even the protection of UN and regional collective security measures in the event of an invasion, might likewise be made conditional on democratic government. Tesón advocates modifications of treaty and diplomatic law that would place further pressure on governments which do not meet the criteria of liberal democracy. Though Tesón alone would be prepared to sanction unilateral intervention, the other scholars appear to support collective enforcement.

Dire consequences could thus follow where legitimacy is denied. From the perspective of citizens, however, dire – perhaps even direr – consequences could also follow where legitimacy is accorded. This latter danger is easy to overlook. Yet if, in line with the international legal scholarship discussed in this article, liberal millenarianism shapes the criteria used, international law may find itself according legitimacy for what may in some circumstances be the most cosmetic democracy. In so doing, the law may undercut efforts to deepen democracy's purchase in the countries concerned. To the objection that any step in the direction

---

[121] An example is the case of economic, social, and cultural rights, and the way their relative de-emphasis is routinely linked to undeniable, but exaggerated, difficulties of monitoring and enforcement.

[122] However, for an intriguing critique of the significance and "reality" of elections, see Jean Baudrillard (Paul Foss, Paul Patton and John Johnston, trans.), *In the Shadow of Silent Majorities, or the End of the Social and Other Essays* (New York: Semiotexte, 1983).

of democracy is better than unmitigated repression, it may be replied that this is not necessarily so if the conditions upon which power is exercised remain essentially unchanged. Where international law confers on a repressive regime a legitimacy that it formerly lacked, the regime is strengthened and counter-authoritarian forces correspondingly debilitated.

According to former United Nations Secretary-General Boutros Boutros-Ghali, democracy is today an "ideal that belongs to all humanity."[123] To characterize democracy as an ideal is to highlight that it is an engine of criticism and change, necessarily at odds with prevailing realities. To label it as the property of all humanity is to recall, amongst other things, that its institutional complements necessarily reflect the huge diversity of social circumstances to which it is applied. Should international law seek to vindicate efforts animated by such an ideal, then a framework of ideas that posits liberal institutions as history's end scarcely seems an adequate basis on which to proceed.

---

[123] "Democracy: a Newly Recognized Imperative," *Global Governance* 1 (1995), pp. 3, 4. *See* further Boutros Boutros-Ghali, *An Agenda for Democratization* (New York: United Nations, 1996).

Index

accountability, 3, 27, 100, 111, 202–04, 527, 529
 criminal, 457–59, 471–73, 475, 479, 485–87, 489, 490
 in customary law, 467–71, 472, 473
 and democracy, 473–84
 general duty of, 459, 461–73, 484–85
 history of, 451–59
 individuals, 453, 456–58
 minimum standards, 488–89
 non-criminal, 488, 489, 490
 norms, 450–51, 456–59, 470–84, 486–87
 retrospective, 450, 455, 460–61, 468, 474–78, 480, 483
 specific duty of, 458–59, 471
 States and, 459–61, 464–68ff.
 transgovernmental, 218, 227, 231–34
Adams, President John, 364, 365, 378
Admissions case, 128n, 136
Afghanistan, 243, 255n, 265, 267, 296
Africa, 6, 30, 31, 35, 40–41, 56, 68, 117, 143, 154n, 267, 288–90, 347, 376, 508, 519
 democratic change in, 101
 election monitoring standards, 219
 non-democratic governments in 148–150, 246, 247
African Charter on Human and Peoples' Rights, 66–68, 92
African Commission on Human Rights, 67–68
Ago, Robert, 297n
Alarcón, President Fabian, 179, 180, 182
Algeria, 31, 117, 118, 150, 255, 391, 393–95, 399, 442, 445
Allott, Philip, 109
American Bar Association, 212
American Civil War, 354n, 355, 368–71, 378
American Convention on Human Rights (1978), 64–66, 100, 155, 157
 and accountability, 462, 463, 465, 466, 481, 485
 Article 23, 64, 65, 156, 185
 see also Inter-American Commission on Human Rights

American Declaration of the Rights and Duties of Man (1948), 155, 157
 Article xx, 155–56
American Law Institute, 1
American public opinion, 350, 353, 355, 357–59, 362–76, 377, 378
amnesties, 73, 74, 172, 462–63, 464, 465, 466, 468, 472, 477, 481–82, 483–84, 524
 self-amnesties, 476, 478, 480, 486, 489
Amnesty International, 471
Angola, 41, 346, 464
Annan, Kofi, 7–8, 26–27, 30, 253n
anti-democratic actors, 4, 19, 389–92, 395–99, 442–43, 530
 exclusion from political process, 404, 406ff., 416–17, 420–21, 422, 428–30, 446, 447, 448
 in international law, 421–33
 popular support for, 443
 restrictions on, 390, 395, 396, 422–35, 445, 448
 and State practice, 406–20, 423n, 425, 428–30
 tolerance of, 399–406, 411–15, 433
 see also non-democratic governments; non-democratic States
anti-democratic intervention, 197
anti-trust policy, 214, 215, 224
Apartheid Convention (1973), 458
arbitrary arrest and detention, 184, 462, 470
Argentina, 176, 189, 194, 202, 230, 520, 521, 523–24
 and accountability, 461, 464, 468, 476, 477, 489, 524
 privatization, 525–26
 Supreme Court, 206
Aristide, President Jean-Bertrand, 79, 80, 123, 146, 160, 168–71, 182, 190, 191, 194, 195, 196, 197, 248, 284, 285, 287, 294, 301, 320, 321n, 496
Armenia, 132

567

arms control, 132
arms embargo, 282
army *see* military forces
Asia, 222
Association of African Election Authorities, 219
Association of South East Asian Nations (ASEAN), 148, 150
associations, prohibition of, 414, 415, 416, 419
Athens, classical, 359
atrocities, 255, 455, 456, 457, 459, 464, 472
Australia, 102
Austria, 419
authoritarian States *see* illiberal States; non-democratic States
autogolpes, 159, 160, 167, 171–75, 177, 187–88, 190, 446
Azerbaijan, 132

Badinter Commission, 134–36
Baker, James, 356
balance-of-threat theory, 380
Baltic States, 130
Bangladesh, 31, 38
bank networks, 200, 214, 215–16, 220, 229
Barcelona Traction case, 278
Basle Committee of Central Bankers, 200, 215–16, 220, 229
Basques, 126
Bayard, Thomas F., 373
Belarus, 30
Belgium, 52n, 105, 209
Benin, 38
Binaisa, President Godfrey, 45
Bodin, Jean, 239, 340
Bonaparte, Emperor Napoleon, 366, 367–68
Bolivia, 158, 180, 185, 468
Bosnia-Herzegovina, 128n, 132, 134, 135, 136, 137, 138, 151, 316, 318–20, 382, 404n, 458, 479
Botswana, 408
Boutros-Ghali, Boutros, 347–48, 385n, 566
Bowett, D. W., 106–07
Brazil, 176, 194, 464, 486, 520, 521, 522, 524–25, 526, 527, 528
Bremen v. Zapata, 210
Breyer, Justice Stephen, 206, 207, 209
Brezhnev Doctrine, 334
Bright, John, 369, 370
British Guiana, 372–76
British Liberal Party, 63–64
Bucaram Ortiz, President Abdalá, 178–80, 181, 182, 188, 189, 197
Bulgaria, 38, 419–20

bureaucracy, 232
Burma *see* Myanmar
Burundi, 117
Bush, President George, 39, 169, 199, 265, 274, 276, 292
business groups, 181
Bwalya, Peter Chiiko, 58

Calabresi, Justice Guido, 207, 210
Cambodia, 37, 41, 104, 144, 147–48, 314, 346, 382, 458, 464, 470
Canada, 228, 282, 412–14
Canadian Charter on Rights and Freedoms, 412–14
Canadian Supreme Court, 205, 401n, 413
capacity-building, 229
capitalism, 225, 531, 535, 537, 542
  see also market economy
Cardoso, Fernando, 521, 526, 528
Caribbean States, 521
Carothers, Thomas, 562, 563
Carter, Jimmy, 286, 518
Castro, Fidel, 442–43, 448
Central African Empire, 280
Central America, 35–38, 141, 142, 158–60, 185, 186, 230, 332, 420, 496, 518, 521
  see also Latin America; Organization of American States
Cerna, Christina, 547
Chamberlain, Joseph, 375, 376, 379
Chesterman, Simon, 17, 20
Chile, 283, 350, 461, 464, 475, 481, 486, 489, 520, 521, 522–23, 526, 527
China, 3, 40, 43, 116, 117, 127, 129n, 249, 284, 382, 519, 520
  economic growth, 222, 227
  recognition of government of, 143–44, 145
  right to unilateral action, 267, 268
Christianity, 539, 563
citizens, 29, 30, 49, 50, 88, 227, 354, 356, 400, 401, 404, 442, 500, 549, 558
civil law, 205
civil rights, 114, 116, 220, 404, 424–25
  limits to restrictions on, 422–30
civil society, 499, 500, 501
civil wars, 25, 37, 80, 81, 288, 299, 314–15, 341, 347, 503, 560
  see also American Civil War
Cleveland, President Grover, 371–72, 373, 375
Clinton, President William J., 169, 170, 201–02, 225, 226, 348
Code of Offenses against the Peace and Security of Mankind (ILC draft), 454–55
Cold War, 6, 55, 86, 295, 356, 448, 518, 519, 535, 551

Index 569

collective enforcement, 46–47, 327, 549, 563
  see also multilateral intervention
collective will, 14, 15
  see also will of the people
Colombia, 43
colonialism, 1, 32, 34, 35, 56, 71–75, 103, 126, 282, 518
comity, 208–10, 215
common good, 499, 500, 501
common law, 205
common values, 224–25
Commonwealth, 38, 103–04, 149, 220, 221, 304, 305
communal life, 438, 446, 500
Communism, 498, 535, 536, 542
Communist Control Act (1954), 410, 433
Communist party of the United States, 410, 431, 434
competition, political, 513–14
compliance, 29, 34, 46, 99, 100, 151–52, 484–85
conditionality, 8–9, 565
Conference on Security and Co-operation in Europe (CSCE), 38, 42, 44, 46, 68, 104, 133
  see also Organization for Security and Cooperation in Europe (OSCE)
Congo, 117, 126, 146, 150–51
consensus, 25–26, 89, 225, 229, 433, 448, 450, 505, 513, 542
consent, 26–27, 49, 125–26, 239, 294
  see also invitation to intervention
consociational pacts, 336, 338–41
constitutional courts, 205–07
constitutional design, 166, 181, 183–92, 198
  and participation, 192–96
  and textualism, 191
constitutional fidelity, 183, 186–91
constitutional legitimism, 332–33
constitutionalism, 494, 495, 512–15, 516
constitutions, 29, 32, 94, 184, 189–90, 197, 198, 404, 405, 512–13
  changes to, 188, 409
  see also constitutional design
constitutive changes, 250–51, 254, 257
Cook Islands, 32, 72n
cooperation, 224–25, 352n
  in dispute resolution, 207–11
  judicial organizations, 211–13
  transnational regulatory, 214–18
  see also government networks
Copenhagen Declaration (1990), 42, 47, 68, 69, 184–85
Corfu Channel case, 264n
corruption, 8, 181, 189, 243, 527

Costa Rica, 97, 185, 244, 279, 332, 418
Council of Europe, 60, 61, 105, 128, 398n, 547
Council of Freely Elected Heads of Government, 38
counter-majoritarianism, 395, 398
coup d'état, juridical, 178
  see also military coups
courts, 201, 202, 203, 205–11, 214, 224, 234, 552
Covenant of the League of Nations Article 15(8), 240n
Crawford, James, 16, 20, 125, 259, 539n
crimes against humanity, 338, 457
criminal accountability, general duty of, 459, 461ff.
criminal law enforcement, 214, 217
Croatia, 132–33, 134, 135, 136, 137, 151, 419
cross-border military actions *see* external use of force
Cuba, 3, 21, 43, 116, 141, 145, 159, 249, 443, 448
Cubas Grau, Paul, 177, 178
customary international law, 69, 201, 256, 265, 266, 267, 275, 281, 289, 456, 458, 548
  and generalized accountability, 467–71, 472, 473
Cyprus, 126, 316–18, 339
Czechoslovakia, 38, 267, 296, 334, 478, 489

D'Amato, Anthony, 251, 263, 267, 269, 275, 292
Dayton Peace Accords, 137–38, 316, 318–20, 458
de facto control, 69, 139, 146, 147, 150, 153, 244, 300, 309, 310, 321, 322, 324, 325, 327, 332, 342, 506, 507
de jure control, 252, 300, 321, 322, 324, 325, 341, 342
de León Carpio, President Ramiro, 173, 174, 188, 190, 195, 196
decentralization, 200, 203, 232, 254
decision-making bodies, 255
declinism, 540, 543–45
decolonization, 71–75, 94, 127
defamation, law of, 102
democracy, 28, 41, 269
  and accountability, 473–84
  and collective rights, 94, 95
  definitions of, 14–15, 16, 48–49, 91–92, 95, 164–66, 183–84, 335, 336, 389–90, 396, 436–39, 441, 443, 446, 495, 548, 563
  and elections, 49–50, 102, 335–37, 442–43, 517, 564
  ends of, 494, 495–97
  and equality, 501, 503–04
  forms of, 185

democracy (cont.)
　growth of, 100–02
　guarantee of, 115, 184
　higher forms of, 498, 505
　and human rights, 3, 7, 49, 93, 111, 116, 398
　and individual rights, 93–94
　internal view of, 436, 440
　and liberalism, 222–23, 533, 534
　minimum standards of, 92
　problems of, 112–13, 114–15, 497
　protection of, 390–91, 420, 421, 436
　restoration of, 146–47, 246, 248–49, 252–54
　"right to," 114–18
　threats to, 146–50
　unsuitability of, 145
　see also democratic entitlement; democratic norm; democratic States; democratization; liberal democracy; procedural democracy; representative democracy; substantive democracy
democratic deficit, 232, 235
democratic entitlement, 1, 4–5, 26, 259–60, 293
　and accountability, 488
　and anti-democratic parties, 390–91
　arguments against, 13–16
　development of, 35–41
　"emerging" right of, 13, 14, 27–29, 43–45, 47, 302, 441, 442, 448, 532–33, 545–49, 561–62
　implications of, 10–13
　and intervention, 328–29
　legality of, 43–44, 48
　and "liberal millenarianism," 540–45, 553–66
　and "liberal peace," 552–53
　meaning of, 40–41
　opposition to, 43, 44, 45
　origins of, 32–35
　and popular sovereignty, 13–14
　problems of, 114–20
　and recognition of States, 123–24
　sources of, 48
　and treaties of guarantee, 341–42
　and unilateral action, 256
　universality of, 116–17
　see also democracy; democratic norm; political participation, right to
democratic governments, overthrow of see elected governments, restoration of; military coups
democratic norm, 3, 13, 19, 20–21, 40, 47, 390, 493–95, 545–53, 561–62
　and accountability, 449–51, 461, 473–84
　indeterminacy of, 335, 337, 441–42

　and transgovernmentalism, 202
　see also democratic entitlement
"democratic peace," 4, 22, 91, 221, 282
　exceptions to, 355
　and foreign policy, 344, 353–57ff.
　and international law, 549–53
　and liberal elites, 344, 357–59, 361ff.
　and liberal ideology, 344, 351–53, 381
　and liberal institutions, 344, 350, 351, 356–60
　and liberalism, 343–46, 549–53
　and realism, 376–81
　and state sovereignty, 384–85
　theories of, 349–51
　unintended consequences of, 382–84
democratic States, 101, 140, 350, 351n, 553
　intervention by, 106–07
　and non-recognition, 129
　recognition policies of, 143–45ff.
　see also liberal States
democratization, 2, 3, 4, 5–10, 49, 101–02ff., 202, 382, 488
　causes of, 518–19
　and conditionality, 8–9
　external enforcement of, 12–13
　false, 502–03
　and government networks, 226–31
　of international organizations, 112
　and social progress, 20–21
　see also transitional States
Dennis v. United States case, 399n
dependency relations, 561
dependent territories, 119
Derrida, Jacques, 539n, 541–42, 543, 544, 561
despotism, 354, 355
　see also dictatorships; illiberal States; non-democratic States
developing countries, 5, 70, 228, 519, 539
Dicey, Albert Venn, 93–94
dictatorships, 14, 45, 180, 198, 227, 244–49, 252, 254, 298, 310, 355, 393, 443
　see also anti-democratic forces; illiberal States; non-democratic governments
diplomacy, 148, 268, 270, 553
disaggregation of States, 200, 201, 202, 220, 231, 233
disappearances, 455, 457, 462, 472, 481, 485
dispute settlement, 110, 207–11
disruption of democracy, 281–83ff.
domestic government institutions, 201, 202, 203, 223, 229, 235
　see also government networks
domestic jurisdiction, 1, 6, 13, 46, 51, 65, 87, 88, 100, 182, 240, 243, 281, 284, 291, 293, 330, 506

Index

Dominican Republic, 141, 158, 159, 161, 296, 518
Dow Chemical Co. v. Castro, 210n
Doyle, Michael W., 348, 354n, 551, 553
drug trafficking, 162, 274
due process, 330n
duties, 44, 450, 455, 457, 459, 461–73, 480

ECOMOG, 306, 307, 308, 310, 311
East Timor, 103, 267
Eastern and Central Europe, 21, 38, 205, 211–12, 419–20, 498, 504
Economic Community of West African States (ECOWAS), 253, 261, 288, 289, 290, 294, 326
and Sierra Leone, 304–07, 310, 311, 320
economic development, 20, 153, 154, 192–93, 222, 439, 537
economic sanctions, 80, 123, 141, 147, 148, 149, 153, 167, 169–70, 248, 256–57, 274, 282, 284, 286, 301
Economist, The, 272
Ecuador, 141, 159, 178–80, 181, 182, 188–89, 190, 196, 197
effective control doctrine, 1, 108, 125, 139, 151, 152, 244, 294, 300, 331, 333, 342
and consent to intervention, 297–99, 302, 309, 320
El Salvador, 38, 41, 158, 185, 279, 332, 346, 458, 464, 489, 516
elected governments, restoration of, 3, 146–47, 284–90, 293–94, 299–300, 325, 329
election monitoring, 3, 30, 31, 41–46, 69, 70–89, 219, 226, 245, 260, 280, 530, 547, 549, 564–65
and decolonization, 71–75, 103
in Europe, 38
failures of, 41
Haiti, 78–80, 83, 103
and human rights norms, 85
inter-American, 157, 165
legality of, 43–44
multilateral, 76, 80–84
NGOs, 38
Namibia, 73–75, 80, 83, 103
Nicaragua, 76–78, 80, 83, 103
opposition to, 43, 45, 47
parameters of, 40, 41
post-colonial, 75–80
pre-1945, 70–71
refusal of, 40–41
and regional organizations, 38
and treaty norms, 85–89
UN role in, 32, 33, 35–37, 39–41, 70, 71–84, 86, 103, 104, 143, 346

elections, 4, 11, 27, 28, 51–52, 88, 99, 100, 164, 166, 175, 240, 260, 344, 356, 366n, 401, 494, 503, 508, 513, 518, 520, 527–28, 548
abuse of, 65, 66, 244
annullment of, 150, 466
anti-democratic forces in, 180–81, 393, 395–99, 442–43, 445, 446, 447, 448
candidates, 59
criteria for, 84
and democracy, 49–50, 92, 102, 335–37, 517, 529, 564–65
in European Convention, 60–63
fraud, 65, 66, 85, 105, 157, 171, 521
free and fair elections, 83, 84, 89, 183, 184, 223, 242, 254, 397, 425, 511, 530
see also election monitoring; elections
and human rights, 6–7, 70, 546
international standards, 219, 445–46
and liberalism, 558–59
norms, 396–97, 445
observation of, 30, 31, 35, 38, 41, 86, 104; *see also* election monitoring
and one-party States, 56–59, 427
periodic, 57, 69, 445
restrictions, 425, 428, 445
validation of, 30, 31
see also election monitoring; electoral assistance; free and fair elections; right to vote
electoral assistance, 5–6, 30, 31, 39, 80–82, 84, 219
electoral education, 84
electoral systems, 219, 407
electors, will of, 57
see also popular will
elites, 192, 320, 322, 337, 377, 382, 494, 502, 503, 505, 510, 520
liberal, 357–59, 361ff., 501
Elster, Jon, 379–80
Emancipation Proclamation, 369–71, 378
"end of history," 493, 517, 535–38, 542–43, 554, 557, 566
Endara, President Guillermo, 275–79, 293, 302n
enforcement, 10, 46–47, 165, 272, 547, 549, 552–53
see also external use of force; multilateral intervention; pro-democratic intervention; unilateral intervention
England *see* Great Britain
English courts, 209, 210–11
environmental protection, 8, 20, 31, 162, 214, 228, 541
equality, 165, 225, 497, 498, 500, 501, 503–04, 533, 538

Equatorial Guinea, 32, 73
erga omnes obligations, 278
Eritrea, 35, 37, 40
Espionage Act (1917), 409n, 410n
Esquipulas II agreement, 35, 76
Estonia, 130, 482
Estrada Cabrera, Manuel, 188
Estrada Doctrine (1930), 142
Ethiopia, 35, 468
ethnic conflict, 112, 316, 336, 339, 560
Europe, 52n, 70, 140, 211
European Commission, 215
European Commission for Democracy through Law, 398n
European Commission on Human Rights, 2, 59, 61, 63, 64, 85, 105, 423, 428
  see also European Convention on Human Rights
European Community *see* European Union
European Convention on Human Rights, 9n, 42, 97, 422
  Article 3, 119, 120
  Article 11, 62
  Article 14, 63–64
  Article 17, 423n, 424, 428
  Article 56(3), 119
  election rights, 60–63
  First Protocol, 59–63, 92, 104, 118, 119
European Court of Human Rights, 42, 59, 61–62, 63, 64, 85, 93n, 104–05, 205, 207, 397n
  and anti-democratic parties, 422, 423–24, 426, 429, 430
  and justiciability problem, 118–20
  and restrictions, 427
European Court of Justice (ECJ), 205, 206, 207–08, 211
European Parliament, 60, 118–20
European Union (EU), 6, 9, 42, 118–20, 173, 198, 199, 208, 304, 305, 346, 398n, 518
  democratization in, 112
  and former Soviet Union, 131–32
  and former Yugoslavia, 133–38
  and government networks, 220, 234
  and non-intervention, 247
  and State recognition, 133
  see also Maastricht Treaty
  executive, 95, 96, 193, 195, 201, 223, 224
  and government networks, 218–20
Eyre Crowe memorandum (1907), 380

fairness, 83, 84, 86, 90
Farer, Tom, 321, 323–24, 325n, 335n
fascist parties, 390, 393, 418–19, 422, 423
  see also Nazi party

Federalists, 364, 365
Fiji, 107
financial regulation, transgovernmental, 200, 202, 215–16, 231
Finland, 419
Forced Labour Convention (1930), 457
foreign law, 206–11
foreign policy, 111, 140–41, 143, 145, 161, 181, 201, 211, 218, 219, 225, 234
  and "democratic peace," 344, 351, 353–57
  liberal elites and, 357–59
former Soviet Union, 131, 132, 205, 212
former Yugoslavia, 128n, 132–39, 455, 458
forum non conveniens dismissals, 209, 210n
Foucault, Michel, 544–45
Fox, Gregory H., 16, 18, 19, 441, 442–43, 548, 549, 552, 558, 564
France, 280, 295, 300, 354, 383, 428
  relations with America, 362–65, 366, 367, 378
  substantive democracy in, 411–12, 416
Franck, Thomas M., 4, 16, 89–90, 110, 123, 151–52, 256, 280, 293, 328n, 471, 479, 545, 546–48, 549, 552, 555–56, 558, 561, 563, 564, 565
freedom, 352, 353, 381, 383, 499
freedom of assembly, 25, 33, 84, 548
freedom of association, 59, 62, 408, 410, 411, 414, 421, 425, 426, 458
freedom of the press, 25, 166, 183
freedom of religion, 25
freedom of speech, 10, 25, 33, 34, 59, 95, 102, 184, 356, 401n, 408, 410, 423, 548
freedom of thought, 34, 548
Frei, President Eduardo, 521, 523
French courts, 210
French Revolution, 140, 240, 363
French Togoland, 73
Friendly Relations Declaration, 94n
Fujimori, President Alberto, 150, 160, 167, 168, 171–72, 187
Fukuyama, Francis, 534–38, 539, 542, 544, 545, 554, 557, 561–62, 563

Gabcikovo-Nagymaros case, 270n
Gambia, 31, 67, 246–47, 248
General Treaty of Peace and Amity (1923), 185–86
Geneva Conventions, 452, 454, 456 Protocol II, 463–64
genocide, 115, 457, 485
Genocide Convention (1948), 128n, 454, 456, 457, 458, 472, 481
Georgia, 326
German Communist party, 416, 423

Index 573

German Constitutional Court, 205, 206, 207
Germany, 247, 354, 359, 373, 376, 380, 383, 392–93, 395, 399, 429–30, 453, 489
　Basic Law, 404, 405, 415, 417, 419; see also *Grundgesetz*
　militant substantive democracy in, 403–05, 415–17
　restrictions on anti-democratic parties, 416–17, 425, 428
Gershman, Carl, 498, 505
Ghana, 31
Gibraltar, 118–20
Gladstone, William, 370, 371
global networks, 200, 201
　see also government networks; transgovernmentalism
globalization, 222, 234, 530, 531, 533, 541, 560
governance, global, 200, 203, 232, 235
　see also government networks; transgovernmentalism
government, 200, 232, 535, 537
government networks, 200, 202, 203, 204–20
　and accountability, 231–34
　and democratization, 226–31
　national regulators, 214–15
　see also judicial networks; parliaments; transnational regulatory cooperation
government/opposition relationship, 436–37
governments, 29, 88
　accountability of, 451–59ff., 476–77
　authority of, 10, 11, 26, 92, 97, 299, 302, 313–14, 342
　balance of power in, 194–96, 201
　consent to intervention, 297–98, 329
　and lack of democracy, 95–98
　limits of, 93
　new, 142, 476, 486, 487; see also transitional States
　recognition of, 118, 123, 124, 139–51
　strengthening of, 227–29
　validation of, 41–6
　see also elected governments, restoration of; military governments; non-democratic governments; successor governments
Great Britain, 52n, 63–64, 73, 94, 96, 118–20, 144, 247, 279, 288, 295, 378, 379, 380
　American perceptions of, 354n, 355, 362–76
　and Cyprus, 316–18
　relations with USA, 365–76
　and Tanganyika, 246, 300
　tolerant procedural democracy in, 406–07
Greece, 105, 135, 316, 339, 419, 468, 518
Grenada, 106, 158, 255n, 261, 267, 271–74, 275, 292, 296

Grundgesetz, 404, 405, 415, 417 see also Germany, Basic Law
Guarantee Clause, 184, 185
Guatemala, 37, 158, 159, 160, 180, 181, 185, 188, 190, 195, 196, 197, 279, 332, 420, 458
　amnesties, 464, 468, 470
　autogolpe, 172–75
Gulf Oil Corp. v. Gilbert, 210n
Guyana, 31

Haiti, 3, 9, 19, 31, 38, 109, 141, 158, 159, 242n, 253, 282, 292, 327, 382, 496, 521n
　amnesties, 464, 468
　collective intervention in, 47, 117, 123, 181, 182, 248, 252, 261, 284–88, 294, 347
　consent to intervention, 301–03, 308–09, 326
　constitution, 190–91, 194–96, 197
　coup in, 168–71, 248, 284, 293, 294, 301
　elections, 171, 443
　Governors Island Agreement, 285–86, 287
　human rights abuses, 230
　intra-State agreements, 320, 321, 322
　UN election monitors in, 36–37, 43, 78–80, 83, 103, 346
Halperin, Morton, 184
Harcourt, W. V., 107
Heads of State, 38, 218
Hegel, Georg Wilhelm Friedrich, 535
Held, David, 540, 541, 543, 544
Helms–Burton Act, 145
Helsinki Accords, 68, 131
hierarchy, 20–21, 200, 226, 427, 510
history, 535, 536, 538–39, 542, 543, 544–45, 554, 557, 566
Hitler, Adolf, 392–93, 399, 404, 405, 429–30
Hobbes, Thomas, 239, 352
Holy Alliance, 331–32, 333, 334
Honduras, 185, 279, 332, 464
Hong Kong, 144, 211
horizontal relationships, 220, 221
House of Lords, 205, 211
human rights, 1, 2, 10, 20, 27, 41, 69, 115, 193, 247, 483
　and democracy, 3, 7, 49, 111, 116
　and elections, 6–7
　linkage, 47, 85
　and non-intervention, 156–57
　norms, 250–51, 254, 257
　and sovereignty, 243, 246, 250, 258
　violations, 65, 148, 157, 158, 172, 175, 230, 255, 277, 291, 328, 397, 449, 457, 459, 463, 464, 468, 474, 488, 489, 522, 523–24
Human Rights Committee, 2, 34, 42, 44, 94, 105, 397n, 422, 423, 426, 427, 430

Human Rights Committee (cont.)
 and accountability, 462, 466, 467, 471, 477, 489
 and political rights, 54n, 55, 56–59, 60, 85
 human rights law, 111, 391, 397–98, 448, 450, 546
 accountability, 485
 anti-democratic forces, 420–22
 see also human rights treaties
human rights treaties, 10, 25, 46, 48, 92, 102, 281, 421–33, 445–46, 447
 abuse clauses, 422–24, 428
 limitations in, 93
 mission standards, 85–87
 "reasonableness" and "necessity," standards for limitation, 424–28, 435
 substantive democracy, 421–22, 434
humanitarian intervention, 255, 264, 273, 284
Hungary, 108, 130n, 205, 267, 270n, 296, 468
Huntington, Samuel, 202, 543
Hurtado, President Osvaldo, 180, 193–94

IFOR, 319, 320
idealism, 555, 556
ideational theory, 380
ideological competition, 536–37, 542, 543
ideological legitimism, 442, 443, 446
Ikenberry, John, 201, 225, 226
illiberal States, 344, 351, 354, 356, 360–61ff., 379, 381, 382–83, 553, 557, 560, 563
illiberal democracies, 224, 227, 359
 see also non-democratic States
imperialism, 45, 439, 447, 563, 564
impunity, 461, 470, 475, 480, 483, 486–487, 523
 see also amnesties
Independent Elections Commission, 82, 84
India, 127, 202, 205, 414–15, 430
indigenous peoples, rights of, 8, 11
individual liberty, 223
individual rights, 10, 60, 93–94, 192, 227, 428, 438, 540
individuals, 34, 51, 92, 111, 344, 352, 356, 507
 accountability of, 453, 456–58, 472
 protection of, 184, 453–55
 violations against, 451–52
Indonesia, 117, 267
inequalities, 162, 165, 166, 270, 500, 504, 510, 511, 525, 526, 531, 542, 543, 561, 562
information, 14, 219, 224, 228, 229
information technology, 200, 217, 241–42, 537, 541
Ingersoll Milling Machine Co. v. Granger, 209, 210
injury to aliens, law of, 452
instability, 254
insurance supervision, 214, 216

Inter-American Commission on Human Rights, 2, 105, 157, 159, 165, 167–68, 197, 198, 397, 420
 inductive approach, 185
 and political rights, 65–66, 67, 88n
 treaty interpretation, 467, 481
 see also Organization of American States
Inter-American Court of Human Rights, 157, 187, 463, 466, 471
inter-governmental organizations, 2–3, 4, 9, 198
 and state recognition, 127–28
 see also international organizations
internal armed conflict, 7–8
 see also civil wars
Internal Security Act (1950), 410
international aid, 170, 247
International Association of Insurance Supervisors, 216
International Committee of the Red Cross, 453, 464
international community, 28, 31, 42, 46, 90
 collective action by, 47
 and consent to intervention, 300
 and non-democratic States, 129–30
 and Sierra Leone, 304–05, 311
 and unilateral intervention, 279–80
International Court of Justice, 33, 43–45, 87, 99–100, 105, 107, 110, 128n, 251, 266n, 270n, 283, 328n, 337
 and consent to intervention, 298
 and unilateral intervention, 264, 268, 278
International Covenant on Civil and Political Rights (ICCPR), 1, 3, 11, 34–35, 40, 53–59, 88, 90, 97, 100, 102, 126, 462, 465, 466, 485, 518
 Article 1, 94, 95, 105
 Article 2, 54
 Article 5, 422, 423, 424, 427, 428–30
 Article 5(1), 421, 423
 Article 18, 34
 Article 19, 425
 Article 19(2), 34
 Article 20, 429n
 Article 22, 34, 425
 Article 22(2), 421
 Article 25, 10, 42, 44, 53, 54, 55, 57, 58, 59, 64, 92, 94, 95, 105, 115, 116, 397n, 422n, 425, 426, 447
 Article 26, 117
 Optional Protocol, 426, 430
 restrictions on political rights, 421, 422–23
 see also Human Rights Committee
"international crimes," 278n
international criminal trials, 111, 455

Index

international humanitarian law, 453–54
international law, 4, 21–22, 109–10, 113, 565, 566
  and accountability, 451–59, 461–73
  and anti-democratic parties, 421–33
  and democratic principle, 95–102
  democratization and, 5–10
  and domestic jurisdiction, 1, 6
  and emerging norm, 43–45, 48
  and "liberal millenarianism," 553–66
  and "liberal peace," 549–53
  nationalization of, 217–18
  and new States, 124, 125ff.
  pre-1945, 70–71, 98
  pro-democratic changes in, 100–02ff.
  and sovereignty, 87, 90, 239–45, 250
  and transgovernmentalism, 201–02
  undemocratic nature of, 95–99, 115
  uniformity in, 86
  Western bias of, 437–40
  see also customary international law
International Law Commission, 295, 454, 455
international lawyers, subjectivity of, 437–40
International Monetary Fund, 527
International Organization of Securities Commissioners (IOSCO), 216, 220, 229
international organizations, 199, 202, 219, 225, 397, 549, 565
  and accountability, 469, 470, 471, 473, 476, 479
  and democratization, 5–10, 112
  and domestic issues, 2, 3
  election monitoring, 103
  and electoral norms, 86
  and government networks, 220
  and intervention, 108
  and liberalism, 344–46, 381–85
  and non-democratic states, 129
  recognition of governments, 142
  State recognition, 128, 129
  and transgovernmental regulators, 215–17
international peace and security, threat to, 281–83ff., 292
international tribunals, 85, 209, 213
Internet, 212, 219
Interparliamentary Union, 219
inter-State pro-democratic agreements, 323–26
intervention *see* invitation to intervention; multilateral intervention; pro-democratic intervention; unilateral intervention
intimidation, 65, 66
intra-State agreements, 320–23
invasion pacts
  consociational, 338–41
  illegality of, 329–34

pro-democratic, 334–38
  see also multilateral intervention
invitation to intervention, 263n, 267, 276, 277, 295–311, 328–29
  effective control standard, 297–99
  limits to consent, 296–97, 312
  from ousted regimes, 299–311, 325
  Haiti, 301–03, 308–09
  and power-sharing agreements, 316–20
  risks of, 326–27
  Sierra Leone, 303–11
  treaty-based, 311–26
  withdrawal of consent, 315–16, 323, 324–25
Iran, 127, 360, 442
Iraq, 127, 151, 265, 266, 267, 288
Islam, 542
Islamic Salvation Front (FIS), 391, 393–94, 431
Israel, 267, 417–18, 425, 428
Italy, 418, 423

Jackson, Justice Robert, 431–32
Jameson, Frederic, 539n
Japan, 173, 202, 221, 383, 408–09
Jay Treaty (1796), 362, 364
Jefferson, President Thomas, 28, 95, 140, 366, 367, 389
Jennings, Sir Robert, 113
Jonah, James, 307–08
judges, 204–13, 224
judicial comity, 208–09, 210
judicial decisions, cross-fertilization of, 204–07
judicial independence, 166, 184, 224, 227, 229
judicial networks, 204–14, 221
judicial organizations, 211–13
judicial review, 207, 415, 430, 508
jus cogens, 270, 278, 313, 317, 329, 334, 337, 339
justiciability problem, 118–20

Kabbah, President Ahmad Tejan, 252, 253, 294, 303–11, 320, 383
Kabila, President Laurent, 146
Kach party, 418
Kaldor, Mary, 560–61, 562
Kant, Immanuel, 226, 348, 352, 385, 481, 550, 551, 552, 553, 555
Karadzic, Radovan, 479, 480
Kazakhstan, 131
Kelsen, Hans, 405
Kenya, 145
Keohane, Robert O., 221
Koskenniemi, Martti, 18, 446, 447, 448, 562, 563
Kosovo, 132, 265, 288
Kurds, 62–63, 127, 285, 429
Kuwait, 98, 151, 244

Laker Airways v. Sabena, 224n
Latin America, 38, 141, 158, 159–60, 221, 373, 498, 504
  constitutional crises, 175–80
  economic development, 192–93
  economic inequalities, 525–26, 531
  electoral democracy, 526–28, 529
  fragmentation in, 522
  redemocratization, 520–22, 523
  violence in, 522–25
  see also Central America; Organization of American States
Latvia, 38, 130
Lauterpacht, Sir Hersch, 111, 260, 275, 277
law, global community of, 213–14
law enforcement, and regulatory cooperation, 214–15
law schools, 212
Lebanon, 296
legal associations, 212
legal rules, 21, 28, 29, 31, 32, 44, 110, 111, 266, 270, 274
  and accountability, 456–59
  compliance with, 151–52
legislative comity, 208, 209
legislature, 60, 195, 196, 201, 223, 224
  transgovernmental, 218–20
legitimacy, democratic, 19, 26, 29–31, 40, 50, 69, 89, 90, 108–09, 126, 138, 139, 234, 502, 507–08, 565–66
  and consent to intervention, 299–311
  and liberalism, 551–52
  and recognition, 152, 153, 154
  and State practice, 117, 118
Lesotho, 40
liability norms, 456–59
liberal democracy, 10–11, 14, 15, 341, 474, 498, 503, 555
  borrowing of, 227, 229–31
  and "democratic peace," 343–45, 381
  and elections, 558–59
  expansion of, 235
  norms, 225, 226
  opposition to, 541, 542, 548
  and peace, 549–53, 560, 561
  problems of, 497–541, 558, 559–60, 562
  teleology of, 499, 539
  transgovernmentalism, 201–04, 220–26, 235
  triumph of, 535, 536–38
  see also "democratic peace"; liberalism; transgovernmentalism
liberal internationalism, 199, 202, 203, 226, 232, 235, 439, 532, 533, 534, 552, 555
  see also liberal democracy; "liberal millenarianism"; liberalism; transgovernmentalism

"liberal millenarianism," 21, 534, 538–45, 553–64, 565
liberal peace *see* "democratic peace"
liberal States, 343, 359–60ff., 384, 557, 560
  see also "democratic peace"; liberal democracy; liberalism
liberalism, 222–23, 351–53, 381, 441, 497, 539, 549
  and democracy, 359–60, 501–02, 533, 534, 535, 540, 543
  economic, 346
  effects of, 382–84
  elites, 357–59, 361ff., 377, 501
  and foreign policy, 353–57
  institutions, 344, 350, 351, 356–60
  and peace, 344–46, 351–53
  and realism, 376–81
  and state sovereignty, 384–85
  UN and, 346–48
  see also "democratic peace"; liberal democracy
liberalization, 382–85
Liberia, 7n, 31, 81–82, 117, 149–50, 289, 308, 314, 347, 382
Lijphart, Arend, 336
Lincoln, Abraham, 368, 369, 370
lis alibi pendens motions, 209
Lithuania, 130, 250, 419
Locke, John, 28, 29, 352, 499, 507, 509
Lockerbie case, 283
Lomasney, Kristen, 184
lower classes, 514

MERCOSUR, 9, 162, 175, 176, 177, 182, 198
Maastricht Treaty, 9n, 42, 96, 112, 118
Macedonia, 132, 133, 134, 135, 136, 138
Macey, Jonathan, 540
Madagascar, 31
Madison, President James, 28, 365, 367
Maine, Sir Henry, 113
majoritarianism, 92, 93–94, 114, 192, 335, 336, 395, 397, 398, 401, 432, 507–08, 511
Malamud-Goti, Jaime, 477, 478
Malawi, 30, 67n
Mali, 31
"margin of appreciation," 115, 119–20, 426
market economy, 220, 222, 499, 504, 505, 525, 529, 539, 540
Marks, Susan, 18, 21
Marx, Karl, 535, 536, 544
Mathieu-Mohin and Clerfayt case, 119, 120
Matthews, Jessica, 199–200
Matthews v. United Kingdom, 118, 119
media, equal access to, 82, 84, 89
Memorandum of Understanding (MOU), 214–15, 228

mental incapacity, 188, 189
Mexico, 30, 31, 35, 43, 65, 88n, 105, 141, 157, 228
Middle East, 143, 358
militant procedural democracy, 409–11
militant substantive democracy, 415–20
military coups, 3, 9, 67, 107, 141, 246–48, 293–94, 300, 321, 442, 477
  Haiti, 79–80, 123, 146, 168–71, 252, 284, 293, 301
  OAS and, 79, 80, 156, 159–60, 166–67, 168, 180, 183, 185, 186, 190, 191
  and popular will, 325, 335n
  Sierra Leone, 288–90, 303–05
  see also autogolpes
military forces, 174, 175, 180, 190, 191, 192, 246, 523, 524
military governments, 67, 97, 117, 118, 181, 460, 461
Mill, John Stuart, 45, 383, 384
Miller, Geoffrey, 540
minorities, 92, 93, 111, 114, 129–30, 132ff., 336, 340, 395, 403, 429, 511
mission standards, 85–87
"modified skepticism," 114
monarchy, 140, 184, 350, 355, 368, 507
Montenegro, 132, 137, 138, 151
Montesquieu, Baron de, 28, 500
Montevideo Convention on the Rights and Duties of States (1933), 333–34
moral principle, 111, 497, 498, 500, 505, 508, 558
Moscow Document (1991), 46, 69, 146–47
Mozambique, 37, 83, 461
multilateral intervention, 46–47, 98, 108, 123, 252–53, 261, 281–290
  consent to by treaty, 294, 311–26
  threat to peace and security, 281–83, 292
  see also collective enforcement; external use of force; invasion pacts; invitation to intervention
Museveni, Yoweri, 336
Mutual Defense Pacts, 311, 326
Mutual Legal Assistance Treaties (MLATs), 214
Myanmar, 40, 47, 117, 118, 150, 242n

NATO, 219, 221, 225, 265
Nagorno-Karabakh, 132
Namibia, 32–33, 41, 86, 103, 242n, 243n
  UN mission, 73–75, 80, 83
national courts, 142, 205, 207–11, 213–14, 251
National Democratic Institute for International Affairs, 38, 86n
national electoral bodies, 81–82, 84

national law, 96
  and transnational cooperation, 217–18, 219
national regulators, 214–15, 222, 228, 229
nationalism, 541, 560
nationals in danger, 267, 273, 274
Nauru case, 110
Nazi party, 390–91, 392–93, 395, 399, 404–05, 415, 429–30, 431, 453, 475
"necessity standard," 424–28
Nedelsky, Jennifer, 192, 196
neo-colonialism *see* imperialism
neo-realism, 353, 380
Nepal, 231
Netherlands, 52n
networks *see* government networks; judicial networks; transgovernmentalism; transnational regulatory cooperation
New Haven School, 471
"new medievalism," 199, 202, 203, 232, 233, 235
new world order, 199, 202, 235
  see also liberal democracy; transgovernmentalism
Nicaragua, 2, 38, 41, 43–44, 105, 158, 185, 332
  amnesties, 464
  human rights abuses, 230
  and sovereignty, 87
  UN election monitoring, 35–36, 75, 76–78, 80, 83, 103
  US role in, 99–100, 107
Nicaragua case, 265n, 270n, 280, 298, 337
Niger, 146
Nigeria, 4, 68, 117, 126, 148–49, 289, 290, 294, 304, 307–08, 310–11, 327, 383
Nino, Carlos, 477–78, 481
Nobel peace prize, 345–46
Nolte, Georg, 18, 19, 441, 442–43, 548–49, 558
non-democratic governments, 21, 22, 40, 47, 65, 67–8, 354, 532, 537
  and emerging democratic norm, 43, 45
  and government networks, 224
  in international law, 52–53
  lack of accountability, 478
  measures against, 12–13, 117
  and mutual defense pacts, 326
  non-recognition of, 9, 108–09
  and popular will, 14, 335n, 443, 496, 508–09
  recognition of, 139–51, 153
  and sovereignty, 89, 245–50
  and State practice, 117–18
  and successor regimes, 97–98
  see also anti-democratic forces; dictatorships; illiberal democracies

non-democratic States, 459, 460, 469, 475, 519–20, 552, 563
  liberal view of, 354
  non-recognition of, 128–30
  recognition of, 128, 129
  rights of, 269–70
  and sovereignty, 244–45
  and transgovernmentalism, 231
  see also illiberal States
non-discrimination, 53, 54, 63–64, 69
non-governmental organizations (NGOs), 86, 112, 198, 473, 476, 477, 479
  and election monitorng, 38, 41, 103, 219
  and government networks, 230, 233
  and liberal democratic order, 202, 203
non-intervention, 5, 45, 46, 97, 100, 115, 125, 246–47, 334, 338, 384, 443, 506
  and consent to intervention, 298, 313
  in inter-American system, 155, 156, 158, 160
  and right of unilateral action, 267, 269
non-liberal States *see* illiberal States
non-peremptory rules, 270
non-recognition, 9, 20, 108–09, 126, 128–29, 146–54, 243, 332
  emerging norm of, 146, 147, 151, 153
  see also recognition
non-State actors, 200, 203, 232
  see also non-governmental organizations
Noriega, General Manuel Antonio, 250, 251, 269, 274, 293
norms, 8, 11, 20, 21, 26, 31, 115, 124, 146, 147, 151, 153, 187, 202, 225, 313, 328, 338, 447, 449–50, 545
  of accountability, 450–51, 456–59, 470–84, 486–87
  and anti-democratic forces, 434–35, 448
  and democratic theory, 405–06
  human rights, 250–51, 254, 257
  and liberal peace, 349–51, 382, 550
  and structure, 349, 377
  see also democratic norm
North Korea, 40, 359
North Sea Continental Shelf cases, 266n
nuclear weapons, 282
nullum crimen sine lege, 483
Nuremberg trials, 452, 453–54
Nye, Joseph S., 221, 349
Nyerere, President Julius, 56, 246, 300

ONUVEH, 36–37, 43, 79
  see also Haiti
ONUVEN, 35–36, 76–78
  see also Nicaragua
Oakes case, 413
O'Connor, Sandra Day, 206, 207

Office of Fair Elections, 104
Olney, Richard, 371–72, 373, 375
one-party system, 56–59, 427, 496, 508, 509
opinio juris, 13, 48, 247, 266, 267, 274, 290, 469
Oppenheim, Lassa, 95, 97, 295
opposition, 436–37, 438, 445, 447, 448, 503, 511, 541
  see also anti-democratic forces; non-democratic governments
"ordinary meaning," 85–86
Organization for Security and Cooperation in Europe (OSCE), 2, 38, 68–69, 219, 346
  and constitutional fidelity, 186–87
  and electoral assistance, 6
  Office for Free Elections, 68–69, 104
  see also Conference on Security and Cooperation in Europe; Copenhagen Document; Moscow Document; Paris Charter
Organization of African Unity (OAU), 149, 252, 304, 305
Organization of American States (OAS), 2, 4, 6, 9, 46, 79, 80, 99, 100, 106, 196, 323, 337, 457, 547
  Charter, 155, 156, 157, 163
  and constitutional design, 166, 181, 182, 183–92
  Declaration of Asuncion, 167
  Declaration of Nassau, 167
  Declaration of Santiago, 156, 183–84
  election monitoring, 38, 40, 76
  General Assembly, 156, 157, 162, 163
  and Guatemala, 174, 187, 195
  and Haiti, 169–71, 248, 284, 285, 301
  and human rights, 156–57, 162
  and non-democratic States, 129
  and non-intervention, 155, 156–57, 160
  and Panama, 278–79, 293
  and Paraguay, 176
  Permanent Council, 157, 278
  and Peru, 172, 181, 184, 187
  Resolution on Representative Democracy, 104, 162–63, 164, 166
  support for democracy, 159–60, 162, 183–84ff.
  Unit for the Promotion of Democracy (UPD), 157
  United States and, 158, 159, 161, 186
  weakness of, 155, 157, 158, 160, 166, 181, 183
  see also Protocol of Washington; Santiago Commitment
Organization of Eastern Caribbean States (OECS), 272
Organization of Economic Cooperation and Development (OECD), 220, 222

Index

Organization of the Supreme Courts of the Americas (OCSA), 212–13, 221, 229
organizations, right to join, 59
Oviedo, General Lino, 175–78, 182, 183, 189–90

pacta sunt servanda, 266
Pakistan, 116
Palmerston, Lord, 370–71, 378
Panama, 38, 46, 106, 158, 194, 251, 255n, 261, 263, 265, 267, 268–69, 274–79, 292, 293, 298
  consent to intervention, 302n
  democratic elections, 279n
  sovereignty of, 250, 253
Panama Canal Treaty, 274
Paraguay, 38, 146, 159, 175–78, 180, 181, 182, 198
  constitution, 183, 189–90
  human rights abuses, 230
Paris Charter (1990), 40, 42, 46, 47, 68–69, 104, 131
Parliamentarians for Global Action, 219
parliaments, 38, 96, 185, 191, 195, 201, 406–07
  and government networks, 218–20
participation, 11, 166, 192–96
  see also political participation, right to
Pascal Trouillot, President Ertha, 78, 79
peace, 8, 22, 25, 36, 115, 153, 201, 226, 269, 343–46, 438, 447, 550
  and election monitoring, 43, 80
  and liberalism, 351–53, 560, 561
  threat to, 281–83
  see also "democratic peace"
people, the, 14, 26, 291, 292
  see also popular sovereignty; will of the people
perceptions, 350, 354–56, 360–61ff.
  see also American public opinion
peremptory rules, 270, 312, 313, 338
Perón, Isabel, 189
Peronists, 521, 527
Peru, 38, 150, 160, 167–68, 171–72, 184, 193, 194, 197, 198, 464, 477
petition, rights of, 96–97, 430
Philippines, 230, 250, 255n, 398
Pinochet, General Augusto, 489, 522, 523, 524
plebiscites, 35, 70, 71, 72, 85, 103, 278
pluralism, 7, 55–56, 66, 77, 82–83, 93, 94, 225, 400
Poland, 398, 419, 475
political community, rights of, 331, 340
political participation, right to, 1, 2, 10, 25–26, 27, 34, 70, 92, 114, 165, 185
  and accountability, 488
  and constitutional design, 192–96
  and elections, 60–63, 70–89
  in Europe, 59–63
  indeterminacy of, 90
  and non-discrimination, 63–64
  opponents of, 88, 89
  pre-1948, 50–53
  restrictions, 425–28
  sources of, 48, 90
  and sovereignty, 87–89
  treaty-based, 53–69, 85–89
  uniformity of, 86
  see also democratic entitlement
political parties, 55–59, 61, 62–64, 74, 77, 82–83, 84, 89, 112, 337
  anti-democratic, 395–99, 402, 422ff.
  restrictions on, 407, 410, 413, 414, 416, 418, 419, 422–35, 445
political progress, 497, 512, 515–16
political rights, 53, 61–62, 114, 116, 118, 220, 425
  limits to restrictions on, 422–30
  see also political participation, right to
political theory, 6, 14–15
politics, 14, 18–22, 336, 564
  see also political rights; political participation, right to
polyarchy, 494, 495–97, 504, 511, 514, 515
popular sovereignty, 10, 13–14, 49, 72, 90, 240–43, 262, 291, 332, 333, 342, 441, 494, 495, 505–12, 515, 516
  and anti-democratic forces, 395, 396
  difficulties of, 254–57
  and non-democratic regimes, 508–09
  and unilateral intervention, 268–70
  violation of, 243–45, 249–50, 257, 258
popular will *see* will of the people
Portugal, 141, 419, 518
positive comity, 215
poverty, 162, 164–65, 524
power, 199–200, 201, 232, 330, 351, 354, 376, 378, 499, 512, 519–20, 527, 545
power-sharing agreements, 316–20
presidential system, 185, 201
Printz v. United States, 206
prior regimes, accountability for, 450, 451, 455, 460–61, 463, 468, 474–75, 476–77, 478, 480, 488
  see also successor governments
private sector, 519, 526, 528, 529
privatization, 173, 192, 193, 195, 525–26, 528
procedural democracy, 15, 16, 49, 112, 389, 400–01, 403, 404, 405, 406–11, 422, 430, 433, 437, 438, 439, 440, 442, 446, 494, 513, 514
  see also polyarchy

pro-democratic intervention, 9, 13, 46, 153,
    245–49, 383, 385
  approval of, 300
  collective, 46–47, 98, 108, 123, 252–53, 261,
    281–90, 327
  inter-State agreements, 323–26
  intra-State agreements, 320–23
  legality of, 249, 263–68, 270, 279–81,
    287–88, 290–92, 294–95
  problems of, 254–58, 291–92
  retrospective authorization of, 277–78, 289,
    290
  and sovereignty, 268–70
  treaty-based, 311–26, 329–38
  unilateral, 46–47, 106–07, 115, 251, 255–57,
    260, 261–81, 327
  see also invasion pacts; invitation to
    intervention
professionalism, 224, 227, 228
progress, 515–16, 543, 544, 554, 556, 561
  see also political progress
proportional representation, 62, 64
proportionality, 426
prosecution, duty of, 472
protection against arbitrary action, 184
Protocol of Cartagena de Indias (1985), 156
  see also Organization of American States
Protocol of Washington, 163–64, 166, 167
  see also Organization of American States;
    Santiago Commitment
public affairs, right to participate in, 53, 54–55
  see also political participation, right to
public opinion, 350, 354–55, 377
  see also American public opinion
public sector, 519, 525, 526, 529
Pulitzer, Joseph, 372, 373, 374

racial discrimination, 1, 24n, 418, 422
rationality, 535, 537, 543
Rawls, John, 389, 402–03, 420, 443
Reagan Doctrine, 106, 442
realism, 351, 353n, 376–81, 551, 555
"reasonableness" standard, 424–28, 435
recognition, 242–43, 331
  and democratic legitimacy, 152, 153–54
  of governments, 118, 123, 124, 139–51
  inconsistencies in, 138
  of non-democratic States, 128–29, 153
  and past practice, 125–28, 139–42
  and rule compliance, 151–52
  of States, 123–39
reconciliation, 476–77, 482, 487
referenda, 1, 70, 126, 129n, 132, 136, 153, 172,
    174, 180

refugees, 169, 284, 285, 287, 347
regional balances of power, 383
regional organizations, 38, 64–69, 86, 108, 112,
    161, 219, 549, 565
regulatory cooperation, transnational, 214–18,
    230
Reisman, W. Michael, 11, 17, 39, 90, 154n,
    261–62, 263, 268–70, 275, 287, 292
remedies, 96–97, 465
removal from office, 188–89
representation principle, 109
representative democracy, 156, 162, 165,
    183–84, 193, 397n, 508
republicanism, 140, 185, 332, 350, 353, 355,
    362–68, 378, 385, 409, 412, 509, 550, 551
revolution, 273, 432–33, 440, 502, 542, 563
Richardson, Elliot, 36, 39
right of resistance, 404, 432
right to democratic governance see democratic
    entitlement
  see also democratic norm
right to free elections, 53, 55–59, 425, 427,
    546–47, 548, 555
right to vote, 11, 55, 59, 66, 92, 95, 184, 442,
    546
rights, 25–26, 46, 93–94, 114, 115, 116, 255–56,
    269, 401–02, 425, 540, 548, 549, 558
  see also civil rights; human rights; political
    rights
Ríos Montt, Efraín, 174–75, 185
Risse-Kappen, Thomas, 221, 225
Romania, 40, 130n, 250, 419, 468
Rome Statute of the International Criminal
    Court (1998), 455
Root, Elihu, 21–22
Roth, Brad, 17, 18, 289, 446–47, 448
Rousseau, Jean-Jacques, 340, 352, 500–01,
    510
rule of law, 28, 166, 183, 184, 193, 194, 220,
    460, 461, 474, 475
Russell, Lord John, 370, 371
Russia, 21, 98, 117, 230, 356, 372, 373, 376, 419,
    496
Rwanda, 73, 285, 455, 468, 478

safe havens, 285
Salisbury, Lord, 372, 374, 375, 376, 378
Sandinistas, 99
Santiago Commitment (1991), 155, 158, 159,
    160, 161, 194, 197–98, 338, 398n
  adoption of, 162–64
  definition of democracy, 164–66
  evaluation of, 180–98
  implementation of, 168–80

and "interruption of democracy," 164, 166–68
limitations of, 180–81
see also Organization of American States; Protocol of Washington
Sao Tome and Principe, 146
Scalia, Justice Antonin, 206, 208
Schachter, Oscar, 262, 264
Schmitt, Carl, 402, 403–05, 441
Schumpeter, Joseph, 400
secession, 126–27, 136
secret ballot, 55, 57, 59, 67, 69, 71, 85, 92, 254
Securities and Exchange Commission (SEC), 228
securities fraud, 202, 211, 214, 216, 217
and global regulation, 230–31
security, 91, 115, 220–21, 281–83
self-defense, 98, 260, 262, 264, 266, 273, 274–75, 307, 338, 436
self-determination, 33, 34, 70, 71–72, 94–95, 116, 126–27, 135, 240, 242n, 506, 507, 546, 547, 555
and pro-democratic intervention, 269, 270, 291, 302, 313, 317, 326, 329, 337, 339–40
self-government, 72, 345, 346, 356, 533
self-help, 262, 265, 266, 267
self-interest, 352, 354, 356
self-protection, 420, 421, 434
Senegal, 30
separation of powers, 184, 201, 220, 223
Serbia, 128n, 132, 133, 134, 137–38, 151, 265, 266
see also former Yugoslavia
Serrano Elias, President Jorge, 172–74, 187–88, 190
Sierra Leone, 3, 9, 117, 149, 242n, 252–53, 261, 282–90, 293, 294
consent to intervention, 303–11, 324, 326, 327
intra-State agreements, 320–21, 322
and liberalization, 382, 383
Slaughter, Anne-Marie, 17, 439, 550–53, 554, 555, 567, 557, 558, 559, 563
slavery, 355n, 360, 369–71, 373, 457, 458
Slavery Convention (1956), 458
Slovenia, 132, 133, 134, 135, 136, 419
Smith Act (1940), 409–10, 433
social contract, 29, 500, 558
social justice, 498, 500, 510
social movements, 541
social reform, 503, 504
social stratification, 504
socialism, 504
Sofaer, Abraham, 275–76, 277

Somalia, 108, 285, 288, 314
South Africa, 19–20, 30, 32–33, 35, 37, 73, 74, 243n, 282, 461, 464
amnesties, 468, 481–82, 483, 487, 489
Supreme Court, 205, 229, 481–82
Southern Rhodesia, 126, 243n, 249–50, 282
see also Zimbabwe
Southern Yemen, 330n
South-West Africa case, 251
sovereign equality principle, 1, 270, 313, 335, 338, 341, 506
sovereignty, 11, 14, 50, 99, 228, 233, 262, 291, 330–31, 340
and "democratic peace," 384–85
human rights and, 243, 246, 258
in international law, 87, 90, 239–45, 250
meanings of, 239–40, 249
and right to political participation, 87–89
and unilateral intervention, 268–70
violations of, 251, 257, 258
see also popular sovereignty
Soviet Union, 46, 69, 98, 130–32, 141, 250, 355, 356, 518, 519
interventions by, 267, 296, 334
see also former Soviet Union
Spain, 52n, 118–20, 126, 282, 350, 355, 418, 475, 480, 518, 524
Spanish-American War, 355, 358
spiritual and economic well-being, 438, 446
stability, 153, 154
State of Madras v. V. G. Row, 414–15
state of public emergency, 186
State practice, 4, 48, 69, 86, 445, 464–67, 468, 472–73
and anti-democratic forces, 420, 423n, 425, 428–30
consent to intervention, 299
and democratic models, 399
inconsistencies in, 115, 117–18
multilateral intervention, 290
and State authority, 314
unilateral intervention, 266, 267, 274
States, 8, 12, 25, 90, 94, 108, 199, 203, 232, 270, 451, 499
accountability of, 459–61, 464–67ff., 472–73
community of, 26, 28, 42, 89
consent to intervention, 295–311
disaggregation of, 200, 220, 231, 233
and economic life, 192–93, 194
electoral assistance to, 39
independence of, 312
inter-State agreements, 323–26
intervention by, 294–97

States (*cont.*)
  intra-State agreements, 320–23
  and liberalism, 353–56ff., 380, 556–57
  merger of, 197
  motivation of, 197
  and national law, 96
  new, 124, 125, 152, 455
  one-party, 56–59, 66
  and participatory rights, 86
  recognition of, 123–39, 151–54
  responsibility, 110, 278, 281, 295, 297n, 452, 456
  sovereignty, 44, 46, 50, 51, 87–89, 99, 259, 313, 330–31, 384–85
  and successor governments, 97–98
  and transgovernmentalism, 232, 235
  unsuitability of democracy to, 145
  will of, 313–16, 320, 324, 340
  withdrawal of consent, 315–16
  see also illiberal States; liberal states; non-democratic States; State practice; transitional States
Statism, 51, 251, 269, 291
Steiner, Henry, 89
structural adjustment programs, 192, 194, 197
structuralism, 349–51, 377, 493, 496
sub-communities, 340, 341
substantive democracy, 112, 401–06, 434–35, 437, 438, 439, 440, 442, 446, 494–95, 497, 512, 513, 516
  in human rights treaties, 421–22, 434
  and liberalism, 498–505
  militant, 415–20
  paradox of, 509–10
  tolerant, 411–20
Subversive Activities Control board, 410, 433
successor governments, 97–98, 115, 142, 277–78
  accountability of, 450, 451, 455, 460–61, 463, 474–75, 476–77
Sudan, 265
summary execution, 459, 470
supranational courts, 205, 213

Taft, Chief Justice William Howard, 9, 142, 244
Taiwan, 143
Tanganyika *see* Tanzania
Tanzania, 106, 205, 245–46, 279, 300
teleology, 14, 495–97, 535, 538–39, 554–56
term limits, 183, 193–94, 198, 508
territorial boundaries, 97, 127, 132
territorial control, 109–10
terrorism, 265

Tesón, Fernando, 269, 286, 292, 439, 550–51, 553, 558, 563, 565
third parties, 109, 280
Third World *see* developing countries
Tinoco case, 9, 97, 110, 142, 244
Tobar Doctrine (1907), 141–42, 332, 333–34
Tokyo Tribunal, Charter of, 453
toleration, 225, 352, 353, 381, 399–409, 411–15, 433, 434, 548
torture, 455, 457, 462, 470, 472, 485, 522, 524
Torture Convention (1984), 457, 481
trade, 12, 20, 145, 162, 192–93, 194, 198, 218, 225, 550, 565
trade unions, 166
transgovernmentalism, 200
  and accountability, 231–34
  advantages of, 234–35
  constraints on, 204
  and liberal democracy, 201–04, 220–26, 235
  and non-democratic states, 224, 227
  regulatory organizations, 215–17
  see also government networks
transitional States, 145, 154, 242, 382, 446, 455, 516, 557
  accountability of, 451, 460–61ff., 473, 480, 482, 486, 487
transnational constitutional law, 183–86, 191
transnational judicial networks *see* judicial networks
transnational regulatory cooperation, 214–18
  see also transgovernmentalism
transparency, 3, 7, 8, 27, 227
treaties, 8n, 9, 96, 185, 297, 457–58
  accountability, 461–67, 471, 472, 481, 484–85
  consent to intervention, 294, 311–26, 329
  election monitoring, 70, 85–89
  inter-communal power-sharing agreements, 316–20
  inter-State agreements, 323–26
  intra-State agreements, 320–23
  law of, 110
  as legal authority for intervention, 312–16
  mutual defense, 311, 326
  national regulators, 214, 215
  prohibition on unilateral action, 260, 261–62, 266, 270
  right to political participation, 50, 53–69, 85–89
  withdrawal of consent, 315–16, 323, 324–25
  see also human rights treaties; invasion pacts

treaty of guarantee *see* invasion pacts
Treaty of Versailles (1919), 70, 453
Treaty of Washington, Additional
  Convention, 241n
Trent affair, 368–69
trials, 461, 477, 478, 479, 487
Tripartite Group, 216
trust territories, 72
truth commissions, 450, 455, 457, 464, 475,
  481, 482, 488, 489
Turkey, 42n, 62–63, 127, 316–18, 339, 424, 426,
  429, 430
"two-level" game, 218

UNOMSIL, 289
UNTAG, 32–33
Uganda, 45, 106, 279
unilateral intervention, 46–47, 106–07, 115,
  251, 255–57, 260, 261–81, 292, 296, 327,
  549, 553, 563
  counterintervention, 308, 309
  see also external use of force; pro-democratic
    intervention
unitary will, 340
United Communist Party of Turkey, 424, 426,
  429, 430
United Kingdom *see* Great Britain
United Nations, 14, 31, 106, 108, 169, 198, 199,
  225, 242, 317, 470, 530, 549
  admission to, 128, 138, 152
  Centre for Human Rights, 83
  Economic and Social Council, 470, 471
  election monitoring, 3, 32, 33, 35–37, 39–41,
    70, 71–84, 103, 104, 143
  electoral assistance, 5–6, 80–82, 84, 346
  and former Yugoslavia, 128n, 135, 136–37,
    138
  and Grenada, 273
  and Haiti, 78–80, 83, 103, 170, 171, 181, 182,
    248, 284–88, 301, 302
  and liberalism, 346–48, 381–85
  Liberia mission, 81–82
  mission standards, 85–87
  and miltilateral intervention, 252–53, 260,
    261, 281–90
  Namibia mission, 73–75, 80, 83
  Nicaragua mission, 75, 76–78, 80, 83, 103
  and Panama invasion, 279, 283
  peacekeeping force, 171
  and Sierra Leone, 304, 305–07, 310–11
  and sovereign States, 1–2, 384–85
  see also Human Rights Committee;
    International Court of Justice;
    International Covenant on Civil and
    Political Rights; United Nations Charter;
    United Nations Commission on Human
    Rights; United Nations General
    Assembly; United Nations Secretary-
    General; United Nations Security
    Council
United Nations Charter, 71–72, 98–99, 128,
  131, 136, 137, 146, 243, 292, 329, 384
  Article 1, 240
  Article 2(4), 260, 261, 262, 263–68, 269, 273,
    295, 328n, 506
  Article 2(7), 269, 281, 283, 330, 506
  Article 24, 283
  Article 39, 286, 338
  Article 42, 338
  Article 51, 274, 283
  Article 52, 272
  Article 53, 272
  Article 103, 328n, 334
  Chapter VII, 261, 283, 286–88, 302
  Chapter XII, 32, 33
  Part VIII, 108
United Nations Commission on Human
  Rights, 47, 116, 470
  and right to democracy, 3–4
United Nations Development Programme, 39
United Nations Economic Commission for
  Europe, 8n
United Nations General Assembly, 3, 32, 33,
  34, 35, 36–37, 40, 42, 43, 71, 78, 80, 118,
  137, 138, 269, 273, 275, 279, 284
  and Cambodia, 470
  contradictory position of, 44–45
  Credentials Committee, 142
  Declaration of Friendly Relations, 127, 264,
    329
  election monitoring standards, 73, 104
  and self-government, 72
United Nations Secretary-General, 3, 35, 39,
  40, 49, 199
  Electoral Assistance Division, 81
  and Liberia, 82, 289
United Nations Security Council, 9, 33, 47, 74,
  138, 143, 262, 273, 275, 300, 305ff., 327,
  382, 455
  and armed intervention, 98, 295
  and Bosnia, 319
  Chapter VII powers, 2, 117, 248, 253, 261,
    264, 281, 282, 283, 284, 285, 286–88, 290,
    302, 303
  Chapter VIII powers, 264, 272, 289
  and collective intervention, 281–90, 294
  inconsistency of, 117–18
  and non-recognition, 151

United Nations Security Council, (cont.)
  Resolution 841, 117, 285
  Resolution 940, 252, 261, 286, 287–88, 302n
  Resolution 1132, 288
  retrospective validation by, 289, 290
  and threat to international peace and security, 283, 289–90
United States, 21, 22, 26, 38, 43, 47, 52n, 139, 140, 144, 148, 172, 221, 223, 230, 231, 318, 332–33, 350, 359, 361–76, 378, 390, 391, 518, 521, 540
  anti-democratic intervention by, 197
  and Chile, 282
  Confederacy, 355, 371
  Constitution, 184, 188, 192, 409, 410
  and Cuba, 145
  Department of Justice, 215
  and Ecuador, 179, 181, 182
  and foreign law, 206–07, 208–11, 234
  foreign policy, 141, 143, 145, 181, 225, 348, 362–76
  and former Soviet Union, 131, 132
  and former Yugoslavia, 133, 136, 137
  and Gambia, 247
  Grenada intervention, 106, 271–74
  and Guatemala, 173, 174, 181–82, 188, 195
  and Haiti, 169, 170–71, 194–96, 197, 286, 294
  militant procedural democracy in, 409–11, 428, 433, 434
  and Nicaragua, 99–100
  and non-democratic States, 129n
  and OAS, 158, 159, 161, 186, 198
  Panama intervention, 46, 106, 251, 265, 266, 267, 269, 274–79, 302n
  and Paraguay, 176, 177, 182, 183
  recognition of States by, 141, 142
  and unilateral action, 106, 265, 266, 267, 269, 279, 280, 292, 296
  see also American Civil War; American public opinion
United States Supreme Court, 205–06, 209, 211, 285n, 410, 411, 428, 431
United States v. Then, 207
Universal Declaration of Human Rights, 11, 33, 46, 52, 55, 125, 241, 428, 450
  Article 19, 33
  Article 20, 33
  Article 21, 10, 53n, 92, 102
  Article 21(3), 118, 240, 396, 506
universal suffrage, 52, 55, 57, 59, 69, 72, 73, 85, 88n, 260, 360, 499, 501, 502, 514
universality, 86, 116–17, 421, 437–38, 439, 440, 447, 535, 563, 564

Uruguay, 176, 461, 464, 475, 481, 482, 483, 523, 524, 525, 527–28
use of force, 3, 9, 98–99, 106–07, 221, 246, 248–49, 252–54, 258, 313, 323, 549
  arguments against, 256, 267–68, 269, 279–81, 287–88, 291–92, 337–38
  consent to, 309–10
  legitimate, 263, 294–95
  and popular sovereignty, 268–70, 291, 309
  prohibition on, 260, 263–68, 270, 279, 292, 506
  risks of, 326–27
  see also pro-democratic intervention; unilateral intervention
uti possidetis, 127, 153, 269

validation, 28, 29, 30, 31, 39, 41–46, 152, 329, 334
  see also election monitoring
values, 224–25, 436–38
vanguardism, 509–10
Vanuatu, 32
variables, 351, 359, 361–62, 380
Velasquez-Rodriguez case, 463
Venezuela, 159, 372–76, 378
verification, 84
vertical relationships, 221
Vienna Convention on the Law of Treaties, 85, 110, 270, 334, 338, 465
Vietnam, 144, 267, 279, 358
violence, 522–25, 560, 561
Virginius affair, 350
voluntary rule, 44
voter registration, 79, 84

waiver *ex post facto*, 278
Walzer, Michael, 290, 291
war, 25, 91, 98, 343, 344, 350, 439, 447, 562
  and actors' perceptions, 350, 353, 355, 357–59, 361–76
  changes in, 560–61
  law of, 452–53
  and liberalism, 382–83, 550, 551
  renunciation of, 408
  see also civil wars; "democratic peace"
war crimes, 452–55, 457, 479, 485
War of 1812, 355, 365–68, 378
Warsaw Pact, 334
Wasmosy, President Carlos, 175–77, 182, 189, 190
Wedgwood, Ruth, 256
West Africa, 148–50, 252–53, 326
  see also Liberia; Sierra Leone

Index

West Irian, 32, 72
Western democratic model, 142, 225, 228, 437–40, 493, 497, 502, 503, 533, 535, 562–63
  see also liberal democracy
Western Sahara, 41, 103
Western Samoa, 73
Westlake, John, 113
will of the people, 10, 11, 14, 15, 89, 92, 95, 102, 115, 140, 240, 254, 258, 261, 325, 335, 502
  see also popular sovereignty
will of the State, 313–16, 320, 324
Wilson, President Woodrow, 141, 142, 202, 240, 555
women, 52n, 95, 396, 397n, 541

World Bank, 148, 215
World Conference on Human rights, 398n, 470
World Trade Organization, 199
World War I, 452–53
World War II, 551

Yemen, 31
Yugoslavia *see* former Yugoslavia

Zaire, 117, 146
Zakaria, Fareed, 222–23, 227
Zalaquett, Jose, 481
Zambia, 38, 41, 58
Zimbabwe, 202, 250, 282
  see also Southern Rhodesia